American Politics
A Field Guide

American Politics
A Field Guide

Jennifer L. Lawless
University of Virginia

Richard L. Fox
Loyola Marymount University

W. W. NORTON & COMPANY
Independent Publishers Since 1923

W. W. Norton & Company has been independent since its founding in 1923, when William Warder Norton and Mary D. Herter Norton first published lectures delivered at the People's Institute, the adult education division of New York City's Cooper Union. The firm soon expanded its program beyond the Institute, publishing books by celebrated academics from America and abroad. By midcentury, the two major pillars of Norton's publishing program—trade books and college texts—were firmly established. In the 1950s, the Norton family transferred control of the company to its employees, and today—with a staff of five hundred and hundreds of trade, college, and professional titles published each year— W. W. Norton & Company stands as the largest and oldest publishing house owned wholly by its employees.

Editor: Pete Lesser
Senior Associate Editor: Anna Olcott
Senior Project Editor: Linda Feldman
Editorial Assistant: Tichina Sewell-Richards
Managing Editor, College: Marian Johnson
Senior Production Manager: Sean Mintus
Media Editor: Spencer Richardson-Jones
Associate Media Editor: Alexandra Malakhoff
Media Project Editor: Marcus Van Harpen
Managing Editor, College Digital Media: Kim Yi
Ebook Producer: Sophia Purut
Marketing Manager, Political Science: Ashley Sherwood
Design Director: Rubina Yeh
Book Designer: Jillian Burr
Director of College Permissions: Megan Schindel
Permissions Specialist: Joshua Garvin
Photo Editor: Mike Cullen
Composition: Graphic World
Manufacturing: Transcontinental

Permission to use copyrighted material is included on p. C-1.

ISBN 978-0-393-53918-9 (pbk.)

W. W. Norton & Company, Inc., 500 Fifth Avenue, New York, NY 10110
wwnorton.com

W. W. Norton & Company Ltd., 15 Carlisle Street, London W1D 3BS

1 2 3 4 5 6 7 8 9 0

Brief Contents

Contents

SECTION I. CREATING THE GOVERNMENT: FROM THE FOUNDING TO TODAY

SECTION IV. POLITICAL INFORMATION, KNOWLEDGE, AND NEWS

Why did we write this book?

We first met in January 1995 in an introduction to U.S. politics class. One of us was a brand-new professor teaching the class for the first time; the other was a student just beginning to study U.S. politics. We didn't realize it at the time but that class planted the seeds of a long-lasting partnership. Since then, we've conducted national surveys together; coauthored academic books, journal articles, policy reports, and op-eds; and shared our research with organizations, political leaders, and the media.

And now, all these years later, we've returned to the scene of our first discussions about U.S. politics. Even though we've steadily collaborated on research projects through the years, we've always been grounded by our teaching—regaling each other with stories about our triumphs and challenges in the classroom. We sometimes have different pedagogical approaches, but we've always shared a sense of dissatisfaction with the materials available to introduce students to U.S. government. So, we decided to try our hand at writing a textbook—the kind we wish had been available to us.

We're well aware that almost all U.S. politics textbook authors believe in their hearts that they have come up with an innovative or better way to present the material. On this front, we are no different. But we really think we've done it! (Perhaps that actually makes us no different either.) The "How do you use this book?" segment elaborates on the rationale for our approach and the format we employ. But, in a nutshell, this textbook rethinks how to present information—no lengthy chapters with dozens of subheadings, no seemingly endless lists of terms, no dry academic prose. Instead, it contains engagingly written short chapters (which we call segments) that cover everything we think is vital for students to have a solid introduction to U.S. politics. Our approach relies on two central features: (1) an organizational framework built around engaging key questions, and (2) a focus on practicing skills that are necessary for becoming a knowledgeable citizen.

First, we present the material consistent with how young people today read and process information. Students read less, get news on their cell phones, learn by watching online videos, communicate via text and images, and instantaneously look up facts. We get that. But we still believe in the merits of an actual textbook—whether it's an ebook or a printed copy that students hold in their hands. So we've tried to find a happy medium by breaking up the course content into short, digestible readings framed around a key question that students may find interesting. Rather than 15 or 16 long textbook chapters, this book comprises 48 segments that pose a question and offer an answer. "Can people say offensive things whenever they want?" covers freedom of speech. "Should you believe the polls?" addresses public opinion. "What does the president do all day?" sheds light on the presidency and the powers of the executive branch. "Why was your T-shirt made in China?" sets the stage for learning about trade policy. Students can read this book with a much clearer sense of purpose. If they can answer the question posed by each segment, it's a win.

Second, we embedded into each segment a focus on the essential skills that knowledgeable citizens must possess. The reality is that years, or even months, after leaving an introductory class on U.S. politics, students will remember few of the specific facts and concepts we all work so hard to present carefully and creatively. This is perhaps more true now than ever before, as students know they can always just do a quick search online to answer any question they may have. Who was Marbury again? Google it. What was the Civil Rights Act of 1964? Ask Siri. How does the Electoral College work? You get the drift. We prioritize giving students the skills they need to be engaged citizens—skills they can practice in the class and carry with them once it ends: reading and digesting quantitative data, identifying reliable sources of information, articulating and defending an argument, and engaging the political system. Being able to do these things—let alone do them well—requires practice. Each segment of this book provides that practice.

During the five years that it's taken to produce this book, we've had the opportunity to test this approach on hundreds of our own students. They have responded enthusiastically to the shorter readings focused around questions, been engaged by our style of presentation, enjoyed the skills-building activities (well, most of them anyway), demonstrated an understanding of how the U.S. government works, and in some cases, even become more politically active. We hope your students react the same way.

Who helped us get here?

When we began this endeavor, we had no idea how long the writing would take. Or how many decisions we'd have to make. And not only about content. We dealt with difficult decisions about what to include in a U.S. politics textbook and what to leave on the cutting room floor. And we faced choices about layout, color scheme, online supplemental materials, photo selection, glossary terms . . . the list goes on. At times it was overwhelming. Fortunately, we were surrounded by lots of people who helped us think through these decisions, improve the finished product, and keep us sane.

First, we are grateful to our colleagues, even if most of them were dumbfounded when we excitedly told them that we were thinking about writing a new intro to U.S. politics textbook. "Really, I don't think either of you know enough to do that," "Don't do it! The process is endless and will crush your soul," and "Wow, you must really have nothing going on in our lives" were among the amusing reactions we received. Even though they questioned our abilities and judgment, once we took the plunge, our colleagues and friends regularly acted as sounding boards, made helpful suggestions, and occasionally talked us off the ledge. In particular, we thank Feryal Cherif, Adriana DiPasquale, Kathy Dolan, Paul Freedman, Michael Genovese, Samantha Guthrie, Danny Hayes, David Leblang, Jan Leighley, John Parrish, Janie Steckenrider, and Matt Wright.

We also thank the many people at Norton who helped turn our idea for a new kind of textbook into a reality. We are especially grateful to Peter Lesser, who approached us and gave us the opportunity to write a truly different kind of textbook. Anna Olcott and Tichina Sewell-Richards kept the manuscript moving and managed the schedule. Spencer Richardson-Jones, Alexandra Malakhoff, and Quinn Campbell developed the media package. Alice Vigliani copyedited the manuscript, and Linda Feldman made sure it was complete and consistent. Mike Cullen wrangled the many photos. Sean Mintus managed all things production. Jillian Burr created the interior design. Ashley Sherwood managed the advertising and marketing effort. And Faceout Studio designed the cover. Thanks to all for their efforts.

As soon as we began working on the book, we realized that a textbook is a collaborative endeavor that must speak to multiple audiences: students, instructors, and the broader field of political science. So we are grateful to the many reviewers who read and commented on early drafts of every segment. Together, they helped us create a textbook that, we hope, breaks new ground and works for a wide range of classes and students:

Matthew Atkinson, Long Beach City College
Alexa Bankert, University of Georgia
Nathaniel Birkhead, Kansas State University
Clare Brock, Texas Woman's University
Jennifer Hayes Clark, University of Houston
Cory Colby, Lone Star College–Tomball
Brett Curry, Georgia Southern University
Anthony Daniels, University of Toledo
Rebecca Deen, The University of Texas at Arlington
Darin DeWitt, California State University, Long Beach
Bryan Dubin, Oakland Community College
Emily Erdmann, Blinn College
Megan Ming Francis, University of Washington
Daniel Fuerstman, State College of Florida
Bobbi Gentry, Bridgewater College
Stephen Goggin, University of California, Irvine
Jessica Gracey, Northwest Missouri State University
Matt Guardino, Providence College
Annika Hagley, Roger Williams University
Clinton Jenkins, Birmingham-Southern College
Christy Woodward Kaupert, San Antonio College
Kellee Kirkpatrick, Idaho State University
Rebecca Kreitzer, University of North Carolina at Chapel Hill
Eric Loepp, University of Wisconsin–Whitewater
Alyx Mark, Wesleyan University
Matthew Murray, Dutchess Community College
Patrick Novotny, Georgia Southern University
David O'Connell, Dickinson College
William Parent, San Jacinto College–North Campus
Andre Robinson, Bunker Hill Community College
Michelle Rodriguez, San Diego Mesa College
Michael Rudy, Truman State University

Richard Rupp, Purdue University Northwest
Cynthia Rugeley, University of Minnesota Duluth
Hans Schmeisser, Abraham Baldwin Agricultural
Ronnee Schreiber, San Diego State University
Jennifer Selin, University of Missouri
Jason Sides, Southeast Missouri State University
Janie Steckenrider, Loyola Marymount University
Candis Watts Smith, Duke University
Rorie Solberg, Oregon State University
Jennie Sweet-Cushman, Chatham University
James Benjamin Taylor, Kennesaw State University
Linda Trautman, Ohio University Lancaster
Sarah Treul, University of North Carolina
John Vento, Antelope Valley College

When we work together on a project, we really work together. We send every outline back and forth numerous times. We revise tables and figures endlessly. We write and rewrite nearly every sentence of every paragraph more times than we can count. (We even sent these acknowledgments back and forth a dozen times!) It takes a lot of time and effort to master overkill in the drafting and revision process, but we've done it. This means countless lengthy phone calls (often early in the morning and late at night to account for living in different time zones), constant self-imposed deadlines (no weekend or holiday is spared), and a propensity to debate the most mundane details (World War III has nearly broken out over section titles, punctuation, and sentence order). To say that we were not that fun to be around while writing this book is to put it mildly. So our next batch of thanks goes to our families and furry friends, all of whom had to put up with a lot (and even more than usual given that we couldn't really leave the house for 15 months): For Jen it was Margie, John, and Viola; for Richard, it was Dominique, Lila, Miles, seven foster dogs, Maple, and Pippy.

Finally, we thank the city of Palm Springs. Although we were in constant Zoom, phone, text, and email contact while working on this project, we couldn't have written this book without spending significant chunks of pre-pandemic time in person—spit-balling ideas, drafting outlines, identifying compelling examples, and realizing that this endeavor was actually a lot of fun. Palm Springs was the scene of many of these meetings, and we can't wait to get back there to work on the second edition.

Jen Lawless | **Richard Fox**

About the Authors

Jennifer L. Lawless (University of Virginia) is the Leone Reaves and George W. Spicer professor of politics at the University of Virginia. She also has affiliations with UVA's Frank Batten School of Leadership and Public Policy and the Miller Center. Jen's research focuses on political ambition, campaigns and elections, and media and politics. She is the author or coauthor of seven books, including *Women on the Run: Gender, Media, and Political Campaigns in a Polarized Era* (with Danny Hayes) and *It Still Takes a Candidate: Why Women Don't Run for Office* (with Richard L. Fox). Her research, which has been supported by the National Science Foundation, has appeared in numerous academic journals, and is regularly cited in the popular press. She is the coeditor in chief of the *American Journal of Political Science*. Jen graduated from Union College with a BA in political science, and Stanford University with an MA and PhD in political science. A long time ago (2006), she sought the Democratic nomination for the U.S. House of Representatives in Rhode Island's second congressional district. Although she lost the race, she remains an obsessive political junkie. That campaign also inspired her to make sure that every student who leaves her classroom knows just how important civic engagement is for a healthy democracy.

Richard L. Fox (Loyola Marymount University) has spent decades teaching intro American government to students that have become less and less engaged by traditional approaches. He teaches in the areas of U.S. Congress, elections, courts, and media and politics. He has spent time teaching at the University of California, Santa Barbara; University of Wyoming; Union College, California State, Fullerton; and Loyola Marymount University. His research, which has been funded by the National Science Foundation, focuses on political ambition, electoral behavior, and gender politics. He is the coeditor of *Gender and Elections: Shaping the Future of American Politics*, 5th edition (2022). He is also the coauthor of *Women, Men, and U.S. Politics: 10 Big Questions* (2017); *Running from Office: Why Young Americans Are Turned Off to Politics* (2015); *It Still Takes a Candidate: Why Women Don't Run for Office* (2010); and *Tabloid Justice: The Criminal Justice System in the Age of Media Frenzy*, 2nd edition (2007). His work has appeared in journals, including the *American Political Science Review, Journal of Politics, American Journal of Political Science, Political Psychology, PS*, and *Politics & Gender*. He has also published op-eds in the *Washington Post, New York Times*, and *Wall Street Journal*. After graduating from Claremont McKenna College, he earned his MA and PhD from the University of California, Santa Barbara.

American Politics
A Field Guide

How do you use this book?

#HowToGetAnA

A former president telling anyone who will listen that he was cheated out of the last election. Partisan warfare in Congress that doesn't stop even amid an insurrection. Conspiracy theories all over the internet about rigged voting machines, Covid-19, and sex-trafficking politicians. Bitter debates over mask mandates, health care, racial justice, immigration, and climate change that regularly paralyze the political system. Uncertainty, turbulence, and confusion characterize U.S. politics more now than perhaps at any time in contemporary history. The enormous range of readily available sources of political information — some accurate, some not — only confounds how we understand and critically analyze politics. If you're interested in public affairs or simply just trying to follow what's going on, it's hard to know how to begin.

Complicating things further is that students today are different from those of previous generations. Many of you have grown up as digital natives; from the time you were old enough to touch a screen, you've been "connected." You read news on cell phones, communicate via direct message, and look up facts with the click of a button. You're more likely than older generations to read shorter pieces and to read for less sustained periods of time.[1] You prefer intense or provocative presentations of material.[2] And you benefit from active learning that involves more than endless pages of text and dense lectures filled with facts and academic jargon.[3]

Some people condemn your generation as having the attention span of a gnat. Not us. Sure, you could read a little more (couldn't we all?). And it wouldn't kill you to put your devices away during class.

Do

**Read
this book**

**Focus on the
key questions**

**Complete the
skills exercises**

Don't

**Eat
this book**

**Fight tigers
with this book**

**Use this book
as a mask**

But overall, we commend your ability to communicate and multitask in a way that previous generations could only have dreamed of. In fact, we think it's time to take these generational changes seriously and integrate them into how we teach U.S. politics. After all, rapid and dramatic changes in politics make it more important than ever for you to know about the government and laws under which you live and your rights and responsibilities as citizens. That's why we've written what we believe is a new kind of textbook to help you learn about U.S. politics — how we got here, how to make sense of what's going on, how to think about the future — and encourage you to be invested in and knowledgeable about the political system.

A New Approach to Learning about U.S. Politics

Most textbooks—those about U.S. politics as well as those in other disciplines—include lengthy chapters crammed with facts, definitions, and concepts. There's rarely a clear narrative. And by the time you get to the end, you're often left wondering what exactly you were supposed to take away from each chapter. Should you memorize all dates and historical facts? Should you know the definitions of every highlighted term? Should you try to remember all the data presented in the tables and figures? And what about all those photos, textboxes, and activities? Are they important parts of each chapter, or can you skip them? We don't like this approach for presenting information about U.S. politics, and most of our students over the years haven't liked it either.

This textbook rethinks how to present information—no lengthy chapters with dozens of subheadings, no seemingly endless lists of terms, no dry academic prose. Instead, this book contains engagingly written short chapters (which we call segments) that cover everything we think is vital for giving you a solid introduction to U.S. politics. Our approach relies on two central features: (1) an organizational framework built around key questions, and (2) a focus on skills. As we elaborate a bit on these two features, we'll also give you a few tips on how to get the most out of this book.

A Focus on Questions

You'll soon see that this isn't an ordinary textbook. We organize the material into 48 short segments. Each one—typically 9 to 12 pages—focuses on a single key question about U.S. politics. The questions serve as the titles of the segments (just like this introductory segment is posed as a question). Right below the title, you'll see a hashtag that summarizes each segment's topic (like #HowToGetAnA). Some of the questions pertain to straightforward nuts and bolts about U.S. government and politics (How doesn't a bill become a law? Should you believe the polls? How does a case get to the Supreme Court?). Others shed light on why the U.S. political system operates the way it does (If everyone hates Congress, why do so many members get reelected? What is the Electoral College anyway? Why do Fox News and CNN viewers see the world so differently?). And still others encourage you to consider competing arguments (Did the Founders believe in democracy? Are the rich too rich? Is there too much money in elections?).

By dividing the content into digestible key questions, we make it very clear what you should know when you're done with the segment: *the answer to the question.* We include key terms, photos, tables, and figures in each segment as well. They're part of helping you answer the segment's question more thoroughly. If you finish reading a segment and the answer still seems a little murky, or if you want to confirm what the answer is, then you can check out the Did You Get It? box. This box provides a succinct answer to the segment's central question. At the end of this course, if you can answer the 48 questions the book poses, then you'll know more about U.S. politics than the vast majority of Americans do. (You don't have to take our word for this; just look at the data we present in Segment 22!)

A Focus on Skills

To be an engaged, active participant in and consumer of politics, you need more than an understanding of how government operates. You also need to be adept at consuming information about politics, evaluating arguments, analyzing data, and engaging with the political system. Being able to do these things—let alone doing them well—doesn't come naturally to most people. These are skills that require practice. And each segment of this book gives you that practice.

The first page of each segment identifies the skill (in words and with one of the icons pictured below and on the next page) that we'll be covering and that you'll practice when you reach the end. Here's a preview of what you'll encounter and what you'll do to sharpen the four political science skills we want you to develop:

 Consuming Political Information: Trying to gain a complete understanding of almost any political topic—guns, abortion, the environment—can be daunting. You can easily find yourself sorting through scholarly books, news articles, TV stories, social media posts, emails from a wacky uncle, even conspiracy-focused websites. How do you navigate this information environment? How do you gather information to make a reasonable assessment of the issue at hand? We want you to have the tools to work through the information onslaught and distinguish facts from opinions, reliable sources from dubious ones, and systematic research from anecdotal accounts.

To develop this skill, you'll check the facts behind political claims and statements; consider political sources' quality, credibility, and ideological bent; and navigate important government and political websites.

 Persuasive Argumentation: Politics is all about arguments. Candidates argue that they're the best person for the job. Elected officials argue over which policy to pursue. Judges issue opinions that lay out the arguments behind their decisions. Media outlets air and publish political analysts' arguments. Regardless of the context, persuasive political arguments rely on evidence, which comes in many forms: statistics, survey data, historical facts, legal precedent, expert analysis, and logical reasoning. If you are to follow political debates, evaluate hot-button topics in U.S. politics, or thoughtfully discuss political issues, then you need to develop your persuasive argumentation skills.

To develop this skill, you'll craft and identify different types of political arguments, choose a side on a range of political topics, and evaluate various kinds of evidence.

 Quantitative Literacy: "Polls Reveal That Race for the White House Is a Tie." "Senate Republicans Pledge to Kill Gun Control Legislation." "President Proposes $2 Trillion in New Spending to Jumpstart Economy." "Women Still Underpaid Relative to Men." So many political stories you'll read and political discussions you'll have involve numbers. Sometimes they're in the form of public opinion polls or survey data. Other times, they involve studies of voters and elections or reports about public policies. Being an informed citizen requires understanding and analyzing many types of quantitative data so that you can draw substantive conclusions.

To develop this skill, you'll read and interpret statistical information in tables and figures, identify trends in data and use that information to forecast political phenomena, and occasionally do a little simple math.

 Citizen Engagement: You're really excited about a candidate. Or really passionate about changing a law—the drinking age, or the death penalty, or the minimum wage. Maybe you even want to run for office. Being politically engaged is a fundamental component of democratic citizenship. Otherwise, you can't shape the political process or hold elected leaders accountable. But that's often easier said than done. Many people just don't know how to get involved.

To develop this skill, you'll answer questions that push you to know your rights, familiarize you with the nuts and bolts of how to participate in politics, and help you stay informed about public affairs.

At the end of each segment, you'll answer three multiple choice questions that help develop one of the skills. An open-ended activity—called Figure It Out—also appears at the end of each segment. These questions provide you with an opportunity to put into practice the skill the segment highlights. If you don't think you've mastered the skill right away, don't worry! The book provides numerous opportunities to work on each skill. More complex questions often include hints. And we've developed exercises for each skill, which you can find in the online supplements. When you leave this class, many facts and even some key concepts will fade with time. But if all goes well, you'll carry your mastery of the four skills with you forever.

A Little Bit about Us

We hope that as you read this book, you'll see that learning about politics and preparing to be engaged citizens are, well, fun. We definitely had fun writing it, especially trying to figure out the most important topics and questions to present. So we figured that we'd end these opening pages by sharing some of the "bests" as we produced this book (see Table 1). We included some worsts, too, because—let's face it—they're more fun to read about. At the end of the book, you can see which of us produced the better list. (Hint: Jen)

TABLE 1. Jen and Richard's Reviews of the Book

	Jen	Richard
Favorite segment	"How do you run for president?" I love George Clooney.	"Is America a racist country?" Feels like we are finally starting to grapple with this key question as a nation.
Least favorite segment	"Can the federal government tell the states what to do?" Federalism is important, but kind of boring.	I love them all.
Easiest to write	"How did the Supreme Court get its power?" *Marbury v. Madison* is like a reality TV show.	"How doesn't a bill become a law?" Having taught a Congress class for two decades, this one practically wrote itself. (Jen doesn't remember it that way.)
Most challenging to write	"Are all Americans equal under the law?" The Fourteenth Amendment and its applications are complex! Slimming it down to 12 pages was nearly impossible.	"How can the U.S. government be $32 trillion . . . whoops . . . $33 trillion in debt?" Turns out we had to learn this topic from scratch.
Segment we fought most about	"Is there too much money in elections?" We didn't agree.	Agreed. Jen is way off on this one. (You can guess which side she's on.)

TABLE 1. Jen and Richard's Reviews of the Book — cont'd

	Jen	Richard
Most original segment	"What happens if you're charged with a crime?" We really tried to be creative in teaching civil liberties.	They're all original. No one has written a textbook quite like this.
Segment with best photo	"Should you worry about terrorist attacks?" The post-9/11 photo is incredibly powerful. It looks like Europe in World War II.	"Where do people get their political beliefs?" The photo of kids wearing "Kids for Trump" shirts shows the power of socialization in the family.
Segment with best joke	"Can the federal government tell the states what to do?" C'mon — it's my least favorite segment; we needed to include a little wit.	None. We need more jokes in this book.
Skill most likely to impress your friends	Quantitative Literacy. Who isn't wowed by people doing simple math on the fly?	Consuming Political Information. You'll be able to swat away misinformation and conspiracy theories with authority.
Best thing about coauthor	Sense of humor	Passion for producing excellent work
Worst thing about coauthor	Spelling and grammar	Very unforgiving if you miss a deadline, or misplace a comma

Source: Jen and Richard's phone calls, texts, and emails.

If you have any comments, suggestions, or feedback, feel free to email us (lawless@email.virginia.edu or richard.fox@lmu.edu). You can even send Richard a text: (310) 621–8514. He doesn't have much to do and would love to hear from you.

DID YOU GET IT?
How do you use this book?

Short Answer:

- Actually read the segments your instructor assigns. They're short and straightforward for a reason. You might actually like them. You might even occasionally smile or laugh.

- Remember the primary goal of each segment: stay awake, and don't pick up your phone. Kidding, kidding. Use the concepts, photos, tables, and figures to answer the segment's opening question.

- Complete the skills exercises at the end of each segment. They'll help you excel in the class and become an informed citizen while you're at it.

Creating the Government:

From the Founding to Today

Start Here!

When you think of the Founders of the United States of America, you probably think of a group of old men from the late 1700s (if you think of them at all). And they were. But beyond that, assessments of who the Founders were and what they achieved vary greatly. Some see them as a group of White, elitist, sexist slaveowners who tried to design a system of government that would protect their own interests. Others view them as visionary leaders with high ideals and morals who set out to create a just and democratic nation.

Regardless of where you come down on the Founders, one thing is indisputable: they designed a **government**—institutions, rules, and procedures that organize and structure a group of citizens—that has been very durable. The **constitution** they drafted more than 230 years ago to lay out our nation's system of government is still around today. And that's quite rare. The United States is the only country in the world with a constitution written in the eighteenth century. Most constitutions were drafted or substantially revised within the last 50 years. In fact, only one country has a governing document that's older than ours: the Republic of San Marino, a tiny country within the borders of Italy that boasts a population of just more than 33,000.

But focusing on the Founding period is important not only because the U.S. Constitution has withstood the test of time. The system of government the Founders created has also led to a style of **politics**—the actions, practices, and policies employed in the struggle to achieve and maintain power—that continues to play out today. It's almost impossible to understand the present without having a sense of the past. Do you want to know why Congress can't seem to get anything done? Or why presidents can't just do whatever they promised in their campaigns? Do you ever wonder why the death penalty is legal in some states but outlawed in others? Or why the Supreme Court gets to decide whether gay people can get married? By the end of this section, you'll have answers to these questions. You'll see how those answers are rooted in decisions made centuries ago. And you'll realize that the Founders didn't see eye to eye when it came to the role of the federal government, the power of large versus small states, slavery, or individual rights. The Constitution we live under today is the product of vigorous disagreements and hard-won compromises.

Together, the eight segments reinforce three key themes:

1 **The framework of government the Founders created is still largely intact today.** Separation of powers, checks and balances, and federalism remain central features of the U.S. political system. The onerous constitutional amendment process suggests that these features are here to stay.

2 **The last 230-plus years have seen significant shifts in powers and responsibilities among the branches and levels of government.** None of these changes contradicts the Constitution's original design, but they demonstrate evolution in how the government addresses the nation's problems and shapes public policy.

3 **The Founders' version of representative government included many undemocratic elements, several of which we continue to grapple with.** As the Founders drafted the Constitution, only White men — and not even all of them — enjoyed liberty and equality. The United States continues to struggle with the legacy of slavery and inequality.

1.
What is the American Dream?

#PoliticalCulture

On October 12, 2018, word of a "caravan" of migrants heading from Honduras to the United States captured journalists' attention. The *Washington Post*, the *New York Times*, Fox News, and many other outlets began tracking the progress of a growing mass of people fleeing violence and a lack of economic opportunity in their Latin American homelands. What started as a group of 160 people in Honduras swelled to roughly 7,000 as the caravan crossed Guatemala and made its way to the Mexican border. Traveling mostly by foot, and hitching rides whenever they could, the women, men, and children — often with only the clothes on their backs — averaged 20 to 30 miles each day. Once in Mexico, the migrants still had more than 1,000 miles to go before they reached the closest U.S. border.

News organizations weren't alone in tracking the caravan. U.S. political leaders became laser-focused as well. And many of them, especially then-president Donald Trump, vowed to stop the migrants before they reached the United States. As part of the heated rhetoric of the 2018 midterm elections, Trump tweeted, "Please go back, you will not be admitted into the United States unless you go through the legal process. This is an invasion of our Country and our Military is waiting for you!"[1] Trump then ordered the deployment of more than 5,000 U.S. troops to await the caravan at the U.S.-Mexico border. He warned the migrants that if they tussled with U.S. border forces — some allegedly

Like this caravan of migrants originating from Honduras in 2018, people for centuries have made their way to the United States in search of the American Dream.

threw rocks at Mexican officers — the border patrol would treat the rocks as firearms, paving the way for a military response.[2] Not exactly the welcoming words epitomized on the base of the Statue of Liberty.

But Trump's words did little to deter people trying to flee their countries for the United States. Indeed, following the 2020 presidential election, another migrant caravan headed for the U.S. border assembled in Honduras and Guatemala.[3] While the Biden Administration's rhetoric may be less aggressive than Trump's, their policies aren't altogether different. In 2021, at a news conference in Guatemala, Vice President Kamala Harris issued a warning to those who might be considering a dangerous trek to the United States. "Do not come. Do not come," the vice president implored. "The United States," she went on to say, "will continue to enforce our laws and secure our border."[4]

So why do thousands of people join caravans heading to the United States? Why endure intense physical hardship to get to a country whose leaders tell you — very explicitly — that you're not welcome? Why risk your life, possible separation from your children, and potential deportation? The answer might sound a little cliché. Well, actually, it sounds a lot cliché: many migrants are in search of the **American Dream**. Coined by historian James Adams in 1931, the term reflects the "dream of a land in which life should be better and richer and fuller for everyone, with opportunity for each according to ability or achievement."[5] In many ways, it embodies the **political culture** of the United

States — that is, it represents the general set of beliefs, attitudes, and values on which our political system is based. The American Dream includes the promise of liberty that brought the pilgrims to Plymouth Rock in 1620, the promise of equality that prompted the colonists to declare independence in 1776, the promise of limited government that guided the drafting of the Constitution in 1787. Essentially, it symbolizes the promise of opportunity that, for centuries, has fostered the idea that the United States is a place where anyone with ambition and a strong work ethic can achieve safety, success, and happiness. For many, the United States is a beacon of hope and possibility.

It's not only people trying to immigrate to the United States who feel this way. The bars in Figure 1 represent the percentage of Americans within each category who believe their family "has already achieved" or "is on the way to achieving" the American Dream. The overwhelming majority of U.S. citizens believe the American Dream is within reach.[6] Although Republicans and people with college educations are especially likely to hold on to this hopeful ideal, more than 8 out of 10 people overall contend that their families have achieved or will achieve the promise of America.

This segment examines the origins of the values at the heart of American political culture: liberty, equality, and limited self-government. (We cover democracy, which many people also consider a core American

FIGURE 1. People Who Believe In the American Dream

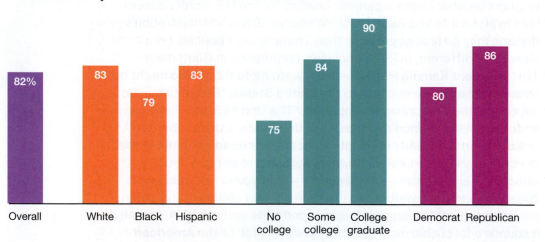

Note: The bars above represent the percentage of Americans who believe their family "has already achieved" or "is on the way to achieving" the American Dream.

Source: Samantha Smith, "Most Think the 'American Dream' Is within Reach for Them," Pew Research Center, October 31, 2017.

value, in Segment 6.) You'll see that these concepts were alive from the moment the colonists set foot on American soil, shaped the nation's founding, and remain key American principles today. But you'll also come to realize that despite widespread support for these three central pillars of political culture in the United States, the American Dream and all it entails is often more an ideal than a reality.

Pillar 1: "Give Me Liberty, or Give Me Death"

Liberty—the freedom from excessive government restrictions imposed on your political views or way of life—has been part of the American spirit since the pilgrims fled the British government's religious persecution in 1620. They arrived on the North American continent and, for the first time, had the freedom to pursue their religious beliefs. Throughout the course of the next 150 years, the call for freedom extended well beyond religious liberty. The freedom to pursue economic and political interests served as the basis for declaring independence from British rule. George Washington motivated the troops during the Revolutionary War by telling them: "Remember, officers and soldiers, that you are fighting for the blessings of liberty."[7] Washington was but one of many Founders to extol the virtues of freedom. Perhaps most notable was Patrick Henry, who urged Virginia to commit more troops to the war with a fiery and impassioned speech that ended with the words "Give me liberty, or give me death!"[8]

Once the country won its independence from Britain, self-reliance and independence emerged as critical aspects of American political culture. The settler. The cowboy. The frontiersman. The entrepreneur. They all worked to expand the nation's territory and achieve economic success along the way. (That they were almost all White and almost all men doesn't escape us; more on that in segments to come.) Their **individualism** embodied personal liberty, resourcefulness, and self-reliance. And it laid the groundwork for a **free market system**—an economy with little government regulation that allows businesses and individuals to compete to determine what goods are produced, who buys them, and at what price.

Liberty, individualism, and market competition remain central to the American philosophy in the twenty-first century. Take a look at Figure 2. The top two bars gauge the extent to which people support religious freedom, even when it means that they might hear things that offend their own religious beliefs. More than three-quarters of citizens are on board. The figure's middle two bars reveal strong support for individualism.

FIGURE 2. People's Attitudes about Freedom, Individualism, and Free Markets

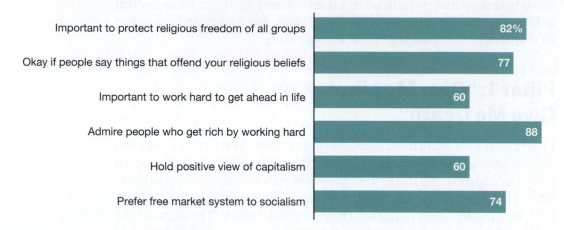

Statement	Percentage
Important to protect religious freedom of all groups	82%
Okay if people say things that offend your religious beliefs	77
Important to work hard to get ahead in life	60
Admire people who get rich by working hard	88
Hold positive view of capitalism	60
Prefer free market system to socialism	74

Note: Bars reflect the percentage of Americans polled who agree with each statement.

Source: Data come from public opinion polls conducted between 2014 and 2021; see Note 9 for full source information.

Six out of 10 people think it's important to work hard if you want to get ahead in life, and almost 9 out of 10 admire those who get rich doing so. The story is largely the same when it comes to economic competition. A majority of Americans support free markets, especially when compared to a system of socialism (see the bottom two bars).[9]

Pillar 2: "We Hold These Truths to Be Self-Evident, That All Men Are Created Equal"

By the mid-1760s, the colonists could no longer tolerate their second-class status. They didn't think they should have to pay taxes to Britain yet receive no representation in the British government. They didn't like the way the British managed westward expansion. They didn't want to be forced to open their homes to British troops. All told, the Declaration of Independence listed dozens of grievances against the king of England. But one particular sentence in the document became an enduring value of American political culture: "We hold these truths to be self-evident, that all men are created equal." The colonists thought they were equal to their British counterparts and were willing to go to war to establish it.

But "equal" was narrowly defined. Wealthy, White men? Equal. Non-land-owning men, women, Native Americans, and enslaved persons? Not equal. It wasn't until nearly 100 years later that the Fourteenth Amendment guaranteed all citizens "equal protection under the law." It took 50 years after that to grant women the right to vote. Nevertheless, the broad value of **equality**—the idea that people should be treated similarly under the law and have the same opportunities to get ahead—has been part of the American value system since the nation's beginning.

Equality and all it represented helped pave the way for America to become a **melting pot**. This term originates from a 1908 Israel Zangwill play that celebrates the diversity of the more than 15 million European immigrants who came to the United States between 1880 and the early 1900s.[10] That's not to say that immigrants were always welcomed with open arms (or that they are today). But the idea of bringing together people from many different backgrounds and cultures to become the people of one nation—with equal rights and opportunities—was uniquely American.

When it comes to general attitudes, citizens today continue to value the basic principles of equality and diversity. The data presented in Figure 3 make it clear that large majorities of Americans believe that everyone—regardless of where they came from or how they got here—should have an equal opportunity to succeed.[11] They think racial equality (which was the goal of the Civil Rights Act) and women's rights are important. And they view immigration as something that strengthens the country. Nearly 7 in 10 people even feel sympathy toward undocumented immigrants—people who didn't follow the legal procedures required to enter the nation.

FIGURE 3. People's Attitudes toward Equality and Diversity

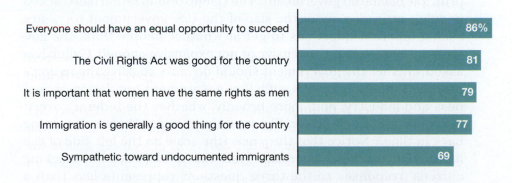

Everyone should have an equal opportunity to succeed	86%
The Civil Rights Act was good for the country	81
It is important that women have the same rights as men	79
Immigration is generally a good thing for the country	77
Sympathetic toward undocumented immigrants	69

Note: Bars reflect the percentage of Americans polled who agree with each statement or hold that view.

Source: Data come from public opinion polls conducted between 2012 and 2020; see Note 11 for full source information.

Pillar 3: "We the People . . . Establish This Constitution for the United States of America"

American political culture, right from the start, valued **self-government**: the belief that people should have a say in determining their nation's laws and rules. In fact, while the pilgrims were on their way to America—literally, while they were on the boat searching for a place to land—they drafted the Mayflower Compact. Aware that there might be chaos upon trying to organize a new colony, the settlers drew up this short document to put forward a set of rules that would govern them. Among the rules was that the colonists collectively would decide the laws.[12] This first attempt at democratic self-government spread across many of the new settlements. And 150 years later, the U.S. Constitution's preamble made the same point: "We the People of the United States, in Order to form a more perfect Union . . . do ordain and establish this Constitution for the United States of America." The document, which lays out the structure of government and allocates its responsibilities and powers, was drafted by citizens who would be legally bound by it.

Beyond self-government, the United States was founded on the principle of **limited government**. In other words, the power rests in the rules, not the rulers. Written laws serve as the basis for governmental authority, and these rules and laws apply to everyone. Because no leader is above the law, no leader can pursue a course of action that violates the law. A government with written rules is also limited because those powers not granted to the government remain in the hands of individual citizens. These values formed much of the thinking that went into writing the Constitution.

Centuries later, American citizens continue to believe in the principle of limited government. The Gallup organization has tracked people's attitudes about the size of the U.S. government for years, asking different questions to get at whether people think the government's reach is too extensive or not expansive enough. Gallup has asked whether the government should do more to solve the nation's problems, whether there's sufficient government regulation of business and industry, and, more broadly, whether the federal government has too much power. Figure 4 summarizes the results, going back in time.[13] Notice that the y axis (the scale on the left side of the figure) only reaches 50 percent. That means that each line tracking citizens' responses to the three questions represents less than a majority of the population—and in some cases, way less. Most Americans do not think the government should do more to solve our problems, two-thirds don't want to see more government regulation

FIGURE 4. People's Attitudes toward Limited Government

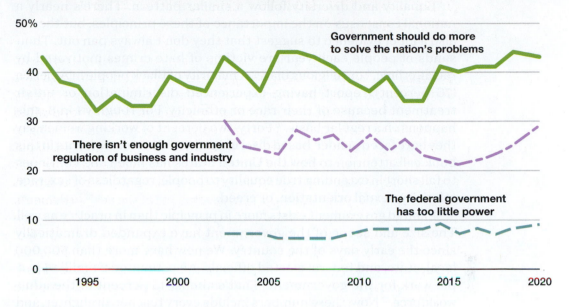

Note: Lines represent the percentage of people who agree with each statement.

Source: Data come from Gallup polls conducted each year from 1992 through 2020; see Note 13 for full source information.

of business, and 9 out of 10 people don't think the government needs more power. These views have held steady over time, indicated by lines that show only moderate fluctuation.

Is the American Dream a Reality?

Most Americans cherish the ideals of liberty, equality, and limited government. But these ideals are not the lived experience for many Americans. There's a big difference between the American Dream and American reality.

Take liberty and individualism. Economic opportunity abounds, and people value the ideals of hard work and the success it can bring. But economic inequality is staggering. The richest 1 percent of families now earn roughly 25 times as much as the other 99 percent of the population.[14] Or consider this: in 2020, CEOs of the 350 biggest publicly traded companies in the United States averaged compensation of $24.2 million per year. That's 351 times the income of the average American.[15] As a result of these income disparities, more than one-third of Americans (35 percent) don't believe that hard work guarantees success.[16] In fact, more than 80 percent believe that the rich get richer while the poor get poorer.[17]

Equality and diversity follow a similar pattern. There's nearly a national consensus on the importance of these principles, but there's also a lot of evidence to suggest that they don't always pan out. Thousands of people each year are victims of hate crimes motivated by racial, ethnic,[18] or religious bias.[19] A majority of Black people in America (76 percent) report having experienced discrimination or unfair treatment because of their race or ethnicity. For roughly 1 in 8, this happens on a regular basis.[20] Forty-two percent of working women say they have faced gender-based discrimination.[21] Several segments in this book call attention to how the United States has fallen and continues to fall short in extending true equality to people, regardless of sex, race, ethnicity, sexual orientation, or creed.

Limited government exists more in principle than in practice as well. The size and scope of the government have expanded dramatically since the early days of the country. We now have more than 500,000 local, state, and federal elected officials. An estimated 24 million people work for the government. That's almost 15 percent of the adult workforce.[22] Now, these numbers include every teacher, firefighter, and IRS agent out there—all of whom perform important work and without whom the day-to-day operations of the country would be compromised. So falling short on the "limited government" dimension isn't necessarily the same problem as it is when we fall short with liberty or equality. But the scope of government is much broader than it was envisioned in the early days of the country, when society was far less complicated.

None of these observations is meant to suggest that the values undergirding the American Dream are no longer core principles of our political culture. Quite the contrary. The promise of the Dream is so deeply embedded in the American psyche—and has been for so long—that the reality of whether it materializes doesn't detract from the belief in the ideals it represents.

DID YOU GET IT?
What is the American Dream?

Short Answer:
- "The American Dream" refers to the idea that everyone has the opportunity to succeed in this country. The concept captures many of the central values of American political culture, including liberty, equality, and limited self-government.

- Not only did these values shape America's political development, but most citizens today still believe in them.
- Although the ideal remains intact, the execution of the American Dream has been much less successful.

DEVELOPING YOUR SKILLS

Quantitative Literacy

Make predictions: Determining the prospects for achieving the American Dream requires relying on public opinion data to gauge trends in people's attitudes. Look at the figures presented in this segment to assess the extent to which the American Dream seems attainable, and for whom.

1. Take a look at Figure 1. Which change over the next decade would represent the biggest shift in beliefs that the American Dream is attainable?
   a. College graduates become the most likely group to believe the Dream is attainable.
   b. Black people become the least likely racial group to believe the Dream is attainable.
   c. Roughly 80 percent of all citizens become convinced that they will achieve the Dream.
   d. Democrats become more likely than Republicans to believe the Dream is attainable.

2. Figure 3 displays recent attitudes on several issues pertaining to equality and diversity. If you wanted to predict whether citizens' support for inclusivity will increase over the next few years, what information would be most helpful?
   a. Data that present people's attitudes on these issues in the 1970s
   b. Data that present people's attitudes on these issues in the 1980s, 1990s, and 2000s
   c. Recent data on other measures of citizens' attitudes about civil rights and equality
   d. The same data presented in Figure 3, but broken down by race and ethnicity

3. Given trends in public opinion about the federal government (see Figure 4), which attitude is most likely to remain stable for the foreseeable future?
   a. The belief that the federal government has too little power
   b. The belief that the government should do more to regulate business and industry
   c. The belief that the government should do more to solve people's problems
   d. All three seem equally likely to remain stable.

The Democracy Project, a bipartisan organization dedicated to promoting and defending democratic values, commissioned a poll in 2018 to assess whether Americans supported democratic norms. The results are summarized in six "findings" in the report posted on the organization's website: https://www.democracyprojectreport.org/. Take a look at the report, and answer the following questions:

- Identify two findings in the study that could be a cause of worry if they get worse over the next 10 years. In a sentence or two, explain why these findings concern you. Be sure to cite specific numbers from the report.

- After perusing the report, are you more or less concerned about the future of U.S. democracy? Again, a sentence or two is all you need to explain your answer. Cite some specific statistics if possible.

Want to Know More?

Pop culture is filled with rags-to-riches movies that epitomize the idea that with hard work and determination, anyone can succeed in America. Some of our favorites are *The Pursuit of Happyness*, *The Social Network*, and *Hidden Figures*. *Forrest Gump* is terrific, too (albeit completely unrealistic). If you don't like our recommendations, google "best rags-to-riches movies" or "best American Dream movies" and you'll find a bunch of top-10 lists.

2.
How did 55 guys hammer out the Constitution?

#FoundingDebates

On a hot night in the summer of 1787, the City Tavern in Philadelphia was hopping. Among the revelers were the nation's Founders, including George Washington and Benjamin Franklin. Fifty-five delegates from 12 of the 13 states had convened a Constitutional Convention four months earlier because the **Articles of Confederation** — the nation's first governing document — had become unworkable. With no president, no power to tax citizens or build a military, and a system that required all 13 states to agree to any changes to the document, the Articles were ill-equipped to respond to either domestic or international threats. The Founders quickly realized, however, that it was one thing to agree that the Articles of Confederation didn't work. It was another to achieve consensus over what a new government should

Established in 1773, City Tavern in Philadelphia is the nation's oldest bar. Today's cocktail menu includes many of the Founders' favorites, which they enjoyed as they celebrated drafting the Constitution, which was no easy feat.

look like. At times, tempers flared. Some of the controversies seemed so difficult to navigate that the prospects of forming a new government approached the brink of failure. But the delegates persevered. After working, debating, and arguing in a hot, poorly ventilated room over the course of 115 days, their work finally neared completion. And they needed a drink.

So two days before the Convention ended, the Founders descended upon the city tavern and appeared to have quite a night. To commemorate their accomplishments — they had drafted a new constitution, after all — the men consumed 54 bottles of Madeira wine, 60 bottles of claret wine, 8 bottles of whiskey, 22 of porter, 8 of hard cider, 12 of beer, and 7 bowls of alcoholic punch.[1] The bill from that evening? £89 (pounds sterling), which is equivalent to about $16,230 today.[2] Although this bar tab might seem excessive — actually, there's no other word to describe it; it is excessive — by the end of this segment you'll see why they felt such a celebration was in order. More specifically, you'll come to understand the four main controversies the Founders confronted in writing the Constitution, and you'll see how the compromises they struck more than two centuries ago bear directly on the way the U.S. government functions today.

How did 55 guys hammer out the Constitution?

Controversy #1: The Strength of the National Government

It is obviously impractical in the federal government of these states, to secure all rights of independent sovereignty to each, and yet provide for the interest and safety of all.

George Washington,
President of the Constitutional Convention[3]

An elective despotism was not the government we fought for; but one which should not only be founded on free principles, but in which the powers of government should be so divided and balanced among several bodies of magistracy.

Thomas Jefferson,
Principal author of the Declaration of Independence[4]

It might not be totally clear from these two quotes (the Founders could be a little formal and verbose), but perhaps the most fundamental debate at the Constitutional Convention centered on the power of the national government. The whole reason the colonists had declared independence in the first place was because of a too-powerful British monarchy. They were taxed by the king but not represented in Parliament, persecuted on religious grounds, and denied the same rights that British citizens enjoyed. So upon declaring independence, they deliberately created a weak national government—one with no executive or judicial branch, no power to raise an army, and no authority to regulate interstate commerce. All of that was left to the states. Each had its own militia, currency, and foreign policy.

But life under the Articles of Confederation was a mess. The country had no money, no way to ward off external threats, no system to manage trade, and no ability to temper internal strife. In 1786, the federal government couldn't even help quash the efforts of Daniel Shays, a Massachusetts farmer who led 4,000 Revolutionary War veterans to rebel against the national government. The government had seized land from farmers who couldn't afford to pay their taxes, so Shays and his men launched a series of violent attacks on federal courthouses in Massachusetts. Soon they escalated to other federal properties. Things came to a head when they made plans to procure weapons by raiding a federal arsenal in Springfield. A privately funded militia ultimately suppressed the effort, but the lesson of **Shays's Rebellion** was clear: the country lacked an effective national government.

Where to strike the balance between an exceedingly strong and a virtually powerless national government was an overriding concern at the Constitutional Convention. Many delegates, including Alexander Hamilton and James Madison, advocated for a strong federal government that could steer the direction of the young nation. Other delegates worried that with too much power concentrated at the top, the new nation could evolve into a monarchy. Ultimately, they agreed to create a stronger national government than what would have prevailed under the Articles of Confederation, but they included two central features to diminish the possibility that a tyrant could rise to power.

First, the new national government embodied a **separation of powers** in which responsibilities were divided among a legislature, an executive, and a judiciary. We detail the specific powers of each branch in Segment 3, but it's important to note here that among the powers given to each branch were ways to monitor the other two. The system of **checks and balances** sought to ensure that no one branch of the national government, and no one elected leader, would ever become too powerful. A president with aspirations to act like a king, for instance, could be thwarted by Congress. But Congress didn't have all the power either. The president's signature was required to pass a law.

Second, the Founders created a system of **federalism**, which meant that the national government would share power with the states. The federal government had fundamental powers—such as conducting foreign policy, regulating interstate commerce, and raising an army—so that never again would an incident like Shays's Rebellion be a threat. But under the system of federalism, any powers not specifically assigned to the federal government were left to the states.[5] (We elaborate on this arrangement in Segment 7.)

Controversy #2: The Influence of Large States versus Small States

Every idea of proportion and every rule of fair representation conspire to condemn a principle, which gives to Rhode Island an equal weight in the scale of power with Massachusetts, or Connecticut, or New York.

Alexander Hamilton,
Advocate of the Virginia Plan[6]

Every State in the Union as a State possesses an equal right to, and share of, sovereignty, freedom, and independence.

William Paterson,
Author of the New Jersey Plan[7]

If you translate Hamilton and Paterson's quotes into modern English, then you'll see the battle lines of what turned out to be one of the most difficult issues to resolve at the Convention: how to determine states' representation (or power) in the new government. In 1787, like today, state population varied substantially. The estimates in Figure 1 illustrate that Virginia, the largest state, had a population 16 times that of the smallest state, Georgia.[8] So it should come as no surprise that small and large states had different ideas about how many representatives each state should get in the national legislature.

Under the Articles of Confederation, each state—regardless of its population—had one vote in the national government. The small states

FIGURE 1. Population Estimates, 1787

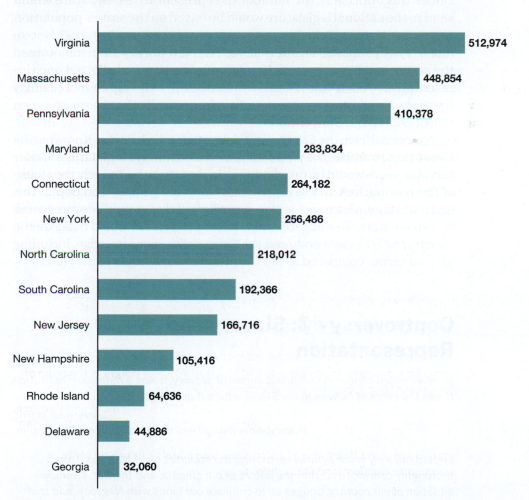

Note: Bars represent the population estimates for each state at the time of the Constitutional Convention.

Source: Lee Ann Potter, "Population Estimates Used by Congress during the Constitutional Convention," *Social Education*.

were determined to keep it that way. They worried about being run over by bigger states and didn't want to relinquish any of their power. In fact, the Delaware delegation was under strict orders from their state legislature not to approve any design that didn't preserve the one-state/one-vote rule. Larger states, in contrast, did not want their voices diluted. Based on what logic, they wondered, should a citizen in Rhode Island have seven times the representation of a citizen living right next door in Massachusetts? (Based on the estimates in Figure 1, Rhode Island's population was only about one-seventh the size of that of Massachusetts'.)

To begin the process of deliberation, James Madison, as part of the **Virginia Plan**, advocated for a system of **proportional representation**. Under this approach, the number of representatives any state would send to the national legislature would be based on the state's population. As you might guess, the large states loved it. The small states? Not so much. They proposed an alternative. The **New Jersey Plan** maintained the status quo from the Articles of Confederation and allotted one representative to each state. Madison and his supporters grew increasingly frustrated, and tensions escalated so dramatically that there was even talk of ending the Convention.

A proposal from the Connecticut delegation saved the day. Known as the **Great Compromise**, the plan established a **bicameral legislature**. Under this plan, there would be two chambers in the legislative branch: the House of Representatives, where representation would be based on population, and the Senate, where each state—regardless of size—would be represented by two senators. To mitigate concerns that the House would bulldoze the Senate, the Founders endowed the Senate with more prestige, including six-year terms, compared to two-year terms for members of the House.

Controversy #3: Slavery and Representation

[I] never would concur in upholding domestic slavery. It was a nefarious institution. It was the curse of heaven in the States where it prevailed.

Gouverneur Morris,
Pennsylvania delegate to the Constitutional Convention[9]

I would raise my voice against restricting the importation of Negroes. I am . . . thoroughly convinced . . . that the nature of our climate, and the flat, swampy situation of our country, obliges us to cultivate our lands with Negroes, and that without them South Carolina would soon be a desert waste.

Charles Pinckney,
South Carolina delegate to the Constitutional Convention[10]

How did 55 guys hammer out the Constitution?

When the delegates convened in Philadelphia, the United States was a slave nation. At the time, approximately 700,000 enslaved persons, constituting close to 20 percent of the total population, lived in the 13 states. Almost half the delegates to the Convention, including James Madison and George Washington, were slaveowners. And the slave trade was going strong. Domestic and international slave traders were still capturing and transporting Africans and selling them as labor in the United States. The movement against slavery, however, was also well underway. Delegates Alexander Hamilton, John Jay, and Benjamin Franklin (a former slaveowner himself) were members of antislavery societies.[11] The abolitionists' fiery rhetoric versus the dispassionate, but resolved, arguments of the proslavery forces ultimately posed two dilemmas for the Founders: (1) how to deal with the moral controversy of slavery, and (2) how to count enslaved persons for the purposes of representation in the new House of Representatives.

The Founders resolved the first dilemma—the moral one—by choosing not to resolve it at all. Some of the states, including Virginia and South Carolina, insisted that slave labor was critical to their economic well-being. Five others—Massachusetts, Pennsylvania, Connecticut, Rhode Island, and New Hampshire—had already ended slavery or passed laws to phase it out. Given the states' deep-seated and competing beliefs, the Founders essentially kicked the can down the road, consciously choosing not to put the word "slavery" in the Constitution. Anywhere. In fact, they were so eager to avoid a debate over slavery that they restricted the new government from addressing the slave trade for at least 20 years. Article I, Section 9, of the Constitution states: "The Migration or Importation of such Persons as any of the States now existing shall think proper to admit, shall not be prohibited by the Congress prior to the Year one thousand eight hundred and eight." That means no national law banning slavery could be passed until 1808. Hardly a bold move, and definitely a significant blemish on the document today.

The Founders agreed to address the second dilemma much more directly, although the solution wasn't obvious. States with enslaved people wanted them counted as part of the population because that would mean more representation in the new government. States that prohibited slavery, in contrast, opposed slavery and couldn't justify counting enslaved persons simply for the purposes of representation. They also knew that their own power in the new government would be diluted if slave states were allowed to use enslaved people to bulk up their population counts. This debate had real ramifications for determining each state's population. Take a look at the data in Table 1.[12] The leftmost column rank orders the states according to the population of recognized "citizens"—in

TABLE 1. State Rankings, Depending on Who Gets Counted

⬆⬇ State Population Ranking

Non-Slave Population		Total Population (including slaves)		Non-Slave Population + Three-Fifths of Slaves	
Virginia	512,974	Virginia	805,601	Virginia	688,550
Massachusetts	448,854	Massachusetts	448,854	Massachusetts	448,854
Pennsylvania	410,378	Pennsylvania	414,085	Pennsylvania	412,602
Maryland	283,834	Maryland	386,870	Maryland	345,656
Connecticut	264,182	⬆ North Carolina	318,795	⬆ North Carolina	278,482
New York	256,486	⬆ South Carolina	299,460	New York	269,202
North Carolina	218,012	⬇ New York	277,679	⬇ Connecticut	265,771
South Carolina	192,366	⬇ Connecticut	266,830	South Carolina	256,622
New Jersey	166,716	New Jersey	178,139	New Jersey	173,570
New Hampshire	105,416	New Hampshire	105,416	New Hampshire	105,510
Rhode Island	64,636	Rhode Island	65,594	Rhode Island	65,211
Delaware	44,886	⬆ Georgia	61,324	Delaware	50,218
Georgia	32,060	⬇ Delaware	53,773	Georgia	49,618

Note: Entries reflect population estimates for each state at the time of the Constitutional Convention.

Source: Lee Ann Potter, "Population Estimates Used by Congress during the Constitutional Convention," Social Education 70:50 (2006): 270–72.

other words, nonslaves. The middle column rank orders the states when we count both citizens and enslaved persons.

Notice that states like Virginia and Maryland see substantial increases in their populations when enslaved persons are counted. North and South Carolina even move up in the rankings (indicated by the green text). New York, Connecticut, and Delaware, however, all fare worse when enslaved people are counted (indicated by the red text). Depending on the rules for counting the population, states could gain or lose representatives.

To resolve the controversy over how to count enslaved persons, the delegates struck perhaps the most abhorrent political deal of the Convention. Delegates James Wilson and Roger Sherman introduced the **Three-Fifths Compromise**: for the purposes of determining a state's population, each enslaved person would count

How did 55 guys hammer out the Constitution?

as three-fifths of a person, but would still have zero-fifths of the rights of a citizen. The rightmost column in Table 1 reports population sizes based on the compromise, which resulted in only two changes in state rankings and more of a middle ground for population counts.

Controversy #4: Protecting Individuals' Rights from an Oppressive Government

The question then will be, whether a consolidated government can preserve the freedom and secure the rights of the people. If such amendments be introduced as shall exclude danger, I shall most gladly put my hand to it.

George Mason,
Virginia delegate to the Constitutional Convention[13]

The powers delegated by the proposed Constitution to the federal government are few and defined. Those which are to remain in the State governments are numerous and indefinite.

James Madison,
Arguing in *Federalist 45* against a Bill of Rights[14]

You might not be able to tell from Mason and Madison's words, but another key debate at the Convention focused on whether the new Constitution did enough to protect individuals and states from the reach of the federal government. Virginia's George Mason had drafted the Virginia Declaration of Rights in 1776. It had affirmed citizens' rights to life, liberty, and property and described the government as a "servant of the people."[15] Mason wanted to include similar language in the U.S. Constitution. James Madison, among other delegates, was unpersuaded about the need to include these protections explicitly. He believed that the Constitution already limited the federal government's power, and he worried that itemizing individual rights could erroneously signal that the rights included in the list were the only rights that were protected.

This was one controversy the Founders did not resolve at the Convention. With heels dug in on both sides of the debate, the Constitution's fate hung in the balance. After all, the Founders agreed that in order for the new Constitution to become law, two-thirds of the states—9 out of 13—had to approve it in their legislatures. And this **ratification process** was no sure thing. The Federalists, who famously stated their case in a series of essays entitled the ***Federalist Papers***, tried to reassure skeptics about the structure and features of the government they had designed. But Mason, one of three delegates at the Convention who refused to sign the new Constitution, didn't leave his opposition in Philadelphia. He helped lead the anti-Federalists in the lengthy debate over ratification, arguing that it was necessary to include a **Bill of Rights** that specified citizens' protections from the government.

Nearly 10 months after the Convention ended, New Hampshire became the ninth state to ratify the Constitution. But Virginia still wasn't on board. Without support from the largest state, it probably wouldn't be feasible to implement. So at a rancorous ratification debate in the Virginia state legislature, James Madison promised, as a first order of business in the new government, to propose to amend the Constitution with a Bill of Rights. Virginia voted for ratification, and Madison was true to his word. In the opening session of Congress, he proposed 12 amendments to the Constitution. Ten of these, including amendments that guaranteed freedom of speech and the press, protected religious freedom, and placed limits on the police power of the state, were added in 1791.

Ending on a Celebratory Note

Completing a draft of the Constitution was no easy task, and the controversies the Founders had to resolve were deep and far-reaching. But at 230 years and counting, the U.S. Constitution is among the longest-standing governing documents in the world. So perhaps the Founders did deserve a drink at City Tavern. Or 20.

DID YOU GET IT?
How did 55 guys hammer out the Constitution?

Short Answer:

- They prevented too powerful a national government by developing a system of separation of powers, checks and balances, and federalism.
- They allocated representation of small versus large states with a bicameral legislature.
- They dealt with controversies related to slavery by agreeing to delay any new federal laws on slavery until 1808 and adopting the Three-Fifths Compromise.
- They addressed protections for individuals' rights with a promise to add a Bill of Rights.

DEVELOPING YOUR SKILLS

Consuming Political Information

Check the facts: Politicians love quoting the Founders because they think it gives their arguments more weight. But that doesn't mean they quote them correctly. One of the best ways to fact-check is by consulting original documents. Give it a shot.

1. At a political fundraiser, President Barack Obama quoted from the Declaration of Independence. He said, "We hold these truths to be self-evident, that all men are created equal, that each of us are endowed with certain inalienable rights, that among these are life, liberty, and the pursuit of happiness." Did Obama quote the Declaration of Independence correctly?

   a. Yes, the quote is correct.

   b. No, he left out a few key words.

   c. No, he changed many of the words around.

   d. No, this quote is from the Preamble to the Constitution.

2. Herman Cain, who ran for president in 2012, regularly told supporters that the Constitution provides for "the right of the people to alter or abolish" the government. Based on your read of the key documents from the Founding, did Cain get it right?

   a. Yes, he quoted the Constitution correctly.

   b. No, this is a quote from the Declaration of Independence.

   c. No, this is a quote from *Federalist 10*.

   d. No, this is a quote from the Articles of Confederation.

3. At a 2017 political rally in Florida, President Donald Trump quoted Thomas Jefferson as saying, "Nothing can be believed which is seen in a newspaper." Read the original source of this quote — an 1807 letter written by Jefferson to John Norvell, who later became a newspaper editor and U.S. senator — here: https://founders.archives .gov/documents/Jefferson/99-01-02-5737. Did Trump characterize Jefferson's words accurately?

   a. Yes, Trump and Jefferson are kindred spirits. They both want to ban the news media.

   b. No, Trump made this quote up.

   c. No, Jefferson's quote really had nothing to do with newspapers.

   d. Sort of, but Jefferson's quote was really about how newspapers no longer distinguish between facts and conjecture.

FIGURE IT OUT

Fact-check these three contemporary politicians quoting the Founders. More specifically, for each quote: (1) determine whether the quote is accurate — both in terms of the words themselves and the person to whom it's attributed; (2) identify the source(s) you used to make your determination; and (3) explain why you can trust the source you consulted.

- Speaking in Greenville, South Carolina, Senator Rand Paul once quoted anti-Federalist Patrick Henry like this: "The Constitution is about restraining the government, not the people."

- In a congressional primary debate against Congressman Jerry Nadler, Oliver Rosenberg quoted Alexander Hamilton as saying, "This is not a moment, this is the movement. Foes oppose us, we take an honest stand. We roll like Moses, claiming our promised land. Rise up, rise up, and vote."

- Texas congressman Louie Gohmert, in a speech opposing health care legislation, read this quote from George Washington: "Government is not reason. It is not eloquence. It is force. Like fire, it is a dangerous servant and a fearful master."

Want to Know More?

Comedy Central's *Drunk History* series offers a fun take on the Constitutional Convention and many of the Founders themselves. The episodes entitled "Hamilton," "Philadelphia," and "Boston" are especially relevant to the content in this segment. You might also be interested in taking two BuzzFeed quizzes: "Which Founding Father Are You?" (https://www.buzzfeed.com/jamesgrebey/which-founding-father-are-you) and "Which Founding Father Is Your Soulmate?" (https://www.buzzfeed.com/kristinchirico/alexander-hamilton-was-a-total-babe).

3.
Which branch of government did the Founders intend to be the most powerful?

#SeparationOfPowers

I am not running for office to be King of America. I respect the Constitution. I've read the Constitution. I've sworn an oath to it many times.

President Joe Biden[1]

Just because a couple of people on the Supreme Court declare something to be "constitutional" does not make it so.

Senator Rand Paul[2]

When somebody is the president of the United States, the authority is total and that's the way it's got to be. . . . It's total.

President Donald Trump[3]

Throughout U.S. history, the three branches of the federal government have battled for power. Although the Founders had a clear vision for which branch should be most powerful, the three branches have always battled for power.

On any given day, the most powerful branch of government can seem like a moving target. Just take a quick look at the news. Some headlines — like "Congress Steamrolls Obama's Veto"[4] or "Biden's Agenda Hits Senate Slowdown"[5] — would lead you to believe that Congress has the upper hand and can readily impose its will on the president. Others, including "U.S. Supreme Court Rules Half of Oklahoma Is Native American Land"[6] and "In Blow to Trump, Supreme Court Won't Hear Appeal of DACA Ruling,"[7] imply that the judiciary can make sweeping rulings and even thwart the will of the White House. Still other news alerts point toward a different answer. How could you read "Biden Will Withdraw All U.S. Forces from Afghanistan by September 11, 2021"[8] or "Biden Expands 'Obamacare' by Cutting Health Insurance Costs"[9] and not think that presidents can simply do whatever they want? It can be dizzying even thinking about which branch of government has the most authority.

This would come as no surprise to the Founders. They expected the legislature, the president, and the judiciary to compete for power. That's why they granted specific powers to each branch of government. And it's why they embedded checks and balances as a defining feature of the system they designed. The goal was to keep any individual, small group, or branch from becoming too powerful. As

Which branch of government did the Founders intend to be the most powerful?

James Madison put it in *Federalist 51*, "Ambition must be made to counteract ambition."[10]

We realize that if you grew up in the United States, the concepts of separation of powers and checks and balances have been drilled into your head since about third grade. We know that reading about them again might be painfully dull. But these concepts are among the most foundational elements for understanding how the government was designed and how it functions today. So this segment tries to do two things: (1) lay out the specific powers and the checks and balances the Constitution assigns to the legislature, executive, and judiciary; and (2) keep you from falling asleep. To that end, we use the national drinking age — an issue you may care at least a little bit about — to assess the powers of each branch of government. You'll soon see that the Founders did not create a government with three equally powerful branches. Rather, they designed a document and a form of government that — in at least three ways — prioritizes legislative authority. But you'll also leave the segment with an awareness that although most of the Founders intended for Congress to be the most powerful branch, things have changed quite a bit in the last 230 years.

Assessing the Relative Power of the Three Branches, and Using Alcohol to Do It

The national drinking age in the United States is 21. Penalties for underage drinking vary from one state to the next—from fines, to driver's license suspensions, to community service, to jail time[11]—but in almost all circumstances, it is illegal for people under the age of 21 to purchase or consume alcohol. To put the U.S. law into perspective, no other advanced democracy sets the drinking age at 21. In fact, 10 percent of countries actually have no drinking age at all. Most others set it at age 18. Overall, 86 percent of nations have a drinking age lower than the United States; more than half of those that don't are majority-Muslim countries that ban alcohol entirely.

For the purposes of this segment, imagine that you and most of your friends think this law makes no sense. After all, 18-year-olds are otherwise considered adults. You can vote. You can serve in the military. You can be approved by a bank to borrow tens of thousands of dollars to pay for college. Is it too much to ask that as an 18-, 19-, or 20-year-old you should be able to have a beer? (Yes, we know that not all college students drink. Just humor us.) Now imagine that you—like lots of students throughout the country—want to change this law. Which branch

College students call for a lower drinking age. At the University of Kansas (left), students from the National Youth Rights Association held a rally to advocate for reducing the drinking age to 18. The school newspaper at Boston University used this image of a frothy beer glass (right) in a series of articles that debated the proper drinking age on campus.

of government should you turn to? Which branch has the most authority to help you get it done?

The Layout of the Constitution: The Legislative Branch Is Number One

The first step in trying to figure out which branch of government would be most helpful in your quest to lower the drinking age is to look at the Constitution. A cursory glance at the document suggests that if you want to change the drinking age—or for that matter, do almost anything—the legislative branch may be your best bet. The most obvious indication that the Founders intended for the legislative branch to be most powerful is the way they organized the Constitution. Consider the facts listed in Table 1.[12]

From the order of the articles, to the number of words and sections in each, to the listing of powers and responsibilities, the legislative branch comes out on top. Not only did the Founders literally place Congress ahead of the executive and judicial branches in the Constitution, but they devoted more than twice as many words to describing the legislature and defining its responsibilities than they did to the president. The same is true when we focus on the **enumerated powers**—those specifically laid out in the Constitution—of each branch. Congress has two and half times the number of powers as the president and more than 10 times the number given to the judiciary.

Which branch of government did the Founders intend to be the most powerful?

TABLE 1. The Constitution by the Numbers

	Legislative Branch (Article I)	Executive Branch (Article II)	Judicial Branch (Article III)
Placement in the Constitution	First	Second	Third
Number of words in the article	2,266	1,023	375
Number of sections in the article	10	4	3
Number of specific powers and responsiblities	32	13	2

Note: Data come from the transcript of the United States Constitution housed at the National Archives. Powers and responsibilities entries are based on items specifically enumerated in the document.

Source: "The Constitution of the United States: A Transcription," National Archives.

A Closer Look at the Enumerated Powers: The Legislative Branch Wins Again

Determining which branch of government is the most powerful also involves assessing the substantive responsibilities allocated to each. Table 2 lists 48 powers granted to the federal government by the Constitution (in the order they appear in the document). In short, Congress makes the laws. The executive branch carries out the laws. And the judicial branch interprets the laws. Beyond its lawmaking authority, notice that two-thirds of the federal government's powers and responsibilities belong to Congress, including many of the most important. That's why, for our purposes, Congress looks best positioned to change the national drinking age.

Right off the bat, because Congress initiates bills and establishes laws, it can use its power to write a national piece of legislation to lower the minimum drinking age. If Congress passes a bill and the president signs it, that's it. The law is changed. In fact, Congress's central lawmaking authority established the current drinking age: in 1984, Congress passed the National Minimum Drinking Age Act, which set the age at 21.[13]

But passing a law isn't Congress's only option. The legislative branch can also propose constitutional amendments. These are really hard to pass (see Segment 5), but Congress is the only branch authorized to try. In this case, an amendment could permanently change the

TABLE 2. Powers Enumerated by the Constitution to Each Branch

Legislative Branch *(makes the laws)*

1. Impeach president and judges
2. Organize federal elections
3. Initiate appropriations bills
4. Override presidential vetoes
5. Impose and collect taxes
6. Pay debts
7. Borrow money
8. Regulate trade with other nations
9. Regulate interstate commerce
10. Establish immigration laws
11. Establish bankruptcy laws
12. Coin money
13. Regulate currency
14. Punish counterfeiters
15. Establish post offices
16. Issue patents and copyrights
17. Organize lower-court system
18. Punish piracy
19. Punish offenses against international law
20. Declare war
21. Capture enemy war combatants
22. Punish war combatants
23. Raise and support an army
24. Build and maintain a navy
25. Fund, arm, and discipline the military
26. Fight insurrections and invasions
27. Legislate over federal property
28. Make all laws necessary and proper to carry out enumerated responsibilities
29. Declare and punish treason
30. Approve treaties
31. Issue advice and grant consent for presidential appointments
32. Propose constitutional amendments

Executive Branch *(carries out the laws)*

1. Vice president is president of the Senate
2. Sign bills into law
3. Veto legislation
4. "Take care" that the laws are faithfully executed
5. Serve as commander in chief
6. Grant pardons
7. Enter into treaties
8. Appoint ambassadors, federal judges, executive branch officials
9. Report on the state of the Union
10. Convene Congress
11. Adjourn Congress
12. Receive ambassadors
13. Commission officers of the United States

Judicial Branch *(interprets the laws)*

1. Chief justice presides over presidential impeachment
2. Holds original jurisdiction over certain cases
3. Exercise judicial review*

Note: Powers for each branch are listed in the order they appear in the Constitution.
* The power of judicial review was not specifically listed in the Constitution. It became a formal power only after the 1803 decision in *Marbury v. Madison*.

Which branch of government did the Founders intend to be the most powerful?

Constitution to reflect the new drinking age. Congress can also use the power to appropriate money to strip all funding from federal agencies that enforce underage drinking laws. As part of its responsibility to regulate interstate commerce, Congress can make it easier to transport alcohol to states that support lower drinking ages. And because Congress regulates all federal lands, it can lower the drinking age on federal properties, such as national parks.

Changing the minimum drinking age is only one example of how Congress often has the upper hand. Who controls the nation's purse strings—from collecting taxes, to coining and borrowing money, to regulating international trade? Congress. Who declares war? Congress. Who builds and maintains the military? Congress. We'll spare you a tedious naming of the remaining powers. You can see them for yourself in Table 2. But it's worth mentioning one more. The **necessary and proper clause** establishes that Congress has the power "to make all laws which shall be necessary and proper for carrying into execution the foregoing powers." Simply put, Congress has authority to pass whatever laws it deems necessary to carry out all of its explicitly assigned powers.

The Constitution is far less generous in assigning explicit power to the other two branches of government. What can the president really do to get the drinking age raised? Not much. The president can suggest legislation during the annual State of the Union address. But that's really only the power to ask for, not to enact, a law. The president can use the appointment power to fill the courts and government agencies with people who support a lower drinking age. But it's not clear whether these officials would have much authority to enact any change. The president could order the Justice Department, which includes the FBI, not to assist with the enforcement of underage drinking laws. But these actions would fall short of actually changing the drinking age. That's because at the end of the day, the executive branch's primary responsibility as outlined in the Constitution is to "take care that the laws be faithfully executed." This **take care clause** means that presidents must implement the laws Congress enacts, regardless of whether they like them.

Beyond the formal powers we've already discussed, the Constitution confers to the president several additional responsibilities: acting as commander in chief of the military, conducting U.S. foreign policy (receiving ambassadors and making treaties), and issuing a veto when Congress passes a law the president opposes (see middle of Table 2). These powers are probably not helpful for your purposes, but they demonstrate that the Founders did give the executive branch critical roles.

Compare that to the way the Founders envisioned the Supreme Court. If you want to enlist the judiciary to help you change the minimum drinking age, your options are really limited. The Constitution tasks the Court with only two explicit powers: (1) to hear "all cases affecting ambassadors, other public ministers and consuls, and those in which a state shall be party"; and (2) to preside over the trial should the president ever be impeached. That's it. Neither of these is very helpful for your cause. But not long after the Constitution was ratified, the Supreme Court determined that it also had the power of **judicial review**—it could determine whether local, state, and federal actions and laws are consistent with the Constitution. So you could argue that laws setting the national drinking age at 21 are unconstitutional, perhaps making the case that 18-year-olds are considered full adult citizens in so many other domains. It's a long shot, but if the Court agreed to hear the case (very unlikely) and ultimately ruled in your favor, that could do it.

Checks and Balances: The Legislative Branch Comes Out on Top Yet Again

The system of checks and balances the Founders created is a way for the three branches to restrain one another. On this dimension, the differences among the branches aren't as stark. But overall, Congress still has more tools to check the executive and judicial branches than either of them has to check Congress.

This becomes clear when we turn back to the national drinking age. Assume that Congress passed a law to lower the age to 18, but the president vetoed it. That's not the end of the game. Congress can override a president's veto if two-thirds of the members of each branch vote to do so. Then the president has no recourse. Or let's say that the president refuses to implement the new drinking age law. Congress can play hardball and try to impeach the president for refusing to implement the new law. The Senate can also reject the president's appointments of anyone opposed to lowering the drinking age. If the Supreme Court gets involved and declares the new national drinking age law unconstitutional, that would likely be the last word. But even then, it doesn't have to be final. Congress could propose a constitutional amendment to nullify the judicial decision.

We know these circumstances are far-fetched. But they reveal that Congress generally has the potential to have the last word as far as new laws are concerned. In fact, even separate and apart from its lawmaking authority, Congress has more tools to combat the other two branches than they each do. Take a look at Table 3. Each row lists the checks enumerated in the Constitution that each branch has over the other two.

Which branch of government did the Founders intend to be the most powerful?

TABLE 3. Summary of Constitutionally Enumerated Checks and Balances

	. . . the Legislature	. . . the Executive	. . . the Judiciary
Legislative checks on . . .		• Power to impeach • Override vetoes • Approve treaties • Confirm appointments • Conduct investigations into the executive branch • Refuse to fund president's initiatives	• Power to impeach • Organize lower courts • Change size of the Supreme Court • Introduce a constitutional amendment
Executive checks on . . .	• Vice president is president of Senate (and casts tie-breaking votes) • Veto legislation • Call Congress into session • Adjourn Congress • Determine how and to what extent to implement a law		• Grant pardons • Appoint federal judges
Judicial checks on . . .	• Use judicial review to declare a law unconstitutional • Chief justice presides over Senate during a president's impeachment trial	• Use judicial review to declare an action of the executive unconstitutional • Preside over a president's impeachment trial	

In the first row, for example, you'll see that Congress can directly check the executive branch in six ways. Four of these checks—impeachment, overriding vetoes, investigating the executive branch, and refusing to fund the president's initiatives—happen after the president engages in behavior or decision making that Congress opposes. The other two checks—approving treaties and confirming appointments—are ways Congress can constrain the president from the outset. The final column in that row itemizes the four congressional checks over the judiciary.

Compared to Congress's 10 direct checks, the executive branch has only seven, and the judicial branch just four. Don't get us wrong—some are very important. The president's veto power can stop a bill from becoming a law, and the pardon power can undo a federal court's decision. Similarly, the Supreme Court's power to strike down a law or presidential action as unconstitutional cannot be overstated. But on balance, the Founders gave Congress more direct checks.

Changing Times: The Legislature Isn't So Clearly Number One

A lot has changed since the Constitution was ratified. First, the Supreme Court regularly exercises judicial review. In doing so, the Court has become the final arbiter on a range of major policy issues—gay rights, abortion, gun laws, and voting rights, to name just a handful. Yet Article III doesn't explicitly give the Court this power. There's no question that the Supreme Court is on far more level footing with the other two branches now than when the Founders drafted the Constitution.

Second, and perhaps more striking, is the rise of executive power. With 15 cabinet departments and roughly 2.7 million employees, the scope and authority of the modern presidency certainly exceeds what was listed in Article II of the Constitution. Much of the executive branch's expansion resulted from Congress creating federal departments and agencies. But presidents have played a role in broadening the scope of their power, too. They've come to read provisions like the take care clause in an increasingly proactive way. The clause authorizes the president to make sure the laws of the land are fully implemented. Because this general directive is so vague, presidents have determined that executing the duties of the presidency can include proposing a budget, calling for major legislation, creating regulations, assembling a cabinet, and issuing executive orders. These **implied powers** are not written anywhere specifically, but they've served as the basis for the executive branch to accumulate more authority and responsibility.

DID YOU GET IT?

Which branch of government did the Founders intend to be the most powerful?

Short Answer:

- Most Founders were leery of executive power, so they prioritized the legislative branch.

- How the Constitution is organized, the specific powers delegated to each branch, and the ways each branch can check the other two all point to a strong legislature.
- Since the Founding, executive and judicial power have grown considerably, shifting the balance of power outlined in the Constitution.

DEVELOPING YOUR SKILLS

Persuasive Argumentation

Identify an argument: We argue that the Founders intended for the legislative branch to be the most powerful. But just because we say it doesn't mean that our argument is persuasive. Many arguments can be refuted by two other types of arguments:

- *Competing arguments* arrive at the same conclusion but for different reasons or based on different evidence.
- *Counterarguments* rely on evidence to arrive at a different conclusion.

Practice identifying competing arguments and counterarguments about the Founding.

1. Which statement is a reasonable *counterargument* to our claim that the Founders intended the legislature to be the most powerful branch?
   a. The Founders wanted the president to introduce legislation.
   b. The Constitution does not list all of the constitutionally enumerated powers of each branch. It focuses only on the powers given to Congress.
   c. There's nothing specific written in the Constitution to suggest that listing the legislative branch first was meant to demonstrate that it is the most powerful.
   d. Over time, the president has expanded the size of the executive branch.

2. We argue that the number of words in Article I suggests that the Founders wanted the legislative branch to be most powerful. Which statement is the most persuasive *competing argument*?
   a. Article II actually has more words.
   b. The historical record shows that the Founders' contempt for the British monarchy led them to favor a more powerful legislative branch.
   c. The system of checks and balances means the branches are equally powerful.
   d. Historians have uncovered documents indicating that several Founders wanted the judiciary to be the most powerful branch.

3. If you want to argue against our claim that the legislative branch is the most powerful, what could be the basis for a persuasive *counterargument*?

   a. The veto is the single greatest power because it can't be overridden.

   b. Carrying out the law is more important than making the law.

   c. The power to finalize treaties without any input from Congress allows the president to shape foreign policy single-handedly.

   d. If you add together the number of executive branch powers and checks on the other branches, then the president actually has more powers than Congress or the courts.

FIGURE IT OUT

Let's say that you just don't agree with the argument in this segment. You've read it twice and think that the Supreme Court's power to declare acts of Congress and the executive branch unconstitutional makes the judiciary the most powerful branch. Use the information presented in this segment to develop a *counterargument*. More specifically:

- Identify two facts or points that support the notion that the judiciary is more powerful than Congress. You can rely on enumerated powers, checks and balances, whatever evidence you think allows you to make the most persuasive case.

- For each point, explain why the power you identify gives the courts an edge over Congress.

Want to Know More?

The West Wing, a television drama from the 2000s, chronicles a fictional president's trials, tribulations, and successes going head to head with both Congress and the Supreme Court. The entire series offers a great account of the power struggles among the three branches of government. But if you have time to watch only one episode, then go for "Separation of Powers" from Season 5. It features a potential Supreme Court nomination, budget negotiations with a Congress that opposes the president, and a series of compromises among the branches in order to keep the government up and running.

4.
How did the Supreme Court get its power?

#JudicialReview

In May 1999, U.S. customs agents seized more than 30 gallons of hoasca tea at the New Mexico border. The shipment was en route to a U.S.-based branch of União do Vegetal, a religion that originated in Brazil. Followers of the religion drink hoasca tea as a central part of their services. The problem, according to law enforcement, was that one of the active compounds in the tea is an illegal narcotic. In a battle that pitted federal drug laws against religious freedom, the church members came out on top. They could receive shipments of hoasca tea, and they could drink it during religious services.[1]

In 2010, Congress passed and President Barack Obama signed the Affordable Care Act. You might know it as "Obamacare." A key provision of the federal health care legislation required citizens to have health insurance. If they refused, then they'd have to pay a fine when filing their taxes. The government argued that this provision of the law, known as the "individual mandate," was necessary for keeping health care affordable. Opponents — including small business owners — viewed the mandate as coercive and expensive. The government won this one: the mandate was valid law and fell under Congress's power to tax its citizens.[2]

When the Court is in session, the justices meet twice a week in this chamber. At these conferences, they exercise the power of judicial review.

In 2018, New York prosecutors opened an investigation into Donald Trump's potentially illegal business dealings. When they subpoenaed financial records from the Trump Organization's accounting firm, President Trump's personal lawyers immediately sued to block the release of the documents. They argued that the Constitution gives a sitting president immunity from any criminal process. One of President Trump's lawyers asserted — in court — that even if the president shot someone on Fifth Avenue in New York City, he could not be prosecuted for the crime. It turns out that Trump's lawyers were wrong. Presidents, just like private citizens, can be subject to criminal investigations.[3]

Who settled these disputes? Who decided the winners and the losers? Who established the line between citizens' rights and the government's authority? The Supreme Court! But how the Court acquired the power to make these decisions was quite the feat. After all, Article III of the Constitution does little to elaborate on the responsibilities and powers of the judiciary. The Constitution does set up a federal court system with a single Supreme Court at the top of the judicial branch. But the actual powers of the Court as described are vague, and nowhere does the Constitution specifically grant it the authority to review the constitutionality of laws.

So the justices took that power for themselves. That's right. The Supreme Court gave itself the power to be the final arbiter of legal disputes. In the 1803 case ***Marbury v. Madison***, the justices interpreted

How did the Supreme Court get its power?

Article III to mean that they could exercise **judicial review** — the power to determine whether local, state, and federal actions and laws are consistent with the Constitution.[4] This segment explains the background and enduring implications of the justices' actions.

An Historic Power Grab: The Story of *Marbury v. Madison*

Commentators often refer to particular Supreme Court cases as "the most important of all time." That's how they've described *Gideon v. Wainwright* (1963), *Brown v. Board of Education* (1954), and *U.S. v. Nixon* (1974), among others. Don't get us wrong—these are all very important cases, and we discuss each of them in later segments. But in fact, only *Marbury v. Madison* can really be considered the most important case of all time. It laid the foundation for almost every major Supreme Court case that would follow.

The backstory is quite dramatic, the stuff of movies. It all started with the election of 1800, which pitted President John Adams against his own vice president, Thomas Jefferson. The two men had long been close friends, but they found themselves at the center of America's first bitter and partisan presidential election campaign. Back then, the president and vice president were elected separately, so they could be members of different political parties. Adams, a Federalist, believed in a strong national government. Jefferson belonged to the Democratic-Republican Party, which favored a more limited role for government. The campaign was nasty. Jefferson hired a propagandist to sell the false story that Adams wanted to go to war with France. And his surrogates referred to Adams as a fool, hypocrite, criminal, and tyrant. Meanwhile, Adams characterized Jefferson as "a mean spirited, low-lived fellow" and "God-hater."[5] Even Martha Washington (George's wife) got involved. She characterized Jefferson as "one of the most detestable of mankind."[6] Don't let anyone tell you that there weren't personal attacks in politics in the "good old days."

In the end, Jefferson defeated Adams in a nail-biter of a race. The Federalists suffered substantial losses in the congressional elections, too. But there was a four-month lag between Election Day and when the new administration would take over. During this period, Congress passed and Adams signed the Judiciary Act of 1801, which established 58 new federal judgeships. Seizing the opportunity for the Federalists to shape the judiciary on their way out the door, Adams quickly got to work making appointments to fill all 58 positions. The Federalist-controlled Senate eagerly confirmed all the nominees.

There were just two final steps in the process of filling the judgeships. First, Adams had to sign the judicial commissions. Historians refer to them as "midnight appointments" because Adams was still completing the paperwork on his last day in office. It was down to the wire, but he got it done. Second, Secretary of State John Marshall had to deliver the commissions to the new judges. This is where things began to go off the rails. Time was short, so Marshall employed the help of his brother James. Together, they managed to deliver most of the commissions, including one to John Marshall, whom Adams had appointed chief justice of the Supreme Court. But four people never received the signed documents. Among them was William Marbury, who awaited a commission as a justice of the peace in the District of Columbia.

Under different circumstances, the new administration might have considered delivering the remaining commissions. But Jefferson was upset with the Federalists' attempts to pack the courts with their nominees. Thus, he instructed his new secretary of state, James Madison, not to deliver any of the judicial commissions that remained in Marshall's office. Jefferson's party now controlled the executive and legislative branches of government. He certainly didn't want to help the Federalists take control of the judiciary.

William Marbury, though, would not go quietly. He had been appointed by President Adams and confirmed by the Senate, exactly as the Constitution requires. He wanted his judgeship. So Marbury filed a suit with the Supreme Court and asked it to issue a **writ of mandamus**— an order directing a government official to take a particular action. Marbury's suit relied on Section 13 of the Judiciary Act of 1789. This federal law authorized the Supreme Court to issue such writs. In this case, Marbury sought a writ of mandamus demanding that Madison deliver the commission. (To help you keep track of all the names and moving parts, Table 1 lists the key players and summarizes their roles in the Supreme Court case of *Marbury v. Madison*.)[7]

The case paved the way for a tense moment of political drama. And we don't mean whether or not Marbury would become a justice of the peace. Rather, the very power of the Supreme Court was at stake. After all, the Court depends on the other branches of government to carry out its decisions. If the Court sided with Marbury and ordered Madison to deliver the commission, the Jefferson administration would likely ignore the ruling. That would send a signal to the states and the other branches of the federal government that they could disregard rulings they didn't like. The Supreme Court would be rendered powerless. But if the Court didn't side with Marbury, then it would be dismissing the constitutional basis by which judicial appointments are made.

TABLE 1. Key Players in *Marbury v. Madison*

John Adams	John Marshall	Thomas Jefferson	James Madison	William Marbury
	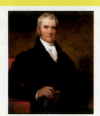	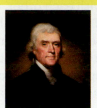		
President who lost the election of 1800. Before leaving office, he appointed a group of Federalist judges. One appointment was John Marshall as chief justice of the Supreme Court. Another was William Marbury as justice of the peace.	Adams's secretary of state. Responsible for delivering the commissions to all of Adams's newly appointed judges. Didn't have time to deliver four of the 58 commissions. Became chief justice of Supreme Court, appointed by Adams.	Defeated Adams in the presidential election of 1800. Ordered his secretary of state, James Madison, not to deliver the four judicial commissions that Marshall did not deliver before President Adams left office.	Jefferson's secretary of state. Complied with Jefferson's order not to deliver the commissions left by Adams and Marshall. Was sued by William Marbury for not delivering his commission to become a justice of the peace.	Appointed by Adams as justice of the peace. One of the four people who never received their commission. Sued Madison at the Supreme Court, asking the Court to issue a writ of mandamus ordering Madison to give him the judgeship.

Marshall found a clever way out of what seemed like an impossible situation. Writing for a unanimous Court, Marshall explained that Marbury was duly entitled to his judgeship; the appointment process had been carried out in accordance with the Constitution. But Marshall also explained that there was nothing the Supreme Court could do for Marbury. The Court determined that it did not actually have the power to issue writs of mandamus. Why? Because Section 13 of the Judiciary Act of 1789 was unconstitutional. In its first use of judicial review, the Supreme Court reasoned that the Judiciary Act, in empowering citizens to ask the Court to issue the writs, conflicted with Article III of the Constitution. Article III grants the Court **original jurisdiction** only in cases involving "ambassadors, other public ministers and consuls, and those in which a state shall be a party." "In all other cases," Article III continues, "the Supreme Court shall have **appellate jurisdiction**," which means that it cannot be the court of first resort. Marbury had the right to sue for his commission, but not at the Supreme Court. The law that gave him **standing**—the right to sue—was unconstitutional. If Marbury wanted to seek a legal remedy to the situation, he would have to initiate the case in a lower court.

But Marshall wasn't done. His opinion concluded: "It is emphatically the province and duty of the judicial department to say what the law is. . . . If two laws conflict with each other, the courts must decide on the operation of each." The Court decided that the Constitution always trumps local, state, and federal laws. In limiting its power in this one case by denying itself the authority to issue the writ, the Supreme Court granted itself the far more important power of judicial review. Jefferson grumbled about the decision, worrying that having the power to decide what laws are constitutional across the entire government could make the judiciary a "despotic branch" of government.[8] But the ruling went unchallenged.

Applying the Power of Judicial Review

You might think that given this newfound power, the Court would begin striking down federal laws left and right. Not quite. It took 54 years before the Court again exercised the power of judicial review over an act of Congress. In **Dred Scott v. Sandford** (1857), the justices struck down the **Missouri Compromise**, a federal law that sought to maintain the balance of power between free states and slave states. In short, the Compromise amounted to a geographic division such that any new state north of Missouri would be a free state, and Missouri, along with any states entering to its south, would be slave states. The issue for the Court was that Dred Scott, an enslaved person in Missouri, had previously resided in Illinois, a free state. Scott sued for citizenship. The Court ruled that African Americans were not, and could never be, citizens of the United States. The Missouri Compromise, in other words, was unconstitutional.[9] This odious decision legalized slavery throughout the country and helped precipitate the Civil War.

As time went on, though, the Court clearly became comfortable exercising its power of judicial review. By the 1950s, the justices were using the power quite regularly. Just take a look at Figure 1. The x axis (the horizontal line at the bottom of the figure) tracks every year between 1950 and 2021 . The y axis (the scale on the left) shows the total number of laws the Supreme Court declared unconstitutional each year. Between 1950 and 2021, the justices determined that 1,287 laws and actions were unconstitutional. Of these, 33 percent were federal laws, 59 percent were state laws, and the remaining 8 percent were local laws. Although some years saw more action than others, as indicated by the peaks in Figure 1, the Court has employed judicial review to strike down an average of 18 laws per year during the last seven decades.[10]

How did the Supreme Court get its power?

FIGURE 1. Number of Laws Struck Down as Unconstitutional by the Supreme Court, 1950–2021

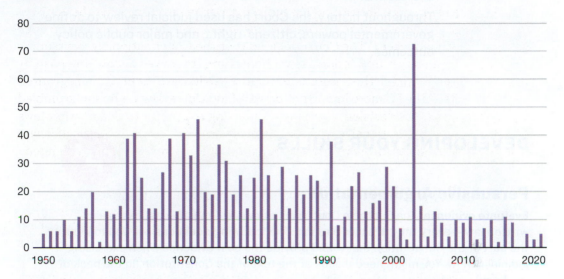

Note: Annual counts reflect the total number of local, state, and federal laws the Supreme Court struck down as unconstitutional.

Source: Supreme Court Database, Washington University Law School; and "Table of Laws Held Unconstitutional in Whole or in Part by the Supreme Court," Constitution Annotated.

Eighteen might not seem like a large number, but given the substance of these laws, the Court's power is remarkable. The Supreme Court has been the final arbiter in almost every major policy issue in American politics. The examples we used to open this segment make this clear, as do the final decisions the Court has issued when it comes to free speech, war, gun control, voting rights, marriage, and racial discrimination, just to name a handful of today's hot-button issues. What seemed like a legally expedient way out of the political conundrum involving William Marbury's judicial commission turned out to be a pretty sensational clarification of the Supreme Court's power.

DID YOU GET IT?

How did the Supreme Court get its power?

Short Answer:

- The Supreme Court established its power of judicial review in *Marbury v. Madison*.

- This decision established the Supreme Court's authority to determine the constitutionality of local, state, and federal laws and actions.
- Throughout history, the Court has used judicial review to define governmental powers, citizens' rights, and major public policy outcomes.

DEVELOPING YOUR SKILLS

Persuasive Argumentation

Evaluate evidence: The Supreme Court uses evidence — mostly past cases and written law — every time it issues a ruling. The following questions ask you to identify the part of the Constitution that would provide the best evidence when exercising judicial review. You might need to look at the text of the Constitution (in the back of the book).

1. A small town in California is trying to build better community relations and improve neighborhood civility. So the town council passed a law banning citizens from putting up political signs in their front yards, windows, or anywhere the signs are visible to the general public. Many citizens have protested the law. If a Supreme Court justice wants to use judicial review to strike down the law, which part of the Constitution should he or she rely on to make the most persuasive argument?

   a. Article I, Section 4, which gives each state the right to run its own elections

   b. The First Amendment's protection of freedom of speech

   c. The First Amendment's protection of freedom of the press

   d. The Nineteenth Amendment, which gives women the right to vote

2. In an address from the Oval Office, the president states: "I am making a formal declaration of war against Canada." Alarmed by this announcement, several members of Congress ask the Supreme Court to declare the president's action unconstitutional. What section of the Constitution would provide the strongest basis for the justices to side with Congress?

   a. Article I, Section 6

   b. Article I, Section 8

   c. Article II, Section 2

   d. The Ninth Amendment

3. Elected leaders in several states have passed laws that ban physician-assisted suicide for terminally ill citizens. But citizens, doctors, and patient rights groups often disagree. If supporters of physician-assisted suicide want the Supreme Court to declare the bans unconstitutional, what provision of the Constitution would likely provide the most persuasive evidence?

   a. The First Amendment's protection of free speech

   b. The First Amendment's protection of the free exercise of religion

   c. The Eighth Amendment's ban of "cruel and unusual punishment"

   d. The Fourteenth Amendment's due process clause

FIGURE IT OUT

In *Federalist 78*, Alexander Hamilton argues that the judicial branch is an essential component of the system of separation of powers. He even suggests that the Supreme Court should have the power to declare acts of the legislative branch null and void.

He's basically arguing for the power of judicial review (although he doesn't use those exact words). Is Hamilton's argument persuasive? More specifically:

- Identify two pieces of evidence Hamilton uses to support giving the Supreme Court the power to declare laws unconstitutional. (Hint: The argument about judicial review begins in paragraph 10 of the essay.)

- For each, explain in a couple of sentences whether the evidence is persuasive. Be specific in explaining your answer.

You can find *Federalist 78* reprinted in the back of this book. It's a little challenging to read because it's written in dry, formal English. But give it a shot.

Want to Know More?

For some examples of the Supreme Court's use of judicial review to shape how the government functions and how citizens live, read Michael Trachtman's *The Supremes' Greatest Hits: The 44 Supreme Court Decisions That Most Directly Affect Your Life*. Richard Beeman and Jay Feinman's *Supreme Court Classics* is another good one, covering 30 landmark cases.

5.
Why is the Constitution so hard to change?

#AmendmentProcess

In the 230-plus years since the Constitution was ratified, nearly 12,000 amendments have been proposed to change it.[1] Some of them are quite amusing, at least by today's standards. In 1838, for example, several members of the U.S. House of Representatives responded to a lethal duel between two members of Congress with a proposed amendment that would have banned dueling.[2] In 1878, a proposed amendment would have replaced the president with a three-person commission to run the executive branch.[3] In 1888, a congressman from Illinois proposed an amendment that would grant voting rights to property-owning "widows and spinsters."[4] He thought this was a good alternative to an amendment that would have gone so far as to give all women the right to vote. Lucas Miller, a member of Congress from Wisconsin, once proposed an amendment to rename the country "The United States of Earth." He also proposed an amendment to abolish the army and the navy.[5] Other amendments have tried to make divorce illegal, ban drunkenness, and limit personal wealth to $1 million.[6] Perhaps reassuringly, none of these amendments passed. (Although an amendment banning dueling doesn't seem so bad.)

Patrons of a St. Louis–area bar toast the pending passage of the Twenty-First Amendment. The amendment repealed the Eighteenth Amendment, which prohibited the sale and consumption of alcohol. That's right: liquor was illegal in the United States from 1920 to 1933.

Not all attempts to change the Constitution have been frivolous, though. Quite the contrary. Figure 1 lists six of the more popular amendments that have been proposed since the 1970s. In each case, public opinion polls reveal that a clear majority of people would have supported the change to the Constitution.[7] In two cases — establishing equal rights for women and limiting the number of terms members of Congress can serve — more than 8 out of 10 citizens backed the proposed change. Yet none of these amendments was adopted. In fact, the Constitution has been amended only 27 times. Ever. And not at all since 1992.

Why do 99.8 percent of proposed amendments fail? Largely because the Constitution, in Article V, lays out an arduous process that requires broad support at both the national and state levels to change the document. This segment describes that process and identifies the types of amendments that have passed. You'll see that the system the Founders designed protects against silly and dangerous amendments, but it also makes revising the Constitution all but impossible — especially in a highly partisan political climate.

The Onerous Amendment Process: The Actual Procedure

In his farewell address as the first president of the United States, George Washington acknowledged that the structure of the government wasn't perfect. He knew that the Constitution would undoubtedly

FIGURE 1. Public Support for Proposed Constitutional Amendments

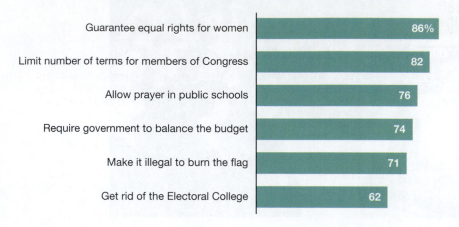

Guarantee equal rights for women	86%
Limit number of terms for members of Congress	82
Allow prayer in public schools	76
Require government to balance the budget	74
Make it illegal to burn the flag	71
Get rid of the Electoral College	62

Note: Bars represent the peak percentage of the population that supported each amendment in national public opinion polls.

Source: Data from the Huffington Post, McLaughlin and Associates, and Gallup. See Note 7 for full source information.

require some revisions. Thomas Jefferson agreed. He assumed that as a matter of good governance the Constitution should be revised every 20 years.[8] Doing so, according to Jefferson, would ensure that each generation had the "solemn opportunity" to update the document and hand it down "with periodical repairs . . . to the end of time."[9]

The Founders did more than acknowledge that the Constitution would need to be revised. They also came up with a process by which to revise it. In designing the process, they emphasized two principles: (1) that states and the federal government were both fully empowered to propose amendments, and (2) that amendments would be adopted only with widespread agreement at both the state and federal levels. Indeed, unlike much of the language in the Constitution—where the specific meaning of clauses and phrases is open to some interpretation— the language outlining the amendment process is crystal clear. Just a single paragraph, **Article V** establishes four specific ways to amend the Constitution. Table 1 describes the four options.

Amending the Constitution is hard because it's procedurally oner- ous. Only Option 1 is straightforward: get two-thirds of the members of both chambers of Congress to vote for the amendment, and then get a majority in three-quarters of the state legislatures to support it. We'll discuss the political feasibility of this option in a minute. But at least the process is clear. Twenty-six of the 27 amendments to the Constitution took this path.

TABLE 1. The Constitutional Amendment Process

	Step 1: Proposing an Amendment	Step 2: Ratifying an Amendment
Option 1 (really the only option)	Amendment is introduced in one chamber of Congress and supported by two-thirds of the members of both the House and Senate.	Amendment passes with a majority vote in three-quarters of the state legislatures (today that means a majority vote in 38 states).
Option 2 (used only once, when the country really needed a drink)	Amendment is introduced in one chamber of Congress and supported by two-thirds of the members of both the House and Senate.	Amendment passes with a majority vote in state-level constitutional conventions in at least three-quarters of the states (today that means a majority vote in 38 states).
Option 3 (never used and almost inconceivable in today's political environment)	Two-thirds of states petition Congress to call a national constitutional convention for proposing amendments (today that means 34 states must make the request).	Amendment passes with a majority vote in three-quarters of the state legislatures (today that means a majority vote in 38 states).
Option 4 (never used and entirely inconceivable in today's political environment)	Two-thirds of states petition Congress to call a national constitutional convention for proposing amendments (today that means 34 states must make the request).	Amendment passes with a majority vote in state-level constitutional conventions in at least three-quarters of the states (today that means a majority vote in 38 states).

As for the other three options, the time, effort, and procedural complexities make them highly implausible. Option 2 starts in Congress but then sends the amendment out to state constitutional ratifying conventions. And that's a messy business. Some states, including Vermont, New Mexico, and Florida, have very specific procedures for how to assemble a state ratifying convention. Many other states, however, haven't updated their procedures since 1933, the one time this path was taken. Still other states have no codified rules whatsoever. Options 3 and 4 require states to petition for a national constitutional convention. The problem is that the Constitution doesn't provide any guidelines for how to organize or operate a national convention. Even though interest groups on both sides of the political spectrum have advocated for a convention from time to time, it has never happened.

The Onerous Amendment Process: The Politics

Beyond procedural complexities, amending the Constitution is difficult because of politics. The threshold of support necessary for proposing an amendment is very high—in fact, so high that it's virtually impossible to reach. To get past the first step of the amendment process, either two-thirds of the members of both the House and the Senate must support it or two-thirds of the states must call for a national convention. The second step of the process—ratifying an amendment—requires an even higher threshold of support: all four options require three-quarters of the states to be on board.

To put these requirements into perspective, just consider the raw numbers necessary to succeed with Option 1. You'd need two-thirds of the members of both the House and the Senate to support the amendment. These are not easy numbers to come by. Only 63 percent of members of the U.S. House of Representatives voted for the popular Clean Air Act of 1963.[10] Just 53 percent of members of the House supported President Ronald Reagan's bipartisan immigration reform package in 1986.[11] In 1996, Democratic president Bill Clinton couldn't quite muster 60 percent of the House vote for a bipartisan welfare reform package.[12] It's easy to compile a very long list of initiatives like these that all became law—with support from both Democrats and Republicans—but that fell short of the two-thirds vote an amendment requires.

Then there's the second step of the amendment process: a majority vote in 38 state legislatures. Again, extremely difficult to achieve. Since 1982, Democrats have never controlled both chambers of the state legislature in more than 35 states at the same time. Republicans reached peak control in 2017, but even then they held a majority of seats in both houses in only 32 states.[13] Because Democrats and Republicans have become increasingly unwilling to cooperate, it's difficult to foresee how 38 states would ever come together to pass an amendment.

The 27 Amendments That Made It

Given the procedures and politics involved in the constitutional amendment process, it's hardly surprising that only 27 amendments have successfully been added to the Constitution. Well, really, only 17 have traversed the process we outlined. The first 10 amendments—the Bill of Rights—were all ratified at the same time in 1791 as part of the original agreement to adopt the Constitution. Beyond the Bill of Rights, the 17 amendments that have passed mainly fall into four general categories:

- *Civil War amendments:* The Thirteenth, Fourteenth, and Fifteenth Amendments ended slavery, made former enslaved persons citizens, and extended voting rights to citizens of all races.

- *Prohibition:* In 1920, the Eighteenth Amendment prohibited the sale and distribution of liquor in the United States. Thirteen years later, the Twenty-First Amendment repealed the prohibition of alcohol.

- *Government functioning:* Another group of amendments established and/or clarified who could bring a suit in the judiciary (Eleventh); how the Electoral College functions (Twelfth); the rules for the transfer of power after an election (Twentieth); presidential term limits (Twenty-Second); presidential succession if a president is no longer able to perform the duties of the office (Twenty-Fifth); and limits on congressional pay raises (Twenty-Seventh).

- *Expanding democracy:* Five amendments expanded democratic practices by moving to the popular election of senators (Seventeenth); extending the right to vote to women (Nineteenth), residents of the District of Columbia in presidential elections (Twenty-Third), and 18-year-olds (Twenty-Sixth); and banning poll taxes (Twenty-Fourth).

Perhaps because of the politics involved, only one amendment deals specifically with a public policy as we tend to think of it today: the Sixteenth Amendment gives the government the right to tax personal income.

A Twenty-Eighth Amendment?

It's so difficult to amend the Constitution that it just doesn't happen anymore. The last amendment to follow any sort of regular protocol was the Twenty-Sixth Amendment, which granted 18-year-olds the right to vote. It passed both houses of Congress on March 23, 1971, and within four months 39 states ratified it. That was more than 50 years ago. The Twenty-Seventh Amendment, which prohibits congressional pay raises from taking effect until the start of the next Congress, was adopted in 1992. But it had actually been introduced in 1789. It just took more than 200 years before enough states ratified it.[14]

James Madison in *Federalist 43* characterized the process for amending the Constitution laid out in Article V as striking the perfect balance between making the Constitution "too mutable" —that is, too easy to change—and making it too difficult to "correct."[15] But that characterization was likely a product of the times, including far fewer states and no political parties. Today's political circumstances make amending the Constitution so challenging that the process we're stuck with—the process devised by the Founders themselves—may actually run counter to their intent. A Twenty-Eighth Amendment—of any kind—is not on the horizon.

DID YOU GET IT?

Why is the Constitution so hard to change?

Short Answer:

- It's really only been amended 17 times because the first 10 amendments were ratified as the Bill of Rights.
- The four options for how to amend the Constitution are difficult to implement, both procedurally and in terms of the political support required by Congress and the states.
- The Founders sought to ensure a rigorous amendment process, but heightened partisanship has made the process nearly impossible.

DEVELOPING YOUR SKILLS

Quantitative Literacy

Do the math: Gauging the likelihood of amending the Constitution involves figuring out how many members of Congress and how many state legislatures support the proposal. The following questions require some basic math and a clear understanding of the different ways to amend the Constitution.

1. For a constitutional amendment to pass Congress, Article V of the Constitution requires at least two-thirds of both chambers of Congress to vote for it. What is the minimum number of votes needed in the House and Senate for an amendment to pass?

    a. 290 in the House and 66 in the Senate
    b. 290 in the House and 67 in the Senate
    c. 291 in the House and 66 in the Senate
    d. 291 in the House and 67 in the Senate

2. Suppose that an amendment just passed Congress and has been sent to the states. As of today, 23 states have passed it, four have rejected it, and the rest are still debating it. How many of the states that have not yet voted must pass it for the amendment to be ratified?

   a. 2   **c.** 15

   b. 11   **d.** 24

3. An organization called the Balanced Budget Amendment Task Force has been working since 2010 to call for a national convention to propose a balanced budget amendment to the Constitution (mandating that the federal government can't spend more than it takes in each year). Currently, 28 states have passed resolutions requesting that a convention be held. How many more states are required to petition Congress before a convention must be convened?

   a. 6   **c.** 34

   b. 10   **d.** 38

FIGURE IT OUT

One reason it's so difficult to change the Constitution is that three-quarters of state legislatures must agree on any proposed amendments, and the states are very politically divided. The map below indicates whether each state legislature is controlled by Democrats, Republicans, or is split. (Nebraska has only one state legislative chamber, and it is not partisan.) Use the map to answer the following questions about amending the Constitution:

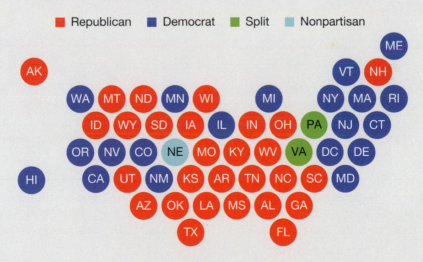

Note: Party control in AK and AZ represents a projection based on election results as of November 13, 2022.

- If all of the unified Democratic states vote together, what is the fewest number of other states that would have to join the Democratic states to pass a constitutional amendment? Explain how you arrived at your answer.

- If all of the unified Democratic states and half of the unified Republican states approved an amendment, would that be enough support for it to pass? Explain your answer.

Want to Know More?

For a gripping portrayal of how Abraham Lincoln coerced the House of Representatives to pass the Thirteenth Amendment, watch Steven Spielberg's 2012 film *Lincoln*.

6.
Did the Founders believe in democracy?

#DemocraticPrinciples

For much of recent history, asking whether the Founders believed in democracy might have seemed silly. Of course they did, right? Political leaders regularly invoked the democratic principles of the Founding in all sorts of settings. Former Speaker of the House Paul Ryan, during a very contentious debate over gun control, assured the public that as "the oldest democracy" in the world, there was no doubt that "we can peacefully settle our issues."[1] Hillary Clinton, during the final debate of the 2016 presidential campaign, pledged to accept the outcome of the race, regardless of what it might be. "We've been around 240 years," Clinton told the audience. "We've had free and fair elections and we've accepted the outcomes when we may not have liked them."[2] In his farewell address to the nation in January 2017, Barack Obama referred to democracy 20 times. "Our Founders quarreled and compromised, and expected us to do the same," the president explained. "But they knew that democracy does require a basic sense of solidarity — the idea that for all our outward differences, we are all in this together; that we rise or fall as one."[3] Even President Donald Trump once called Americans the "the luckiest people in history," largely because the United States is "a democracy that is enviable throughout the world."[4]

On January 6, 2021, thousands of protesters stormed the U.S. Capitol to stop Congress from certifying the 2020 presidential election. By the time order was restored, hundreds of people — including Capitol police officers — had sustained injuries. Several even died. These events threatened the peaceful transfer of power, a hallmark of democratic government.

But then January 6, 2021, happened. As Congress was set to certify Joe Biden's victory in the 2020 presidential election, Donald Trump held a large rally within walking distance of the U.S. Capitol. In a contradictory set of remarks, he urged the crowd to "peacefully and patriotically" march to the Capitol but also to "fight like hell" to stop Congress from certifying a corrupt election.[5] Despite no evidence of voter fraud — the Trump campaign had filed and lost dozens of lawsuits contesting the outcome[6] — protesters breached the Capitol to disrupt the counting of electoral votes. They broke through police barricades, forced members of Congress into hiding, and occupied Speaker of the House Nancy Pelosi's office. Order was eventually restored, but not until hundreds of people sustained injuries and several died.[7] The peaceful transfer of power, a hallmark of American democracy since the Founding, was in question. You'd have to go back to the War of 1812 to find the last time the U.S. Capitol was under siege.

Donald Trump and many of his supporters characterized the insurrectionists as protesters simply exerting their freedom of speech.[8] But many others, including Congresswoman Liz Cheney, lamented the blow to the U.S. governing system. "Our election was not stolen, and America

Did the Founders believe in democracy?

has not failed," the Republican told her colleagues in a floor speech. "Remaining silent and ignoring the lie emboldens the liar."[9] Democrats, led by President Biden, believe that the events of January 6 reveal that "democracy itself is in peril, here at home and around the world."[10]

As the debate over the state and fate of U.S. democracy rages on, it's important to consider whether the United States ever really embodied the democratic ideals that leaders of all political stripes regularly claim. Most historians and political scientists would agree that democracies, at the very minimum, embody three central elements. First, democratic governments allow citizens to choose their leaders through open and direct elections. Second, all citizens are eligible to vote, and all of their votes carry equal weight. Third, there is a free marketplace of ideas — typically, in the form of a news environment where citizens and leaders can share their views and also be held accountable for them. This segment assesses how the Founders score on each of these dimensions, and it suggests that contemporary political leaders often view the nation's democratic foundation more positively than might be warranted.

The Founders on Democracy: In Their Own Words

The term **democracy** comes from two Greek words: *demos*, which means "people"; and *kratos*, which means "power." So democracy literally means "people power." Democratic governments generally take one of two forms. In a **direct democracy**, citizens make decisions by voting on specific issues and policies. In a **representative democracy**, citizens vote for leaders whom they trust to consider all the issues and choose a course of action on the people's behalf. At the time of its conception in ancient Greece, a form of government that vested power in the people—either directly or through representatives—stood in stark contrast to the aristocracies and monarchies that were the norm of the time.

Given that the Founders worked to create a government that minimized the likelihood of a king or other tyrant coming to power, direct democracy should have been right up their alley. But debates at the Constitutional Convention and later commentary from the Founders reveal that nothing could be further from the truth. Just look at what some of them had to say. Benjamin Rush, one of the people to sign the Declaration of Independence, equated a simple democracy with "the devil's own government."[11] John Adams and James Madison both warned that democracies tend to be short-lived. According to Adams, "Democracy never lasts long. It soon wastes, exhausts, and murders itself. There is never a democracy that did not commit suicide."[12] Madison remarked that direct democracies have been "as short in their lives as they have been violent in their deaths."[13]

These Founders didn't trust voters to use good judgment, and they worried that citizens could be easily manipulated by power-seeking, unprincipled leaders. Massachusetts convention delegate Elbridge Gerry epitomized this concern: "The people do not want virtue, but are the dupes of pretended patriots. . . . They are daily misled into the most baneful measures and opinions by the false reports circulated by designing men."[14] John Jay, one of the most outspoken advocates for the new constitution, put it a bit more colorfully. "Too many . . . love pure democracy dearly," he said. "They seem not to consider that pure democracy, like pure rum, easily produces intoxication, and with it a thousand mad pranks and fooleries."[15]

The trick for the Founders was to create a system of government that honored the ideals of the Declaration of Independence—that "just powers" come from "the consent of the governed"—but that also quelled their concerns about relying too heavily on the voters' judgment. The result? A representative democracy, also known as a republic. But the version of a republic the Founders created sought to diminish the direct influence of the people.

Open and Direct Elections: The Founders Get a D

The first central component of a democracy is a fair electoral system through which people can influence the government's actions. The democracy the Constitution laid out, however, was at best a mixed bag when it came to open and direct elections. The system was open in that the Founders placed few restrictions on who could run for federal office. They virulently opposed monarchical or aristocratic rule, so they steered clear of privileging birthright leadership. Rather, as indicated in Table 1, the delegates to the Convention identified only three basic requirements for federal officeholders: age, citizenship, and residency. The threshold for each increased with the stature of the office. Still, there were only three requirements.

But don't take these lax stipulations to mean that the Founders supported a broad array of people running for office. At the time, it was a given that only land-owning White men were eligible to seek positions of political power. Because the Constitution didn't

TABLE 1. Constitutional Requirements for Federal Officeholders

House of Representatives	Senate	President
• Must be at least 25 years old when term begins. • Must be an inhabitant of the United States for at least seven years. • Must live in the state you represent at the time you're elected.	• Must be at least 30 years old when term begins. • Must be an inhabitant of the United States for at least nine years. • Must live in the state you represent at the time you're elected.	• Must be at least 35 years old when term begins. • Must be a natural-born citizen. • Must be a resident of the United States for at least 14 years.

specify or codify these requirements, the document didn't stand in the way of allowing for a more diverse group of candidates as societal norms evolved. But the Constitution wasn't written to ensure "open" elections.

Elections were also far from direct. People voted for candidates for only one of the three federal offices—the House of Representatives. The selection process for the Senate and presidency severely limited citizen input. The original Constitution required each state legislature to choose the state's U.S. senators. To select the president, the Founders created the Electoral College. We cover the Electoral College extensively in Segment 30, but for now you should know that the original conception involved state legislators choosing the members. Those members of the Electoral College then voted for the president.

In the centuries since the Founders drafted the Constitution, federal elections have become much more democratic. In the mid-1800s, as more and more people became eligible to vote (more on that in a minute), states began adopting systems that allowed people to vote directly for members of the Electoral College. And the Seventeenth Amendment, passed in 1913, implemented direct election of U.S. senators. Citizens today play a direct role in choosing all federal elected officials.

Direct democracy has also flourished, probably to many of the Founders' dismay. Twenty-six states now have laws that provide for citizens to propose a policy or law and bring it directly to the voters through a **ballot initiative**.[16] Through this form of direct democracy, states have passed election reform, legalized marijuana, improved the transportation infrastructure, made it more difficult to abolish the death penalty, and raised the minimum wage.[17] A 2016 ballot measure in California even asked voters to weigh in on whether actors in pornographic films should be required to wear condoms. (Voters said no.[18])

Equal Voting Rights for All: The Founders Get an F

The original Constitution did not establish any rules for who could vote. The Founders couldn't agree on who should be eligible, so they left the decision up to the states. Just because the document didn't explicitly limit voting rights doesn't mean that it was consistent with true democratic principles. Most states restricted voting to land-owning White men. Whether the Founders expected these restrictions to fade away over time is unclear. What is clear is that in the beginning, voting was reserved for the elite.

Figure 1 traces the percentage of the population eligible to vote dating back to the first national elections in 1789. Pinning down specific numbers of eligible voters is very difficult, both because states set their own rules and because early population figures are hard to come by. But in almost every state, land-owning White men constituted the entire population of eligible voters. And they made up just 6 percent of the overall population. So only 6 percent of people living in the United States were definitely eligible to vote in the first national elections. In most states, the remaining 94 percent of the population—made up mostly of enslaved persons, women, indigenous people, and non-land-owning men—had no say in choosing their representatives. Keep in mind, too, that not everyone who was eligible actually cast a ballot. In Delaware and New York, for instance, less than 3 percent of the population voted in the 1789 election.[19]

Over time, the Constitution was amended to extend voting rights to previously excluded groups. The Fifteenth Amendment, adopted at the end of the Civil War, stated that the right to vote "shall not be denied or abridged by the United States or by any State on account of race, color, or previous condition of servitude." In other words, formerly enslaved men could cast ballots. This, of course, did not mean that they weren't blocked from voting by other means. This amendment, plus the fact that by 1870 states no longer required property ownership, tripled the proportion of the voting-eligible population, bringing it up to 18 percent (see the second bar in Figure 1).

The remaining bars in Figure 1 represent the three other times that constitutional amendments broadened the electorate. Women

Did the Founders believe in democracy?

FIGURE 1. Percentage of the U.S. Population Eligible to Vote

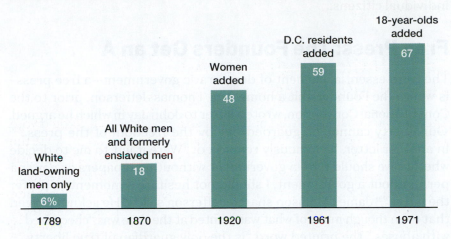

Note: Bars reflect the percentage of the U.S population constitutionally eligible to vote at each point in time.

Source: U.S. Census Bureau.

received the right to vote with the Nineteenth Amendment in 1920. Forty-one years later, the Twenty-Third Amendment conferred the right to vote in federal elections to residents of the District of Columbia. The jump between 1920 and 1961 isn't only a result of enfranchising D.C. residents. During this time, Congress passed a law that allowed indigenous people to vote, and states began abolishing other voting requirements as part of the civil rights movement. Finally, in 1971, the Twenty-Sixth Amendment lowered the voting age from 21 to 18. Today roughly two-thirds of the U.S. population is eligible to vote. The vast majority of those who aren't eligible are minors (younger than 18).

It's not only because the Founders limited the voting-eligible population that we give them an F on equal voting rights for all. They also created a system in which all votes were not equally weighted. And this system persists today. Regardless of a state's population it has two U.S. senators. That means, for example, that residents of Delaware, where the population is a little less than a million, send the same number of senators to Washington as do residents of New York, where the population is roughly 20 million. A Delaware voter, then, has almost 20 times the representation in the U.S. Senate as a voter from New York does. These inequities carry over to presidential elections because the number of electoral votes allocated to each state is equal to the size of the state's congressional delegation—House and Senate combined. The Founders' version of a republic valued the representation of each state over the equal representation of individual citizens.

Free Press: The Founders Get an A

The third essential element of democratic government—a free press— is where the Founders hit a home run. Thomas Jefferson, prior to the Constitutional Convention, wrote a letter to John Jay in which he argued: "Our liberty cannot be guarded but by the freedom of the press."[20] In another letter, he famously remarked: "Were it left to me to decide whether we should have a government without newspapers or newspapers without a government, I should not hesitate a moment to prefer the latter."[21] James Madison shared Jefferson's view. He acknowledged that even though much of what was printed at the time was "chequered . . . with abuses," the printed word "is the only guardian of true liberty."[22] That's probably why the Constitution never mentions political parties, labor unions, corporations, schools, or any of the other major institutions in the United States—but does mention "the press." In fact, the press is the only nongovernmental institution mentioned anywhere in the document. The First Amendment prohibits Congress from making any law abridging the freedom of the press.

Despite the Founders' strong defense of a free press, the U.S. government has episodically attempted to curtail it. The first major challenge came less than a decade after ratification of the Constitution. In 1798, Congress passed and President John Adams signed the **Alien and Sedition Acts**—a set of four laws designed to protect the United States from internal insurrection in what was thought to be a pending war with France. The Sedition Act outlawed "false, scandalous and malicious" writing against the president or the Congress and made it illegal to conspire to oppose any "measures of the government." It was criminal to "defame" the government or to cause the "hatred" of the people toward it.[23]

And that went for newspaper editors who opposed the Federalist government's policies. Benjamin Franklin's grandson, for example, was the editor of the *Philadelphia Aurora* newspaper. He was arrested for describing President Adams as "old, querulous, bald, blind, crippled, toothless." (The 29-year-old died of yellow fever before he went to trial.) James Callender, a journalist for the *Richmond Examiner*, spent nine months in prison for writing that Adams "never opened his lips, or lifted his pen, without threatening and scolding."[24] All told, more than two dozen journalists who expressed opinions just as innocuous as these were sentenced to up to five years in prison and fined as much as $5,000

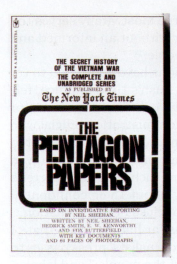

In a blow to the Nixon administration, the Supreme Court's 1971 decision in *New York Times Co. v. United States* protected freedom of the press. The justices ruled in favor of the *New York Times* and the *Washington Post,* both of which were allowed to continue printing excerpts of the Pentagon Papers.

(about \$100,000 today).[25] The controversy over the law likely contributed to Adams's defeat in 1800. Shortly thereafter, most of the Acts' controversial provisions expired.

Fast-forward almost 200 years, and you'll still see efforts to curtail press freedom. In the early 1970s, the federal government tried to prevent the *New York Times* and the *Washington Post* from publishing a classified report about U.S. involvement in the Vietnam War. The report was embarrassing for the government because it revealed a long history of U.S. leaders lying to the public about what was really going on in Vietnam and the prospects for winning the war. How did the newspapers get it? From Daniel Ellsberg, a military analyst who had been commissioned by the Defense Department to write the report years earlier. Ellsberg had become disillusioned with the war and thought the American people had a right to know what was really going on. When the *Times* and the *Post* began publishing excerpts of Ellsberg's materials—which became known as the **Pentagon Papers**—President Nixon tried to block the publication of any further excerpts, claiming that publishing the classified information jeopardized national security.

The Supreme Court sided with the press. The justices upheld the papers' right to print the material, ruling that the First Amendment severely limits **prior restraint**—government action that prohibits the press from reporting potentially harmful information. Justice Potter Stewart's concurrence didn't sound that different from the Founders' argument for a free press. He wrote that especially in the areas of national defense and international affairs, the press is the "only effective restraint" on executive power. He continued: "It is perhaps here that a press that is alert, aware, and free most vitally serves the basic purpose of the First Amendment. For without an informed and free press there cannot be an enlightened people."[26]

More recently, presidential administrations have continued to try to limit press freedom. During George W. Bush's time in office, federal prosecutors jailed Judith Miller, a *New York Times* reporter, for refusing to identify the name of the Bush administration official who leaked the identity of a CIA agent.[27] The Obama administration adopted a zero-tolerance policy when it came to leaking. The administration even got a federal appeals court to rule that there's no such thing as "reporter's privilege"; indeed, journalists must testify about their confidential sources in criminal cases, including leaks of classified information.[28] Donald Trump's pushback on the press was far harsher than that of previous presidents. Trump removed some journalists' press passes to the White House, called them "the enemy of the people," and labeled some of the most esteemed news organizations in the country "fake news." The Trump Justice Department even seized the phone records of reporters from the *New York Times*, the *Washington Post*, and CNN with the hopes of uncovering their sources.[29]

The Founders' support for a free press is not always popular among contemporary presidents. But despite attempts by the government to block the news media from reporting on unfavorable stories, the Constitution's vision of a free press generally remains intact.

DID YOU GET IT?
Did the Founders believe in democracy?

Short Answer:

- Only in a very limited capacity. They favored a government based on the consent of the people, but they worked to minimize and dilute the people's direct impact.
- The Founders didn't allow for the direct election of senators or the president, and they excluded the vast majority of people from voting.
- They did establish the sanctity of a free press, which is a critical component of a democracy.

Consuming Political Information

Navigate political websites: This segment focused on the extent to which the Founders created a democratic government. Freedom House is an organization that tracks and monitors the degree to which countries around the world adhere to democratic principles today. Familiarize yourself with its website — https://freedomhouse.org — to answer these questions about the current state of U.S. democracy.

1. One of the ways that Freedom House rates a country's democratic qualities is by measuring citizens' political rights. What's the United States' Political Rights Score?

    a. 32
    b. 53
    c. 86
    d. 100

2. On Freedom House's ranking of countries and territories, which three countries have a higher Internet Freedom Score than the United States?

    a. Iceland, Italy, and the United Kingdom
    b. Australia, Canada, and Argentina
    c. Iceland, Estonia, and Germany
    d. Iceland, Canada, and Armenia

3. Freedom House makes numerous policy recommendations to specific countries and international organizations. Which is *not* one of the policy areas it focuses on?

    a. Combating government corruption
    b. Internet freedom and securing elections
    c. Strengthening democracy abroad
    d. Global civic engagement

FIGURE IT OUT

Freedom House is not the only organization rating democratic values around the world. The Global Democracy Ranking is another. Go to their website (http://democracyranking .org/wordpress/) and compare it to Freedom House. More specifically:

- How does each organization measure democracy?
- Under each ranking system, what rating does the United States receive?

- Based on the information provided by each organization's website, what accounts for the different rankings of the United States? (Note: The systems used by the organizations are quite different, so you will really need to think about what factors they use to draw their conclusions.)

Want to Know More?

The 2017 movie *The Post* offers a dramatic retelling of the *Washington Post*'s decision to publish the Pentagon Papers. The Oscar-nominated film celebrates freedom of the press and highlights how government leaders and journalists can butt heads around this democratic ideal.

Did the Founders believe in democracy?

7.
Can the federal government tell the states what to do?

#NationalSupremacy

A flashpoint in the debate over immigration policy occurred shortly after a bullet hit and killed Kate Steinle in San Francisco on July 1, 2015. As Steinle, a 32-year-old local resident, walked with her father along the waterfront in one of the city's tourist areas, José Ines García Zárate fired the fatal gunshot. The gunman had a long criminal history. He'd previously been convicted of seven felonies. He was well known to customs and immigration agents as someone from Mexico who was in the United States illegally. And just months before the shooting, he had been in police custody for a drug charge. But upon his release from jail, local authorities did not turn García Zárate over to federal immigration officials for deportation.

Local law enforcement never informed the feds that they had García Zárate in custody, or that they released him, because San Francisco is a **sanctuary city**. A San Francisco ordinance directs the local police department not to assist federal law enforcement officials with the deportation of people living in the country illegally.[1] These local laws — which are on the books in roughly 140 cities across the United States — stand in direct opposition to a federal law that requires state and local governments to cooperate with the federal Immigration and

Immigration policy is one example of the tension between the federal government and the states. California refuses to enforce federal immigration laws that require state and local governments to cooperate with the federal Immigration and Customs Enforcement Agency. If federal agents want to to take undocumented workers into custody, they need to do it themselves.

Customs Enforcement Agency (known as ICE). So sanctuary cities, when they refuse to assist ICE, fail to comply with a federal law. For decades, though, sanctuary cities received little attention. San Francisco actually became one in 1989.[2]

That changed a couple of weeks before Steinle's death. In the speech that launched his 2016 presidential campaign, Donald Trump promised to "build a great, great wall on our southern border" because, he claimed, the Mexicans coming to the United States are "bringing drugs. They're bringing crime. They're rapists."[3] For the next year and a half, Trump spoke relentlessly against illegal immigration and promised a zero-tolerance policy for sanctuary cities.

Supporters of sanctuary cities had a different perspective. During her U.S. Senate campaign, now vice president Kamala Harris urged the nation to "get smart" and realize that the vast majority of undocumented immigrants are "following the law, working hard, raising their children, paying taxes."[4] Libby Schaff, the mayor of Oakland, California — also a sanctuary city — issued a press release warning

Can the federal government tell the states what to do?

undocumented immigrants about a possible federal deportation raid.[5] A group of sheriffs in Texas even wrote an op-ed citing FBI statistics to show that sanctuary cities have lower crime rates than other cities.[6]

Within a week of taking office, President Trump issued an executive order stating that "sanctuary jurisdictions" that don't follow federal immigration laws would not receive federal funds.[7] California, which had sanctuary designations in 14 counties and six cities, hit back. The governor signed into law a bill making California a sanctuary state. "We're not soldiers of Donald Trump or the federal immigration service," the governor told CNN.[8]

"Yes, you are," responded the federal government, which filed suit in federal court to block the California law. Federal district court judge John Mendez ruled that the sanctuary law didn't actually violate the federal law. He concluded that "standing aside does not equate to standing in the way." In other words, the California law didn't bar federal officials from enforcing immigration policies in California. It just meant that the state didn't have to help.[9]

The conflict surrounding sanctuary cities and states highlights the difficulty in identifying where one level of government's power ends and another's begins. These tensions have been a defining feature of U.S. politics since the very beginning. At the Constitutional Convention, those Founders who wanted the states to retain much of their independence butted heads with those who supported a more powerful national government. They ultimately created a system of **federalism** whereby the national and state governments would share power. But from the conflicts over ending slavery and extending civil rights to more recent debates about how to deal with immigration, climate change, and health care, the federal and state governments have always jockeyed for power. This segment illustrates that even though the Constitution grants the federal government supremacy

In October 2017, California governor Jerry Brown signed into law a bill making California a sanctuary state.

over the states, the states have wide discretion and latitude over many key issues and policy areas.

I'm the Boss of You: The Constitutional Basis for Federal Supremacy

Donald Trump's view that the federal government can tell the states what to do is rooted in Article VI of the Constitution. It reads: "This Constitution, and the laws of the United States which shall be made in pursuance thereof . . . shall be the supreme law of the land." Known as the **supremacy clause**, these words suggest that federal laws consistent with the Constitution are the final word. If state or local laws conflict with the federal law, the federal law must be followed. But as is the case with so many of the Constitution's clauses, it took two major Supreme Court cases to interpret what the words really meant and how broadly they applied.

The first major test of federal versus state authority can be traced back to 1816. That year, the federal government established the Second National Bank of the United States, and it put a branch in Baltimore. Political leaders in Maryland didn't want the branch because it would compete with the state's local banks. They were also unconvinced that the federal government had the power to set up a national bank in the first place. Nowhere does the Constitution grant that specific authority. To show its objections to the federal bank, the state of Maryland passed a law that taxed the national bank. And when the bank clerk, James McCulloch, refused to pay the $15,000 tax (about $262,000 today), Maryland sued. *McCulloch v. Maryland* made it to the Supreme Court three years later.

In a unanimous ruling, the justices came down on the side of McCulloch and the federal government. First, the Court concluded that Congress had the right to establish a national bank even though the word "bank" never appears in the Constitution. Because the Constitution explicitly grants Congress the powers to tax, borrow money, and regulate commerce, the Court determined that creating a bank was an implied power consistent with the "letter and spirit of the Constitution."[10] Second, the justices interpreted the supremacy clause to mean that states "have no power, by taxation or otherwise, to retard, impede, or . . . control" the "appropriate" and "legitimate" laws of the federal government. Creating the bank was a lawful exercise of federal authority, so Maryland would have to suck it up. The bank stayed, and Maryland couldn't tax it.

Five years later, in *Gibbons v. Ogden* (1824), the Supreme Court affirmed federal authority over the states.[11] It all started with the

Can the federal government tell the states what to do?

Licensing Act of 1793. (Doesn't everything?) That law granted the federal government the sole power to issue licenses to shipping and ferry companies that wanted to use the waterway between New York and New Jersey. But the state of New York, increasingly aware of the economic opportunities of steamboat navigation, wanted to get into the licensing game, too. The New York state legislature passed a law that essentially granted Aaron Ogden an exclusive license to offer ferry service between New York and New Jersey. Things seemed to be going well until one of Ogden's business partners, Thomas Gibbons, began operating another steamboat on the same route. For that boat, Gibbons had a federal license granted under the 1793 Licensing Act. So Ogden sued Gibbons, arguing that he was in violation of the state law that granted Ogden exclusive rights on the waterway. Gibbons contended that the state law granting the monopoly conflicted with federal law, so it was invalid from the start.

The Supreme Court agreed with Gibbons. The state of New York did not have the power to issue licenses on the waterway, given the federal law already in place. The decision did more than affirm the supremacy clause, though. It dramatically increased federal authority over the states. Article I, Section 8, of the Constitution gives Congress the power "to regulate commerce . . . among the several states." In defining the scope of what is known as the **commerce clause**, the Court ruled that the power to regulate commerce "may be exercised to its utmost extent, and acknowledges no limitations, other than are prescribed in the Constitution." The federal government could regulate businesses in any state if those businesses shipped or received goods to or from any other state. And if those federal regulations conflicted with state laws, the federal laws won out. Virtually every business today—big or small—engages in interstate commerce in some way or another. The federal government's reach applies to every single one of them.

The net impact of these two Supreme Court cases early in U.S. history cannot be overstated. Together, they established the basis of federal supremacy over the states, and they made it clear that the federal government has wide latitude in carrying out its powers and responsibilities.

You're Really Not the Boss of Me: State Powers in a Federal System

Just because the supremacy of federal laws is well established does not mean that the federal government has complete power over the states. The Founders developed a system that clearly anticipated distinct roles and responsibilities for the different levels of government. The federal government's main powers are all either enumerated in or implied by the Constitution itself (see the first column of Table 1). The document doesn't actually list any specific powers for the states.

The **Tenth Amendment**, however, establishes the potential for the states to exercise broad authority over a range of policy areas. The amendment reads: "The powers not delegated to the United States by the Constitution, nor prohibited by it to the States, are reserved to the States respectively, or to the people." Essentially, states have the power to manage their economic, education, election, and criminal justice systems (see the middle column of Table 1). They can also more broadly promote their residents' public health and safety (sanctuary laws fall into this category). The federal government cannot interfere with the way states choose to do so as long as a state's policy doesn't violate a federal law.

The rightmost column in Table 1 identifies **concurrent powers**—those that both the federal and the state governments can exercise in their respective domains. In some cases, the federal and state governments act completely independently of one another. That's the case with income tax. The federal income tax is based on your income regardless of where you live. The state income tax is unrelated to the federal tax. (Seven states don't even have one.) In other cases, such as building and maintaining interstate highways, the federal and state governments work collaboratively. Often the federal government builds a highway and the state maintains it.

TABLE 1. Federal, State, and Concurrent Powers

Federal	State	Concurrent
• Declare war • Conduct foreign policy • Enter into treaties • Regulate international trade • Regulate interstate commerce • Build and maintain the military • Print money • Issue copyrights and patents • Establish post offices • Make laws necessary and proper to carry out these powers	• Regulate intrastate commerce • Conduct elections • Establish local governments • Oversee public education • Promote public health and safety • Issue licenses (professional, marriage, driver's, etc.) • May exert powers not delegated to the federal government and not prohibited to the states	• Make and enforce laws • Collect taxes • Borrow money • Build roads • Establish courts • Charter banks and corporations • Take private property for public purposes, with just compensation (eminent domain) • Provide for the common good

Source: U.S. Constitution and the U.S. Government Printing Office.

The key point here is that the Constitution does not confer all power—either enumerated or implied—to the federal government. States have far-reaching powers themselves, and in several domains the federal government cannot interfere with them.

Federal-State Relations Today: The Evolution of Federalism

The evolution of federalism has taken a long and winding path. A few specific historical twists and turns demonstrate how we wound up with the system of federalism we have today—one that features separate federal and state roles but also involves a great deal of cooperation between the two levels of government.

Soon after the Civil War ended in 1865, the United States entered into an era of **dual federalism**. The federal and state governments operated within their own spheres of influence. The federal government took care of national defense, negotiated treaties, and governed on broad issues of economic policy, as the Constitution directs. States generally managed commerce within the state, individual rights of the state's residents, and local issues such as transportation and criminal justice. When state and federal laws conflicted, the federal law prevailed. In general, though, the two levels of government kept to themselves.

This system changed dramatically in response to the Great Depression, which began in 1929. Often considered the worst economic collapse in the industrialized world, the Depression began with a stock market crash. Substantial declines in consumer spending and investments followed. As a consequence, companies had no choice but to lay off workers. Within five years, the national unemployment rate had grown from 3 percent to 25 percent.[12] In addition, more than half the banks had failed.

In an attempt to end the Depression, President Franklin Delano Roosevelt worked with Congress to implement the **New Deal**—a series of federal programs that focused on economic recovery. With unemployment in some cities reaching a staggering 90 percent, the federal government began regulating and funding banks and investing in infrastructure.[13] The government developed jobs programs and a system of unemployment insurance. And perhaps most notably, it created the Social Security program, which continues to serve as a pension system for senior citizens. Between 1933 and 1938, federal grant dollars to fund these programs in the states more than tripled.[14] Given the size and scope of the New Deal, the federal government needed the states to help administer and implement the programs. Thus began the era of **cooperative federalism**, in which all levels of government work together to solve problems.

Since the New Deal era, the amount of money allocated to the states for federal programs has continued to grow—exponentially. Figure 1 plots, in billions of dollars per year, the total amount the federal government grants to state and local governments. Whereas states received only about $15 billion in federal grant money in the 1940s, by 2010 the amount neared $600 billion. That's a forty-fold increase. Grants to local and state governments have come to constitute a greater share of federal dollars spent, too (as indicated by the dotted lines). The majority (about 60 percent) of federal grant money helps with health care, subsidizing what the states spend on Medicaid, Medicare, and Obamacare. Income security is the next largest category; one out of every six dollars is devoted to a range of programs aimed to alleviate poverty by providing assistance for housing, heat, and food.[15]

Although the designated roles of the state and federal governments under cooperative federalism are quite clear and have remained largely intact since the New Deal, political leaders have periodically attempted to shift power to the states. Since the 1970s, Republicans have typically favored **devolution**, arguing that allowing state and local governments to run federal programs with little interference from Washington is more efficient and effective. Democrats generally prefer the federal government to play a major role in shaping and implementing the kinds of programs created during the New Deal because they want to

FIGURE 1. Federal Grants to State and Local Governments, 1940–2020

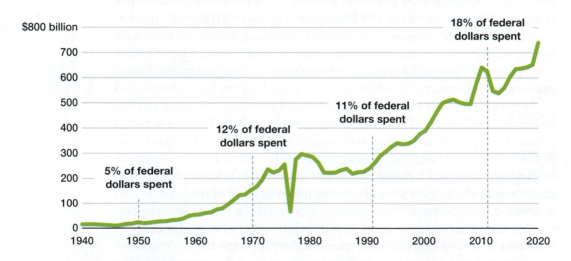

Note: Entries are in fiscal year 2012 dollars, which allows for direct comparisons.

Source: "Summary Comparison of Total Outlays for Grants to State and Local Governments, 1940–2026," Office of Management and Budget.

Can the federal government tell the states what to do?

ensure that people have access to government resources regardless of where they live.

This philosophical difference between the parties has generally not changed the distribution of powers listed in Table 1. Rather, the chief tool in ceding more power to the states has been a change in how federal programs are funded. Over time, the size and scope of **block grants** have increased substantially. These grants from the federal government come with few specific instructions. The states, in essence, are free to decide how to run the program. Temporary Assistance to Needy Families (TANF)—typically referred to as "welfare"—falls into this category. The federal government provides cash to citizens living in poverty. But each state decides how to implement the program, including who's eligible to participate. Block grants stand in stark contrast to **categorical grants**, which provide states with very specific instructions and lots of strings attached for how to spend federal money. The food stamp program is a prime example. The federal government uses a formula to determine food stamp eligibility, and states must use the money in accordance with the federal government's eligibility guidelines. Thus, the move to more block grants shifts the balance of power, leaving the states with increasing latitude over key policy areas that have traditionally been operated by the federal government.

All of this is to say that even though the federal government has the constitutional authority to be more powerful than the states, it is often not involved in the day-to-day operations of even its signature programs. So it's not necessarily the case that the federal government can't tell the states what to do, but more that the federal government—at least for some programs—chooses not to.

DID YOU GET IT?
Can the federal government tell the states what to do?

Short Answer:

- Based on the Constitution (Article VI) and early Supreme Court decisions, the answer is yes. The federal government has supremacy over the states.
- But the federal government doesn't control everything. The Tenth Amendment reserves certain powers for the states.
- Today's federal government also cedes some power to the states, relying on them to implement certain federal programs at their own discretion.

Civic Engagement

Stay informed: Living under a system of federalism means you must know which level of government to approach for assistance. Use the information presented in this segment, as well as the websites of the various government agencies mentioned in each question, to identify the best place to resolve each issue.

---

1. You just moved to California. Where can you register your car?
   a. A branch of the federal Department of Transportation
   b. A branch of the California Department of Motor Vehicles
   c. Either A or B. You can register your car in both places.
   d. It depends on what city in California you live.

2. You live in Virginia and are excited to travel to Canada for your cousin's wedding. But you don't have a passport. Where can you get one?
   a. The Virginia Department of Consumer Affairs
   b. The Virginia Secretary of State's Office
   c. A United States post office
   d. Any federal courthouse

3. You started a new job in Texas, and now that you're a resident, you want to register to vote. According to the Texas secretary of state's website, which would *not* qualify as a valid form of identification when it comes time to vote?
   a. U.S. passport
   b. Texas handgun license
   c. Texas hunting license
   d. Texas election ID certificate

FIGURE IT OUT

If you are aware of a problem in your community, state, or even country, and you want to voice your concern, it is important to know whom to contact. In that spirit, compile a contact list for some of your key federal, state, and local elected officials. More specifically:

- When you have a concern about something the federal government is doing, you can contact your member of Congress or one of your two U.S. senators. Choose one of these individuals, and based on where you live, list the district (local) office address and phone number; the Washington, D.C., office address and phone number; and the email address and Twitter handle.

- When you're concerned about something the state government is doing, you can get in touch with your governor, state senator, or member of the State House or Assembly (unless you live in Nebraska, which has only one legislative chamber). Choose one of these individuals, and based on where you live, list the phone number, local mailing address, email address, and Twitter handle.

- Local concerns require contacting local officials. Identify your mayor, and provide contact information: phone number, mailing address, email address, and Twitter handle. If you live in a place without a mayor, then identify the name, title, and contact information of an elected official you think would be able to help you address a problem in your community.

Want to Know More?

For an amusing look at how federalism plays out in terms of health care and Medicaid, watch this segment of *Last Week Tonight with John Oliver*: https://www.youtube.com/watch?time_continue=6&v=5d3nASKtGas. It demonstrates the unevenness that can occur across the country when Congress and the president leave it to the states to implement federal policy.

8.
Why can you smoke pot in Colorado, but could go to jail for smoking it in Oklahoma?

#FederalismMatters

Scenario 1: In college, you hung out with Jimmy Tyler all the time. He was really funny, played in a band, and did pretty well in school. Senior year, you took a couple of classes together, went to a lot of parties together, and attended school basketball games together. The one thing you didn't do together was smoke pot. Jimmy really liked pot. You wouldn't call him a pothead exactly, but he smoked quite a bit. It just wasn't your idea of fun. After graduation, Jimmy left Florida, where you both lived, and headed off to graduate school. He enrolled in a master's program in political science (of course) at the University of Colorado. You keep in touch but aren't as close as you used to be. Still, you're very concerned when Jimmy texts you that he just had a run-in with the police.

"What happened?!?" you reply immediately. Well, it turns out that after spending a few weeks getting situated in his new apartment and

While some states have legalized recreational marijuana and allow dispensaries to sell marijuana products, others continue to treat marijuana possession as a serious crime. This is an example of how federalism allows for significantly different public policies depending on where you live.

adjusting to his classes, Jimmy decided it was time to have a little fun, Jimmy style. In college, he had always gotten pot from his roommate, who sold him small amounts whenever he wanted it. But now he wasn't sure where to get it. Steve, a guy in his master's program, seemed in the know, so Jimmy broached the subject with him. Steve looked at Jimmy like he had two heads. "Man, you live in Colorado. You can buy it anywhere." So Jimmy googled nearby marijuana shops — often called dispensaries — and headed off to a spot a couple of blocks from campus.

As the story unfolds over multiple texts, you have a feeling you know where it's headed. Jimmy writes that the dispensary was "amazing, nothing like Florida." He went on to describe the variety and packaging of the many marijuana products. He purchased several grams of pot, some edible gummies, and a batch of fresh-baked brownies. Jimmy also bought a baby marijuana plant to keep at his apartment. That night, he brought the "goodies" to a small party at a friend's apartment. They could all share in the "fun."

As everyone began to try Jimmy's merchandise, they heard a loud knock on the door. When Jimmy's friend opened it, two police officers greeted him on the other side. The officers entered the apartment, smelled marijuana, and saw the products on the table. Jimmy's heart started racing. "I was sure we were going to get busted," he writes. But that's not what happened. The officers told Jimmy and his friends that a neighbor had complained about noise. They'd have to turn down the music and be a little quieter. The officers left and the party continued, just with a little less volume.

Scenario 2: In college, you hung out with Jimmy Tyler all the time. He was really funny, played in a band, and did pretty well in school. Senior year, you took a couple of classes together, went to a lot of parties together, and attended school basketball games together. The one thing you didn't do together was smoke pot. Jimmy really liked pot. You wouldn't call him a pothead exactly, but he smoked quite a bit. It just wasn't your idea of fun. After graduation, Jimmy left Florida, where you both lived, and headed off to graduate school. He enrolled in a master's program in political science (of course) at the University of Oklahoma. You keep in touch but aren't as close as you used to be. Still, you're very concerned when Jimmy texts you that he just had a run-in with the police.

"What happened?!?" you reply immediately. Well, it turns out that after spending a few weeks getting situated in his new apartment and adjusting to his classes, Jimmy decided it was time to have a little fun, Jimmy style. In college, he had always gotten pot from his roommate, who sold him small amounts whenever he wanted it. But now, he wasn't sure where to get it. Steve, a guy in his master's program, seemed in the know, so Jimmy broached the subject with him. Steve told him about a friend who lived near campus who could probably sell him some. He then gave Jimmy the number.

As the story unfolds over multiple texts, you have a feeling you know where it's headed. Jimmy writes that he took the friend's number and arranged to go to his house. He bought a few grams of pot and a marijuana plant. That night, he brought the pot to a small party at a friend's apartment. They could all share in the "fun."

As everyone began to try Jimmy's merchandise, they heard a loud knock on the door. When Jimmy's friend opened it, two police officers greeted him on the other side. The officers entered the apartment, smelled marijuana, and saw the products on the table. Jimmy's heart started racing. "I was sure we were going to get busted," he writes. And that's exactly what happened. The officers told Jimmy and his friends that a neighbor had complained about the noise. But once they saw the pot, their tone changed. The officers asked who it belonged to. Jimmy admitted that it was his. The police left, along with Jimmy, whom they arrested for possession of marijuana. One officer looked at Jimmy and said, "You're in big trouble."

It's true. What's perfectly legal in Colorado could actually land you in jail in Oklahoma. And not just for a night or two. Table 1 compares the penalties for possession and distribution of marijuana in both states.[1] In Oklahoma, Jimmy could get sentenced to one year for possession and two more years for giving marijuana to his friends. If the police found the

Why can you smoke pot in Colorado, but could go to jail for smoking it in Oklahoma?

TABLE 1. Marijuana Penalties: Oklahoma versus Colorado

	Oklahoma	Colorado
Possession of one ounce or less of marijuana	One-year incarceration	Legal
Giving a friend one ounce or less of marijuana	Two-year minimum incarceration	Legal
Growing up to six marijuana plants in your home	Two-year minimum incarceration	Legal
Possession of "marijuana paraphernalia"	One-year incarceration	$100 fine

Source: Compiled from Colorado and Oklahoma state laws.

marijuana plant in his apartment, he could get two years on top of that. That's right. For a night of completely legal marijuana use in one state, Jimmy could receive a five-year, life-altering prison sentence in another.

How is it possible for such different consequences to apply to the exact same behavior in two states, perhaps even just a few miles apart? The Tenth Amendment — that's how. Because the Constitution reserves certain powers for the states, they can shape public policy on a wide range of issues. And as this segment demonstrates, very different state cultures influence what's legal in one place and illegal in another.

The Tenth Amendment: Paving the Way for Different State Policies

During the drafting and ratification process of the Constitution, some of the Founders worried that the federal government was too strong and would crush the states' autonomy. To ensure that wouldn't happen, they required the inclusion of the Tenth Amendment, which created a broad range of **reserved powers** for the states. Basically, the states had substantial authority to do anything that wasn't specifically delegated to the federal government or prohibited by the Constitution.

To see how this plays out, consider a couple of contemporary Supreme Court cases. In 1993, Congress passed and President Bill Clinton signed the Brady Handgun Violence Prevention Act.[2] In a nutshell, the bill required federal background checks on gun purchases in the United States. Simple enough, right? Not quite. The federal government had not yet developed a system or a database to enable these background checks. So the bill mandated that local law enforcement officers had to perform the checks themselves. Local authorities weren't having it. Sheriffs from Montana and Arizona challenged the law, claiming that the federal government did not have the authority to order cities or states to carry out a federal law.

In *Printz v. United States*, the Supreme Court agreed.[3] In the majority opinion, the justices explained that Congress does indeed have the authority to regulate the purchase of guns and that imposing background checks falls within its powers. But nothing in the Constitution empowers the federal government to force states to carry out its policy objectives. Referring to the *Federalist Papers* and debates at the Constitutional Convention, Justice Antonin Scalia wrote in the majority opinion that federalism in the United States means that the states retain "a residual and inviolable sovereignty" over internal matters. The federal government cannot "compel the states to enact or administer a federal regulatory program."

More recently, the Court weighed in on a conflict between state and federal laws over sports gambling. First, a little background. In 1992, Congress passed the Professional and Amateur Sports Protection Act. The law prohibited sports gambling in any state that didn't already permit it. Twenty years later, the New Jersey state legislature wanted to expand legal gambling. So it passed a law to permit sports betting. Several major sports leagues opposed this move. Although sports organizations might benefit from the increased interest that gambling can generate among sports fans, the leagues were concerned that expanding sports betting could corrupt the integrity of the games.[4] To prevent this from happening, they sued New Jersey for violating the federal law. New Jersey argued that the federal law violated the Tenth Amendment.

The case, *Murphy v. National Collegiate Athletic Association,* reached the Supreme Court in 2018. In a 7–2 decision, the justices ruled in favor of New Jersey. Justice Samuel Alito explained that the Constitution "confers on Congress . . . only certain enumerated powers. Therefore, all other legislative power is reserved for the States." "Absent from the list of powers given to Congress," Alito continued, "is the power to issue direct orders to the governments of the states."[5] In other words, Congress cannot tell state governments what to do unless the order is part of the federal government's enumerated powers. And regulating whether a state permits betting on sporting events doesn't fall within that realm.

These cases affirm that the Tenth Amendment carries broad implications for what states can do within their own borders. The federal government has the authority, for example, to require background checks for gun purchases, but it does not have the power to force states to help enact these policies.[6] When it comes to policy areas that are not part of the federal government's enumerated powers—such as gambling—the federal government cannot command a state to adopt a particular policy.

Why can you smoke pot in Colorado, but could go to jail for smoking it in Oklahoma?

Even when state policies explicitly contravene a federal law, the federal government sometimes chooses not to do anything about it. Legalizing marijuana falls within this realm. The Controlled Substances Act, signed into law by President Nixon in 1970, classifies marijuana as a Schedule 1 drug. This distinction places it in the category of the most dangerous illegal drugs, including heroin.[7] Federal law enforcement officers, therefore, could opt to enforce the federal law. They could shut down dispensaries and arrest users and distributors even in the 36 states where medical marijuana is legal.[8] The federal government, however, has generally taken a hands-off approach, leaving marijuana policy to the states.

Big Differences in Policies across States

Given the Court's interpretation of the Tenth Amendment, different state political cultures can generate some huge disparities in public policy. Think about the dramatically different political outlooks across states. In the 2020 presidential election, for instance, Donald Trump beat Joe Biden in Oklahoma by a whopping 33 percentage points (he received 65 percent of the vote, compared to Biden's 32 percent). But Biden blew Trump out of the water in Hawaii (he received 64 percent of the vote to Trump's 34 percent). As you might expect, the Oklahoma state government is dominated by Republicans, who, for decades, have controlled the governor's office and the state legislature. The opposite is true in Hawaii, where Democrats are in full control of the state government.

These disparate political preferences across states can lead to some very different laws. The columns in Table 2 summarize how five states address eight policy areas over which states have considerable discretion.[9] We chose these states because they range from very Republican (Wyoming) to very Democratic (California). Their overall partisanship rankings appear in the bottom row of the table.

Not only are each state's residents governed by different polices—from how much they have to pay in income tax, to the minimum wage, to access to abortion, to transgender rights—but state laws about basic ways of life differ, too. Take getting married. Four states actually have no minimum age for marriage. In most others, you have to be at least 16, and usually 18, years old. But in New Hampshire, for example, minors can marry at age 13 if their parents give permission. In Mississippi, 15-year-olds can get married, even without parental consent.[10] Divorce laws vary, too. If you need a fast divorce, then Alaska is the state for you; it takes only a few weeks. Arkansas makes you wait 18 months, and if you live

TABLE 2. Differences in Public Policy across the United States

	Wyoming	Alabama	Ohio	Illinois	California
Minimum wage	$7.25 per hour	$7.25 per hour	$9.30 per hour	$12.00 per hour	$15.00 per hour
Top individual state income tax rate	None	5%	3.99%	4.95%	13.3%
Death penalty	Yes	Yes	Yes	No	Yes (but the governor imposed a moratorium)
Marijuana legalization	Illegal	Medical only	Medical only	Recreational and medical	Recreational and medical
Adopted Medicaid expansion	No	No	Yes	Yes	Yes
Legal abortion	No	No	No	Yes	Yes
Must teach evolution in public schools	No	No	No	Yes	Yes
Prohibit transgender discrimination	No	No	No	Yes	Yes
Partisanship ranking	1	8	22	41	48

Note: For partisanship ranking, 1 is the most Republican state, and 50 is the most Democratic.

Source: Data from National Conference of State Legislatures, Tax Foundation, Death Penalty Information Center, Henry J. Kaiser Family Foundation, Guttmacher Institute, Evolution: Education and Outreach, Movement Advancement Project (MAP), and Cook Political Report. See Note 9 for full source information.

together at any point during that waiting period, the clock resets.[11] Driving is another example. Depending on where you live, you might be able to get your learner's permit when you turn 14. That's right—when you're in eighth grade! Or you might be unlucky and live in a state that forces you to wait until your sixteenth birthday. In South Dakota, you can be 14½ years old and drive with a license that carries few restrictions. You can't do that until you're 17 in New Jersey.[12] Or look at how states responded to the Covid-19 pandemic. South Dakota never issued a statewide mask mandate or required businesses

Why can you smoke pot in Colorado, but could go to jail for smoking it in Oklahoma?

The driving age isn't the only transportation-related issue that varies across states. States also differ in their traffic laws, including speed limits, cell phone restrictions, headlight use, and seatbelt requirements.

to close at any point during the pandemic.[13] California, in contrast, implemented a mask mandate that lasted well over a year and forced businesses to close or reduce capacity several times as virus case counts spiked.[14]

The disparities in what policies govern citizens in different states will likely only continue to grow—for two reasons. First, Democrats' and Republicans' attitudes toward a broad array of issues have grown further apart, even since 2000. And not by just a little. When it comes to gun control, for example, 60 percent of Democrats and 45 percent of Republicans in 2001 thought that gun control laws should be stricter. By 2021, that 15 percentage point difference had more than quadrupled. Immigration is another example. In 2003, 53 percent of Republicans and 42 percent of Democrats thought that immigration into the United States should decrease. That 11-point gap grew to 35 points by 2020. The partisan gap has also expanded when it comes to health care, public education, the death penalty, abortion, and taxes.[15] Second, state legislatures have become increasingly dominated by one party or the other. In 2000, 12 states had "split" state legislatures—one chamber was controlled by Republicans and the other by Democrats. By 2023, the number of states in that category had fallen to two (Pennsylvania and Virginia). The other 48 were dominated by one political party.[16]

Together, these trends make it more likely that Republican and Democratic states will adopt different public policies spanning the wide range of issues on which the Tenth Amendment gives them discretion. And it accounts for why Jimmy Tyler's graduate school days could be filled with pot-filled parties in Colorado but jail time in Oklahoma.

DID YOU GET IT?

Why can you smoke pot in Colorado, but could go to jail for smoking it in Oklahoma?

Short Answer:

- The Tenth Amendment reserves for the states powers that are not delegated to the federal government or prohibited by the Constitution.
- States have broad freedom to develop different positions on a wide range of public policies, including marijuana.
- The laws and regulations that states develop are often rooted in their political cultures, which vary dramatically across the country.

DEVELOPING YOUR SKILLS

Civic Engagement

Know your rights: The typical American will spend time living, working, or traveling in 12 states across a lifetime! Knowing the rules and laws of whatever state you're in is critical to being an engaged citizen.

1. Congratulations! You're getting married. To avoid family drama, you and your partner want to do it quickly. Which state can marry you the fastest? (Hint: Check out the marriage laws by state at https://www.law.cornell.edu/wex/table_marriage.)
   a. Illinois
   b. Oregon
   c. Wisconsin
   d. Wyoming
2. If you don't want to pay a lot in state and local income tax, where should you consider moving when you graduate? (Hint: Taxfoundation.org usually has an up-to-date map of state and local income tax burdens under its "State Taxes" tab.)
   a. New Jersey
   b. North Dakota
   c. Oregon
   d. Wisconsin

3. You drive fast — too fast, according to your many speeding tickets. If you want to avoid getting pulled over, which state's highways are best for you?
    a. Arkansas
    b. Delaware
    c. Idaho
    d. Vermont

FIGURE IT OUT

Do you want to live in a state that's tough on crime? Maybe you want to live in a state where there's no death penalty, a higher minimum wage, few restrictions on abortion, and relatively high spending on education. Given your political beliefs, determine one state that is a good political match for you and one state that does not fit your values. More specifically:

- List three issues that are important to you and where laws vary by state. Choose any three issues you care about — the environment, taxes, guns, etc.

- Identify a state that's a match on all three issues you chose. For each law or policy, note the source you relied on to determine the state law. (Hint: Searching "death penalty by state" should yield a reliable source for information.)

- Now identify a state that isn't a match on any of your three issues. Again, for each law or policy, note the source you relied on to determine the state law.

Want to Know More?

Driving laws differ across states. If you think there's a road trip in your future, then you might want to check out the website Is It Illegal to Drive . . . ? (https://www.justpark.com/creative/is-it-illegal/). In some states you can drive while wearing headphones, in a car without a bumper, or with a cracked windshield. In others, it's illegal to drive with a dog on your lap or past a funeral procession. (Spoiler alert: In Mississippi, you can drive while drinking alcohol, as long as you stay under the legal limit.)

Liberties and Rights

Start Here!

Citizens' rights are a fundamental component of any democratic government. Only if people are ensured basic freedoms can they prosper and engage meaningfully in civic and political life. This is part of what sets democracies apart from other political regimes. Whereas democratic governments strive to protect citizens' freedom and rights, many other forms of government severely regulate and restrict them. What are the freedoms and rights that are so essential to democracy? What are your fundamental protections under the law? They fall into two categories: civil liberties and civil rights. People often confuse these two terms, so let's be clear about what each means.

Civil liberties are the basic freedoms that protect citizens from undue government intrusion into their lives. The Bill of Rights guarantees many of them. The First Amendment, for example, establishes your freedom of speech and religion. The Fourth Amendment protects you from an unlawful search of your home. The Eighth Amendment ensures that the government doesn't subject you to cruel and unusual punishment. And although the Constitution doesn't explicitly refer to a "right to privacy," the Supreme Court has determined that the Bill of Rights implies that many of your most personal decisions — such as whether to use birth control or whom to marry — should be yours alone to make, free from government interference.

Civil rights are basic protections from unfair or unequal treatment based on demographic characteristics, such as race, ethnicity, or gender. They protect citizens from discrimination by fellow citizens or the government. The Supreme Court's interpretation of the Constitution, particularly the equal protection clause of the Fourteenth Amendment, has played a central role in defining civil rights, many of which are embodied in federal laws enacted by Congress. Civil rights laws guarantee citizens the right to vote; equal access to public facilities such as schools, hospitals, and parks; and fair treatment in housing and employment. A landlord, for instance, can't refuse to rent an apartment to you just because you're Black, or Jewish, or a man.

Despite what might seem like straightforward words — "free speech," "free exercise of religion," "equal protection under the law" — your rights actually aren't so clear-cut. You'll see the complexities in defining them in the segments that follow, which cover freedom of speech, freedom of religion, the right to privacy, rights of the accused, and the application of civil rights based on race, gender, and sexual orientation. Although not an exhaustive list, these topics offer a strong foundation for you to develop an understanding of civil liberties and civil rights, the general freedoms they provide, and the ways in which they're limited.

Ultimately, the content in this section drives home three core ideas:

1 **Civil rights and civil liberties can sometimes clash.**
There are times when one person's rights are pitted against another's civil liberties. Freedom of speech, for example, can lead to racist and sexist language that encroaches on civil rights. Business owners' free exercise of religion can result in discrimination against gay and lesbian customers. When conflicts like these arise, the Supreme Court faces the difficult task of determining which rights to prioritize.

2 **Evolving social norms and new technologies make defining civil liberties and civil rights a fluid process.**
The ubiquity of the internet, the prevalence of social media, and the emergence of gay and transgender rights are only some of the many changes our society has experienced in recent decades. These developments have required the Supreme Court to apply constitutional language written centuries ago to situations the Founders never could have imagined.

3 **Extending civil liberties and civil rights to all citizens has been, and continues to be, a slow process.**
When the Constitution was written, the many freedoms and protections it included applied only to White men. Over time, Congress, state governments, and the courts have extended rights to people of color, women, and to a lesser extent, gay and lesbian citizens. Still, we've yet to achieve full equality for everyone in all domains.

PERSUASIVE ARGUMENTATION

9.
Why can't kids pray in public schools?

#EstablishmentClause

Roy Costner, the valedictorian at Liberty High School in South Carolina, stood at the podium to address his graduating class, their families, teachers, and community members. But rather than deliver his preapproved remarks, Costner ripped up the document, looked out at the audience, and said: "One thing I am certain of is we're all a sum of our experiences, both good and bad."[1] Before school administrators could breathe a sigh of relief at what seemed to be an innocuous opening, Costner explicitly defied the school principal who had told him weeks earlier that he was not permitted to advocate a religious point of view in the speech. Costner thanked his parents for leading him "to the Lord at a young age" and began to recite a Christian prayer. By the time he made it to the second verse, no one could even hear him; thunderous applause had drowned out the words. Later, when asked why he did it, Costner responded: "I wanted to stand up for God. This is what God wanted me to do."[2]

It turns out that just like the majority of people who attended Costner's graduation, most Americans would have had no problem with the religious content of Costner's speech. Approximately 60 percent of people believe that state and local governments should be able to require reading the Lord's Prayer or Bible verses in public schools.[3] That's not to say there aren't some big differences among groups of people. People over the age of 75 are almost twice as likely as 18- to

Despite the separation of church and state, the Supreme Court has ruled that high school football players and their coaches, like this team in Palm Beach, Florida, have the right to pray on the field.

29-year-olds to support prayer in public schools (see Figure 1).[4] Residents of northeastern and western states are about 30 percentage points less likely than southerners to support it.

So what's the big deal? Why did the principal forbid Roy Costner from including a prayer in his graduation speech? The answer is rooted in the principle of separation of church and state, a bedrock tenet of American democracy that dates back to the Founding. The concept is embedded in two clauses of the First Amendment. The **establishment clause** reads: "Congress shall make no law respecting the establishment of religion." The **free exercise clause** states that there shall be no laws "prohibiting the free exercise" of religion.

But as is the case with so many of the civil liberties listed in the Bill of Rights, the actual meaning of the language is fuzzy. There's little question that the establishment clause and the free exercise clause prohibit a state-sponsored church or the adoption of a national religion. Beyond such obvious violations, though, the entanglement between church and state is pretty common. "In God We Trust" appears on every piece of American currency. The Pledge of Allegiance includes the phrase "One nation, under God." Christmas trees and menorahs regularly adorn government property. Public schools take breaks for Christmas and Easter. And the U.S. Congress, as well as many state legislatures, begins its proceedings with a prayer.

FIGURE 1. Support for Prayer in Public Schools

Overall	57%
Northeast	42
Midwest	55
West	44
South	73
18–29 years old	38
30–44 years old	58
45–59 years old	65
60–74 years old	63
75 and older	71

Note: Bars represent the percentage of Americans who disapprove of the Supreme Court ruling that no state or local government may require reading the Lord's Prayer or Bible verses in public schools.

Source: General Social Survey, National Opinion Research Council.

How is it that religion is permitted in some areas of public life and not others? What's permissible and what's not comes down to the Supreme Court's interpretation of the First Amendment. This segment focuses on religion in public schools to demonstrate how the Court has grappled with where to draw the line when it comes to the establishment clause. (We elaborate on issues related to the free exercise clause in Segment 16.)

Religion in Public Schools: Setting the Guidelines

If you had been a student in public school during the 1940s, then there's a good chance that you would have spent at least part of the school week focused on religious education. In Champaign, Illinois, for example, the local board of education implemented a program that devoted one hour each week during the regular school day to religious instruction. Public school students could take a class taught by approved Catholic, Protestant, or Jewish instructors. Those students who chose not to participate in the program were sent to classrooms that focused on secular studies.

Vashti McCollum, an atheist parent of a student in one of the district's elementary schools, objected to this arrangement. Not only did her son suffer from embarrassment and ridicule because she wouldn't let him attend the religion classes, but the program itself, she argued, represented an unacceptable blurring of church and state.[5] McCollum, who sued the school board, was widely ostracized. She received physical threats. She lost her job. Mobs of Halloween trick-or-treaters threw rotten tomatoes and cabbages at her entire family. The McCollums' cat even turned up dead.[6]

But the hardships McCollum sustained weren't for nothing. In 1948, eight Supreme Court justices agreed that the use of taxpayer-funded school property for religious instruction "falls squarely under the ban of the First Amendment."[7] In *McCollum v. Board of Education*, the Court ruled that the establishment clause didn't simply mean that public schools had to treat all religious sects equally, as this district had attempted to do by providing instruction for Protestants, Catholics, and Jews. Rather, it meant that belief and non-belief had to be treated equally, too. As such, Justice Hugo Black advised that "both religion and government can best work to achieve their lofty aims if each is left free from the other in its respective sphere." Four years later, in *Zorach v. Clauson*, the Court permitted a similar program in New York, but only because it took place off of school grounds.[8]

Even if religious instruction wasn't permitted on school grounds during school hours, the Court hadn't said anything specific about prayer. And in New York in the 1950s, that's how the school day began. The New York State Board of Regents, which oversees all public education in the state, had authorized a short, voluntary, nondenominational prayer to be recited each morning. It was just 19 words: "Almighty God, we acknowledge our dependence upon Thee, and beg Thy blessings upon us, our teachers, and our country." At the time, the question of school prayer was becoming increasingly controversial, with some school districts and communities being adamantly opposed to it and others compelling the recitation of very specific Christian prayers. So the Regents' prayer was an attempt to diffuse the issue.

Steven Engel, along with several other parents whose children attended Herricks High School in New Hyde Park, New York, didn't like it. Because the prayer invoked God, they argued that reciting it in school violated the establishment clause. So in 1959 they sued William Vitale, the school board president. They didn't win in either the New York State trial or appellate court. Because reciting the prayer was a voluntary act, the New York Court of Appeals concluded that "there was a sufficient separation of church and state so that the First Amendment was not infringed."[9] Engel and the other parents petitioned the U.S. Supreme Court to hear the case.

Given the Court's previous interpretation of the establishment clause, it wasn't a tough call for the justices. Once again writing for the majority, Justice Black was unequivocal:

> There can be no doubt that New York's state prayer program officially establishes the religious beliefs embodied in the Regents'

prayer. . . . Neither the fact that the prayer may be denominationally neutral nor the fact that its observance on the part of the students is voluntary can serve to free it from the limitations of the Establishment Clause.[10]

Black added, however, that the ruling should not be interpreted as sacrilegious or antireligious. The ruling, after all, did not stop students from praying in school on their own time—whether before or after school, at recess, or during lunch. It applied just to prayer that was in any way organized by the school itself.

The circumstances in *Engel v. Vitale* were quite clear-cut. But, some cases involving church and state are more complex. In the 1971 decision of *Lemon v. Kurtzman*, the Court developed what the justices hoped would be a clear standard for what's permissible under the establishment clause and what's not.[11] Known as the **Lemon Test**, three requirements would determine whether a law passes constitutional muster (see Table 1). In the particular case of *Lemon v. Kurtzman*, the Court found that providing state funding to teachers who taught core subjects like math or English at religious schools violated the third requirement of the test. The Supreme Court relied on the Lemon Test for decades to determine whether a law had the effect of establishing religion.

Religion in Public Schools: Applying the Guidelines

The Court applied the Lemon Test when considering several potential entanglements between church and state in public schools. *Engel v. Vitale* made it clear that a school-sanctioned morning prayer is

TABLE 1. The Lemon Test

Requirement 1	The law must have a secular purpose.
Requirement 2	The law's principal or primary effect must be one that neither promotes nor inhibits religion.
Requirement 3	The law must not foster "excessive government entanglement with religion."

Note: In order for a law to be constitutional, it must meet all three requirements set out by the Supreme Court in *Lemon v. Kurtzman*.

Why can't kids pray in public schools?

unconstitutional. But what about a one-minute moment of silence for "meditation and voluntary prayer"? That's how the Alabama state legislature tried to get around the school prayer ban. The Supreme Court didn't see the distinction and ruled that the Alabama law's intention was to establish religion in public schools. It lacked a secular purpose and, accordingly, violated the Lemon Test.[12]

The guidelines applied outside the classroom, too. Clergy—regardless of their denomination—may not recite a prayer at public school graduation ceremonies, even though these occur only once a year. A graduation prayer, Supreme Court Justice Anthony Kennedy wrote, "places subtle and indirect public and peer pressure on attending students to stand as a group or maintain respectful silence during the invocation and benediction."[13] Similarly, the Court ruled against a Texas school district that allowed a student to recite a Christian prayer over the loudspeaker prior to varsity football games.[14]

Beyond prayer, the Court's view about religion in public school varied. Consider religious documents and decorations. In the late 1970s, when the Kentucky legislature passed a law requiring every public school classroom to post the Ten Commandments, the Supreme Court struck down the statute for violating the first requirement of the Lemon Test: it had no secular purpose.[15] But holiday decorations, religious songs in school music classes and at school concerts, and Christmas parties in the classroom are generally okay. As long as these activities were part of a broader curriculum designed to teach religious and cultural heritage, they didn't violate the establishment clause.[16]

More recent Supreme Court rulings on the question of state funding for private religious schools, however, revealed more support for merging government and religion. In the 2017 decision of *Trinity Lutheran Church of Columbia, Inc. v. Comer*, the Court ruled that the state of Missouri could not deny a church state funding to improve the playground of its preschool simply because the school was a religious entity. Chief Justice John Roberts wrote in the majority opinion that excluding the church from "a public benefit for which it is otherwise qualified, solely because it is a church . . . cannot stand."[17] In a strongly worded dissent, Justices Sonia Sotomayor and Ruth Bader Ginsburg argued that violating the establishment clause leads the nation "to a place where separation of church and state is a constitutional slogan, not a constitutional commitment." Roberts's interpretation of the establishment clause, however, carried the day. In 2022, the Court struck down a Maine law that prevented students from using funds from a state tuition-assistance program to attend private religious schools.[18]

A New Day at the Supreme Court: Replacing the Lemon Test

Interpreting the establishment clause has been a difficult balancing act for the Supreme Court. Despite the standards set forth in *Lemon v. Kurtzman*, it's hard to assess what constitutes a "secular purpose" or an "excessive entanglement" of church and state. In fact, many of the more conservative justices believe that the establishment clause does little more than prohibit a state-sponsored religion.

So in 2022, when the Court had an opportunity to rethink the Lemon Test, rethink they did. *Kennedy v. Bremerton School District* involved Joseph Kennedy, an assistant football coach at a public high school in Bremerton, Washington. He often knelt and prayed at midfield with some of the players at the end of the games. The school asked him to curtail the practice—public school officials leading prayer on public school grounds violated the Lemon Test. Coach Kennedy refused to stop and was fired. The Court sided with Kennedy, arguing that the free exercise of religion protected his right to pray with his team.

But that wasn't all. In a sweeping decision, the Court discarded the Lemon Test altogether, calling it an "abstract, and ahistorical approach to the Establishment Clause." The Court instructed that the establishment clause must be applied using "reference to historical practices and understandings" and that the government must faithfully "reflec[t] the understanding of the Founding Fathers."[19] In other words, the historical record and religious practices of the 1780s replaced the Lemon Test as the guide for deciding what behavior is permissible under the establishment clause.

With a conservative majority now entrenched on the Supreme Court—*Kennedy v. Bremerton* was a 6–3 decision—it may well be that within a few years, the Court will even reverse its position on school prayer. Future Roy Costners might very well be able to include a prayer in their graduation speeches without giving it a second thought.

DID YOU GET IT?
Why can't kids pray in public schools?

Short Answer:
- They actually can pray in school. They just need to do it on their own time.
- Prayer in public schools explicitly violates the establishment clause when it is organized or promoted by school officials on school property.

- When it comes to other ways religion makes its way into schools, including holiday celebrations and state funding for religious activities, the line dividing what's allowed from what's not is quite fuzzy.

DEVELOPING YOUR SKILLS

Persuasive Argumentation

Evaluate evidence: School prayer has always been controversial, and people on both sides of the debate have tried to assemble strong evidence to support their position. Consider possible evidence for arguments favoring and opposing prayer in public schools to answer the following questions.

1. You have to write an essay arguing that school prayer should be allowed because it provides positive societal benefits. Which piece of evidence would most help support your point?
   a. Public opinion polls revealing that people overwhelmingly support school prayer
   b. Academic studies showing that teenagers who pray regularly do better in school
   c. Research that finds no relationship between the rate at which young people pray and the number of disciplinary problems in their high school
   d. The majority opinion in *Lemon v. Kurtzman*

2. You want to convince the Supreme Court to reverse its long-held opposition to school-sanctioned prayer in public schools. You plan to argue that the Court has decided previous cases incorrectly. Which two cases should you make sure to use as evidence of incorrect decisions?
   a. *Engel v. Vitale* and *Zorach v. Clauson*
   b. *McCollum v. Board of Education* and *Engel v. Vitale*
   c. *Kennedy v. Bremerton School District* and *Trinity Lutheran Church of Columbia, Inc. v. Comer*
   d. *Kennedy v. Bremerton School District,* and *Zorach v. Clauson*

3. Your friend is angry about what she perceives as violations of the establishment clause at your public high school. But when she tells you her examples, you explain that only one is evidence of a violation. Which of your friend's examples is compelling evidence of her claim?

   a. A teacher who reads the Bible at his desk during his lunch break

   b. A Christian prayer club that holds meetings on school grounds after school hours

   c. A school principal who prohibits a science teacher from discussing the theory of evolution in class

   d. A vice principal who uses her spare time to serve as a minister at her church

FIGURE IT OUT

A group of public school students decides to hold a review session for a math test in an empty classroom. A teacher passes by the classroom and stops in to tell them some bad news: a classmate was just in a car accident and is on the way to the hospital. One student — quite shaken by the news — asks everyone to take a moment to pray for their friend. The students and the teacher all bow their heads in a moment of silence. The teacher then crosses herself and exits the classroom. Based on the cases we've discussed throughout this segment:

- Identify two aspects of this scenario that you could use as evidence to argue that it violates the establishment clause.

- Identify two aspects of this scenario that you could use as evidence of activities protected by the First Amendment.

- Explain which set of evidence is more persuasive. A few sentences is fine.

Want to Know More?

If you're interested in what the Founders meant when they wrote the establishment and free exercise clauses of the Constitution, then Gregg Frazer's book *The Religious Beliefs of America's Founders: Reason, Revelation, and Revolution* is for you. It provides a fascinating account of the Founders' deliberations and intent in defining the relationship between church and state.

**CONSUMING
POLITICAL
INFORMATION**

10.
Can people say offensive and hateful things whenever they want?

#FreedomOfSpeech

If the freedom of speech is taken away, then dumb and silent we may be led, like sheep, to the slaughter.

George Washington
First president of the United States[1]

To suppress free speech is a double wrong. It violates the rights of the hearer as well as those of the speaker.

Frederick Douglass
Former enslaved person and leader of the abolitionist movement[2]

Free speech is the whole thing, the whole ball game. Free speech is life itself.

Salman Rushdie
Author[3]

White nationalists carry torches at the University of Virginia on the eve of a 2017 Unite the Right rally in Charlottesville. Although this speech was constitutionally protected, the Supreme Court has made it clear that freedom of speech is not absolute.

Free speech is central to a democratic government. Throughout the history of the United States, political figures, authors, and activists have considered it one of the most fundamental civil liberties an open society can bestow upon its citizens. Indeed, the framers of the U.S. Constitution enshrined the importance of **freedom of expression**—the right to hold opinions and to communicate them freely—explicitly in the First Amendment: "Congress shall make no law . . . abridging the freedom of speech, or of the press. . . ."

American history, however, reveals that free expression is not as absolute as the words of the First Amendment might suggest. Soon after the Founding, and on the brink of a war with France, Congress passed the Sedition Act of 1798, which criminalized making false statements that criticized the government. In 1918, socialist and perennial presidential candidate Eugene V. Debs went to jail for giving a speech opposing World War I.[4] In the 1960s, courts found several men guilty of breaking the law when they burned their draft cards in protest over the Vietnam War. It doesn't take a war to curtail freedom of expression, though. Courts have upheld bans on public nudity,[5] found a young woman who sent text messages encouraging her boyfriend to commit suicide guilty of involuntary manslaughter,[6] and sentenced a filmmaker to five years in prison for producing "crush videos" that depict the gruesome deaths of small animals, including puppies, chickens, and kittens.[7]

Can people say offensive and hateful things whenever they want?

So how "free" are free speech and expression? The answer almost always comes down to whether the expression is simply "too" threatening or offensive. Societal norms evolve, and new modes of communication emerge. What's threatening or offensive, therefore, is a moving target. To gain a better handle on how this civil liberty has evolved—and to differentiate what's protected by the Constitution from what's not—we focus on three areas of potentially offensive speech: (1) speech that incites lawless behavior, (2) libel and slander, and (3) symbolic speech.

Imminent Lawless Action

The First Amendment guarantees free speech; but not until the early part of the twentieth century—more than 100 years after the Bill of Rights was ratified—did the Supreme Court begin to weigh in on it. The first landmark case on speech involved Charles Schenck, who mailed pamphlets to men who were drafted to serve in World War I. The pamphlets read: "Do not submit to intimidation." Schenck advocated only peaceful resistance to the draft, but he was charged with conspiracy to violate the Espionage Act of 1917. In the 1919 case of *Schenck v. United States*, the Supreme Court upheld the conviction, ruling that Schenck's words and actions posed a "clear and present danger."[8] Military disobedience and insubordination, after all, could interfere with the defense of the country, so Schenck's speech was not protected.

In 1969, the Court modified the clear and present danger test in *Brandenburg v. Ohio*.[9] The justices protected the right of Clarence Brandenburg, a Ku Klux Klan leader, to deliver a speech to hooded Klansmen—some armed with guns—and urge them to consider taking action to bring about political change. "We're not a revengent organization," Brandenburg told his followers, "but if our President, our Congress, our Supreme Court, continues to suppress the White, Caucasian race, it's possible that there might have to be some revengeance taken."[10] Brandenburg also urged the return of African Americans (he used the N-word) to Africa and Jews to Israel. The Court concluded that Brandenburg's speech, while offensive, did not incite "imminent lawless action"— that is, it didn't promote lawbreaking behavior in the immediate future. The Court later clarified that advocacy of illegal action at "some indefinite future time" does not meet the imminence requirement.[11]

This standard has continued to guide restrictions—or the lack thereof—on free speech. In 1978, for example, neo-Nazis were allowed to stage a march in Skokie, Illinois. Their expression was protected

Members of the Westboro Baptist Church, a fringe religious group headquartered in Topeka, Kansas, often protest with offensive signs to condemn people, groups, and institutions they believe support LGBTQ rights. The Supreme Court has upheld Westboro's right to protest, even at military funerals and weddings.

even though the town was home to an unusually large population of Holocaust survivors, and even though town officials had voiced concern that the appearance of Nazi demonstrators might lead to violence.[12] More recently, in 2011, the Supreme Court upheld the right of members of the Westboro Baptist Church to protest at military funerals with signs reading "Thank God for Dead Soldiers" and "Fag Troops."[13] The Westboro Church links the death of American soldiers to the expansion of gay rights. Racist, antisemitic, anti-gay hate speech, while repugnant, is protected because rarely does it incite imminent lawlessness.

In fact, even hateful threats typically receive protection. Anthony Elonis's 2010 online behavior is a case in point. Shortly after his wife left him, Elonis logged on to Facebook and posted: "There's one way to love you but a thousand ways to kill you. I'm not going to rest until your body is a mess, soaked in blood and dying from all the little cuts." When a coworker accused Elonis of sexual harassment, he posted a photo of himself holding a knife at the coworker's neck, with the caption "I wish." And after an FBI agent came to speak to him about his online comments, Elonis posted: "Little Agent Lady stood so close, Took all the strength I had not to turn the bitch ghost. Pull my knife, flick my wrist, and slit her

Can people say offensive and hateful things whenever they want?

throat."[14] A district court found Elonis guilty of making criminal threats and sentenced him to nearly four years in prison.[15] But Elonis appealed the conviction, arguing that because the posts were not "true threats" or a "serious expression of intention" to hurt or kill anyone, his words were protected by the First Amendment. In the 2015 case *Elonis v. United States*, the Supreme Court agreed.[16]

The only notable restriction on hateful, threatening speech is when it's directed at the president of the United States or anyone protected by the Secret Service. It's a federal crime to "knowingly and willfully threaten to kill, kidnap, or inflict bodily harm upon" anyone with this protection,[17] and the Supreme Court has done nothing to chip away at that restriction. Even so, only people with detailed plans and the capacity to carry out their threats tend to be arrested.[18] Donte Jamar Sims, for example, served jail time for repeatedly tweeting—with specificity—about his intent to assassinate Barack Obama at the 2012 Democratic National Convention.[19] Travis Luke Dominguez was indicted after posting this threat on a Salt Lake City tip line: "I'm a Navy SEAL . . . I woke up and decided to kill the president Donald Trump today. Please forgive me and then I will die by suicide by cop."[20] As for the tens of thousands of more generic threats on presidents' lives, former Secret Service agent Tim Franklin told a reporter: "It's an American right to be able to express those opinions."[21]

Libel and Slander

The challenges of regulating offensive speech also emerge when people communicate falsehoods and lies about other people. Just consider the behavior of an eighth-grade honors student at a public school in Pennsylvania. Upset with her principal, she created a fake social media profile meant to humiliate him. It included a picture of the principal with a bio that described him as a "hairy sex addict" and "pervert" who enjoys "hitting on students" in his office. It featured the quote "Kids rock my bed." Comments on the site mocked his wife and children. The principal identified the student who made the profile and suspended her for 10 days. But that wasn't the end of the incident. Supported by the American Civil Liberties Union, the student and her family filed a lawsuit against the school district claiming that the suspension violated her right to free speech. And they won.[22] According to a circuit court ruling, not only did the speech occur off school grounds (in cyberspace) and not during school hours, but the fake profile was satirical, so it didn't really threaten or defame the principal. This is just one of the many "cyber defamation" cases that have entered the federal court system in recent years. Students have used social media platforms to mock their teachers and principals as drug users, created lewd Twitter accounts in teachers' names, and generated online sites that ridicule fellow students for being promiscuous, stupid, or gay.[23]

The courts have made it clear, however, that the right to free speech can be regulated in cases of **libel** or **slander**—false written or spoken statements that damage a person's reputation. Limits on what you can write or say about another person vary according to the location, intent, and target of the speech.

Take, for example, public figures. In the Supreme Court's 1964 landmark ruling in *New York Times Co. v. Sullivan*, the justices unanimously held that the First Amendment protects almost any statements that describe the behavior of public officials, even if the statements are not true. The case involved a libel suit brought by L. B. Sullivan, a Montgomery, Alabama, city commissioner who was offended by a full-page ad in the *New York Times*. The ad accused the Montgomery police department of arresting Martin Luther King Jr. as a way to disrupt the civil rights movement and discourage African Americans from voting. Sullivan identified factually incorrect statements in the ad and claimed that he had been personally defamed by it. But the Supreme Court concluded that the First Amendment protects all statements—even false ones—about public officials.

Libel in these cases occurs only when the false statements meet the legal definition of "malice" (that is, knowledge that the statements are false or made with a reckless disregard for the truth).[24] That's why, in 2021, an appeals court dismissed Virginia lieutenant governor Justin Fairfax's slander suit against CBS. Fairfax sued for $400 million in damages after the network aired interviews with two women who claimed that Fairfax had sexually assaulted them years earlier—allegations Fairfax denied. The Court found, however, that Fairfax failed to disprove the allegations or demonstrate that CBS ever doubted the women's accusations.[25]

When the target of offensive speech isn't a public official, the bar for libel is lower. The 1974 case of *Gertz v. Welch* involved a private attorney who was criticized harshly in a magazine for representing a family that sued the police department for the wrongful death of their child. The article railed against the attorney's ideology and ethics and implied that he had a criminal record. The attorney sued the magazine for libel. The Court sided with the attorney, reasoning that ordinary citizens like him deserve more protection from libelous statements than public figures do.[26]

Libel standards become fuzzier when the speech includes offensive insults, jokes, or satire. The Supreme Court first weighed in on this issue in the 1988 case of *Hustler v. Falwell*.[27] A 1983 edition of *Hustler* magazine

Can people say offensive and hateful things whenever they want?

included a mock interview with Jerry Falwell, a prominent religious leader, about his first sexual encounter. The piece, entitled "Jerry Falwell Talks about His First Time," had Falwell admit, among other ridiculous things, that the first time he had sex was with his mother in an outhouse. Falwell sued the magazine for libel, arguing that the patently offensive material caused him emotional distress. But the Court ruled that restricting speech was too high a price to bear in cases where no reasonable person would think the story is based in fact. The decision provides broad protection for satirical material directed at public figures as well as private citizens.

Symbolic Speech

Freedom of expression also applies to nonverbal forms of communication. These types of **symbolic speech** include waving the flag; displaying signs, buttons, and bumper stickers; attending sit-ins or protests; and making gestures. Just like verbal speech, many of these forms of expression have tested how far the First Amendment extends.

Consider the story of Annie Caddell, a White woman who moved to the predominantly African American neighborhood of Summerville, South Carolina, in 2010. To the horror of many of her neighbors, Caddell flew a full-sized Confederate flag from the front porch of her house. Her neighbors asked her to remove the flag because they considered it overtly racist and tantamount to celebrating slavery. One of them, 74-year-old Violet Saylor, wanted the flag taken down because it reminded her of "the Ku Klux Klan that used to ride through the town and we used to have to turn our lights off and hide behind the shades."[28] Caddell refused to take down the flag, explaining that it is a tribute to her southern heritage and "not a racial thing."[29] The neighbors held marches and demonstrations and eventually took a signed petition to a town council meeting asking that Caddell be forced to remove the flag.[30] But the city of Summerville could find no legal grounds on which to do so. Freedom of expression meant that Caddell had the right to fly the flag, and her neighbors had the right to protest it.

For the most part, the Supreme Court tends to come down on the side of allowing symbolic speech, even during times of war. In 1965, for example, a group of high school students devised a plan to wear black armbands to school to protest the Vietnam War. When school officials learned of the plan, they told the students that anyone who wore an armband would be asked to remove it. When the students who wore the armbands were suspended, they filed suit claiming that school officials had infringed on their right of expression. The Supreme Court agreed.

In *Tinker v. Des Moines*, the majority opinion asserted that students do not lose their speech rights when they set foot on school grounds. Moreover, "They may not be confined to the expression of those sentiments that are officially approved."[31] These rights also extend to speech that might be perceived as more visually offensive. In *Cohen v. California*, the Court ruled that a 19-year-old store clerk could not be arrested simply for walking through a California courthouse wearing a jacket that read "Fuck the Draft. Stop the War." If the state is going to prohibit symbolic speech, then it must show real evidence that the speech is disruptive or dangerously provocative.[32] The jacket didn't meet that bar.

Perhaps the most famous symbolic speech case of the modern era occurred in 1989 with the Supreme Court's decision in *Texas v. Johnson*.

This poster, which shows Vietnam War protester Bill Greenshields burning his draft card, became an iconic symbol of the antiwar movement in the 1960s and 1970s. The Supreme Court ruled that burning the card was not a protected form of symbolic speech.

Can people say offensive and hateful things whenever they want?

As a way to protest the policies of the Reagan administration, Gregory Lee Johnson burned an American flag outside the 1984 Republican National Convention in Dallas. Many Americans find flag burning abhorrent, and a large majority of the population believes that it should be illegal.[33] That was certainly the case in Texas in the 1980s, where the law prohibited burning the flag. Johnson was arrested, convicted, fined $2,000, and sentenced to one year in jail. In a 5–4 decision, though, the Supreme Court overturned the conviction. With strong language, the justices upheld flag burning as an act of free speech: "If there is a bedrock principle underlying the First Amendment, it is that the Government may not prohibit the expression of an idea simply because society finds the idea itself offensive or disagreeable."[34]

That's not to say that the Court always favors symbolic speech. During the Vietnam War, David O'Brien's rights did not include burning his government-issued draft card at an antiwar demonstration. O'Brien's free expression ran counter to another critical government function: maintaining the military in a time of war.[35] The Supreme Court has also banned or curtailed cross burning when the intent is to intimidate.[36] And it has restricted symbolic speech in the form of nudity. The Court ruled that an Erie, Pennsylvania, ban on public nudity—even within the confines of a strip club—does not violate erotic dancers' freedom of expression. Because the dancers are still free to perform (they just have to wear pasties and G-strings when they do it), the ban "leaves ample capacity to convey the dancers' erotic message."[37]

DID YOU GET IT?
Can people say offensive and hateful things whenever they want?

Short Answer:

- No, not whenever they want. But the Supreme Court tends to protect offensive and hateful speech most of the time.
- The Court has, however, limited the right of free expression in some instances, such as communication that directly incites violence, targets a private citizen with libel or slander, or prevents the government from carrying out its central functions.

Consuming Political Information

Navigate Supreme Court decisions: To analyze the laws surrounding free speech, you need to be able to read and apply Supreme Court decisions. Two highly regarded websites that house and summarize Supreme Court cases are https://www.oyez.org and https://supreme.justia.com. Visit these websites to answer the following questions about various types of free speech protections.

1. The Supreme Court has placed limits on obscene or pornographic materials. In providing a legal framework for defining and restricting obscenity, the Court developed a three-part test in *Miller v. California*. Based on that case, which of the following forms of expression would be *least* likely to be restricted?
   a. Child pornography
   b. A billboard depicting nudity as a way to sell a skin care product
   c. An art exhibit that features nude photos of adult women and men
   d. A video game with explicitly sexual content that is marketed to teenagers

2. Imagine that the president of the United States finds out that a major news network is planning to report a series of unfavorable stories about the administration. The president orders the network to cancel the report, and the president's lawyer tells network executives that the stories are libelous. Which Supreme Court case speaks directly to this issue?
   a. *Debs v. United States* (1919)
   b. *Near v. Minnesota* (1931)
   c. *Rust v. Sullivan* (1991)
   d. *Citizens United v. Federal Election Commission* (2010)

3. Advertisements are entitled to less First Amendment protection than other types of speech. Based on the landmark ruling in *Central Hudson Gas & Electric Corp. v. Public Service Commission*, under what circumstances can the government regulate commercial speech?
   a. Almost always. Commercial speech receives very little protection under the First Amendment.
   b. When the commercial speech can harm a particular industry economically.
   c. When regulating the speech directly advances a substantial government interest.
   d. Rarely. The First Amendment almost always protects commercial speech.

Want to Know More?

The People vs. Larry Flynt is a 1996 film that chronicles the life of Flynt, the publisher of *Hustler* magazine. The central free speech controversy depicted in the movie is the conflict with Jerry Falwell, which—as we discussed in this segment—made its way to the U.S. Supreme Court.

**CIVIC
ENGAGEMENT**

11.
What happens
if you're charged
with a crime?

#RightsOfTheAccused

Ever since you received a new iPhone as a birthday present from your rich uncle, you've had problems with it. Sometimes the facial recognition feature glitches and you can't unlock the phone. Sometimes the Wi-Fi won't connect. Sometimes your calls disconnect with no rhyme or reason. Something is clearly wrong with the phone. On what's become an almost daily basis, you call the customer service line, reset the phone, and search for online solutions. But you can't stand this anymore. You need to suck it up, go to an actual Apple store, and talk to a real person.

When you walk into the very crowded store on a Tuesday afternoon, a greeter tells you that it'll be about 30 minutes before someone can help you. You give her your name so that she can call you to the counter when it's your turn. In the meantime, you walk over and pick up an iPhone from the display. As far as you can tell, this phone seems to work much better than yours. So you grab a piece of paper from your backpack and scribble down some of the information from the settings tab. You put the paper back in your bag, zip it up, and leave the store. You'll try to fix the phone by yourself, or maybe you'll come back later. Thirty minutes has already turned into an hour, and you have to get to class.

Police arrest a University of Kentucky student in Lexington for disorderly conduct after a celebration of the school's men's basketball team's victory in the NCAA national championship game.

Your decision to leave the store sets into motion a series of events you'll find hard to believe for years to come. The clerk eventually calls your name, and when you don't approach, she walks over to the iPhone display to look for you. You're not there, but neither is one of the phones. What remains is a dangling security cord. She alerts her manager, and they check the security camera footage. The camera is often blocked by other customers, but they have clear shots of you holding the phone, reaching into your backpack, zipping it up, and leaving the store. The manager calls the police, shows them the footage, and asks to press charges if they find that you took the phone.

Your soon-to-be foray into the criminal justice system is not unusual. Just consider some statistics about how frequently U.S. citizens interact with law enforcement:

- In a typical year, 24 percent of people report having face-to-face contact with the police.[1]
- Each year, 1 in 10 drivers is pulled over and ticketed for a traffic violation.[2]
- Police arrest more than 10 million people every year.[3]
- Roughly one-third of adults will have been arrested by the time they're 23 years old.[4]
- Today's young adults are 30 percent more likely to be arrested than were young adults of previous generations.[5]

These numbers don't mean that all people who are arrested or pulled over are charged with a crime, let alone convicted of one. But they do demonstrate how often citizens are accused of breaking the law. Think about it this way: in the United States, more people have criminal records than have college degrees, and more households in the United States include someone with an arrest record than include a dog. Even if you're not accused of a crime at some point in your life, the odds are that you'll know someone who is.[6]

A key part of being an informed citizen is knowing your rights when interacting with law enforcement. The Bill of Rights includes four amendments that protect people accused of crimes from an overreaching government. It's important to know your rights not only because you might need to assert them but also because the government has not always honored them. Indeed, many constitutionally secured protections were not fully recognized or enforced until the second half of the twentieth century. And still today, their application is uneven based on the race and socioeconomic status of the people involved. Table 1

TABLE 1. The Supreme Court's Landmark Rulings Interpreting the Rights of the Accused

Protection from unlawful search and seizure	Fourth Amendment	• *Weeks v. United States* (1914): evidence obtained without a warrant is unlawful and must be excluded at trial. • *Mapp v. Ohio* (1961): evidence of illegal activity obtained through an unlawful search is inadmissible at trial.
Protection against self-incrimination	Fifth Amendment	• *Miranda v. Arizona* (1966): suspects must be made aware of their rights when they're arrested, including the right to remain silent; unlawfully obtained confessions are inadmissible.
Right to an attorney to assist with your defense	Sixth Amendment	• *Gideon v. Wainwright* (1963): your right to a lawyer is absolute, so one must be appointed for you if you cannot afford to hire one. • *Escobedo v. Illinois* (1964): your right to counsel is immediate, beginning as soon as the police arrest you.
Protection against cruel and unusual punishment	Eighth Amendment	• *Gregg v. Georgia* (1976): the death penalty constitutes cruel and unusual punishment only if it is applied in a capricious or arbitrary way.

What happens if you're charged with a crime?

identifies several of these fundamental rights as well as the Supreme Court's interpretation of them. We use the stolen iPhone scenario to illustrate how the courts have interpreted the rights of the accused, as well as the important ways they have evolved.

The Police Arrive at Your Door

Shortly after the Apple employees show the police the security footage, two officers arrive at your apartment to look for the stolen merchandise. You don't have to let them in unless they have a warrant. The Fourth Amendment protects you and your property from **unreasonable searches and seizures**. Only with a warrant—a document typically signed by a judge and specifying the location or person to search and the items they're looking for—can government officials proceed to look for the phone and seize it if they find it. The Supreme Court has ruled that evidence obtained without a warrant is unlawful and, thus, must be excluded as a case moves forward.[7]

When it comes to searching a residence, the need for a warrant is clear-cut. But other situations aren't always so straightforward. If officers believe that there's evidence of a crime in your vehicle, then they don't need a warrant. Moreover, the Supreme Court has taken a broad view of what can be included in a warrantless car search. It's not just items in plain view, or even those in the glove compartment or the trunk of the car. When police in Wyoming pulled over a driver for a faulty brake light, they noticed a syringe in his shirt pocket and track marks on his arms. They searched the car—including passenger Sandra Houghton's handbag—for drug paraphernalia. When they found drugs in her bag, the police arrested Houghton. The Supreme Court held that the search was valid. As long as there is probable cause to search a vehicle, then searches of most of its contents, including passengers, are legal, too.[8]

Public schools are another venue where warrantless searches are sometimes permitted. The Supreme Court has determined that public school officials can conduct random drug tests on student athletes[9] as well as search students' bags if they suspect them of having cigarettes, marijuana, or other items not permitted on school property.[10] When schools officials strip-searched an eighth-grader based on a tip that she had ibuprofen, however, the Court ruled that they had gone too far. The safety of minors under a school's supervision trumps student privacy; but according to the Court, warrantless searches must not be "excessively intrusive in light of the age and sex of the student and the nature of the infraction."[11]

The Police Arrest You

In your case, the officers have a warrant that permits them to search your apartment for an iPhone. They open your backpack, but there's no phone in it. When they open your desk drawer, bingo. They find a phone that looks just like the one that has been stolen. But they're not done. One of the officers tells you: "We're going to keep looking around because stealing smartphones might be your thing." When they search your bathroom, they find a pill box with ecstasy tablets in the medicine cabinet. The officers arrest you for possession of stolen materials *and* illegal drugs.

At this point, you need to be aware of two key provisions of the Fifth Amendment. Perhaps most notable, it protects you from **self-incrimination**: you have the right to remain silent. Beyond ensuring that citizens cannot be compelled to testify against themselves, the Fifth Amendment also states that citizens "cannot be deprived of life, liberty, or property without **due process** of law." In other words, your constitutional rights cannot be infringed by the government.

That's not to say, of course, that for much of U.S. history states and local communities didn't regularly ignore these constitutional protections. But in the 1960s, the Supreme Court became more assertive in establishing that suspects must be made aware of their rights. If they are not, even an explicit confession to a crime will likely be inadmissible at trial.[12] That's what happened to Ernesto Miranda. Following two hours of questioning by police, he confessed to committing a rape. But he was neither informed of his right to remain silent nor told that his admission of guilt would be used against him. Ultimately, in *Miranda v. Arizona*, the Supreme Court overturned the conviction because Miranda's confession hadn't been lawfully obtained, so it should not have been used as evidence at his trial.

The Court has, however, recognized a "public safety exception" in which incriminating information can be obtained even if a suspect hasn't been issued a **Miranda warning**. In the case of *New York v. Quarles*, an officer received a tip that a rape suspect carrying a gun had just entered a grocery store. The officer entered the store, stopped the suspect, frisked him, and asked where his gun was. The suspect told the officers he had placed the gun in some empty boxes. He later argued that both the statement about the gun's location and the gun itself should be inadmissible because when he responded to the officers, he had not yet been read his rights. The Supreme Court disagreed. According to Justice William Rehnquist, who wrote the majority opinion, "So long as the gun was concealed somewhere in the supermarket, with its actual whereabouts unknown . . . an accomplice might make use of it, a customer or employee might later come upon it." Because the police officer's question about the location of the gun was prompted by an immediate interest in public safety, no constitutional violation had occurred.[13]

In your case, the police officers inform you of your right to remain silent. As they're leading you out of your apartment, you keep telling them that it's your phone and that they've made a mistake. You can even get the receipt from your uncle to prove it. But they don't seem interested in your explanation. You decide to exercise your Fifth Amendment right against self-incrimination and accompany them to the police station without saying another word.

You Arrive at the Police Station for Questioning

You arrive at the station, where the police will interrogate you about the iPhone and the ecstasy. You're lucky because when you call your parents, they tell you that they'll be there right away and they're bringing a criminal defense lawyer with them. They're very clear: do not answer any questions until you speak with the attorney. Your parents' instructions are grounded in your Sixth Amendment right to have a lawyer assist with your defense.

Here, too, exactly what this right entails wasn't fully determined until the 1960s, when the Supreme Court issued two landmark rulings. First, the Court's decision in *Gideon v. Wainwright* firmly established that your right to a lawyer is absolute. Clarence Gideon was charged with breaking into a Florida pool hall with the intent to commit a misdemeanor. Prior to his trial, Gideon, who couldn't afford a lawyer, asked to have one appointed to assist with his defense. The judge presiding over his case denied the request because under Florida state law only people charged with murder had the right to an appointed lawyer. Gideon had no choice but to act as his own lawyer—he made his own opening and closing arguments and cross-examined witnesses. Not surprisingly, the jury returned a guilty verdict, and the judge sentenced Gideon to five years in prison. Once again acting on his own behalf, Gideon petitioned the Supreme Court, arguing that his Sixth Amendment rights were being violated. In a unanimous decision, the Court agreed and vacated Gideon's conviction. The state of Florida retried the case but appointed a lawyer to assist with Gideon's defense. A jury deliberated for only an hour before acquitting him of all charges.[14]

If your parents can't provide a lawyer for you—maybe they don't know one; maybe they don't have the money to pay for one—then one must be appointed for you. That doesn't mean that your representation will be as effective as it would be if you hired your own lawyer, though. Certainly, many court-appointed public defenders are excellent at what they do. But lawyers appointed by the state tend to have large caseloads that spread them much too thin to provide the kind of quality defense that private lawyers can offer.[15]

The Supreme Court also decided in the 1960s that your right to a lawyer is immediate, beginning the moment you're taken into custody. When Danny Escobedo, a suspect in a fatal shooting, was arrested, the police questioned him in the police car and at the police station even though he kept asking for his lawyer (and his lawyer was in the building waiting to see him). The police allowed the lawyer in only after Escobedo made some incriminating statements. Escobedo was convicted of murder in part because of the damaging statements. The Supreme Court subsequently threw out the conviction, affirming that the right to counsel begins from the moment the police make an arrest.[16]

You Have a Preliminary Hearing

After the police question you about the crimes they believe you've committed, your lawyer explains that you're entitled to **habeas corpus**. This protection requires that a person placed under arrest be brought before a judge to determine whether there is just cause for the arrest and detainment. Typically, this takes the form of a preliminary hearing within 24 hours of the arrest. At the hearing, the state informs the court of the charges it plans to bring against you. In your case, your parents produced a copy of the iPhone receipt from your uncle, so the theft charge is dismissed. But the charge for illegal possession of drugs remains.

In the vast majority of cases, when the government decides to press ahead and charge a citizen with a crime, there's no trial. At this point in the process, more than 90 percent of federal and state criminal proceedings end with a **plea bargain**—that is, the defendant pleads guilty to a lesser crime in exchange for a reduced sentence.[17] But when your lawyer raises the option of a plea bargain, you turn him down. You know you are innocent and won't plead guilty to anything!

So at the preliminary hearing your lawyer requests bail, which is meant to serve as collateral to ensure that someone charged with a crime appears in court for the trial. If you don't show up for your court date, you lose the bail money. Many criminal justice reform advocates oppose cash bail because of inequity. If you can afford bail, great. You can await your trial from the comfort of your home and basically go about your daily life until the trial. But if you don't have the money, then you

What happens if you're charged with a crime?

remain in jail awaiting trial. And even a few days in jail can result in a loss of income, employment, or child custody.[18] In 2021, Illinois became the first state to eliminate cash bail, and the movement is picking up steam.[19] Still, the traditional cash bail system remains in place for most of the country.

In your case, there's no reason for the judge to deny bail. You didn't commit a violent crime, and you have no criminal record. You need to get home to finish studying for your midterms! The judge has some discretion over the bail amount, but the Eighth Amendment requires that it not be "excessive." In fact, when judges impose fines and bail amounts that fail to take into account the crime and the financial circumstances of the suspect, they can be reprimanded. The Michigan Supreme Court, for example, censured Judge Norene Redmond for setting "grossly excessive" bail. On one occasion, Redmond raised the bail amount for a woman after she was told that the woman's son had called the judge an asshole outside the courtroom. In another, she set bail at $1 million for a man who had overbilled an elderly woman for a paint job.[20]

The judge at your hearing sets bail at $2,000, which is typical for possession of an illegal substance. Your parents are able to post it, and you can go home until the trial date. It won't be too long before you're back in court because the Sixth Amendment guarantees your right to a fair and speedy trial. The logic behind this protection is twofold: (1) it prevents suspects—whose guilt has not yet been established—from being imprisoned for an indefinite period awaiting trial, and (2) it decreases the likelihood that witnesses will forget what happened or that evidence will be lost or destroyed. The Constitution doesn't define "speedy." The U.S. Congress has, however, passed a law that requires trials for federal crimes to take place within 70 days. In most states, the maximum wait for a speedy trial is between 60 and 120 days.[21] Of course, for people sitting in jail, this doesn't feel very speedy. Your trial date is set for 45 days from now.

The Trial Begins

As you walk into the courtroom, you're really worried. A guilty verdict for possession of drugs? You never even tried the ecstasy. You should have just thrown the pills away when you realized that your friend had left them at your apartment. Now, you could face some serious penalties, including a permanent mark on your record. You just hope that the Sixth Amendment's guarantee to an impartial jury, as well as the right to confront the state's witnesses and present witnesses of your own, will result in an acquittal. If it does, then this whole ordeal will be over. The Fifth Amendment bars **double jeopardy**, so you cannot be tried again for the same crime if you are acquitted.

Before the jury selection process begins, your attorney makes a motion to dismiss the case. She tells the judge that the drug charge and the evidence on which it is based resulted from an illegal search of your apartment. The search warrant allowed the police to look for an iPhone. It did not authorize them to continue the search of your medicine cabinet after they found the phone. The evidence, she argues, was illegally obtained and, thus, inadmissible.

Your lawyer bases her argument on the Supreme Court's decision in the 1961 case of *Mapp v. Ohio*.[22] Officers arrived at Dollree Mapp's house looking for a fugitive wanted in connection with a bombing. Mapp wouldn't let them in because they didn't have a search warrant. A few hours later, and still without a warrant, the police came back and forcibly entered her home. They searched the entire house and found nothing pertaining to the fugitive. But they arrested her for possession of obscene materials—which were illegal in Ohio at the time—that they found in a trunk in her basement. Mapp's lawyer argued that evidence of illegal activity obtained through an unlawful search must be excluded. The Court agreed. The justices established the **exclusionary rule**, which prohibits illegally obtained evidence from being used at trial. Dollree Mapp's case was dismissed.

Determining whether a search violates the Fourth Amendment can be a close call for a judge. Police officers can make many plausible arguments about why they felt they had probable cause to continue searching beyond the specific parameters of the warrant. In your case, the judge agrees with your lawyer's argument that the search that turned up the ecstasy wasn't valid. He dismisses the drug charge. You are free to go.

If You Had Been Found Guilty

If you had been found guilty of stealing an iPhone worth about $1,000 and possessing illegal drugs, these criminal offenses would have resulted in substantial penalties. Most states would punish you with some combination of a fine, restitution, probation, and short prison sentence. The Eighth Amendment prohibits **cruel and unusual punishment**, so a long sentence, or a fine that greatly exceeded the value of the merchandise, would be unlikely for a first conviction.

But not impossible. It turns out that determining what constitutes "cruel and unusual punishment" can be quite challenging. The Supreme

Court has upheld what might seem like some pretty excessive penalties. In 1973, for instance, William Rummel was convicted of obtaining $120.75 under false pretenses—a felony in Texas. Because this was Rummel's third felony (he had been found guilty of fraudulent use of a credit card in the amount of $80 in 1964 and had forged a check for $28.36 in 1969), he was sentenced to life in prison. Texas had an anti-recidivism statute on the books to try to discourage repeat offenders, so the nature of the crimes didn't matter, only that they were felonies. The third crime meant a life sentence. Period. Rummel brought suit claiming that in light of the crimes he had committed, a life sentence was cruel and unusual. After all, his total theft—over the course of nearly a decade—amounted to less than $250. But a deeply divided Court upheld the sentence, arguing that the state has a right to adopt strong measures to discourage repeat offenders.[23]

The Supreme Court has also established the constitutionality of the death penalty—the greatest sanction a government can administer. In its 1976 decision in *Gregg v. Georgia*, the Court upheld the death sentence for a convicted murderer: in "extreme criminal cases," capital punishment is lawful as long as it is "careful and judicious."[24] This means that a state may not impose it in an "arbitrary" or "capricious" manner.[25] But that's a pretty high bar. The Supreme Court has acknowledged racial discrimination in the application of the death penalty. Black people are more likely than White people to be sentenced to death for committing the same crime. But even systemic racism does not make capital punishment cruel and unusual. Only racism in an individual's case, not the system itself, rises to that level.[26] The Court has determined that the death penalty is cruel and unusual—and thus unconstitutional—when it is imposed on minors;[27] on people who, in the Court's words, are "mentally retarded";[28] or in cases that do not involve a capital murder conviction.[29]

Luckily, your case was dismissed, so you won't face any sanctions. As you'll see in Segment 14, though, your entire experience navigating the criminal justice system and asserting your rights can be significantly shaped by your race and socioeconomic status.

DID YOU GET IT?

What happens if you're charged with a crime?

Short Answer:

- You're entitled to protection against unreasonable searches and seizures, protection against self-incrimination, a lawyer to assist with your defense, information about the charges against you, a fair and speedy trial, and protection from cruel and unusual punishment.
- These fundamental rights — as stated in the Bill of Rights — have been enforced and further defined by the Supreme Court.
- It is critical to know these rights so that you can hold police and the legal system accountable for upholding them.

DEVELOPING YOUR SKILLS

Civic Engagement

Know your rights: Being an engaged citizen means understanding the law. This can be particularly important when it comes to interacting with the criminal justice system. Use the following scenarios to see how your rights would apply in each situation.

1. You're pulled over for speeding. The police officer approaches your car, looks at you, asks if you have been drinking, and then asks you to pop the trunk. Are you required to comply?

   a. Yes, the officer has a right to look anywhere in the vehicle after pulling you over.

   b. No, the officer can only search anything in clear sight in the car itself.

   c. No, the officer cannot look in the trunk without a warrant.

   d. No, the officer can never look in the trunk.

2. The police arrive at your house with a warrant to search for stolen credit cards. You tell the police that they can't look for the items until your lawyer arrives. Did you properly assert your Sixth Amendment right?

   a. Yes, your right to a lawyer kicks in the minute the police arrive at your house.

   b. No, your right to a lawyer is guaranteed only after the police arrest you.

   c. No, your right to a lawyer applies for the first time at the preliminary hearing.

   d. No, your right to a lawyer pertains to the trial only.

3. After the police arrest you for committing a crime, which of the following rights can you exercise before they start asking you questions?

   a. Right to an impartial jury

   b. Right protecting you from an unlawful search and seizure

   c. Right to a speedy trial

   d. Right protecting you from self-incrimination

FIGURE IT OUT

Imagine that the iPhone scenario happens again, but this time it's your best friend who is arrested for stealing the phone and possessing illegal drugs. You happen to be at your friend's apartment when the police arrest him. As he's being led out of the apartment, he asks you to find him a lawyer and meet him at the police station. Help your friend exercise his Sixth Amendment right to an attorney to assist with his defense (and assume for this exercise that you don't personally know a lawyer or anyone who can help you find one). More specifically:

- Go online to find two lawyers or law firms in your area you could contact to help your friend. For each, list the appropriate contact information and why you chose the firm. Was it the online reviews? quality of the Web page? experience with drug cases? Be specific in explaining your choices.

- Now, assume that your friend could never afford to hire the lawyers you identified in your search. In your area, are there any low-cost alternatives to relying on a court-appointed public defender? If so, explain what they are. If not, summarize how you arrived at this conclusion.

Want to Know More?

The Netflix documentary *Making a Murderer* follows the case of Steven Avery, who served 18 years in prison before being exonerated of sexual assault and attempted murder. Shortly after he sued Manitowoc County, Wisconsin, for his wrongful conviction, he and his nephew were prosecuted and convicted of another murder. The 10-part series highlights the rights of the accused as well as how it's difficult to prove that those rights have been violated.

12.
Can the government regulate your sex life?

#RightToPrivacy

Andrew Andrade, a 25-year-old graduate student studying criminal justice, tried to purchase emergency contraception for his girlfriend. But a Jersey City Rite Aid refused to sell him the over-the-counter drug. Although Andrade explained that his girlfriend worked full-time and couldn't make it to the pharmacy herself, two Rite Aid employees claimed that the law prohibited men from buying that kind of birth control.[1] Andrade left the store and bought the drug at another nearby pharmacy. Recounting the incident to a reporter, he said: "In a stressful situation where time is of the essence, the last thing anyone needs is to feel demoralized by having their rights violated."[2]

In Peoria, Arizona, Nicole Arteaga, age 35, dropped off a prescription at her local Walgreens. She had just learned that her nine-week-old fetus had stopped developing and had no heartbeat.[3] Her doctor prescribed misoprostol, a drug designed to induce a miscarriage. That way, Arteaga could avoid a surgical procedure.[4] But the Walgreens pharmacist — citing ethical objections to abortion — refused to fill the prescription. A teary-eyed Arteaga explained the situation while her seven-year-old son and a line of customers looked on. But to no avail. Reflecting on the experience, Arteaga said she left the store feeling

The government has long tried to regulate sexual conduct among consenting adults, from birth control, to reproductive rights, to same-sex marriage.

"ashamed" and "humiliated." Walgreens later apologized for the incident and prepared her prescription for pick-up at a different store location.

The list of examples goes on and on. There's Megan Kelly, a married mother in Illinois whose local pharmacist refused to fill her monthly prescription for birth control.[5] There's Amanda Phiede, who encountered a Kmart pharmacist in Wisconsin who not only refused to fill her prescription for birth control but also refused to transfer it to a pharmacy that would.[6] There's a Lebanon, Pennsylvania, rape victim who had to drive to the next county to fill a prescription for emergency contraception. The emergency room and pharmacy where she was initially treated refused to dispense the drug on religious grounds.[7] The National Women's Law Center has chronicled incidents of pharmacists declining to fill birth control prescriptions in at least 26 states.[8]

Can pharmacists do this? Can they deny citizens the right to purchase legal drugs, even with a prescription? In eight states, the answer is no; laws prohibit pharmacists from refusing to dispense legal drugs, including birth control. But in six others, the law explicitly grants pharmacists with moral or religious objections the right to refuse to provide contraceptives.[9] In the remaining states, it's up to pharmacies to establish their own policies. Although the Supreme Court has yet to weigh in on this particular issue, the justices have spent quite a bit of time thinking about your sex life. By that, we mean that the Court has attempted to define the boundaries of personal freedom — including your most intimate decisions — by identifying a constitutional "right to privacy." To understand how this right has evolved — and to highlight the controversies it has fueled — we focus on three areas: (1) birth control, (2) abortion, and (3) consensual sex.

Establishing the Right to Privacy: The Case of Birth Control

In 1954, Estelle Griswold became the director of the Planned Parenthood League of Connecticut. In that capacity, she organized "border runs." An 1879 Connecticut law banned the sale or manufacture of contraception to anyone—including married couples—within the state. So Griswold took women to New York and Rhode Island to get birth control. Even these border runs technically violated the law because it was a crime to assist in providing contraception. But Griswold figured that it was virtually impossible for the state to prove what she was doing.[10]

By the early 1960s, Griswold decided to challenge the law head-on. Rather than continue her out-of-state trips, she opened a clinic next door to the Planned Parenthood office and, with the help of physician C. Lee Buxton, began dispensing contraception to married couples. When a local resident protested the clinic and police followed up, they found sufficient evidence to make an arrest. Griswold argued that the Connecticut law violated the due process clause of the Fourteenth Amendment, which guarantees protections for citizens' basic rights. She claimed that among those rights was privacy in intimate relationships. Unfortunately for Griswold, the word "privacy" appears nowhere in the Fourteenth Amendment (or anywhere in the Constitution, for that matter). The trial court convicted Griswold and Buxton of violating the Connecticut law that made it illegal to provide contraception, and the appellate court upheld the conviction.[11] Griswold appealed the decision to the U.S. Supreme Court.

After hearing the case in 1965, the Court issued one of the most far-reaching decisions of the twentieth century. Even though the Constitution makes no explicit mention of it, the justices determined that citizens have a fundamental **right to privacy**, which is alluded to in the "shadows" of the First, Third, Fourth, Fifth, and Ninth Amendments. After all, people's religious beliefs are private, people are protected from unlawful searches of themselves and their homes, and people can keep information private if it might incriminate them. Justice William Douglas, who wrote the majority opinion in *Griswold v. Connecticut*, concluded that the right to privacy is "older than the Bill of Rights—older than our political parties, older than our school system." Applying it to intimate decisions within a marriage, he reasoned, is as "noble a purpose as any involved in our prior decisions."[12]

Still, the decision was highly controversial. Those who thought the Connecticut law was archaic or even silly praised the outcome, whereas the Court's creation of a new right gave others pause. Indeed, it didn't take long for the right to privacy to extend beyond married couples. In 1972, the Supreme Court invalidated a Massachusetts law that prohibited single people from using birth control.[13]

Although the right to privacy includes adults' decision to use birth control, it's important to note that it doesn't guarantee access to contraception. The Court has allowed nonprofit religious organizations and for-profit companies, on the grounds of their religious objections, to deny employees health coverage that includes contraception.[14] And as the stories that opened this segment reveal, depending on where they live, pharmacists and medical professionals can refuse to prescribe or dispense birth control.

Extending the Right to Privacy: The Case of Abortion

Did the right to privacy include the right to have an abortion? On January 22, 1973, the U.S. Supreme Court provided an initial answer. At issue was the constitutionality of a Texas statute that outlawed abortion in all cases except when the procedure was necessary to save the pregnant woman's life. In a 7–2 decision in *Roe v. Wade*, abortion became a constitutional right. The Court ruled that the right to privacy applied to the decision to terminate a pregnancy. Under the decision, during the first three months of a pregnancy, a woman's right to an abortion was fully protected. In the second and third trimesters, states could regulate and even restrict abortion as long as they were acting to protect the mother's health or the "potentiality of human life."[15]

The decision in *Roe v. Wade* launched one of the most controversial and enduring political debates in contemporary U.S. politics, as activists on both sides of the issue came to see themselves in a life-or-death struggle. For pro-choice organizations, liberals, and most Democrats, keeping abortion safe and legal became synonymous with protecting women's rights more broadly. On the other side of the debate, religious conservatives and most Republicans believed the Court's decision was tantamount to state-sanctioned murder.

As the political battle over abortion raged on for the next half century, more than 30 cases that addressed some aspect of abortion law made their way to the Supreme Court. Most involved a challenge to a state law that restricted or regulated first-trimester abortion access. These restrictions took many forms: mandatory waiting periods after a woman sought an abortion, parental consent requirements for minors, mandatory counseling to inform women about alternatives to abortion, to name just a few. As long as the restriction didn't severely limit the fundamental right to an abortion during the first trimester, the Court tended to allow it.

But conservative judges and political leaders continued to argue vehemently that *Roe v. Wade* was a mistake and that it should be overturned. So when the Supreme Court had the opportunity to rethink *Roe* in 2022—now with a majority of conservative justices—they took it. The case, *Dobbs v. Jackson Women's Health Organization*, involved a Mississippi law that banned almost all abortions after 15 weeks of pregnancy. This contravened *Roe*, which allowed access to abortion well beyond 15 weeks.

The Court ultimately made one of the most monumental decisions of the 21st century: they upheld the Mississippi law and overturned *Roe v. Wade*. Justice Samuel Alito's majority opinion stated

Protesters march outside Supreme Court Justice Brett Kavanaugh's home in response to his vote to overturn *Roe v. Wade.*

emphatically, "Roe was egregiously wrong from the start. Its reasoning was exceptionally weak, and the decision has had damaging consequences." The Court's argument rested on the notion that the right to an abortion is not mentioned in the Constitution and the Court had no authority to create such a right. Justice Alito concluded his 108-page opinion with words that shook the pro-choice side to its core: "We now overrule [Roe]" and return decisions about the legality of abortion to the states, or as he put it, "to the people and their elected representatives."[16] In their dissent, Justices Stephen Breyer, Sonia Sotomayor, and Elena Kagan expressed "sorrow [. . .] for the many millions of American women who have lost a fundamental constitutional protection" that they had been granted almost 50 years earlier.[17]

The *Dobbs* ruling immediately threw decisions about laws regarding abortion to the states. And many states had been waiting for this moment for years. In fact, 13 states had trigger laws in place that made abortion illegal the moment *Roe v. Wade* was overturned.[18] The Guttmacher Institute, a think tank that monitors reproductive rights, estimates that more than half the states will ban abortion now that they can.[19] Although many states immediately began working

FIGURE 1. Abortion Restrictions and Rights by State

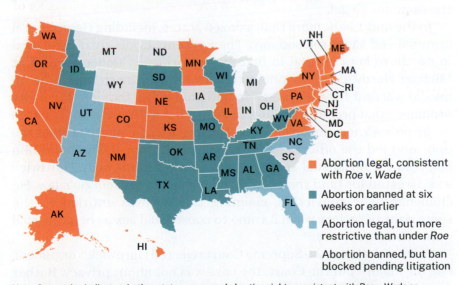

Abortion legal, consistent with *Roe v. Wade*

Abortion banned at six weeks or earlier

Abortion legal, but more restrictive than under *Roe*

Abortion banned, but ban blocked pending litigation

Note: Categories indicate whether states preserved abortion rights consistent with *Roe v. Wade* or limited them following the 2021 Supreme Court decision in *Dobbs v. Jackson Women's Health Organization*. List is current as of October 22, 2022.

Source: "After Roe Fell: Abortion Laws by State," Center for Reproductive Rights.

to impose bans on abortion, several others—such as New York, New Jersey, and Connecticut—moved to strengthen abortion rights and make it easier for women from out of state to access abortion services.[20] The future of abortion access will likely be fought out in states across the country and the result will be a crazy quilt of divergent state laws (see Figure 1).[21] In some states, seeking an abortion or assisting someone seeking an abortion—regardless of the reason or how far along the pregnancy is—will be a felony; in others, it will be a fully protected right.

Solidifying the Right to Privacy: Consensual Sex

The third major application of the right to privacy concerns state laws that regulate consensual sex among adults. Throughout the history of the United States, first settlers, then colonists, and finally state governments regularly passed laws that banned specific types of sex (see image on the next page).[22] Most common were those banning sodomy. In their original form, these laws were directed at all sexual relationships. As the twentieth century progressed, though, they came to target gay Americans. In essence, the types of sex acts the laws regulated effectively made intimate relationships between people of the same sex illegal.

In the mid-1980s, more than a dozen states, including Georgia, still criminalized same-sex sodomy. The Supreme Court finally weighed in on these laws in 1986 in *Bowers v. Hardwick*. Police arrived at Michael Hardwick's apartment to serve what turned out to be an invalid warrant for his arrest. He had paid a fine for violating a city ordinance that prohibited public drinking, but a clerical error resulted in the police knocking on his door. Hardwick's roommate opened the door and led the officers to Hardwick's bedroom. They found him engaged in consensual sodomy with another adult man. Hardwick was arrested for (and then convicted of) violating Georgia's law. He challenged the conviction, claiming that he was entitled to the same right to privacy when it came to consensual sex as heterosexual women and men were.[23]

In a 5–4 decision, the Supreme Court rejected Hardwick's argument. For the majority of the Court, the case was not about privacy. Rather, Justice Byron White's majority opinion reasoned that the Constitution did not confer "a fundamental right to engage in homosexual sodomy." Chief Justice Warren Burger concurred, referring to the "ancient

MAXIMUM PUNISHMENTS FOR CERTAIN SEX CRIMES IN THE U. S. A.

	ADULTERY	FORNICATION	SEDUCTION	SODOMY
Ala.	1st conviction—$100 and/or 6 months; 2nd—$300 and/or 1 year; 3rd—2 years	same as adultery	1-10 years	2-10 years
Ariz.	3 years	no crime; cohabitation—3 years	1-5 years	1-5 years
Ark.	1st conviction—$20-$100; 2nd—$100 and/or 1 year; 3rd—1-3 years	same as adultery	1-10 years and $5000	5-21 years
Cal.	1 year and/or $1000	no crime	5 years and/or $5000	1-10 years; oral perversion—15 years
Colo.	1st offense—$200 or 6 mos.; 2nd—double; 3rd—treble	same as adultery	10 years	1 year to life
Conn.	5 years	$100 and/or 6 mos.	5 years and $1000	30 years
Del.	1 year and/or $500*	no crime	no crime	$1000 and 3 years
D. C.	$500 and/or 1 year	$100 or 6 mos.	3 years and/or $200	no crime
Fla.	2 years or $500	3 mos. or $30; with a minor, 10 years or $2000	no crime	20 years
Ga.	$1000 or 1 year	same as adultery	2-20 years	life; bestiality—5-20 years
Idaho	$100-$1000 or 3 mos.-3 yrs.	$300 or 6 mos	no crime	5 years
Ill.	1st conviction—$500 or 1 year; 2nd—double; 3rd—treble	same as adultery	$1000-$5000 and/or 1 year	1-10 years
Ind.	$500 and/or 6 mos.	same as adultery	6 mos.—5 years and $100-$500	$100-$1000 and/or 2-14 years
Iowa	3 years or 1 year and $300	no crime	5 years or $1000 and 1 year	10 years
Kan.	6 mos and/or $500	$500-$1000 or 30 days-3 mos.	no crime	10 years
Ky.	$20-$50	same as adultery	1-5 years	2-5 years
La.	no crime	no crime	no crime	$2000 and/or 5 years
Me.	5 years or $1000	$100 and 60 days; cohabitation—$300 or 5 years	no crime	1-10 years
Md.	$10	no crime	no crime	1-10 years

An image from a 1948 magazine chronicles — state by state — laws pertaining to sexual conduct at that time. Notice the severe penalties that used to be imposed on personal conduct. Of course, many remnants of these laws remain intact. Today, adultery is still a criminal offense in 17 states.

roots" of prohibitions against same-sex and concluding that protecting same-sex sodomy as a fundamental right "would be to cast aside millennia of moral teaching." The minority, in contrast, argued that the right to privacy established in *Griswold* extended to consensual sex between same-sex adults. Justice Harry Blackmun's dissent accused the Court of an "almost obsessive focus on homosexual activity" and a "refusal to consider the broad principles that have informed our treatment of privacy."

Seventeen years later, Blackmun's position gained traction. This time, police arrested John Lawrence and Tyron Garner, two gay men living in Houston, Texas, for criminal sodomy. (The officers entered the house because of a report of someone waving a gun.) Both men were convicted of violating the Texas anti-sodomy law. In challenging their convictions, the men asserted that the right to privacy covers consensual sex acts in one's own home. And the Supreme Court, with several new members, agreed. In *Lawrence v. Texas*, the Court overturned *Bowers v. Hardwick*.[24] Justice Kennedy wrote for the majority:

"The Texas statute furthers no legitimate state interest which can justify its intrusion into the personal and private life of the individual." It had taken a long time, but with this decision the Court established a zone of privacy around intimate relationships for all consenting American adults.

DID YOU GET IT?

Can the government regulate your sex life?

Short Answer:

- Not when it comes to using birth control, which is protected by the right to privacy.
- Much more so when a pregnancy is involved. The government can place restrictions on a woman's right to have an abortion, with regulations increasing at later stages of pregnancy.
- Not when sexual conduct is consensual, among adults, and in the confines of one's home.

DEVELOPING YOUR SKILLS

Civic Engagement

Know your rights: Laws and restrictions pertaining to abortion vary dramatically by state. Take a look at the map in Figure 1, which categorizes each state by whether it prohibits, restricts, or permits abortion. Then answer the following questions about the right to privacy as it applies to abortion law.

1. Your friend, an ardent supporter of abortion rights, has been offered jobs in four different states. She had no idea that state laws regarding abortion vary so dramatically. Which state's laws best reflect her strong support of abortion rights?

   a. Missouri

   b. Vermont

   c. Wyoming

   d. Ohio

2. Another friend is an evangelical Christian who strongly opposes abortion rights. Which of the following states' abortion laws best reflect this friend's values?

   a. Arizona

   b. Montana

   c. South Dakota

   d. Minnesota

3. When the Supreme Court overturned *Roe v. Wade*, it effectively put states in charge of abortion law. Based on the Court decisions described in this segment, which state regulation on abortion might still be an unconstitutional violation of the right of privacy?

   a. A state law that requires women to wait 24 hours before getting an abortion

   b. A state law that bans all abortions after six weeks

   c. A state law that denies public funding for abortion to women who can't afford it

   d. A state law that bans the "morning-after pill"

FIGURE IT OUT

The Findlaw website identifies abortion restrictions in every state. Visit the site at https://statelaws.findlaw.com/family-laws/abortion.html and answer the following questions:

- What restrictions on the right to have an abortion exist in your home state?

- Compared to your home state, identify one state where it's easier to access abortion services. Explain how you arrived at your answer.

- Compared to your home state, identify one state where it's more difficult to access abortion services. Explain how you arrived at your answer.

Want to Know More?

The Center for Reproductive Rights collects data on the abortion policies in countries throughout the world. Take a look at the Center's website — http://worldabortionlaws.com — to compare abortion laws in the United States to those of countries from around the world.

13.
Are all Americans equal under the law?

#FourteenthAmendment

"Hello, Chicago!" thundered Barack Obama, as he delivered his 2008 presidential victory speech to hundreds of thousands of people in Grant Park. "If there is anyone out there who still doubts that America is a place where all things are possible, who still wonders if the dream of our Founders is alive in our time, who still questions the power of our democracy, tonight is your answer. . . . Change has come to America."[1] Despite its long history of slavery and racial discrimination, the United States had elected a Black man president.

The historic nature of Obama's win couldn't be overstated. *New York Times* reporter Adam Nagourney commented that the victory represented "a strikingly symbolic moment in the evolution of the nation's fraught racial history, a breakthrough that would have seemed unthinkable" only a few years before.[2] John Lewis, a civil rights leader and member of Congress from Georgia, told MSNBC that the outcome showed that "America is a different nation, a better nation," a country "prepared to lay down our dark past and look to a bright future."[3] Even Obama's opponent, Senator John McCain, captured the magnitude of the moment in his concession speech: "This is a historic election, and I recognize the significance it has for African Americans. . . . We have

Americans have been fighting for equality since the Founding. In one of the most iconic moments of the civil rights movement, Martin Luther King Jr. and civil rights leaders arrived in Washington, D.C., where King delivered his "I Have a Dream" speech (left). Congresswoman Bella Abzug led feminist activists in a protest to urge Congress to adopt the Equal Rights Amendment (center). Until her death in 2020 at the age of 95, Frances Goldin carried a sign at pride parades ever since her daughters came out to her in 1972 (right).

come a long way from the injustices that once stained our nation's reputation."[4] People throughout the country sensed that American society had finally moved beyond its history of division and was ready to become inclusive of all Americans, regardless of race, gender, or sexual orientation.

The push for civil rights had been underway — albeit on a rocky road — for 150 years. The legal foundation for equality began shortly after the Civil War, with three amendments to the Constitution. The Thirteenth Amendment abolished slavery, the Fourteenth Amendment made formerly enslaved persons citizens, and the Fifteenth Amendment extended the right to vote to citizens of all races. These **civil war amendments** were instrumental in establishing the basis for civil rights. But one particular part of the Fourteenth Amendment — the **equal protection clause** — became the impetus in the push for legal equality. It guarantees all citizens "equal protection of the laws."

Equality can be measured in lots of ways — equal opportunities, equity in outcomes, similar societal experiences, to name just a few. And we address these types of equality in the next three segments of this section. Here we focus on equality under the law, which is a central tenet of any civil rights movement. By highlighting critical moments in political history, as well as landmark Supreme Court decisions, we demonstrate that legal equality has been slow to come and that "equal protection under the law" even today is applied unevenly to people of color, women, and the LGBTQ community.

The Struggle for Racial Equality under the Law

The Emancipation Proclamation, delivered by President Abraham Lincoln in 1863, called for an end to slavery. The Civil War came to a close in 1865. And the civil war amendments were all ratified by 1870. But civil rights and equal protection under the law for Black people did not immediately follow. Rather, the country entered an era of **Jim Crow laws**—state and local statutes that sanctioned racial segregation—in hospitals, restaurants, barbershops, liquor stores, cemeteries, libraries, schools, prisons, park playgrounds, the list goes on.[5]

Louisiana's Separate Car Act of 1890, which required Black and White people to ride in separate train cars, was one such example. And in 1892, Homer Plessy, who was one-eighth Black (and, therefore, technically Black under Louisiana law), sat in a Whites-only train car in Louisiana. When he refused to move, police arrested him. Plessy's lawyers, in what would be the first real test of the equal protection clause, argued that the Separate Car Act violated the Fourteenth Amendment. The U.S. Supreme Court didn't see it that way. In **Plessy v. Ferguson**, one of the most odious decisions of the nineteenth century, the Court determined that equal protection under the law did not require racial integration. It required only that Black and White people be entitled to facilities of equal quality.[6] This **"separate but equal" doctrine** would stand for nearly 60 years.

Not until the Supreme Court heard **Brown v. Board of Education** in 1954—fully 90 years after the end of the Civil War—did the laws begin to change. Linda Brown, an eight-year-old Black girl who lived in Topeka, Kansas, was forced to walk across railroad tracks and take a bus to a Black elementary school. Yet an all-White school was located just a few blocks from her house. Because this situation was fairly common across many southern states, the National Association for the Advancement of Colored People (NAACP) decided to challenge the constitutionality of school segregation. The NAACP asked Brown's father, as well as other parents in similar situations, to try to enroll their children in closer all-White schools. When the children were denied admittance, the parents, with the help of the NAACP, sued the schools, arguing that "separate but equal" violated the equal protection clause of the Four-teenth Amendment. This time, the Supreme Court agreed. In the field of public education, the justices ruled, "The doctrine of separate but equal has no place. Separate educational facilities are inherently unequal."[7] Even if the schools provided exactly the same facilities and curricula (which they rarely did), segregation could instill a sense of inferiority among Black students. Commenting decades later on her own children's racially diverse education, Linda Brown said: "They are advancing much more rapidly than I was at [that] age. . . . And I think that children are relating to one another much better these days because of integration."[8]

As the fight for racial equality made its way through the court system, the arrest of Rosa Parks in 1955 for refusing to give up her bus seat to a White passenger served as the symbolic beginning of the civil rights movement.[9] Parks's arrest elevated the leadership of Martin Luther King Jr., who organized a bus boycott in Montgomery, Alabama, and set into motion a wave of protest and civil disobedience throughout the South. Black college students staged sit-ins at "Whites-only" lunch counters in Greensboro, North Carolina. Freedom Riders—civil rights advocates of all races—rode buses across the South to ensure that local officials enforced the desegregation of interstate bus travel. These activists confronted violence from White counterprotesters and faced fire hoses, attack dogs, beatings, and arrests at the hands of the local police. The Southern Poverty Law Center identifies several dozen activists who were actually killed between 1954 and 1964.[10] King himself was arrested 29 times, either for peaceful protest or on trumped-up criminal charges.[11]

Police officers unleash attack dogs on civil rights demonstrators, arrest Martin Luther King Jr., and use fire hoses to break up an act of civil disobedience. These images characterized the police response to the civil rights movement in many southern states.

Are all Americans equal under the law?

It was against this backdrop that King led the march on Washington, D.C., where more than 200,000 people listened to his "I Have a Dream" speech. But their call to end racial discrimination and urge Congress to pass civil rights legislation wasn't immediately embraced on Capitol Hill. Segregationists and southern Democrats in the almost all-White Congress spent 75 days trying to block such legislation. Senator Richard Russell, a Democrat from Georgia, promised to "resist to the bitter end any measure or any movement which would have a tendency to bring about social equality and intermingling . . . of the races."[12] South Carolina senator Strom Thurmond put it more bluntly. Passing the Civil Rights Act, he said, "will mark one of the darkest days in history."[13]

Ultimately, Congress passed and President Lyndon Johnson signed the **Civil Rights Act of 1964**.[14] The law had three major features. First, it prohibited segregation on the grounds of race, sex, religion, or national origin, and it banned discrimination in all places of "public accommodation." This meant that parks, restaurants, theaters, sports arenas, and hotels could no longer refuse service based on skin color. Second, the law barred discrimination in hiring and employment. Third, it created the Equal Employment Opportunity Commission, a new division of the Justice Department that had the power to help citizens file racial discrimination lawsuits.

The final step in the road to legal equality occurred the following year. Although the Fifteenth Amendment extended the right to vote regardless of race, tactics such as voter intimidation, literacy tests, and even poll taxes remained common ways to turn Black voters away. (Take a look at an excerpt of a literacy test below, and see how many questions you can answer correctly.) Following a particularly egregious event in March

---

THE STATE OF LOUISIANA

Literacy Test (This test is to be given to anyone who cannot prove a fifth grade education.)

Do what you are told to do in each statement, nothing more, nothing less. Be careful as one wrong answer denotes failure of the test. You have 10 minutes to complete the test.

1. Draw a line around the number or letter of this sentence.

2. Draw a line under the last word in this line.

3. Cross out the longest word in this line.

4. Draw a line around the shortest word in this line.

5. Circle the first, first letter of the alphabet in this line.

6. In the space below draw three circles, one inside (engulfed by) the other.

An example of a perfectly legal literacy test used prior to the passage of the Voting Rights Act of 1965.

1965—Alabama police used nightsticks and tear gas on people demonstrating for the right to vote—President Johnson delivered a speech to Congress and demanded action. The **Voting Rights Act of 1965**, which was passed later that year, outlawed literacy tests and required federal oversight of voter registration.[15] The Supreme Court has since issued rulings that have watered down this law,[16] but the act made these primary tools of voter suppression illegal.

The decision in *Brown v. Board of Education*, the Civil Rights Act, and the Voting Rights Act went a long way toward solidifying racial equality under the written law. But it took until 1967 for the Supreme Court to invalidate state laws banning interracial marriage.[17] Voter suppression tactics continue today in the form of requiring ID, purging voter files, moving polling sites to hostile locations, and limiting the number of polling places.[18] All of these tactics ultimately make it more difficult for people of color living in poorer communities to vote. And not until 2021 did Juneteenth—which commemorates the emancipation of enslaved African Americans—become a federal holiday.[19]

The Struggle for Gender Equality under the Law

The march to women's equality under the law has also been a long struggle. As early as 1776, Abigail Adams wrote a letter to her husband, John, who was a member of the Continental Congress in Philadelphia. She implored him to "remember the ladies" as he drafted the documents that would govern the nation:

> Be more generous and favorable to them than your ancestors. Do not put such unlimited power into the hands of the husbands. . . . If particular care and attention is not paid to the ladies, we are determined to foment a rebellion, and will not hold ourselves bound by any laws in which we have no voice, or representation.[20]

Despite Abigail's plea, the Constitution made no mention of women and conferred no rights to them. It took another 133 years—many of them filled with marches, picket lines, hunger strikes, and imprisonment—for women even to win the right to vote.[21] Citizenship and equal protection under the Fourteenth Amendment, according to the Supreme Court in 1874, didn't include women's suffrage.[22] The Nineteenth Amendment finally granted women this right in 1920.

Voting was only part of the historic struggle for legal equality, and both before and after 1920, women and men were not on equal legal footing. In 1873, for example, Myra Bradwell applied to practice law in the state

The fight for women's right to vote was a long political battle dating back to the Founding. It wasn't until the Nineteenth Amendment was ratified in 1920 — fully 133 years after the Constitution was adopted — that women received the right to vote.

of Illinois. Her application was denied because of a state law prohibiting women from becoming attorneys. When Bradwell's case made it to the Supreme Court, she argued that as a citizen she was entitled to practice law under the protections of the Fourteenth Amendment. The Court disagreed, reasoning that the right to practice law isn't part of citizenship.[23] In his concurring opinion, Justice Joseph Bradley went even further in denying Bradwell's claim: "Man is, or should be, woman's protector and defender. The natural and proper timidity and delicacy which belongs to the female sex evidently unfits it for many of the occupations of civil life." The notion that the law needed to protect women wasn't just an antiquated position held by justices in the late 1800s. It carried over well into the twentieth century. In 1948, for instance, the Supreme Court upheld a Michigan law that prohibited women from working as bartenders unless the business was owned by their father or husband. The Court defended this seeming violation of the equal protection clause because, the justices argued, allowing women to bartend could "give rise to moral and social problems."[24]

The movement for women's legal equality gained momentum as more and more women began working outside the home in the 1950s and 1960s and confronted unfair hiring practices, pay discrimination, and sexual harassment in the workplace. They won legal protection against wage discrimination with the Equal Pay Act of 1963 and protection from discrimination on the basis of sex with the Civil Rights Act of 1964. The National Organization for Women, founded in 1966, then pushed for better enforcement of these antidiscrimination laws. Women's rights activists also began to coalesce around the importance of passing an **Equal Rights Amendment (ERA)**. Amending the Constitution to state that "Equality of Rights under the law shall not be denied or abridged by the United

States or any state on account of sex" would ensure that women and men were treated as social, economic, and political equals.[25] Congress passed the amendment in 1972 and sent it to the states for ratification. But in a big setback for women's rights, the ERA failed to muster support in the minimum number of states required and was never adopted.

At around the same time, though, the Supreme Court took a turn toward recognizing legal equality for women. In the 1971 case of *Reed v. Reed*, a unanimous Court invalidated an Idaho statute that automatically made a male parent the executor of a child's estate. The justices ruled that "to give a mandatory preference to members of either sex over members of the other . . . is to make the very kind of arbitrary legislative choice forbidden by the Equal Protection Clause of the Fourteenth Amendment."[26] In 1976, the Court ruled on the same grounds that states could not establish different drinking ages for men and women.[27] And 20 years later, the justices extended the logic to military schools, striking down all-male admission policies.[28]

The Court's interpretation of the equal protection clause and the Civil Rights Act, however, has not been as complete when applied to women as it has been for people of color. When the federal government reactivated the draft registration process in 1980 and restricted it only to men, a number of men challenged the law's constitutionality. They didn't think they should have to register for the draft if women didn't have to. They lost. In *Rostker v. Goldberg*, six justices accepted the government's argument that because women and men are not "similarly situated" when it comes to combat roles, and because "military problems" can arise when drafting women for noncombat roles, equal treatment was not required.[29]

The same is true for statutory rape. Consider the case of a 17-year-old boy who had sexual relations with a 16-year-old girl. He was found guilty of violating a California law that made men—and only men—criminally liable for statutory rape if they had sex with anyone under the age of 18. The boy, referred to as Michael M. in the case, challenged the law, arguing that it discriminated on the basis of sex. But the Court found no "equal protection" violation because, according to the majority, "Young men and young women are not similarly situated with respect to the problems and the risks of sexual intercourse." The justices went on to explain that while the "risk of pregnancy itself" deters women from committing statutory rape, "no similar natural sanctions deter males."[30]

In most domains, however, women and men are generally equal under the law. That's not to say, of course, that sexism and sexual harassment don't remain common in many arenas (just turn on the news or search #MeToo on Twitter). Or that sexual assault isn't prevalent and underreported, including on many college campuses.[31] Legal equality and equal treatment are often not the same thing.

The Struggle for Gay Rights under the Law

In 1952, the American Psychiatric Association's diagnostic manual classified "homosexuality" as a "sociopathic personality disturbance."[32] The following year, President Dwight D. Eisenhower issued an executive order banning gay men and lesbians from working in the federal government because they posed a "security risk."[33] Gay marriage and adoption, or serving openly in the military, weren't even on the horizon as legal rights at the time. There was little societal acceptance of citizens who identified as gay and little activism on behalf of their rights.

This began to change on June 28, 1969, when police raided the Stonewall Inn, a gay club in New York City. Gay bars and clubs were among the only places where gay men and lesbians could express themselves openly. Even then, the New York State Liquor Authority regularly shut them down, both for serving liquor without a license and because gay and lesbian gatherings were considered "disorderly."[34] When police entered the Stonewall Inn at 3 A.M., patrons, who for years had felt harassed by the police, started throwing bottles at the officers. The riot police put an end to the incident, but that evening's events set into motion the modern civil rights movement for gay and lesbian Americans. Several days of demonstrations outside the club followed, with protesters demanding that gay people receive equal treatment under the law. On the one-year anniversary of the riot, activists staged the first gay pride parade, which many cities have replicated every year since.

From a legal standpoint, though, there was little activity and little progress for the next 30 years. In 1975, several Democratic members of Congress proposed bills to prohibit discrimination against gay men and lesbians, but they didn't receive much.[35] In 1982, Wisconsin became the first state to outlaw discrimination based on sexual orientation, but it took another seven years for a second state (Massachusetts) to follow suit.[36] In early 1993, President Bill Clinton altered the ban on gay people serving in the military. But his "don't ask, don't tell" policy still precluded openly gay citizens from taking part in military service. The military could just no longer ask if you were gay, so gay people who chose not to tell anyone about their sexual orientation could serve.

The question of equal protection under the law for gay and lesbian citizens finally reached the Supreme Court in 1996. At issue was a Colorado law known as Amendment 2. This voter-approved ballot initiative prohibited towns and cities in Colorado from passing antidiscrimination ordinances. In other words, the law restricted towns and cities from protecting citizens from discrimination on the basis of their sexual orientation. The Court sided with gay rights activists, noting that while no federal civil rights law explicitly protected gay men and

When police officers stormed the Stonewall Inn, a gay bar in New York City, in 1969, they set into motion the modern gay rights movement.

lesbians, "If the constitutional conception of 'equal protection of the laws' means anything," it prohibits a law that singles out a group and prevents that group from having any legal protection.[37] Still, the decision was narrow. It said nothing about whether gay men and lesbians were entitled to civil rights more broadly. In fact, that same year, in response to individual states allowing same-sex marriage, Congress passed and President Clinton signed the Defense of Marriage Act. This federal law defined marriage as "the union of one man and one woman" and allowed states to refuse to recognize same-sex marriages granted under the laws of other states.[38] There was little public outcry; only 27 percent of citizens supported same-sex marriage at the time.[39]

But attitudes rapidly began to change. The Human Rights Campaign, a gay rights advocacy organization, launched National Coming Out Day in 1988, an annual event that aims to provide a safe space for LGBTQ individuals to announce their sexual identity.[40] In 1997, Ellen DeGeneres became the first lead character on a mainstream television show to come out as a lesbian.[41] The hit sitcom *Will & Grace*, which premiered in 1998, featured two gay lead characters. By 2007, more than 40 percent of people said they had a close friend or family member who was gay.[42]

As familiarity with the LGBTQ community grew, laws started to change. In 2010, President Obama signed a law ending "don't ask, don't tell." In making the historic announcement, the president remarked: "No longer will our country be denied the service of thousands of patriotic Americans who were forced to leave the military—regardless of their skills, no matter their bravery or their zeal, no matter their years of exemplary performance—because they happen to be gay."[43] By 2013, 12 states had legalized same-sex unions. And in 2015 the Supreme Court, in *Obergefell v. Hodges*, struck down the Defense of Marriage Act. In the majority opinion of the contentious 5–4 ruling, the justices concluded that marriage is a fundamental right protected for all citizens by the Fourteenth Amendment.[44] With this ruling, same-sex marriage became the law of the land. As of 2022, 71 percent of people supported same-sex marriage, a truly dramatic change from only 20 years before.[45]

Despite marriage equality, gay men and lesbians have not achieved the same level of civil rights protections as racial and ethnic minorities or women. Twenty-seven states have no antidiscrimination laws that protect LGBTQ individuals.[46] Two 2020 landmark decisions, however, represented a major advance in establishing civil rights for LGBTQ individuals.[47] In two simultaneous decisions, the Supreme Court ruled that Title VII of the 1964 Civil Right Act, which explicitly prohibits employment discrimination on the basis of sex, also applies to sexual orientation and gender identity. No longer can someone be fired simply for being gay or transgender. Although the opinion very clearly extends protection from discrimination in matters of employment, the Court acknowledged that discrimination pertaining to housing, bathroom use, and serving customers will have to wait to be resolved in future cases.

Different Frameworks for Applying Civil Rights

Civil rights have not been extended equally to people of color, women, and gay men and lesbians. Instead, the Supreme Court has established a three-tier framework to assess claims of unequal treatment under the law. In cases where a law treats people differently by race, the Court employs **strict scrutiny**. It assumes the law is unconstitutional and violates the Fourteenth Amendment unless the government can demonstrate a "compelling interest" to treat people of different racial backgrounds differently. A less rigorous standard—and one that is applied to cases of sex—is **intermediate scrutiny**. Here laws are assumed to be unconstitutional if they treat men and women differently unless there is an "important governmental reason" for the disparate treatment. The lowest tier of the framework is the **rational basis test**. The Court assumes that a law is constitutional as long as it meets a "legitimate government interest" standard. Laws that treat people differently by age (e.g., driver's license requirements) or income level (e.g., eligibility for public housing) fall into this category. Although the Court hasn't formally placed sexual orientation under this classification, some case law on gay rights has relied on the rational basis test. The application of these different standards is imperfect and regularly tweaked by the Court, a process that is sure to continue as cases concerning transgender rights begin to work their way through the justice system.

DID YOU GET IT?
Are all Americans equal under the law?

Short Answer:

- In terms of race, yes. There are almost no circumstances in which people of different races can be treated differently under the law.
- In terms of women, mostly yes. The Supreme Court has carved out a few exceptions in the law where women and men can be treated differently.
- In terms of sexual orientation and gender identity, sometimes. The Supreme Court established marriage rights and protection against employment discrimination. But other types of antidiscrimination laws remain up to the states to pass and enforce.

DEVELOPING YOUR SKILLS

Persuasive Argumentation

Evaluate evidence: In pushing for legal equality, advocates rely on many different types of evidence, including case law, employment and crime statistics, and public opinion data. For the following questions, consider what information would help you make the strongest arguments having to do with legal equality.

1. In its 1954 decision in *Brown v. Board of Education*, the Supreme Court outlawed school segregation. More than 65 years later, many scholars and activists contend that the decision failed to desegregate the public schools. What information would be most helpful if you wanted to provide evidence for this argument?

    a. The percentage of students in today's public schools who are Black

    b. The percentage of students in today's public schools who are White

    c. The percentage of Black students who attended majority-Black public schools between 1954 and 2022

    d. The ratio of public to private school students between 1954 and 2022

2. If the Supreme Court wants to rely on a precedent that allows women and men to be treated differently under the law, which case provides the best supporting evidence?

   a. *Brown v. Board of Education*

   b. *Reed v. Reed*

   c. *Obergefell v. Hodges*

   d. *Rostker v. Goldberg*

3. Twenty-seven states have no law protecting gay men and lesbians against housing discrimination. Often, political leaders in these states argue that these protections are unnecessary. Which piece of evidence supports their argument?

   a. Housing statistics showing that gay men and lesbians are well represented in all neighborhoods

   b. Crime statistics about violence toward gay men and lesbians in every state

   c. Public opinion data about citizens' attitudes toward equality for gay men and lesbians

   d. Public opinion data comparing the attitudes of gay and straight people

FIGURE IT OUT

In 2019, the U.S. Congress considered a bill entitled the Equality Act. It would have amended the Civil Rights Act of 1964 to guarantee legal equality for LGBTQ citizens. In short, it would have outlawed discrimination against gay and transgender people when it comes to employment, housing, and other key areas established in the Civil Rights Act.

Debate over the bill was very contentious. To some members of Congress, passing it into law was the obvious right thing to do. They thought it was high time Congress acted to protect gay and transgender citizens from discrimination. To other members of Congress, the Equality Act looked like an unnecessary attempt to impinge on religious freedom and give special rights to a group of citizens who are not entitled to these protections. Identify clear evidence for both sides. More specifically:

- Imagine your job is to help a member of Congress write a speech arguing in favor of the Equality Act. Identify two pieces of evidence provided in this segment that could be the basis of the argument.

- Now imagine that you need to help a member of Congress write a speech arguing against the Equality Act. What two pieces of evidence would be most compelling? Again, you can rely on the content of this segment to answer the question.

Want to Know More?

Several critically acclaimed movies depict the fight for racial justice in the 1960s. *Mississippi Burning* is a fictional account of the circumstances surrounding the murder of three civil rights activists in Philadelphia, Mississippi; *Selma* focuses on the struggle for voting rights; and *In the Heat of the Night* offers a fictional account of a Black police detective who becomes involved in a murder investigation in the South in the late 1960s. You should also watch Spike Lee's documentary *4 Little Girls*, which records the events leading up to the Ku Klux Klan's 1963 bombing of an Alabama church, resulting in the deaths of four young Black girls.

CONSUMING
POLITICAL
INFORMATION

14.
Is America a racist country?

#RacialJustice

Throughout the spring and summer of 2020, roughly 20 million Americans took to the streets to protest police violence against people of color. On June 6 alone, more than 500,000 people attended one of more than 500 protests, many organized by the Black Lives Matter movement.[1] Despite the fact that much of the nation was locked down during this time — the Covid-19 pandemic was surging — a civil rights movement was underway in small towns and big cities alike. And it had broad public support. Two-thirds of Americans supported the protests, including more than 60 percent of White people.[2]

The protests were a response to the murder of George Floyd, a 46-year-old Black man. Derek Chauvin, a White police officer, had apprehended Floyd on a Minneapolis street and intended to arrest him for allegedly using a counterfeit $20 bill. Floyd offered little resistance, but Chauvin handcuffed him, forced him to lay prone on the ground, and held Floyd down with a knee on his neck. Floyd begged for help and repeatedly told Chauvin he couldn't breathe. But to no avail. After nine minutes with Chauvin's knee on his neck, Floyd suffocated and died. The entire incident, captured on video, took place in broad daylight amid onlookers pleading for Floyd's life. The footage unleashed a wave of political activity unlike anything the country had seen since the civil rights movement of the 1960s.

157

In the wake of George Floyd's murder, activists in hundreds of cities across the country —
such as these pictured in St. Louis, Missouri — took to the streets in the summer of 2020
to protest police violence against Black citizens.

The death of a Black man (or woman) at the hands of a White police
officer was nothing new. Just google the names Michael Brown,[3] Walter
Scott,[4] Freddie Gray,[5] Philando Castile,[6] or Breonna Taylor for details
of some of the most recent high-profile incidents.[7] But Floyd's murder
was so brazen, so public, and so fully documented on camera that it
prompted millions of Americans to take action.

The initial national consensus around the importance of addressing
and preventing police brutality that led to Floyd's murder soon gave way
to partisan political debate over policing and race relations. In the 2020
presidential election — just six months after Floyd's death — 92 percent
of people concerned about racial inequality voted for Joe Biden. Donald
Trump received the overwhelming support (84 percent) of voters who
believed that the criminal justice system treats all people fairly.[8] Perhaps
it's no surprise that citizens believe race relations in the country are getting
worse. In 2013, almost 60 percent of people thought race relations were
"generally good." By the summer of 2020, that number had fallen to 31 percent.[9]

So where are we on the road to **racial justice** — a term we define to
mean fair and equal treatment for people of all races? The Civil Rights
Act of 1964, the Voting Rights Act of 1965, and landmark Supreme
Court cases — most notably *Brown v. Board of Education* — established
racial equality under the law. It is illegal in the United States to
discriminate based on race. But this segment demonstrates that legal

Is America a racist country?

equality alone cannot undo the deep racial divisions and animosities that have always dominated life in the United States. From income and wealth, to educational opportunities, to various aspects of the criminal justice system, significant racial disparities remain.

Economic Injustice: Racial Divisions in Poverty and Wealth

One of the most important barometers for assessing racial equality is standard of living—the degree of wealth and material comfort a person enjoys. After all, money can determine, among other things, where you live, how you live, and your ability to weather a financial setback, such as losing your job or dealing with a medical emergency. We focus on differences in the standard of living among the three largest racial and ethnic groups in the country: White people (59 percent), Latinos (19 percent), and African Americans (14 percent). (The remaining 8 percent of the population comprises Asian Americans, Native Americans, and Pacific Islanders.[10])

Table 1 presents three categories of statistics that gauge standard of living: (1) poverty and income, (2) home ownership, and (3) wealth and savings.[11] Given the different histories of White people, Black people, and Latinos, we expect some differences. When slavery ended in 1865, most free Black people and formerly enslaved people had little or no wealth. Thus, they began from a starting point well behind White people. Latinos have also suffered from a lagged start. In 1960, only 3.5 percent of the U.S. population was Latino. Today, after a period of substantial immigration, Latinos constitute almost 20 percent of the population. And they are on track to reach 25 percent of the population by 2045.[12] Because Latino immigration has been so recent, they've had far less time to develop economic security.[13] Indeed, the comparisons in Table 1 reveal striking racial and ethnic differences.

Just consider poverty and income statistics. In 2020, the median household income was $67,521. This means that half the households in the United States earned more than that amount in a year, and half earned less. As the first row in Table 1 indicates, though, the median income in White households exceeded that of Black and Latino households substantially. If we break down the annual income data into weekly paychecks, White households earned nearly $560 more *each week* than Black households and $377 more than Latino households did.

Another way to assess standards of living is with the **poverty rate**—the percentage of people who live on less than half the median income of a four-person household. In 2022, that meant a family of four living on

TABLE 1. Citizens' Economic Circumstances, by Race and Ethnicity

	White	Latino	Black
Poverty and Income			
Median household income	$74,912	$55,321	$45,870
Poverty rate	8%	17%	20%
Child poverty rate	11%	28%	34%
Home Ownership			
Home ownership rate	71%	46%	46%
Median home value	$230,000	$200,000	$150,000
Wealth and Savings			
Percentage with no bank account	3%	12%	14%
Percentage with retirement savings	65%	28%	44%
Average retirement savings	$50,000	$20,000	$20,000
Median net worth	$188,200	$36,100	$24,100

Note: Data reflect the most recent information provided by the U.S. Census Bureau and poverty-related nonprofit organizations and think tanks.

Source: United States Census Bureau, National Center for Education Statistics, Board of Governors of the Federal Reserve System, and Federal Deposit Insurance Corporation. See Note 11 for full source information.

an annual income of less than $27,750.[14] For African Americans and Latinos, the poverty rate is roughly twice the rate among White people. It's not only that people of color are more likely than White people to live in poverty; they also have a more difficult time getting out of it. Childhood poverty is greater among people of color and more likely to carry over into adulthood.[15]

Home ownership and wealth and savings statistics paint a similar picture. Whereas more than 7 out of 10 of White people own a home, fewer than half of African Americans and Latinos do. And those homes that people of color do own are worth significantly less than those homes owned by White people. When it comes to net worth (the value of everything you own, minus your debts), the disparities are even more dramatic.

White people's median net worth ($188,200) is almost eight times higher than Black people's ($24,100) and more than five times higher than Latinos' ($36,100).[16] The average retirement savings of people of color is less than half that of White people. Given these realities, it's hardly surprising that African Americans and Latinos are more than four times as likely as White people not to have a bank account.

Disadvantaged from the Start: Racial Inequities in Education

Although myriad factors contribute to the racial disparities in standards of living, educational opportunity plays a major role. Jonathan Kozol, an author, activist, and former fourth-grade teacher in Boston, has been studying the racial dynamics of public schools for 50 years. His books, including *Shame of the Nation*, compare the experiences of children of color attending low-quality urban public schools to White children's experiences in affluent, suburban public schools, often just a few miles away. According to Kozol, we are "running an apartheid education system in which funding for schools and resources for schools are savagely unequal. . . . It's obvious that there's no level playing field in the United States. The game is rigged before it even starts."[17]

How does Kozol arrive at this conclusion, given that the Supreme Court—in its 1954 decision in *Brown v. Board of Education*—held that laws segregating schools are unconstitutional? Well, schools reflect the neighborhoods where they're located. And for a series of reasons—ranging from economic circumstances, to historically discriminatory housing policies, to people's preferences for less diversity in where they live[18]—residential segregation is prominent.[19] Public schools reflect this. According to data from the Department of Education, the average White student attending public school goes to a school where 73 percent of the students are White. Meanwhile, nearly half of African American and Latino public school students attend schools where 80 percent of the students are people of color.[20]

These patterns are important because they're linked to school funding and school performance. Researchers at the University of California, Los Angeles, have found that Black people and Latinos represent more than half the children in the most impoverished schools but just 11 percent of students in the most well-funded ones.[21] Data from the Education Trust, a nonprofit organization that focuses on education equity, reveal that school districts serving the largest populations of African American and Latino students receive about 13 percent less in state and local funding (about $1,800 per student) than those serving the fewest students of color.[22] In a school district with 3,600 students (the average size of a district in the United States), a gap of $1,800 per student amounts to a shortage for the district of nearly $6.5 million per year. Funding allows for higher teacher salaries, the most up-to-date instructional materials, better facilities, and more electives and extracurricular activities. Black and Latino students, therefore, are more likely to encounter poorly paid teachers, outdated materials, and dilapidated buildings.[23]

Public school funding also correlates with student performance. African American and Latino students are less likely to graduate from high school (see Table 2).[24] They also, on average, don't perform as well as White students on college entrance exams.[25] Wealthier schools often provide SAT preparation classes, and when they don't, wealthier parents can pay for the classes themselves. These scores can affect students' college acceptances as well as the financial aid packages they receive.

Racial disparities in education don't disappear when students step onto college campuses. Even when they go to college, African American and Latino students are less likely to attend the most selective and prestigious schools, including flagship state universities. At the University of Virginia, for example, just 7 percent of the students are Black,[26] yet 22 percent of graduating high school seniors in Virginia are Black.[27] The gaps are even bigger in states like Delaware and Georgia. College students of color are also less likely to graduate. Given that the average college graduate earns about 56 percent more each week than someone with just a high school diploma and more than twice as much as someone who didn't graduate from high school, racial inequalities in education contribute to economic inequalities over a lifetime.[28]

TABLE 2. Educational Experiences, by Race and Ethnicity

	White	Latino	Black
High school graduation rate	89%	81%	79%
College enrollment rate (for 18-to 24-year-olds)	41	36	37
Graduation rate for those who enter college	62	42	41

Note: Data come from reports issued in 2020 and 2021 and reflect the most recent information provided by education-related nonprofit organizations and think tanks.

Source: *Journal of Blacks in Higher Education,* National Center for Education Statistics, and EducationData.org. See Notes 24 and 25 for full source information.

Colleges and universities are aware of these realities and, dating back to the 1970s, have often attempted to use **affirmative action programs** to diversify their student bodies. These programs aim to address the consequences of prior discrimination by making efforts to provide opportunities based on race or other markers of identity. Opponents consider these policies to be "reverse discrimination" that unfairly advantages applicants of color over White applicants, and the Supreme Court has struck down many of them. In the 1978 case of *Regents of the University of California v. Bakke*, the Court concluded that colleges and universities could take race into account as a positive attribute when considering applications, but they could not establish a quota or percentage of slots for members of historically disadvantaged groups.[29] The Court reaffirmed this principle when it reviewed the University of Michigan's admissions criteria in 2003.[30] Today's increasingly conservative Supreme Court is likely to declare all affirmative action programs unconstitutional, so closing racial disparities in higher education will have to take another path.

Racial Disparities in the Criminal Justice System

Racial disparities in the criminal justice system suggest yet another dimension on which we have a long way to go on the road to racial justice. The United States has the highest incarceration rate in the world, with roughly 2.1 million people confined in either state or federal prisons or local jails.[31] But the racial composition of the prison population does not mirror the overall population. It's not even close. Figure 1 compares three racial or ethnic groups' percentages in the U.S. population (purple bars) to their percentage of the prison population (orange bars).[32] If the prison population reflected the U.S. population, then the purple and orange bars for any given racial group would be the same height. That's never the case. African Americans, for example, make up 14 percent of the overall population, but their prison population (33 percent) is roughly two and a half times greater. Latinos are also overrepresented in prisons, though by a smaller ratio. All told, the likelihood of being incarcerated at some point in their lives is 1 in 3 for Black men and 1 in 6 for Latinos, but only 1 in 17 for White men.[33]

Many scholars point to these incarceration statistics as evidence of a racially biased criminal justice system. They note, for instance, that the War on Drugs, launched in the 1980s, increased the police presence in Black and Latino neighborhoods. Accordingly, the implementation of laws requiring longer prison sentences for drug-related crimes has

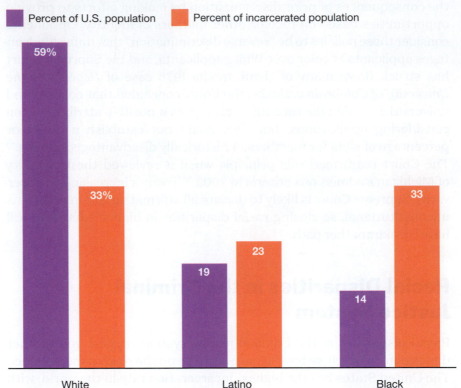

FIGURE 1. U.S. Population Compared to Incarcerated Population, by Race and Ethnicity, 2018

■ Percent of U.S. population ■ Percent of incarcerated population

	White	Latino	Black
Percent of U.S. population	59%	19	14
Percent of incarcerated population	33%	23	33

Sources: Quick Facts, U.S. Census Bureau; John Gramlich, "Black Imprisonment Rate in the U.S. Has Fallen by a Third since 2006," Pew Research Center.

had a disproportionate impact on people of color. Arrest rates for marijuana are a prime example. African Americans are 3.6 times more likely than White people to be arrested for marijuana use, even though marijuana use is similar across races.[34] After they're arrested, Black people are also more likely than White people to be jailed while awaiting trial,[35] serve longer sentences for committing the same crime,[36] and have their probation revoked.[37]

How police officers do their jobs is an additional area of concern for civil rights advocates. **Racial profiling**—the practice of using race or ethnicity to make assumptions about possible criminal behavior—is common in much of the United States. Nowhere is the practice explicitly written into the law, but it is a norm for many police departments. A Justice Department study of the Ferguson, Missouri, police department found that Black people are twice as likely as White people to be stopped by police. In Chicago, Black people and Latinos are four times more likely to be stopped, even though drugs and other illegal substances are found with White people more than twice as often. Similar studies have uncovered disparate treatment in North Carolina, New York, and Arizona. Nationwide, 65 percent of Black people have felt targeted by the police because of their race.[38]

Most troubling, perhaps, is that the disparate treatment carries over into deadly shootings by police. From 2015 to 2021, roughly 6,000 people were killed by police officers in the United States. The rate at which Black people were killed was more than twice as high as the rate for White people.[39] For Latinos, the rate was almost double that of White people. Statistics like these have led civil rights and Black Lives Matter activists to conclude that when it comes to people of color, the police shoot first and ask questions later. Based on citizens' experiences, it's hardly surprising that when asked whether they worry about being the victim of police violence, 63 percent of Black people, but only 21 percent of White people, express concern.[40]

The Black Lives Matter movement has shed a light on the role race plays in various aspects of the criminal justice system and spawned numerous legislative efforts at the state and federal levels to address inequality and inequity. The George Floyd Justice in Policing Act is a prime example. The bill would, among other things, ban police chokeholds, end no-knock warrants, and prohibit racial profiling.[41] Moreover, it would remove qualified immunity for police officers, which means they could be held personally liable for violating victims' constitutional rights.

But prospects for quickly ending racial inequities in the criminal justice system are not good. The Biden administration supports widespread reform and championed the George Floyd Justice in Policing Act. But partisan politics and ideological differences regarding the role of the police make passing federal legislation like this doubtful.[42] Indeed, when the House of Representatives voted on the bill in March 2021, not a single Republican supported it.[43] But the effort to pass a reform bill collapsed in the Senate when negotiators could not find a compromise.[44] Moreover, the Supreme Court has yet to decide whether racial profiling violates the Constitution. And it has reaffirmed that police officers are, for the most part, immune from excessive-force lawsuits.[45] In other words, they cannot be sued for using what turns out to be unreasonable force if they demonstrate that they behaved like any competent police officer would when facing a similar situation.

The Political Landscape and the Road to Racial Justice

The civil rights movement delivered something close to legal equality by the middle of 1960s, but racial inequities in income and wealth, educational opportunities, and the criminal justice system persist. How and whether the government can do anything to close these gaps is at the center of a long-standing political debate over how best to achieve the goal of equality.

Scholar and author Cornel West, in his seminal work *Race Matters*, describes the two sides of the debate.[46] On one side are civil rights activists, progressives, and some Democrats, whom West labels "liberal structuralists." They believe that racism continues to plague much of American life and that the way forward is to invest in government programs that help ensure equal opportunities for members of traditionally marginalized groups. Education, job training, and day care, for example, would provide people of color with an improved infrastructure to help them get ahead. On the other side are most Republicans, who tend to fall into what West labels the "conservative behavioralist" camp. They believe that the playing field in America is basically level, that legal equality is well established, and that "cultural values" in communities of color are to blame for their living conditions. The government, therefore, has little or no responsibility to close the racial divides we've identified. Though West's analysis is now three decades old, it continues to ring true today as Democrats and Republicans debate the existence of structural racism and what, if any, role the government should play in combating it. Because these two sides are so well entrenched, so linked to partisan politics, and so obviously speaking past each other, concrete steps to remedy racial inequities remain caught in a quagmire.

DID YOU GET IT?
Is America a racist country?

Short Answer:

- Most civil rights advocates think so.
- An analysis of today's economic conditions, educational opportunities, and experiences with the criminal justice system reveals significant racial disparities.
- Prospects for closing these gaps are linked to heated political debates that are unlikely to be resolved anytime in the near future.

Consuming Political Information

Consider the source: Finding reliable and credible information about race and racial dynamics in the United States can be challenging. Google "race relations" or "racism in America" and you'll get literally thousands of hits. Try your hand at evaluating various sources for information you can rely on.

1. You read in a blog post that there are more White people in prison than people of color. But you're a little skeptical because of other information you have heard. You find a 2015 Bureau of Justice Statistics (BJS) report that confirms your suspicion. There are almost 24,000 more Blacks than Whites in the prison system. Should you trust the BJS report?

   a. No. Online blogs tend to report more accurate data than the government.

   b. Probably not. Government statistics likely don't account for everyone in prison.

   c. Probably not. Government agencies usually lie in statistical reports like these.

   d. Probably. Official government reports tend to include accurate statistics.

2. If you want to know more about income and wealth disparities across races, which of these is the most reliable source of information?

   a. A report on CNN.com

   b. A report on Sean Hannity's Fox News television program

   c. A report from the Census Bureau on income and home ownership

   d. A U.S. Chamber of Commerce report on race and income disparities

3. While political leaders claim that the educational experience for all students is improving throughout the country, liberal columnists and pundits often lament how the public school system is failing students of color. If you wanted unbiased, nonpartisan information to help you determine what is really going on with students of color in the public school system, which of the following sources would probably be the most objective? (Hint: Visit the website of each organization or outlet to get a better sense of its mission.)

   a. A speech from Miguel Cardona, the secretary of the Department of Education

   b. A front-page article printed in the *Wall Street Journal*

   c. An editorial printed in *The Nation*

   d. An editorial printed in *The National Review*

FIGURE IT OUT

Use credible sources to learn more about high-profile victims of police brutality. More specifically, from the list below, choose two and: (1) identify a credible journalistic or academic source that summarizes the course of events; (2) explain, in a sentence or two, how you determined that the source was credible; (3) summarize what happened in the confrontation between the police officer and the individual; and (4) note whether the officer(s) was charged with committing a crime.

*   Rodney King (Los Angeles, 1991)
*   Amadou Diallo (New York City, 1999)
*   Eric Garner (New York City, 2014)
*   Freddie Gray (Baltimore, 2015)
*   Breonna Taylor (Louisville, 2020)
*   Daunte Wright (Minneapolis, 2021)

Hint: Because there's so much information about these cases, you might try including the name of a source you trust in your search terms.

Want to Know More?

If you are interested in a candid discussion of racial dynamics on today's college campuses, read Beverly Daniel Tatum's *Why Are All the Black Kids Sitting Together in the Cafeteria? And Other Conversations about Race*. You might also like *Between the World and Me*, by Ta-Nehisi Coates. The influential commentator writes about race, society, and his personal journey.

15. Why do women earn less money than men?

#GenderEquality

On June 10, 1963, President John F. Kennedy signed into law the **Equal Pay Act**. Surrounded by influential champions of the bill — including female members of Congress, Vice President Lyndon Johnson, and leaders of women's organizations — the president denounced gender discrimination in the workplace:

> I am delighted today to approve the Equal Pay Act of 1963, which prohibits arbitrary discrimination against women in the payment of wages. This act represents many years of effort . . . to call attention to the unconscionable practice of paying female employees less wages than male employees for the same job. This measure adds to our laws another structure basic to democracy.[1]

The law mandated that employers pay men and women the same wages and benefits for performing jobs that require the same skills and responsibilities.[2] At a time when the average woman earned only 60 percent of the average man's pay, the legislation represented, in Kennedy's words, "a significant step forward."

Fast-forward 51 years to the summer of 2014. In upstate New York, the airwaves were abuzz with Congressman Dan Maffei's new campaign ad.

President John F. Kennedy signs into law the Equal Pay Act. The law aimed to abolish wage disparities based on sex.

It featured an eight-year-old boy named Fred, an aspiring entrepreneur in a business suit who operates a lemonade stand where two of his "employees" (also eight-year-olds) just finished a shift. "Great work," Fred tells Jason, handing him $10. "And Sally, since you did the same work, here's $8 for you." Across the street, Maffei, a Democrat, turns to the camera and says: "You don't have to be a grownup to know that isn't fair. We've got to make sure that women get equal pay for equal work."[3]

Maffei wasn't alone in his rallying cry. Democrats throughout the country had called attention to women's lower pay for decades and have continued to do so in the decade following the lemonade stand ad. After all, whereas the typical man earns $989 per week, the average woman earns just $900. When it comes to median annual earnings for full-time work, men make a little less than $58,000. Women? Just a little more than $47,000. The gap is even bigger when we compare single-parent households. There, men's median earnings are $56,458 per year; women's come in at just $35,287. That means that the average single mother relies on an annual income that's only about 63 percent of what a single father can depend on.[4] "Closing the pay gap," according to President Joe Biden, "is more than just an economic imperative — it's a moral imperative as well."[5]

Why do women earn less money than men?

There are many ways to track women's progress in the march for equality — the extent to which women have secured reproductive rights and physical autonomy, efforts to combat sexual harassment in the workplace and on college campuses, the number of sex discrimination lawsuits filed, and women's representation in U.S. political institutions, to name just a handful. But comparing women and men's economic equality has become a central barometer for measuring women's advancement. Indeed, economists regularly link economic freedom and prosperity to gender equality. The more economic opportunities women have, the more they are empowered socially and politically.[6] That's why the National Organization for Women places pay equity right up there with reproductive rights when listing the key policy issues in the fight for gender equality. And it's why the National Women's Law Center characterizes the pay gap as a "harsh reality," one that costs the average woman in the workforce more than $10,000 per year.[7]

Closing the pay gap is clearly a fundamental issue to resolve in the struggle for equality. So how far away are we from gender equality in the economic sphere? Didn't the Equal Pay Act — which was passed more than 50 years ago — bar employers from paying women and men different wages for performing the same job? This segment explains what the pay gap is, what causes it, and why it's legal. Answering these questions also underscores the fact that despite the legal equality they've already achieved, full equality for women in U.S. society remains elusive.

The Wage Gap: What Is It and How Do We Measure It?

Several government agencies and research organizations release statistics regarding people's annual incomes. The U.S. Census Bureau and the Bureau of Labor Statistics report the yearly earnings of male and female full-time workers. Some are paid with an annual salary, others at an hourly rate, but all work full-time. The Pew Research Center, in contrast, documents the pay awarded to men and women regardless of whether they work full-time or part-time. Figure 1 presents data from all three agencies and organizations; the lines represent the **pay gap**, which is a calculation of women's wages as a percentage of men's.[8]

To determine whether women earn less money than men, it's critical that you understand how to analyze and interpret these data. If women and men earned the same incomes, then the lines in Figure 1 would reach

FIGURE 1. Women's Pay as a Percentage of Men's Pay, 1960–2020

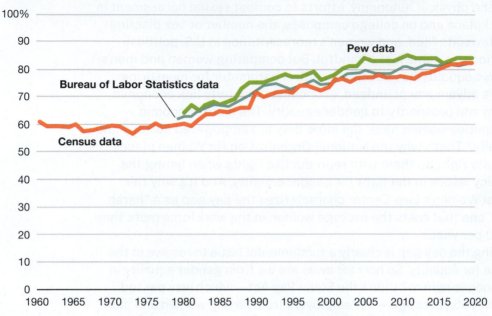

Note: U.S. Census Bureau and Bureau of Labor Statistics data reflect women's earnings as a percentage of men's earnings among full-time workers. Pew data reflect women's earnings as a percentage of men's among hourly wage workers, including part-time workers.

Source: Jessica Semega, Melissa Kollar, Emily A. Shrider, and John Creamer, "Income and Poverty in the United States: 2019," U.S. Census Bureau, September 15, 2020; Amanda Barroso and Anna Brown, "Gender Pay Gap in U.S. Held Steady in 2020," Pew Research Center, May 25, 2021.

the 100 percent mark on the *y* axis (the vertical scale). But they don't. Women's pay is always less than 100 percent of men's. Although the size of the pay gap varies slightly depending on the data source, all of the statistics point to women making somewhere around 82 percent of what men do. That means that women earn roughly 82 cents for every dollar earned by men. The trend lines also indicate that women's pay made steady gains starting in about 1980. But the progress stalled in the early 2000s.

As we consider the magnitude of the pay gap, it's important to be explicit about what the data collected by these agencies represent and what they don't. We want to be very clear about this because it's a distinction that's often lost in political debates on the topic. The statistics gathered by the Census Bureau, the Bureau of Labor Statistics, and Pew paint a compelling picture of women earning less money than men. But we cannot assume that these differences are a result of pay disparities for doing the same job. That's because pay gap statistics reflect the difference in what the average female and average male worker earn overall, even when they're doing different jobs.

Why do women earn less money than men?

FIGURE 2. Median Hourly Earnings, as Pennies on the Dollar of White Men's Earnings, 2019

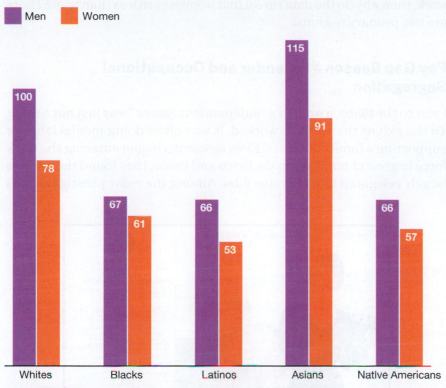

Source: "The Simple Truth about the Gender Pay Gap," AAUW, 2019.

Figure 1 represents average pay for all women and men. But women of color face a double disadvantage.[9] Consider the comparisons illustrated in Figure 2.[10] Here we set the base level of pay as the average hourly earnings of a White man. That's represented by the 100 in the figure's leftmost bar. The 100 signifies one dollar (or 100 pennies). The other bars indicate the pay for everyone else as pennies on the dollar of what White men earn. White women, for example, make 78 cents for every dollar earned by a White man. Black women and Latinas earn significantly less. Within each racial group, women also fare worse than men. Black women, for example, earn 61 cents on the dollar, compared to Black men, who earn 67 cents. This means that Black women's hourly wages are just 91 percent of Black men's. (We calculated that by dividing Black women's wages by Black men's.) A similar calculation shows that Native American women earn only 86 percent of what Native American men do. Latinas earn just 80 percent of what Latinos do. And although Asian women and men earn the most, the gender gap in pay among them is still 24 cents on the dollar.[11]

If it is illegal to compensate women differently from men for the same work, then why do the data reveal that women earn less than men? There are two primary reasons.

Pay Gap Reason #1: Gender and Occupational Segregation

Prior to the 1950s, a woman's "independent career" was just not a thing. To the extent that women worked, it was often doing menial labor or supporting a family business. Even as women began entering the workforce in greater numbers in the 1950s and 1960s, they found themselves largely relegated to low-status jobs. Among the most prestigious was

In the 1950s, women's career options were severely limited. But as airline travel became a thing, a new job opportunity emerged: stewardess. It wasn't open to all women, though only those with a cheerful disposition who could meet ideal height and weight requirements.

Why do women earn less money than men?

airline stewardess. The job offered the possibility of traveling the world. It also required women to be between 5'2" and 5'7" and weigh no more than 135 pounds.[12]

A lot has changed since the 1960s. Women today have access to educational and professional paths that once were open only to men, as well as legal recourse to fight wage discrimination. Beyond the Equal Pay Act, the Civil Rights Act of 1964 broadly prohibits gender discrimination in the workplace.[13] And the Lilly Ledbetter Fair Pay Act of 2009 makes it significantly easier for women to file wage discrimination lawsuits.[14]

Nevertheless, many jobs continue to be dominated by either women or men. Table 1 lists the 20 jobs that, based on Department of Labor statistics, are the most gender-segregated. The top half of the table rank orders the 10 jobs with the most male-dominated workforces. In each of these positions, men constitute at least 98.5 percent of the workers. The bottom half of Table 1 presents the most female-dominated jobs. In each of these, women represent at least four out of every five employees. Next to each job, we note the average annual pay.

These occupational divisions serve as a central explanation for the pay gap. Notice that the male-dominated jobs pay, on average, about 50 percent more than the female-dominated positions. The key point here is that women in general aren't paid less because they work less or because they don't perform as well as men. They're paid less because jobs typically held by men, at all skill levels, pay more than jobs dominated by women. That's why the wage gap narrowed throughout the 1980s and 1990s, decades when women were breaking into traditionally male occupations. And that's why, as women's integration into the full range of male professions began to stall in the 2000s, so did their pay relative to men's.[15]

It's also important to note that even when women and men work in the same career field, women still often earn less than men do. It's against the law for employers to pay women less for doing the same job, but most jobs have salary ranges. In many cases, part of arriving at a salary involves negotiations between employer and employee, and here significant gender differences emerge. Studies of salary negotiations reveal that when there's no explicit statement that a salary or wage is negotiable, women are more likely than men to accept the salary they're offered. Men, even without being told that it's appropriate or possible to ask for higher pay, tend to do so.[16] In fact, surveys find that when asked to select metaphors that describe the idea of negotiating a salary, men choose winning a ball game. Women equate the experience with going to the dentist.[17]

TABLE 1. Average Annual Pay for Jobs with the Highest Rates of Gender Segregation

	Percent Female Employees	Average Annual Pay
10 Most Male-Dominated Jobs		
Brick, block, and stonemason	0.1%	$39,640
Drywall and tile installer	0.3	40,470
Mining machine operator	0.3	49,270
Bus and truck mechanic	0.5	46,110
Home electronics installer/repairer	0.5	55,160
Firefighter supervisor	0.5	74,970
Tool and die maker	0.8	42,110
Heavy vehicle servicer	1.0	47,120
Auto technician or mechanic	1.2	37,850
Construction equipment operator	1.3	49,110
Mean Salary		**$48,173**
10 Most Female-Dominated Jobs		
Secretary/administrative assistant	95.3%	$36,500
Childcare worker	94.1	20,320
Receptionist	91.5	28,430
Teacher's assistant	91.1	26,550
Registered nurse	90.6	67,490
Bookkeeping/accounting clerk	89.1	38,990
Maid/housekeeper	88.1	22,990
Home health aide	87.9	21,920
Personal care aide	84.7	20,980
Office clerk	83.4	31,890
Mean Salary		**$31,606**

Sources: Data compiled from the Department of Labor and the Bureau of Labor Statistics' 2015 report.

Pay Gap Reason #2: The Exorbitant Cost of Childcare

The cost of childcare also contributes substantially to the pay gap. When two parents work full-time, families often need to find full-time childcare. And it's not cheap. On average, one young child's full-time enrollment in a private childcare center in the United States costs $216 per week (which amounts to more than $11,000 per year).[18] That number, in and of itself, is high. But when considered as a percentage of an individual's annual income, it is often prohibitive. Childcare is most affordable in South Dakota, where it eats up "only" 11 percent of an average full-time worker's pay. At the other end of the continuum, Washington, D.C., is the most expensive; childcare costs there constitute 26 percent of a typical annual income. The national average is 17.1 percent. And these figures are based on one child. Multiply them by two or three for larger families, and costs become untenable. Figure 3 displays childcare costs by state. The more darkly shaded the state, the greater the expense.[19]

Because women earn, on average, only 80 percent of what men do, it's often women who leave the workforce, even temporarily, to provide childcare that they otherwise can't afford. Given that roughly 40 percent of women either take significant time off or reduce their hours to care for their children, they stymie their potential for career advancement and

FIGURE 3. Childcare Expenses (for One Child) as a Percentage of Mean Annual Income, by State

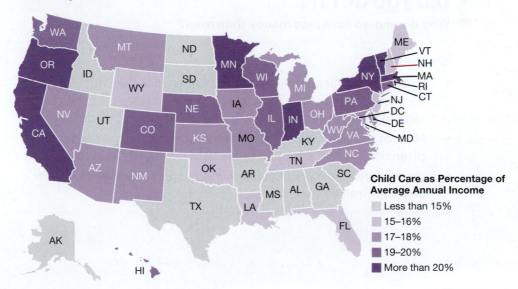

Child Care as Percentage of Average Annual Income

- Less than 15%
- 15–16%
- 17–18%
- 19–20%
- More than 20%

Source: Trevor Wheelwright, "The Top 10 Most Expensive (and Least Expensive) States for Child Care," Move.org, 2021.

the higher incomes that come with it. Indeed, the wage gap is smallest among those under the age of 35, many of whom are not parents.[20]

Women's Equality on the Horizon

Since President Kennedy signed the Equal Pay Act in 1963, women have made substantial advances across a broad spectrum of professions. In 1950, only 6 percent of doctors were women. Today that number is close to 40 percent.[21] Similar gains are true for lawyers, managers in the business world, and college educators. But we remain far off from women and men earning similar incomes overall. And the reasons for the pay gap suggest that achieving full equality for women will be difficult. After all, occupational segregation results from historical patterns that are deeply embedded in U.S. culture. Childcare is a deeply partisan issue with no solution in sight—Democrats tend to support more government funds for childcare, while Republicans generally think that the private sector should step in to provide more options. Whereas legal equality can generate advances when it comes to sexual harassment and discrimination, it cannot ensure women's economic parity. Given that economic freedom is perhaps the most fundamental component of women's overall equality, the outlook for getting there anytime soon doesn't look too promising.

DID YOU GET IT?
Why do women earn less money than men?

Short Answer:
- It is not legal for employers to pay women less than men for doing the same job, although most jobs do have a salary range and men tend to negotiate for higher wages more than women do.
- Most of the pay gap results from the fact that women and men often do different jobs, and those held by women tend to pay less.
- Women are also more likely than men to leave the workforce for childcare-related reasons.

Quantitative Literacy

Do the math: This segment featured various statistics about the pay gap and the causes for it. Rely on the tables and figures from the segment to compute the implications of the data we present.

---

1. Look closely at Figure 1. Which of the following statements is accurate?
    a. In the 1970s, if the average man earned $500 per week, then the average woman earned about $300.
    b. The difference in women's and men's wages increased by about 20 percent throughout the 1980s and 1990s.
    c. The pay gap is about one-third larger today than it was in the early 1960s.
    d. The pay gap for salaried workers is about 40 percent smaller than it is for hourly workers.

2. A White man works 40 hours per week and earns $20 per hour. Assume that he gets paid for working 52 weeks a year. Based on the data presented in Figure 2, how much less would a Black woman's annual income be if she also worked 40 hours a week all year?
    a. $34,112
    b. $25,376
    c. $14,560
    d. $7,488

3. According to Figure 3, which move would lead to an increase in the proportion of income spent on childcare?
    a. Moving from Arkansas to Mississippi
    b. Moving from Oregon to Washington
    c. Moving from Iowa to Wisconsin
    d. Moving from Vermont to New Hampshire

Want to Know More?

In *Meet the Parents*, a goofy comedy released in 2000, Ben Stiller plays Gaylord Focker, a male nurse. When he spends the weekend meeting his fiancée's parents, he experiences quite a bit of derision for working in this historically female-dominated field. His portrayal generated social commentary from experts within the field of nursing as to whether Stiller's character refuted or perpetuated stereotypes about men in the nursing profession.

16.
Do you have to bake a gay couple's wedding cake?

#ConflictingRights

On March 13, 2014, William Jack walked into Azucar Bakery in Denver, Colorado, and tried to order two custom cakes. He described his vision for the cakes to pastry chef Lindsay Jones. Each would be shaped like a Bible and feature an image of two groomsmen with a red X through them. On one cake, he wanted the words "God hates sin. Psalm 45:7" and "Homosexuality is a detestable sin. Leviticus 18:22." On the other, "God loves sinners" and "While we were yet sinners, Christ died for us. Romans 5:8." Before Jones offered a price quote, she consulted with the bakery's owner, Marjorie Silva. Silva spoke to Jack and decided that his request made her uncomfortable. She told him that the bakery "does not discriminate" and accepts "all humans."[1] Silva said that she would bake the Bible-shaped cakes but that she couldn't decorate them with the images and verses Jack wanted. Instead, she offered to sell him icing in a pastry bag so that he could design and write whatever he wanted on the cakes. Jack filed a grievance against Azucar Bakery with the Colorado Division of Civil Rights, claiming he had been discriminated against because of his devout Christian viewpoint.

It wasn't a coincidence that Jack tried to place his order at Azucar Bakery. It had been listed on an LGBTQ website as gay-friendly. As an

Many churches across the country grapple with the tension between LGBTQ rights and religious doctrine. Some churches fly a pride flag on occasion to show that religion and LGBTQ rights can coexist.

evangelical Christian activist, Jack had been offended the previous year when the Division of Civil Rights ruled against a cake shop owner who refused to make a wedding cake for a same-sex couple because of his religious beliefs (a case we discuss later in this segment). Jack hoped to make the point that it was unfair to force bakers to support same-sex marriage but not force them to support the religious views of devout citizens. The Division of Civil Rights didn't see it that way. It concluded that Silva's refusal to decorate the cakes stemmed from the "derogatory language and imagery" Jack requested, not from his religious beliefs.[2]

    This case and others like it symbolize how the civil rights of gay men and lesbians can clash with **religious freedom** — the right to exercise religious beliefs in all aspects of life. This conflict has become far more prevalent as society has become more accepting of gay citizens. To see how fundamentally public opinion has changed throughout the last 30 years, take a quick glance at the polling data presented in Figure 1. The solid orange line tracks people's placement of gay and lesbian citizens on what political scientists call a "feeling thermometer." The thermometer ranges from 0 to 100 degrees, with higher numbers indicating "warmer" or more positive assessments and lower numbers indicating "cooler" or more negative reactions. In the early 1990s, citizens were rather "cool" toward gay citizens (the average rating was 45 degrees). But by the

FIGURE 1. Public Attitudes toward Gay and Lesbian Citizens

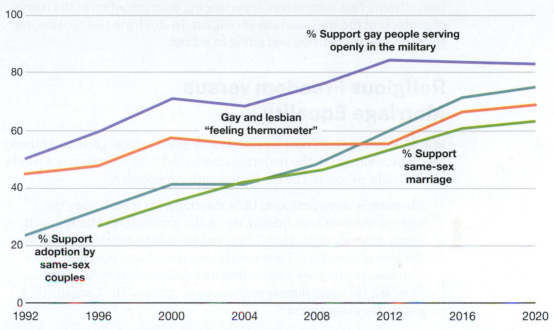

Note: "Feeling thermometer" ratings range from 0 to 100 "degrees." Lower numbers represent "cooler" feelings, and higher numbers represent "warmer" feelings. The figure displays the mean rating for each year. The marriage, military, and adoption lines reflect the percentage of respondents who support the policy.

Sources: Gallup, "LGBT Rights"; American National Election Studies, Time Series Cumulative File.

middle of the decade, the average rating hit 50. And in the 20 years that followed, it inched up to around 69. Ratings for gay men and lesbians are now similar to ratings for Whites (71), Blacks (67), and Latinos (66). As support for gay people has increased, so too has support for allowing them to marry, adopt children, and serve openly in the military (indicated by the dotted and dashed lines in Figure 1).[3]

But even as attitudes toward gay and lesbian citizens have become much more favorable, the teachings of major religions have largely stayed the same. And whereas no mainstream religions in the United States make discriminatory distinctions about people based on race or ethnicity, churches across the nation teach millions of their followers that being gay is morally wrong. The two largest religious faith traditions in the United States — Catholicism and Evangelical Protestantism — explicitly identify being gay as a sin. A combined 46 percent of the U.S. population identifies with one of these religions.[4]

All of this means that as gay rights evolve, strong adherents to certain religious faiths find themselves in situations where following the law makes them feel as though they are violating their religious beliefs. Conversely, when religious freedom takes priority, gay and lesbian citizens find themselves experiencing discrimination in the name of protecting the free exercise of religion. To illustrate this tension, we focus on getting married and going to school.

Religious Freedom versus Marriage Equality

In 2015, the Supreme Court legalized same-sex marriage. Justice Anthony Kennedy, writing for the majority, concluded that marriage is a fundamental right protected by the Fourteenth Amendment:

> No union is more profound than marriage, for it embodies the highest ideals of love, fidelity, devotion, sacrifice, and family. . . . It would misunderstand [gay] men and women to say they disrespect the idea of marriage. Their plea is that they do respect it, respect it so deeply that they seek to find its fulfillment for themselves. . . . They ask for equal dignity in the eyes of the law. The Constitution grants them that right.[5]

This ruling required that all states issue marriage licenses to same-sex couples and recognize same-sex marriages performed in other states.

But if you've ever known anyone who has gotten married, then you know that acquiring the license is often only a small part of it. More than $72 billion every year goes into wedding-related expenses like invitations, catering, flowers, photographers, DJs, and wedding planners.[6] So as same-sex marriage has become more common, a simmering conflict between the religious views of small business owners and gay and lesbian couples seeking wedding-related services has bubbled to the surface. In New Mexico, for example, a lesbian couple sued a photographer for refusing to shoot their wedding. The photographer regularly served gay and lesbian clients, taking portraits and other types of photos, but she believed that marriage is a sacred religious act reserved for opposite-sex partners.[7] Barronelle Stutzman, the 73-year-old owner of Arlene's Flowers in Richland, Washington, refused to provide flowers for the same-sex wedding of a longtime customer. The couple sued her for violating a Washington State law prohibiting discrimination on account of sexual orientation.[8] Similar legal conflicts have arisen involving an inn in Vermont[9], a photography business in California,[10] wedding chapels in Nevada and Idaho,[11] and an accounting firm in Kentucky[12]—all of which, because of their owners' opposition to same-sex marriage, denied services to gay and lesbian couples.

Do you have to bake a gay couple's wedding cake?

Despite the prevalence of such conflicts, the courts have not yet established any clear constitutional framework for deciding these cases. In most of the cases we mentioned, state courts sided with the gay and lesbian customers over the business owners—but only because these cases occurred in states or cities that have antidiscrimination ordinances on the books. In states with no such ordinances, gay and lesbian customers have no avenue of legal recourse against business owners with strong religious convictions.[13]

That's why it was such an important development when the conflict between gay rights and religious freedom reached the Supreme Court in 2018. Six years earlier, Charlie Craig and David Mullins had gone to the Masterpiece Cakeshop in Lakewood, Colorado, to order a cake for their wedding reception. Jack Phillips, the owner, told the couple that he could not put his artistic talent behind making them a cake because same-sex marriage violated his religious beliefs. Mullins said the conversation with the baker made him feel "mortified and embarrassed." For Craig, the interaction conjured up childhood memories of bullies who taunted him for being gay.[14] The two men filed a complaint with the Colorado Civil Rights Division, and they won. The division found that Phillips had violated a state law prohibiting discrimination. Phillips appealed, arguing that the Colorado law violated his First Amendment right to the free exercise of religion.

From the minute the Supreme Court agreed to hear the case, legal scholars and court watchers expected a historic ruling. Mullins summarized the stakes as far bigger than a cake: "It's about the right of people to receive equal service in places of public business. It's about having equal access to public life."[15] Tony Perkins, the head of the Family Research Council, an organization that advocates for religious freedom, said the decision in the case could end "the days of persecution against believers."[16] Put simply, the case presented the Court with the opportunity either to advance gay civil rights or to side with religious freedom.

But it did neither. The justices issued a 7–2 decision in favor of the cake shop owner, but not explicitly because religious freedom was more important than gay rights.[17] The Court determined that one of the Colorado civil rights commissioners had shown hostility toward religious freedom during the initial hearing. According to the majority opinion, these disputes "must be resolved with tolerance, without undue disrespect to sincere religious beliefs, and without subjecting gay persons to indignities when they seek goods and services in an open market." Because the Civil Rights Commission had violated this premise, the Court would not weigh in on the merits of the case. The justices acknowledged that they were not ready or willing to make a broader ruling: "The outcome of cases like this in other circumstances must await further elaboration in the courts."

The likelihood that the Supreme Court will have another chance to weigh in is a certainty. Just one day after the *Masterpiece Cakeshop* decision, an Arizona state court ruled against devout Christian business owners who refused to design wedding invitations for a same-sex couple.[18] State courts are hearing arguments from a bakery in Oregon and a graphic design firm in Colorado that don't believe they should be compelled to serve gay clients. And a wedding photographer has filed suit against the city of Louisville, Kentucky, over its antidiscrimination ordinance that prohibits her from refusing to serve same-sex couples.[19] Whether the Supreme Court will issue a broader ruling in any of these cases or leave these questions up to the states will likely be determined in the coming years.

Religious Freedom in Schools versus Gay Students' Civil Rights

Tensions between religious freedom and civil rights have also become increasingly prevalent in schools across the country. Fifteen-year-old Alexandria Kraft, for example, was expelled from an evangelical Christian high school in California after telling her friends on Facebook that she was bisexual.[20] Jeffrey Woodard, a gay high school senior at Jupiter Christian High School in Florida, was given the choice of working with the school to "overcome his problem" or being expelled.[21] Coventry Christian Academy in Texas expelled high school senior Devin Bryant, who had attended the school since kindergarten, when he disclosed that he was gay. The headmaster acknowledged that Bryant was an "outstanding student"[22] but said that the expulsion was what "Jesus would want [the headmaster] to do."[23] Danielle Powell, who had come out as a lesbian, was expelled from Grace University, a small Bible college in Omaha, Nebraska, just one semester before she was set to graduate. School officials said that her "immoral sexual behavior" made it "impossible" for the faculty of Grace University to affirm Powell's "Christian character," a requirement for graduation.[24] According to Campus Pride, a nonprofit organization working to make college campuses safer for LGBTQ students, 151 colleges across the country take action against LGBTQ youth in the name of adhering to religious doctrines.[25]

When it comes to navigating tensions between LGBTQ students' civil rights and religious freedom in schools, courts have offered little direction. One conflict that did reach the Supreme Court, though, involved a public law school and a religious student group. The Christian Legal Society (CLS) is a national organization with a presence on more than 150 law school campuses. Its mission is "to nurture and encourage

Austin Wallis, a 17-year-old gay student at Lutheran High North School in Houston, Texas, came out on his YouTube channel. The school told him that his behavior violated the "moral clause" of the student handbook. He could delete the channel or leave the school. Despite not wanting to go, Wallis felt he had no choice but to leave.

Christian law students" by providing mentors, Bible study, and discussion groups about how to apply their faith when practicing law.[26] The organization requires members to sign a statement that affirms a series of religious beliefs, including the position that the Bible is "the inspired word of God."

In 2004, CLS wanted to renew its chapter at the University of California, Hastings College of the Law.[27] The law school denied the request. California state law requires student groups to allow "any student to participate, become a member, or seek leadership positions, regardless of their status or beliefs."[28] Hastings determined that CLS's membership guidelines, which required a repudiation of "homosexual conduct," violated the state law. The CLS chapter sued Hastings on the grounds that the nondiscrimination policy for student groups violated the religious students' freedom of speech and freedom of religion.

In *Christian Legal Society v. Martinez*, a deeply divided Supreme Court ruled in favor of Hastings.[29] But as in the Colorado bake shop case, the Supreme Court's decision was quite narrow. The five justices in the majority reasoned that the nondiscrimination policy was "reasonable" and did not try to advance any particular point of view. Hastings hadn't singled out CLS for its beliefs (that wouldn't have been okay) but, rather, had treated all student groups the same. The decision, however, applied only to the California law mandating that student clubs in public schools be open to all students. The Court provided no guidance as to what types of membership and leadership requirements are permissible when state law isn't so explicit.[30] Even then, the four justices in the minority vehemently disagreed, characterizing the decision as prohibiting expression when it "offends prevailing standards of political correctness."

More Conflict on the Horizon

As societal acceptance of LGBTQ citizens continues to grow, civil rights continue to collide with ardent support for religious liberty. Conflict is inevitable because of the substantial role religion plays in American life. One-sixth of all hospital beds in this country are in Catholic hospitals.[31] More than 600 religiously affiliated colleges and universities operate across the country.[32] Upward of 23,000 private religious schools serve more than 3.5 million K–12 students annually.[33] And religious organizations regularly provide social services to communities grappling with poverty.[34]

The Supreme Court has not explicitly said that religious liberty trumps LGBTQ civil rights, but recent decisions suggest that the Court is moving in that direction. In 2021, the justices ruled unanimously that the city of Philadelphia could not end a Catholic group's contract to provide foster-care services simply because the organization refused to allow same-sex couples to become foster parents.[35] The Court has also sided with religious organizations when it comes to exempting them from providing birth control coverage as part of employee health care plans[36] and in striking down Covid-19 social distancing guidelines and capacity restrictions for religious services.[37]

The conflict has also already begun to expand in scope as transgender rights become the next frontier in the battle over civil rights and religious freedom. Transgender students have been expelled from religious schools and suspended for using the "wrong" bathroom in public schools.[38] State legislatures have introduced "bathroom bills" to restrict transgender citizens' access to restrooms and locker rooms based on their biological sex.[39] And they've proposed dozens of bills to prevent transgender girls and women from playing on girls' and women's sports teams.[40] One court has ruled that physicians have "religious freedom" to refuse to treat transgender patients.[41] Although the Supreme Court ruled in 2020 that federal law prohibits workplace discrimination against gay and transgender employees, Justice Neil Gorsuch in his majority opinion wrote that the Court was not addressing "bathrooms, locker rooms or anything else of the kind."[42] How to balance a broad array of transgender rights with religious liberty, therefore, remains an open question.

DID YOU GET IT?
Do you have to bake a gay couple's wedding cake?

Short Answer:

- Probably, at least until the Supreme Court takes up the issue again.
- Conflicts between gay and lesbian civil rights and religious freedom affect small businesses, religious schools, and other religious institutions, such as hospitals.
- The Supreme Court has offered little guidance on how to resolve the conflict, which continues to grow as calls for equality under the law for the LGBTQ community expand and the push for transgender civil rights gains momentum.

DEVELOPING YOUR SKILLS

Persuasive Argumentation

Identify an argument: The Supreme Court issues critical rulings concerning civil liberties, civil rights, and conflicts between the two. When analyzing and critiquing Supreme Court decisions, scholars and analysts generally make two types of arguments:

- *Legal arguments* — which focus on the consistency of the law — rely on evidence from prior Supreme Court decisions, legal reasoning by judges and scholars, and the written law, such as the Constitution or laws passed by Congress.
- *Policy arguments* — which try to demonstrate the benefit or harm of a law or action — rely on evidence in the form of empirical studies, anecdotes, and philosophical reasoning.

Differentiate between these types of arguments as you answer the following questions about the collision course between gay rights and religious freedom:

1. If you want to write an essay making a *policy argument* that little harm is caused by devoutly religious business owners turning away gay customers, what type of evidence would be best?
   a. The text of the First Amendment
   b. The Supreme Court's ruling in *Obergefell v. Hodges*
   c. A survey of gay citizens that reveals that the overwhelming majority say they would not patronize "anti-gay" businesses anyway
   d. A survey of gay citizens that reveals that they feel humiliated when being refused service at a business because they are gay

2. If you want to make a *legal argument* that civil rights for gay people should be prioritized over religious freedom, which piece of evidence would be most persuasive?

   a. The Fourteenth Amendment's equal protection clause

   b. A national survey that finds that almost 50 percent of Americans have a gay family member or friend

   c. Political leaders' speeches about why religious freedom is the most important citizen right

   d. All of the above would be good evidence for making this legal argument.

3. If you are writing a paper and need to identify one *legal argument* for prioritizing civil rights for LGBTQ citizens and one *legal argument* for prioritizing religious freedom, which two pieces of evidence would respectively provide the most solid basis for your paper?

   a. A close reading of the Fourteenth Amendment and case law supporting same-sex marriage

   b. The *Masterpiece Cakeshop* opinion and social science evidence demonstrating that devout Christians in the United States feel alienated

   c. Arguments from the majority opinion in the case supporting same-sex marriage and Supreme Court decisions that establish the fundamental nature of the right to free exercise of religion

   d. A study showing that discrimination causes deep pain for many gay people and a powerful anecdote from a Christian business owner who had to close the family business to remain true to his religious beliefs

FIGURE IT OUT

A married lesbian couple is preparing to have a baby. They had hoped to give birth at a highly regarded Catholic hospital close to where they live. But the physician in charge of the maternity ward told the women that they cannot have their baby at the hospital because delivering a child of a gay married couple violates the hospital's religious principles. The lesbian couple files a complaint against the hospital claiming unlawful discrimination. Use legal and policy arguments to make both sides of the case. More specifically:

- Identify one *legal argument* and one *policy argument* the couple's lawyer could use to claim that they've been unlawfully discriminated against. You can draw the legal argument from the cases presented in this segment or one of the other segments in this section. For the policy argument, you can refer to hypothetical evidence that shows the potential harm of not letting gay couples give birth at this hospital.

- Now do the same thing for the hospital's lawyers. That is, identify one *legal argument* that supports the hospital's position of excluding gay patients and one *policy argument* that points to the potential harm of forcing the hospital to accept gay patients.

Want to Know More?

For an amusing take on the "gay wedding cake" cases, watch this clip from *Jimmy Kimmel Live*. The sketch highlights how we tend to think about gay and lesbian civil rights differently from the way we think about civil rights for women, people of color, or people of different religious faiths: https://www.youtube.com/watch?v=kTVA9PRHe4E.

Political Engagement

Start Here!

"You've gotta vote!" "You have to participate!" "You need to be engaged!" These are just some of the enthusiastic pleas that educators, policy makers, and elected officials regularly issue to their fellow citizens. That's because the United States' system of government relies on direct citizen action. Citizens vote to select the people who write the nation's laws. Citizens work on campaigns and join political interest groups to shape the country's policies. Citizens run for office to become elected leaders themselves.

A democracy, of course, depends not only on citizens performing their roles but also on candidates and elected officials performing theirs: representing their constituents. Whether political leaders fulfill their duties is certainly an important question. And we address it in Sections V and VI of this book, where we cover campaigns, elections, and representation. But first, in the next five segments, we assess whether citizens are doing their part to contribute to a healthy democracy. We do this by taking a close look at how they develop their political views and how politically engaged they are.

We define political engagement broadly. It includes acquiring political beliefs about government and politics. And it encompasses fundamental acts of political participation, like voting, engaging in political dialogue and debate through social media, contributing money to campaigns, attending political rallies, and joining political interest groups.

In an ideal democracy, almost all citizens would be politically interested and participatory. Although that might not be realistic, the segments in this section highlight how well the United States fares in meeting that goal.

When we look at political engagement in the United States, three core themes emerge:

1 **There are many ways to participate in the political system.**
From voting, to contacting an elected official, to joining a political organization, citizens have many opportunities to be politically engaged. The internet and social media provide additional ways for people to participate.

2 **Most people aren't super interested in politics.**
Although most people have some partisan affiliation — they consider themselves either Democrats or Republicans — their participation in most political activities is low. Voting in presidential elections is the only political act in which a majority of those eligible to participate actually do, and sometimes it's only a slim majority.

3 **People with more resources are more likely to engage the political system.**
Older, wealthier, and more educated citizens participate at much higher rates than those who are younger and have less income and education. These differences raise serious concerns about whether all citizens' voices are heard.

17.
Where do people get their political beliefs?

#PoliticalSocialization

In 2018, Democratic congressional candidate David Brill released a series of attack ads against his Republican opponent, Congressman Paul Gosar. Like many conservative members of the U.S. House of Representatives, Gosar supported gun rights and tax cuts, opposed reproductive freedom and gay rights, and advocated for clamping down on illegal immigration. So Brill's first 60-second ad seemed pretty run-of-the-mill. Six people — including a lawyer, a physician, a private investigator, and an engineer — look into the camera and tell Arizona voters that casting a ballot for Gosar would be a mistake. From immigration and health care to jobs and the environment, they assert that "Paul's absolutely not working for his district."[1] It was the kind of ad that almost any Democrat could run against almost any Republican in almost any district across the United States.

Except for one thing. The six people featured in the ad condemning Gosar's record were six of the congressman's nine siblings! That's right. Six of Gosar's own brothers and sisters opposed his conservative agenda so strongly that they openly supported his opponent.

Children pose for a picture at a Trump rally in Costa Mesa, California. Every election season, it's easy to find political events featuring young kids who have presumably adopted their parents' political views, evidence of political socialization within the family.

Gosar's brother David states in the first ad: "We gotta stand up for our good name. . . . This is not who we are." His sister Joan tells viewers: "I think my brother has traded a lot of the values we had at our kitchen table." Another sister, Grace, concludes that given Gosar's hard-line position on immigration, "It would be difficult to see my brother as anything but a racist." The siblings just can't fathom how their brother, who grew up with the same parents in the same Wyoming household, developed political views so different from their own. The congressman's brother Pete had actually twice run for governor of Wyoming — as a Democrat. David, the attorney featured in the ad, describes himself as a progressive.

Perhaps because he knew he was a shoo-in for reelection in his solidly Republican district, Congressman Gosar took it all in stride, tweeting:

> You can't pick your family. We all have crazy aunts and relatives etc. and my family is no different. I hope they find peace in their hearts and let go all the hate.

> To the six angry Democrat Gosars — see you at Mom and Dad's house! #AZ04 #MAGA2018.[2]

But that didn't end the family tension. The siblings were back at it in 2021, accusing their brother of treason for his role in encouraging the insurrection at the U.S. Capitol on January 6.[3]

The level of political disagreement among the Gosars is pretty unusual. Typically, family members tend to have similar political views. Just look at some of the most famous political families in the United States. The Kennedys produced one president, two U.S. senators, several members of the U.S. House of Representatives, a lieutenant governor, ambassadors, and multiple state and local elected officials — every one a Democrat.[4] The Bush family generated two presidents, a U.S. senator, two governors, ambassadors, and several lower-level office-holders. In their case, all Republicans.[5]

How does this happen? Why is there so much political disagreement in some families but political harmony in most others? And what about the many families that don't much care about politics at all? The answer comes down to **political socialization** — the process by which people acquire their political beliefs and values, including whether to participate and be politically engaged. This segment begins by focusing on family. But family doesn't explain everything — if it did, the Gosar siblings would have filmed an ad for, not against, their brother. So we then examine how experiences at school and with government shape people's political beliefs. You'll also see that adults' life circumstances often reinforce the political beliefs they've held since childhood.

All in the Family? How Socialization Affects Political Attitudes

Exposure to politics begins with the family. After all, people come into the world with no pre-formed political opinions or values, but by the time they turn 18—voting age—they usually have some sense of what they think and whether they care about politics. People can certainly develop an interest in politics later in life, political views can change and evolve over time, and specific circumstances and events can motivate adults to become politically engaged.[6] But more than 50 years of research shows that the basis for most political attitudes and behaviors is formed at home from a young age.[7]

Experiences within the family lay the groundwork for political beliefs in at least two key ways. First, parents and guardians instill in their children a broad framework of political views. When young people register to vote, for example, they tend to choose their **party identification**—whether to be a Republican, a Democrat, or something else—based on their parents' affiliation. Other, more specific, political beliefs—such as

Though humorous, this bumper sticker illustrates the important influence families tend to have on political beliefs and party identification. (For the record, D.A.D.D.D is not a real organization.)

whether they support or oppose gun control—are also often passed on from one generation to the next. The same even applies to specific political leaders. Odds are that if your parents are big fans of President Biden, you have a pretty favorable view of him, too. And if they're not, you're probably not a fan either. In fact, less than one-third of people report that they've ever had a serious disagreement over politics with a family member.[8]

Family socialization is about more than a parent creating a "mini-me" when it comes to political views. The second way parents socialize their kids is by sending clear signals about good citizenship and the value of political engagement. Young people whose parents vote, emphasize the importance of voting, or take them to the polls are much more likely to be regular voters later in life. Teenagers who discuss politics with their parents know more about public affairs and are more likely to be politically active than people who aren't raised this way. They're also more likely to attend community meetings, sign petitions, participate in boycotts, and contribute money to candidates and political causes.[9] They're even more likely to express interest in running for office as adults.[10]

But the opposite is also true. Families that don't pay much attention to politics transmit that disinterest to their children. A survey of high school and college students revealed that many families fall into this category (see Table 1). Only 1 in 5 young people reported that they regularly talked about politics at mealtimes while growing up. Roughly 50 percent said they rarely or never discussed politics with their mother or father. And the overwhelming majority didn't remember engaging in any political activities, like voting or attending a political event, with their parents.[11] So another part of the reason families don't disagree much about politics is that they never talk about politics in the first place. In these households, a lack of political engagement is passed on from one generation to the next.

TABLE 1. Political Engagement in Young People's Families

Politics in the Household	
My parents often talk about politics with friends and family.	25%
We often talk about politics at mealtime.	21

Political Discussion with Parents	
Growing up, spoke about politics with mother rarely or never	51
Growing up, spoke about politics with father rarely or never	49

Political Activity with Parents	
Watched election coverage with parents	37
Went to vote with parents	26
Shared a story on email, Facebook, or a social networking site with parents	20
Attended a political event with parents	6

Note: Data come from a national sample of 4,102 high school and college students.

Source: Jennifer L. Lawless and Richard L. Fox, *Running from Office: Why Young People Are Turned Off to Politics* (New York: Oxford University Press, 2015). Reproduced with permission of the Licensor through PLSclear.

Family Doesn't Explain Everything: Two Additional Agents of Political Socialization

Family clearly influences your political beliefs and engagement. But many other factors and experiences—including school, peer groups, religion, the media, interactions with government, and major political events—can substantially affect your political values, too. This list isn't exhaustive. Political scientists, however, have identified some of these factors as especially important for shaping political attitudes. We cover one of them—the media—extensively in Section IV. So here we focus on two others: experiences at school and with peers and experiences with government.

Experiences at School and with Peers

Schools across the United States make a concerted effort to teach young people about the political system and the importance of being engaged citizens. A majority of states (31) require that public schools offer at least one civics class—usually, a course on government that also emphasizes citizens' rights and responsibilities.[12] Some even require students to take a civics exam in order to graduate from high school. Although these efforts don't turn all students into politically engaged citizens, young people who attend high schools that include political activities or assignments as part of the curriculum are more likely to say they will vote when they turn 18.[13]

School-based political socialization continues in college. Many states, including California and Texas, require students enrolled in public colleges and universities to complete at least one government class that covers both national and state politics. Moreover, when students major in social sciences (such as psychology, sociology, political science, or economics), they are more likely to develop **civic skills**—which include communication skills, knowledge of the political system, and critical thinking. Armed with these skills and a familiarity with the political system, they are more likely to participate politically.[14]

Outside the classroom, extracurricular activities, usually undertaken with friends or peers, can also spur political interest and engagement later in life.[15] If you were one of the weird kids in high school who liked to talk about politics (our favorite kind of student!), then odds are that you hung around other kids who liked politics. You also might have volunteered with your peers and friends on community projects, political causes, or election campaigns. Maybe you even ran for student government or participated in model UN. These political experiences with your peers often lay the groundwork for what you'll do in college and whether you'll be politically active later in life.

Just like with family, though, nonpolitical experiences at school can have a socializing effect. And just like with family, nonpolitical experiences are prevalent. The same national survey of young people that revealed high levels of political disinterest in most families found a similar pattern at school. Nearly two-thirds of high school students said they discuss politics in their classes less than once a week. One-third said that political discussions in the classroom occur "rarely" or "never." Just 9 percent of high school students considered their classmates "very interested" in politics and current events. College students reported more political exposure in the classroom. Nearly 7 out of 10 had taken at least one government or political science class. But weekly political discussions in the classroom were still quite rare, and only 20 percent described their classmates as very interested in politics and current events.[16]

Much like their classroom experiences, young people's friendships also tend to be pretty devoid of political content. Just take a look at Figure 1, which shows the percentage of young people who discuss a variety of topics with their friends at least once a week. School is the most

FIGURE 1. Topics Young People Discuss with Friends on a Weekly Basis

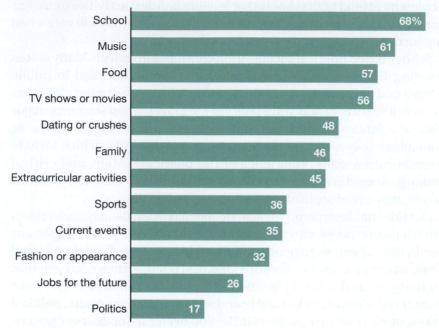

Topic	Percentage
School	68%
Music	61
Food	57
TV shows or movies	56
Dating or crushes	48
Family	46
Extracurricular activities	45
Sports	36
Current events	35
Fashion or appearance	32
Jobs for the future	26
Politics	17

Note: Bars indicate the percentage of high school and college students who discuss each topic with their friends at least once a week. Sample size = 4,208.

Source: Jennifer L. Lawless and Richard L. Fox, *Running from Office: Why Young People Are Turned Off to Politics* (New York: Oxford University Press, 2015).

popular topic of conversation, followed by music, food, and TV shows or movies.[17] Current events, in general, rank toward the bottom of the list, behind dating, family, and sports. And by today's standards, talking about current events more likely includes a discussion of the latest celebrity breakup than a conversation about world politics or public affairs. Politics comes in dead last.

Experiences with Government

Americans interact with government all the time. You might not realize it, but when you register a car, apply for a student loan, or try to convince a police officer not to give you a speeding ticket, you're interacting with government. When people file for unemployment, Social Security, or Medicare, they're interacting with government. Even a simple trip to the post office typically involves an interaction with a government worker.

For many people, these experiences shape their attitudes about government. Such experiences can even influence whether they choose to participate in the political system. If public assistance recipients feel disrespected or treated poorly by government social workers, for example, they're more likely to express distrust for government in general. As a result, they're less likely to vote.[18] On the other hand, when people in poverty have access to government-subsidized health care, their satisfaction with government increases, and they're more likely to go to the polls on Election Day.[19] Interactions with the police affect political participation, too. In the case of the urban poor, people who had negative interactions with the police were more likely to become politically engaged, perhaps because they wanted to ensure that others weren't treated by a representative of the government as poorly as they had been.[20] Similarly, Black Lives Matter protests are more likely to occur in communities where citizens are exposed to prevalent police brutality.[21]

Political socialization can also occur through the government's response to major events. Wars, natural disasters, and political scandals fall into this category. When Republican president Richard Nixon resigned in 1974 following the Watergate scandal (his 1972 presidential campaign was found responsible for breaking into the Democratic National Committee's headquarters, stealing papers, and bugging the office), citizens' trust in government decreased. The scandal also turned many voters off to the Republican Party, for at least a period of time.[22] Following the terrorist attacks in the United States on September 11, 2001, many citizens came to favor a more militaristic national security policy.[23] They were also willing to give up long-held political beliefs about the importance of protecting citizens' privacy in the name of heightened security, at least temporarily.[24] The government's mixed performance in responding to the Covid-19 pandemic beginning in 2020 will also likely be a formative event for many citizens. With so much death, illness, and economic hardship caused by the health crisis, some people will form broad opinions about whether government can competently address a national (and global) crisis.

Early Political Beliefs Tend to Stick

Early political socialization in the family and at school is important because the political values young people adopt tend to stick with them throughout their lives. Some people's views change and evolve, but that's not very common—largely because people's life experiences as adults end up reinforcing their beliefs. When people get married, for example, less than 10 percent cross party lines.[25] Democrats tend to marry Democrats, and Republicans tend to marry Republicans. The same is true when it comes to where people live. Those who grow up in rural areas generally remain in rural areas. And in doing so, they tend to live among White working-class citizens who are likely to identify as Republicans. People who grow up in cities typically prefer to continue an urban lifestyle, so they wind up living in more racially diverse communities that are predominantly Democratic.[26] These trends have become even more pronounced in the last couple of decades. All of this means that when most people go out to dinner, stop at the grocery store, or even have a conversation with their spouse, they're usually interacting with politically like-minded people. Early political attitudes and experiences—or the lack thereof—set into motion many of the political beliefs and actions that follow people throughout their lives.

DID YOU GET IT?
Where do people get their political beliefs?

Short Answer:

- People acquire their political values through the political socialization process.
- Family is most important, but experiences at school and with peers, as well as interactions with government, are also central sources of citizens' political beliefs.
- Although people's political views can change over time, people often make choices as adults that reinforce the beliefs they developed as children.

Persuasive Argumentation

Evaluate evidence: Family is the most influential factor shaping political values, but other factors matter, too. Determine the type of evidence necessary to make persuasive arguments about how different agents of socialization affect political beliefs.

---

1. A classmate tells you that she's "super passionate about gun control" and thinks that it's the most important issue facing the country. If you want to collect the most compelling piece of evidence for how this 18-year-old came to have such strong feelings, and you can only ask her one question, which would likely be most helpful?

   a. What classes did she take in high school?

   b. How do her parents feel about gun control?

   c. Where did she grow up?

   d. Which news programs does she regularly watch?

2. Two sisters grew up in the same family with the same Republican parents and went to the same schools. Yet one is a 20-year-old liberal Democrat and the other is a 24-year-old conservative Republican. Which piece of evidence might help explain how these sisters turned out so different politically?

   a. The educational philosophy of the schools the sisters attended

   b. Their parents' experiences dealing with government workers

   c. A profile of each sister's peers and friends

   d. Their parents' party affiliation

3. In most states, people think of the Department of Motor Vehicles (DMV) as an inefficient government bureaucracy. If you were trying to study the impact of citizens' experiences at the DMV on their political attitudes, what type of evidence would allow you to craft the most persuasive argument?

   a. The total number of DMV offices in each state

   b. A survey of DMV employees assessing their experiences at work

   c. A survey that compares attitudes about politics between those who have visited the DMV and those who have not

   d. A public opinion survey about people's experiences at the DMV

FIGURE IT OUT

Is your life consistent with the political socialization process outlined in this segment? In other words, do your experiences provide good anecdotal evidence for the segment's main argument? To answer this question, make a chart that summarizes your political experiences with your family, school and peers, and government. More specifically, list responses to the following questions (many require just a yes or no):

How political was your family?

- Did anyone in your family ever take you to vote?
- Did anyone in your family ever take you to a political rally or meeting?
- How frequent were political discussions in your household when you were growing up?
- Do your parents or guardians clearly identify as Republicans, Democrats, something else, or nothing at all?

How political were your experiences at school and with your friends?

- Did you have many political discussions in your high school classes?
- Were your friends interested in politics?
- Are the majority of your friends Republicans, Democrats, something else, or nothing at all?

Do you remember any politically relevant experiences with government?

- During your childhood, did any major events — such as a particular presidential election, terror attack, or natural disaster — shape your family's view of the government?
- Do you remember any members of your family talking about interactions with a government worker or official, such as the police, an employee at the DMV, or a member of Congress?

Now, answer two questions about yourself:

- Do you consider yourself a Republican, a Democrat, something else, or nothing at all?
- How politically engaged are you?

Based on your answers to all of these questions, would you say that your life provides good anecdotal evidence for this segment's claims, or not so much? Explain your answer in a few sentences.

Want to Know More?

In *Family Ties*, a long-running 1980s sitcom, political socialization was on full display. But it was also a little complicated: the parents were 1960s hippie liberals, but their son, Alex, was a conservative Republican. If you want to watch some vintage television — including entire episodes devoted to the Equal Rights Amendment, U.S.-Soviet relations, and sexual harassment — and see a fictional family as politically divided as Paul Gosar's, then it's worth streaming.

18.
Are you a Democrat or a Republican?

#PartyID

Have you ever taken an online quiz that's supposed to tell you something about yourself? You can find out your celebrity soulmate,[1] which *Star Wars* character is most like you,[2] or the superhero you most resemble.[3] You can learn where you should take your next vacation,[4] the exact age you'll be when you get married,[5] where you should live,[6] even whether you're "hot or not."[7] And if you don't know whether you're a Democrat or a Republican, there's a quiz for that, too.[8] All you need to do is answer a few questions — about things like your daily mode of transportation, how you take your coffee, your favorite animal — and the internet will spit out your party affiliation.

Online quizzes, of course, aren't the only way to try to determine which political party you align with. If your favorite store is Banana Republic, REI, or Forever 21, then you're likely a Democrat. Republicans tend to prefer Sam's Club, Dick's Sporting Goods, and Hobby Lobby.[9] When it comes to cars, the most popular ride for Democrats is the Honda Civic hybrid. Republicans favor the Ford Mustang convertible.[10] Whereas Democrats often like hip-hop and rap, Republicans prefer country music.[11] The differences go on and on — from favorite singers (Democrats like Adele and Beyoncé; Republicans like Ted Nugent and George Strait), to favorite actors (George Takei and Will Smith for

Polarization between the two parties has become such a dominant theme in U.S. politics that no aspect of life — even a depiction of commuter rail benches — seems immune to it.

Democrats; Adam Sandler and John Wayne for Republicans), to favorite movies (Democrats choose *Harry Potter*; Republicans favor *God's Not Dead*).[12]

Republicans and Democrats don't even like to eat the same things! *Time* magazine and Grubhub, an online food delivery service, partnered to analyze the most frequently ordered dishes in hundreds of congressional districts throughout the country. Results varied dramatically based on the number of Democrats and Republicans in each district. Whereas Republicans often go for Chinese and Italian food, Democrats tend to prefer Thai and Mexican. Republican and Democratic districts don't share one favorite food among the top 10 (see Table 1).[13]

Clearly, many aspects of cultural and social life in the United States are divided along political party lines. And online quizzes and consumer preferences often do a pretty good job identifying differences in Democratic and Republican tastes. But the kinds of tendencies and preferences we just highlighted don't tell us much about who identifies with each party or what each party's identifiers believe when it comes to important issues. This segment does just that. By the end, you'll have a clear idea of where you fall on the political spectrum and how consistent your political views are with both major political parties' positions on the issues.

TABLE 1. Partisan Foods

Most Popular Dishes in Republican Congressional Districts	Most Popular Dishes in Democratic Congressional Districts
1. Sweet and sour chicken	1. Massaman curry
2. Cannoli	2. Veggie burger
3. Brownie	3. Summer roll
4. Egg roll	4. Guacamole
5. Boneless wings	5. Pancake
6. Lo mein	6. Green curry
7. Sesame chicken	7. Burrito
8. Gyro	8. Turkey burger
9. Calzone	9. Basil fried rice
10. Mozzarella sticks	10. Avocado salad

Note: Rankings are based on the number of times 175 dishes were ordered in 214 congressional districts across the country.

Source: Chris Wilson, "The Most Political Foods in America," *Time*, July 18, 2016.

Party Identification in the United States

Determining whether someone supports a particular party is perhaps the most important piece of political information there is to know about a person. After all, **party identification**—whether you're a Republican, Democrat, or something else—dictates much of what happens in contemporary politics. Candidates and campaigns rely on the support of people who share their party label.[14] Voters make judgments about what politicians will do when they're elected based on whether there's a D or an R after the person's name.[15] And knowing someone's party affiliation can often tell you about their broader value system.[16] Because party identification—party ID, for short—tells us so much about voters, political researchers and campaign practitioners have been asking about it since the advent of modern polling.

Most measures of party ID rely on a series of questions. First, people are asked whether they consider themselves a Democrat, a Republican, an Independent, or something else. A recent survey indicates that most people identify with one of the two major parties: 33 percent consider themselves Democrats and 29 percent identify as Republicans.[17] A large chunk of the population (35 percent), however, reports identifying as **Independent**—they don't have a loyalty or affiliation to either of the two major political parties. But it turns out that the overwhelming majority of Independents aren't actually independent at all. When pollsters ask Independents a follow-up question—"Do you think of yourself as closer to the Republican or the Democratic Party?"—most report that they "lean" toward one of the two major parties. And those partisan leaners tend to have the same policy views and voting records as people who said they were Democrats or Republicans in the first place.[18] After accounting for the leaners, more than 9 out of every 10 people are Democrats or Republicans. Less than 10 percent of the population, in other words, are true Independents. There are other political parties in the United States, too—such as the Libertarian, Green, and Reform parties—but they attract few identifiers (only about 1 percent of the voters). So, this segment focuses on the two major parties.

Figure 1 reveals that party identification in the United States has been closely divided for the past several decades.[19] That's part of the

FIGURE 1. Party Identification of Registered Voters, 1992–2022

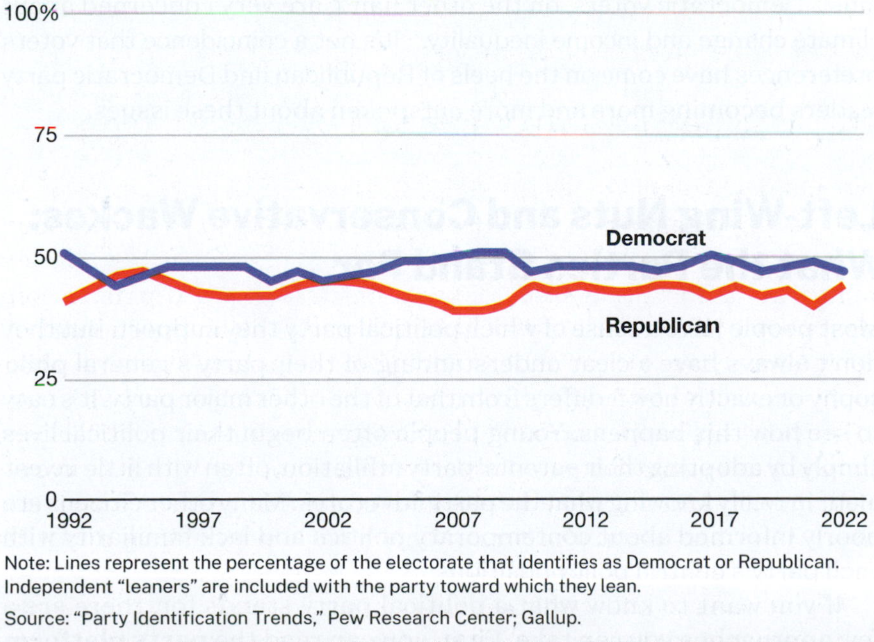

Note: Lines represent the percentage of the electorate that identifies as Democrat or Republican. Independent "leaners" are included with the party toward which they lean.

Source: "Party Identification Trends," Pew Research Center; Gallup.

reason many recent presidential elections have been so close—the public is almost evenly divided between people who vote for Republicans and those who vote for Democrats. If one party's candidate is able to appeal to even just a small fraction of citizens who identify with the other party, then that can be enough to sway an election.

Although the share of the population that affiliates with each party is similar, the citizens who identify as Democrats and Republicans are dramatically different. Just take a look at Table 2. The Democratic coalition includes women, people of color, younger voters, and those living in urban areas. The Republican Party appeals more to older people, White Evangelicals, and citizens who live in rural areas. In the next few pages, you'll begin to get some clues as to why certain demographic groups are more supportive of one party than the other. In some cases, the party supports policies that are favorable to that group. In others, people identify with the party whose central positions seem to be most consistent with their own values.

Regardless of their motivations, knowing which groups of people constitute each party's **base voters**—core supporters who almost always support candidates from that party—can tell you a lot about the policies political leaders pursue. That doesn't mean, however, that citizens' preferences shape the party's positions. It's usually the other way around. That is, citizens take their cues from their party's leaders.[20] A majority of Republican voters, for instance, do not believe environmental protection is a top priority but feel strongly that strict immigration laws are a must. Democratic voters, on the other hand, are very concerned about climate change and income inequality.[21] It's not a coincidence that voters' preferences have come on the heels of Republican and Democratic party leaders becoming more and more outspoken about these issues.

Left-Wing Nuts and Conservative Wackos: What the Parties Stand For

Most people have a sense of which political party they support. But they don't always have a clear understanding of their party's general philosophy or exactly how it differs from that of the other major party. It's easy to see how this happens. Young people often begin their political lives simply by adopting their parents' party affiliation, often with little investment in really knowing what the party advocates. Many other citizens are poorly informed about contemporary politics and lack familiarity with each party's central policy positions.

If you want to know what a political party stands for, there are a few approaches you can take. First, you can read the **party platform**.

Are you a Democrat or a Republican?

TABLE 2. Party Identification, by Demographic Groups

	Republican	Democrat
Gender		
Men	48%	44%
Women	37	56
Race		
White	51	43
Black	8	84
Latino	28	63
Asian	27	65
Age		
21 to 38 years old	32	59
39 to 52 years old	43	48
53 to 71 years old	46	48
72 to 89 years old	52	43
Education		
High school diploma or less	47	45
Some college	45	47
College degree	39	54
Advanced degree	31	63
Income		
Less than $30,000 per year	32	60
$30,000 to $75,000 per year	48	45
More than $75,000 per year	49	45
Religion		
White Evangelical	77	18
Catholic	46	47
Jewish	31	67
Unaffiliated	22	68
Community		
Rural	54	38
Suburban	45	47
Urban	31	62

Source: Pew Research Center.

Every four years, during the summer before a presidential election, the Democratic and Republican parties articulate in a formal document their positions on dozens of issues, underlying principles, and goals for the future. Second, you can look to a party's current leaders. Statements from the president and congressional leaders reflect the party's priorities and policy positions. Third, you can examine public opinion data. Polls summarize what ordinary voters from each party believe about a wide range of issues.

All three sources provide valuable, generally consistent information, which is exactly what we'd expect. Party leaders and activists write the platforms, and elected officials lead the way in shaping voters' attitudes about specific issues. Here we focus on public opinion data to highlight that Democrats and Republicans differ substantially when it comes to (1) the economy, (2) social and domestic policy, and (3) diversity and inclusion. The parties aren't monolithic, of course—Democrats don't all hold the same views, and Republicans don't all believe the same things—but large majorities within each party do agree on many issues and principles.

The Economy

Democrats typically support an active role for government in managing the economy. Republicans, by contrast, tend to believe in a **free market system**—one in which privately owned businesses operate free from government control. The public opinion data presented in Figure 2 illustrate how these broad principles play out.

Approximately 4 out of 5 Democrats believe that the government should actively work to reduce income inequality—both by raising taxes on corporations and wealthy people and by providing government assistance to poor citizens through programs like Medicaid and SNAP ("food stamps"). Four out of 5 Republicans, however, think that if the government taxes businesses at lower rates, then the wealth and jobs these businesses create will improve the overall economy and ultimately benefit all Americans. Further, Republicans don't believe that the government has a responsibility to ensure a basic standard of living to all Americans. Quite the contrary. They tend to hold the view that providing assistance to the poor can create a cycle of dependence that makes it even more difficult to climb out poverty. It's not surprising, then, that 60 percent of Americans with an annual income of less than $30,000 consider themselves Democrats (see Table 2). They are the very people who benefit from the party's commitment to providing a safety net.[22] Nor is it a shocker that many of the nation's wealthiest Americans—those with incomes of at least $500,000 per year—identify as Republicans.[23]

FIGURE 2. Party Differences on Economic Policy

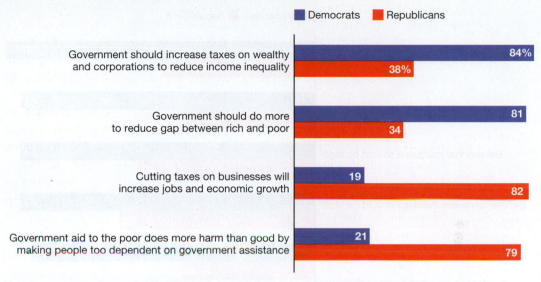

Democrats ■ Republicans ■

Government should increase taxes on wealthy and corporations to reduce income inequality
- Democrats: 84%
- Republicans: 38%

Government should do more to reduce gap between rich and poor
- Democrats: 81
- Republicans: 34

Cutting taxes on businesses will increase jobs and economic growth
- Democrats: 19
- Republicans: 82

Government aid to the poor does more harm than good by making people too dependent on government assistance
- Democrats: 21
- Republicans: 79

Note: Bars represent the percentage of Democrats and Republicans who believe each statement or support each policy.

Source: PollingReport.com surveys conducted from 2015 to 2019.

Social and Domestic Policy

Partisan differences are just as stark across a broad range of social and domestic policies. Indeed, on five controversial issues that all tap into individual freedom, Democrats are far more supportive than Republicans of four of them: transgender rights, legalization of marijuana, same-sex marriage, and access to abortion (see Figure 3).[24] In only one case—gun control—do the parties swap positions. Here Republicans overwhelmingly favor an individual's right to purchase and own a gun with few, if any, laws governing the process. Democrats support stricter gun control. These policy differences reflect the fact that Democrats favor more personal freedom and choice in how people live. Republicans espouse more traditional values—including "appropriate" roles for women and men—that are often supported by religious beliefs. That's part of the reason why more than two-thirds of people unaffiliated with any religion are Democrats, but three-quarters of White Evangelicals are Republicans (see again Table 2).

Opinions on issues pertaining to individual freedom aren't the only domestic policy differences between the parties. Similar to the way that Democrats support a role for government in managing the economy, they also see a role for government in establishing broad

FIGURE 3. Party Differences on Individual Freedom

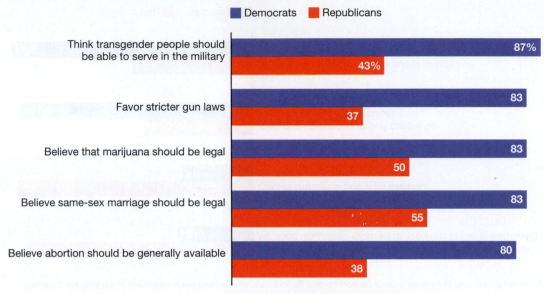

Note: Bars represent the percentage of Democrats and Republicans who believe each statement or support each policy.

Source: Surveys conducted in 2021 and 2022. See Note 24 for full source information.

policies on the environment. More specifically, 91 percent of Democrats support policies to combat climate change. Republicans, consistent with their support for free market principles, are much less likely (40 percent) to favor broad environmental protection because those laws would place additional regulations on businesses and corporations.[25] The same is true for health care for all Americans. Democrats are approximately 5 times more likely than Republicans (69 percent compared to 14 percent) to support a single-payer health care system.[26] That's a system in which the government funds a program that provides health care for all citizens.

Diversity and Inclusion

Finally, the parties hold starkly different views regarding race and gender in contemporary society. Democrats are much more likely than Republicans to believe that prejudice and discrimination against women and people of color are major problems (see Figure 4). It follows, therefore, that they're more likely to support policies that promote equal pay for women and reforms aimed at rooting out racism in the criminal justice system. Republicans consider these policies unnecessary because they don't see the race- and gender-related

FIGURE 4. Party Differences in Attitudes toward Diversity and Inclusion

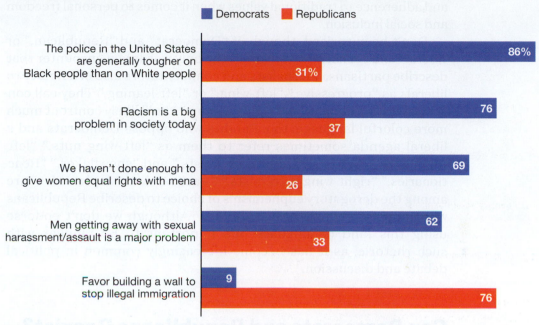

■ Democrats ■ Republicans

Statement	Democrats	Republicans
The police in the United States are generally tougher on Black people than on White people	86%	31%
Racism is a big problem in society today	76	37
We haven't done enough to give women equal rights with mena	69	26
Men getting away with sexual harassment/assault is a major problem	62	33
Favor building a wall to stop illegal immigration	9	76

Note: Bars represent the percentage of Democrats and Republicans who believe each statement or support each policy.

Source: PollingReport.com surveys conducted from 2015 to 2021.

discrimination in society that such proposals aim to address. Consistent with Democrats' support for diversity and inclusion, they are less concerned about restricting immigration—which is often a top priority for Republicans. The vast majority of Republicans support building a wall along the southern border to prevent illegal immigration. Less than 10 percent of Democrats support such an approach. The parties' disparate views pertaining to diversity and inclusion undoubtedly play a role in accounting for the fact that women and people of color are significantly more likely than men and White people to identify as Democrats (again, see Table 2).

Labels and More Labels

For the most part, the three categories of policy positions we outlined cohere into general political philosophies. Democrats believe that it's the government's job to promote economic and social equality. They think it's the government's responsibility to make sure that all citizens are treated fairly. These values are the core of a **liberal political philosophy** in the United States. Conversely, Republicans in the United

States embrace a **conservative political philosophy**—one that favors a much more limited role for government intervention in the economy and adherence to traditional values when it comes to personal freedom and social inclusion.

Don't be surprised, though, if "Democrat" and "Republican," or "liberal" and "conservative," aren't the only words you encounter that describe partisans. Journalists and commentators also often refer to liberals as "progressive," "left-wing," or "left-leaning." They call conservatives "right-wing" or "right-leaning." You'll likely confront much more colorful language, too. Pundits who oppose Democrats and a liberal agenda sometimes refer to them as "left-wing nuts," "left-wing loons," "leftists," "radical socialists," and "snowflakes." "Reactionaries," "right-wing extremists," "wackos," and "deplorables" are among the derogatory euphemisms of choice to describe Republicans who support a conservative agenda.[27] Although we don't endorse using this kind of language, it's important to be familiar with such rhetoric, as it has become increasingly common in political debate and discussion.

Can Democrats and Republicans Coexist?

After reading this segment, you may have concluded that the vast majority of Democrats and Republicans are hopelessly divided. On contemporary issues like abortion, immigration, tax policy, the environment, and guns, the parties do have very different visions for the country. And many Democrats and Republicans find themselves living in different places with different cultural habits. But despite these divisions, Democrats and Republicans have historically agreed on many of the fundamental values upon which the American system of government rests (see Segment 1). Citizens of all political persuasions, after all, overwhelmingly support a democratic form of government, free speech, freedom of religion, and capitalism.

That said, it's unclear whether these foundational values can withstand the deep partisan division and rancor that developed in the face of the 2020 presidential election. A majority of Democrats and Republicans claim to support democratic governance, but a majority of Republicans believe the Democrats stole the election and that Joe Biden is not a legitimate president. If millions of people are willing to cast aside core political values for short-term political victories, then it might not matter that partisans on both sides of the political aisle subscribe to the same abstract beliefs about free and fair democratic elections.

DID YOU GET IT?

Are you a Democrat or a Republican?

Short Answer:

- It depends on how you feel about the role of government, personal freedom, and diversity and inclusion.
- If you support a philosophy of government intervention in the economy, individual freedom, and social inclusion, then you're a Democrat. If you believe in less government intervention in the economy and a more traditional outlook on personal freedoms, then you're a Republican.
- Although Democrats and Republicans differ on many public policies, they both still support — at least for now — many of the general political values upon which the U.S. system of government rests.

DEVELOPING YOUR SKILLS

Consuming Political Information

Navigate party platforms: Platforms are good sources for identifying differences between what Democrats and Republicans believe and figuring out which party you most closely align with. You can find platforms dating back to 1840 on the website of the American Presidency Project. Current platforms are available on each party's official website. Use these sources to gain a better handle on party differences.

1. If you're interested in finding out what the Democrats support when it comes to foreign policy, which section of their 2020 party platform should you read?
   a. Restoring and Strengthening Our Democracy
   b. Healing the Soul of America
   c. Renewing American Leadership
   d. Creating a 21st Century Immigration System

2. Policy priorities change over time. Which topic appeared in the 1980 Republican platform but was gone by 2000?
   a. Taxes
   b. Veterans
   c. Women's rights
   d. LGBTQ rights

3. Party platforms have changed quite dramatically. Which statement best characterizes how their length in recent years compares to decades past?

   a. Platforms for both parties have generally gotten shorter.

   b. Platforms for both parties have generally gotten longer.

   c. The Democrats have shortened their platforms, but the Republicans have lengthened theirs.

   d. The Republicans have shortened their platforms, but the Democrats have lengthened theirs.

FIGURE IT OUT

Political scientists, pollsters, and pundits often claim that Americans are more divided now than they have ever been. Use party platforms to determine whether this characterization is accurate. More specifically:

- Choose one issue you care about, and summarize where the Democrats and Republicans stood in 2020. For the Republicans, use their 2016 platform (they chose not to update it in 2020).

- Now find what the parties' platforms said about the issue in 1972, if anything.

- Have the parties become more divided? Explain in a couple of sentences how you arrived at your answer.

Want to Know More?

For an amusing take on what happens when a Hollywood liberal travels through Republican areas of the United States, you should watch comedian Sarah Silverman's *I Love You, America*. The show's mission is to force people to speak with others who aren't like them. Silverman, a self-proclaimed liberal, spends a lot of time talking to Trump supporters and evangelical conservatives. Her intent is to promote more harmony among citizens with different political views. (Warning: Some of the humor in the show can be quite crude!)

QUANTITATIVE
LITERACY

19.
Why doesn't everyone vote?

#LowTurnout

If you woke up on November 8, 2022, having forgotten that it was Election Day, celebrities on social media quickly alerted you. Pop singer and actress Selena Gomez told her followers: "Today is the last day to vote. Your voice matters!!!"[1] Actress Kerry Washington made an enthusiastic plea: "We're so much stronger together! We will not back down! #ELECTIONDAY. BABY LETS DO THIS!!!!!"[2] Singer Billie Eilish posted a video urging her 106 million Instagram followers to "Please vote."[3] Lin-Manuel Miranda, Katy Perry, Halle Barry, John Legend, and Mindy Kaling participated in last-ditch social media efforts to encourage people to go to the polls. Even Krispy Kreme got in the game. They offered, without irony, a free "original glazed donut" on Election Day because "a healthy, vibrant democracy depends on engaged citizens who vote."[4]

   It's not only celebrities who plead with people to vote. Every election season, citizens are inundated with candidates' recorded messages on their phones, campaign workers at their doors, emails in their inboxes, and political ads on their screens, all trying to convince them to go to the polls. Why? Because a lot of people in the United States don't vote. And low **voter turnout** — the percentage of the voting-age population

Every election season, images like this one from outside a polling place in Austin, Texas, in 2022, suggest that Americans are eager to vote. This segment shows how misleading these types of photos can be.

that casts a ballot — raises some concerns about the health of American democracy.

The very essence of a democratic government, after all, is that it's chosen by the people. President Ronald Reagan summed up this argument well in 1982 as he signed into law an extension of the Voting Rights Act: "The right to vote is the crown jewel of American liberties, and we will not see its luster diminished."[5] Voting doesn't only signal a vibrant democratic system, though. It's also a way for people to express their preferences for laws, policies, and elected leaders. President Barack Obama made this point at a town hall meeting following the 2014 midterm elections, in which turnout for a national election had fallen to its lowest level in 75 years (just 36 percent of eligible voters turned out[6]). "Why are you staying home? . . . Why are you not participating?" the president asked the audience in Miami, Florida. "There are war-torn countries, people full of poverty, who still voted 60, 70 percent. If here in the United States of America, we voted at 60 percent, 70 percent, it would transform our politics."[7] Obama tried to convey to the crowd what scholars, politicians, and political organizations have long argued: if more people voted, then the political system would better reflect the will of the people.[8]

If voting is so important to the health of democracy and the policies the government pursues, then why don't more people do it? And why do those who *do* vote often need to be coaxed and cajoled? There's no one simple answer, but this segment presents three of the leading explanations: (1) the way elections are run, (2) the laws regulating who is allowed to vote, and (3) the feeling that one person's vote doesn't really matter anyway.

Voter Turnout in the United States

There are several ways to gauge voter turnout in the United States—how we fare relative to other countries, the percentage of people who vote in national elections, the proportion of citizens who cast ballots in local contests, to name just a few. But no matter how we measure it, voter turnout is well below what most people would hope for in a democratic country.

Figure 1 lists voter turnout rates for most of the developed democracies throughout the world. For each nation, the bar represents the percentage of the voting-age population that turned out in the most recent election for president or prime minister. In 2020, 62 percent of the voting-age population in the United States cast a ballot in the presidential election. That places the United States in a three-way tie for 21st out of the 35 nations listed in the figure. Five of the countries that surpass us (marked with an asterisk on the figure) have **compulsory voting**—a system in which citizens are legally required to vote or else face fines or penalties. But the other 15 don't, and many still outpace the United States in voter turnout.[9]

The United States' unimpressive ranking after the 2020 election actually represents a marked improvement from previous elections. There was a 7 percentage point jump in turnout from 2016 (from 55 to 62 percent). One reason for the increase is the record number of people who either really liked or really disliked Donald Trump.[10] If you are passionate about a candidate (love or hate), you're more likely to show up to vote.[11] Typically, the United States falls even closer to the bottom of the global ranking each election cycle. To be sure, when people are enthusiastic—like when Barack Obama first ran for president in 2008—turnout goes up a bit (see Figure 2). And when there's less public interest—such as Bill Clinton's 1996 reelection campaign—turnout drops a little. But these fluctuations aren't very dramatic.[12] In the last 10 presidential elections, turnout has averaged 54.1 percent.

The picture is worse when we move beyond presidential elections. In **midterm elections**—national elections that take place two years into a president's term—turnout over the last 100 years has been, on average, a

FIGURE 1. Voter Turnout in National Elections across the Globe

Country	Turnout
*Turkey	89%
Sweden	82
*Australia	81
Israel	78
South Korea	78
*Belgium	78
Netherlands	77
Denmark	76
Hungary	72
Norway	71
Germany	69
Finland	69
France	68
*Mexico	66
Italy	65
Slovakia	65
Poland	65
Austria	64
New Zealand	63
*Greece	63
United States	62
United Kingdom	62
Canada	62
Portugal	61
Spain	60
Lithuania	59
Czech Republic	58
Ireland	57
Colombia	57
Estonia	56
Slovenia	55
Latvia	54
Chile	52
*Luxembourg	48
*Switzerland	36

Note: Data are based on the voting-age population that cast a ballot in the most recent national election in each country (all of which took place between 2017 and 2020). An * indicates a compulsory voting requirement.

Source: Drew Desilver, "In Past Elections, U.S. Trailed Most Developed Countries in Voter Turnout," Pew Research Center, November 3, 2020.

little more than 40 percent. Despite the fact that the entire House of Representatives and one-third of the U.S. Senate is up for reelection every two years, in the last century, never has a majority of the voting-age population turned out to vote in the midterms.

If you think these numbers are low, consider turnout in **primary elections**—those in which members of a political party choose among their party's candidates for the general election. Democrats pick a winner among Democrats, and Republicans pick a winner among Republicans. In 2020, just 23 percent of the voting-age population participated in either the Democratic or the Republican presidential primary.[13] In other words, more than three-quarters of voting-age Americans played no role in the process that resulted in Donald Trump and Joe Biden competing in the head-to-head contest to become president of the United States. Turnout is even lower in congressional primaries.[14]

As far as local races are concerned—and there are literally hundreds of thousands of them on the ballot every election season—typically only about 20 percent of people show up to choose their city council members or mayor.[15] In many school board elections, hardly anyone votes. Turnout can be as low as 5 percent.[16]

FIGURE 2. Voter Turnout in the United States, 1920–2022

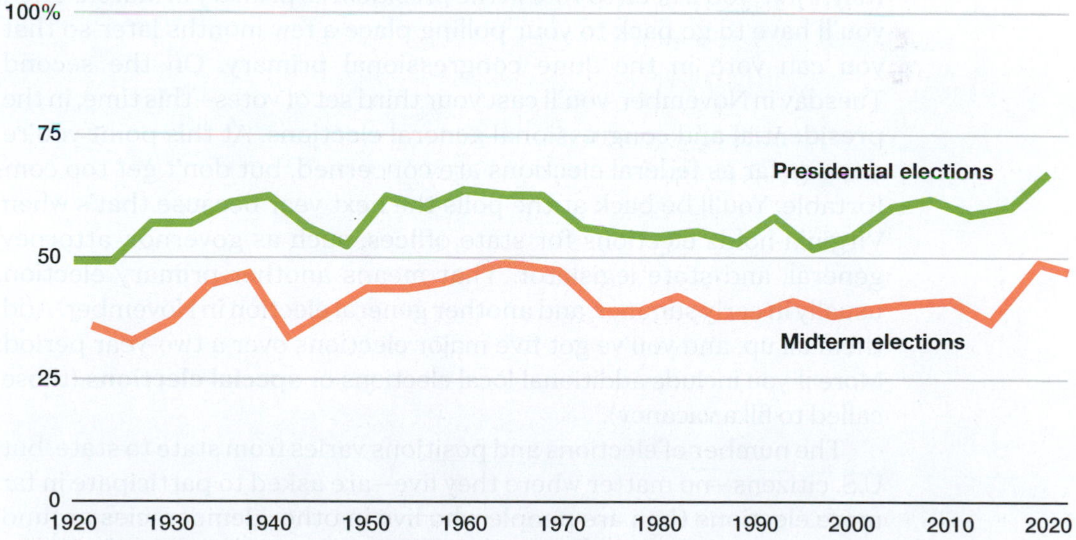

Note: The data presented represent the percentage of the voting-eligible population who cast a ballot in each election.
Source: "Voter Turnout," United States Elections Project.

Why Don't People Vote?

A few years ago, National Public Radio (NPR) interviewed dozens of people who don't vote. The goal was to understand why so many citizens stay on the "sidelines of democracy."[17] Megan Davis, a resident of Rhode Island, explained that she doesn't go to the polls because she doesn't think her voice matters. "People who suck still are in office, so it doesn't make a difference," she concluded. Jonas Rand of Las Vegas agreed: "I don't believe it is actually effective to vote. . . . The system is stacked against the citizenry." Others, including Shelby Mabis of Missouri, don't think they're sufficiently informed about the process or rules for voting. "I don't know what I need to bring. I don't even know what happens," Mabis told the reporter. Others attributed staying away from the polls to dishonest politicians, a complicated system, and too little time to follow politics. These sentiments embody three of the top reasons people do not turn out to vote.

Reason 1: Too Many Elections, Too Many Offices

Imagine that you live in Virginia. Imagine that your parents and teachers always impressed upon you the importance of voting. And now imagine that it's a presidential election year. What do you have to do to live up to your civic responsibility? A lot—at least if you want to participate fully. First, you'll need to vote in the presidential primary in March. Then, you'll have to go back to your polling place a few months later so that you can vote in the June congressional primary. On the second Tuesday in November, you'll cast your third set of votes—this time, in the presidential and congressional general elections. At this point you're done as far as federal elections are concerned, but don't get too comfortable. You'll be back at the polls the next year because that's when Virginia holds elections for state offices, such as governor, attorney general, and state legislator. That means another primary election, usually in early summer, and another general election in November. Add them all up, and you've got five major elections over a two-year period. More if you include additional local elections or **special elections** (those called to fill a vacancy).

The number of elections and positions varies from state to state, but U.S. citizens—no matter where they live—are asked to participate in far more elections than are people who live in other democracies around the world. Most democratic countries have one national election every five years. The United States has one every two years. In most of the countries listed in Figure 1, the political parties select the candidates for the general election. In the United States, voters choose the finalists by voting first in primary elections.

It's not just the frequency of elections that is onerous for citizens, though. The sheer number of elected positions can be overwhelming, too. In Virginia, not only might you have to show up to vote five times in two years, but you also have to select candidates for at least 15 different offices, ranging from president of the United States at the top of the ballot down to town treasurer at the bottom. But that's nothing compared to California. In 2020, citizens in some counties voted in as many as 20 different electoral contests. In addition, because California has **ballot initiatives**—specific laws put to a direct vote by the citizens—voters also had to weigh in on 13 statewide policy proposals, some of which were rather complex budgetary and tax measures.[18] Voters had no need to feel overwhelmed, though. They could simply download the 112-page election guide available on the California secretary of state's website prior to the election. (That's not a typo; the guide really was 112 pages![19]) Expectations of voters are similar in Texas, where citizens often have to consider candidates for a couple dozen different elected positions, including governor, probate judge, member of the board of education, railroad commissioner (which has very little to do with railroads), and county treasurer.[20]

All of this is to say that one of the reasons voter turnout is low in the United States is that expectations of good citizenship are too demanding for many people. It's just not feasible to find the time or exert the effort required to keep up with so many candidates and election dates.

Reason 2: Rules for Voting

In most countries, the government automatically registers citizens to vote. In the United States, it's up to you to register. But that's only the first step. Even if you want to become a registered voter, you might not be eligible. The Constitution sets the voting age at 18, but beyond that, each state determines its own registration requirements. Some states don't let you vote unless you've registered 30 days prior to an election, whereas others allow you to register on Election Day. Some states ban people who have ever been convicted of a felony from voting for their rest of their lives, others reinstate voting rights the minute they get out of prison, and a handful of others allow voting while in prison. Overall, about 20 million people in the United States who are of voting age are not voting eligible. In fact, if we calculate voter turnout among only the voting-eligible population, which is often how it is reported in the news, then it was close to 67 percent in 2020.[21]

It's not only registration requirements that vary. States also determine how easy it is for registered voters to cast a ballot. Some states don't let you vote without a valid government-issued picture ID. Others request, but don't require, an ID. Still others take your word that you are who you say you are when you show up at the polling place. Some states allow early voting so that if you can't make it to the polls on Election Day, you can vote in the days or weeks leading up to it. Others don't offer an early voting option. Some states issue absentee ballots to any voter who requests one. Other states require a documented excuse.

Table 1 illustrates several differences in voting laws across states.[22] We focus on Oregon, Iowa, Florida, and Mississippi because they range from having very open (Oregon) to very restrictive (Mississippi) voting rules.[23] Notice that the easier a state makes it for citizens to register and vote, the higher that state's voter turnout will be in both presidential and midterm elections. In Oregon, turnout was roughly 13 points higher in the 2020 presidential election and 15 points higher in the 2018 midterms than it was in Mississippi. More broadly, in the 2018 midterm elections, average

TABLE 1. Differences in Voting Requirements across the United States

	Oregon	Iowa	Florida	Mississippi
Voter registration deadline	21 days before the election	Election Day	29 days before the election	30 days before the election
Voting rights for people convicted of felonies	Yes, upon release from prison	No (permanently disenfranchised)	Yes, after probation and parole (for most crimes)	No (permanently disenfranchised)
ID requirement	None	ID required	Photo ID required	Photo ID required
Early voting	Begins 18 days before the election	Begins 20 days before the election	Begins 10 days before the election	None
Absentee voting	All voting is by mail	Approved for any reason	Approved for any reason	Must provide a documented excuse
Turnout in 2020	**70.9%**	**69.7%**	**63.5%**	**58.1%**
Turnout in 2018	**56.9%**	**54.9%**	**48.0%**	**42.2%**

Source: See Note 20 for full source information.

turnout in the 10 least restrictive states was 7 percentage points higher than turnout in the 10 most restrictive.[24]

Part of the reason voter turnout was unusually high in 2020 was because many states made it easier to vote. With the Covid-19 pandemic sweeping across the nation, states worked to implement safety measures for casting a ballot. Nine states mailed ballots to every voter in the state, and 34 others allowed fear of Covid-19 to serve as a reasonable excuse for requesting a mail ballot.[25] In most cases, though, these changes to ballot access were not permanent.

Reason 3: "There's No Point"

The vast majority of citizens—91 percent, according to a recent survey—believe that voting is important, but far fewer say they're excited to do it.[26] That's often because people's perceptions of the electoral system suggest that going to the polls just isn't worth it.

First of all, people are more likely to vote when they think the outcome isn't a foregone conclusion.[27] Yet most elections are not very competitive. Members of the House of Representatives who sought reelection in 2022, for example, defeated their challengers by an average of almost 30 percentage points. In presidential elections, the Electoral College system means that winning a majority of a state's voters is the name of the game (see Segment 30). That leaves just a handful of competitive states. If you live in California, a state that votes overwhelmingly for Democrats, what's the point of going to the polls? If you're a Republican, you figure your candidate has no chance. If you're a Democrat, you know your side is going to win even if you don't show up. The reverse is true in states that almost always vote Republican. Democrats in Utah, Tennessee, or Wyoming can rightfully conclude that their party's presidential candidate probably doesn't have a fighting chance. Republicans can rest easy knowing that even if they stay home, their side will claim victory. This is the reality in about 40 of the 50 states.

Second, even when a race is competitive, people are often not excited about the choices. Take the 2016 presidential race. On Election Day, 61 percent of Americans viewed Donald Trump unfavorably and 58 percent viewed Hillary Clinton unfavorably. A majority of people said they didn't trust either candidate. And voters didn't find either of them likeable.[28] Even though the stakes were very high and the two candidates had different visions for the country, millions of people just didn't feel compelled to go to the polls. More broadly, all sorts of survey results show that voters are not very excited about the political system overall. A majority of Americans don't have a favorable impression of either the Democratic or the Republican Party.[29] Almost three-quarters of Americans have little confidence in the way elected officials perform their job, regardless of their party.[30] So many voters conclude that no matter the election outcome, it'll be undesirable.

Third, many voters toss up their hands because they don't think votes from "regular people" make much of a difference. In other words, many citizens—especially those with lower incomes and less education—have a low sense of **political efficacy**. That is, they don't believe that their voice will be heard and can influence government. In fact, surveys reveal that roughly three-quarters of the population doesn't think that the government cares about the views of ordinary citizens.[31] Roughly 80 percent of citizens believe that the wealthy and corporations have too much influence in the U.S. system.[32] The irony is that when people vote, their sense of political efficacy increases.[33]

Finally, some people conclude that one vote in a sea of thousands, sometimes millions, will never affect the outcome of an election. Technically, this is true—the odds are virtually zero that your one vote will be decisive. But that's not to say that there haven't been some important elections where very few votes could have made a difference. Donald Trump would have defeated Joe Biden in 2020 if he had received just 0.5 percent more of the vote in Arizona, Georgia, and Wisconsin.[34] In a 2017 state legislative race in Newport News, Virginia, one vote could have mattered. The race ended in a tie: each candidate received 11,608 votes.[35] So the members of the State Board of Elections wrote the candidates' names on pieces of paper, placed them in a ceramic bowl, and chose the winner that way. That's right—the district's representative was ultimately selected by the equivalent of flipping a coin. If voter turnout in any of these contests had been just a little bit higher, it's certainly possible that the outcomes would have been different. But these kinds of close outcomes are rare, and voters know that the chances of their vote tipping the balance are slim.

The Politics of Voter Turnout

If voter turnout is low, and we know that the way we administer elections and impose registration requirements is part of the reason, then why not reform the system? It turns out that rules governing ballot access are the subject of one of the biggest debates between the two political parties in contemporary politics. Democratic leaders tend to embrace the argument that low turnout threatens democracy, and as a result they push for fewer restrictions and easier access. In fact, after retaining control of the House of Representatives following the 2020 elections, Democrats introduced the For the People Act as their first bill. It would have created national standards for voting across the country and made it much easier for citizens to register to vote.[36] Two-thirds of Republicans, by contrast, believe that potential voter fraud is a much bigger problem than low voter turnout.[37] Accordingly, they tend to favor mandatory voter ID laws, shorter periods of early voting, and sometimes laws requiring citizens to re-register if they haven't voted in a while. It's not surprising, then, that all but one House Democrat voted in favor of the For the People Act, and every Republican opposed it.[38] The Senate never voted on the bill.

These debates will rage on for years to come because the parties' positions on voter access aren't only about promoting democracy or protecting against fraud. They're also part of a political calculation. Democrats generally believe that if more people vote, more Democrats will be elected. After all, some of the citizens least committed to showing up at the polls are young people, poor people, and Latinos — all likely Democratic voters. Democrats worry that any additional hurdles to voting will only further deter members of these groups from casting ballots. Republicans, for their part, believe that when fewer people vote, Republican candidates do better. Because Republican voters tend to be older, White, and wealthier, a few more regulations pertaining to identification or registration will likely not deter them. Recent electoral outcomes seem to support the parties' calculations. In the 2020 presidential election, 13 of the 15 most restrictive states voted for Republican Donald Trump. Thirteen of the 15 least restrictive states went for Democrat Joe Biden.[39] As long as voting reform is a partisan issue, significant upticks in voter turnout in U.S. elections are unlikely.

DID YOU GET IT?

Why doesn't everyone vote?

Short Answer:

- The frequency of elections, restrictive voting rules, and negative attitudes toward the political system all contribute to low voter turnout.
- Reforms that make it easier to register and vote tend to increase turnout, but they're often politically controversial.
- Among advanced democracies, the United States ranks near the bottom in the percentage of citizens who turn out to vote.

Quantitative Literacy

Interpret the numbers: Drawing conclusions about voter turnout requires a careful look at the data because there are many ways to analyze turnout statistics. These questions ask you to delve a little deeper into the tables and figures presented in this segment.

1. Most countries have one national election every five years. The United States has at least two national elections every five years — one presidential and one midterm. Given what you now know about midterm voter turnout, what would happen if we re-created Figure 1 so that the United States was ranked based on an average of the most recent presidential and midterm elections?

    a. The United States would move up a couple of spots.

    b. The United States would move up one spot.

    c. The United States would stay in the same position.

    d. The United States would drop even lower on the list.

2. Experts don't agree on the best way to calculate voter turnout. Some think it should be based on the voting-age population (VAP) — the number of people age 18 and older. Others think it's better to use the voting-eligible population (VEP) — the number of people age 18 and older who are *allowed* to vote (this measure excludes noncitizens, people convicted of felonies in many states, etc.). Which statement is true about these two measures when it comes to calculating turnout?

    a. The turnout rate using VEP is always higher than when using VAP.

    b. The turnout rate using VEP is always lower than when using VAP.

    c. The turnout rate is often the same, regardless of whether you use VEP or VAP.

    d. In some states the VEP is higher than the VAP, but in others it's lower.

3. Which statement most accurately describes the presidential and midterm election turnout trends in Figure 2?

    a. Voting in presidential elections has remained stable since 1920, but voting in midterm elections has declined.

    b. Turnout in both presidential and midterm elections has been slowly increasing over time.

    c. Turnout in both presidential and midterm elections has been slowly decreasing over time.

    d. Except for some minor fluctuations, turnout in both presidential and midterm elections has remained generally stable since 1920.

Want to Know More?

The website of the United States Elections Project (http://www .electproject.org/) is a treasure trove of information about voter turnout — some of it going as far back as 1789! If anything in this segment sparked your interest, then this website is for you. You can see which elections have had the highest or lowest turnout throughout history, or you can check out turnout rates by state. Beyond historic and state numbers, if you're interested in turnout rates across different demographic groups, then we recommend Bernard Fraga's *The Turnout Gap: Race, Ethnicity, and Political Inequality in a Diversifying America*. We cover some of this in Segment 20, too.

20.
Who participates in politics?

#PoliticalParticipation

Sonia ImMasche felt crushed after Donald Trump defeated Hillary Clinton in the 2016 presidential election. She didn't wallow in political misery, though. Instead, the 72-year-old Democrat began sending money to Democratic congressional candidates throughout the country. Every time Trump said or did something that made ImMasche angry, she turned on the computer, went to ActBlue's website — which connects Democratic candidates to donors everywhere in the United States — and made a contribution.[1] By the end of the 2018 election cycle, she had made literally hundreds of donations to candidates in Virginia, California, Kansas, and Texas. If a Democrat had a chance to unseat a Trump-supporting Republican, ImMasche was all over it. Her average contribution was just $10.16. But every dollar helps. Democrats regained control of the House of Representatives in part because of victories from candidates who received a lot of small contributions.[2]

Nine-year-old Dane Best wanted to have a snowball fight with his friends. But a 98-year-old law in his hometown of Severance, Colorado, actually banned throwing snowballs.[3] So the third-grader organized a letter-writing campaign among his classmates to urge the town board to change what he considered a "silly" law. Best even attended a town board meeting and delivered a prepared three-minute speech. Dressed in a button-down shirt and bow tie, he told

Nine-year-old Dane Best exemplified how political participation can matter. He appeared before the city council in Severance, Colorado, where he successfully persuaded them to overturn a city law that banned throwing snowballs.

the board that "today's kids need reasons to play outside." Citing research his parents helped him find, Best explained that "a lack of exposure to the outdoors can lead to obesity, ADHD, anxiety, and depression." He implored the city officials to strike down the ban because, as he put it: "The children of Severance want the opportunity to have a snowball fight like the rest of the world."[4] It worked. The board voted unanimously to overturn the ban.

Twenty-five-year-old Ned Alexander spent many nights at a boarded-up restaurant in Ferguson, Missouri. The site served as a camp-ground and headquarters for Lost Voices, a group that formed in 2014 after Michael Brown, an unarmed Black 18-year-old, was shot and killed by a police officer. The officer claimed that he had acted in self-defense, but the shooting sparked a national wave of protests over race relations and police misconduct.[5] Members of Lost Voices gathered daily in Ferguson to protest peacefully for justice for Michael Brown and other unarmed victims like him. "I never imagined myself doing anything like this," Alexander told a reporter.[6] He knew the protests wouldn't guarantee a conviction of the officer who shot Brown. In fact, criminal charges were never even filed against the officer. But Lost Voices members felt it was important to take a stand.[7] In time, Ferguson replaced its city manager and hired its first Black police chief to help combat racist police practices.[8]

We could easily recount many more examples of **political participation** — the ways citizens actively engage with their government and make their voices heard in the political system. Some give money, contact elected officials, or attend marches and protests. Others vote, go to rallies, post comments or forward stories on social media, volunteer for candidates or causes they believe in, or sign petitions. Political participation doesn't always produce the desired outcomes, but it's a necessary part of ensuring that the government responds to citizens.

This segment focuses on two aspects of political participation: (1) how — and how much — people engage with the political system, and (2) who those people are. You'll see that for many political activities, rates of participation are quite low. And the people who do participate are often older, wealthier, and more educated than the citizens who tend not to get involved. These patterns raise questions about **political representation** in the United States — how well the political system reflects the demographics, preferences, and priorities of its citizens.

Political Participation: How Citizens Do It

It's no exaggeration to say that political participation is the lifeblood of democracy. The First Amendment to the Constitution, after all, guarantees the "right of the people peaceably to assemble, and to petition the government." In other words, citizens have the right to hold political meetings, demonstrations, and rallies. The right to vote, though extended only to White men in the original constitution, has also been a fundamental freedom for all adult citizens for more than 50 years.

Yet the scorecard is undoubtedly mixed when it comes to whether citizens are active participants in American democracy. **Voter turnout**— the percentage of the voting-age population that casts a ballot—is much lower in the United States than it is in many other democratic nations. Advocates of voter participation might have been gratified to see that in the 2020 presidential election, 62 percent of the voting-age population cast a ballot.[9] That's the highest share of voters coming to the polls since the election of 1900[10] and the first time since 1968 in which turnout in a presidential election exceeded 60 percent. Even though millions of Americans don't vote, voting is far and away the most prevalent form of political participation (see Figure 1).[11]

Why is voting the most popular political activity? First, it's ingrained in many of us from an early age that a sense of civic duty requires turning out on Election Day. It's the one political act that even little kids know about. Second, candidates can only win elections if they get their supporters to the polls. Accordingly, many campaigns spend a lot of

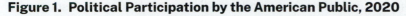

Figure 1. Political Participation by the American Public, 2020

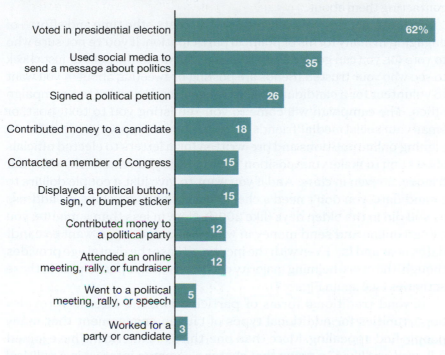

Voted in presidential election	62%
Used social media to send a message about politics	35
Signed a political petition	26
Contributed money to a candidate	18
Contacted a member of Congress	15
Displayed a political button, sign, or bumper sticker	15
Contributed money to a political party	12
Attended an online meeting, rally, or fundraiser	12
Went to a political meeting, rally, or speech	5
Worked for a party or candidate	3

Note: Bars represent the percentage of Americans who reported engaging in each political activity during 2020. The "Voted" bar isn't based on self-reports; it's the actual percentage of the voting-age population that turned out in 2020.

Source: United States Elections Project; 2020 American National Election Study.

time and money on **voter mobilization**—initiatives aimed at registering people and urging them to vote. Third, compared to other political acts, voting usually requires relatively little effort. We don't want to minimize the challenges that voters sometimes face. After all, casting a ballot in some states and counties is much more difficult than in others—it might require showing a form of government identification or even waiting in line for many hours. And sometimes voters are asked to weigh in on dozens of races. But for most Americans, especially compared to other types of political participation, voting is pretty straightforward.

The more onerous the activity, the lower the rate of participation. Notice in Figure 1 that the second and third most popular forms of participation—using social media to send a message about politics and signing a petition—are also relatively easy. You don't have to step away from your keyboard or smartphone to do either. Most of the other activities listed in the figure require a much greater commitment of resources and effort. To contribute to candidates or political parties, you need money. To volunteer for a candidate, you need time. And to write letters to elected officials, you need information and knowledge concerning the issue you're contacting them about.

The internet dramatically reduces the costs—the time and effort—of engaging in many forms of political participation. If you're not sure who to vote for, you can google a candidate on the way to the polls or just check to see who your trusted friends are posting or tweeting about. If you want to volunteer for a candidate, you no longer need to travel to a campaign office. The campaign will come to you—enlisting you to text, post, or email your social media "friends" urging them to support your candidate. Signing online petitions and pre-written form letters to elected officials allows you to make your position known while you're at work, with your friends, or even in class. And if you want to give just a couple dollars to a candidate, you don't need a checkbook, stamp, envelope, or address as you did in the olden days (like 2006). Now, in less than a minute, you can go online and send money in whatever amount you want to candidates near and far. Even with the increased ease the digital age provides, though, the overwhelming majority of citizens do not participate in these activities (see again Figure 1).

Beyond traditional forms of participation, the internet provides opportunities for additional types of citizen engagement that many people find appealing. More than one-third of Americans have joined, followed, or "liked" a group that shares a common interest in a political issue or cause. Roughly the same proportion have encouraged others in their social media networks to take action on a political issue. Nearly

Sometimes politically active citizens can get a little carried away. Putting bumper stickers on your car, yard signs on your lawn, or buttons on your jacket are time-honored ways of participating. Transforming your house into a monument to support your candidate, as Leslie Rossi of Youngstown, Pennsylvania, did, is somewhat more unusual.

one-fifth of people use profile pictures and hashtags to make political statements.[12] The most popular conservative hashtag, #MAGA, appeared more than 200,000 times a day on social media during the first year of Trump's presidency.[13] #MeToo has become synonymous with supporting women's rights. And #BlackLivesMatter indicates support for racial justice. In the aftermath of George Floyd's murder at the hands of police in June 2020, the hashtag appeared in an average of 3.7 million tweets a day.[14]

Overall, more than half of all Americans (53 percent) report using social media to engage in at least one of the political activities listed in Figure 2.[15] Although these rates of participation are not extremely high, they are far higher than the rates for most non-internet-based political activities listed in Figure 1.[16] Seven times as many people, for example, have posted a picture to show support for a cause than have attended an actual political rally for the same purpose.

Some scholars argue, however, that we should not equate participation through social media, which requires little true commitment or effort, with more traditional forms of engagement.[17] Taking a few seconds to post a political meme on Instagram about a candidate you support isn't the same as volunteering for that candidate's campaign. Joining a social media group to support a cause isn't as effective as actually

Figure 2. Political Activity through Social Media

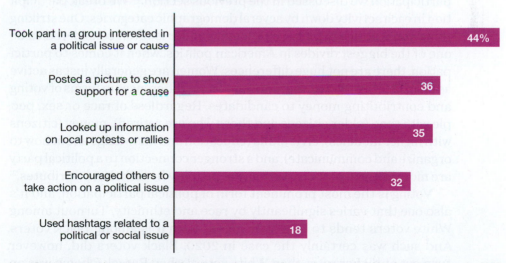

Activity	Percentage
Took part in a group interested in a political issue or cause	44%
Posted a picture to show support for a cause	36
Looked up information on local protests or rallies	35
Encouraged others to take action on a political issue	32
Used hashtags related to a political or social issue	18

Note: Bars represent the percentage of Americans who reported engaging in each political activity during the 2020 election season.

Source: Brooke Auxier, "Activism on Social Media Varies by Race and Ethnicity, Age, Political Party," Pew Research Center, July 13, 2020.

showing up to a political meeting. Signing an online petition protesting an action by the government isn't as powerful as participating in a real live protest. These skeptical scholars derogatorily refer to this type of point-and-click political participation as **slacktivism**. Social media, without a doubt, allows more people the opportunity to organize and communicate about politics, and that sense of engagement is important in and of itself. But online activism is perhaps most meaningful when used to augment traditional methods of participation, like those used by Sonia ImMasche, Dane Best, and Ned Alexander.[18]

Political Participation: Who Does It?

Do you ever wonder why politicians in Washington, D.C., spend a lot more time talking about Social Security and Medicare (government programs for older Americans) than they do discussing student loans and the cost of college tuition? Do you ever think about why elected officials devote more attention to lowering taxes for wealthy people than to making housing more affordable for low-income people? Are you ever curious about why members of Congress are so wedded to partisan warfare even though poll after poll indicates that citizens favor compromise? Actually, there's a good chance that you've never thought about these things. But you should! In each case, the answer comes down to who participates. Elected leaders are most responsive to citizens who are politically active.[19]

So who participates? Table 1 presents six of the methods of political participation we discussed in the previous section.[20] We break participation in each activity down by several demographic categories. One striking thing you'll notice is that even though gender is often considered to be one of the biggest divides in American politics, when it comes to participation, there are not huge differences. Women are generally just as active as men. In terms of race, there are important differences in terms of voting and contributing money to candidates. Regardless of race or sex, people with time (older citizens and those who are retired), money (citizens with higher incomes), **civic skills** (education and knowledge about how to organize and communicate), and a stronger connection to a political party are more likely to participate than are people who lack these attributes.[21]

Voting is the most prominent form of political participation, and it's also one that varies significantly by race and ethnicity. Turnout among White voters tends to be a little higher than it is among Black voters. And such was certainly the case in 2020. Black voters did, however, turn out at higher rates than White voters when Barack Obama was on the ballot in 2008 and 2012. Voter turnout is lower among Latinos.[22] In 2020, White citizens were 17 percentage points more likely than Latinos to go to the polls; Black citizens were 9 points more likely.[23]

TABLE 1. Differences in Political Participation across Demographic Groups

	Voted in the presidential election	Signed a political petition	Contributed money to a candidate	Displayed a button, sign, or sticker	Attended meeting, rally, or speech	Used social media to talk about politics
Gender						
Male	65%	22%	19%	16%	5%	32%
Female	68	29	17	15	5	37
Race						
White	71	26	20	17	5	36
Black	63	23	13	14	5	28
Latino	54	23	11	13	5	31
Age						
18 to 29	53	34	8	10	7	38
30 to 44	64	28	12	13	5	38
45 to 59	73	24	15	13	5	36
60 and over	78	23	27	17	5	22
Education						
Less than a BA	60	21	11	15	4	32
4-year degree	77	30	22	15	5	37
Advanced degree	90	34	31	17	6	39
Income						
Less than $50,000	50	24	12	14	5	33
$50,000 or more	69	28	22	17	5	37
Partisanship						
Not "strong" partisan	no data	23	12	9	3	25
"Strong" partisan	no data	29	25	23	7	30

Notes: Entries represent the percentage of Americans who reported engaging in each political activity during the year of the 2020 presidential election. Voter turnout is based on the voting-eligible population, and the income comparisons for voting are from 2016. "Strong" partisans are people who identified as "strong Republicans" or "strong Democrats."

Source: "Voter Turnout Demographics," United States Elections Project; U.S. Bureau of the Census; 2020 American National Election Study.

Some of this difference reflects fewer voter mobilization efforts in Latino communities.[24]

Some of the gaps in voter turnout rates can also be explained by differences in people's access to money and civic skills. Notice that turnout rates vary considerably by education, income, and age. The data in Table 1 reveal a 30-point gap in turnout between people with an advanced degree and those without a college degree. The gap is almost 20 points when we compare people who earn more than $50,000 per year to those who earn less. Overall, the more educated and wealthier you are, the more likely you are to vote. This also helps explain why only a slim majority of people under the age of 30 cast ballots, compared to the more than three-quarters of people over the age of 60 who do.

People with more education and money are also more active when it comes to the five other activities listed in Table 1. People living in households that earn more than $50,000 a year are more likely to contribute money to political candidates than those living in households that earn less than $50,000 a year are. People with a college degree are more likely than those without one to engage across the board, as they typically know more about the issues, how the political system works, and how to communicate with political leaders. And people who consider themselves either "strong Republicans" or "strong Democrats"—are almost twice as likely as everyone else to donate money, display campaign paraphernalia, and attend a meeting, rally, or speech.

Lower rates of political activity among younger, lower-income, and less educated citizens, as well as people of color, wouldn't be as concerning if they shared the same general views as older, wealthier, White, college graduates. But they don't. People under the age of 30, for instance, are much more supportive of transgender rights than people over the age of 65 are.[25] Older citizens are more likely than younger ones to prioritize strengthening the military and defeating terrorism.[26] People with lower incomes are more likely than those with higher incomes to say that combating income inequality should be a top priority.[27] Black people are twice as likely as White people to believe police violence is a "serious problem."[28] White people are more than twice as likely as Latinos and four times more likely than Black people to oppose raising the minimum wage.[29] These are just a handful of examples.

The issues and policies that different groups of people care about get more attention from politicians if the group is politically active. In other words, elected officials tend to follow the lead of people who are the most engaged. As a result, elected leaders are representing some citizens' interests at the expense of others'. A representative's job in a democracy is to represent all constituents, not just the most vocal. But political leaders' priorities make it clear that who participates matters.[30]

Who participates in politics?

Short Answer:

- People participate in the political system in many ways — from voting, to donating to candidates, to communicating about politics on social media.
- Political activities that are relatively easy — those that require less time, money, and knowledge — are more common than those that require more resources.
- White, older, wealthier, more educated citizens are the most politically active, and this raises questions about the quality of political representation in the United States.

DEVELOPING YOUR SKILLS

Quantitative Literacy

Interpret the numbers: The news media present citizens with a lot of information about voters every election season. Sometimes the data are presented in a simple figure or chart. Other times, you'll find yourself staring at a dizzying blur of statistics. Take a close look at Table 1, and use it to practice interpreting busy tables.

1. Which of the following four political activities has the largest gap between "strong" partisans and not "strong" partisans?
   a. Voting
   b. Contributing money to a candidate
   c. Signing a political petition
   d. Using social media to communicate about politics

2. Which group has the highest rate of political participation on all dimensions?
   a. People who are at least 60 years old
   b. People with an advanced degree
   c. People with household incomes of at least $50,000
   d. Men

3. Of the six types of political activities listed, in how many do women participate at a higher rate than men?
   a. 0   b. 2   c. 3   d. 5

FIGURE IT OUT

This table from the Pew Research Center provides a typical presentation of voter statistics. The table lists the percentage of people, broken down by their level of education, who think that each issue should be a priority for the president and Congress to address. Analyze the table's information, and then answer the questions that follow.

Percentage of citizens who believe the following issues should be a top priority of the president and Congress:

	HS or less	Some college	College grad+	Low-high diff
Strengthening military	46%	36%	24%	+22
Social Security	65	60	44	+21
Terrorism	66	54	47	+19
Reducing crime	61	50	42	+19
Criminal justice system	52	44	35	+17
Drug addiction	38	28	22	+16
Improving job situation	57	51	42	+15
Reducing budget deficit	50	48	35	+15
Global trade	42	33	28	+14
Immigration	55	48	42	+13
Health care costs	66	63	57	+9
Problems of poor people	48	45	39	+9
Education	57	62	52	+5
Race relations	40	37	36	+4
Strengthening economy	71	72	70	+1
Climate change	42	39	45	−3
Improving political system	51	52	56	−5
Dealing with Covid-19	59	58	67	−8

Note: Survey of U.S. adults conducted in Jan. 7, 2022.

Source: "Public's Top Priority for 2022: Strengthening the Nation's Economy," Pew Research Center, February 16, 2022.

- Compare people with a high school diploma or less to those with more than a college degree. In how many cases does a majority of one group think the issue should be a priority for the government to address but the majority of the other group does not? List all of the issues where this is the case.

- Identify the top three priorities for people who attended some college. For each issue, determine whether citizens with some college education hold beliefs more like people who never attended college or more like people with more than a college degree. Be specific in explaining how you came up with your answer, and show the calculations you made in each case.

Want to Know More?

Did reading this segment make you think "Hey, I should get a little more involved"? Maybe it sparked you to think you should do something about an issue that has always bothered you. Here are a couple of books that can give you the tools to become a more participatory citizen: Eric Liu's *You're More Powerful than You Think: A Citizen's Guide to Making Change Happen* and Morgan Carroll's *Take Back Your Government: A Citizen's Guide to Grassroots Change.*

21.
Why do people join interest groups?

#NationOfJoiners

From the minute you and your college roommate met, you hit it off. You both cared a lot about school and were always prepared for class. You both preferred to study late at night rather than early in the morning. You both played sports — one tennis, the other soccer. And you both shared one of the most important qualities when it comes to roommates: neither of you could stand a messy room or an unmade bed. In short, you got along great — definitely not a "roommate from hell" story like you might find on YouTube.

Until politics came up. One night a couple of weeks into the semester, you decided to make a late-night pizza run. Stopped at a traffic light, you called your roommate's attention to a "ridiculous" bumper sticker on the car in front of you. It read: "The Second Amendment: Protecting the U.S. from Oppression since 1791." Your roommate looked puzzled and asked: "What's the problem with that? It's true." It turned out that your roommate also believed in cutting taxes, outlawing abortion, and building a wall on the southern border to deal with illegal immigration. You couldn't believe it. Even though you'd never discussed politics, you assumed that you shared the same worldview — that you both supported abortion rights, health care for all, efforts to fight global warming, and citizenship for undocumented people.

Public interest groups like the Sierra Club and the National Rifle Association regularly call on their members to attend rallies and protests, meet at annual conferences to affirm their goals, and contribute money to the cause.

By the time you got back with the pizza, you realized that you didn't see eye-to-eye on any political issue — not guns, not immigration, not abortion, certainly not climate change. But you did learn that you had at least one thing in common when it came to politics — you both believed that people were too disengaged. You'd been living together for several weeks and had never had even one brief conversation about anything political. Most of your friends didn't seem to know or care much about politics. And your classmates didn't either.

So you made a pact to get more involved. You'd each join an organization that would allow you to become active around an issue you cared about. Your roommate decided to find a group that works to protect citizens' gun rights — which made sense, having come from a family of hunters who worried that the government would impose unfair restrictions on law-abiding gun owners. You chose to focus on the environment. Your mom, a high school science teacher, always talked about the importance of addressing climate change. The two of you agreed to keep each other posted on your quests to become more politically active.

This segment tracks your and your imaginary roommate's interest group participation as a way to highlight (1) the many types of groups citizens can join, (2) the reasons people become members of interest groups, and (3) how members of interest groups influence the political process.

Interest Groups in America

In the early 1830s, French diplomat and historian Alexis de Tocqueville observed that citizens in the United States were more "supportive of association" than people just about anywhere else in the world.[1] Wherever he traveled in America, he saw citizens (mostly White men at the time) creating and joining social clubs, community and church groups, and debating societies. Although Tocqueville didn't use these exact words, he basically concluded that America was a "nation of joiners." And that's still true today. The *Encyclopedia of Associations* identifies roughly 23,000 organizations that operate in the United States.[2] About 6 out of every 10 of adults belong to at least one group that focuses on social issues or civic life.[3]

Indeed, when you began investigating groups to join, you quickly learned that there's a group for almost everything. Your roommate found the American Cheese Society, a group that supports small cheese manufacturers and whose membership is open to "anyone who enjoys great cheese,"[4] as well as the U.S. Association of Reptile Keepers, a group of "veterinarians, researchers, breeders, manufacturers, feed producers, hobbyists and pet owners; collectively known as the Reptile Nation."[5] You were more drawn to the Catfish Farmers of America. Who doesn't like a group whose purpose is to "develop, stimulate, and encourage harmony, goodwill, and understanding among catfish farmers"?[6] The longer you stayed online, the more you came to appreciate the amazing breadth of groups that exist. If you're in the balloon industry and want to prevent helium shortages, a drone enthusiast who wants to ensure responsible recreational drone use, or a sports fan who thinks seats at sporting events should be more affordable, there's a group for you.[7]

Although many of the thousands of groups out there are amateur sports leagues, religious organizations, and clubs for people with similar hobbies, there are also lots of **political interest groups**—official associations of people with similar concerns who seek to influence public policy. Your searches also revealed that the most high-profile political interest groups are linked to people's professions or jobs. To join the American Medical Association, for example, you need to be a doctor. To join the National Realtors Association, you need to be, well, in the real estate business. Only teachers can be members of the National Education Association.

Of the five broad categories of political interest groups (see Table 1), four work very specifically on issues that advance the financial or professional interests of their members. Consider ExxonMobil. The oil company has a division charged with advocating for positions that can benefit the company and the energy industry. The company's website states: "We have a responsibility to our customers, employees, communities, and shareholders to represent their interests in public policy discussions that impact our business."[8] The American Bar Association is another example. The organization's Governmental Affairs Office serves as the "focal point for advocacy efforts before Congress, the Executive Branch,

Why do people join interest groups?

TABLE 1. Five Main Types of Interest Groups

Business or corporation	Division of a business or corporation devoted to influencing public policies to benefit the company.	**Examples:** ExxonMobil, Google, Walmart
Professional association	Organization of individuals who are licensed members of the same profession. Mission includes advocating for policies that promote and benefit the profession.	**Examples:** American Bar Association, American Medical Association, National Exercise and Sports Trainers Association
Trade association	Founded and funded by businesses that work in a particular industry. Seeks to influence policy on issues that affect members.	**Examples:** American Advertising Federation, American Gaming Association, Motion Picture Association of America
Labor union	Organization of workers formed to advance members' interests pertaining to wages, benefits, working conditions, and public policies.	**Examples:** Service Employees International Union, National Education Association, International Brotherhood of Teamsters
Public interest group	Pursues goals that benefit the broader population, not just the group's members. Anyone can join. Can focus on one or a broad range of issues.	**Examples:** American Civil Liberties Union, National Organization for Women, Habitat for Humanity

and other governmental entities" on issues including independence of the legal profession, independence of the judiciary, and citizens' access to legal services.[9]

Groups like these would be of no use to the two of you, and neither you nor your roommate would be eligible to join them anyway. You needed to find **public interest groups**, which are open to anyone. These groups mobilize citizens to take action around a particular policy issue and would offer you an opportunity to get out into the community and really do something to protect gun rights and the environment.

Your roommate's Google search eventually led to a list of more than 15 national gun rights groups and dozens of state-level organizations. The websites of Gun Owners of America, the Second Amendment Foundation, and the National Association for Gun Rights were all appealing. But ultimately, the biggest and most famous gun rights group of them all—the National Rifle Association (NRA)—seemed to be the best fit. Upon joining the national group (which required filling out an online application and paying the annual membership fee of $45), your roommate received an e-newsletter that listed all the ways to get involved.

Your own search was a bit more complicated. After googling "environmental interest groups," you found yourself immersed in lists of literally hundreds of international, national, and local groups fighting to protect the environment. Some focused specifically on protecting animals and wildlife. Others concentrated on fighting pollution—air, water, or land. Some made it their mission to ban plastic and other environmentally harmful items. Others were all about preserving local or national parks. And still others devoted their efforts to fighting climate change. After a long search, you chose the Sierra Club, one of the oldest and most well established environmental groups in the United States. The group's mission is broad: "To explore, enjoy, and protect the planet." You paid a $15 membership fee and looked forward to learning about ways you could get involved with your local Sierra Club chapter.

The Benefits of Membership

Interest groups can succeed only if they can attract and maintain members. The more members they have, the more time, energy, and resources they can devote to their mission. And the more clout they have with political leaders shaping the policies the group cares most about. Indeed, politicians take the NRA and the Sierra Club seriously largely because of their membership base—5 million people belong to the NRA, and 3 million are members of the Sierra Club. Not only do these members engage in direct citizen action, which we'll get to in a couple of pages, but they also pay dues. Multiply the 5 million NRA members by the annual $45 membership fee, and suddenly you've got a substantial operating budget of $225 million a year. This money allows the organization to maintain a headquarters, pay professional staff, and donate to political campaigns.

Interest groups try to attract members by enticing them with an array of benefits. The most straightforward is a **purposive benefit**—a sense of reward or purpose that comes from contributing to an important cause and working to achieve the group's goal.[10] That's why you and your roommate joined your respective groups. You feel a sense of purpose by contributing to the mission. And if the group succeeds, then your roommate maintains the right to purchase and use firearms, and you enjoy a cleaner environment.

For most of the economic groups listed in Table 1—labor unions, trade and professional associations, and businesses and corporations—

purposive benefits are basically all they need to attract members. These groups have relatively narrow goals that, if reached, provide their members with substantial advantages. If a teacher's union negotiates for higher salaries, only the teachers in the union benefit. So there are clear incentives for teachers to join. If the ExxonMobil oil company convinces the government to allow it to drill for oil on public lands that were previously off-limits, then only the corporation, its executives, and its shareholders reap the rewards.

For public interest groups, relying on the mission as the sole benefit to attract and sustain members is often not enough. Sometimes a group's mission and goals are so broad—such as "preserving democracy" or "reforming the criminal justice system"—that it's hard for citizens to grasp what being a member even means. Moreover, it's often the case that if a public interest group succeeds, even nonmembers benefit. If your roommate's membership in the NRA helps block laws that ban assault weapons, then everyone can buy an assault weapon, not just NRA members. If you help the Sierra Club pass a law that reduces air pollution, then everyone, not just Sierra Club members, gets cleaner air. To use a little political science jargon, public interest groups face a **collective action problem**—everyone benefits from the group's efforts regardless of whether they join. So rather than pay a membership fee and help the group advocate for gun owners' rights or wildlife protection, you can **free ride** on the efforts of the people who do join. You get the benefit without doing anything.[11]

Public interest groups are well aware of this problem, so they often try to entice potential members with more than a mere appeal to their sense of purpose.[12] Many groups provide a range of **selective benefits**—those that are available only to group members. There are two types. **Solidary benefits** include the friendships, networking opportunities, and camaraderie that people get by associating with a group of like-minded people. When your roommate attends an NRA rally or goes to an NRA-affiliated gun club, part of the experience involves meeting fellow gun rights supporters. When you show up at the Sierra Club's Environmental Film Festival or go on one of its many organized nature hikes, you'll get to know people who are just as concerned about environmental issues as you are. Solidary benefits are among the most important that an interest group can offer.[13] In fact, two of the main reasons people say they join interest groups are to work on issues that are important to them and because they know someone in the group.[14]

Beyond solidary benefits, public interest groups typically offer **material benefits**, too—actual goods and services provided only to group members. When you joined the Sierra Club, you received an insulated cooler

Members of the NRA and the Sierra Club receive material benefits as part of their membership.

tote and a subscription to *Sierra* magazine. As a member, you'll also get offers to attend group environmental trips at discounted rates.[15] Your roommate's NRA membership comes with the choice of one of four magazine subscriptions (*American Rifleman*, *American Hunter*, *America's 1st Freedom*, or *Shooting Illustrated*) and an NRA swag item. A $1,500 lifetime membership would come with a brushed leather jacket with an NRA logo.[16]

Material benefits are critical to some public interest groups' very existence. AARP (formerly the American Association of Retired Persons)—which focuses on improving the quality of life for older citizens—attracts its members by offering discounts on prescription drugs, travel, insurance, and entertainment.[17] AAA (or the American Automobile Association)—which plays an active role in shaping transportation policy—sustains itself by offering its members roadside assistance, maps, travel discounts, and reduced-rate car insurance.[18]

Your Role as an Interest Group Member

As soon as you joined your groups, you and your roommate began looking for ways to be active. Your roommate immediately became one of the more than 4 million members of the NRA's Facebook group, which provides updates on gun laws around the country. The "NRA Events" link on the drop-down menu of the main website also lists NRA activities in the area. So your roommate quickly found a "Friends of NRA" meeting just a couple of miles from where you live. Friends of NRA raises money to give grants to local organizations that teach about gun safety and the importance of the Second Amendment. Your roommate attended the meeting—which included dinner, guest speakers, a raffle, and games for kids—and also downloaded the NRA-ILA app (ILA stands for Institute of Legislative Action). The app delivers emergency alerts and links that allow members to send letters to political leaders about pending gun legislation. That night, your roommate contacted two members of Congress urging them to oppose a law that would require universal background checks for anyone who wants to buy a gun.

Your cause was different, but many of your interest group activities were the same. After joining the Sierra Club, you immediately followed the group on Twitter and Facebook. You also scrolled through your state's Sierra Club website to learn about volunteer opportunities. You chose to become part of the Clean Energy and Gray Wolf Recovery "teams." You signed up for online tutorials on how to contact and communicate with state and national elected leaders when they're considering important environmental legislation. You registered for a free Letter to the Editor Training Lunch, where you'll learn to draft and submit letters to the editor of the local newspaper.[19] And you were really excited about meeting fellow members at an upcoming creek cleanup event.

These experiences are typical techniques public interest groups use to exert influence over the political process. They tend to rely on **outside strategies**, which are ways that groups build broad public support by rallying their members to pressure elected officials. Letter-writing and email campaigns attempt to convince politicians to vote a certain way on legislation the group cares about. Protests and rallies make it clear to elected leaders that an energized group of citizens is concerned about a particular issue. And information campaigns are important, too. The more that people know about the dangers of environmental degradation, for example, the more likely they'll be to factor that issue into how they vote. Beyond these citizen pressure tactics, all groups—no matter the type—rely on **inside strategies**, which involve engaging directly with people at the center of power. These tactics include meetings with, and financial contributions to, elected officials. Inside strategies are especially common among the many types of economic and professional groups listed in Table 1.

You and your roommate hadn't been aware of all the ways you could get involved when you made your pact. But you both quickly learned that if you wanted to devote yourselves to your respective causes, you could be kept very busy—maybe even too busy—with NRA and Sierra Club activities. So you made another pact: you wouldn't comment on political bumper stickers again anytime soon!

DID YOU GET IT?
Why do people join interest groups?

Short Answer:

- Even though most Americans aren't very politically active, the vast majority belong to some sort of political, community, or social group.
- People often join public interest groups because they support the organization's mission.
- Because of the collective action problem, a sense of purpose may not be enough for a group to survive. Groups often offer selective benefits — solidary and material — to attract and maintain members.

DEVELOPING YOUR SKILLS

Civic Engagement

Engage with politics: Joining an interest group is one of the best ways to get involved with an issue you care about. And you have lots of options because thousands of political groups work to shape public policy. These questions allow you to spend some time exploring the interest group universe.

1. If you're interested in working to promote democracy and the integrity of the electoral process, which public interest group should you join? (Hint: Interest groups' official websites are the best way to learn about their priorities and positions.)

   a. Club for Growth

   b. Americans for Prosperity

   c. Common Cause

   d. Population Council

2. Your friend is an intern at the Family Research Council, a group that tries to influence abortion laws. If you fundamentally disagree with her views on abortion, which group should you join to push back against her efforts?

    a. People For the American Way

    b. NOW

    c. Susan B. Anthony List

    d. NAACP

3. If you want to start an interest group to fight for lower interest rates on student loans, which selective benefit would likely attract the largest membership?

    a. An email to the entire student body letting them know that student loan debt is a problem for your generation

    b. A compelling website with videos of recent graduates talking about the difficulties that come with large student loan payments

    c. A monthly happy hour open to all students with college debt to meet and commiserate with each other

    d. A one-on-one meeting with a financial planning expert who helps members of the group figure out how to consolidate their loans and get lower interest rates

FIGURE IT OUT

Given your interests and political views, identify an interest group in your community or state you could join or become involved with. To get started, google the issue you're interested in — like "gay rights" or "lower taxes" — along with "interest groups" and the state where you live. You'll likely get several options to consider. Once you've done this preliminary search, answer the following questions:

- List the issue you're interested in and the group that would provide you with an opportunity to work on it. Note the group's website, too.

- How did you determine that the group was a good fit for your beliefs? (One sentence is fine.)

- What, if any, specific purposive and selective benefits does the group offer?

- Describe the process you would follow to join or connect with the group.

Want to Know More?

Vote Smart compiled a directory of interest groups. The directory is great for political science students because it only lists groups that take an active role in campaigns and elections. When you select a particular group, you'll be able to see the candidates the group has endorsed (if any) as well as which elected officials share the group's positions.

Political Information, Knowledge, and News

Start Here!

When Speaker of the House Nancy Pelosi agreed to participate in an event hosted by the Center for American Progress, a liberal think tank in Washington, D.C., she never could have predicted what would happen next. Shortly after her remarks, which centered on her long-standing disputes with then-president Donald Trump, a three-minute clip of her speech began circulating online. And it wasn't good. The clip showed Pelosi slurring her words, swallowing the ends of sentences, and speaking very slowly. What had happened to the then-78-year-old Speaker? Maybe she was showing signs of age? Perhaps she was intoxicated or having a problem with prescription drugs? Had her escalating tensions with Trump caused her to lose it?

Regardless of the reason, something was very wrong with the Democratic leader of the House. That was clear to the more than 1 million people who viewed the speech on Facebook within the first 24 hours of the posting — a number that more than doubled by the next day. And it was clear to Trump. "She's a mess. . . . She's lost it," he concluded.[1]

There was just one small problem with the video. It was fake. An unknown source had doctored footage of the speech to slow down

Pelosi's cadence and give the false impression that she was impaired. Within a few days, news organizations began reporting on the manipulated video. Some even posted the actual speech and the doctored clip side-by-side. But the damage was done. Millions of people had already seen it without knowing the truth.

This example illustrates the complexity of navigating the contemporary universe of political news and information. Advanced technology, tech-savvy citizens, and online platforms are all it takes to make something real into something fake, to take information and turn it into fabrication. Yet democracy depends on an informed citizenry with access to quality information. Otherwise, people can't make appropriate decisions about who to vote for, how to hold elected leaders accountable, or what they think is the best direction for the country. As you'll see in the next five segments, diverse, readily available political information comes at people from all directions. And this onslaught complicates how we understand and critically analyze politics.

Three key features of the current information environment pose challenges for citizens who want to stay informed.

1 **Political information is everywhere.**
People have access to an array of political information and choose whether and how much political news to follow. Just as political junkies can indulge their interest nonstop, people who aren't politically interested can avoid political information altogether, selecting instead entertainment, sports programs, or even cat videos.

2 **Assessing the quality of news and information is difficult**.
Amid the dizzying array of information, facts sometimes seem incidental. To be an informed citizen today, it's not enough just to follow the news. You also need to consider news organizations' motivations for presenting information.

3 **The contemporary information environment can undercut democratic ideals.**
The internet promised to make it easier to get information and improve citizen engagement. But by heightening competition in the news business, blurring the lines between journalism and commentary, and facilitating the distribution of fake news, the expanded news environment often makes informed debate and deliberation difficult.

22.
Do people know anything about U.S. politics?

#PoliticalKnowledge

On Sunday, December 4, 2016, Edgar Maddison Welch burst into the Comet Ping Pong pizzeria in Washington, D.C., waving an assault rifle. The 28-year-old had driven from North Carolina to investigate a story that had been circulating on the internet. Hillary Clinton, the recently defeated Democratic presidential candidate, was allegedly running a satanic child sex ring out of the back room of the pizza place. One anonymous online post claimed: "Hillary has a well-documented predilection for young girls."[1] A labyrinth of underground tunnels supposedly connected the pizzeria to other shops and restaurants on the block, which made it easy to smuggle children around D.C. Welch couldn't stand by. He entered the pizza shop, terrorized the employees, and fired one shot. Welch surrendered after his search of the premises failed to turn up any hidden rooms or evidence of sex trafficking. He later told law enforcement officials that he "came to D.C. with the intent of helping people" and to relieve "the suffering of a child."[2]

The idea that Clinton was operating a pedophilia ring out of a pizzeria had started a couple of months earlier when a right-wing conspiracy theorist with 2,800 Twitter followers made the claim. As it began circulating on the internet, several websites took up the story and cited "credible sources" who confirmed the existence of an "international child enslavement and sex ring" run by Clinton and her campaign manager.[3] The sites even claimed — falsely — that the New York City Police Department had raided Clinton's home.[4] These online articles offered no verifiable evidence whatsoever — no photos, no eyewitness accounts, no police reports.

But Pizzagate, as it came to be known, was not just a fringe story for internet trolls, Hillary-haters, or deeply misguided individuals like Edgar Welch. Even after Welch found nothing at the pizza parlor, the story didn't die. A couple of weeks later, an *Economist*/YouGov poll found that 38 percent of people overall — and nearly half of Republicans (49 percent) — thought that some or all of the story was true. In fact, only 29 percent of people believed that it was definitely not true.[5]

And the legacy of Pizzagate lives on. Ten months after Edgar Welch fired his shot, someone calling himself "Q" began posting messages on 4chan — an anonymous online forum where people can post almost any content they want. He claimed that the Democrats' operation went

In March 2017, protesters arrived at the White House to demand further investigation into the unfounded allegations that Hillary Clinton was using a pizza place as headquarters for a child sex-trafficking ring. Misinformation about politics has only ramped up as Americans continue to embrace wild conspiracy theories about the 2020 election and the Covid-19 pandemic.

well beyond Comet Ping Pong; they were operating a worldwide network of child sex-trafficking and satanic rituals that involved drinking children's blood.[6] According to the theory, which came to be known as QAnon, top military generals had recruited Donald Trump to run for president in 2016 to break up this pedophilia ring and bring its members to justice.[7] A poll conducted just before the 2020 election found that 25 percent of all voters, and 50 percent of Republicans, believed that top Democrats were involved in child sex trafficking. Another third of Republicans said they weren't sure.[8]

How does this happen? How can so many people believe any portion of a patently absurd story for which there is absolutely no evidence? Commentators like comedian Bill Maher, the host of HBO's political discussion show *Real Time*, have a simple answer: it's because America is "a stupid country with stupid people who don't pay attention."[9] Google "Are Americans stupid?" and you'll see an avalanche of news articles, polls, snarky blog posts, and editorials that share Maher's view, including "We Are a Deeply Stupid Country"; "Why Are Americans So Stupid — And So Proud of It?"; "Dumb and Dumber Americans"; and "The Era of Stupid?"[10]

But is it fair to characterize Americans as not so smart when it comes to politics? This is an important question for at least two reasons. First, a well-functioning democracy requires an informed citizenry. After all, citizens who don't know much about politics often cannot perform the essential democratic task of holding elected officials accountable. Second, people who know more about politics are more likely to vote and participate in a broad range of political activities.

This segment offers an assessment of **political knowledge** — what citizens know about politics and government. You'll see that on some topics, the majority of the public has a basic familiarity with the U.S. political system. But on many others, the electorate is uninformed — often unable to answer simple questions about the U.S. government and how it operates. You'll also see that beyond being uninformed, many Americans are misinformed — they believe stories like Pizzagate. This is especially true when the story, as far-fetched as it might be, is consistent with their political views or espoused by political leaders they support.

Today's Poorly Informed Electorate

Demonstrating that Americans are terribly uninformed about politics is pretty easy. Americans know a lot more about reality TV stars and pop singers than they know about the members of Congress and cabinet secretaries who pass and implement the laws and policies that govern the nation. If you have any doubt, then just ask your friends whether they know anything about Billie Eilish, Lady Gaga, or Simon Cowell. Then ask them what they can tell you about Nancy Pelosi, Mitch McConnell, or Lloyd Austin. Or consider some striking survey results:

- 22 percent of Americans can name all five members of the Simpsons (yes, the cartoon family), compared to only 1 percent who can identify the five freedoms granted by the First Amendment.[11]

- 25 percent of citizens think the United States declared independence from a nation other than Great Britain.[12]

- 77 percent of Americans can name at least two of Snow White's seven dwarfs, compared to only 24 percent who can name at least two Supreme Court justices.[13]

- Only 34 percent of adults could find Ukraine on a map, a country that played a role in the first impeachment of Donald Trump and made constant headlines in its war with Russia.[14]

More broadly, a national survey of more than 40,000 Americans found that a majority of citizens in 49 states would flunk a U.S. citizenship test— an exam that includes basic questions about U.S. history and the government that all people applying for U.S. citizenship must pass. (Congrats to Vermont. You're the only state with a majority of citizens who can pass the test.)[15]

Survey questions like these begin to help us understand the limited extent of Americans' political knowledge, but they don't tell the whole story. We can't assess whether people are informed about politics simply by cherry-picking survey questions that would lead us to conclude that Americans are idiots. Rather, Table 1 presents three types of information that political scientists identify as key components of political knowledge.[16] The table's entries suggest that it's not fair to say that Americans know nothing about U.S. politics. More than three-quarters know the Electoral College formally selects the president. More than 8 out of every 10 Americans correctly identify the majority party in the Senate. And an overwhelming majority (86 percent) know the First Amendment guarantees the right to free speech. Not bad, right? That depends on whether you think it's a problem that three-quarters of Americans can't name the three branches of government. Or that only about one-third of people can name their mayor, state attorney general, or member of Congress.[17]

Table 1 also highlights why assessing whether the American people are uninformed is complicated. First of all, they know some things and not others. Second, it's not clear how much political knowledge is reasonable

TABLE 1. What Do Americans Know about Politics?

Knowledge of Institutions and Processes

Know the Electoral College formally elects the president	76%
Know the vice president casts the tie-breaking vote in the Senate	54
Know 60 votes are needed to end a filibuster in the Senate	41
Can name the three branches of government	26

Knowledge of Political Parties and Public Figures

Know the majority party in the Senate	83
Can identify the party of their member of the House of Representatives	53
Can name their member of Congress	35
Can identify their city's or town's mayor	35
Know how many Supreme Court justices are women	33
Can identify their state's attorney general	27

Knowledge of Political Issues and Public Policies

Know the First Amendment guarantees free speech	86
Receive Medicare but say they've never used a government social program	40
Receive food stamps but say they've never used a government social program	25
Know less than 1 percent of the federal budget is spent on foreign aid	5

Note: Entries indicate the percentage of people who can answer each question correctly or know the fact.

Source: Data from Pew Research Center, Annenberg Public Policy Center, *The Washington Post*, Weldon Cooper Center for Public Service, The Kaiser Family Foundation, and research from Danny Hayes and Jennifer L. Lawless. See Note 17 for full source information.

to expect. Take the filibuster as an example. Only 40 percent of Americans know that 60 votes are required to end a filibuster and pass a bill in the Senate. In an ideal, vibrant democracy, every citizen would know this. But that's not a realistic expectation. So how many people need to know it to make for a "healthy" democracy—50 percent? 70 percent? 90 percent? The answer's not obvious. And third, it takes only a split second to look up information on a smartphone. Just because people don't know a lot about politics off the top of their head doesn't mean that they can't easily become informed.

Of course, even though information is easy to come by, most people don't seek it out. So the fact that 95 percent of people think the United States spends more on foreign aid than it actually does, or that 40 percent of Medicare recipients don't realize they're benefiting from a government program, means that their opinions about the government's spending priorities will be based on incorrect assumptions, not facts. Despite the challenges involved in defining a clear standard for whether the electorate is informed, it's probably safe to conclude that in all three categories of political knowledge, Americans come up short.

Today's Misinformed Electorate

Beyond being uninformed, Americans are often willing to believe things about political figures and policies that fly in face of actual evidence or facts. We discuss where people access political information, as well as the advent of "fake news," in later segments. But suffice it to say, the internet and social media are providing citizens with immediate and unlimited access to an array of rumors, accusations, allegations, and falsehoods like never before. In 2009, for example, 30 percent of voters believed that the health care legislation that eventually became the Affordable Care Act ("Obamacare") created "death panels"—groups of bureaucrats who would decide who would get life-saving medical treatment and who wouldn't.[18] The bill included no such panels. More recently, roughly 20 percent of Americans reported believing in at least one far-fetched and unsupported claim about the Covid-19 vaccine—that it causes infertility in women, or implants a microchip in recipients, or is made from aborted fetuses, or has the power to alter human DNA.[19] Approximately 50 percent of the U.S. population thinks that immigration leads to higher crime rates.[20] In reality, researchers have found no connection between immigration—legal or illegal—and crime.[21]

The fact that Americans believe these sorts of falsehoods is important because these beliefs can shape people's views of policies and politicians. People worried about death panels were less likely to support health care reform. Parents concerned about the Covid-19 vaccine won't inoculate their children against the deadly disease. Citizens who think that immigrants are more likely to commit crimes tend to support stricter immigration policies.

Now, conspiracy theories are certainly not unique to politics. Polls continue to reveal, for example, that more than one-third of Americans believe that the U.S. government carried out the attacks on September 11, 2001.[22] Yep. They believe that the United States attacked itself. As many as 20 percent of Americans think the 1969 moon landing was a hoax.[23] That famous footage of astronaut Buzz Aldrin saluting the U.S. flag on the surface of the moon? Fake.

But many of the false stories people believe are influenced by their political beliefs. Democrats are more willing than Republicans to believe a negative story about a Republican politician, regardless of how implausible it might be. The reverse is true for Republicans.[24] Just take a look at Figure 1, which compares the percentage of Democrats and Republicans who believed four widely circulated stories that lacked any credible evidence.[25] Roughly equal proportions of Democrats and Republicans (about 1 in 4 people) viewed one story—that the U.S. government helped plan the September 11 terrorist attacks—as true. But the other three saw strong partisan divides. Democrats were almost 3 times more likely than Republicans to believe that the Russians literally tampered with the vote count in 2016 to ensure that Donald Trump won the presidency. In 2020, Republicans were 20 times more likely than Democrats—yes, this one is super polarized—to believe that Joe Biden became president only because the election was rigged and stolen.[26] When it came to the January 6 insurrection at the Capitol, Republicans were 5 times more likely than Democrats to believe that the rioters were a left-wing mob trying to make President Trump look bad.[27]

FIGURE 1. Political Conspiracy Theories Americans Believe, 2015–2021

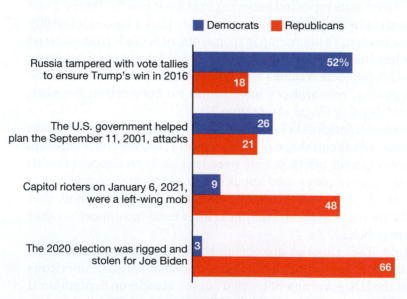

Note: The bars above represent the percentage of Democrats and Republicans who believed each statement was "definitely" or "probably" true.

Sources: *Economist*/YouGov poll and CNN poll.

Many of these stories may sound ridiculous to you. But it's impossible to overstate the extent to which false stories based on misinformation can gain a life of their own. A perfect example is the belief held by many Americans that former president Barack Obama was born in Kenya and not the United States. Non-native-born citizens aren't constitutionally eligible to serve as president, so "birthers," as they came to be called, thought that Obama's presidency was illegal. A number of forged Kenyan birth certificates even began circulating on the internet. Obama tried to put an end to the conspiracy theory by releasing his real birth certificate—which confirmed that he was, in fact, born in the United States.[28] But even five years later, 51 percent of Republicans still didn't believe it.[29]

Political conspiracy theories aren't new. Following President John F. Kennedy's assassination in 1963, rumors began to emerge that the gunman, Lee Harvey Oswald, had acted on behalf of foreign leaders, mobsters, or even the disgruntled husband of a woman with whom Kennedy had allegedly had an affair.[30] In the early 1990s, conservative commentators pushed out the story that Bill and Hillary Clinton had orchestrated the murder of White House counsel Vince Foster because he knew too

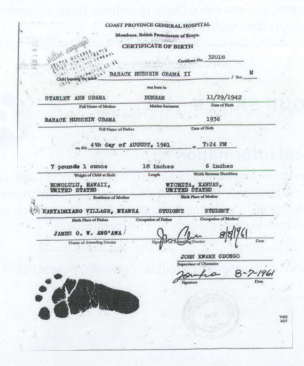

One of the numerous copies of Barack Obama's forged Kenyan birth certificate floating around the internet. This forger even took the trouble to include a baby footprint of the former president.

much about the couple's "shady" business deals.[31] With limited technology, though, conspiracy theorists had a more difficult time communicating with one another. The internet and social media now make it easy to circulate rumors or downright lies in a way that wasn't possible prior to the mid-1990s.[32] Today, stories like Pizzagate, election fraud, and killer vaccines can gain steam in a matter of days, quickly taking hold among people inclined to believe them.

DID YOU GET IT?
Do people know anything about U.S. politics?

Short Answer:

- People are quite uninformed about the way the U.S. political system works, key political figures, and public policy.
- Many Americans are also misinformed about politics, often willing to believe false claims and rumors even when there's no evidence to support them.
- Many Americans are more likely to believe false statements when they're about their political opponents.

DEVELOPING YOUR SKILLS

Consuming Political Information

Check the facts: Regardless of whether we're talking about government rules, political figures, or public policy, Americans are often uninformed. And that lack of information can make people more susceptible to believing falsehoods. Try to identify correct, verifiable facts about some controversial political and policy questions.

1. According to most experts and researchers, roughly how many people live in the United States illegally?

   a. 1 million

   b. 5 million

   c. 11 million

   d. 24 million

2. How did the violent crime rate change in the United States between the 1990s and 2020?

   a. It almost doubled.

   b. It increased by almost 50 percent.

   c. It stayed the same.

   d. It decreased by almost 50 percent.

3. In a typical year, roughly how many people die in the United States from gun violence?

   a. 30,000

   b. 40,000

   c. 60,000

   d. 300,000

FIGURE IT OUT

A friend tells you that without a doubt, Vice President Kamala Harris was involved in a sex scandal. Your friend even shows you a headline from the internet: "Kamala Harris Now at Center of Sex Scandal. . . ." Investigate your friend's claims to determine whether the story is true. More specifically:

- Come up with three different search terms to track down the information you'll need. Provide the exact wording of each search along with the search engine you used.

- List three sources (the names of the websites or organizations that discuss the story) you encountered when you conducted your search. For each source, note whether there's a lot, some, or no evidence of the Harris sex scandal.

- Based on your research, is your friend well-informed, uninformed, or misinformed? How did you arrive at this conclusion? (A couple of sentences is all you need.)

Want to Know More?

To become a U.S. citizen, you have to take a civics test. You receive 128 questions in advance, and when you go for the test you're asked a random set of 20 of them. If you answer at least 12 correctly, you pass the test. Go to the U.S. Citizenship and Immigration Service's website and see how you do: https://www.uscis.gov/sites/default/files/document/crc/M_1778.pdf.

23.
Should you believe the polls?

#MeasuringPublicOpinion

On any given day, you can find out what the American public thinks about almost any political issue or policy. Just google the topic you're wondering about, add the word "poll," and chances are you'll get a list of hits that tell you what people believe. Is climate change in the United States a crisis? Fifty-nine percent of Americans think so.[1] Should schools require eligible students to get Covid-19 vaccinations? Not according to 54 percent of parents.[2] Do people favor spending $1 trillion to improve U.S. infrastructure — roads, bridges, rail service, internet access? Most do, although they also worry about where the money will come from.[3] The death penalty, health care, legalization of marijuana, energy policy — name an issue, and there's a poll. Two-thirds of people favor stricter gun control laws;[4] 62 percent support making it easier for people to vote;[5] 47 percent think it was a mistake to send troops to fight in Afghanistan 20 years ago.[6]

During election years, you don't even have to look for polls. It's almost impossible to avoid them. In 2020, more than 1,000 polls monitored the presidential race. In the week leading up to Election Day, 122 polls — that's an average of 17 every day! — told people who was up, who was down, who was gaining ground, and who was falling behind in key states.[7] Sometimes pollsters even rush out to see how the public feels about people who have unequivocally said they won't run for president. Oprah Winfrey, you might be interested to

2020 DEMOCRATIC PRIMARY
NBC NEWS | THE WALL STREET JOURNAL

JOE BIDEN	31%	KAMALA HARRIS	5
ELIZABETH WARREN	25%	YANG	
BERNIE SANDERS	14%	AMY KLOBUCHAR	
PETE BUTTIGIEG	7%	CORY BOOKER	2

STEVE KORNACKI | MSNBC NATL. POLITICAL CORRESPONDENT

MSNBC

Public opinion polls are a constant feature of American politics. They're regularly the basis of news stories about campaigns, elections, and policy debates. But you shouldn't assume that poll results are accurate. Instead, you should run through the checklist we develop in this segment to help you assess whether you should believe the polls.

know, regularly defeated Donald Trump in match-ups heading into the 2020 election, sometimes by double digits. But she regularly lost to Joe Biden.[8]

Poll results represent much more than interesting tidbits of information about what citizens think about a political issue or figure. They play a fundamental role in shaping how politics plays out. When polls reveal that a president, senator, or governor's approval rating is slipping, high-quality challengers are more likely to enter the race.[9] When candidates do well in the polls, they generate more media attention and, as a result, typically raise more money for their campaigns.[10] Polls signal to voters whether a race is going to be close or a blowout, which is important because people are more likely to participate in competitive contests. And when polls indicate that voters care a lot about an issue, political leaders tend to emphasize it. Donald Trump's hard-line stance on immigration, opposition to gun control, and dismissal of climate change were all consistent with his most enthusiastic supporters' views. How did he know? He looked at the polls.

Given their prevalence and their influence, do polls accurately reflect public opinion? Can a survey of a thousand people really tell us anything meaningful about the views of more than 250 million American adults? Most people doubt it. In fact, a recent poll — note the irony — found that a majority of citizens don't trust polls.[11] Although that's understandable in light of the many pollsters who underestimated support for Donald Trump in both 2016 and 2020, polls — when conducted appropriately — are usually accurate. And that's important because in a democratic system, elected leaders need to know what the people think.

This doesn't mean, however, that you should blindly accept all poll results you see reported in the news, touted by campaigns, or promoted by political organizations. Quite the contrary. A healthy dose of skepticism is in order. This segment presents a 10-item checklist to use whenever you encounter **public opinion polls** — surveys of citizens that gauge the preferences and beliefs of the U.S. population or a subset of it. Keep in mind that one segment in this book can't cover every aspect of polling, which, when done well, is a complex, scientific process. But after reading the next several pages, you'll have the tools you need to think more critically about polls and to determine which results you should believe and which ones you should take with a grain of salt.

1. Is the pollster talking to the right people?

When you want to know what people think about a political topic, it's not feasible to ask every single person whose opinion you'd like to gather. Instead, pollsters identify a **sample**—a group of people whose responses they'll use to estimate the views of the population they're interested in. The poll's results, therefore, are only as good as the sample on which they're based.

If you're interested in finding out Americans' views on immigration reform, gun control, taxes, or any other public policy issue, then a national sample of the entire country works just fine. But for many other questions, a national sample would do you no good. How enthusiastic are young voters about the upcoming presidential election? You'd need to assemble a sample of 18- to 29-year-olds. Which candidate do voters prefer in the 2024 presidential race? The sample should consist only of people who are eligible to vote in that election. How are the presidential primaries shaking out? The sample should include only potential primary voters—and that can be tricky because different states have different rules for who can vote in primaries. In some states, only Republicans can vote in the Republican primary and only Democrats can vote in the Democratic primary. In others, voters choose the primary they want to vote in when they show up on Election Day.[12] The sample should be a subset of the group of people you want to study—and that's often *not* a subset of the entire U.S. population.

2. Is the sample representative?

Accurate poll results require a **representative sample**—one that approaches a microcosm of the population whose opinions you're trying to measure. If your sample doesn't reflect key demographic and political characteristics such as gender, race, age, income, education, religion, and party affiliation, you can wind up with skewed results. Imagine that you want to get a sense of whether the public favors cutting Social Security benefits. Roughly 16 percent of the U.S. population is age 65 or older.[13] And older Americans are more likely than younger people to oppose cuts to Social Security. After all, seniors often rely on these benefits in their retirement. If your sample overrepresents people who are 65 or older—perhaps they constitute 25 or 30 percent of it—then your poll might uncover greater opposition to the cuts than is actually the case.[14]

How the sample is compiled matters, too. You'll undoubtedly encounter a lot of online polls soliciting your opinion on everything from politics to your favorite movie, singer, or car. They might be fun, but the results typically don't provide an accurate picture of the overall public's preferences; they just represent the views of a group of people who opted to participate in the poll. The best way to achieve a representative sample is through **random sampling**—each member of the larger population has an equal chance of being chosen. The most common technique for assembling a sample like this is **random digit dialing**—a process in which a computer generates every possible 10-digit phone number in the United States and then randomly chooses which numbers to call. Anyone with any kind of phone has an equal chance of being called.

3. Does the poll include enough people?

For any poll, the **sample size** must be large enough to establish meaningful results. It's often indicated by the letter N followed by a number. But what is "large enough"—50 people? 100? 500? For most large populations—voters, residents of a city or town, the U.S. population—pollsters and statisticians have determined that a sample size of 1,000 ($N = 1,000$) is about right. This might sound dubious. The views of 1,000 people can really capture the opinions of millions? The answer is yes! Probability theory and pollsters' ability to weight the sample allow for pretty accurate results. We don't go into these concepts in depth here, but **weighting** means adjusting the poll results to ensure that the sample reflects the characteristics of the population of interest. It doesn't involve changing the answers to any survey questions, but it means counting some people's responses more heavily and others' less.

Just because a representative sample of 1,000 can do a good job gauging the opinions of 250 million adult Americans does not mean that the sample size required for a smaller population can be smaller. Polls of voters in the small town of Alpine, Texas, or the city of New York, or the state of Wyoming, or the entire country should all have about 1,000 respondents. And if you want to compare the responses of subgroups of the sample—say, you want to check for differences between women and men, Black people and White people, young people and senior citizens—then you need to have an adequate sample size for each subgroup as well. That's why in many cases the sample size exceeds 1,000.

4. Are the poll questions clear?

Pollsters have many choices for how to word a question. Typically, they go for closed-ended questions with yes/no, multiple choice, or "check all that apply" response options. Regardless of the question format, it's vital to step back and carefully consider whether the words themselves are straightforward and easy to understand. As obvious as this might sound, even professional pollsters sometimes fail miserably on this dimension.

One of the best examples of unclear question wording dates back to 1992, when Roper, a well-regarded polling firm, asked people whether they were sure the Holocaust—the German government's systematic imprisonment and murder of 6 million European Jews during World War II—actually happened. One-third of the people polled said it was either impossible or they weren't sure that this catastrophic event had ever occurred (see Table 1).[15]

TABLE 1. The Importance of Question Wording: The Holocaust Example

1992: Does it seem possible or does it seem impossible to you that the Nazi extermination of the Jews never happened?		1994: Does it seem possible to you that the Nazi extermination of the Jews never happened, or do you feel certain that it happened?	
Possible	22%	Possible that it never happened	1%
Impossible	65	Certain that it happened	91
Not sure	2	Not sure	91

Source: Michael R. Kagay, "Poll on Doubt of Holocaust Is Corrected," *New York Times*, July 8, 1994.

The results dismayed many historians and commentators, who concluded that our education system must be failing. It turned out that the problem wasn't the education system. It was the wording of Roper's question, which included a poorly constructed double negative. Indeed, when Roper used much clearer language to ask the question differently in 1994, 91 percent of people reported that they were sure the Holocaust had happened. Clearly, changes to the words in questions and answer choices can lead to very different results.

5. Do people know enough to answer the questions?

Polls often try to measure public opinion on complex political issues. And most people who agree to be polled will provide responses to the questions they're asked even if they don't know much about the topic. So you need to think about whether people have the baseline level of information required to answer the poll's questions in a meaningful way.

To see how this plays out, consider a 2018 poll that asked people whether they thought the United States should remain in the Iran nuclear deal. Only 21 percent of Americans favored continuing the agreement.[16] But when pollsters defined the deal in the question itself—noting that it's an agreement that the United States and five other countries entered into with Iran to prevent Iran from developing nuclear weapons—public support for remaining in the deal tripled (to 63 percent).[17] A lack of baseline knowledge doesn't apply only to foreign policy questions. When asked whether they favored a legislative agenda that would reduce the size of government, 71 percent of Americans reported that they did. But that was likely because they didn't know what a legislative agenda to reduce the size of government would entail. Indeed, the same people who wanted to reduce the size of the government also opposed cuts to Medicare (81 percent), Social Security (78 percent), and Medicaid (71 percent)—which constitute the three largest government programs.[18] When pollsters assume that people know about or understand the nuances of policies and programs, poll results can be misleading.

6. Do the questions reveal people's actual beliefs?

Poll questions can be general or specific. And response options can be limited or wide-ranging. So a little vagueness in a question or greater specificity in the possible answers can fundamentally shift public opinion.

Consider people's attitudes about the importance of having a strong military. When asked simply whether they agree or disagree that the best way to ensure peace is through military strength, 55 percent of Americans agree. But when the question asks whether the best way to ensure peace is through military strength or through diplomacy, a majority of people choose diplomacy. Only one-third choose military strength.[19] When the response option did not include diplomacy, many people just didn't think about it as a way to prevent war.

The same is even true for highly controversial issues that people have thought more about. Broad questions about abortion tend to find that roughly half of people consider themselves "pro-choice" and the other half "pro-life."[20] When pollsters ask more specific questions on the topic—such as when abortion should be legal or illegal—public opinion is much less divided. If a woman's physical health or life could be endangered by carrying a pregnancy to term, more than 8 out of 10 people support her right to end the pregnancy. The same is true if the pregnancy was caused by rape or incest. At the other end of the spectrum, a majority of the public opposes abortion when a woman doesn't want or can't afford to raise a child.[21] The more specific questions yield a much clearer picture of public opinion about abortion.

7. Does the question have a "right" answer?

Questions that elicit what researchers call **social desirability bias** can lead to inaccurate poll results. In these cases, people feel like there's a "right" or socially acceptable answer to the question. And they worry that if they don't give that answer, they'll be judged negatively by the pollster. That's why many people do not admit to pollsters that they watch pornography, cheat on their partners, or use drugs. The same dynamic applies to controversial or unpopular political attitudes and behaviors.

Asking about voting is a good example. People don't want pollsters to think that they've shirked their civic responsibility, so many say they've voted even when they haven't.[22] We know that people stretch the truth because we know how many people actually vote in a given election. And time and time again, the percentage of people who turned out to vote is considerably lower than the percentage who claim to have done so.

Social desirability bias also comes into play when gauging levels of prejudice. Citizens don't want to admit to being racist or sexist, for instance, so almost everyone reports that they're willing to vote for a woman or a candidate of color for president (see Table 2).[23] Yet some studies find a discrepancy between the percentage of people who tell

TABLE 2. Social Desirability Bias toward Different Demographic Groups

"If your party nominated a generally well-qualified person for president who happened to be _____ would you vote for that person?"	Yes	No
Black	96%	3%
Hispanic	95	5
A woman	94	6

Note: *N* = 1,024 adults nationwide. Margin of error ± 4.2.

Source: Gallup poll, April 17–30, 2019.

pollsters that they would support a Black candidate and the vote share that candidate actually receives. It's not always the case, but the effect does emerge in some political contexts.[24] Pollsters encountered a similar dynamic when it came to Donald Trump. Many polls underestimated support for Trump because voters—especially wealthy, educated ones—didn't want to admit that they planned to vote for such a divisive candidate.[25] All of this is to say that you should be careful when interpreting poll results around controversial topics that put respondents in a position to admit something unfavorable about themselves.

8. Did you consider the margin of error?

Polls are only an approximation, not a perfect reflection, of public opinion. When a poll uncovers that 60 percent of people disapprove of the Supreme Court's decision to overturn *Roe v. Wade*, for instance, it's unlikely that exactly 60 percent of Americans hold that view.[26] It's some number close to 60 percent. In other words, there's uncertainty surrounding every result. As soon as you see a poll, it's vital to determine the **margin of error**—an estimate of how close the poll result from the sample is to the actual population's opinions. The margin of error usually appears with the poll results.

To see how the margin of error affects the interpretation of poll results, look at Figure 1, which tracks public approval and disapproval for President Biden throughout the first six months of 2022.[27] At first glance, it looks like Biden's approval rating jumped around quite a bit. It was at a low of 37 percent in January but jumped to 45 percent in April. Upon closer inspection, though, that 8-point fluctuation might actually be nothing at all. And the margin of error is why.

As the note underneath Figure 1 indicates, these Gallup polls have margins of error of plus or minus 4 points. That means that the 37 percent approval rating in January could have been as low as 33 percent (37 minus 4) or as high as 41 percent (37 plus 4). Similarly, the 45 percent approval rating in April could have been as low as 41 percent (45 minus 4) or as high as 49 percent (45 plus 4). Notice that both estimates include a 41 percent approval rating. In other words, it's possible that in both January and April, Biden's approval rating was roughly the same. This was also the case for his disapproval ratings—from January to June, all of the fluctuations from one month to the next fell within the margin of error.

The margin of error relates to the sample size. A sample size of about 1,000 can provide reliable results—it has a margin of error of about 4 points. If you increase the sample to 1,500, the margin of error falls to 3 points. Beyond that, there's really little added value when it comes to the margin of error. For a sample size of 2,000, it's still close to 3 points (2.7 to be exact). Samples smaller than 1,000, however, have margins of error that lead to very imprecise estimates. With a sample size of 100, the margin of error is plus or minus 10 points. A sample size of 50? You're dealing with a 14-point margin of error.

FIGURE 1. President Biden's Approval Ratings, January–June 2022

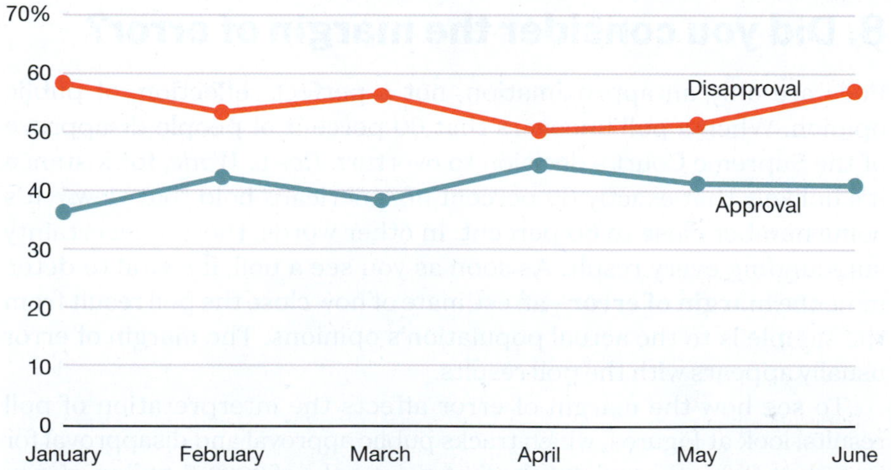

Notes: Question read: "Do you approve or disapprove of the way Joe Biden is handling his job as president?" Sample sizes approximately 1,000 adults nationwide. Margin of error ± 4.

Source: Gallup.

9. Did a trustworthy source conduct the poll?

Candidates and their campaigns release poll results. Political organizations with specific policy agendas release them, too. As do news organizations—some mainstream and some you've probably never heard of. So you need to assess whether a poll is from a source you can trust. As a general rule, almost any poll conducted in conjunction with a major news organization or university upholds the scientific standards of polling—the sample, question wording, and reporting of results tend to be reliable. This doesn't mean the poll is flawless, but it was likely carried out using appropriate techniques. If you're not sure which polling firms to trust, look at Table 3, which lists some of the most reputable pollsters as well as some of the worst-performing ones.[28] You can also google the name of a pollster to learn more about the quality of the poll.

Beyond considering who conducted the poll, it's important to think about the media source reporting on it. Partisan news outlets tend to pick and choose, reporting only on polls and poll questions that support their political positions. Liberal outlets, like MSNBC and the Huffington Post,

TABLE 3. Pollster Report Cards, 1998–2021

"A" Grades	"C," "D," and "F" Grades
ABC News / *Washington Post*	American Research Group
Fox News	ccAdvertising
IBD/TIPP	McLaughlin & Associates
Landmark Communications	Mitchell Research & Communications
Marist College	SoonerPoll.com
Monmouth University	SSRS
Research & Polling Inc.	SurveyMonkey
Selzer & Company	Swayable
Siena College/*New York Times* Upshot	
SurveyUSA	

Note: Entries represent the complete list of polling firms that conducted more than 25 polls from 1998 to 2021 and received from Nate Silver an "A+" or "A" or a grade of "C+" or worse for accuracy in predicting election outcomes.

Source: "FiveThirtyEight's Pollster Ratings," FiveThirtyEight.

often highlight polls that show solid approval ratings for President Biden and the agenda he's trying to enact. The opposite is true for conservative outlets, such as Fox News and the Drudge Report. They tend to cover polls that emphasize low favorability of Democratic politicians and their policies. For any poll, be sure to look at the questions and the margins of error to confirm that the news outlet doesn't misrepresent the results.

10. Does the poll's timing raise concerns?

Polls are typically conducted over the course of a week, and any good poll identifies the dates. It's important to consider the timing and political context of those dates. Polls about gun control reveal higher levels of support for new gun restrictions when they're conducted soon after a highly publicized mass shooting.[29] Similarly, when people are polled in the aftermath of a terrorist attack, their attitudes about refugees, fear of terrorism, and trust in government can shift.[30] This doesn't mean that these poll results are inaccurate, but it does suggest that they can reflect short-term fluctuations in public opinion linked to political events.

Timing also matters for election polls. The news media often start conducting polls and reporting on voters' preferences more than a year before Election Day. The results might be interesting, but they probably don't mean much because most people haven't even begun to think about the election a year ahead of time. That's why these early polls don't have much predictive capacity. They didn't favor future president Barack Obama in 2007. And they certainly didn't forecast future president Donald Trump in 2015. In fact, political analyst and statistician Nate Silver is skeptical of polls conducted more than three weeks out from an election.[31]

Evaluating Your Checklist

The checklist we provide gives you the necessary tools to think critically about poll results and how to interpret them. If a poll fails to meet one of the criteria we lay out, it doesn't mean you should disqualify it altogether. No poll is perfect. But you also shouldn't automatically decide that a poll that checks off 8 or 9 boxes on the 10-item list is excellent. One big mistake in question wording or timing can render meaningless an otherwise perfectly executed poll. Basically, you just need to be thoughtful and deliberate when you see a news report about poll results. Now that you're familiar with some common missteps, you can decide how much confidence you want to place in the polls you come across.

DID YOU GET IT?
Should you believe the polls?

Short Answer:

- Yes. Most polls reported in the news media have been carried out by organizations that use scientifically valid methods.
- Still, you should consider the sample and question wording, both of which affect the results.
- It's also important to assess the source and margin of error, which can influence how you should interpret the results.

DEVELOPING YOUR SKILLS

Quantitative Literacy

Interpret the numbers: Quantitative literacy is particularly important for analyzing poll results. The following questions ask you to consider a series of specific polls and interpret them in light of the checklist we presented in this segment.

1. *New York Times*/Siena College conducted a poll of registered voters nationwide in July 2022. Based on the results below — which appeared in this format on PollingReport.com — what can you conclude about Biden's lead over Trump?

   New York Times/Siena College Research Institute Poll. July 5–7, 2022. N = 849 registered voters nationwide. Margin of error ± 4.1.

   "If the 2024 presidential election were held today, who would you vote for if the candidates were Joe Biden, the Democrat, and Donald Trump, the Republican?" Options rotated

	Joe Biden (D)	Donald Trump (R)	Someone else (vol.)	Would not vote (vol.)	Unsure
	%	%	%	%	%
7/5–7/22	44	41	4	6	4

   a. Biden is leading Trump by 3 points.
   b. Biden is leading Trump, but the lead could be as little as half a percentage point.
   c. Given the margin of error, the candidates are statistically tied.
   d. It's impossible to conclude anything about Biden's lead because the sample is too small.

2. Here's a screenshot of a Fox News poll from 2018. It tracks people's views on legalizing marijuana. What additional information would give you more confidence in the trend revealed in the poll?

FOX NEWS POLL

LEGALIZING MARIJUANA

	FAVOR	OPPOSE
NOW	59%	32%
2015	51%	44%
2014	50%	43%
2013	46%	49%

JANUARY 21-23, 2018
REGISTERED VOTERS ± 3% PTS.

a. Poll results for 2012

b. Information on the sample and margin of error for each year, not just 2018

c. The percentage of people who responded "don't know" or "unsure" each year

d. Specific dates for the 2013, 2014, and 2015 polls

3. On the following page are the results of an OZY/SurveyMonkey poll about the things people associate with patriotism. Would you say these results are probably accurate, or should we be skeptical of them? (Hint: You'll have to look up OZY and SurveyMonkey for information about their methods.)

a. It's probably accurate. The graphic provides all the information necessary to evaluate the poll.

b. It's probably accurate. The question is clear and doesn't invite social desirability bias.

c. Be skeptical. The percentages don't add up to 100 percent.

d. Be skeptical. The polling firm doesn't rely on national random samples.

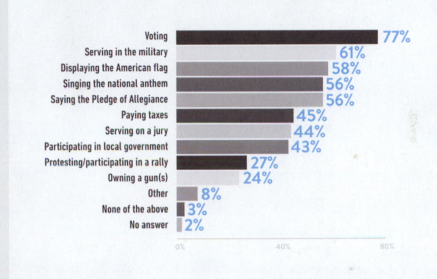

OZY ASKED: WHICH OF THE FOLLOWING THINGS DO YOU ASSOCIATE WITH BEING PATRIOTIC? (RESPONDENTS COULD SELECT MORE THAN ONE ANSWER.)

Voting	77%
Serving in the military	61%
Displaying the American flag	58%
Singing the national anthem	56%
Saying the Pledge of Allegiance	56%
Paying taxes	45%
Serving on a jury	44%
Participating in local government	43%
Protesting/participating in a rally	27%
Owning a gun(s)	24%
Other	8%
None of the above	3%
No answer	2%

POLL CONDUCTED BY OZY AND SURVEYMONKEY 2018

FIGURE IT OUT

The best way to apply what you've learned about proper polling techniques is to draft your own poll questions and apply parts of this segment's checklist to them. So choose a political topic you're interested in — immigration, race relations, the environment, you name it — and try your hand at being a pollster. More specifically:

- Compose two closed-ended questions about the issue you've selected. Make one a leading question where you try to guide the respondent to a particular answer. The other should be a question that is written as objectively as possible.

- Explain how you think the same respondent might answer the two questions differently.

- If you actually conducted your survey among your fellow classmates, would the results be generalizable? In developing your answer, be sure to consider the composition of the sample and the sample size.

Want to Know More?

For an amusing take on why you need to be skeptical of polls, check out Anderson Cooper's RidicuList from February 8, 2019. The two-minute segment offers an analysis of a poll the Trump campaign sent to supporters following the former president's State of the Union address (https://www.cnn.com/videos/politics/2019/02/08/trump-state-of-the-union-survey-ridiculist-cooper-sot-ac360-vpx.cnn).

24.
Why do you hear more about politicians' sex scandals than the bills they propose?

#Newsworthiness

Political events happen all day, every day. The latest tweet or statement from the president. Developments in U.S. relations with North Korea, China, Russia, and Afghanistan. Reports on the economy (Will it tank?), climate change (How serious is it?), crime (Is it on the rise?), the opioid crisis (What can we do about it?). Upcoming elections. Proposals to address mass shootings, exploding health care costs, and illegal border crossings. Supreme Court decisions. You get the point: the number of possible stories about government, politics, and policy is endless. So the **news media** — journalists, editors, and commentators who deliver information to citizens — ultimately decide which news stories to cover and emphasize. They determine what's newsworthy. Without them, citizens wouldn't have the information they need to participate in the democratic system.

Anthony Weiner, a disgraced former Democratic member of Congress, leaves a New York courthouse after pleading guilty to texting inappropriate photos to underage girls. Matt Gaetz, a Republican member of Congress from Florida, is under investigation for sex trafficking a minor. The media determined that both stories were newsworthy and, as a result of sustained coverage, Weiner and Gaetz became household names.

From the 1940s to the 1980s, news organizations, which were almost exclusively daily newspapers and television stations, deemed something newsworthy if it would likely have a direct impact on a significant number of people. A journalist's job was to provide citizens with information about key political leaders, war, the economy, major legal or policy changes, and critical developments in campaigns and elections. As Walter Cronkite, the lead anchor for the *CBS Evening News* from 1962 to 1981, summarized: "The profession of journalism ought to be about telling people what they need to know."[1] During this "golden age of journalism," deciding what people needed to know wasn't always easy, but the goal was clear.

Also clear was the industry norm of **objectivity**, which required that journalists present information in a nonbiased, balanced, fair way. If you search YouTube for news clips from the 1960s and 1970s, you'll find newscasters reading dry, fact-based descriptions of the day's main events — even highly controversial and dramatic ones. That's how they covered the Vietnam War in the 1960s. It's how they reported on President Richard Nixon's resignation a decade later.

So rare was it for a journalist to take a clear position on a political issue that when Walter Cronkite did, the nation listened. Upon returning from a trip to Vietnam in February 1968, he concluded, while delivering the evening news, that it "seems now more certain than ever that the bloody experience of Vietnam is to end in a stalemate."[2] Contrary to reports from the president and other political leaders, Cronkite told the American people that the United States was not winning the war. His words mattered because 81 percent of Americans considered Cronkite "someone you could really trust."[3] Following the broadcast, antiwar sentiment increased, and the public's attitudes toward U.S. involvement in Vietnam began to change. Although many commentators now question the extent to which objective coverage of important issues really did dominate this so-called

Why do you hear more about politicians' sex scandals than the bills they propose?

golden age, the news media generally aspired to these ideals.[4] Indeed, news organizations sought to keep people hooked by serving as trustworthy sources that delivered important information to the public.

The appeal of that brand of news began to change in the 1980s — for at least two reasons. First, more competition. CNN burst on the scene as the first 24-hour cable news network. Political talk radio became a thing, and Rush Limbaugh skyrocketed to fame and fortune by offering conservative political commentary to almost 20 million listeners every week. Rollouts of Fox News and MSNBC followed in the mid-1990s. By the early 2000s, Yahoo and Google began aggregating news stories as part of their web browsers. And when Facebook launched in 2004, Twitter in 2006, and Instagram in 2010, citizen journalists, bloggers, and a mushrooming number of political pundits were eager to use these new social media tools to transmit their own analysis of all things political. Nightly newscasts and daily newspapers were no longer the only game in town. News organizations had to fight for audiences.

Second, large conglomerates began buying up broadcast networks, local television stations, and newspapers. In 1983, 50 companies owned 90 percent of the TV stations, radio stations, magazines, and newspapers in the United States. By 1992, that number was down to 25. By 2000, only 6 companies controlled 90 percent of the media.[5] The new owners — many of whom had no background in journalism — rejected the idea that it was "enough" for a news organization to report on important events and build trust with an audience. Rather, they insisted that their news divisions generate large and growing profits.[6]

As the news environment radically changed in just a couple of decades, so did the industry's definition of newsworthiness and the value it places on objectivity. Although many news outlets espouse high journalistic standards (for example, major newspapers, television networks, and internet news sites often have codes of ethics), increasing competition and consolidation demand a laser focus on how to maximize viewers, readers, clicks, and, ultimately, profits. That's the only way a news organization — regardless of whether it's local or national, objective or partisan — can stay in business. This segment demonstrates how news organizations' profit-seeking motives shape what they cover and how.

News as a Business: Attracting an Audience

With the expansion of the media environment—first with the introduction of cable TV and then with the internet—consumers' news preferences have come to matter more than ever.[7] Outlets don't survive if they don't provide consumers with what they want or need. Newspapers are a perfect example. In 1990, newspaper publishers employed about 455,000 people around the country. By 2020, thousands of papers had closed or merged, and Sunday circulation—the biggest day of the week for newspapers—was roughly half of what it had been 30 years earlier.[8] The number of newspaper jobs was down to less than 175,000.[9] Why the decline? Because there are so many other ways people can learn what's going on. If you want to know who won the special election, how your favorite sports team did, or whether it's going to rain, you can find out in real time. Why wait for the morning paper when CNN.com, ESPN.com, and Weather.com are at your disposal? Indeed, internet news and information sites have been adding jobs at twice the rate newspapers have been cutting them.[10]

Consumer preferences also affect the content of news. When given a choice about which news to consume, most people don't choose politics. They prefer stories that shock, titillate, and entertain. Throw in a celebrity, and it's even more appealing. To get a sense of the market for "news," take a look at Table 1, which lists the top internet searches and stories that went viral in 2021.[11] The top 10 Google searches involved a real crime drama, a celebrity death, sports highlights, and a TV show.

TABLE 1. Internet Searches in 2021

Top News Stories Based on Google Searches	Top Viral Internet Stories
1. NBA Highlights	1. Man trapped by grizzly bear
2. Death of rapper DMX	2. Gorilla glue girl
3. Disappearance and death of Gabby Petito	3. Biden removes Trump's Diet Coke button
4. Trial of Kyle Rittenhouse	4. Gabby Petito's disappearance
5. Murder suspect Brian Laundrie	5. UFOs
6. Mega Millions lottery	6. Oprah's interview with Prince Harry
7. AMC Stock	7. Iceland's four-day workweek
8. Stimulus check	8. Bernie Sanders's mittens
9. Georgia Senate race	9. Ship stuck in the Suez Canal
10. *Squid Game*	10. Flight attendant duct tapes passenger

Sources: "NBA, DMX, Gabby Petito Stand Out on Google's 2021 Year in Search Trends," ABC7 News, December 8, 2021; Michelle Butterfield, "Year in Review: The Most Viral News Stories of 2021," Global News, December 31, 2021.

Why do you hear more about politicians' sex scandals than the bills they propose?

Politics? Just the special election for a U.S. Senate seat in Georgia, which would determine party control of the chamber. A couple of political stories made it into the top 10 viral videos, but they were puff pieces about the removal of a Diet Coke on demand button from the Oval Office and a senator's mittens.

Because many citizens have little taste for serious political stories, news organizations attract audiences by dramatizing the political news of the day. Even news executives, editors, and reporters who might long for the golden age of journalism have a business to run. That's why determining what's politically newsworthy in this day and age often comes down to content that can be portrayed as negative, conflictual, or sensational.

"The Sky Is Falling!"
If It's Negative, It's Newsworthy

When was the last time you saw a headline that read "Medicare Provides Health Care to 44 Million Americans"? How about "Air Pollution Down due to Enforcement of the Clean Air Act"? The answer is probably never. That's not because good news never happens. It's because people just aren't that interested in it. Research shows that citizens are more likely to read, watch, and click on negative stories. One study found that news headlines containing the words "never" or "worst" have much higher click rates than headlines with the words "always" or "best."[12] Another found that words like "cancer," "bomb," and "war" attract far more attention than "baby," "smile," or "fun."[13]

Competition for viewers means that political coverage reflects this **negativity bias**. Depending on the topic, as much as 90 percent of political news is negative.[14] And it doesn't really matter what the source is—network news, cable news, and the internet all highlight death, despair, destruction, and dysfunction (see Table 2). What's more, they have a tendency to produce a negative story even when a positive one is possible.

"You're an Idiot!" "You're a Pathetic Tool!"
If It's Conflictual, It's Newsworthy

Conflict is a second central feature of contemporary political news coverage. Part of the reason is that politics is often about competing interests. Congress versus the president. The president versus the media. Democrats versus Republicans. Citizens versus corporations. Name the issue, institution, or idea, and it can almost always be conveyed as two sides standing in stark opposition ready to debate. The news media present the news this way for a reason: psychologists have long known that people navigate toward conflict; they just can't look away.[15] So news

TABLE 2. A Typical Day's Political Headlines

ABC News	CNN	Politico
Jurors See Gruesome Video of Parkland Shooting	Ted Cruz Says Supreme Court Was 'Clearly' Wrong about 2015 Same-Sex Marriage Ruling	It's Not Just Hunter Biden: Prepare for a 2023 Packed with House GOP Investigations
Never-Ending GOP Primaries Mark New Republican Normal	Why the US Is So Horribly Incapable of Meaningful Climate Action	Pandemic Overdose Deaths Spiked among People of Color
Democrats' Infighting Threatens to Overshadow Remaining Agenda	Biden Lashes out at Reporter over Polling Question	Without Congressional Action 29 Million Americans Could Lose Access to Care
Army Likely Won't Meet Recruiting Goals this Year	Guantanamo Detainee Cleared for Release after 20 Years of Detention without Trial	False Georgia Electors Are Deemed Targets of DA Criminal Probe
House Democrats Arrested at Abortion Protest at Supreme Court	Trump-Backed Arizona Senate Candidate Escalates Election Fears ahead of GOP Primary	Chill from SCOTUS Climate Ruling Hits Wide Range of Biden Actions
Biden Executive Actions on Climate to Fall Short of What Activists Want	CNN Poll: Most Voters Say Neither Republican nor Democratic Congressional Candidates Have the Right Priorities	Indiana Doctor Moves toward Suing AG Who Threatened to Charge Her over 10-Year-Old's Abortion

Note: Entries are based on political coverage included on each news source's website for July 19 and 20, 2022.

organizations, eager for an audience, place a premium on pitting one side against the other in both the delivery and content of political information.

More specifically, heightened competition has fundamentally changed the format of news. In the 1980s, there were very few political debate programs. Only CNN's *Crossfire* had much of a following. The program had two co-hosts—one liberal and one conservative. The hosts and their guests duked it out over the issues of the day. Now, every single night, CNN, Fox News, and MSNBC air hours of programming filled with opinionated and argumentative guests, from politicians to political commentators to reporters themselves.[16] Sometimes the hosts just give

Why do you hear more about politicians' sex scandals than the bills they propose?

Bickering and extreme rhetoric are typical of prime-time cable news programs. Eye-rolling, anger, shock, and surprise are all on vivid display as these programs try to ramp up the entertainment value of the news they cover.

up, sit back, and enjoy the fireworks as angry, rowdy, disruptive guests fight it out on air. As long as both sides are represented—no matter how loud or superficial the debate—some programs can claim that they've provided balanced coverage. Other programs don't even attempt to be balanced. But that doesn't mean that conflict isn't alive and well. These programs assemble panels of like-minded commentators who discuss their political opponents' positions and usually arrive at the same conclusion: regardless of this issue, they're right, and their political foes are either utterly evil or completely incompetent.

Consumers' thirst for conflict affects not only the style but also the content of news. Health care reform, immigration policy, Supreme Court appointments, taxes—pretty much all substantive issues—tend to be treated as a contest between two sides. Politics and strategy suck up far more of the storylines than the nuts and bolts of proposed legislation.[17]

Elections are another prime example. Because campaigns in the United States drag on for so long, the news media fixate on winners versus losers, who's ahead versus who's behind in the polls. **Horse race coverage**—which focuses on the competition involved in an election rather than details of the candidates' policy positions—dominates the presentation of election information. One study of presidential elections found that roughly two-thirds of all news stories focus on who is up and who is down.[18] Another calculated that in the 2016 presidential primaries, 89 percent of coverage focused on the polls, campaign strategy, and tactics.[19] Even in 2020, as the nation grappled with the Covid-19 pandemic and Donald Trump and Joe Biden a rticulated very different ways to address the crisis, horse race coverage dominated broadcast and cable news networks' reporting on the presidential election.[20]

"'Bigfoot Erotica' Takes Center Stage"
If It's Sensational, It's Newsworthy

In a consumer-driven market, news organizations that can make people gawk have a better shot at building and sustaining an audience. **Sensationalism**—the use of exciting language, visuals, and content to attract people's attention—serves as the third principle undergirding the presentation of news. And it can take many forms.

Writing headlines that highlight unusual or surprising events is perhaps the simplest way to draw attention. In a hotly contested race in Virginia's 5th congressional district, for example, reporters couldn't resist covering candidate Denver Riggleman's interest in the legendary creature Bigfoot.[21] In particular, they were drawn to his self-published book entitled *The Mating Habits of Bigfoot and Why Women Want Him*.[22] Reporters delighted in writing articles with titles like the one that opened this section. This and other stories from campaigns—such as "Candidate Pepper Sprays Himself in Ad"[23] and "Candidate Spends Campaign Funds for Rabbit Air Travel"[24]—don't carry much in the way of national importance but certainly turn heads.

Hyping the immediate importance of "new" news is another technique. Television stations flash "news alert" or "breaking news" across their screens to signal to viewers that whatever they're about to tell them is really important. News alerts sent to smartphones provide people with "important" information as it happens. Yet we've reached the point where almost none of these stories contains critical pieces of information that citizens must have right away (see photos on the next page). CNN actually returns from *every* commercial break with a screen that reads "BREAKING NEWS." It also sends an average of 10 smartphone news alerts—every day—to people who have downloaded its app. The *Wall Street Journal*, Buzzfeed, Fox News, and *USA Today* also send out multiple alerts to their subscribers daily. The gold medal goes to the *New York Times*, though, which has been known to send out as many as 16 alerts on a single day.[25]

Finally, the news media love truly salacious stories. Google the names of politicians like Gary Hart, Bill Clinton, David Vitter, and Mark Foley and you'll see what we mean. Letting the American public know when high-profile politicians get caught up in scandals is important. But the amount of attention devoted to these scandals is striking. In 2017, for instance, porn star Stormy Daniels alleged that she'd had an affair with Donald Trump and that he paid her hush money to keep the story quiet during his presidential campaign. There's no question that the allegations were newsworthy; they involved a sitting president who may have violated campaign finance laws and lied about it. But did the allegations really merit pictures of Daniels—alone, with Trump, strapped

Why do you hear more about politicians' sex scandals than the bills they propose?

To help hold viewer interest, television news stations often run a stream of bold, conflictual, and sometimes absurd chyrons across the bottom of the screen.

to a polygraph machine—all over the media for months? Did they really require her lawyer to do more than 120 news interviews?[26] If you google "Stormy Daniels" and "Trump," you get more than 6.3 million hits.

The news media also became obsessed with the story of disgraced congressman Anthony Weiner, who pled guilty and was sentenced to prison in 2017 for sexting with underage girls. Again, the story was objectively newsworthy. The behavior began when Weiner was a member of Congress and continued as he tried to resurrect his political career as a candidate for mayor of New York City. But the news media couldn't get enough of the story—or the fodder it provided for headlines. "Pop Goes the Weiner,"[27] "Too Hard to Stop,"[28] and "Weiner's Pickle"[29] were among the most eye-catching. So, too, was the up-close shot of Weiner's bulging underwear that he had intended for a private message but mistakenly posted publicly on Twitter.

And we'd be remiss not to mention the barrage of news coverage that centered on Katie Hill, who was elected to Congress in 2018. Allegations arose that Hill had sex with a member of her staff, which violates ethics rules in the House of Representatives. The media loved the story because it came with pictures. Millions of people viewed nude photos of Hill in compromising positions and smoking marijuana. The story was also juicy because it involved "revenge porn"—Hill accused her estranged husband of leaking the photos. The congresswoman decided not to stick around for a full investigation and more embarrassing media coverage. Instead, she resigned less than a year after winning the seat.[30]

Any Chance This Will Change?

The short answer: no. Citizens claim they want the news to focus on serious topics. They report that they want to see more coverage of education, science, and corruption. They want to hear more about the economy and foreign policy.[31] They say they're tired of celebrity gossip and trivial stories. They believe the news media select the wrong stories to cover and that the coverage is often too dramatic and too negative.[32] On an abstract level, perhaps people do want more serious stories presented in a less splashy way. But as long as their viewing habits favor what's negative, conflictual, and sensational, that's what news organizations will continue to deliver. Because that's where the money is.

DID YOU GET IT?

Why do you hear more about politicians' sex scandals than the bills they propose?

Short Answer:

- Because news organizations are businesses that compete to attract consumers.
- Economic imperatives mean that consumer preferences play a major role in how the media decide what to cover and how to cover it.
- Most citizens are not very politically interested, so news organizations appeal to them by presenting politics as negative, conflictual, and sensational — all characteristics that Americans tend to seek out when following the news of the day.

Civic Engagement

Stay informed: Engaged citizens must understand the news landscape and distinguish substantively important political news from sensationalized coverage. In other words, you need to be on the lookout for coverage that can inform you versus coverage that is simply trying to grab your attention with drama and conflict.

---

1. Which of the following news stories should you read if you want information about a policy issue that might affect millions of people?

   a. "Proposed Changes to Health Care Law to Affect People with Pre-Existing Conditions"

   b. "Polls Show Republicans and Democrats Agree on Little as Congress Convenes"

   c. "Progressive and Moderate Democrats Exchange Snipes While Debating the Future of the Party"

   d. "Trump Developing Policy Message as He Contemplates Running in 2024"

2. You just read CNN's politics page and saw a bunch of sensationalistic headlines. Upon a closer look, though, which of the following headlines actually does offer news value for people trying to follow politics?

   a. "Congresswoman Uses Profanity to Argue That President Biden's Election Was Not Legitimate"

   b. "Republicans Accuse Democrats of Hypocrisy in Battle over Immigration Policy"

   c. "Congressman Throws Wife under Bus in Dispute with Neighbor"

   d. "Don't Drink the Water! The Environmental Protection Agency Says H_2O Quality in the U.S. Worse Than Expected"

3. Congress is debating a bill that would ban assault rifles. If you wanted to get the facts and avoid sensationalism, what's the best way for you to follow the debate?

   a. By watching evening political talk shows on both CNN and Fox News

   b. By reading a CNN.com story about which party will benefit from the bill in the next election

   c. By consistently scanning breaking news alerts from MSNBC on your phone to see how the debate is progressing

   d. By reading coverage of the debate published by the Associated Press

FIGURE IT OUT

Even engaged citizens don't always know how to follow the news in their communities. And once they figure out how to access local news, they still need to scroll through headlines and make choices about which stories to read. Are the news outlets in your community dramatic, or are they more like what we would expect in the golden age of journalism? In order to answer this question, do the following:

- Go to the website of one local newspaper and one local TV station in the area where you live.

- Identify the first three political stories you encounter on each site.

- For each story, note whether the headline is sensationalized and how you arrived at your determination.

Want to Know More?

The Newsroom, an award-winning television drama that ran on HBO from 2012 to 2014, chronicles the trials and tribulations of ACN, a fictional news network that finds itself caught between the lofty goal of providing serious news coverage of important events and the ever-present quest to attract viewers. (The romantic relationships among the news anchor, editors, and reporters are pretty captivating, too.)

Why do you hear more about politicians' sex scandals than the bills they propose?

25.
How do you know if you're reading fake news?

#SoMuchPoliticalInformation

Your alarm buzzes. When you pick up your phone to turn it off, you notice two news alerts — one from CNN ("North Korea Tests a Weapon") and one from Apple News ("Celebrate the Pulitzer Prize Winners").

You open your web browser on the way to check email and see the morning's headlines on Google News — "How Much Money a Single Person Needs to Get By in Every U.S. State," "Violence Erupts in Ukraine," and "Biden Pledges to End Gun Violence."

When you scan your email, you notice that your mom sent you an article about terrorism in the Middle East. It's a Breitbart.com opinion column entitled "Biden's Disastrous Foreign Policy Is Spiraling Out of Control." She's always sending you anti-Biden stuff, which is hardly surprising given that she thinks the 2020 election was rigged and that Donald Trump actually won the race. She also included a second link — this one to an article entitled "Hillary Clinton Sold Weapons to ISIS." You've never heard of the source but make a mental note to read the article later.

You stop for coffee on your way to school. Waiting for your order, you peruse the headlines of a local newspaper that someone left on

CPAC
NATIONAL HARBOR, MD
10:29 AM ET

2017

AMERICAN
CONSERVATIVE
UNION

CPAC
2017

FOX NEWS channel

PRES TRUMP: FAKE NEWS IS THE ENEMY OF THE PEOPLE

FOX NEWS ALERT

Donald Trump regularly labeled NBC, CNN, the *New York Times*, and the *Washington Post* as "fake news" and the "enemy of the people." But just because a politician labels a story "fake" doesn't mean that it is.

the counter. Apparently, the state education department bungled an investigation, candidates for county executive will hold a debate tomorrow night, and state police are cracking down on drivers who use cell phones. Heading out the door, you catch a snippet of an MSNBC program playing on the TV above the counter. The show's host gleefully speculates that the Justice Department will pursue criminal charges against Trump for trying to pressure election officials to overturn the results of the 2020 election. Not exactly your mother's view!

Back in the car, your regular music station does its usual two-minute summary of news at the top of the hour. More on the situation in Ukraine, as well as the president's approval rating, the latest unemployment numbers, and last night's NBA scores.

Throughout the school day, your friend keeps DMing you about a news report that popped up in her feed. It's about how the polar ice caps are melting faster than anyone realized. As a science major, she's obsessed with this story. So obsessed, in fact, that when you get back in the car to go home, you discover that your beloved music station has been replaced with National Public Radio (NPR). The same friend borrowed your car at lunch and probably hoped to catch a polar ice cap story.

At home, you flip on the TV and head to the kitchen to grab some food. When you come back, *ABC World News Tonight* is on. You catch about three seconds of a story about a Justice Department press conference and then quickly look for something else. This is what old people watch. As you're flipping through the channels, your roommate comes in and tells you to turn to the local news: "There was a suspected shooter on campus today! TV cameras were all over the place." (It turned out to be a false alarm.)

So far on this regular school day, you've come into contact with 12 different news sources without even trying. And the day's not over yet. You often watch at least part of *The Daily Show with Trevor Noah* or *Late Night with Seth Meyers*—both of which focus on the day's headlines—before going to bed. Your experience isn't unusual. Many citizens report getting news multiple times throughout the day—some from social media and news websites, others from TV, radio, and newspapers (see Figure 1).[1] TV is the main source of news for people over the age of 50. By contrast, a majority of young people consult online news sources regularly.[2] Regardless of the source, citizens can get news updates constantly if they want them—and often even when they don't.

With so much news coming from so many sources, how are you supposed to navigate this avalanche of often-conflicting information? What are facts, what's just opinion, and how do you distinguish between the two? How can you differentiate a balanced news outlet from one that's pushing a particular perspective? And what about "fake news"? What is it, and how do you identify it? This segment prepares you to traverse the increasingly complex news landscape.

FIGURE 1. Americans' Main Sources of News, 2021

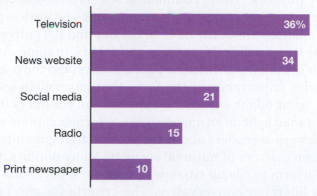

Note: Bars represent the percentage of people who report that they get news "often" from each source.

Source: Elisa Shearer, "More than 8 in 10 Americans Get News from Digital Devices," Pew Research Center, January 12, 2021; Mason Walker and Katerina Eva Matsa, "News Consumption across Social Media in 2021," Pew Research Center, September 20, 2021.

Straight News versus Pure Punditry

News and information come in many forms—from lengthy, detailed newspaper articles (in print and online) to podcasts, panels of "experts" arguing on cable TV, and 45-second TikToks. And the quality of this news and information varies considerably. So the first thing you need to do when confronting political information is determine whether it's fact-based journalism or commentary.

The gold standard for political news is authentic **journalism**—information that's produced after a rigorous process of research and verification. Quality journalism involves at least three elements:

1. The reporter, when possible, relies on multiple sources to gather facts and draw conclusions.

2. The reporter corroborates the accuracy of the story and the facts provided by sources.

3. Before the story is published or aired, a professional news editor reviews it to make sure the reporter followed appropriate and ethical journalistic practices.[3]

The news divisions of most major local and national newspapers, television networks, and news magazines adhere to the practices of quality journalism. But in the internet age, it's common for unconventional news sources that don't follow these practices to publish articles, too. Keep in mind that these stories often don't have multiple sources and haven't undergone review by a professional editor.

A lot of political information you'll encounter is not the result of quality journalism. Rather, it's analysis of political developments delivered by **pundits**. These commentators—typically social critics, policy experts, former political leaders, or people who work in politics—share their opinions about the news of the day and tell citizens how to interpret the latest political headlines and events. In some cases, pundits use their experience to help the public understand the background or the broader importance of the facts that journalists uncover. A former FBI agent might explain how the bureau conducts investigations so as to shed light on an ongoing case. A former cabinet secretary might tell viewers or readers about the process that goes into briefing a president on matters of national security. Many pundits, however, use their platform to rile up citizens to fight for a particular political cause, be it liberal or conservative. The criteria for good punditry often include who has the inside scoop, who is the most entertaining, who makes the most provocative argument, or who says or writes the most outlandish things.

How do you know if you're reading fake news?

CNN politics   The Biden Presidency   Facts First   US Elections

LATEST HEADLINES

Risks abound for both parties in uncertain Senate races

ANALYSIS

A January 6 committee witness was just censured by the Arizona Republican Party

Another election denier just won a big GOP primary

New post-Roe reality hits home in Texas, while Democrats move to protect marriage and contraception from Supreme Court

Most major news organizations now blur straight news and punditry. On CNN's Politics homepage, straight news appears in the left column and analysis and opinion pieces appear on the right. Headlines for both are similar in style, though, so many readers may not see a clear distinction between the two types of information.

The distinction between journalism and punditry can be quite blurry because the same outlets often include both. You can watch a hard-hitting interview with a politician on a network news program, like *Meet the Press*, and then watch a roundtable of pundits—on the very same program—dissect and critique every word of the interview. You can click on CNN's website and see, often in the same list of stories, an article summarizing an important news event and an opinion piece offering a perspective on it (see images below). If you rely on Google News, Yahoo, or another **news aggregator**—an internet-based news source that compiles stories and commentary from other news organizations—then the situation is even more complicated. The source appears alongside each article, but sometimes it's a journalistic account and other times it's pure opinion.

To evaluate the quality and accuracy of the news you're consuming, think about whether what you read or see is based on documented and verified evidence or simply someone's opinion. And if it's commentary, consider whether those opinions are based on genuine knowledge and expertise. Remember those 12 news sources you encountered throughout your day? The NPR segment you heard in the car on the way home from school, the local newspaper you skimmed at the coffee shop, and the evening news program you quickly turned off all adhere to journalistic practices. The Breitbart article your mom sent you bashing Biden as well as the cable news host's speculations about Trump are commentary. You might find some pundits' analysis quite persuasive, but you need to remember that it often fails to meet journalistic standards for accuracy.

Balanced Reporting versus Ideological News

The next critical step in being an informed news consumer involves determining whether an outlet strives to present an independent, balanced assessment of the day's events. In other words, are the news organization and its reporters committed to a fair presentation of political issues and developments?[4] Offering a balanced assessment doesn't mean that the news source treats all sides of every issue equally or that it never arrives at a conclusion. It simply means that the journalist will consult a variety of sources, consider competing perspectives, and write or air a story based on where the facts lead.

Major newspapers' coverage of the 2021 Covid-19 relief bill proposed by President Biden and passed by Congress serves as a good example. The *Washington Post* ran a story entitled "Congress Adopts $1.9 Trillion Stimulus, Securing First Major Win for Biden."[5] The piece laid out the various components of the package—$1,400 to most Americans, an extension of unemployment benefits, and money for Covid-19 testing, contact tracing, and vaccine deployment—and the largely partisan vote. The reporter provided quotes from Democratic members of Congress explaining why they supported the bill as well as comments from Republican members explaining their opposition. The *Wall Street Journal* offered a similar set of facts to readers in "House Passes $1.9 Trillion Covid-19 Stimulus Bill; Biden to Sign Friday."[6] Most of the stories you'll read in major newspapers or watch on network news broadcasts follow a similar model—they offer a balanced presentation of information based on verifiable facts.

Ideological news sources, in contrast, embody a clearly political perspective. This often means that they're explicit in their support for, or opposition to, certain policies and political leaders. The Huffington Post, a liberal online news source, falls into this category. In an article entitled "Thanks to the Covid-19 Relief Bill, Parents Could Soon Be Getting Regular Checks," the reporters focused entirely on how the bill helps the middle class and lifts people out of poverty. Nowhere did they raise Republicans' concerns about wasteful spending or the logistics involved in distributing the money.[7] The approach doesn't mean that the story lacked accurate economic and health data, well-sourced facts, or in-depth reporting. But the accurate data and well-sourced facts included in the piece were only those that helped promote a liberal viewpoint. In a similar vein, outlets like Breitbart ("Democrats Want Covid Welfare Provisions to Last Well beyond the Pandemic Itself"[8]), Newsmax ("Dems' Covid Bill Dedicates $36 Billion Subsidy to Obamacare"[9]), and Fox News ("Toomey Calls Out Covid Relief Bill's 'Litany of Outrageous Items'"[10]) serve up a steady diet of news emphasizing only the conservative perspective.

How do you know if you're reading fake news?

TABLE 1. Ideological News Outlets

Liberal	Conservative
CNN.com opinion pages	American Spectator
Daily Beast	TheBlaze
Huffington Post	Breitbart
The Intercept	The Daily Caller
Mother Jones	The Federalist
MSNBC	Fox News
The Nation	*National Review*
New York Times opinion pages	*New York Post*
Slate	Newsmax
Vox	*Wall Street Journal* opinion pages

Classifying news outlets as liberal or conservative isn't an entirely straightforward process. Reporters at major newspapers—the *New York Times*, the *Washington Post*, and the *Wall Street Journal*, for instance—strive to offer balanced coverage of political developments. This is also true of most daily local newspapers in cities across the country. But the papers' editorial boards, political columnists, and opinion pages tend to skew either liberal (the *Times* and the *Post*) or conservative (the *Journal*). Still, most observers agree that certain outlets are clearly ideological. Table 1, while not exhaustive, can serve as a guide when you're consuming news.

Fake News versus "Fake News"

Ten days prior to his inauguration in January 2017, Donald Trump held a press conference. In the course of answering reporters' questions, the president-elect denied allegations that Russia had compromising information on him and condemned the U.S. intelligence agencies that had "leaked" details about it. He used the press conference as an opportunity to criticize the news organizations that covered the story. Trump singled out BuzzFeed, which he called a "failing pile of garbage," as well as CNN, whose reporting he labeled a "disgrace." When CNN's White House correspondent, Jim Acosta, attempted to ask a question, the president refused the request. "Your organization is fake news," he told Acosta, ushering in what quickly became a well-known refrain.[11] Over the course of the next year, the president used the term "fake news" more than

150 times in speeches, interviews, press conferences, and tweets.[12] Its use was so prevalent that *Collins Dictionary* and the American Dialect Society both named it 2017's Word of the Year.[13] A Google search of "fake news" returns more than 70 million hits.

If you're going to be an informed consumer of the news, then you obviously have to know whether a story is real or fake. What makes this distinction somewhat complicated is that the term "fake news" has two definitions. The first one—which we'd call **fake news** with no quotation marks—traces back to 1890. It refers to stories that have no factual basis or those that represent major distortions of a kernel of truth. These sorts of false stories are much more prevalent in the internet age than they were when the term first originated because today anyone can create a web page, publish a fake news story that looks and sounds very real, and have it reach potentially millions of citizens. Recent examples include a Somali immigrant throwing a boy off a balcony in a mall in Minnesota (not true), a Muslim woman's arrest for planning an attack on the Notre Dame Cathedral in Paris (didn't happen),[14] and Congresswoman Alexandria Ocasio-Cortez's proposal to ban motorcycles (doesn't exist).[15] These stories—which gained traction in some media outlets, especially online—are simply not true. Social media sites like Twitter and Facebook try to clamp down on fake news by shutting down the accounts of users who regularly traffic in misinformation. In the last three months of 2020 alone, Facebook banned more than 1 billion accounts.[16]

The second definition of **"fake news"**—in quotation marks—is actually a misuse of the term. Here politicians label stories and news organizations they don't like as "fake news." It doesn't matter whether the stories are true or the outlets legitimate.[17] Trump regularly used the term "fake news" to describe, well, everything. News reports critical of his interactions with foreign leaders? Fake. Investigations into his presidential campaign? Fake. Stories about people quitting his administration? Fake. Accounts of his administration's response to a devastating hurricane in Puerto Rico? You guessed it—fake.[18]

It's not just Trump who invokes the term "fake news" when stories are unflattering or could potentially tarnish his image. Congressman Mo Brooks, on his official website, referred to the "Fake News Media" multiple times when defending himself against claims that he played a role in inciting the January 6, 2021, insurrection at the Capitol.[19] Priscilla Giddings, an Idaho state legislator, told her constituents that reports of her primary residence being outside her district were "fake news."[20] Florida state legislative candidate Melissa Howard accused a local newspaper of pushing "fake news" after it reported—based on evidence provided by Miami University—that Howard had lied about graduating from the school.[21] There's no question that politicians disliked these stories. But they were all true and based on accurate reporting.

If you're not sure whether to believe something you read, we offer two recommendations. First, consider the type of news it is and the outlet it appears in. One analysis published in *Forbes* magazine identifies 10 news sources you should feel comfortable trusting (see Table 2).[22] It's unlikely that you'll come across falsehoods, misstatements, or spin when dealing with these outlets. And when they do make mistakes, reputable news outlets like these are careful to print or air corrections. Some political leaders don't like the names on this list, but each has an excellent reputation for fact-based, fact-checked, well-sourced reporting. Second, as a basic rule of thumb, be skeptical when a political leader claims something is "fake news" or "media misinformation," especially if the story paints the person in a negative light. Candidates and elected officials often condemn news reports as fake, misinformed, or unreliable as a way to distance themselves from undesirable coverage.[23]

Navigating the news landscape involves an attentive eye and a series of considerations. And even then, you might feel unsure of exactly what to believe. But at the very least, you should now be better equipped than you were yesterday to deal with all of the news that comes at you tomorrow.

TABLE 2. Organizations with a Reputation for Presenting Fact-Based News

The New York Times

The Economist

The Washington Post

BBC

THE WALL STREET JOURNAL.

POLITICO

REUTERS

Bloomberg NEWS

AP Associated Press

FOREIGN AFFAIRS

Source: Paul Glader, "10 Journalism Brands Where You Will Find Real Facts Rather than Alternative Facts," *Forbes*.

DID YOU GET IT?

How do you know if you're reading fake news?

Short Answer:

- Content coming out of major news organizations tends to adhere to journalistic standards that involve research and verification.
- But you still need to assess whether the material you're looking at is well-researched journalism or political commentary, as well as whether the news organization you're consulting provides balanced or ideological coverage.
- As for "fake news," most of it isn't fake. It's a term used by politicians to discredit news stories they don't like.

DEVELOPING YOUR SKILLS

Consuming Political Information

Consider the source: The news and information universe is vast. Build your skills as a news consumer by differentiating among sources and applying the core concepts we covered to some online searches for political information.

1. Increasingly, news aggregators offer people a convenient way to follow the day's events. Which of these websites is a news aggregator?
   a. CNN.com
   b. Breitbart.com
   c. DrudgeReport.com
   d. Newsmax.com

2. FoxNews.com and CNN.com use the same technique for classifying political stories as news versus commentary. Go to the home page of each, and determine which of the following statements is accurate.
   a. Both websites mix commentary and news stories on their home pages with no distinction between articles based on opinion and articles based on fact.
   b. Both websites mix commentary and news stories on their home pages, but they cue readers with a color-coded scheme as to which stories are news and which are opinion.

c. Both websites have separate Politics and Opinion pages. The two types of news never appear on the same page.

d. Both websites have separate Politics and Opinion pages, but their home pages frequently mix news stories and opinion pieces.

3. The story below is typical of the news coverage you'll see on The Political Insider's website (thepoliticalinsider.com). Based on the information you can glean from the headline, coupled with your assessment of the news practices of the website, is it fake news?

NEWS

Utah students who are caught without masks in school may be hit with criminal charges, even kindergarteners

BY POLIZETTE STAFF
AUGUST 22, 2020

MARIE CREVIS, SHUTTERSTOCK

a. No, it's real. The website's stories are generally well sourced, and most of its news reporting is balanced and conducted by professional journalists.

b. No, it's real. The headline is a bit provocative, but that's just how the website grabs readers' attention. The site generally provides balanced reporting.

c. It's probably not entirely made up, but the provocative headline is an extreme interpretation of the facts. The website is known for pushing conspiracy theories.

d. It's fake news. Most of the stories featured on the site don't even include real people.

What kind of political information do these three popular news sites offer?

1. HuffingtonPost.com (internet-based news source)
2. FoxNews.com (cable TV news source)
3. NBCnews.com (network TV news)

More specifically, for each site:

- Identify a headline for a political story that follows the practices of authentic journalism.
- Identify a headline for a political story that is commentary, not journalism. For each, note the author, that person's relevant background, and whether it's balanced or ideological.
- Identify a political story on each site that a contemporary politician might claim is "fake news." For each, explain why he or she might do that.

Want to Know More?

If you want to have a little fun with fake news, check out the satirical newspaper *The Onion* (theonion.com). You'll never have to wonder whether stories are fake because they are all absurd. Here are some of our favorite recent political headlines: "Infrastructure Talks Come to a Halt after Giant Sinkhole Swallows Capitol Building," "Supreme Court Votes 5–4 to Reclassify Women as Service Animals," and "Men Fired in Wake of #MeToo Movement Come Forward about How It Took Them Several Hours to Find New Jobs."

26.
Why do Fox News and CNN viewers see politics so differently?

#MediaEffects

If you turn on Fox any night, it is the CNN, MSNBC criticism channel. They almost always lead with something we are doing that they hate, and they hate [it] because we're actually talking about real news.

Don Lemon,
CNN host[1]

They never talk about America's greatness, America's success . . . [They] just hate Trump all day long. That's what the world sees through the CNN lens.

Sean Hannity,
Fox News host[2]

One of the biggest challenges we have to our democracy is the degree to which we don't share a common baseline of facts. If you watch Fox News, you are living on a different planet than you are if you are listening to NPR.

President Barack Obama[3]

News organizations have discretion over what to cover and how to cover it. Fox News and CNN present and shape the news to tell very different stories about what's happening in the political world.

If you want to know what's going on in the political world, all you need to do is check a website or two, turn on the news, or read the paper. Armed with the day's headlines, you'll be good to go, right? Not quite. These days, the news you get all depends on where you look. According to longtime journalist Ted Koppel, "The day's events are conveyed to the viewing public by way of alternate universes." Citing an example of this phenomenon, Koppel concludes that "the Fox News cable channel conveys its version of reality, while at the other end of the ideological spectrum MSNBC presents its version."[4]

How is it possible for two news organizations — observing the same political events and the same cast of political characters — to portray the news of the day so differently? The answer lies in the discretion that news organizations have when deciding what to cover and how to cover it. Certainly, economic concerns drive the news business — that's why negative, conflict-ridden, and sensational political stories have such an easy time making their way into the headlines. But how much to emphasize any one story or topic, which aspects of it to cover, and how to discuss its consequences depend on the news organization's goals and the composition of its audience.

This segment compares CNN and Fox News to demonstrate how the media can shape content to affect and reinforce citizens' perceptions of political news. We focus on these news sources for a couple of reasons. First, they're among the most popular outlets for national news about politics and government in the United States.[5] Second, their prime-time programs, comprising both journalism and commentary, are

Why do Fox News and CNN viewers see politics so differently?

so different from one another that comparing the two outlets allows for a clear illustration of the choices news organizations make when presenting news to viewers. Although this segment uses Fox News and CNN as primary examples, the central concepts we cover apply to any news outlet — newspapers, broadcast TV, radio, websites — you might encounter.

By the end of the segment, you'll have a clear understanding of how the news media can affect (1) the political news citizens see, (2) the way people evaluate politicians, (3) how the public views various policies, and (4) Americans' attitudes about people who don't share their political views. Essentially, you'll develop a sense of how it's possible for two citizens to be avid news consumers yet have completely different perceptions of the nation's biggest political problems, who's to blame, and what the government is doing to address them.

Deciding What's News

News organizations have tremendous discretion in deciding what to publish or broadcast. And if no one reports on a political topic, figure, or event, then it never becomes "news." Just think about it. If the news media didn't report on events in your city, state, Washington, D.C., or around the world, you'd never know what occurred. The news media's power of **agenda setting**—determining what to cover and, thus, what's important—is essentially the power to tell people what to think about. Crime is a good example. When television news focuses on crime instead of other issues, people think a lot more about it. So much so that if you want to know how concerned citizens are about crime, the amount of attention the evening TV news devotes to it does a better job of predicting citizens' fear of crime than the actual crime rate does.[6]

To see how agenda setting plays out on cable news, consider Fox News and CNN's prime-time political coverage. One typical day in October 2022, Tucker Carlson, the top-rated host on the Fox News channel, opened his broadcast by condemning President Biden's Ukraine policy for leading to fuel shortages that will destroy the global economy. Beyond this lead story, Carlson and the other two prime-time news program hosts on Fox featured stories entitled "Kids Forced to Endure Sexualized Performances," "Athlete Complained to School about Male in Locker Room," "The Most Uninteresting Candidates are Democrats," "RNC Wins Slew of Legal Challenges before the Election," and "Townhall with Florida Governor Ron DeSantis."

If you want to see the "different planets" that President Obama referred to in the quote that opened this segment, compare these

FATHER FIGHTS BACK AGAINST TRANSGENDER BATHROOM RULE IN DAUGHTER'S MIDDLE SCHOOL

FOX NEWS 8:24 MT | THE INGRAHAM ANGLE

MIDTERM ELECTIONS
BIDEN BLASTS ELECTION DENIERS AS THREAT TO U.S. DEMOCRACY
LIVE
DOW ▼ -133.04

▶ JIM BANKS (R) | INDIANA CONGRESSMAN
BIDEN, DEMS HAVE SPENT $3.8 TRILLION SO FAR

The two cable networks emphasize different news stories, often at the exact same moment in time. Agenda setting is evident in the two leading headlines on Fox and CNN on June 21, 2022.

Fox News stories to some of those that ran during the same three prime-time hours on the same night on CNN. These stories covered the following content:

- Parents of Uvalde Shooting Victims Demand Answers
- January 6 Rioter Who Attacked Capitol Police Officer Sentenced to 7 Years in Prison
- Republicans Vow Policy Changes, Probes If They Win Control of Congress in the Midterm Elections
- Biden Seizes on Rebounding Economy 12 Days to Midterms

Depending on which channel you watched, you'd have an entirely different perception of the most important political issues and problems facing the country. The upcoming midterm elections were the only topic to receive substantial coverage on both networks.

Setting the Criteria for Evaluating Politics

Most people aren't political junkies who follow the inner workings of government and know intimate details about the players. Rather, they rely on the news media to provide them with critical information about politics. Because there are so many ways to think about political figures and policies, the news media engage in **priming**—establishing the criteria by which people assess political candidates, elected officials, and issues. When the *Wall Street Journal* or the *Washington Post* mentions quarterly jobs reports in a story about the

FOX NEWS 3:42 PT
GAS PRICES HAVE DOUBLED SINCE BIDEN TOOK OFFICE
INFLATION ‣NATION‣

BREAKING NEWS
DR. ANTHONY FAUCI GIVES UPDATE ON BIDEN ADMIN'S VACCINE EFFORT

The two cable networks regularly cover the president by priming different contexts and topics. The criteria you're encouraged to use to evaluate political leaders depend on what you're watching.

president, for example, it's cuing audiences to think about the president in relation to the economy. When there's coverage of decreasing unemployment rates, a president may get a bump in the polls. Bad economic news, in contrast, can often cause a president's approval rating to take a hit.[7]

One way to highlight how news networks prime citizens to think about political leaders is by taking a look at the banners—also called chyrons—that run across the bottom of the screen. That's how Fox News, CNN, and most cable news stations summarize the stories they're covering and emphasize how viewers should think about them. As an example, Figure 1 compares the frequency with which certain words were included in each network's chyrons during a five-month period of Donald Trump's presidency.[8] For each word, the bar represents the percentage of chyrons including the word that appeared on CNN compared to Fox News.

Notice that CNN regularly primed viewers to evaluate President Trump by linking him to controversial figures from his campaign, his administration, and beyond. For example, of the total number of banners the two networks ran that mentioned Trump's scandal-plagued former national security advisor, Michael Flynn, 73 percent appeared on CNN. CNN was also far more likely than Fox News to cover President Trump in relation to Vladimir Putin, Russian interference in the 2016 election, and Special Counsel Robert Mueller's investigation of it. Fox News, on the other hand, primed viewers to think about the Trump presidency through the lens of the economy (wages, economic growth, the Dow Jones, and gross domestic product). In fact, whereas Fox News featured the Trump tax cut policy more than 130 times in news banners, CNN never did. Not even once. Whether viewers evaluated Trump in relation to scandals or as presiding over a strong economy depended on their news source.

FIGURE 1. Fox News and CNN Chyrons Priming Evaluations of President Trump

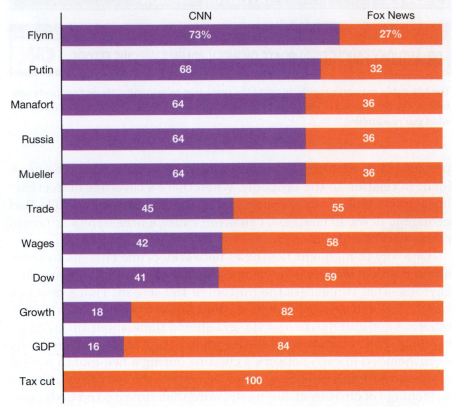

Note: For each word, the bar represents the percentage of news banners (chyrons) including that word that appeared on CNN compared to Fox News from August 25, 2017, to January 21, 2018.

Source: Charlie Smart, "The Differences in How CNN, MSNBC, and Fox Cover the News," The Pudding.

Shaping the Way People Think about Politics

Most public policy issues have many facets. And covering all of them is neither practical nor useful for presenting complex issues to the public. So when the news media cover politics, they engage in **framing**—providing the context of an issue so as to emphasize certain aspects over others. CNN and Fox News's coverage of policing policy epitomizes the concept. Both news organizations' prime-time programs covered the topic extensively in the wake of the 2020 murder of George Floyd, a Black man killed by a White police officer. And as protests erupted around the country, the networks devoted substantial

Why do Fox News and CNN viewers see politics so differently?

The two networks often frame policy issues differently. The aspects of the issue that one network emphasizes may not even be acknowledged by the other.

attention to Black Lives Matter, police reform, and the racial dynamics of the criminal justice system. Both networks covered the topic widely, and each had a tab on its website where much of its coverage could be found. Fox News labeled the tab "Crime"; on CNN.com, it was "Crime + Justice."

But attention to these topics and a navigable website tab are where the similarities end. Prime-time hosts on Fox News regularly depicted Black Lives Matter (BLM), the organization leading the call for police reform, as a violent group trying to "defund the police." Throughout 2020 and 2021, FoxNews.com presented more than 8,500 articles employing the phrase "defund the police." During the same period, CNN.com published only about 200 pieces using that phrase. Fox News stories were also 3 times more likely than CNN's to associate BLM with riots and looting. CNN stories about police reform, by contrast, were more than twice as likely as Fox News stories to mention "systemic racism" and "police misconduct." In short, whereas Fox News framed the issue of police reform as a dire threat to personal security and associated it with skyrocketing crime, CNN covered the topic with an emphasis on racial justice. Both networks' hosts and experts framed their coverage and analysis of police policy this way, too.[9]

Selective Exposure: The News You Choose

With so many news sources, types of news, and smart technology options, consumers have an almost unlimited set of choices. Interested in straight news presented by professional journalists? Then broadcast news and print and online newspapers can satisfy that thirst. Prefer pundits yelling over each other on cable TV? You can choose from a multitude of programs. Drawn to partisans who share your views? You're always just a few clicks away from like-minded bloggers and commentators. Social media makes it even easier to filter news this way, whether you want to or not. Do an internet search on a political topic or policy issue, and the next thing you know your newsfeed will be filled with stories about those topics. "Like" a friend's social media post about a news article or news photo, and you'll find yourself inundated with related items. Computer algorithms constantly track your digital footprint and ensure that your news is consistent with your preferences.

It's very easy to engage in **selective exposure**—consuming only the news you want and avoiding the information and viewpoints you don't.[10] In fact, this phenomenon is so prevalent that scholars have given it lots of different names: "echo chamber,"[11] "personal infosphere,"[12] even "the daily me."[13] This last one highlights the fact that people can customize their news alerts, feeds, and sources so that they're exposed only to content they agree with or topics they're interested in. Basically, politically interested citizens can intentionally narrow their news choices so that they wrap themselves in a news cocoon of their own choosing. And that cocoon is often driven by partisan preferences. More than half the people who consider themselves Democrats rely on CNN for political news, whereas less than a quarter of Republicans do. Instead, Fox News is the outlet of choice for a whopping 60 percent of Republicans. It comes in a distant ninth place for Democrats (see Table 2).[14]

As a result of selective exposure, the effects of agenda setting, priming, and framing can generate a set of circumstances whereby a news consumer who relies on National Public Radio or CNN will have trouble even agreeing on basic political facts with someone who gets news from conservative talk radio or Fox News. And people know it. Almost 80 percent of both Democrats and Republicans believe that members of opposing parties cannot even agree on basic facts.[15]

A steady diet of ideological news also contributes to the growing contempt that Democrats and Republicans have for each other. People who consume partisan news are regularly exposed to coverage that paints their political opponents in an entirely negative light. And when you repeatedly hear that people on the other side of the aisle are "radical," "extreme," "trying to destroy America," "willing to trash the Constitution," or "want take your rights away," it can harden your views and drive up animosity toward them.[16] **Affective polarization**—the mutual and growing dislike between Democrats and Republicans—has become so severe that today more than 75 percent of Democrats and 64 percent of Republicans consider

Why do Fox News and CNN viewers see politics so differently?

TABLE 2. Most Popular Sources of Political News

Overall U.S. Population		Democrats		Republicans	
Fox News	39%	CNN	53%	Fox News	60%
CNN	39	NBC News	40	ABC News	30
NBC News	34	ABC News	37	NBC News	28
ABC News	33	CBS News	33	CBS News	26
CBS News	30	MSNBC	33	CNN	24
MSNBC	24	*New York Times*	31	Sean Hannity (radio)	19
NPR	20	NPR	30	Rush Limbaugh (radio)	17
New York Times	20	*Washington Post*	26	MSNBC	14
Washington Post	17	BBC	22	PBS	11
PBS	16	PBS	22	*Wall Street Journal*	11

Note: Entries indicate the percentage of people who reported getting news about politics and government from each outlet in the previous week.

Source: Mark Jurkowitz, Amy Mitchell, Elisa Shearer and Mason Walker, "U.S. Media Polarization and the 2020 Election: A Nation Divided," Pew Research Center, January 24, 2020.

people who affiliate with the opposite party to be more "closed-minded" than other Americans. Roughly 40 percent of Democrats and Republicans think their partisan opponents are "unintelligent." Six out of 10 Republicans believe that Democrats are "unpatriotic." Meanwhile, only 9 percent of Democrats think Republicans are "respectful and tolerant of others."[17]

The Media's Power Isn't Unlimited

News organizations face a complex political world with finite human and financial capacities. They simply can't cover every story from every angle even if they want to. Agenda setting, priming, and framing are inevitable consequences of news production. But they also mean that the news media have the power to shape how people receive and process political information.

It's important to keep in mind, though, that media effects are limited. They generally can't persuade someone to adopt a particular viewpoint or change someone's already strong preexisting beliefs. A progressive Democrat doesn't tune in to Fox News and suddenly become politically conservative. A conservative Republican who lands on CNN doesn't walk away an hour later aren't ready to join the AOC fan club. Selective exposure can take run-of-the-mill Republicans and Democrats and shape them into more ideologically extreme citizens.[18] But the media don't create these citizens' partisan views in the first place.

That's not to say, of course, that people never change their minds about political figures, political events, or policy issues as a result of media exposure. Citizens who don't know much about politics, or who don't have strong political views, are the most susceptible to persuasion as well as to priming and framing. And this isn't an insignificant portion of the population. But because these people aren't super interested in politics to begin with, they tend to consume less news, which limits the extent to which media exposure can affect them.

DID YOU GET IT?

Why do Fox News and CNN viewers see politics so differently?

Short Answer:

- Because the two networks use agenda setting, priming, and framing to tell very different stories about what's happening in the political world.

- Because of the many choices people have for getting political news, citizens are often exposed only to the stories and commentary they already agree with. So each network's coverage reinforces its viewers' beliefs.

- Selective exposure can also cause people to demonize those who don't share their political beliefs.

Persuasive Argumentation

Evaluate evidence: When news organizations use agenda setting, priming, and framing, they shape the way their audiences receive the news of the day. The following questions ask you to identify evidence of these key media concepts.

1. Which would provide the best evidence that cable news networks use their agenda-setting power to present different takes on the most important political news?

   a. An analysis of how each covers a particular issue, such as health care, over the course of a month

   b. A study of the adjectives each uses to characterize the president during one month of coverage

   c. A comparison of the total number of stories on a range of topics each network focuses on for a one-month period

   d. An analysis of the partisan breakdown of each network's commentary during the same month

2. Which headline is the best evidence of a news organization trying to prime viewers to have a positive view of the president?

   a. "Republican Voters Unimpressed with Democratic Presidential Candidates"

   b. "President's Policy on Tariffs Has Achieved Mixed Results, but Is More Popular Than Many Expected"

   c. "President Meets with Russian Leader"

   d. "President Presides over Growing Economy"

3. If you want to argue that selective exposure has a negative impact on the public — such as fostering anger toward people with opposing views — what's the best potential source of evidence to support your claim?

   a. Data on the race, age, gender, and income level of people who watch CNN and Fox News

   b. Data examining how viewership of ABC, CBS, and NBC nightly news broadcasts has changed over time

   c. A study comparing how many people each month read stories on CNN.com versus FoxNews.com

   d. Data comparing the political attitudes of people who rely on partisan news sources and people who rely on more objective news sources

FIGURE IT OUT

Imagine that you're a journalist applying for a job to write for CNN.com, the *New York Times* news pages, and FoxNews.com. You have to demonstrate that you can write headlines consistent with each organization's approach to presenting the news. Although each outlet would probably consider itself objective and unbiased, for the purposes of this exercise you should follow the classifications offered in this segment: CNN is liberal, the *New York Times* is neutral, and Fox News is conservative.

First, choose one of the following stories:

1. A report that shows climate change occurring at a faster rate than previously thought

2. A congressional debate on banning assault weapons

3. A decision by President Biden to suspend building a wall on the U.S.-Mexico border that had begun under the Trump administration

Now, for the topic you choose:

- Develop three realistic headlines for your story — one liberal, one neutral, one conservative. The headlines should provide evidence of each outlet's ideological bent. Your headlines can be up to 15 words.

- Now draft a chyron for a segment about the story — again, one liberal, one neutral, one conservative. Each chyron should serve as evidence of the outlet's political ideology and not exceed six words.

In total, you'll be drafting three headlines and three chyrons.

Want to Know More?

When Fox News burst onto the scene in the 1990s, it provided people with a brash approach to news with a decidedly conservative twist. None of it would have been possible without Roger Ailes, the network's founder. Many political analysts believe that his impact on American politics cannot be overstated. To get a sense of his life, read Gabriel Sherman's book *The Loudest Voice in the Room: How the Brilliant, Bombastic Roger Ailes Built Fox News — and Divided a Country*; and watch Showtime's *The Loudest Voice*, a seven-part series starring Russell Crowe as Ailes. You'll see the rise of Fox News as well as Ailes's downfall, brought on by his sexual harassment of many of the network's employees.

Campaigns and Elections

In the United States, it seems like someone is always running for office. On the day of his inauguration as president of the United States, Donald Trump filed paperwork to run for a second term — an election that wouldn't take place for almost four years. Most members of Congress solicit contributions for their reelection bids within days of declaring victory. Elected officials at the state and local levels use Twitter, Facebook, Instagram, and their own websites to let voters know that the next election is right around the corner. And the news media eagerly cover what's basically a permanent campaign. Turn on cable news on any given day and you're likely to encounter campaign coverage, no matter how far off the next election is.

Despite constant exposure to seemingly endless political campaigns, what you see on TV, read in the paper, or view online tends to focus on the sensational and dramatic aspects of the electoral process. Strategists stealthily using social media to convince, coerce, and manipulate voters. Billionaires spending lavishly to support particular candidates and causes. Viral footage of candidates' gaffes and provocative statements, often taken out of context. What you probably hear much less about are the rules and norms governing U.S. elections. Where did the Electoral College come from? Why can rich people spend so much to help candidates win elections? How does redistricting actually work? These questions might sound boring, but they're critical for evaluating the electoral process. Elections, after all, are the heart of our democratic system — they determine the nation's leaders, public policies and priorities, and direction for the future.

The seven segments in this section demonstrate the unique — some might say downright bizarre — way we conduct elections in the United

States. Before you start reading, though, it's important to familiarize yourself with the definitions of some key terms that will come up throughout the segments. You've probably heard them many times but not thought much about them. First, it's essential to differentiate between the two stages in most elections. The first stage is the **primary**, where in most cases voters registered with a political party choose among their party's candidates. Once the parties have their respective nominees, the **general election** follows. That's when candidates from opposing parties square off to determine who will win the elective office. The second distinction you need to make has to do with the candidates. **Incumbents** already hold the position and are seeking reelection. Most of them win their races. **Challengers** try to unseat incumbents and typically face very long odds. **Open seats** are just that — there are no incumbents, so there's usually more competition.

Together, the segments in this section highlight how many aspects of modern campaigns pose three fundamental challenges to "democratic" elections.

1 **Winning a majority of votes doesn't always mean winning an election.**
The Electoral College can produce a president who received fewer citizens' votes than the losing candidate did. Moreover, because of the process by which states draw congressional district lines, one party can win a majority of seats in a state's congressional delegation without winning a majority of the statewide vote.

2 **The rich and the powerful have an edge in the electoral process.**
Our elections present opportunities for certain people — typically, those with money and political resources — to exert outsize influence in the political system. We see this in how candidates are recruited and campaigns are financed, the entrenched two-party system, and incumbents' advantages over challengers.

3 **Intense partisanship structures electoral competition.**
How people vote and the way congressional and presidential candidates campaign point to a system in which partisanship drives voters and candidates' choices. Policy stalemates over the Electoral College, third parties, and campaign finance reform also reveal how partisan considerations often trump thoughtful debate and deliberation.

27.
Who will you probably vote for?

#VoteChoice

Candidates running for office make all sorts of promises. They'll cut taxes. They'll combat climate change. They'll provide health care for all Americans. They'll create more jobs. Name a major issue, and you'll find a candidate promising to do something about it.

Sometimes the promises are over the top, even astounding. In 2004, Democratic vice-presidential candidate John Edwards promised to "stop juvenile diabetes, Parkinson's, Alzheimer's, and other debilitating diseases."[1] Four years later, Democratic presidential candidate Dennis Kucinich promised to arrest members of the Bush administration for going to war in Iraq.[2] In 2012, former Speaker of the House Newt Gingrich promised to build a colony on the moon,[3] former U.S. senator Rick Santorum promised to ban hard-core pornography,[4] and business-man Herman Cain promised to veto any bill that was longer than three pages.[5] And who can forget Donald Trump's campaign promise to "build a great, great wall" on the southern border? A wall he promised Mexico would pay for.[6]

Regardless of whether campaign promises are plausible or outlandish, they're all aimed at attracting more voters. That's the entire purpose of campaigning for elective office — candidates try to convince as many people as possible to vote for them. As you'll see in this segment, though, the most important factor that voters consider is whether a candidate belongs to the same political party as they do. Sure, candidates'

In Silver Spring, Maryland, voters have to choose among dozens of candidates for city, county, state, and federal offices.

positions on key issues — from health care to the economy to the environment — certainly matter to some voters. And candidates' professional experience and personal background can be relevant, too. But at the end of the day, party identification is really how most voters decide in most elections. So when candidates make bold campaign promises to end certain diseases, colonize outer space, or build beautiful walls, they might get media attention, but rarely do they win over new voters.

Almost Everyone Loves a Party

People don't pay much attention to politics. They usually don't know all the details of the candidates' issue positions. They probably don't follow the nuances of the campaign. And they likely aren't very familiar with the candidates' life stories. This is especially true once we move beyond presidential elections. In lots of low-profile races—such as for state legislature, mayor, town council, or school board—people often know next to nothing about the candidates. Yet for most citizens, deciding how to vote is actually pretty easy, particularly when an election pits a Republican against a Democrat. When they step into the voting booth and see the word "Democrat" or "Republican" next to each name, voters use these party labels.[7] Voters use party identification as a shortcut or cue to infer all the things they don't know about the candidates. And it usually works. People who rely predominantly on a candidate's party affiliation to determine their vote tend to make the same choice they would have made if they'd been very informed about the candidate's background, personality, and issue positions.[8]

Table 1 illustrates the importance of party identification in presidential elections.[9] The left two columns report the percentage of Democrats and Republicans who voted for the Democratic presidential candidate in the last 11 elections. The right two columns display the same information for the Republican candidate. On average, 87 percent of Democrats voted for the Democratic presidential nominee, and 90 percent of Republicans voted for the Republican. Even in 1984, when Walter Mondale won only one state (Minnesota, his home state), almost 80 percent of Democrats nationwide still chose him over Ronald Reagan.

Most people simply vote for their party's candidate. Some voters do this out of a deep sense of shared purpose or common values. Others do it because they were raised to support candidates of one party and that preference has taken hold. And for some citizens, **negative partisanship**—a visceral dislike of the opposing party—plays a role as well. The 2016 election is a perfect example. Democrat Hillary Clinton

TABLE 1. Presidential Vote Choice, 1980–2020

	Voted for the Democratic Candidate		Voted for the Republican Candidate	
	Democrats	**Republicans**	**Democrats**	**Republicans**
1980	69%	8%	26%	86%
1984	79	4	21	96
1988	85	7	15	93
1992	82	7	8	77
1996	90	10	6	85
2000	89	7	10	92
2004	93	5	7	95
2008	93	7	7	93
2012	95	3	5	97
2016	89	8	8	88
2020	94	5	6	94

Note: Percentages do not always sum to 100 because of votes for third-party candidates.

Source: "U.S. National Election Day Exit Polls," Roper; "2016 Exit Polls," CNN; "2020 Exit Polls," CNN.

and Republican Donald Trump shared the honor of being the two most disliked presidential candidates in modern history. Still, both candidates received support from almost 90 percent of their party's voters.[10]

This isn't the case only in presidential elections. In the last 10 midterm elections, an average of 90 percent of Democrats and 90 percent of Republicans voted for their party's candidate, too.[11] For most people, deciding how to vote in a general election isn't much of a decision at all. Crossing party lines just isn't a thing most voters do.

It's Not Always a Party

Voters can't always rely on a candidate's party affiliation to help them make decisions in the voting booth. In primary elections, all the candidates are from the same party. In **nonpartisan elections**—typical for local offices such as city council, school board, or sheriff—candidates don't run as members of a party. And for **swing voters**, party affiliation doesn't matter. They don't have an allegiance to either party and don't consistently support one party's candidates. Most swing voters are Independents (somewhere in the neighborhood of 10 percent of voters fall into this category[12]). But a small sliver of Democrats and Republicans cannot be counted on to back their party's nominee either (see Table 1). When partisanship isn't a factor, voters often rely on issues and candidate characteristics to decide their vote.

How Issues Matter

Candidates' positions on issues can help citizens decide how to vote in three general ways. The most basic involves assessing the candidates' specific policy views and figuring out which person is the best overall match. Take a look at Figure 1, which lists a series of policy positions for four candidates who sought the 2020 Democratic presidential nomination.[13] The differences among the candidates weren't that dramatic. Nor would we expect them to be—they were all Democrats, and they were all seeking support from Democratic voters.

But the differences that do exist can help voters narrow their choices. After all, even though all four Democrats believed in providing health care to all Americans and raising taxes on the wealthy, only three believed in allowing late-term abortions or legalizing marijuana. We're down to two when it comes to free tuition at public colleges. If a Democratic voter had check marks in all four rows, then only Bernie Sanders and Elizabeth Warren were a perfect match. If that voter had a more moderate position on marijuana, free public college tuition, or abortion, then those two candidates weren't ideal choices.

FIGURE 1. Four 2020 Democratic Presidential Candidates on the Issues

	Joe Biden	Bernie Sanders	Elizabeth Warren	Pete Buttigieg
Legalize marijuana	✗	✓	✓	✓
Universal health care	✓	✓	✓	✓
Free public college	✗	✓	✓	✗
Late-term abortion	✗	✓	✓	✓
Tax the rich	✓	✓	✓	✓

Source: Beatrice Jin and Caitlin Oprysko, "Here's Where the Democratic Candidates Stand on the Biggest 2020 Issues," Politico, April 25, 2019.

This sort of calculus assumes that each issue is equally important. But that's not always the case. Some people are **single-issue voters**— their vote is dictated by a candidate's position on one particular policy. This is a second way issues can play a role in shaping voters' decisions. This type of behavior is limited to a small subset of issues—mainly, those on which voters have strong moral convictions.[14] Roughly one out of every four voters, for example, would never support a candidate who doesn't share their view on abortion.[15] If those people support full abortion rights through the entire pregnancy, or if their single issue is legalizing marijuana, then Biden wasn't their guy. Again, they might not wind up with just one candidate, but they'll likely be able to eliminate some options.

A third way that issues can help voters make decisions has to do with priorities, especially in the literally tens of thousands of nonpartisan local elections every year. Consider a recent election for a seat on the Jefferson County school board in rural Oregon. In interviews with the local newspaper, the five candidates identified their most important priority if elected. Casandra Moses, the mother of a dyslexic daughter, wanted to make it easier for parents to advocate for children with disabilities. Taylor Lark, who coaches youth sports in the district, prioritized expanding extracurricular offerings. Carina Miller wanted to push for additional career and technical education options. Courtney Snead planned to focus on closing the achievement gap between wealthy and poor students. And Kevin Richards's priority was to have no priorities at all.[16] Without party at their disposal, voters can support the candidate who shares their priorities.

Issue priorities matter in partisan elections, too. It turns out that when people like the direction the country is going on the issues that matter most to them, they tend to vote for the party (or person) in power. When things aren't going well, voters are more likely to opt for someone new. Making decisions based on whether you're better or worse off now than you were the last time you voted is called **retrospective voting**. In 2022, this method of voting advantaged the Republicans. Heading into the midterm elections, voters cared most about the economy, which saw record inflation under the Democratically controlled government (see Figure 2).[17] People who prioritized health care

FIGURE 2. Voters' Issue Priorities in the 2022 Midterm Elections

Note: The bars above represent the percentage of people who said that each issue would be "extremely important" to them when deciding how to vote. *N* = 900 registered voters. Margin of error ± 3.3.

Source: Gallup, June 1–20, 2022.

were concerned about rising costs and efforts to eliminate coverage of preexisting conditions—both of which were taking place under the Trump administration and the Republican-controlled Congress. That's part of the reason the Democrats managed to retake control of the House of Representatives.

Who Do You Want to Have a Beer With?

Candidates, particularly for high-level office, often try to cultivate a particular personal image. They emphasize their experiences by highlighting roles that voters value: member of the military, business owner, devout family person.[18] They call voters' attention to character traits that people like to see in elected officials: honesty, toughness, patriotism, humor. This last one might surprise you, but 40 percent of voters think a sense of humor is an important trait in a candidate.[19] And candidates try to appear ordinary and authentic. That's why they go on comedy shows, drink beer in neighborhood bars, fill out March Madness brackets, and trade jokes with late night talk show hosts.

Candidates spend time developing an appealing persona because experience and character can help some citizens decide how to vote. Indeed, ever since TV became an important part of political campaigns in the 1950s and 1960s, almost 30 percent of voters have regularly identified personal characteristics as an important part of their decision-making process when selecting a presidential candidate.[20] According to Gallup polls that ask people whether they have a favorable or unfavorable view of the presidential candidates—these polls basically measure whether people like the candidates or not—the candidate with the higher favorability rating has won 14 of the last 17 presidential elections.[21]

To get at likeability, pollsters sometimes ask voters which presidential candidate they'd rather have a beer with. In 2000, voters thought Democratic candidate Al Gore had better experience and better policy proposals. But George W. Bush won the beer drinking question[22]—and the election. In 2016, Trump beat Clinton in the beer contest 45–37. That said, nearly one out of every five voters didn't want to have a beer with either of them.[23] Indeed, Trump lost the beer contest and the election to Biden four years later.[24] Candidate evaluations can't be divorced from partisanship, though. Democrats find Democratic candidates to be more competent, honest, and likeable than Republican candidates. The reverse is true for Republicans.[25]

Who will you probably vote for?

Presidential candidates want you to like them. Clockwise from top left, Democratic presidential candidate Joe Biden eats ice cream with Stephen Colbert; Hillary Clinton downs a pint of Guinness and kisses babies while visiting an Irish pub; Donald Trump allows late-night talk show host Jimmy Fallon to determine whether Trump's famous mane of hair is real; and while seeking a second term, President Barack Obama fills out his NCAA March Madness bracket on ESPN.

Other Stuff That Helps Voters Decide

Candidates' partisan affiliation, issue positions, and personal characteristics are, far and away, the most important factors citizens rely on when deciding how to vote. But additional factors are sometimes important, too. Some people, for example, have what's called a baseline gender preference.[26] All else equal, they prefer either male or female candidates. It turns out that the proportion of people who favor women is roughly the same size as the group that discriminates against them. So even though some voters exhibit these biases, women are just as likely as men to win elections overall.[27] A small group of voters applies racial considerations in the same way.[28] And some voters with strong evangelical convictions look for candidates who share their religious values.[29] Ultimately, though, it's difficult to disentangle preferences for candidates based on race, gender, and religion from preferences for a particular party. As it turns out, most female candidates and candidates of color are Democrats, and the most ardently evangelical candidates are Republicans. So partisanship plays a role even when it seems like it doesn't.

DID YOU GET IT?

Who will you probably vote for?

Short Answer:

- The candidate who shares your party affiliation.
- When voters can't rely on partisanship, they turn to candidates' positions on the issues and their priorities if elected.
- Candidate characteristics influence voters' decisions, too.

DEVELOPING YOUR SKILLS

Civic Engagement

Stay informed: Being a thoughtful voter often involves having a familiarity with candidates and the issues they stand for. Acquaint yourself with some online sources that can help you find the information you need to make informed decisions.

1. Gun legislation is important to many voters. Some favor more restrictions on gun ownership, and some want to keep things the way they are. If you're a single-issue voter on guns, which website will be most useful for helping you decide whether to reelect your member of Congress?

    a. Dailykos.com

    b. Votesmart.org

    c. CNN.com

    d. NRA.org

2. If extending health care to all citizens is your highest priority, which website will help you figure out which candidates share your views?

    a. KFF.org

    b. Ballotpedia.org

    c. Ontheissues.org

    d. Politico.com

3. Which piece of information would probably be the most useful if you wanted to determine what the candidates stand for in a nonpartisan city council race?

   a. The number of campaign signs you see for each candidate

   b. National media coverage of the candidates

   c. Which candidate is the incumbent

   d. Each candidate's website

FIGURE IT OUT

When you don't have party labels to rely on — or even when you do — you might want to consider other factors when deciding the best candidate for you. Maybe you care about abortion rights or student loan debt. Perhaps transgender rights or gun rights matter most to you. Or maybe you care a lot about foreign policy. Consider how to select your preferred candidate for president, governor, and mayor. More specifically:

- Identify one issue that is important when you think about voting for president, governor, and mayor. Remember, local, state, and federal governments have different responsibilities, so you should come up with three different issues.

- For each issue, identify your position.

- Now, for each of the three offices, list the character trait or type of experience that you think is most important in a candidate.

- What resources could you rely on to figure out if a candidate holds the position and possesses the traits you've listed?

Want to Know More?

For an amusing take on how people decide how to vote, watch the 2001 episode of the classic comedy television show *Will & Grace* entitled "Star-Spangled Banter." Will, a gay man, is supporting a gay mayoral candidate. And Grace, a Jewish woman, is supporting a Jewish female candidate. They quickly come to learn that selecting candidates based on their shared identity doesn't always work out. If the episode inspires you to up your game as a voter, then check out this list of 10 websites to make you an informed voter: https://lifehacker.com/top-10-election-tools-to-turn-you-into-an-informed-vote-1787886914

28.
How do Democrats and Republicans fight to control the government?

#PartyPolitics

In fall 2018, all signs pointed to Congressman Ruben Gallego entering the U.S. Senate race in Arizona. On paper, he looked like the perfect candidate for 2020. Ivy League degree? Check. Combat veteran? Check. Rising Democratic star with a lot of energy? Check.[1] Who could possibly be better suited to unseat Republican Martha McSally?

Mark Kelly, that's who — at least according to top Democratic Party leaders in Washington, D.C. Democrats had been recruiting Kelly to run for office ever since his wife, Gabby Giffords, resigned from Congress after surviving a mass shooting in 2011. Beyond showing himself to be a loving and devoted spouse during his wife's recovery, Kelly's biography was straight out of central casting. He was an astronaut, decorated navy veteran,[2] and outspoken gun control advocate with a national profile.[3] But perhaps Kelly's greatest asset was how he described himself: "Not as a partisan, but as a patriot."[4] The national party was convinced that a message of moderation, unity, and bipartisanship was the Democrats' path to victory in Republican strongholds like Arizona.[5]

As is common for political party leaders, Democratic Party chair Jaime Harrison and Republican Party chair Ronna Romney McDaniel often take to the national airwaves to advocate for their respective visions for the country.

They thought Gallego was a great fit for his district but simply too liberal to win statewide.

Following a series of meetings in Washington with high-ranking Democratic strategists and elected officials, Kelly agreed to give it a shot. With the party's help, Kelly assembled a team of experienced political consultants and campaign staffers well-known for helping Democrats win elections. His campaign manager had been chief of staff to a Democratic member of Congress. His finance director had previously worked for the Democratic Party. His fundraising consultants worked for a half-dozen Democratic senators. And Kelly's direct mail, digital advertising, and polling firms touted dozens of Democratic politicians as their clients.[6]

In February 2019, Kelly announced his campaign with a four-minute video entitled "My Next Mission."[7] Overlaying footage of himself in a spacesuit, a military uniform, and at his wife's side, Kelly narrates his life story. He never says he's a Democrat, never mentions Donald Trump, never condemns the Republican Party. Instead, he bashes partisanship, gridlock, and divisiveness and argues that relying on science, data, and cooperation is the way to get things done.[8] Within the first month of announcing his candidacy, Kelly raised more than $3 million, a whopping sum for a first-time candidate.[9] Seeing the writing on the wall, Gallego decided to sit out the race.

From start to finish, the Democratic Party's leaders, donors, and consultants launched Kelly's campaign (a little astronaut humor). They recruited him, helped ensure that he wouldn't face a competitive primary, and worked with him to build an experienced campaign team for the general election. But even with all this, Kelly was no shoo-in. He faced a Republican opponent with similar resources: campaign funds, expert consultants, and the full backing of her political party. Ultimately, Kelly won the race, besting Martha McSally by fewer than 80,000 votes out of more than 3.5 million cast.[10]

The race for the U.S. Senate seat in Arizona is just one example of this segment's central point: political parties are broad-based organizations on a mission to control the government. Winning as many elections as possible is the party's goal. Electing candidates, of course, isn't the only thing political parties do. They also embody a set of values and positions that simplify choices for voters. And as you'll see in Section VI, they play a fundamental role in organizing political institutions and the governing process. But in order to implement their agendas, political parties first need to win elections, so this segment walks you through how the major parties are organized and how they fight to control the government by (1) developing political messages, (2) recruiting candidates, and (3) supporting their candidates' campaigns.

Political Party Organizations

The political party infrastructure has three levels—national, state, and local. At the top sit the **national party organizations**: the Democratic National Committee (DNC) and the Republican National Committee (RNC). These committees focus heavily on the presidential election process, closely monitoring the primaries, determining rules for amassing delegates, setting the debate schedule, hosting the national conventions, and raising and spending gobs of money to get their nominee into the White House (see Table 1).

But the DNC and RNC's roles extend beyond presidential elections. They develop the parties' platforms, oversee fundraising efforts nationwide, and implement an election strategy for the whole country. All of these efforts involve coordinating with an elaborate network of political strategists and elected officials as well as state and local party leaders who have their fingers on the pulse of the political landscape. Roughly 300 people—200 national leaders and the top 2 members of each state party organization—make up the DNC.[11] The RNC is smaller, with just 168 members—50 state party leaders and 118 national and regional leaders.[12] Every few years, each national party organization meets to choose a chair, who serves as the public face of the party and shapes its agenda and direction. Both major parties also have separate national organizations that focus on winning control of each chamber of Congress.

In addition to the official party organizations, literally hundreds of firms and companies employ thousands of political consultants who work to elect Democrats and Republicans. The directory on the Campaigns & Elections website (campaignsandelections.com), a popular resource in the world of political campaigns, identifies more than 70 types of consultants.[13] Some are pretty standard for any serious

TABLE 1. Formal Political Party Organization

	Democrats	Republicans	Broad Responsibilities
Nationwide	Democratic National Committee (DNC)	Republican National Committee (RNC)	Coordinate party message and election strategy nationwide; run presidential elections; raise money to support party's candidates.
U.S. Senate	Democratic Senatorial Campaign Committee (DSCC)	National Republican Senatorial Committee (NRSC)	Recruit and support U.S. Senate candidates.
U.S. House	Democratic Congressional Campaign Committee (DCCC)	National Republican Congressional Committee (NRCC)	Recruit and support U.S. House candidates.
States	50 Democratic state parties	50 Republican state parties	Work with national party to implement party message in state campaigns; recruit and support candidates for state and local offices.

presidential or congressional candidate: campaign managers, fundraisers, and get out the vote (GOTV) specialists; social media, website, and mobile app strategists; polling, advertising, and opposition research firms. Others might seem a little obscure, but candidates and campaigns often hire consultants for crisis management, legal advice, photography, transportation, outreach to key voting groups (like African Americans, senior citizens, or veterans), voter registration, and even voiceovers in campaign ads. In most cases, consultants work exclusively for Democrats or Republicans. Regardless of their area of expertise, the mission for most consultants is the same as it is for the official party organization: to defeat the opposition and help their party's candidates win enough elections to take control of the government.[14]

Fighting for Control

Step 1: Develop a Winning Message

The major national party organizations constantly try to shape how citizens think and talk about politics. Party officials work with elected leaders, candidates, and political consultants to figure out the best way to portray themselves as the only ones fighting to improve the lives of the American people. The national parties rely on pollsters, graphic designers, and web developers to formulate compelling language and create effective images. When they're confident their message will resonate, they take it to the public and promote it through the media. A winning message can improve a party's chances of gaining public support.[15]

One of the most basic ways parties engage in this rhetorical battle is by developing and circulating **talking points**—a set of clear, succinct ideas that outline a party's positions and arguments. The parties often craft broad messages that they hope will appeal nationwide. In 1994, for example, the Republican Party campaigned on what it called the Contract with America—a 10-point plan that laid out what Republicans would do if they won control of Congress.[16] Republican candidates across the country signed the contract, which focused on cutting spending and reducing the size of government. They rode this national message to recapture the House of Representatives for the first time in 40 years. In the 2020 election, Republicans emphasized the idea that Democrats want to move the country toward socialism.[17] The Democratic Party, by contrast, homed in on a narrower set of issues. In particular, Democratic candidates campaigned on health care and, more specifically, how Americans can only count on Democrats to protect it.[18]

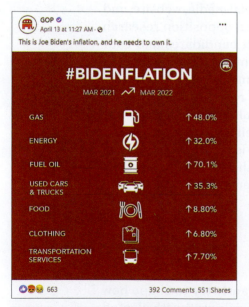

Political parties try to shape the debate by releasing talking points. The party organizations use Facebook and other social media platforms to tout their successes and condemn their opponents.

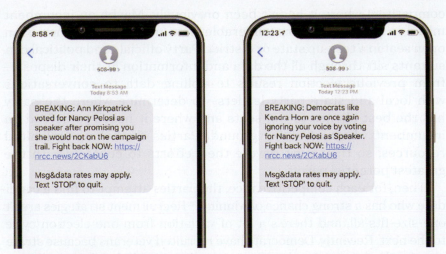

In 2020, the National Republican Congressional Committee targeted voters in swing districts across the country by linking incumbent Democrats to Speaker of the House Nancy Pelosi. The text messages were all the same; only the name of the incumbent varied.

In order for national messages to resonate in specific districts and states, the party organizations personalize them. Heading into the 2022 election season, for instance, the Democratic Congressional Campaign Committee (DCCC) and the National Republican Congressional Committee (NRCC) launched text message campaigns with very different narratives. Republicans blamed Democrats for inflation and supporting the failed leadership of President Biden. Democrats focused on gun violence and abortion bans.[19] The text a voter received identified that voter's member of the House, so the national message took on a local flavor.

Step 2: Identify and Recruit Candidates

In their quest to control the government, the Democratic and Republican parties are laser-focused on the congressional political landscape. Each election cycle, 435 House seats and 33 or 34 Senate seats are up for grabs. In the overwhelming majority of cases, though, incumbency and the party composition of each district mean that, in many races, the winner is a foregone conclusion even before campaign season begins. Usually, only about 10 percent of seats could really go either way. The congressional campaign committees figure out which seats are in play and the best potential candidates to seek them.[20] The stakes are high. A successful recruitment strategy can mean maintaining or regaining power in Washington. A lackluster strategy can mean losing it.

The parties begin by identifying districts and states where they can win. Maybe a demographic shift or redistricting has made a district competitive where it hadn't been previously. Maybe an incumbent mired in scandal is more vulnerable than usual. Maybe there's an open seat in a toss-up state or district. Party officials and political consultants sift through all the data and information at their disposal—from previous election results to polling data to conversations with local and state party leaders—to determine where the party has the best chance to win seats and where it needs to defend an incumbent who's on shaky ground. Parties don't have unlimited resources, so they must devote their efforts to contests with the greatest potential payoff.

Then, for each competitive race, the parties attempt to find a candidate who has a strong chance of winning.[21] Recruitment strategies aren't one-size-fits-all, and there's a lot of variation from one election cycle to the next. Recently, Democrats have recruited veterans because strategists for the congressional party organizations concluded that candidates with a military background appeal to moderate voters in swing districts and states.[22] Republican Party officials, meanwhile, often work behind the scenes to steer clear of extremely conservative candidates who would face a tough road in the same places.[23] As a general rule, candidates with high name recognition, the ability to raise money, campaign experience, and a political philosophy that matches the district or state's voters are hot commodities.

In their efforts to recruit candidates who can win, party representatives fan out across the country to speak with potential candidates, assess people who have expressed an interest, and invite top contenders to come to Washington, D.C. And when they find their dream candidate, if that person needs convincing, then the parties enlist the help of political bigwigs to make the case. That's why, with the raging battle for control of the U.S. Senate in the 2022 midterm elections, Republican Minority Leader Mitch McConnell actively worked to find the strongest candidates. In Arizona and New Hampshire, he recruited popular Republican governors to take on incumbent Democrats.[24] In other key states, McConnell tried to fend off candidates he viewed as too extreme. He told reporters he had only one criterion for choosing candidates: "Can you win in November?"[25] Despite these efforts, extreme and/or inexperienced candidates still won the Republican nominations in Pennsylvania, Missouri, and Georgia.[26]

Once the party solidifies its lineup of candidates, it publicizes them. By showcasing its successful recruits, the party subtly—or maybe not so subtly—discourages other candidates from running. As was the case with Ruben Gallego, it's hard to take on an opponent who benefits from the support of the party apparatus.

Step 3: Raise and Spend Lots of Money

Running the national party organizations requires a lot of money. The parties spend on advertising, research and recruitment, and GOTV efforts. They also support candidates in targeted races. So the parties actively raise funds to ensure that they have the money required to run successful operations. In 2022, the two major parties raised more than $1 billion each (see Figure 1).[27] All told, party money amounted to about one-third of all the money raised and spent in national elections.

Federal law limits political parties' direct contributions to federal candidates to $5,000 per election cycle. But parties can get around these limits by making **independent expenditures** on behalf of a candidate. The expenditures are "independent" because the parties do not coordinate these expenditures with a candidate's campaign. This means that parties are free to come into a congressional district or state and spend as much as they want. They can use party money to conduct polls, bombard the airwaves with ads for or against a candidate, launch social media and text message campaigns, deploy

FIGURE 1. Money Raised by the Two Major Political Parties, 2022

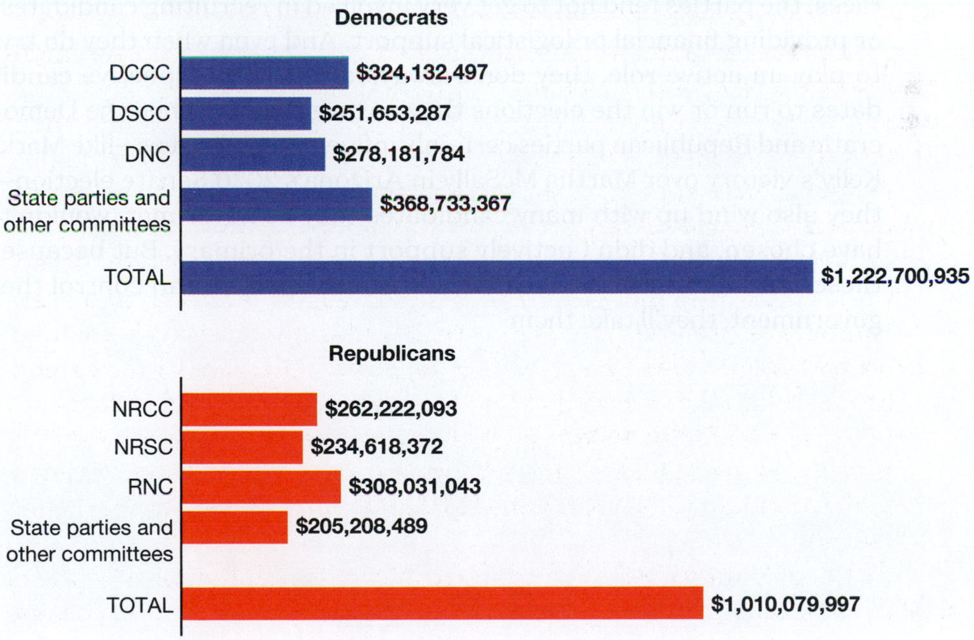

Democrats

DCCC	$324,132,497
DSCC	$251,653,287
DNC	$278,181,784
State parties and other committees	$368,733,367
TOTAL	$1,222,700,935

Republicans

NRCC	$262,222,093
NRSC	$234,618,372
RNC	$308,031,043
State parties and other committees	$205,208,489
TOTAL	$1,010,079,997

Source: Federal Election Commission filings as of November 9, 2022.

canvassers to knock on thousands of doors—anything to help their candidates win.

Not all campaigns receive party resources. But when parties decide to get involved, they pour a lot of money into targeted races and close contests and conduct very elaborate campaigns. When the Democrats saw an opportunity to knock off Senator Cory Gardner, a Republican, in Colorado in 2020, for example, they spent $15 million to do it.[28] The Republican Party spent almost $7 million to defeat Senator Joe Donnelly, a Democrat, in Indiana during the same cycle.[29] The parties spend lavishly in competitive House races, too, sometimes as much $5 million in one district.[30]

The Limits of Party Influence

Although it might seem like political parties exert a lot of control over who seeks and wins public office, it's important to put their influence into context. In many other democratic countries, political parties have total control over the selection of candidates. But the United States actually has a **weak party system**—parties exert only loose control over the candidate selection process.[31] Anyone can run for office and choose which party to affiliate with. With the exception of targeted competitive races, the parties tend not to get very involved in recruiting candidates or providing financial or logistical support. And even when they do try to play an active role, they don't always convince prospective candidates to run or win the elections they've targeted. So while the Democratic and Republican parties certainly influence some races—like Mark Kelly's victory over Martha McSally in Arizona's 2020 Senate election—they also wind up with many candidates they've never met, wouldn't have chosen, and didn't actively support in the primary. But because these candidates are the means by which the parties can control the government, they'll take them.

How do Democrats and Republicans fight to control the government?

DID YOU GET IT?

How do Democrats and Republicans fight to control the government?

Short Answer:

- Both the Democratic and Republican parties have large national party organizations engaged in a constant battle to win elections and control the political system at all levels of government.
- Supported by an army of political consultants, parties develop messages, recruit candidates, and fund campaigns.
- Although the parties can be very influential, they are strategic in choosing where to get involved and do not have complete control over the electoral process.

DEVELOPING YOUR SKILLS

Persuasive Argumentation

Evaluate evidence: Party politics involves making strategic decisions based on compelling evidence. Determine what evidence would best assist party leaders in identifying and supporting candidates.

1. In recent election cycles, Democratic Party leaders have tried to recruit military veterans to run in swing congressional districts. What is the strongest evidence that they should continue this strategy?
   a. An increase in the total number of veterans who agree to run for office
   b. Election results indicating that Republican veterans perform no better than Republican non-veterans in swing districts
   c. Election results indicating that Democratic veterans outperform Democratic non-veterans in swing districts
   d. Election results indicating that Republican candidates with military experience are most competitive in the South
2. What piece of evidence would best help party leaders decide whether to make a sizable independent expenditure on behalf of a Senate candidate?
   a. The quality of the opposing party's message
   b. Poll results showing that the candidate has low name recognition among voters
   c. Poll results showing that the race is very close
   d. Poll results showing that the candidate is way behind

3. Local party leaders want to help a Republican candidate knock off a vulnerable Democratic incumbent for a U.S. House seat in a rural district. What information would likely be most useful in helping the Republican candidate come up with a winning message?

   a. A memo summarizing messages the party is using to help other rural Republican House candidates across the country

   b. A poll showing the job approval ratings of the president

   c. A national poll revealing the issues voters say they care most about when deciding how to vote in the upcoming presidential election

   d. Conversations with Republican House candidates who lost to Democrats running in urban districts

FIGURE IT OUT

Party leaders create talking points that show their party in the most favorable light possible. Consider the following information about the 2020 elections:

- Democrats won the presidency and picked up five states that they lost in 2016 (AZ, GA, MI, PA, and WI).

- Republicans picked up 12 House seats, reducing the size of the Democrats' majority in the chamber to a mere 5 seats. They even knocked off Democratic incumbents in eight states, including CA and MN.

Based on these details, come up with two talking points that paint the 2020 outcomes as favorable for Democrats. Keep each to just a sentence or two. Then do the same thing for the Republicans. This is an exercise in selecting and interpreting evidence to make different arguments about the same event. Feel free to have a little fun with the language; talking points are often colorful.

Want to Know More?

Lots of great movies reveal how political consultants do their jobs. The 1993 documentary *The War Room* is one of the best. It's a behind-the-scenes look at how a team of strategists made Bill Clinton, a little-known Arkansas governor, the president of the United States. *Boogie Man*, a 2008 film about Lee Atwater — considered by many to be a master of negative campaigning — is another good choice. And if you're looking for some pure fun (or stupidity), then check out *The Campaign*. It revolves around a North Carolina congressional race between a fictional congressman (Will Ferrell) and the son of a political big shot (Zach Galifianakis). Political consultants and lobbyists try to keep the undisciplined candidates on message.

29.
Is there too much money in elections?

#CampaignFinance

In January 2015, Colleen Bradley Bell became ambassador to Hungary. In appointing her to the position, President Barack Obama highlighted Bell's success in "the business world" and her ability to maintain relationships "with the government and people of Hungary."[1] But Bell's critics, including many Republican senators, weren't impressed with her credentials. They thought the ambassadorship probably had less to do with her primary professional achievement — producing the long-running soap opera *The Bold and the Beautiful*[2] — and more to do with the $2.1 million she'd raised for Obama's 2012 campaign.

Obama's decision to nominate Noah Bryson Mamet as ambassador to Argentina also raised eyebrows. Unlike Bell, Mamet was fully immersed in the political process. He'd worked on political campaigns for years before starting a consulting firm in California. But with the exception of a short stint as an election monitor in Sierra Leone in 2007, Mamet had little foreign policy experience.[3] More to the point, he'd never been to Argentina and didn't speak Spanish. Mamet did, however, raise more than $3.2 million for Obama in 2012.[4]

Barack Obama wasn't the first president to reward major campaign donors with cushy appointments, nor was he the last. Donald Trump's ambassador to Iceland had never set foot in the country.[5] His ambassador to the Bahamas thought the island nation was part of

Given the billions of dollars spent on U.S. elections every cycle, portrayals of rich donors who try to control the political system are common. But efforts to enact meaningful campaign finance reform typically don't go very far.

the United States.[6] And his choice for ambassador to Morocco? A car dealer from Michigan.[7] What these nominees lacked in foreign policy experience they made up for in the hundreds of thousands of dollars they had raised for Trump's inauguration.[8] Rewards to big donors included more than just ambassadorships, though. Trump's secretaries of Commerce, Education, and the Treasury had all made large contributions to his campaign.[9]

With high-profile political favors like these popping up all the time, it's no surprise that the public thinks there's too much money in elections. More than 9 out of 10 Americans believe that politicians prioritize their major donors' interests over those of regular voters. And overwhelming majorities of citizens favor new laws to curb the prevalence of money in politics (see Figure 1).[10] Joe Biden pledged to rein in the practice of rewarding political donors with plum government jobs. At least a little bit. Early in his administration, he promised to cap his number of politically connected ambassadors to a mere 30 percent.[11]

In reality, though, the role money plays in campaigns and elections is more complex than first meets the eye. When you see how much money is raised and spent by candidates running for president and Congress, you might be blown away — especially because, in many

FIGURE 1. Public Attitudes about Money in Politics

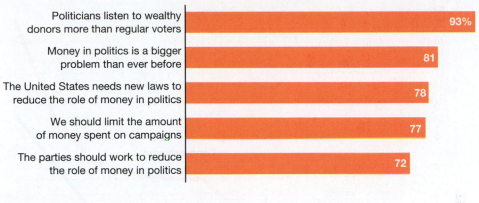

- Politicians listen to wealthy donors more than regular voters — 93%
- Money in politics is a bigger problem than ever before — 81
- The United States needs new laws to reduce the role of money in politics — 78
- We should limit the amount of money spent on campaigns — 77
- The parties should work to reduce the role of money in politics — 72

Note: Bars represent the percentage of survey respondents who agree with each statement.

Source: Pew Research Center 2018; Ipsos/Reuters 2016.

cases, campaign finance laws don't do much to limit donations to political campaigns. But you'll also read competing perspectives about whether the infusion of money into the electoral process poses a serious threat to democracy. By the end of this segment, you'll be able to judge whether too much money is spent on U.S. elections and whether politicians should do something about it.

Money in Elections: A Quick Overview

Elections are expensive. Campaigns hire staff, rent office space, hold events, produce ads, and conduct polls. And as campaigns have become increasingly complex—broad social media strategies, in-house poll- sters, and elaborate get out the vote operations have become the norm—they've also become more costly. Even adjusting for inflation, Barack Obama's 2008 presidential campaign cost 77 times as much as John F. Kennedy's 1960 race for the White House.[12] The amount of money campaigns spent on federal elections more than quadrupled just from 2000 to 2020 (see Figure 2).[13]

Congressional elections have also seen record price tags. In the 2020 elections, members of the House of Representatives running for reelection raised an average of $2.7 million each. Incumbent U.S. senators running for reelection spent an average of $28 million.[14] In highly competitive races, spending was off the charts. Total spending exceeded $510 million in the hotly contested U.S. Senate race in Georgia

FIGURE 2. Spending in Elections (in billions)

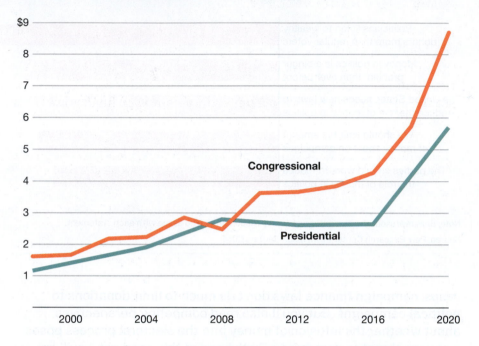

Note: The dollar amounts above include money spent directly by presidential, Senate, and House candidates, as well as by political parties and independent interest groups on behalf of federal candidates.

Source: "Total Cost of Election, (1998–2020)," OpenSecrets.

in which incumbent Republican David Purdue narrowly lost to Democratic challenger Jon Ossoff.[15] The most expensive House race of the 2020 cycle took place in New Mexico's 2nd congressional district: the contest in which Republican Yvette Herrell unseated Democrat Xochitl Torres Small cost more than $37 million. To put that figure into perspective, it equates to spending $94 on each of the district's 393,812 registered voters.[16] All told, the 2020 federal elections cost roughly $14.4 billion.[17]

The money that candidates raise and spend usually pays off. In 9 out of the last 10 presidential elections, the candidate who raised the most money won the election.[18] The same was true for congressional elections: 92 percent of House candidates and 80 percent of Senate candidates who outspent their competitors claimed victory.[19] Money doesn't necessarily guarantee a win, but candidates with more money have more resources to run successful campaigns.

Contributing to Political Campaigns: Who Can Give What?

Where does all the money come from? The overwhelming majority of candidates rely on political donors, so they must adhere to regulations that govern political giving. In 1971, Congress passed the Federal Election Campaign Act. Although it has been amended several times, the act still serves as the basis of current federal campaign finance law. This federal law doesn't apply to local or state candidates, which we'll get to in a minute.

Under the law, citizens may contribute to federal election campaigns in several ways. First, they can give directly to candidates. These donations were initially limited to $1,000 per candidate in a primary election and another $1,000 per candidate in the general election. In 2002, Congress modified the law to increase the limit and link it to inflation. By 2022, individuals could contribute a maximum of $5,800 to a candidate ($2,900 in the primary and another $2,900 for the general election). Second, people can contribute to **political action committees (PACs)**—organizations that exist for the sole purpose of influencing elections, both by endorsing candidates and by donating to their campaigns. Third, contributors can give to political parties, which may then use the funds to advance the party's interests.[20] Under the current rules, donors are limited in how much they can give to candidates, PACs, and parties (see Table 1). It doesn't matter who you are or how much money you have; you're held to these limits.

Federal election law does more than limit individuals' political contributions. It also sets up a reporting system. Every quarter, candidates, PACs, and parties must list the total amount they've raised. In addition,

TABLE 1. How Much Can You Donate in the 2022 Federal Election Cycle?

To a candidate	$2,900 for primary and $2,900 for general election
To a PAC	$5,000 per year
To a political party	$156,000 per year
To a Super PAC	Unlimited
To your own campaign	Unlimited

for every donor who gives more than $200, campaigns must disclose the donor's name and employment information. The law's intent is to bring transparency to the process. These reports are public and easy to access online, so citizens can find out where candidates get their money.

On the basis of these reports, we know that in 2020 roughly 40 percent of all contributions to Democratic and Republican congressional candidates came from individuals making large contributions (more than $200). Small donors—people contributing no more than $200 to the candidate throughout the election cycle—accounted for less than a quarter of the contributions to Democratic and Republican candidates. PAC contributions amounted to one-fifth of the money raised by House candidates and 5 percent of the dollars raised by Senate candidates. And the candidates' contributions to their own campaigns—which can be unlimited—rounded out their war chests. Overall, 36 candidates for the House and Senate contributed at least $1 million to their own races in 2020.[21]

Although the campaign finance framework set up by the 1971 law remains in effect today, two federal court decisions in 2010 facilitated an additional path for money to make its way into federal elections. In *Citizens United v. Federal Election Commission*, the Supreme Court, in a 5–4 decision, struck down limits on how much corporations and unions could spend in federal elections. A few months later, a federal appeals court applied the ruling to individuals.[22] These two cases led to the creation of **Super PACs**, which are political action committees that can accept unlimited contributions from individuals, unions, and corporations.[23] And by unlimited, we mean unlimited. In the 2020 election cycle, conservative billionaire Sheldon Adelson and his wife, Miriam, gave more than $215 million to Super PACs supporting Republican candidates. Michael Bloomberg and Tom Steyer donated $98 million and $64 million, respectively, to Democratic Super PACs. Overall, Super PACs funneled more than $2.1 billion into the 2020 elections.[24]

Only two restrictions govern Super PACs: they can't donate directly to candidates, and they can't coordinate their activities with a candidate's campaign.[25] But they can run a parallel campaign to elect or defeat a candidate. And the restriction on coordination doesn't mean that candidates—especially those running for president—can't woo billionaire donors to fund Super PACs on their behalf.[26] If these distinctions seem fuzzy, it's because they are. It doesn't take much for a Super PAC—which can be funded by just one person or several thousand donors—to figure out a candidate's official campaign message and run political ads or develop a social media strategy that's completely consistent with it. In essence, Super PACs allow wealthy donors, corporations, and unions to work around campaign finance limits on direct donations to candidates and infuse unlimited amounts of money into the electoral process.

Federal laws governing campaign contributions apply only to congressional and presidential candidates and national PACs. When it comes to state elections—such as those for governor, attorney general, or state legislator—state laws apply. And those rules vary significantly (see Table 2).[27]

In Virginia, as well as in 10 other states with no limits on political giving, you can literally hand a candidate for governor a check for $1 million (or more).[28] Corporations and unions can do the same thing. In the state of Washington, it's a different story. You're limited to no more than $2,000 per gubernatorial candidate. Corporations and unions are held to the same limit. And if they aren't active in the state, then corporations and unions can't give at all. Some states also limit contributions to state legislative candidates. In Colorado, Maine, and Montana, those limits are set at less than $500. Reporting requirements vary as well. Only 13 states require state political parties to disclose their contributions. Just 5 states require campaigns to report any loans they've taken out. All 50, however, mandate that campaigns report what they spend and receive during an election cycle.[29]

TABLE 2. Maximum Campaign Contributions in Four States' Elections

	Virginia	Florida	Ohio	Washington
Individual contributions	Unlimited	$3,000 to statewide candidates $1,000 to state legislative candidates	$13,704.41 to any state candidate	$2,000 to statewide candidates $1,000 to state legislative candidates
PAC	Unlimited	$3,000 to statewide candidates $1,000 to state legislative candidates	$13,704.41 to any state candidate	$2,000 to statewide candidates $1,000 to state legislative candidates
Corporate contributions	Unlimited	$3,000 to statewide candidates $1,000 to state legislative candidates	Prohibited	$2,000 to statewide candidates $1,000 to state legislative candidates
Union contributions	Unlimited	$3,000 to statewide candidates $1,000 to state legislative candidates	Prohibited	$2,000 to statewide candidates $1,000 to state legislative candidates

Note: Entries represent the maximum legal contribution each source can make to a state election in VA, FL, OH, and WA.

Source: See Note 27 for full source information.

Is Money a Problem? Two Perspectives

There's no question that money plays a critical role in U.S. politics. And it's clear that the public is convinced money is a problem. But there's no consensus among policy makers as to whether there's "too much" of it floating around. Consider some of the leading arguments on both sides of this debate, and then draw your own conclusion.

There's Not Too Much Money in U.S. Elections

One of the bedrocks of democracy is an engaged citizenry. According to some political observers, money in elections helps grab people's attention and gets them involved in the democratic process. Only with money can candidates conduct polls to find out what voters want. Only with money can they produce campaign ads to inform voters of their ideas and distinguish themselves from their opponents. And only with money can they develop programs to remind voters to go to the polls. In fact, candidates who value small contributions from average citizens often encourage people to become more engaged and connected to the electoral process by donating money. In 2016, Bernie Sanders proudly asserted that the average contribution to his campaign for president was "27 bucks."[30] In 2020, his average contribution was even smaller. Yet he managed to raise $114 million from small donations.[31] Donald Trump, in an unprecedented move for a Republican presidential candidate, raised more than $100 million from people giving less than $200 each in 2016. Four years later, he took in more than $378 million from small donors.[32] In both cases, strong grassroots support—often from people who had never before given to a political candidate—helped propel these candidates' campaigns.

That's not the only reason some people argue that there's not too much money in elections. They also point out that we are too caught up talking about expensive presidential and congressional elections, "fat cat" donors, and wealthy candidates. Yet campaigns for the vast majority of elected positions in the United States cost relatively little. According to Campaign in a Box, a guide for first-time candidates, people who want to run for city council in small to medium-sized cities only need to raise $8,000 to $12,000 to run a campaign.[33] That might still seem like a lot of money, but it's nowhere near the millions of dollars that candidates for federal office need to raise. And it's still enough to create a good website, get voters to the polls, and even do a little local advertising.

State legislative races in many places are pretty inexpensive, too. The average candidate running for the Montana House of Representatives in 2020 raised $7,907. The average state legislative candidate in New

Hampshire? A mere $1,566.[34] For many other positions—school board, judge, county commissioner—depending on where you live, there are often no real campaign costs at all; the only expense is a modest filing fee to get on the ballot.

Finally, it's important to place the amount of money spent on elections in context. Campaigns are essentially advertising plans designed to promote a candidate and close a sale with voters. In 2020, the presidential campaigns spent roughly $4 billion total on selling their candidates. To put that figure into perspective, Comcast spent $5.7 billion marketing phone services, Procter & Gamble spent $4.4 billion selling household products (think toilet paper and shampoo), and Amazon, AT&T, and General Motors each spent close to $3.5 billion on advertising.[35] Some political leaders argue that we're not spending too much if the campaign to elect the leader of the "free world" costs roughly the same as a single company's annual ad budget.

There's Way Too Much Money in U.S. Elections

Concerns about democracy also underpin arguments that there's too much money in elections. Elected officials are supposed to be accountable to all of their constituents, not just to the ones who contribute to their campaigns. But as the stories of the ambassadors that opened this segment suggest, major campaign donors often curry favor with candidates.

Even when they're not explicitly rewarded with a political appointment, most major donors have an agenda and expect their preferred candidates to be responsive. We address whether special interests control the political process more fully in Segment 41. But for now, it's enough to note that when oil tycoons like the Koch brothers donate hundreds of millions of dollars, it's to support candidates who will look favorably on the oil industry and oppose almost all business regulations if elected. Or when billionaire and former New York City mayor and presidential candidate Michael Bloomberg spends tens of millions of dollars supporting candidates who favor gun control, he expects those who win to advocate for stricter gun laws. In the end, the top 100 donors and their families in the 2020 cycle contributed more than $1.5 billion.[36] Compounding the perception of undue influence from billionaires is money pouring in from specific industries: $802 million from banking, $419 million from real estate, $268 million from health care, and $141 million from oil and gas in 2020 alone.[37] We live in a world where super-wealthy donors and well-funded industries can launch and sustain candidates all by themselves.

But the potential consequences of buying access are damning even when we move beyond billionaire donors. One study found that members of Congress and their senior staffers were more likely to agree to a meeting with donors than with local constituents who didn't contribute to their campaigns.[38] Similar dynamics apply to state legislators.[39] This matters because in recent election cycles, only about 13 percent of U.S. adults reported making a contribution to a presidential candidate.[40] And in 2020—as well as in every other federal election dating back to 1990— less than 1.5 percent of citizens made a political donation to a presidential or congressional candidate that exceeded $200. Moreover, money from large donors has come to represent an increasing share of the contributions that candidates receive.[41]

Finally, many people worry about a system increasingly driven by wealthy donors because these donors don't actually represent most Americans. They're older, richer, Whiter, and overwhelmingly male.[42] Consider gender differences as an example. Men, who constitute a little less than 50 percent of the U.S. population, account for approximately 65 percent of direct contributions that exceed $200 to federal candidates. They also account for more than two-thirds of the individuals who "max out"—that is, who give the maximum allowable contribution to candidates in both the primary and the general election.[43] These gender disparities are important because men and women have divergent views on many issues. To the extent that campaign contributions affect the legislative agenda that elected officials pursue, women's underrepresentation as political donors is worrisome.[44] Underrepresentation in political giving along racial, ethnic, or age groups raises similar concerns.

The Future of Campaign Finance

Even though the public thinks there's too much money in elections, sweeping change is unlikely. And not because there are no ideas out there. In fact, the most common proposal—a system of publicly financed elections—has already been adopted in several states. Public financing, which can take multiple forms, typically involves using tax dollars to fund candidates' campaigns. Candidates all receive the same amount of money, and their campaign spending is capped at that level. The idea is to reduce the influence of large donors and wealthy corporations. The problem is that there's no path forward at the federal level. Most Republican elected leaders in Washington, D.C., don't see money in elections as a serious problem. Most Democrats claim they do, but they don't prioritize changing a system that helped them get elected. And even if they did, the Supreme Court has established campaign contributions as a form of free speech. Reforms that limit the right to contribute to campaigns, even in unlimited amounts, will likely be interpreted as unconstitutional. Without a seismic shift in Washington, D.C., the status quo will remain, and many of our ambassadors will continue to know more about fundraising than they do about the countries where they're sent.

DID YOU GET IT?

Is there too much money in elections?

Short Answer:

- Increasingly large amounts of money flow into elections, but whether there's too much is a matter of ongoing debate.
- Federal laws try to regulate the billions of dollars that flow into politics from individuals, parties, and PACs.
- The advent of Super PACs elevates the role of wealthy donors by providing an avenue for individuals, corporations, and unions to contribute unlimited sums to elect candidates.

DEVELOPING YOUR SKILLS

Quantitative Literacy

Make predictions: Quantitative skills are critical when it comes to counting cash! These questions ask you to make projections about the role of money in elections and figure out how individual candidates can achieve their fundraising goals.

1. Assuming the trend since 2008 continues, about how much money is likely to be spent in the 2024 presidential election? You'll need to consult Figure 2 for this one.
   a. About $1 billion
   b. About $4 billion
   c. About $7 billion
   d. About $20 billion
2. Presidential candidates often have to raise tens of millions of dollars to be considered viable contenders. Based on campaign finance laws for federal candidates, which strategy would be the most efficient (and legal) way to get $20 million donated *directly* to their campaigns? (Hint: Refer to Table 1.)
   a. One wealthy donor writing the candidate a check
   b. One billionaire creating a Super PAC
   c. Five billionaires creating Super PACs
   d. 3,449 maximum individual contributions

3. Take a look at the campaign finance rules of the four states listed in Table 2. In which state would a future candidate for governor likely have the hardest time raising money?

    a. Virginia

    b. Ohio

    c. Washington

    d. Florida

FIGURE IT OUT

OpenSecrets.org is a great website that tracks campaign contributions to federal candidates. It allows you to check presidential and congressional candidates' previous fundraising and provides a sense of sources of money for future elections. Choose one of your home state senators, and assess their campaign committee's fundraising profile. If your home isn't in the United States (or maybe it's in Washington, D.C., or Puerto Rico), just choose a state you're interested in. Then answer the following questions, some of which require you to make some simple predictions:

- What senator did you choose? And when was the senator's last election?

- How much money did the senator raise in the most recent election?

- What percentage of the senator's money came from (1) small contributions, (2) large contributions, and (3) PACs?

- What are the top three industries that contributed to this senator's most recent campaign?

- Identify one industry that your senator might be able to go to in order to raise even more money. In a sentence or two, explain why this might be a good source of future fundraising.

Want to Know More?

Campaign finance reform is one of the toughest political issues to tackle. It involves constitutional constraints, powerful interests, and elected officials who have succeeded under the current rules. But lots of interest groups are devoted to reforming the system. Check out the websites of Common Cause (commoncause.org), openDemocracy (opendemocracy.org), and Public Citizen (citizen.org) if you're interested in learning more about proposals for getting money out of politics.

30.
What is the Electoral College anyway?

#PathTo270

In 2000, Democratic presidential candidate Al Gore received 48.4 percent of the vote. Republican George W. Bush? 47.9 percent. Gore received 500,000 more votes nationwide, but Bush won the election.

Fast-forward to 2016. Democrat Hillary Clinton received 48.2 percent of the vote. Republican Donald Trump? 46.1 percent. Clinton received roughly 3 million more votes, but Trump became president of the United States.

Huh? How did this happen? In a democracy, doesn't the person who gets the most votes win the election? If you're running for president in the United States, not necessarily. That's because we employ one of the most unusual methods for electing a political leader of any democratic country in the world: the Electoral College.[1] Which isn't a college. Or even a place. It's the process the Founders established for choosing the nation's leader when they drafted the Constitution. Put simply — we'll get to the details shortly — the states, not the citizens, select the president.

And lots of people don't like it. Most Americans favor replacing the Electoral College with a popular vote system, which would guarantee that the candidate who receives the most votes nationwide becomes president.[2] Not surprisingly, Democrats are significantly more likely than Republicans to feel this way. After all, Democratic candidates

The United Battleground States of America

The rest of you can take a nap or keep looking at TikTok

Presidential candidates win when they get 270 electoral votes, regardless of whether they win the most votes nationwide. As a result, the fight for 270 often means that swing states are the only ones that really matter to the campaigns.

won the popular vote but couldn't claim victory in two of the last six presidential elections.

This segment explains the logic underpinning the Electoral College and walks you through how it works. Prior to the 2020 election, this would have been a pretty straightforward discussion. But when supporters of President Trump stormed the U.S. Capitol on January 6, 2021, in an attempt to prevent Congress from certifying the Electoral College's vote, they heightened major doubts and concerns about our system of electing the president. By the end of this segment, armed with clear information about the process and the challenges the Electoral College poses to democratic presidential elections in the United States, you'll be well equipped to determine whether we should keep it or scrap it.

How Did We Wind Up with Such an Unusual Way to Elect the President?

When the Founders drafted the Constitution, they weren't sure how to choose the president. Should Congress decide? Should it be left to each state's legislature? Maybe the governor of each state should choose? Or perhaps a randomly selected group of congressmen should be tasked with the decision? The Founders considered many options at the Constitutional Convention and couldn't reach an immediate consensus.[3]

But the Founders did agree on two things. First, most of them did not believe that the people themselves should directly select the president. They were leery of too much democracy and wanted a buffer against citizen rule. James Madison, after all, had warned that direct democracies typically end in "violent death."[4] Second, they needed to assure small states that they'd have influence in the presidential selection process. Otherwise, the small states would be reluctant to ratify the Constitution.

To meet these two criteria, the Founders ultimately arrived at the **Electoral College**, which they laid out in Article II, Sections 2 and 3, of the Constitution:

> Each State shall appoint, in such Manner as the Legislature thereof may direct, a Number of Electors, equal to the whole Number of Senators and Representatives to which the State may be entitled in the Congress.... The Electors shall meet in their respective States, and vote by Ballot [to select the president].

The process was unusual, but it achieved the Founders' goals. It minimized direct citizen input in selecting the president by leaving it up to each state legislature to devise a process of choosing "electors." The electors would decide which presidential and vice-presidential candidates the state supported. Because citizens voted directly for their state legislators, the people (or at least land-owning White men in most states at that time) would play a role in selecting the head of the executive branch, but it would be an indirect one. And the process quelled the small states' concerns about having no influence in the process because the number of electors allocated to each state would equal the size of its congressional delegation. The large states would have more electors because they had more members of the House of Representatives. But the small states wouldn't be steamrolled because every state had two U.S. senators. The candidate who won a majority of electoral votes would become president.

No state's electoral votes would be set in stone. Every 10 years, the Constitution calls for a census of the population to be conducted. The results are then used to ensure that every congressional district contains roughly the same number of people. So when a state would gain or lose a member of the House of Representatives, that change would be reflected in its electoral votes as well.

The Electoral College: How It Works Today

The general structure the Founders established for the Electoral College remains intact. Today there are 538 electors. That number equals the size of the U.S. Congress (435 members of the House of Representatives and 100 U.S. senators) plus an additional 3 electors granted to the District of Columbia. In every state, the leaders of each political party with a presidential candidate on the ballot choose a slate of electors prior to the general election. They're usually party activists, former elected officials, or party leaders. In 2020, for example, Hillary Clinton was one of the Democratic Party's electors in New York. Each elector has one vote—that's what it means when you hear the term **electoral vote**. Figure 1 shows the number of electoral votes allocated to each state.[5] More sparsely populated states have fewer electoral votes, and more heavily populated states have more.

According to Article II of the Constitution, it's up to each state to decide how to award electoral votes. In contemporary politics, all 50 states and the District of Columbia follow their citizens' preferences. On Election Day, voters go the polls and cast their ballots for president. Well, sort of. They're technically voting for the slate of electors

FIGURE 1. Electoral Vote Allocations for the 2024 Presidential Election

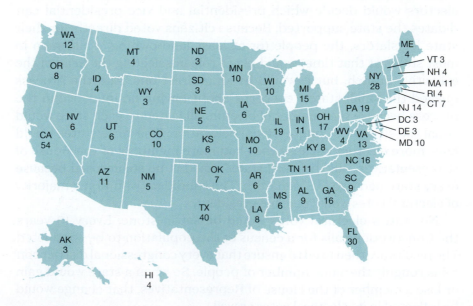

Source: "2024 Presidential Election Interactive Map," 270toWin.

What is the Electoral College anyway?

NBC's Tim Russert (left) and CNN's John King (right) track the electoral vote. The whiteboard and magic marker Russert used in 2000 have given way to the flashier screens and technology King relied on in 2020. But regardless of the graphics, election night is always about which candidate can rack up 270 electoral votes.

associated with the candidate of their choice. In 48 states, the party whose candidate wins the statewide popular vote sends its slate of electors forward. It doesn't matter if the winner barely eked out a victory by a few votes or crushed it. The winner gets all the electoral votes. In Maine and Nebraska, candidates get an electoral vote for every congressional district where they win the popular vote. Each state's remaining 2 electoral votes go to the candidate who wins the popular vote statewide. In the end, a candidate needs 270 electoral votes to win the presidency.

Despite the fact that a winner is usually declared on election night in November, the outcome isn't official until almost two months later. First, each state's winning slate of electors must meet to vote in that state's capital—usually, in the third week of December. It's important to note that nothing in the Constitution requires the electors to cast their votes in line with the state's popular vote. They can literally vote for anyone. David Mulinix, a 2016 Democratic elector from Hawaii, summarized the rules like this: "If all the electors got together and held a conference, and said you know what, we're going to vote for like Donald Duck, they can just do that."[6] But they rarely do; electors typically pledge to support the statewide winner.

The second part of the process takes place in early January at the U.S. Capitol building in Washington, D.C. All the electors' votes from all 50 states and the District of Columbia are tallied. Then, in a ceremony presided over by the vice president of the United States, the members of the House and Senate vote to accept each state's electoral votes. The vice president then declares the winner of the presidential election—the candidate who receives at least 270 electoral votes. In the case of a tie (269–269) or a situation in which no

TABLE 1. Electoral College Cheat Sheet

How many electoral votes are there?	538
How many electoral votes does each state have?	Each state's allocation equals the size of its congressional delegation (the number of members of the House of Representatives plus U.S. senators). The District of Columbia has three electoral votes.
How do candidates win electoral votes?	In every state except Maine and Nebraska, it's winner-take-all. If you win the state's popular vote, then you get all of that state's electoral votes.
How many electoral votes does a candidate need to win the election?	270

candidate reaches 270, the Constitution dictates that the House of Representatives chooses the president and vice president. Under these circumstances, each state's congressional delegation gets 1 vote, and the candidate who receives at least 26 out of 50 votes becomes president.[7]

The Electoral College might seem complicated. That's because it is, at least compared to a popular vote system. It's also very difficult to change. That's because it's embedded in the Constitution. But if you remember just the four essential aspects of the process laid out in Table 1, you'll be prepared to follow the next presidential election.

The Electoral College Poses Challenges to Democracy

The Electoral College settled some controversies and concerns at the Constitutional Convention. But that was 1787, and since then, attitudes about democratic governance have changed. After all, we've expanded voting rights to women, African Americans, residents of the District of Columbia, and 18-year-olds; moved to the direct election of U.S. senators; and banned **poll taxes** (laws designed to suppress the African American vote by charging people a fee to cast a ballot). Twenty-six states allow citizens to vote directly on specific state policies. And almost 80 percent of Americans believe that democracy is the best form of government.[8] Yet the Electoral College remains, despite three fundamental challenges it poses for democratic elections.

Challenge #1: The Person with the Most Votes Doesn't Always Win

A fundamental criticism of the Electoral College is that it can produce a winner who received fewer overall votes than the loser. This has happened five times. In 1824 and 1876, no candidate received a majority of electoral votes, so the House of Representatives chose the winner. And in both cases, they selected the candidate who received fewer votes nationwide. In 1888, 2000, and 2016, the candidate who won a majority of electoral votes lost the popular vote. To a lot of people, this simply doesn't make sense. But it's not too difficult to see how it can happen. Just take a look at Table 2, which displays the election returns from three large states in 2016.

Let's start with California. The entries reveal that Hillary Clinton won the popular vote by a large margin (more than 4 million votes). And because California is winner-take-all, Clinton received all 55 of the state's electoral votes. In Florida and Texas, Donald Trump claimed victory. His popular vote margins were significantly smaller than Clinton's in California, but the winner-take-all system means that Trump received all 38 electoral votes in Texas and all 29 in Florida.

Now, tally the popular vote and the electoral vote across California, Texas, and Florida. Clinton led Trump in the popular vote by more than 3 million. But she trailed him in the electoral vote by 12. The bottom row of Table 2 compiles the total popular vote and electoral vote for all 50 states and Washington, D.C. Because the winner is the person who receives the most electoral votes, it's possible to elect as president someone who didn't win the most votes nationwide.

TABLE 2. The Popular Vote versus the Electoral Vote in 2016

	Popular Vote		Electoral Vote	
	Trump	Clinton	Trump	Clinton
California	4,483,810	8,753,788	0	55
Texas	4,685,047	3,877,868	38	0
Florida	4,617,886	4,504,975	29	0
Total in three biggest states	13,786,743	17,136,631	67	55
National total	**62,980,160**	**65,845,063**	**306**	**232**

TABLE 3. How Much Does One Vote Count?

	State Population	Electoral Votes	Residents per Electoral Vote
Wyoming	590,013	3	196,671
Vermont	648,560	3	216,187
New York	20,200,000	28	721,428

Challenge #2: Citizens' Votes Don't All Count the Same

A fundamental premise of American democracy, and one affirmed by the Supreme Court in the 1960s, is the notion of "one person, one vote."[9] In other words, each legislative district must have approximately the same number of residents so that each person gets the same "amount" of influence in selecting a representative. But with the Electoral College, some citizens' votes literally count more than others'. That's because electoral votes are based on the size of a state's congressional delegation. And although all congressional districts have similar populations, every state—regardless of how many people live there—has two senators. That dilutes the impact of each citizen's vote in states with larger populations.

To see how this plays out, look at Table 3, which lists the population size and electoral vote count for two small states and one large state. In the two small states, each electoral vote represents somewhere in the neighborhood of 200,000 voters. In New York, each electoral vote represents more than 700,000 voters. That means that one citizen's vote in Wyoming or Vermont counts about 3.6 times as much as a citizen's vote in New York. Most of the citizens whose votes count more are White people living in rural states. People of color, in contrast, tend to be concentrated in urban areas of large-population states. So the Electoral College dilutes the power of voters of color in selecting the president.[10]

Challenge #3: Presidential Campaigns Are Distorted

An irony of the Electoral College's reliance on states is that very few states actually matter in contemporary presidential elections. Because of the winner-take-all system, heavily Democratic and heavily Republican states just aren't worth campaigning in. In New York, California, Rhode Island, and Delaware, for example, Democrats significantly outnumber Republicans.[11] A Republican presidential candidate hasn't won any of these states since 1988. With virtually no way to win the statewide popular vote, what's the point of campaigning in those places? And there's no reason for Democratic candidates to spend time there either—they're shoo-ins. The opposite is true in states like Idaho, Utah, Wyoming, and South Carolina. The last time a Democrat won any of these states? 1976. No need for either candidate to make a direct case to the voters there. With so many Republicans, the outcome is a foregone conclusion.

The overwhelming majority of states are **safe states**—those where the outcome of an election is never in doubt. In fact, during the 2020 general election campaign, 33 states saw no public presidential campaign events from either party. No rallies, no speeches, no fairs, no town hall meetings featuring the Republican or Democratic presidential or vice-presidential candidates. Zero.[12] Several of the remaining 17 states didn't see much action either. Five had somewhere between one and three visits from a presidential or vice-presidential candidate. That's hardly a vigorous campaign. Instead, 96 percent of the 212 general election campaign events in 2020 occurred in just 12 states (see Figure 2).[13]

FIGURE 2. Number of Campaign Events in Swing States in 2020

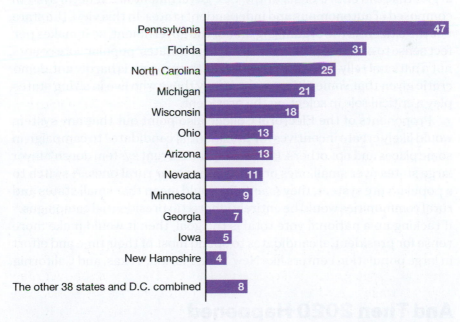

State	Events
Pennsylvania	47
Florida	31
North Carolina	25
Michigan	21
Wisconsin	18
Ohio	13
Arizona	13
Nevada	11
Minnesota	9
Georgia	7
Iowa	5
New Hampshire	4
The other 38 states and D.C. combined	8

Note: In 2020, Donald Trump, Joe Biden, Mike Pence, and Kamala Harris attended 212 public events in the three months leading up to Election Day.

Source: "Map of General-Election Campaign Events and TV Ad Spending by 2020 Presidential Candidates," National Popular Vote.

Candidates spend their time in **swing states**—those where neither party has a consistent edge in voter registration and, thus, whose electoral votes are genuinely up for grabs. But by focusing on the 12 swing states listed in Figure 2, presidential campaigns tend to ignore the 70 percent of the U.S. population that lives in the other 38 states and the District of Columbia. Residents of those states miss out not only on seeing public campaign events but also on the rest of the campaign—television ads, armies of volunteers, and get out the vote operations. A few thousand people in a handful of states are more important than millions of voters nationwide.

The Electoral College Preserves the Influence of All States

Arguments to get rid of the Electoral College because it's antidemocratic are quite prevalent. But is the situation really that bad? Proponents of the Electoral College argue that we should keep it because it embodies fundamental principles on which the U.S. government was founded.

More specifically, many people who support the Electoral College argue that the entire basis of the U.S. government is a federal system composed of autonomous and independent states. In this view, the state, not the citizen, is the organizing unit of the government, so it makes perfect sense to elect the president by relying on states' popular vote counts, not a national tally.[14] Besides, they argue, the process is hardly antidemocratic given that some citizens, especially those who live in swing states, play a critical role in selecting the president.

Proponents of the Electoral College also point out that any system would likely create incentives for presidential candidates to campaign in some places and not others. But at least the current system doesn't favor large states over small ones or urban areas over rural ones. A switch to a popular vote system, they maintain, would mean that small states and rural communities would be entirely ignored in presidential campaigns.[15] If racking up a national vote total is the goal, then it would make more sense for presidential candidates to spend most of their time and effort in large population centers like New York, Florida, Texas, and California.

And Then 2020 Happened

The Electoral College, despite the confusion and controversies that always surrounded it, had been humming along for more than two centuries. Sure, it seemed unnecessarily complex. But for the most part, the system produced undisputed leaders of the country. At least until the 2020 presidential election. At first glance, the outcome didn't seem particularly complicated. Joe Biden won the popular vote; he received roughly 7.5 million more votes than Donald Trump nationwide. That win translated into a clear victory in the Electoral College, too: 306 electoral votes for Biden compared to 232 for Trump.[16] But Trump and his supporters did not accept those results. They claimed that Biden's popular vote victory in at least five states—Arizona, Georgia, Michigan, Pennsylvania, and Wisconsin—was the result of election fraud. And if the results in those states were reversed, then Trump would win in the Electoral College and retain the presidency.

Because there are more than two months between Election Day and the certification of the electoral vote, Trump and his supporters had time to make a case. They filed dozens of lawsuits in local, state, and federal courts contesting the results in the five states.[17] They lobbied election officials charged with counting the votes in several states to change the results. In a recorded call to Georgia's secretary of state, for example, Trump said, "I just want to find 11,780 votes. . . . There's nothing wrong with saying, you know, that you've recalculated."[18] They urged state legislators in the contested states to vote to seat an alternate slate of electors—people who would cast their electoral votes for Trump.[19] In each case, Trump and his allies attempted to disrupt the awarding of electoral votes in ways never seen before. Though Trump had many sympathetic allies in states across the country, the effort ultimately failed because neither election officials (including Republicans) nor the courts (including judges appointed by Trump) uncovered any systematic evidence of voter fraud in any of the states.[20]

Trump's last chance to prevent Biden from taking office was to block certification of the electoral vote. So, on January 6, 2021, approximately 10,000 Trump supporters gathered in Washington, D.C., to rally Congress and Vice President Mike Pence not to certify Biden's win. After listening to speeches by President Trump and several members of Congress—all of which recounted allegations of voter fraud and a stolen election—the protesters marched toward the U.S. Capitol, where the Electoral College certification was underway. Roughly 1,000 of them broke through barricades and stormed the Capitol building. The Capitol police rushed members of Congress to safety, where they waited for hours as protesters destroyed property and rummaged through the offices of Democratic leaders. Some even chanted, "Hang Mike Pence." They considered the vice president a traitor for carrying out his constitutional obligation to preside over the electoral vote certification.[21]

After the police cleared the Capitol of the demonstrators, members of Congress returned to certify the electoral vote in what had always been a symbolic, typically unanimous vote. But not this time. Despite a tumultuous day and hours spent in hiding, 145 Republican members of the House and Senate, many of whom once again raised concerns about election fraud, voted not to certify some of the states' electoral vote counts. By the time Pence ultimately declared Joe Biden and Kamala Harris the next president and vice president of the United States, it was nearly 4 A.M.[22]

The 2020 election highlights the fragility of the Electoral College as an institution. For the first time in contemporary politics, high-profile political leaders—including the president of the United States—and their allies called into question the integrity of various states' voting laws and procedures. They carried out specific efforts to delegitimize the accuracy of state vote counts. State legislators faced, and sometimes succumbed to, pressure to invalidate lawful vote counts in their states. Violent demonstrators disrupted the certification of the electoral vote. And many members of the U.S. Congress refused to accept the electoral vote count submitted by some states. Until 2020, concerns about the Electoral College had predominantly revolved around how the system could produce a president who did not win the national popular vote. But now, individual states' systems for running elections and awarding electoral votes are under attack. The system managed to survive in 2020, but many fear that it won't in 2024 or beyond.

DID YOU GET IT?
What is the Electoral College anyway?

Short Answer:

- The Electoral College is a system the Founders designed to elect the president and vice president of the United States. It limits direct democracy and ensures that all states play a role in the process.
- The Electoral College is controversial because it can result in outcomes in which the winner isn't the candidate who receives the most votes nationwide.
- Whether we should get rid of the Electoral College comes down to which you value more: direct democracy or more balance between the influence of large and small states.

Persuasive Argumentation

Choose a side: The Electoral College is one of the most controversial aspects of the presidential election process, largely because it can result in outcomes in which the candidate who gets the most votes loses the election. These questions ask you to consider persuasive arguments for maintaining and abolishing the Electoral College.

1. If you want to argue against the Electoral College, which sentence could follow a thesis statement that says the system gives small states disproportionate influence?

   a. Wyoming has the same number of senators as Pennsylvania.

   b. Presidential candidates spend more time in Wisconsin than in Vermont.

   c. California has more than 10 times as many electoral votes as Nebraska.

   d. Idaho and Maine have the same number of electoral votes.

2. Which could serve as a persuasive thesis statement in support of the Electoral College?

   a. We should maintain the Electoral College because it forces presidential candidates to focus their time on swing states.

   b. We should maintain the Electoral College because the Founders easily arrived at it as a way to choose the president.

   c. We should maintain the Electoral College because it ensures that everyone's vote counts equally.

   d. We should maintain the Electoral College because it embodies the federal system of government in the United States.

3. If you want to convince your friends that we should scrap the Electoral College, which argument would be most persuasive?

   a. The Electoral College often reduces the presidential election to a contest in a handful of swing states.

   b. The Electoral College incentivizes candidates to spend time campaigning in Massachusetts and California.

   c. The Electoral College is laid out in the Constitution.

   d. Electors almost always follow the popular vote in their states when deciding how to vote in the Electoral College.

FIGURE IT OUT

One criticism of the Electoral College is that it depresses voter turnout in states that are not competitive. In other words, in states that almost always vote either Republican or Democratic, voters are less likely to show up at the polls because the outcome in their state is a foregone conclusion. But is this true? Determine whether this is a persuasive argument against the Electoral College. More specifically:

- Select two safe Republican states, and get the voter turnout rate for each in 2020. You can find turnout statistics on all 50 states at the United States Elections Project website: http://www.electproject.org/2020g. For the purposes of this question, you can rely on the column entitled "VEP Turnout Rate (Highest Office)." Hint: You might need to scroll to the right in the spreadsheet to get to the column you need.

- Select two safe Democratic states, and get the voter turnout rate for each in 2020.

- Select two swing states (you can find these in Figure 2), and get the voter turnout rate for each in 2020.

- For each group of states, calculate the average voter turnout rate.

- Does the information you uncovered help you choose a side in the debate over whether the Electoral College depresses turnout in uncompetitive states? Answer this question by constructing a clear thesis statement.

Want to Know More?

Getting rid of the Electoral College would require a constitutional amendment, which is unlikely given how difficult the amendment process is. But several organizations have proposed reforms to the system that wouldn't require an amendment. James W. Lucas's book *Fifty States, Not Six: A Bipartisan Approach to Reforming the Electoral College and Assuring that Every Citizen's Vote Counts* provides one possibility. The National Popular Vote organization (https://www.nationalpopularvote.com/) offers another.

31.
How do you run for president?

#PresidentialElectionProcess

George Clooney is running for president. Well, not really. Despite regular speculation that he might one day throw his hat into the ring, Clooney denies any such political ambition.[1] But just indulge us for the purposes of this segment.

Actually, a Clooney candidacy isn't that far-fetched. He's been a household name for decades, having appeared in hit television shows and starred in more than 50 films. He's a two-time recipient of *People* magazine's "Sexiest Man Alive" designation. He's also very civically engaged. Clooney grew up in a political family in Kentucky — his mother served on the local city council, and his father ran (unsuccessfully) as a Democrat for the U.S. Congress. He's raised millions of dollars for flood, tsunami, and earthquake victims in the United States and abroad. In the early 2000s, he became an outspoken advocate to end the genocide in Sudan. He served for six years as the United Nations' "Messenger for Peace."[2] And like many Democratic candidates for high-level elective office, he has publicly decried the role of money in politics, lauded the #MeToo movement, condemned Donald Trump, and advocated for widespread masking amid Covid-19.[3]

Just a few years ago, it might have seemed absurd for a liberal Hollywood actor who had never run for any elected position to seek the presidency. The White House had always been reserved for governors, senators, vice presidents, and an occasional war hero. No more. Donald

Actor George Clooney has no aspirations to run for any political office, let alone president of the United States. But the process he'd have to undergo — which we track throughout this segment — is long, arduous, and expensive.

Trump, a high-profile businessman and reality TV show host, had no electoral experience when he ran for president and defeated Hillary Clinton, a former U.S. senator and secretary of state. Oprah Winfrey, Ben Affleck, and Dwayne "The Rock" Johnson have all been touted as possible presidential candidates. Pop singer Katy Perry posted a picture on Instagram with two former presidents and suggested that she, too, would one day occupy the Oval Office.[4] Musical artist Kanye West actually ran for president in 2020.[5] Suffice it to say that a Clooney candidacy is certainly plausible.

So what does George Clooney, or anyone with aspirations for the White House, have to do to get elected president? To have a little fun describing the presidential election process, we show you all it would entail for Clooney to run for president. You'll see that the process is a marathon, not a sprint. It's a two-year endeavor in which Clooney must first seek and win the Democratic Party's nomination and then defeat the Republican Party's candidate in the general election. By the end of this segment, you'll be familiar with the rigorous campaign calendar that candidates must adhere to and the myriad strategic decisions they must make along the way.

 January 2023 ## Clooney for President! Deciding to Run and Building a Campaign

The Constitution doesn't provide many barriers when it comes to eligibility to run for president. You need to be at least 35 years old, be a native-born citizen, and have lived in the United States for at least 14 years. George Clooney checks all the boxes. But beyond these legal requirements,

How do you run for president?

Clooney—like all potential presidential candidates—must assess whether he's got a shot at winning. Political professionals often refer to this pre-stage of a campaign as "testing the waters." And it requires a more systematic analysis than looking at an *Entertainment Weekly* poll from a few years back that deemed Clooney the celebrity best suited to be president.[6]

To assess his prospects, Clooney takes several steps typical of potential candidates. First, he conducts a poll of Democratic voters. It turns out that most of them view him favorably. The poll results also reveal that the issues Clooney cares most about—health care, the environment, and equality—appeal to a broad array of Democratic voters. With positive poll results in hand, Clooney then speaks with several members of Congress and former White House officials, many of whom he came to know when he testified before the Senate Foreign Relations Committee about the humanitarian crisis in Sudan.[7] The conversations go well. No one is quite ready to pledge support, but no one discourages him either.[8] Finally, Clooney considers the depth and commitment of his social media followers and compiles a list of potential donors. Campaigns can't take off without a devoted group of supporters and the ability to raise money early on.[9] Given the favorable reception by voters and politicians, Clooney decides to run. His family is on board, too, fully aware that the campaign will consume almost two years of their lives.

Before sharing with the world his decision to enter the Democratic primary, Clooney needs to assemble a campaign staff. He must move quickly because there's often strong competition among candidates to attract people who have worked on successful presidential campaigns. It turns out that the campaign organization Clooney needs to build isn't all that different from the team he would need to assemble to make a major motion picture. Every movie needs a producer, just like every campaign needs a chairperson. Every movie needs a director, just like every campaign needs a campaign manager. Table 1 summarizes the major campaign positions Clooney needs to fill. If he makes it to the general election, the paid campaign staff will likely swell to as many as 800 people.[10]

February 2023

Clooney Gets in the Race: Deciding on a Message and Making the Announcement

As his campaign team begins to take shape, there's no time to waste. Clooney must develop a message that resonates with voters. A campaign message usually consists of a theme or key policy issue as well as a slogan. You know the message is effective when you can easily recall it. In 2008, Barack Obama ran on "hope" and "change." In 2020, Joe Biden's "Build

TABLE 1. Key Staff Positions on a Presidential Campaign

Role	Responsibility	In Hollywood-Speak
Campaign chair	Well-known person with deep ties to party leaders and donors. Identifies potential endorsements, raises money, and offers input on strategy.	*The producer:* makes sure all the pieces are in place.
Campaign manager	Coordinates the campaign's fundraising, budgeting, and strategy. Oversees day-to-day operations and the candidate's time and schedule.	*The director:* frantically tries to keep all the parts moving in the same direction.
Chief strategist	Works with the candidate and campaign manager to develop and execute the campaign plan. Gathers damaging information about opponents.	*The agent:* promotes the candidate and tries to crush all competitors.
Communications director	Builds relationships with the press, serves as campaign spokesperson, drafts speeches, and provides content for campaign materials and website.	*The publicist:* works to get positive coverage of the candidate in the news media.
Finance director	Works with the candidate to raise money. Oversees all fundraising solicitations and events.	*The studio executive:* secures the money for the project.
Policy advisers	Provide expertise and help develop the candidate's specific plans for addressing domestic and foreign policy issues.	*The writers:* take the candidate's broad ideas and craft them into actual proposals.
Media consultant	Develops and produces campaign ads (for television, radio, internet, and social media) and other campaign materials to get out a candidate's message.	*The promotor:* creates catchy, 30-second clips of the candidate's bio and policies.
Pollster	Conducts polls to determine which messages resonate best with voters, which voters to target, and how to characterize the opponent.	*The critic:* lets the campaign know what the voters are thinking.

Back Better" embodied the many ways he would strengthen the economy in the wake of the global pandemic. Perhaps the most effective message in recent elections was Donald Trump's message in 2016: "Make America Great Again." Campaign merchandise, lines in every speech, and MAGA hashtags made it all but impossible to forget Trump's stated goal.

Clooney and his team of strategists want to run on the issues that voters care most about and build on Clooney's previous political activism. So they decide to focus on "advancing world peace," "restoring democracy," and "taking care of all citizens." He'll apply these themes more specifically to health care, the environment, and equality. As far as a slogan is concerned, they settle on "An America with Heart." "Choose Peace" was a close second. One strategist thought that "Not Too Sexy to Lead" would be memorable and grab headlines. But Clooney vetoed that idea, reminding his staff that he wants to be taken seriously as a candidate, not as eye candy on a debate stage. He does know, however, that his looks certainly can't hurt; candidates perceived by voters to be more attractive often do better at the polls.[11]

Prior to the internet era, candidates almost always announced their campaigns by assembling a large crowd and delivering a speech that laid out the rationale for their candidacy. These days, candidates can skip the speech route if they'd rather announce their intentions via social media, TV interviews, press conferences, or even late night talk shows. Clooney's team decides to build on his strengths. They'll produce a video—Hollywood style—that shows him delivering a passionate speech about the future of America. They'll overlay his words with compelling footage that pushes the theme of "An America with Heart." Clooney helping people after a devastating flood. Clooney talking to immigrants at the border. Clooney meeting with first responders. Clooney speaking with people at a homeless shelter. Clooney at a Black Lives Matter rally. The campaign will distribute the video to millions of voters via social media. With a little luck, it'll be just as compelling to the American people as some of Clooney's Oscar-winning films have been. Or so he hopes.

June 2023

Clooney Hits the Campaign Trail

A full two summers before Election Day, the presidential election season is well underway. And it's around this time when successes and failures begin to show. Televised debates are one reason why. At this stage of the process, Democrats debate Democrats and Republicans debate Republicans. These interactions give voters the chance to see a political party's candidates next to one another for the first time. A sparkling debate performance can lead to increased news coverage, perhaps even a viral video or two. Debates also provide candidates who are languishing in the polls an opportunity to reset their campaigns.

Clooney, as expected, shines in the first debate. He's an actor, after all! He's charming, witty, and knowledgeable. But he demonstrates a willingness to take on his opponents, too. One of the best moments of the evening is Clooney's response to a longtime Democratic senator's criticism of Clooney's priorities. "When people come to my office and tell me what they care most about, they're not talking about women's rights or racial equality," the senator begins. But before he can finish, Clooney interjects, "They don't talk to you about justice and equality because they know they can't count on you to fight for it." Zing! Democratic primary voters love it. His strong performance allows him to continue to build support in the polls.

Clooney's quarterly fundraising reports filed with the Federal Election Commission are impressive as well. Wealthy Hollywood friends are holding fundraisers and donating large sums to the campaign. And thousands of movie fans are giving in small amounts. In fact, Clooney has raised over $30 million—more than any of the Democratic presidential contenders had raised by this point in the 2020 election cycle. Even without using any of his personal funds, Clooney has enough cash on hand to set up campaign offices around the country.

The money also enables Clooney's chief strategist, communications director, and media consultant to develop and refine their multimedia strategy. As in most presidential campaigns, a ton of the money raised goes toward advertising. They air TV ads in states that have early primaries. They pepper social media with campaign ads, videos, and digital flyers. They even send campaign materials through snail mail targeting senior citizens. Clooney's face will be the first thing that older Democratic voters across the country see when they open their mailboxes.

The media strategy involves more than paid advertising, though. Presidential candidates want as much free advertising as they can find. For Clooney's team, it's easy. He has preexisting relationships in Hollywood, so with just a few phone calls he's booked on Seth Meyers, Jimmy Fallon, and Stephen Colbert's late night talk shows, as well as *The Today Show*, *The View*, and *60 Minutes*.

He also takes a page out of previous candidates' playbooks to develop a big social media footprint. In 2008, Barack Obama was the first presidential candidate to use YouTube to reach millions of voters with his inspirational "Yes We Can" speech.[12] By 2016, presidential candidates were embracing hashtags to build a following—#I'mWithHer (Clinton), #FeeltheBern (Sanders), and #MAGA (Trump). In 2020, Democratic candidate Elizabeth Warren stayed after all her speeches—often for hours—to make sure that any supporter who wanted to take a selfie with her got one.[13] The strategy proved ingenious, as thousands and thousands of supporters uploaded the pictures, which were in turn shared with millions of "friends" on social media. And Donald Trump was in a league of his own. A year before the 2020 election, Trump had placed more than 2,000 different ads on Facebook promoting his reelection bid, and he regularly communicated with his more than 88 million Twitter followers, 26 million Facebook friends, and 14.6 million Instagram followers. Clooney's movie star status sets him up well for a major social media campaign, but even he will have trouble coming close to Trump's effective use of Facebook, Twitter, and Instagram.

January 2024

Clooney Focuses on the Early Contests

The presidential primary process entails a series of individual state elections held over the course of several months. Iowa has historically gone first, holding a caucus in January or February. **Caucuses** are old-style political meetings. Voters meet at the local fire station, high school gymnasium, or neighborhood community center (wherever their polling place is) to listen to short speeches from representatives of each candidate's campaign. Attendees then move to the place in the room designated for supporters of each candidate. At that point, they're counted, which is how the votes are tallied. At the conclusion of all these meetings across the state, the candidate with the most supporters overall wins the caucus. A week later, New Hampshire holds the first **primary**: voters go to a polling place, step into a voting booth, and cast a ballot. In 2020, only five states used caucuses, and the cumbersome process means that even fewer might do so in the future.

Every contest provides an opportunity for candidates to amass **delegates**—individuals selected to represent their state's party at the nominating convention the following summer. Each state has a certain number of delegates, generally based on the state's population. A candidate needs to secure a majority of the party's delegates to win the party's nomination. To be the Democratic nominee, a candidate needs to win the majority of the 3,779 Democratic delegates up for grabs nationwide. Republicans have a smaller pool of delegates at stake—the winner only needs a majority of 2,550. Different states have different rules for awarding delegates. Some elections are winner-take-all, and others award delegates based on the proportion of the vote a candidate receives. Most Democratic primaries award delegates in proportion to each candidate's vote share in that state, but to be eligible to receive any delegates, a candidate must receive at least 15 percent of the vote.

The importance of amassing delegates in the early states cannot be overstated. Only one candidate—Joe Biden—has become president in the last 50 years without coming in either first or second in Iowa or New Hampshire. That's why it's no surprise that presidential candidates have focused on Iowa and New Hampshire for decades. During the 2016 presidential campaign, for example, 15 Republican candidates spent a combined 640 days campaigning in Iowa and 681 in New Hampshire. The story was similar for the Democrats in 2020—21 Democratic candidates spent 817 days campaigning in Iowa and 541 in New Hampshire.[14] On any given day in the year leading up to the Iowa caucuses and the New Hampshire primary, multiple candidates visited each state and attended state fairs, snapped selfies, talked to voters in crowded diners, and plastered the airwaves with campaign ads.

Clooney understands this. He spends months in Iowa Falls, Ames, Newton, Council Bluffs, Des Moines, Cedar Rapids, and Ottumwa, kissing

Clockwise from top left, Bernie Sanders, Mitt Romney, Kamala Harris, Andrew Yang, Donald Trump, and Hillary Clinton sample corn dogs, turkey legs, and pork on a stick at the Iowa State Fair.

How do you run for president?

every baby and shaking every hand that comes his way. He doesn't love eating a deep-fried Twinkie on a stick at the Iowa State Fair, but he does it anyway. Like so many presidential candidates before him, Clooney samples the craft brews at the New Hampshire Barley House, participates in the "Politics and Eggs" breakfast forum at Saint Anselm College, and knows his way around the town halls in Strafford, Manchester, and Portsmouth. Voters in each state can't turn on the TV without seeing a Clooney ad touting his plans to create "An America with Heart."

Clooney's compelling message and active campaign in Iowa and New Hampshire work. He wins both contests. Surrounded by his parents, wife, and two young children, the new front-runner for the Democratic nomination delivers a riveting speech after his victory in New Hampshire, telling voters in the other 48 states what he plans to do as president. And then he heads off to compete in more contests.

Clooney Campaigns Everywhere to Secure the Nomination

Clooney now sets his sights on **Super Tuesday**, a day in March when a dozen or so states hold their primaries or caucuses. In 2020, the 13 Super Tuesday states awarded more than a third of the overall delegates in the race. Clooney knows that a strong showing on Super Tuesday could clinch the nomination for him. In 2016, Hillary Clinton won 9 of 12 Democratic contests on Super Tuesday. Joe Biden won 10 of 14 Democratic primaries in 2020. Although the remaining states' elections continued into early June, Clinton and Biden's commanding leads after Super Tuesday made them nearly impossible to beat.

In the lead-up to Super Tuesday, Clooney traverses the country, holding four or five events a day in multiple states. He gives more speeches, shakes more hands, and participates in more town halls than he ever thought possible. His campaign hits social media with hundreds of targeted ads and floods the airwaves with commercials, especially in states where staffers think Clooney needs a boost. He even gets to spend some time at home—with the most delegates at stake, California is the big prize on Super Tuesday (and it's nice to sleep in his own bed).

The strategy works. Clooney triumphs on Super Tuesday, winning 10 of 14 primaries. With an impressive lead in the race for delegates, he steadily marches forward to the remaining states. By early May, he has secured the Democratic Party's nomination. Even though he hasn't yet officially been named the party's nominee—more on that in a minute—his campaign team begins strategizing about how to defeat his Republican opponent in November.

Clooney Heads to the Party Convention

The summer before Election Day, both political parties host four-day conventions. The party not controlling the White House goes first. The incumbent party's convention follows a week or two later. The locations change from election to election, with big cities in key states competing to host the event. The convention's main purpose is to nominate the party's candidate officially. This wasn't always the case. For much of American history, there was no 50-state nominating process. Instead, the convention delegates actually selected the nominee. These conventions were high-drama, often raucous affairs with multiple rounds of voting before a candidate secured the nomination. Today it's still technically possible to arrive at the convention without a clear nominee, but it never seems to play out that way. The last time the Republicans didn't have a nominee prior to the convention was 1976. For the Democrats, it hasn't happened since 1984.

So as Democratic delegates arrive in Philadelphia, the home of this year's convention, they're prepared for a big, loud extravaganza designed to showcase their nominee. What viewers see during the prime-time coverage of the convention each night is a party with goofy hats, crazy signs, noise blowers, balloons, and speeches by the party's rising stars. But officially, the convention is more than that. It's where the party and its candidates must complete four essential tasks:

1. Delegates adopt the **party platform**, which is a statement of the party's formal position on issues.

2. Delegates formally nominate the vice-presidential and presidential candidates, making sure they have secured the majority of delegates.

3. The vice-presidential candidate accepts the party's nomination in a prime-time speech.

4. The presidential candidate accepts the party's nomination in a prime-time speech that lays out the candidate's vision for the country.

The speeches the candidates deliver on the final night of their respective conventions are the most watched events of the campaign. They also provide an opportunity for the nominees to summarize their vision, differentiate one party from the other, and set the terms of debate for the general election.

And that's exactly what Clooney's speech does. His impassioned closing goes viral: "An America with heart is one where every citizen has quality health care. An America with heart is one that preserves the environment and protects the planet for our children. An America with heart is one that values every voice, not just the rich and powerful. An America with heart is who we must always strive to be." As Clooney receives thunderous applause, his running mate, a popular senator from the Midwest, joins him onstage. The Democrats packed into the convention hall go crazy. The ratings for the speech are great. More people watch Clooney than the 23.8 million who tuned in for Donald Trump's speech in 2020[15] or the 24.6 million viewers who watched Joe Biden accept the nomination that same year.[16]

September 2024

The General Election Campaign

Nomination in hand, Clooney turns to the general election campaign. The contest is no longer only about wooing his fellow Democrats. Now it's about making a case to the entire country that he should be elected president. Many of the daily activities are similar to those during the primary campaign, but the pace intensifies. Clooney spends the next three months crisscrossing the country—losing his voice from speaking at so many events, raising hundreds of millions of dollars, and debating his Republican opponent. Although post-debate polls show that voters think Clooney easily won all three debates, he and his team don't get too comfortable. They know that debates during the general election campaign are important—they're a rare opportunity for the candidates to appear together, talk to each other, and critique each other.[17] But the team doesn't need to look further back than to Clinton's debates with Trump in 2016 to be reminded that it's possible to be perceived by more voters as the winner of all the debates and still lose the election.[18]

So Clooney's team keeps pushing ahead, concentrating on swing states. Neither Clooney nor his opponent has an unlimited amount of time, so they don't want to campaign in states where the election outcome is a foregone conclusion. And based on recent elections, there are only 14 states where both parties have a shot at winning. Just take a look at Figure 1.[19] The red states are those that are either very likely or almost sure to vote Republican; the blue are likely or certain wins for the Democrats. These states account for 334 of the 538 electoral votes available. The states shaded in purple aren't sure things for either campaign. Some are pure toss-ups, like Michigan, Wisconsin, and Georgia. Others lean toward one side or the other—like Texas toward the Republicans and Minnesota toward the Democrats—but have the potential to flip.

Although these swing states constitute only about a third of electoral votes, neither party can win the election without claiming victory in some of them. In fact, the strategies that campaigns employ to win electoral

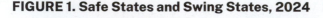

FIGURE 1. Safe States and Swing States, 2024

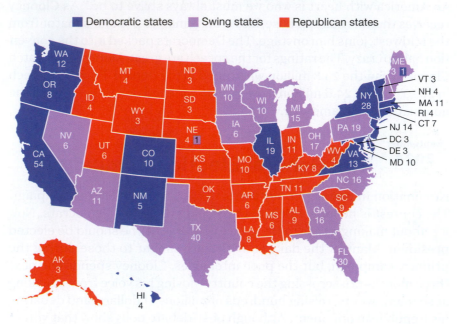

Note: Classifications are based on a consensus of election forecasters prior to the 2024 election.

Source: "2024 Presidential Election Interactive Map," 270toWin.

votes make it seem like swing states are the only states in the country. It's in swing states where the bulk of presidential campaign events occur. It's in swing states where the vast majority of the hundreds of millions of dollars are spent on campaign ads. And it's in swing states where campaigns are laser-focused on making sure that their supporters get to the polls.[20]

This requires a successful **get out the vote (GOTV)** effort—sometimes called the ground game. Campaigns sift through each state's list of registered voters and use every means possible—phone calls, email, door-knocking, offers of rides to the polls—to encourage potential supporters to vote absentee, vote early, or go to the polls on Election Day. They often also try to register as many new voters as possible and remind them—endlessly—to cast a ballot. The general election is all about winning 270 electoral votes, and wooing voters in swing states is the only way to get there. Clooney holds all of his big rallies and airs most of his campaign ads in Florida, North Carolina, Nevada, Arizona, Ohio, Michigan, Wisconsin, Georgia, and Pennsylvania. It's during the last few weeks of the campaign that ads, GOTV, and candidate events matter the most for mobilizing and persuading pivotal voters.[21]

Election Day and Beyond

Election Day finally arrives. Clooney casts his vote near his California home in the morning and then jets off to Michigan and Wisconsin, where he makes final pleas with voters to remember to vote. By 6 P.M., he's surrounded by family, friends, and top advisers in a hotel suite in Philadelphia awaiting the results. Thousands of campaign employees, volunteers, and supporters gather in the hotel ballroom, where they'll shortly be met with either euphoria or despair.

The television news networks begin their coverage early. And as soon as the first polls close (6 P.M. East Coast time), reporters share the results of **exit polls** in those states—surveys of actual voters as they leave the polling place about who they voted for and what issues mattered most to them. The reporting continues as more and more polls close. Early on, there are no surprises. And there shouldn't be—the earliest-closing states are reliably Republican (Kentucky and Mississippi) or Democratic (Vermont). But that'll change soon. Florida, New Hampshire, and Virginia polls close at 7 P.M. East Coast time, followed by North Carolina at 7:30 P.M. Easy wins in these states, especially Florida, often foreshadow how the evening will go. Usually, one candidate crosses the 270 electoral vote line by the wee hours of the morning, at which point the news networks call a winner.

Unfortunately for Clooney, by about 11 P.M. he realizes it's not going to be the night he hoped for. His campaign manager hands him a cell phone to call his opponent and concede the election. So Clooney places the call to the Republican presidential candidate, singer and rapper Kid Rock. (Voters were apparently unhappy with how Democrats had been leading the country and wanted change. Kid Rock's song "American Bad Ass" was his campaign's theme.) Clooney then heads down to the ballroom to thank his supporters and make a gracious concession speech.

For Clooney, the loss stings. It took two years, billions of dollars, dozens of debates, hundreds of speaking engagements, thousands of campaign workers and volunteers, 50 state nominating elections, a national party convention, endless media appearances, a general election, and much more to run for president. And now it's all over, even though Congress won't formally certify Kid Rock as president until it convenes in January 2025.

Within a few weeks of his defeat, though, Clooney manages to pick himself up and brush himself off. He's on a movie set in northern Canada, playing the role of an eccentric environmentalist who thinks he can stop climate change. Under his jacket, the character can be seen wearing a T-shirt that reads "An America with Heart." His agent tells him it's the kind of role that could get him another Academy Award.

DID YOU GET IT?

How do you run for president?

Short Answer:

- Potential candidates embark on a multistep process that can take almost two years.
- Candidates must amass a majority of delegates to win their party's nomination in the primary election. To do so, they develop a campaign strategy and then tend to focus on states with early contests.
- The party nominee then needs to win 270 electoral votes in the general election. This stage is dominated by big campaign events, ads, and GOTV operations in swing states.

DEVELOPING YOUR SKILLS

Quantitative Literacy

Do the math: The race for the White House requires securing a majority of delegates in the primary. These questions rely on the 2020 Democratic delegate count map on the next page. In that election, there were 3,979 delegates. A candidate needed 1,990 delegates to secure the nomination.

1. If a candidate is doing very well and winning all the primaries and caucuses, when is the soonest it would be possible to amass enough delegates to win the nomination?
   a. Super Tuesday
   b. Toward the end of March
   c. Toward the end of April
   d. Not until the final contests in June

2. The five states with the most delegates are California, New York, Texas, Florida, and Pennsylvania. Roughly what percentage of the total delegates are at stake in these five states?
   a. 20 percent
   b. 25 percent
   c. 33 percent
   d. 40 percent

3. Imagine that two candidates are tied after the April primary contests and running head-to-head in the states that haven't voted yet. Which one of the following states should the candidates focus on in order to win the most delegates possible?

a. New Jersey

b. New Mexico

c. Texas

d. Pennsylvania

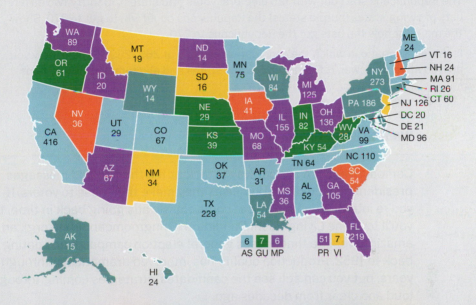

	February	Super Tuesday	March 4-31	April	May	June
Contests	4	16	13	11	7	6
Delegates	155	1,358	1,091	853	300	222
% Delegates	3.9%	34.1%	27.4%	21.4%	7.5%	5.6%
Cumulative %	3.9%	38.0%	65.4%	86.9%	94.4%	100.0%

Source: "2020 Democratic Presidential Nomination," https://www.270towin.com/2020-democratic-nomination/

FIGURE IT OUT

To win the presidency, you need 270 electoral votes. Take a look at the map in Figure 1, and answer the following questions:

- From the outset, the Democrats have 209 electoral votes (blue states). Identify two different lists of swing states (purple states) the Democrats could win to get to 270. Show the math for how the lists get the Democrats to 270.

- The Republicans start out with 125 electoral votes (red states). Identify two different lists of swing states (purple states) the Republicans could win to get to 270. Show the math for how the lists get the Republicans to 270.

- Is there a scenario in which the candidates could tie at 269–269? Explain how you arrived at your answer, referencing specific states and electoral vote allocations.

Want to Know More?

Campaign ads are a great way to look at the themes and messages presidential candidates pursue as they make their case to voters. If you're interested in looking at some classic ads going back in time, then you'll love The Living Room Candidate (livingroomcandidate.org), an amazing website that houses general election campaign ads dating back to 1952. Production quality has improved dramatically through the years, but you can still see the candidates' strategies coming through loud and clear from decades ago.

32.
If everyone hates Congress, why do so many members get reelected?

#IncumbencyAdvantage

It's no secret that most Americans aren't fans of the U.S. Congress. Why would they be? You'd basically have to be living under a rock not to notice partisan warfare, legislative gridlock, the basic inability to address pressing national problems. Just read the paper, surf the internet, or flip on a news program, and you'll see stories pronouncing the latest congressional failure. A search of major news sources — even just between July 2021 and July 2022 — identifies more than 4,000 stories that include the terms "Congress" and "dysfunctional." Searching "Congress" and "gridlock" produces more than 5,000 articles during the same period.[1] Glance at Amazon's list of books about Congress, and it's the same thing. You can order *The Broken Branch: How Congress Is Failing America and How to Get It Back on Track*; *Congress Behaving Badly*; or *It's Even Worse Than It Looks* (updated in the second edition to *It's Even Worse Than It Was*). Assessments like these are now standard practice in how citizens, journalists, and scholars describe congressional politics. And although we can debate their accuracy, we cannot question their ubiquity.

Most citizens don't approve of the job Congress is doing. In fact, they don't think Congress does its job at all. Yet every election cycle, the overwhelming majority of members get reelected — typically with healthy margins.

Not surprisingly, public opinion polls consistently reveal overwhelmingly negative attitudes toward Congress. Congressional approval in recent years has been hovering at around 25 percent (see the dotted line in Figure 1). Just 1 in 4 Americans believe that most members of Congress deserve to be reelected.[2] Roughly half think that if members of Congress were replaced with "random people walking down the street," those everyday Americans could do a better job handling the country's problems.[3]

If these numbers don't adequately convey citizens' disdain for Congress and its members, then a Public Policy Polling survey certainly does. Pollsters asked people whether they had a more favorable impression of Congress or something else that's typically considered unpopular or unappealing. The results of the matchups are amusing — but also depressing. Citizens rated head lice, root canals, traffic jams, cockroaches, colonoscopies, and used car salesmen higher than they did the U.S. Congress.[4] To be fair, Congress outperformed meth labs, playground bullies, and gonorrhea. Yay?

But here's what's puzzling. Take a look at the solid line running along the top of Figure 1.[5] It represents House incumbents' reelection rates. Congressional approval may be in the tank, and people might say they're ready for new political leaders, but in the last 10 congressional elections, 93 percent of members of the House who sought reelection

If everyone hates Congress, why do so many members get reelected?

FIGURE 1. Congressional Approval versus Congressional Reelection Rates

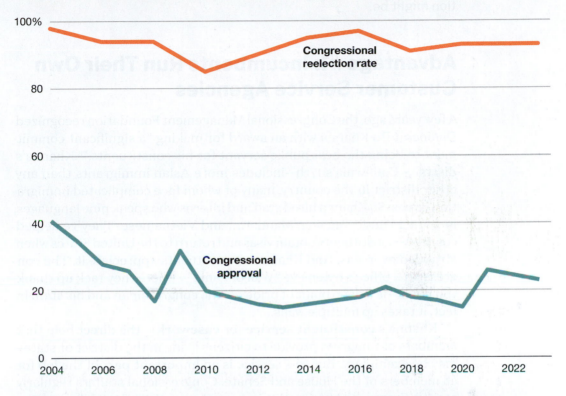

Note: The line for congressional approval reflects responses to the question "Do you approve or disapprove of the way Congress is handling its job?" Congressional reelection rates are for the U.S. House of Representatives.

Source: "Congress and the Public," Gallup; "Reelection Rates over the Years," OpenSecrets; "U.S. Congress Approval Rating," YouGov.

won their races.[6] The numbers aren't much worse even for those implicated in financial or sex scandals. More than 80 percent of those members won reelection, too.[7] Most citizens hold the U.S. Congress in low regard, but they keep sending back the same people to represent them in Washington, D.C.

Why? This segment highlights four advantages incumbents have. Three involve the resources and activities available only to incumbents — all of which help them deter potential challengers and defeat those who do emerge. The fourth advantage is structural. Most congressional districts are not competitive; district lines are rigged to the advantage of one party or the other, and the incumbent almost always belongs to the party that benefits. These four advantages aren't the only ones incumbents benefit from, but together they create an electoral playing field that makes it difficult to defeat a sitting member of Congress, no matter how unpopular the institution might be.

Advantage #1: Incumbents Run Their Own Customer Service Agencies

A few years ago, the Congressional Management Foundation recognized Democrat Ro Khanna with an award for making "a significant commitment to being the best public servant for his constituents."[8] Khanna's district—California's 17th—includes more Asian immigrants than any other district in the country, many of whom face complicated immigration issues. So Khanna hired staff and interns who speak nine languages, including Hindi, Tagalog, Mandarin, and Vietnamese. They've helped countless constituents obtain visas and return to the United States when stranded overseas. And Khanna's constituents appreciate it. The congressional office's extensive "Wall of Fame"—where they tack up thank-you notes—is a deep point of pride for the congressman and his staff. In fact, it takes up multiple walls.

Khanna's **constituent service** (or **casework**)—the direct help that members of Congress provide to citizens living in the district or state—may be exemplary. But this service is an important part of the job for all members of the House and Senate. Congressional staffers regularly assist citizens with immigration issues, veterans' benefits, and programs such as Social Security, food stamps, and housing subsidies. They also provide less essential services to their constituents. Do you want a tour of the White House? Your member of Congress can arrange that. How about passes to watch the House or Senate in action? Your member of Congress can arrange that, too.[9] Overall, members report spending about 17 percent of their time in Washington, D.C., and one-third of their time in their district, attending to constituent service.[10]

When done well, constituent service enhances a representative's image among voters and provides a key advantage over any challenger. It can even deter challengers from emerging. As one expert notes, casework is "all profit" for the member.[11] Assisting district (or state) residents creates goodwill and is generally unrelated to the rancor of the political process. Challengers can't help voters in any official capacity. But members of the House of Representatives can hire up to 22 staff members, many of whom work in a district office that's primarily responsible for assisting constituents, and U.S. senators face no limits on the size of their staff.

Advantage #2: Incumbents Can Build and Tout a Legislative Record

When Republican John Katko challenged Democratic incumbent Dan Maffei in upstate New York in 2014, Maffei's record was a central part of the campaign. Katko criticized Maffei for getting nothing done.[12] During the previous term, Maffei had introduced 13 bills, but none had gone anywhere. And he hadn't secured any major new projects or funding for the district. No Democrat in a Republican-controlled House can do much. But Katko's message resonated. In the swing district, Katko won handily, securing 58 percent of the vote.[13]

Determined to hold on to his seat, Katko made building a legislative record a top priority. During his second term, for instance, he introduced 29 bills, 14 of which the House passed. Donald Trump signed 3 of them into law—pretty impressive, given that only about 2 percent of bills ever become law. Among Katko's accomplishments? Passing a bill to start the process of making Fort Ontario, a major landmark in his district, a national park. If that happens—it's a multiyear process that is still underway—then the district will receive tax incentives, federal jobs, and access to additional benefits. For accomplishments like these, the nonpartisan Center for Effective Lawmaking named Katko, who decided not to seek reelection in 2022, one of the 10 most effective members of Congress in both his first and second terms. In his third term, he ranked third among 205 Republicans in the chamber.[14] And every time he gets the chance, Katko points to the designation—on his website, to reporters, and in newsletters.[15]

It's not just the accomplishments themselves that give incumbents an edge when they seek reelection. It's also the perks that enable incumbents to communicate their records to their constituents. In their official capacity as members of Congress, incumbents have substantial resources to spend on mail (referred to as the franking privilege), phone, email, and social media. These communications must be distinct from campaign materials—they can't explicitly attack political opponents or urge citizens to vote in a particular way. But the line between governing and electioneering is very blurry. As you can see in the photos on the next page, it's often hard to differentiate official congressional communications from campaign mailers. In fact, researchers find that members representing competitive districts send out almost 3 times as many pieces of mail as members representing safe districts do. That suggests that incumbents use their mailing privileges as a way to boost their support in the district and help their reelection chances.[16]

Beyond mail, members often also have elaborate media strategies. They have at their disposal the House or Senate floor, where they can

Republican Marjorie Taylor Greene relies on the franking privilege to communicate to her constituents that they should advocate for impeaching President Biden. Although mailers like this look an awful lot like campaign brochures, incumbents don't have to pay for them.

give a speech on any topic and then tweet the video of it, post it on YouTube and Facebook, or forward the clip to the news media in their state or district. Incumbents have communication directors who issue press releases, manage social media networks, and arrange interviews with journalists and supportive pundits. In other words, when a member of Congress wants media attention to highlight an achievement or publicize a position, it's pretty easy to get it. That's why incumbents receive substantially more media coverage from the local press than their challengers do.[17] This elaborate network of communication resources can support members' reelection efforts—a luxury that challengers simply don't have.

Advantage #3: Incumbents Have Access to Big Money

First elected to represent Washington's 5th congressional district in 2005, Republican Cathy McMorris Rodgers typically sails to reelection. Her prospects are rosy not only because she's a conservative in a conservative district but also because as an incumbent she has access to a lot of money to support her reelection. In the six campaigns she has run since her initial race, McMorris Rodgers raised more than $2 million each time. Her opponents averaged just a little more than $350,000. In 2018, the Democrats took a shot at knocking off McMorris Rodgers and put up a candidate who raised almost $6 million. Not to be outdone, McMorris Rodgers raised even more. She defeated Democratic challenger Lisa Brown by almost 10 points. The Democrats didn't bother to devote resources to the 2020 contest. McMorris Rodgers raised $4.3 million—that's 43 times more than her opponent raked in.[18]

Most candidates bemoan the amount of money it costs to run a successful campaign and the amount of time they need to spend raising it.

But incumbents like McMorris Rodgers have access to a fundraising network that makes the task much easier. They have lists of previous supporters and donors they can go back to every election cycle. They have track records that make them a much surer bet for companies and special interests that want a friend in Congress. And whenever an incumbent appears vulnerable, the national party campaign committees can step in. The Democratic Congressional Campaign Committee (DCCC) and the National Republican Congressional Committee (NRCC) are sometimes described as incumbency protection agencies. One of their key responsibilities is to make sure incumbents who need a boost have all the money they need. Heading into the 2022 midterm elections, the two committees raised a combined $509 million.[19]

These various facets of financial support mean that incumbents almost always have enough money to run successful campaigns. In 2020, incumbents running for reelection raised, on average, about $2.7 million. The average challenger? About one-sixth of that.[20] More than a year out from her next reelection campaign, McMorris Rodgers already had close to $2 million in the bank—a nice chunk of change to discourage would-be challengers, and probably enough to fund her race.

Advantage #4: Incumbents Run in Tailor-Made Districts

Democrat John Sarbanes was an ideal candidate when he chose to run for the U.S. House in Maryland's 3rd congressional district in 2006. Born and raised in Baltimore, he had a successful career at one of the city's prestigious law firms. He served as a liaison to the Baltimore City Public Schools. He spent more than a decade on the board of the Public Justice Center, a Baltimore nonprofit organization that provides legal support to people who can't afford it.[21] And he had a famous name. His father, Paul, served 30 years as a U.S. senator from Maryland. Sarbanes surprised no one when he breezed through the 2006 primary and easily defeated Republican John White in the general election. Since then, he has coasted to victory in all of his reelection bids.[22]

The easy general election wins, however, probably have little to do with Sarbanes's background, credentials, or even his family name. They might not even have much to do with his constituent service, legislative record, or fundraising prowess. Instead, he's a Democrat in a district full of Democrats. And voters almost always vote for their party's candidate.

It's not unusual for congressional districts to lean toward one party or the other. After all, it's common for people to marry, socialize with, and live among people who are politically like-minded. In Sarbanes's case, though, he doesn't just happen to be a Democrat living among other Democrats. He represents a district that was deliberately created to contain a clear majority of Democratic voters. In fact, prior to the redrawing of district lines in 2022, its shape had been referred to as a "crazy quilt," "praying mantis," "blood splatter from a crime scene," and "broken-winged pterodactyl." These bizarre district lines result from

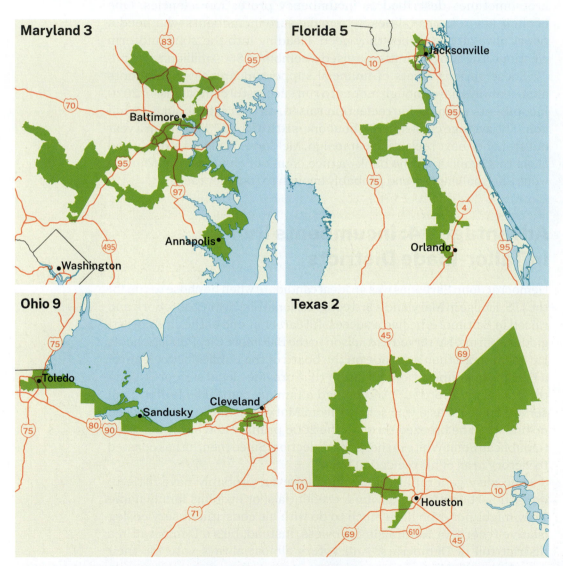

When state legislatures draw congressional district lines, political considerations often play a role. As a result, many districts look like paint splatters or the quixotic drawings of small children, and they certainly are neither compact nor contiguous.

If everyone hates Congress, why do so many members get reelected?

partisan gerrymandering—the process of drawing electoral district boundaries that make it easier for one political party than the other to win an election.

Creating districts this way is possible because every 10 years, in a process known as **redistricting**, state governments redraw congressional districts' lines to reflect population shifts. The Constitution requires that all districts have an approximately equal number of residents—currently, a little more than 700,000 per district. But beyond that, states have substantial latitude.[23] Many states try to draw district lines that are geographically compact; contiguous—all parts of the district connect to one another; and preserve political boundaries—that is, they don't break up small cities, towns, or counties into multiple districts.

But when you see districts like those presented on the previous page—whose maps don't reflect any of these goals—it's likely that they've been created for political purposes. In Maryland, Democrats control the state legislature. So they create districts that connect pockets of Democratic voters from communities across the state, even if other district configurations make more geographic sense. As a result, prior to the 2020 round of redistricting, Democratic voters outnumbered Republican voters in 7 of the state's 8 districts. Republicans do it, too. In North Carolina, for example, the Republican-controlled state legislature carved up the state so that Republicans had a clear advantage in 10 of 13 congressional districts.

Partisan gerrymandering means that incumbents representing these districts face little chance of being knocked off by a challenger from the opposing party—there just aren't enough voters from the opposing party who live in the district. In most election cycles, only about 10 percent of the 435 House districts are competitive. In 2022, the average incumbent member of the House won by roughly 30 points.[24] Aware of their bleak prospects for success, challengers are less likely to run.[25] And because the lopsided nature of these districts makes the outcome seem like a foregone conclusion, the media are less likely to cover these contests, which further limits challengers' ability to make a case to voters.[26]

Although many voters don't like gerrymandering—and lots of candidates challenging incumbents don't either—it will likely continue for the foreseeable future. In 2019, the Supreme Court acknowledged that drawing congressional lines simply to favor one party over another is an undesirable practice in a democracy, but the Court was not willing to strike down partisan gerrymandering as unconstitutional. Writing for the majority in a contentious 5–4 decision, Chief Justice John Roberts concluded that "federal judges have no license to reallocate political power between the two major political parties."[27] Congress has the power to change the rules to prohibit partisan gerrymandering, but the current system works pretty well for incumbents. And they're the people who would have to enact the change.

DID YOU GET IT?

If everyone hates Congress, why do so many members get reelected?

Short Answer:

- Incumbents get reelected at very high rates because the job itself enables them to provide direct service to their constituents, build and tout a legislative record, and raise large sums of money with relative ease.
- Partisan gerrymandering also makes it very difficult for challengers to knock out incumbents, most of whom run in lopsided districts that favor their party.
- These advantages both deter would-be challengers and provide advantages to incumbents who find themselves in a reelection fight.

DEVELOPING YOUR SKILLS

Consuming Political Information

Check the facts: Every campaign season, incumbents and challengers battle to win elections, and in the process they make all sorts of claims. These questions ask you to determine whether accusations that candidates hurl at each other are true.

1. The Center for Effective Lawmaking ranks the effectiveness of all members of Congress. If the opponent of Senator Susan Collins, a Republican from Maine, said that Collins was the least effective senator in 2017–2018, would she be accurate? You can access the data here: www.thelawmakers.org.

   a. Yes, the statement is true.

   b. No, Collins was actually the most effective senator.

   c. No, Collins was near the bottom of the pack, but not the least effective.

   d. No, Collins was among the 20 most effective Republicans in the Senate.

2. Suppose then–Speaker of the House Nancy Pelosi claimed that the majority of the money she raised in her 2019–2020 campaign came from small individual contributions of less than $200 each. But her opponent claimed that the majority of Pelosi's money came from political action committees (PACs). Who is telling the truth? You can access fundraising data by clicking on the "Congress" link in the Candidates and Office Holders section of the homepage of OpenSecrets.org.

   a. Pelosi is accurate.

   b. Her opponent is accurate.

   c. Both are inaccurate; the majority of Pelosi's contributions came from large donors.

   d. Both are inaccurate; Pelosi self-funded her campaign.

3. Political pundits and candidates — regardless of where they live — often claim that their state is one of the most gerrymandered and that elections are unfair. In which of the following states would such a claim be true? (Hint: Consult reputable journalistic outlets like the *Washington Post* and Politico or organizations that do research on gerrymandering to identify which state below is one of the most gerrymandered.)

   a. Louisiana

   b. Illinois

   c. California

   d. North Carolina

FIGURE IT OUT

Members of Congress often boast about their effectiveness and the financial support they receive from their constituents. If your member of Congress made such claims, would the statement be accurate? More specifically:

- How effective a legislator is your member of Congress compared to other members from your state? If you live in a state with only one member, then compare your representative to your state's senators. This information is available at the website for the Center for Effective Lawmaking.

- What percentage of your member's campaign contributions in the most recent election cycle came from small donors? What percentage came from in-state donors? This information is available at OpenSecrets.org.

Want to Know More?

If partisan gerrymandering seems a little confusing, don't worry. You can gain a handle on the process by playing the Redistricting Game, developed by the University of Southern California. It provides a fun and interactive opportunity to draw district lines and assess their consequences for campaigns and elections. Check it out here: http://www.redistrictinggame.org/.

If everyone hates Congress, why do so many members get reelected?

33.
Are third parties doomed to fail in the United States?

#TwoPartySystem

Happy birthday! And what a birthday it is. You just turned 18, it's a beautiful fall morning in central New Jersey, and it's Election Day. A presidential election, no less. You haven't followed the race very closely, but you're excited to cast your first vote. And you're confident that you know enough about the Democratic and Republican candidates to make a good decision.

But when you step into the voting booth, you begin to panic. Who are all these people listed on the ballot? You didn't know that the Constitution, American Delta, Libertarian, Socialism and Liberation, Workers World, and Green parties even existed. You certainly didn't expect to see that each one had a candidate running for president.

You text your friend, who recently moved to Colorado. "Hey," you write. "Did you vote yet? Who are all these people running for president?" He texts back quickly: "I know. I just got back. We've got 22 candidates running for president here. There's a Nutrition Party candidate. A Prohibition Party candidate. It's crazy." You decide to ignore the candidates from all the other parties and choose between the Republican and the Democrat.

"You can try but it's pretty small in here...the water's going cold and the good soap is gone."

The majority of Americans believe that casting a ballot for a third-party candidate is a wasted vote. The two-party system in the United States is structured to make it very difficult for a candidate who isn't a Democrat or a Republican to win elective office.

It turns out that's what most other Americans do, too. There might be lots of political parties floating around, but the only real game in town is between the two major parties. In the past 100 years, only seven candidates from a **third party** — any party other than the Democrats or Republicans — have received 2 percent or more of the vote. Just two third-party candidates have won any electoral votes, and the last time that happened was 1968 (see Table 1). The story is the same beyond the presidency. Only 2 of the 535 members of the 117th Congress (2021–2022) don't affiliate with either the Republican or Democratic Party. None of the 50 state governors is from a third party. And of the roughly 7,400 state legislators across the country, more than 99 percent are either Democrats or Republicans.[1]

These numbers might seem puzzling because majorities of voters have held unfavorable views of the two major parties for decades.

Are third parties doomed to fail in the United States?

TABLE 1. "Successful" Third-Party Presidential Candidates

Year	Candidate	Party	Popular Vote	Electoral Votes
1948	Strom Thurmond	Dixiecrats	2.4%	39
1948	Henry Wallace	Progressive Party	2.4	0
1968	George Wallace	American Independent Party	13.5	46
1980	John Anderson	Independent Party	6.6	0
1992	Ross Perot	Independent Party	18.9	0
1996	Ross Perot	Reform Party	8.4	0
2000	Ralph Nader	Green Party	2.7	0
2016	Gary Johnson	Libertarian Party	3.3	0

Note: Table includes all third-party presidential candidates who received at least 2 percent of the popular vote since 1924. Dozens of others have run, but they have failed to clear the 2 percent popular vote threshold.

Seven out of 10 citizens say that the Democrats and Republicans don't adequately represent the American people. Gallup consistently finds that roughly 60 percent of voters think we need a viable third party in the United States. That number climbs to 70 percent among young voters.[2]

Given public support for the idea of third parties in general, why do they experience so little success in American politics? It's not because the two-party system is written into law. In fact, the Constitution doesn't even mention political parties. It's also not because democracies tend to have two-party systems. Most don't. By the end of this segment, you'll see that third parties typically fail in the United States for two primary reasons: (1) the specific rules that govern elections and (2) the political ideologies of the two major parties we already have. As a result, the United States will likely remain the solidly two-party system it has always been. But you'll also see that third-party candidates influence U.S. politics even though they usually lose their races.

Procedural Obstacles: The Rules of the Game

A political party doesn't succeed if it can't win elections. In the United States, electoral rules help ensure third-party failure in three basic ways.

First, each state establishes its own rules for how candidates qualify to get on the ballot. And lots of specific state laws make it difficult for third parties to compete. In some states, third-party candidates face more onerous requirements—like obtaining more signatures or paying higher fees than those required of the two major parties' candidates. Florida, for instance, doesn't require Democratic or Republican presidential candidates to gather voters' signatures in order to run. They just file the paperwork and they're on the ballot. Not the case for third-party presidential candidates. In order to be eligible, they must collect more than 100,000 signatures by the July before Election Day. That's quite an undertaking—and not something that's feasible without a corps of volunteers or a sizable paid staff.

In other states, ballot requirements are generally the same for Democrats, Republicans, and third-party candidates. But they're so difficult that few third parties can meet the threshold. Massachusetts, for example, requires gubernatorial candidates to get 10,000 signatures to qualify for the ballot. Not so difficult in a state with 4.7 million registered voters, right?[3] Well, there's a catch: the signatures have to be from members of that party or from people with no party affiliation at all. That's easy for Democrats or Republicans. But try to find 10,000 members of the Working Families Party or unaffiliated voters willing to sign the petition for a Working Families candidate. Not so easy.

Or consider Alabama, where a party can get a candidate on a statewide ballot only with a petition signed by at least 3 percent of the people who voted in the most recent gubernatorial election (typically about 50,000 voters). That's challenging in and of itself, but especially for third parties that don't have well-established infrastructures and staffs. And that's not all. If a candidate manages to get the signatures needed, but then doesn't receive 20 percent of the vote in the election, the party must go through the same process and collect signatures all over again for the next election.[4] Democrats and Republicans don't have to worry about this because both parties always get at least 20 percent of the vote. Third-party candidates almost never do, so they face collecting signatures every election cycle.

These are just a few examples of the types of requirements that often make it difficult for third parties to compete. But the examples reflect a much broader set of laws across the country that work to favor

Are third parties doomed to fail in the United States?

the two-party system. In 2022, of the active third parties in the United States—those you can join or affiliate with—only 8 met at least two states' requirements to appear on the ballot (see Table 2).[5] Only the Libertarian and Green parties could compete in elections in a majority of the states. If you're not on the ballot, you certainly can't win the race.

The second way that election rules make it difficult for third parties pertains to candidate debates. Third-party candidates are usually excluded from the debates, and candidates who don't make it onto the debate stage hardly ever receive attention from the news media.[6] As a result, voters don't learn much about them. This is particularly true for presidential candidates. In the 2020 presidential election campaign, the Commission on Presidential Debates—a nonpartisan group that establishes the rules for presidential debates—invited only those candidates polling at 15 percent or better in at least five preelection polls to appear on the debate stage.[7] That threshold is easy for any Republican or Democratic nominee to meet—most people support their party's nominee, and most voters consider themselves either Democrats or Republicans. But it's extremely difficult for a third-party candidate. Indeed, in the 2016 election between Donald Trump and Hillary Clinton, Libertarian Gary Johnson performed quite well in the preelection polls that cycle, at least for a third-party candidate. His support was sometimes as high as 13 percent. But Johnson didn't meet the commission's requirements, so

TABLE 2. Active Third Parties in the United States

Party	Number of States Where the Party Is on the Ballot
Libertarian Party	33
Green Party	17
Independent Party	12
Constitution Party	9
Working Families Party	5
Reform Party	2
Working Class Party	2
Unity Party	2

Note: The list includes the eight third parties that have met at least two states' ballot requirements.

Source: "List of Political Parties in the United States," Ballotpedia.

he wasn't permitted to debate alongside Trump and Clinton. According to Johnson, that guaranteed his loss. "There's no chance without the debate," he told a reporter from the *Morning Consult*.[8]

Third, almost all state and federal elections—and the overwhelming majority of local races—are winner-take-all. That means that in each contest, there's only one winner. And the winner is the person who receives a plurality of the votes. In other words, the person who receives the most votes, regardless of whether they receive a majority of the ballots cast, wins the election. Maurice Duverger, a French sociologist who wrote about political parties in the 1950s and 1960s, concluded that countries with an electoral arrangement like this—those with single-member districts and plurality vote rules—almost always wind up with a strong two-party system.[9] This principle, known as **Duverger's Law**, results from the fact that the two major parties have an incentive to build broad coalitions. That's a way to encourage the most voters to support them.[10] With two broad parties, it's much more difficult for a third party to draw support.

The 1992 presidential election is a case in point. Democrat Bill Clinton won the election by securing victories in 32 states, for a total of 370 electoral votes. Republican George H. W. Bush claimed victory in the other 18 states, racking up 168 electoral votes. The third-party candidate, Independent Ross Perot, won no states and, thus, zero electoral votes. Overall, it was a relatively easy win for Clinton. But when you look at the popular vote, Clinton's win wasn't so impressive. He won only 43 percent of the popular vote nationwide and received a majority of the vote in only one state—his home state of Arkansas.[11] That was enough to win him the White House. Perot's 19 percent of the popular vote nationwide—an unusually strong performance by a third-party candidate—got him nothing. All it did was make it easier for one of the two major-party candidates to win the election with less than a majority of the vote.

Ideological Obstacles: The Parties' Platforms and Positions

A political party's success is contingent on appealing to a significant number of voters. And beyond the procedural hurdles third parties face, ideological factors also make it difficult for them to build a following.

Some third parties try to fight their way into relevance by advocating for a single issue position or policy—typically one that the two major parties don't prioritize. The Marijuana Reform Party, for example, cares only about legalizing marijuana. The Vegetarian Party seeks to end animal cruelty and meat eating. Parties like these advance a cause—and often one that a decent share of voters support. But such parties don't put

Are third parties doomed to fail in the United States?

forward a complete plan for running the government. Without a broad philosophy, these parties tend to attract support only from voters who prioritize a single issue above all else. Because most people tend to care about more than one issue, single-issue parties usually fade after a few election cycles.

Third parties with broad philosophies typically don't do well either—usually because they're too extreme. Communist Party USA attracts few members because the overwhelming majority of citizens support a capitalist system.[12] Anarchy Party USA also hasn't been able to build much of a following. Although most Americans think the government is dysfunctional, they still favor some form of government over none at all.

Even when third parties espouse philosophies that aren't altogether at odds with American public opinion, they still tend to fall outside the mainstream views of most citizens. Many people, for instance, agree with the Libertarian Party's position that government is too big. But to limit the size of government, many libertarians call for abolishing the public school system, legalizing drugs, and ending the minimum wage. That's going too far for most Americans. It's a similar story for Socialist Party USA. Lots of people care deeply about economic inequality and believe that the U.S. system of government favors the interests of wealthy citizens.[13] But the Socialist Party's proposals call for dismantling the nation's economic system and capping how much money people can

Many third parties in the United States focus on a single issue or espouse a political philosophy that's at odds with most Americans' views. The Marijuana Party, Working Families Party, Pirate Party, Libertarian Party (top row), Green Party, Communist Party USA, Women's Equality Party, and Right to Life Party (bottom row) have not been able to build strong followings and compete with the Democrats and Republicans.

earn. Even when people support economic reforms to reduce income inequality, they don't want to do so by completely changing the American way of life.

Further complicating third parties' prospects for success is the fact that the Democratic and Republican parties are willing to evolve if that means appealing to more supporters. The Green Party's emphasis on environmental protection, for instance, resonated with many voters, most of whom were quite liberal. So what did the Democrats do? Rather than risk losing a group of voters who could be key in a close election, the Democrats became the "pro-environment party." Indeed, many Democratic candidates and elected leaders endorsed the "Green New Deal"—a set of proposed social and economic reforms intended to address climate change and economic inequality.[14] We see the same dynamic with the Republican Party's position on immigration. The Constitution Party and Reform Party, both started in the 1990s, advocate for strict anti-immigration policies. Rather than compete for voters, the Republican Party ultimately adopted these positions as well. In fact, Republican presidential candidate Donald Trump's hard-line position and rhetoric regarding illegal immigration appealed to members of the Constitution Party—to such an extent that Virgil Goode, the Constitution Party's 2012 presidential nominee, enthusiastically endorsed Trump in 2016.[15]

Third Parties Still Matter

The various procedural and ideological obstacles we've chronicled certainly contribute to third parties' lack of electoral success. Because third-party candidates rarely win, voters and donors perceive them as unlikely to win. Those perceptions make it more difficult for third-party candidates to attract the kind of funding they need to build the infrastructure and hire the staff that could help them get on the ballot, rise in the polls, participate in debates, and win some elections.

Nevertheless, there's no question that third parties still matter. And they matter beyond just encouraging the two major parties to adopt certain policies. Third parties also sometimes act as spoilers—in essence, changing which of the two major parties wins an election.

In 2000, for example, Green Party candidate Ralph Nader won only 2.7 percent of the popular vote. But if he hadn't been in the race, Democrat Al Gore would have almost surely won the state of Florida, which he lost by only a few hundred votes. Given that a win in Florida would have given Gore enough electoral votes to win the election, Nader's presence was pivotal.[16]

Are third parties doomed to fail in the United States?

The 2016 presidential election was another recent case in point. Libertarian Gary Johnson and Green Party candidate Jill Stein received more votes in the key states of Michigan, Wisconsin, and Pennsylvania than the margin by which Trump defeated Clinton. Although we can never know for sure how those states would have voted if Johnson and Stein hadn't been on the ballot, the Johnson campaign reported that it pulled support equally from Trump and Clinton. Stein appealed to disenchanted Democrats.[17] It's possible that the third parties' presence ultimately helped Trump and hurt Clinton. President Barack Obama certainly thought so, warning voters ahead of Election Day: "If you vote for a third-party candidate who's got no chance to win, that's a vote for Trump."[18]

DID YOU GET IT?

Are third parties doomed to fail in the United States?

Short Answer:

- Probably. We've always had a two-party system, and because of the winner-take-all arrangements in most U.S. elections, it will likely remain that way.
- Procedural obstacles and the ideological flexibility of the two major parties make it hard for third parties to succeed.
- Even though they rarely win elections, third parties still matter — both by encouraging the Democrats and Republicans to adopt some of their positions and by acting as spoilers in close contests.

Persuasive Argumentation

Evaluate evidence: Many citizens, especially young people, believe that sustainable third parties would be a positive addition to the American political system. Others doubt whether a third party could ever succeed in the United States. These questions ask you to examine evidence surrounding the benefits and plausibility of third parties.

1. If you want to argue that a successful third party could improve the governing process, which piece of evidence would provide the strongest support?

   a. A large poll of U.S. citizens revealing that a majority believes that a third party would result in less government dysfunction and more compromise

   b. A large poll of citizens from around the world revealing that people who live in countries with successful third parties have a more favorable view of government

   c. An essay by three distinguished political scientists arguing that viable third parties would improve the functioning of the U.S. government

   d. A study of two dozen democracies that finds that nations with at least three viable parties see less political gridlock than nations with a two-party system do

2. If you are writing an essay arguing that restrictive ballot access laws hurt third-party candidates' chances for success, what quantitative evidence would be most helpful?

   a. A list of the most restrictive ballot requirements in the United States

   b. A comparison of the proportion of third-party candidates in states with the most versus the least restrictive laws

   c. The average vote share that all third-party candidates receive across multiple election cycles

   d. Quotes from third-party candidates who explain the difficulties the system posed for them when they ran for office

3. Which piece of evidence would most strongly suggest that Duverger's Law no longer applies to elections in the United States?

   a. A steady increase in the number of third-party candidates winning elections

   b. A steady increase in the number of Democratic and Republican candidates winning a majority of the vote

   c. A steady decrease in the number of third-party candidates winning at least 10 percent of the vote

   d. A decrease in the number of Democratic candidates winning elections

FIGURE IT OUT

Lots of third parties emerge, but few succeed. Now that you're familiar with the procedural and ideological obstacles that third parties face, develop an idea for a third party that might actually have a chance in contemporary U.S. elections. To do this, you can come up with a completely new idea for a third party or modify one that already exists. More specifically:

- Give your party a name.

- In one sentence, summarize your party's central purpose.

- List three policy positions the party will advocate.

- Identify two reasons your party might actually succeed when so many others fail. Be specific in providing evidence for your argument.

- Now identify two obstacles your party faces. Again, provide specific details to back up your claims.

Want to Know More?

If you want to get a better sense of what third parties stand for and how they pitch themselves, take a look at their websites. Ballotpedia lists all the active third parties (https://ballotpedia.org/List_of_political_parties_in_the_United_States). Or check out *Rigged 2016*, a 3-minute documentary about how third parties are shut out of the political system. You can watch it here: www.rigged2016.com/

Political Institutions

Start Here!

All too often, a mass shooting occurs somewhere in the United States. Elementary schools, nightclubs, shopping centers, churches, military bases — nowhere is off-limits. The motives underlying these random acts of violence vary. The numbers of injuries and fatalities range from a handful to dozens. And the types of weapons used run the gamut from assault rifles to handguns. But one thing about mass shootings is always the same: the government quickly leaps into action. The president takes to the airwaves to condemn the act and reassure the public. The Federal Bureau of Investigation tries to determine the details underlying the crime and whether the perpetrator violated any federal civil rights or gun laws. Members of Congress put forward proposals to prevent gun violence in the future. The federal court system prepares for criminal proceedings and legal challenges over what the Second Amendment's "right to bear arms" really means.

You'll see a similar multifaceted response by the federal government in the face of any crisis or, for that matter, any major public policy debate. Our **political institutions** — the central components of government with the power to craft, implement, and review the nation's laws — play key roles in addressing just about every major event or issue. Understanding what political institutions do and how they operate requires thinking about them in two ways: (1) as distinct players with specific roles and responsibilities and (2) as political actors interacting with one another throughout the governing process. The nine segments in this section elaborate on both dimensions.

Before we lay out the section's key themes, we should explain what we mean by institutions as "players" or "actors." We don't mean specific people who work within political institutions. Instead, we mean the institutions themselves: Congress, the presidency, the bureaucracy, and the courts. Yes, each institution is filled with people who carry out its mission. But political leaders come and go, whereas institutions remain. Think about it like this: members of Congress work on behalf of their constituents — writing laws, advocating for their state or district, providing services to the citizens they represent. When one member retires or loses an election, someone else takes over those responsibilities, but it's still the same job. Or consider the presidency. All presidents oversee the military regardless of whether they have military experience or believe that U.S. troops should be deployed widely or brought home. The job description doesn't change based on who happens to occupy the Oval Office. That's largely because the Constitution, federal laws, and centuries of norms dictate political institutions' organizational structures and responsibilities.

Three broad themes apply to the segments in this section:

1 **Our governing institutions have remained largely intact since the Founding.** The legislative, executive, and judicial branches of the federal government have grown and evolved over 230+ years. Yet each branch maintains the same specific powers laid out in the Constitution, and each relies on the system of checks and balances the Founders devised.

2 **The structure and rules of government can be very inefficient.** In the United States, big changes and bold policy reforms are difficult to implement. Because no one actor has complete control — not Congress, not the president, not the Supreme Court — rarely can any player single-handedly push through sweeping change without careful consideration and some degree of consensus.

3 **Tension between Democrats and Republicans is a defining feature of U.S. political institutions today.** Members of Congress, presidents, government bureaucrats, and judges all exercise their roles in a partisan environment, with each major political party battling to impose its preferences and control the American political system.

34. How well does Congress serve the American people?

#Representation

If the American public held up a mirror to itself, the image staring back certainly wouldn't look like the 535 members of the U.S. Congress. Congress is Whiter, more male, and less likely to identify as LGBTQ than the U.S. population is. Its members are much older, by more than 20 years on average. They're also more Christian, more religious, and have more military experience than the typical citizen. They're a whole lot wealthier. Members of the House have a net worth nearly 10 times that of the average citizen they represent. The average senator's net worth is roughly 33 times the average American's. And whereas almost every member of Congress has a bachelor's degree, only one-third of the public does (see Table 1).[1]

The fact that Congress doesn't look like the American public raises questions about how well it can do its job. Many citizens look cynically at Congress and assume that these old, rich, White guys are hopelessly out of touch. There's no way they could possibly understand the struggles of working people. Others think that representatives and senators are only there for the power and prestige, caring little about the people they serve. These perceptions are troubling because the United States

The 116th Congress (2019–2021) was the most diverse in history, including the youngest congresswoman ever elected, the first Native American and Muslim women to serve in the House, and the first openly bisexual woman to serve in the Senate.

is a **representative democracy** — a system of government in which voters select leaders to advocate on behalf of their interests. The House of Representatives, in particular, is supposed to be "the people's house" — the institution in our federal system where elected leaders most directly reflect citizens' voices.

But determining whether Congress represents the public involves more than looking at its class photo or simply assuming the worst about political leaders. It also involves considering whether Congress takes action on the issues that citizens across the country care about most. It requires assessing whether representatives reflect the values and pursue the goals of their hometown constituents. It demands a fuller assessment of the underrepresentation of certain groups of citizens. Accordingly, we lay out three fundamental aspects of what it means to "represent." By the end of this segment, you'll see that the concept of representation is complicated, and the question of whether Congress represents the American people doesn't lend itself to an easy answer.

TABLE 1. The Face of the 117th Congress (2021–2023)

	U.S. Population	House of Representatives	Senate
Male	49%	73%	76%
Female	51	27	24
White	72	72	88
Black	16	13	3
Hispanic	13	11	7
Asian	5	4	2
Identify as LGBTQ	5	2	2
Christian	74	86	85
Jewish	2	6	9
Muslim	1	1	0
No religion	18	4	6
College degree	33	94	100
Postgraduate degree	13	67	76
Veteran	7	17	16
Median net worth	$97,300	$900,000	$3.2 million
Median age	38 years	58 years	64 years

Notes: Entries include non-voting delegates in the House. Median net worth data is for members of the 116th Congress.

Source: "Membership of the 117th Congress: A Profile," Congressional Research Service, August 8, 2022.

Collective Representation: Reflecting the Will of the People

One fundamental way to gauge whether Congress serves the public is by considering the extent to which it does what the people want. In other words, does it provide **collective representation**—does it adopt policies and take actions that reflect the views of a majority of the U.S. population? The evidence for whether Congress responds to the public mood is mixed.[2]

On one hand, it's easy to come up with a long list of examples in which public opinion and large-scale congressional action are in sync.[3] Look no further than Social Security (cash benefits for retirees) and Medicare (health care for senior citizens). Both programs are very popular. Nearly three-quarters (74 percent) of the public opposes changes to Social Security.[4] Eighty-eight percent oppose cuts to Medicare.[5] Even though these programs are constantly on the brink of serious financial trouble—as of 2021, Medicare is projected to run out of money in 2026 and Social Security by 2033[6]—political leaders on both sides of the aisle consistently vote to maintain them. These programs are just too important to the public.

On the other hand, some policies that are very popular with the public see virtually no congressional action. An overwhelming majority of citizens (84 percent), for example, wants mandatory background checks for anyone who buys a gun;[7] three-quarters of voters support allowing "dreamers"—children whose parents brought them into the country illegally—to stay in the country as legal residents.[8] In the current political climate, this level of consensus is surprising because Democrats and Republicans don't see eye to eye on much. So if there's any easy action for Congress to take, it would be on these issues, right? Nope. Congress hasn't passed anything close to meaningful gun control or immigration reform in decades.

The disconnect between congressional action and public opinion is also evident when members of Congress pursue policies that a majority of Americans oppose. Just consider health care reform. In 2010, most citizens did not support the Affordable Care Act, but the law, also known as Obamacare, passed anyway. Fast-forward to 2017, and public opinion about health care had changed. Nearly three-quarters of people supported the Obamacare provision that no health care plan could penalize people with preexisting conditions. Yet the Republican Congress tried to overturn the law and toss out the provision. Or think about taxes. For decades, roughly two-thirds of citizens have thought that corporations and wealthy people haven't paid their fair share.[9] Yet during the Trump administration, what did Congress do? It passed a major tax cut aimed to benefit wealthy citizens anyway.

Passing major legislation is complex and highly political. The White House, lobbyists, interest groups, and the courts often play pivotal roles. But it's nevertheless fair to conclude that when it comes to collective representation, Congress sometimes rises to the occasion but regularly falls short.

Constituent Representation: Reflecting the Interests of the District or State

Battles over what it means to be a good, responsive representative play out in states and congressional districts across the country. Whether they're talking about health care, the environment, a highway project, or the federal response to Covid-19, members of Congress almost always link their positions and actions to working for and serving their constituents. And that means different things in different parts of the country. Do people who live in California's 12th congressional district, which includes just 39 square miles of land in San Francisco, care about farm subsidies? Probably about as much as voters in Montana, which has just one congressional district that covers 147,000 square miles, care about traffic congestion and urban homelessness. Do voters in New York's 15th District, where Joe Biden received 86 percent of the vote for president in 2020, expect the same things from their members of Congress as voters do in Alabama's 4th District, where Donald Trump secured 81 percent of the vote?[10] Unlikely. So assessing whether Congress serves the American people requires considering **constituent representation**—how well individual legislators advance the interests of citizens who live in their district or state.

One measure of constituent representation is the partisan match between constituents and their members of Congress. Representatives who share the majority of their constituents' party affiliation may better represent their district or state. We see a partisan match in the overwhelming majority of states and districts (see Table 2).[11] In the last Congress, 409 of the 435 districts (94 percent) were represented by a

TABLE 2. Partisan Matches and Mismatches, 2021–2023

	Democratic Representative	Republican Representative
Majority-Democratic District	97.1% (202 districts)	2.9% (6 districts)
Majority-Republican District	8.8% (20 districts)	91.2% (207 districts)

Note: Calculations are based on the partisanship of a majority of the district's registered voters.

Source: "2021 Fully Downloadable PVI State and District List," Cook Political Report, April 15, 2021.

How well does Congress serve the American people?

member who was of the same party as a majority of the district's voters. Eighty-eight of the 100 senators shared the party affiliation of a majority of the citizens in their state.

In most districts, we're talking about a fairly sizable majority of voters, too. Democratic members of the House, for example, represent districts with, on average, a 13.9-percentage-point advantage in Democratic voter registration. Republican members' districts have a 13.6-point Republican advantage.[12] To see how this plays out, consider that just 3 of the 40 purely urban congressional districts have a Republican representative. But 12 of the 15 most rural districts do.[13]

Another way to assess constituent representation is to examine the legislative effort a representative exerts on behalf of the district. The number of bills members write or add their name to often indicates the extent to which they're pursuing goals on behalf of their constituents. But not every member is equally active or effective on the lawmaking front. Take a look at Table 3.[14] Whereas some House members sponsor and co-sponsor nothing—like, literally zero bills—others write dozens and sign on to thousands of others. The differences are just as prevalent in the Senate. Although most bills never become law (we'll get to that in Segment 35), if you don't introduce any, then there's no chance of enacting your ideas and proposals.

Partisan match and legislative productivity aren't the only ways members of Congress can provide constituent representation. **Constituent service**—the direct help members of Congress provide to citizens living in the district or state—is vital. This direct help takes many

TABLE 3. Lawmaking Activity in the 116th Congress, 2019–2021

	Lowest	Highest	Average
Bills Sponsored (Wrote the bill)	0	81	23
Bills Co-sponsored (Added name to bill as a full supporter)	9	1,265	394
Sponsored Bills Enacted into Law	0	7	0.5

Note: Data are based only on voting members of the House of Representatives.

Source: "Sponsors and Cosponsors," Congress.gov and "Download the Data," Center for Effective Lawmaking.

forms, including helping constituents navigate Medicare, Social Security, or immigration programs. Members of Congress can also represent their constituents by securing money in the federal budget to support government projects and programs back in the home district or state. Unfortunately, there are no systematic ratings for how well members of Congress perform on these dimensions.

Descriptive Representation: Reflecting the Face of the People

Congress does not look like the American public. But at least in terms of race, ethnicity, and gender, it's gotten a lot closer, albeit slowly. As of 2021, "only" 67 percent of U.S. senators and "just" 58 percent of House members were White men.[15] Compare that to even the early 1990s, when 9 out of 10 senators and 80 percent of House members fell into that category. In fact, until 1993, no more than two women ever served in the U.S. Senate at the same time. Still, the composition of both chambers continues to undermine **descriptive representation**— the degree to which elected officials reflect citizens' demographic characteristics.[16] And when it comes to wealth and income, there has been no improvement in descriptive representation. Congress continues to be dominated by millionaires.[17]

Although increasing racial, ethnic, and gender diversity in Congress overall has been slow, descriptive representation looks very different for Democrats and Republicans. In the 117th Congress (2021–2023), 73 percent of the female members were Democrats. There's no question that women are still underrepresented numerically—they constitute 39 percent of the Democratic members in the House and 32 percent of Democrats in the Senate. But for the past few decades, women have become a steadily growing proportion of Democratic candidates and representatives (see Figure 1).[18] Not so for Republicans. Across both chambers, only 39 Republican women served in the 117th Congress. That's less than 15 percent of all Republicans serving in the House and 16 percent of Republicans in the Senate.

The partisan differences are just as dramatic when it comes to race and ethnicity. In the 117th Congress, 37 percent of Democratic members of the House and Senate were people of color—exactly on the mark if the goal is to reflect the proportion of the U.S. population that identifies as non-White. But of the 262 Republicans serving in the House and Senate combined, only 21 were people of color. That amounts to just 8 percent of all Republicans.[19]

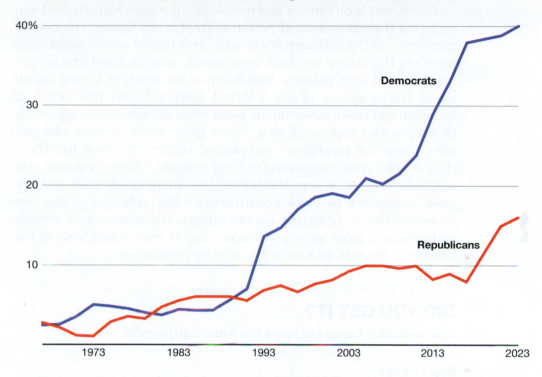

FIGURE 1. Women's Representation in Congress, 1967–2023

Democrats

Republicans

40%

30

20

10

1973   1983   1993   2003   2013   2023

Note: Lines represent the share of each party's seats occupied by female members in the House and Senate combined.

Source: "History of Women in the U.S. Congress," Center for American Women and Politics. Entries reflect estimates for 2023, as of November 15, 2022.

Contrary to what many people believe, numeric underrepresentation of women and people of color today isn't a result of widespread bias or discrimination on the part of voters. Women raise just as much money, receive just as many votes, and are just as likely to win their races as men are.[20] This is true for both Democrats and Republicans and in both congressional primaries and general elections.[21] Research that focuses on the electoral fortunes of Black congressional candidates also uncovers little evidence of overt voter discrimination.[22] Instead, one of the most significant explanations for the underrepresentation of historically excluded groups is incumbency. Members of Congress have tremendous advantages when they seek reelection, making it difficult for anyone who isn't already in Congress to get elected. Moreover, as far as women's underrepresentation is concerned, women are significantly less likely than men—regardless of political party, income level, age, race, profession, or region—to think they're qualified to run for office or to receive encouragement to do so.[23] This has been true over time and across generations.[24]

Given that both women and people of color have historically been excluded from positions of power in the United States, the overall numbers and the partisan differences carry important consequences. After all, the extent to which traditionally marginalized groups are incorporated into political leadership roles sends a strong signal about the openness of the political system.[25] And this sense of inclusion can make government seem more democratic[26]—especially to people who aren't old, rich, White guys. When women and people of color see candidates and elected leaders who look like them, they're more politically interested and engaged.[27] Some research also suggests that Black representatives hire more Black staff and are more responsive to Black constituents.[28] But only one of the two major parties in Congress counts substantial numbers of women and people of color among its ranks—and in many cases, only in the handful of districts with majority-minority populations.

DID YOU GET IT?
How well does Congress serve the American people?

Short Answer:

- It depends on which aspect of representation you consider.
- In terms of collective representation, the evidence is mixed— Congress fails to take action on a lot of issues where there's a public consensus, but it does act on many others.
- As for constituent representation, pretty well. The vast majority of districts and states are represented by members who share the same party affiliation as the majority of their constituents.
- When it comes to descriptive representation, not very well— although in terms of race and gender, that's changing, at least among Democrats.

Persuasive Argumentation

Evaluate evidence: A lot of persuasive evidence in politics comes from systematic data collection. Rely on the data presented in the tables and figures in this segment to identify evidence to support persuasive arguments about congressional representation.

1. If you want to argue that the U.S. government falls short when it comes to descriptive representation, what overall evidence from the tables and figures in this segment is most persuasive?

    a. The gaps in values between the U.S. population and the House of Representatives in Table 1

    b. The gaps in values between the U.S. population and the Senate in Table 1

    c. The entries in Table 3

    d. The "Democrats" line in Figure 1

2. Which policy area discussed in this segment offers the most compelling evidence that Congress does not provide collective representation?

    a. Social Security

    b. Immigration

    c. Education

    d. Medicare

3. Which fact provides the strongest evidence that members of the House of Representatives generally provide good constituent representation?

    a. Members representing majority-Democratic districts sponsor 24 bills on average.

    b. Members representing majority-Republican districts sponsor 54 bills on average.

    c. Almost 100 percent of majority-Democratic districts are represented by a Democrat.

    d. One-sixth of majority-Republican districts are represented by a Democrat.

FIGURE IT OUT

Questions of representation don't just pertain to Congress. All political institutions can be evaluated along these lines, including state legislatures across the country. Find the evidence necessary to make an argument about how well the state legislature where you live descriptively represents the state's residents. More specifically, determine:

- the percentage of the state legislators who are (1) female, (2) African American, and (3) Latino

- the percentage of the state's citizens who are (1) female, (2) African American, and (3) Latino

Based on these data, is your state succeeding or failing in terms of descriptive representation? Or is it somewhere in between? Explain how you arrived at your answer. If you live in Washington, D.C., which doesn't have a state legislature, then you can choose any of the 50 states.

To answer this question, the National Conference of State Legislators website will come in handy: https://www.ncsl.org/research/about-state-legislatures/who-we-elect-an-interactive-graphic.aspx. Governing.com is also useful, as it provides breakdowns of racial categories by state: https://www.governing.com/gov-data/census/state-minority-population-data-estimates.html.

Want to Know More?

If you're interested in the kinds of facts we presented in this segment, then you'll love "Vital Statistics on Congress," a report issued by the Brookings Institution every couple of years: https://www.brookings.edu/multi-chapter-report/vital-statistics-on-congress/. It provides a dizzying array of stats about who serves in the House and Senate. You'll learn everything you ever wanted to know about Congress — and probably quite a bit you didn't.

35.
How doesn't a bill become a law?

#LegislativeProcess

In 2018, U.S. surgeon general Jerome Adams issued a report declaring e-cigarette use among young people "an epidemic" in the United States.[1] The report set into motion a flurry of news coverage about the health risks associated with teen vaping. The Pew Research Center released a study showing that nicotine vaping roughly doubled from 2017 to 2018 among eighth-, tenth-, and twelfth-graders.[2] ABC News ran a lengthy account of a teenager who had damaged her lungs so badly from vaping that she had to be put on life support.[3]

Particularly worrisome was the prevalence of fruity, sweet cereal–flavored, and candy-flavored vaping products that appealed to children and teenagers. According to the Food and Drug Administration, the "overwhelming majority" of the estimated 25 percent of high school students smoking e-cigarettes used these flavored products, the problem didn't subside.[4] Indeed, in 2022, worried that isolation and depression from the pandemic had pushed many young people toward substance abuse, President Biden's surgeon general, Vivek Murthy, also sounded the alarm about teen vaping.[5] Although, more than 300 cities and towns across 10 different states passed restrictions on flavored tobacco products.[6]

The time seems perfect for Congress to outlaw flavored vaping products for the entire country. After all, laws are often a response to societal problems. Social Security sought to curb poverty among the elderly. Transportation bills aim to fix crumbling highways. The Vape

After waking up from a medically induced coma to treat the lung damage brought on by vaping, 18-year-old Simah Herman, who had never even considered herself a smoker, became an advocate against vaping.

No More Act — what we're calling our hypothetical new law — could regulate flavored vaping products and address the growing number of health issues associated with teen vaping.

Of course, that's easier said than done. In the 116th Congress, members introduced 16,601 legislative proposals. But just 344 of them — roughly 2 percent of those submitted — passed and were enacted into law (see Figure 1).[7] That's a pretty typical congressional session. The historic average is 3 percent.

This segment traces the long, complex journey our hypothetical Vape No More Act must travel to become a law. We walk through the conventional legislative process — also referred to as **regular order** — by focusing on the specific rules and procedures involved in turning an idea for legislation into an actual law. The Constitution explicitly spells out very little of this process. Instead, it's based mostly on rules and norms created by Congress during the last 200 years. As you follow the fate of our Vape No More Act, you'll come to see how most bills fall victim to partisan warfare and why even a broadly supported proposal to reduce something as harmful as teen vaping isn't a sure thing.

Step 1: Introduce a Bill

The first step in the legislative process involves introducing a bill, which requires a few steps of its own—most obviously, writing it. Because both the House and the Senate need to pass a bill before it moves on to the

FIGURE 1. Bills Introduced and Number of Bills Enacted, 1979–2021

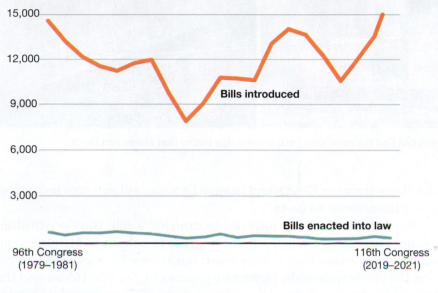

Bills introduced

Bills enacted into law

96th Congress (1979–1981)

116th Congress (2019–2021)

Source: "Statistics and Historical Comparison," GovTrack.us.

president, members in each chamber often work together to introduce similar legislation at similar times.

Typically, members of Congress don't draft bills themselves. They rely on staffers and outside organizations who have expertise on the topic. Depending on the complexity of the issue, bills can be as short as a few pages or as long as a few thousand. The Coronavirus Aid, Relief, and Economic Security Act came in at 880 pages.[8] The 2021 trillion-dollar infrastructure bill to improve and modernize the nation's roads and bridges? 2,700 pages.[9] But those are exceptions. The average bill is about 18 pages.[10] Even short bills typically summarize the rationale for the legislation, how it will be implemented and enforced, and how it will be funded. Once the bill is drafted, the author, known as the sponsor, seeks co-sponsors—other members of Congress who didn't write the bill but who put their name on it to signal their full support.

The Vape No More Act is a straightforward 10-page bill that simply bans all flavored vaping products. If it passes, then the days of Cap'n Crunch–flavored and Trix-flavored vape cartridges will be gone. No more cotton candy or watermelon vape juices either. U.S. companies will no longer be permitted to manufacture these products, and people won't be able to purchase them in the United States. The bill specifies that

Name a flavor and you can find the vape juice (left) or cartridge (right) that tastes just like it.

the Department of Health and Human Services will enforce the law and cover the associated costs.

Regardless of who is involved in drafting a bill, the Constitution permits only sitting members of Congress to submit it. Members can introduce as many bills as they want. But once a bill has been submitted, the challenges of the legislative process begin. The House and the Senate are both organized by political party. The party with the most seats in each chamber, known as the majority party, in effect picks that chamber's party leaders. In the House of Representatives, the whole chamber votes, and the candidate whom the majority party favors is elected **Speaker of the House**. In the Senate, that role goes to the majority leader. These party leaders control the congressional agenda and essentially determine which bills move forward. And they have no obligation to ensure that a bill gets any attention. If the Speaker or the majority leader doesn't like the bill—for any reason—that's almost always the end of it. Majority party leaders can delay or thwart consideration of a bill until the congressional session ends, at which point it's dead.

Without jumping too far ahead in the legislative process, it's worth noting here that even when bills make it through one chamber, there's no guarantee that the other chamber will act. Inaction is particularly likely when Democrats control one chamber and Republicans control the other. In 2019, for example, the House, controlled by Democrats, passed more than 400 bills that never received any action in the Republican-controlled Senate.[11] That's because Senate Majority Leader Mitch McConnell refused to move forward any Democratic bills that Republicans generally disagreed with. He even tweeted, "Let me be clear: I will be the 'grim reaper' in the Senate."[12] In 2014, when Democrats controlled the Senate and Republicans controlled the House, Senate Majority Leader Harry Reid did the same thing. Republicans accused him of sitting on 350 bills passed by the House.[13]

Fortunately for us, the Vape No More Act is a **bipartisan** bill—members of both parties in both chambers support it and have signed on as co-sponsors. The Speaker of the House and the majority leader in the Senate both promise to make it a priority.

Step 2: Navigate the Committee System

After the party leadership has signaled support for a bill, the next stop is a congressional committee, in which a subset of members with expertise or interest in a particular policy come together to take a close look at the proposed legislation. The House has 20 **standing committees**—permanent committees that meet regularly—and the Senate has 16. The committees focus on specific policy areas like agriculture, defense, natural resources, and veterans' affairs. Each committee also has roughly 5 subcommittees associated with it; these are even smaller groups of lawmakers who consider more specific topics and report back to the full committee.

In the House, the Speaker refers bills to the appropriate committee. In our bill's case, that's the Energy and Commerce Committee, which is charged with health care and product safety issues that come before Congress. In the Senate, the parliamentarian—a nonpartisan adviser to the Senate who is an expert on Senate rules and procedures—essentially matches bills to appropriate committees. The Health, Education, Labor, and Pensions Committee takes up the Vape No More Act. Had the content of the bill focused on gun policy or tax reform, it would have been referred to a different committee.

As with the leadership of Congress, political party affiliation determines everything about how committees operate. Members of the majority party, with heavy input from the Speaker or the majority leader, choose each committee chair. That's why the parties work so hard every election cycle to ensure that they hold at least 218 of the 435 seats in the House and 51 of the 100 in the Senate. It doesn't matter the size of the majority. The party with the most members—even by the slimmest of margins—still appoints the chair of every committee. And the committee chair has almost total control over the committee, including decisions about which bills to put on the committee's agenda and which bills never to take up. In fact, roughly 90 percent of the thousands of bills referred to committees in each two-year session never get scheduled by the committee chair for consideration. The majority party's influence doesn't end with the chair. The majority party also holds a majority of seats on each committee, which typically means that the majority party determines a bill's fate.

Committees engage in three essential tasks. First, they gather information about the proposed bill by holding hearings. In the case of the

Top row: Teenage activist Greta Thunberg testifies before a House Foreign Affairs Subcommittee about climate change; Facebook CEO Mark Zuckerberg testifies in front of the House Financial Services Committee about data privacy and cryptocurrency. Bottom row: Comedian Hasan Minhaj pleads with the House Financial Services Committee to address the student loan crisis; Elmo pitches funding for music education programs to the Education Appropriations Subcommittee.

Vape No More Act, the committee hears testimony from doctors and health professionals about the medical risks of vaping, from educators and parents' associations about the social ills of vaping, and from teenagers who suffered serious health problems as a result of using flavored vaping products. But as with almost any policy issue, there's more than one side. So the committee hearings also feature executives from two prominent vaping companies—KangerTech and Geekvape—both of whom say they're willing to work with Congress to address teen health risks but oppose a broad ban. The executives claim that their companies don't market their products to children and that it's illegal for teenagers to buy their products anyway. Several legal experts and libertarians also testify before the committee, arguing that the proposed ban is just one more example of big government telling people how to live.

After the hearings, committees undertake their second task: amending the bill. Minor changes, called markups, modify the language and clarity of the bill but not its substance. To change the substance of a bill, committee members propose amendments. A member from Idaho, for example, moves to exempt "mint" from the Vape No More Act, arguing that it's not a kid-friendly flavor and, thus, doesn't need to be excluded. It's not a coincidence, by the way, that Idaho is one of the top mint-producing states.[14] Another member proposes an amendment that limits the ban to two years, which should be sufficient time for Congress and public health officials to study the issue thoroughly before enacting a permanent ban. Someone else proposes an amendment to ban only flavored vape juices, not flavored vape cartridges.

The full committee must vote on whether to approve any substantive amendments. Majority rules, so once again, the party in control shapes the bill. In this case, the House committee adopts just one amendment— the "mint exemption." Things go a little differently on the Senate side. The Health, Education, Labor, and Pensions Committee votes down the "mint exemption" but approves the amendment to ban just vape juices, not cartridges. (Keep the different versions of the bill passed in the House and Senate committees in the back of your mind. The differences will become important later.)

The third and final task for a congressional committee is to vote on the bill. Any bills that receive a majority of votes from the full committee continue on in the legislative process. Those without it die. Of the 55 members of the House Energy and Commerce Committee, a bipartisan mix of 41 vote in favor of the bill. In the Senate, the committee passes the Vape No More Act in a bipartisan vote of 17–6.

Step 3: Get a Bill to the Floor

The bill got through committee, the biggest obstacle in the legislative process. Yay! Time for the House and Senate to vote on this thing and get it to the president, right? Not so fast.

In the House, the next step is the Rules Committee, which must pass a set of rules governing how the bill will be debated on the House floor. (Just imagine how difficult it would be for 435 members to debate a bill without clear rules.) Rules for bills generally establish how long the debate will last and whether members may offer amendments. But once again, that's only if the committee chair wants to move forward with the bill. If not, then it dies in the Rules Committee. We're in luck. The committee passes a rule allowing for five hours of debate time equally divided between those who favor the Vape No More Act and those who oppose it. Each side will be permitted to propose two amendments. Once the bill has a rule, the Speaker of the House can schedule it for a debate and vote before the full House of Representatives.

In the Senate, after a bill is voted out of committee, it's placed on a list of all bills eligible for debate on the Senate floor. At this point, the majority leader and minority leader negotiate the terms of how to debate the bill. Senators have the right to propose unlimited amendments, so if any senator introduces a controversial amendment, that one change could undermine, delay, or even halt the bill's progress. To avoid this, Senate leaders often enter into agreements to make the floor debate run smoothly. If they can work things out, the bill is scheduled for a vote. If they can't—which is what happens for many controversial bills—the bill will likely never be scheduled for a vote. That's another way a bill can die in this process. Because the Vape No More Act has substantial bipartisan support, the party leaders are able to agree on the terms: two days of floor debate where each side is allowed up to five amendments.

Step 4: Hold Floor Debate and Vote

The floor debate and vote is the first opportunity for all members of Congress to debate a bill and formally register their opposition or support. In the House, floor debates tend to be quite orderly. Members on each side of the issue give short speeches—usually one to two minutes—stating their position on the legislation.

During the debate in the House, members get up to explain how the Vape No More Act will affect their constituents. Those speaking in favor of the bill relay heartbreaking stories about teenagers suffering life-threatening illnesses from vaping. Several even include compelling props in their presentations—enlarged photos of teenage constituents in hospital beds, graphs and charts showing the skyrocketing use of vaping products, and poster-size images of emails from CEOs talking about how much money they're making from vaping products. They also read statements from the American Cancer Society, the American Lung Association, the American Academy of Pediatrics, and the Campaign for Tobacco-Free Kids, all of whom support the bill.

Though it might seem difficult to argue against a bill that would protect sick children and punish greedy tobacco-industry CEOs, there are some opponents. Some claim that government should impose fewer regulations on how people live, not more. They believe that keeping teenagers safe from vaping is up to their parents. One member—a congresswoman who represents a district with a tobacco company that produces many vaping products—offers an amendment to delay implementation of the bill for an indefinite period. But most of the bill's opponents complain about the process that led to consideration of the bill. A few accuse the bill's supporters of unfairly pushing it forward: "The process has been rushed. We're being asked to vote on a bill but haven't

How doesn't a bill become a law?

Sometimes, members of Congress rely on props to hammer home a key point during floor speeches. Senator James Inhofe (R-OK) brought a snowball to the Senate floor to argue that global warming is a fake crisis that requires no government action; Senator Maria Cantwell (D-WA) summarized her concerns about proposed cuts to Medicaid in a poster with an embarrassing spelling error. Critics mockingly called her Senator Cantspell.

been given enough time to read it." In fact, this is a common refrain from opponents of any bill. In some cases, an argument like this might carry water. A vote on a 2,232-page bill to fund the government a few years ago was scheduled for 18 hours after its release from the Rules Committee.[15] Even a speed-reader would have a tough time with that one. But in this case, the criticism falls flat. Members had two weeks to read the 10-page bill, and people on both sides of the aisle support it. Upon conclusion of the five-hour debate, the Vape No More Act easily passes the House, 353–82.

In the Senate, floor debates tend to last much longer. Dubbed the "world's greatest deliberative body," Senate rules allow senators to speak on the floor for as long as they want and to propose as many amendments as they see fit. Party leaders often agree to some limits to help move the legislative process along. But even then, the rights of individual senators to speak take precedence. In fact, senators can engage in a **filibuster**—a speech of unlimited length with the intent of delaying or forcing a vote on specific legislation. The filibustering senator's goal is to tie up the Senate until the leadership agrees to the action sought by the senator. In 2015, for example, Democrat Chris Murphy, who represented Connecticut at the time of the Newtown school shooting, spoke for 15 hours—without a bathroom break—in an attempt to coerce the Senate to vote on two gun control measures.[16] Republican Ted Cruz used a 2013 filibuster to try to stop a vote on a bill that provided funding for Obamacare.

Senators can use their time to talk about anything; content isn't restricted to the bill under consideration. In Cruz's case, his 21-hour filibuster included discussions of his father's cooking, actor Ashton Kutcher, and horror movie character Freddy Krueger. Cruz also sang part of a Toby Keith song and read the Dr. Seuss classic *Green Eggs and Ham*.[17]

To end a filibuster, at least 60 senators must vote for **cloture**, which limits debate to 30 additional hours and then requires the Senate to vote. As partisan tensions have risen, the minority party has increasingly relied on the filibuster to thwart the majority party's legislative goals. Between 2010 and 2020, senators attempted nearly 1,000 filibusters—more than the total number attempted during the preceding 90 years![18] That's because as long as the majority party doesn't have 60 senators willing to end the filibuster—and it's rare that it does—then the filibuster could theoretically go on forever, preventing the Senate from taking up other business. Even the threat of a filibuster is often enough to ensure that a bill never gets scheduled for a floor debate.[19] By 2017, filibusters had become such a central impediment to the legislative process that the Senate changed its rules to limit the filibuster only to debates about major legislation.

The Vape No More Act has no trouble mustering support on the Senate floor. No senators even propose amendments, let alone threaten a filibuster. If the bill were controversial or highly partisan—addressing an issue like immigration, abortion, or tax policy—then both parties' leaders would spend time urging their members to stick with the party position. And they'd likely succeed. In committee and on the floor, members of Congress on both sides of the aisle vote with their party leadership more than 90 percent of the time.[20] Even without pressure from party leaders, though, the Vape No More Act passes with a healthy margin of 82–18.

Step 5: Resolve Differences between House and Senate Versions of the Bill

Getting a positive vote, particularly in the Senate, is a major victory for proponents of the Vape No More Act. But it's still not ready for the president's signature. The bills passed by the House and Senate aren't quite the same. Remember, the House version includes the "mint exemption exemption," and the Senate version bans only flavored vape juices, not cartridges. It's common for bills that work through the House and Senate simultaneously—which most of them do—to look a little different by the time they pass in each chamber. But for a bill to make it to the president, both chambers must pass identical bills. So the House and Senate must resolve the differences in their respective bills.

In ancient times, like before the 2000s, the House and Senate leaders appointed **conference committees** to iron out differences and agree

How doesn't a bill become a law?

on one version of any particular bill. These temporary panels typically included members of the standing committees that originally considered the bill in each chamber. These days, that practice is far less common; only about 5 percent of bills go to a conference committee.[21] Instead, party leaders from both chambers hammer out any differences in closed-door meetings, or they work together to resolve inconsistencies prior to sending the bill back to the floor for final passage.

Reconciling the House and Senate versions of the Vape No More Act turns out to be tough. Senate leaders readily agree to the "mint exemption," but members of the House feel strongly that banning flavored vape juices but not flavored cartridges defeats the whole point. Kids can still get access to appealing flavors. In the end, party leaders strike a deal. They agree to ban the cartridges, but they delay implementation of that part of the ban for two years. When the House and Senate negotiators reconcile their differences, they bring the new compromise version of the bill back to the floor of each chamber for a vote. Ultimately, majorities in both the full House and full Senate vote to support the Vape No More Act.

Step 6: Send to the President

The power to sign a bill into law or **veto** a bill from becoming a law is one of greatest powers enumerated to the president in the Constitution. With the stroke of a pen, the president can invalidate the work of 535 members of Congress. But by the time a bill is ready for the president's consideration, there are few surprises. Members of Congress aren't nervously awaiting the outcome. Presidents sign the overwhelming majority of bills that make it to their desks. After all, they almost always signal support or opposition to a proposed law as it's making its way through Congress. If Congress knows that the president plans to veto a bill, then members have less incentive to push it through the legislative process in the first place. They could override the veto, but that requires a two-thirds vote in each chamber, which is exceedingly rare. Dating back to 1960, presidents on average have vetoed only about 2 percent of the legislation that crosses their desks. In his first two years in office, President Biden did not veto a single bill. Congress musters support to override only a very small proportion of vetoes (see Figure 2).[22]

In our case, the president's support for the Vape No More Act was clear. The president had numerous conversations with members of Congress to express his support for the ban, and invited to the State of the Union address a high school student who had been hospitalized as a result of vaping. The president signs the Vape No More Act into

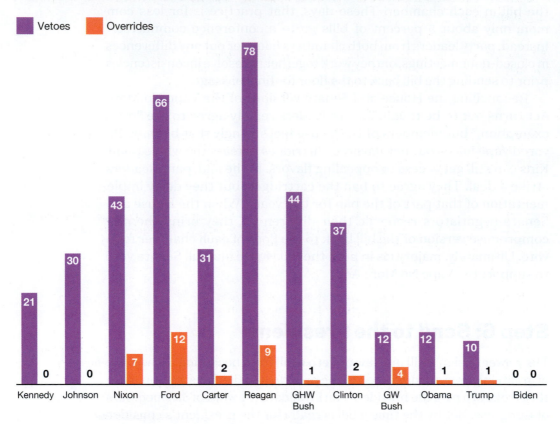

FIGURE 2. Number of Presidential Vetoes and Overrides, 1960–2022

Legend: Vetoes (purple), Overrides (orange)

President	Vetoes	Overrides
Kennedy	21	0
Johnson	30	0
Nixon	43	7
Ford	66	12
Carter	31	2
Reagan	78	9
GHW Bush	44	1
Clinton	37	2
GW Bush	12	4
Obama	12	1
Trump	10	1
Biden	0	0

Note: Bars indicate the total number of vetoes each president issued during his full time in office. For Biden, the count ends on December 31, 2022, representing just his first two years as president.

Source: "Presidential Vetoes," United States House of Representatives.

law at a signing ceremony in the Oval Office. Looking on are the bill's sponsors in the House and Senate as well as several members of Congress who worked hard to drum up support for the act.

Did That Seem So Bad?

The Vape No More Act is now a law! It defied the odds and successfully navigated the six major steps of the legislative process (see Table 1). The process our hypothetical bill followed is the conventional path by which a bill becomes a law. And although many of the steps we outlined affect any bill, **unorthodox legislating** now often disrupts regular order. That

TABLE 1. Estimating the Fate of 100 Typical Bills as They Go through Regular Order

Step 1: Introduce a Bill	The bill's sponsor works with staffers and experts to draft it. The member submits the bill to the Speaker of the House or Senate parliamentarian, who refers it to a standing committee.	100 enter the system
Step 2: Navigate the Committee System	The standing committee chair decides whether to take action on the bill. If so, the chair often refers it to a more specialized subcommittee. The committee holds hearings, amends the bill, and votes on it.	10 get out of committee
Step 3: Get a Bill to the Floor	In the House, the Rules Committee chair decides whether to establish rules of debate for the bill. In the Senate, party leaders play that role. Once a bill has a set of rules for debate, it can be scheduled for the floor.	5 get scheduled for a floor vote in both chambers
Step 4: Hold Floor Debate and Vote	Members speak about the bill and introduce amendments as permitted in the bill's rule. Then the full chamber votes.	4 pass both chambers
Step 5: Reconcile House and Senate Versions	Members of both chambers meet to iron out differences in the versions of the bill they each passed. The new identical versions then go to each chamber's floor for a vote.	3 pass both chambers in identical form
Step 6: Send to the President	The president signs or vetoes the bill. Overriding a presidential veto requires a two-thirds vote in each chamber of Congress.	3 pass into law

is, key decisions about controversial or high-profile legislation are handled outside of the typical process.[23] Sometimes party leaders bypass committee deliberations and make final adjustments to a bill in closed-door negotiations. Other times they run a bill by the president and make changes that will guarantee the president's signature prior to holding a floor vote. There have even been cases—especially in an emergency or to avoid partisan rancor—in which a bill goes straight to the floor after it's introduced. And when members try to make major changes to existing laws through the budget process, passing the bill requires only a majority vote in the Senate. These deviations from regular order have increased as the parties have become increasingly polarized and less inclined to work together in Congress.

DID YOU GET IT?

How doesn't a bill become a law?

Short Answer:

- Most bills die somewhere along the legislative process. Only about 3 percent of proposed bills are ever enacted into law.
- The legislative process is difficult to traverse because it is long and complex, involving powerful special interests, party leaders, committees, both chambers of Congress, and the president.
- The legislative process is also dominated by party politics. This means that bills that are controversial and supported by the majority party often meet strong resistance from the minority party, and the minority party's legislative priorities rarely see the light of day.

DEVELOPING YOUR SKILLS

Civic Engagement

Stay informed: The legislative process lies at the heart of U.S. government. To be an engaged citizen, you need to know how to follow what's going on in Congress.

1. Which of the following websites allows you to search the bills Congress is working on by issue area?
   a. Ballotpedia.org
   b. Census.gov
   c. GovTrack.us
   d. OpenSecrets.org

2. House.gov is the official website of the U.S. House of Representatives. The site provides detailed information about the chamber's business in real time. If you want to keep up with an environmental policy bill that matters to you, where on the website could you look to find out whether it was submitted to the president?
   a. The "Recent Votes" tab under the Legislative Activity banner
   b. The "Bills and Reports" tab under the Legislative Activity banner
   c. The "Leadership" tab on the home page, where you can then see if the Speaker has scheduled any meetings with the president
   d. The "Committees" tab on the home page, where you can then see what bills were sent to the floor for a vote

3. If you want to follow a bill through the committee system, you also need to immerse yourself in the work of subcommittees. Based on the information provided at House. gov, which of these standing committees has the most subcommittees?

    a. Appropriations

    b. Budget

    c. Foreign Affairs

    d. Judiciary

FIGURE IT OUT

Following bills that are up for debate or have recently been voted on is one way to stay informed about congressional action. Visit GovTrack.us or Congress.gov, and draft an email to send to your member of Congress about an issue that interests you. More specifically:

- Identify and get the email address for either of your U.S. senators or your member of the U.S. House.

- Find a bill that the member recently sponsored or co-sponsored.

Craft a short email — a couple of sentences is sufficient — informing your member of either your support for or opposition to the bill. If you're so inclined, feel free to send the email. Now that's citizen engagement!

Want to Know More?

If you haven't seen the famed Schoolhouse Rock video "I'm Just a Bill," then you really need to google it right now! It provides a simplified view of regular order, but it's how millions of elementary and middle-school students are first exposed to the legislative process. In addition to the three-minute cartoon, you'll likely encounter many spinoff videos, mostly by comedians. *The Daily Show*, Stephen Colbert, and *Saturday Night Live* have all riffed on the contemporary legislative process in the vein of the original video.

36.
What does the president do all day?

#PresidentialRoles

As the years passed, most Americans were able to return to life much as it had been before 9/11. But I never did. Every morning, I received a briefing on threats to our nation.

George W. Bush[1]

The most important thing you need to do [in this job] is to have big chunks of time during the day when all you're doing is thinking.

Barack Obama[2]

This is more work than my previous life. I thought it would be easier.

Donald Trump[3]

I've only been president four weeks and, sometimes, because things are moving so fast . . . it feels like four years.

Joe Biden[4]

The president of the United States presides over the most powerful country in the world. The person elected to occupy the Oval Office commands the world's strongest military, oversees the

Despite the daily rigors of the job, the last four presidents found time to play golf, especially Barack Obama and Donald Trump. Obama headed to the golf course more than 300 times during his eight years in office. Trump matched that in one term alone. But both fell short of Presidents Woodrow Wilson and Dwight Eisenhower, who played 1,200 and 800 rounds respectively.

world's largest economy, and executes laws that directly affect the nearly 330 million people who live in the country, not to mention billions of others around the globe. The irony is that the Founders were generally leery of presidential power. That's why they designed a government that put Congress at the center of the political system. But over time, the presidency has evolved, and the U.S. president has become the most powerful actor in domestic and global politics.

What does that mean? What does the president actually do? What authority does the president really have? Pinpointing every specific responsibility and identifying all of the potential ways a president can exercise power is a complex endeavor that can't possibly be covered in just one segment or even one book. The following pages, though, offer a start. We help you gain a handle on the president's major roles and powers by walking you through a hypothetical, but hectic, composite day — one that features the president's key roles. You'll see that the powers of the president fall into two broad categories: **formal powers**, which derive directly from Article II of the Constitution, and **informal powers**, which lack an explicit constitutional basis but still allow presidents to exert considerable influence over the political system. All told, the responsibilities of the presidency are staggering. That's perhaps why many presidents leave office looking so much older, grayer, and more exhausted than when they began, even if they still find time to play a little golf.

6:00 AM *Presidents get up whenever they want. George W. Bush was in the Oval Office by 6:45 A.M. Barack Obama ate breakfast with his family, exercised, and typically made it to the West Wing by 9 A.M. Donald Trump often remained in the living quarters of the White House until about 11 A.M., watching the news. Joe Biden is at his desk by 9 A.M. every day.[5]*

Commander in Chief

7:00 AM *Receive the Daily Intelligence Brief*

Regardless of where a president chooses to spend the early hours of the morning, one thing is always the same: the daily intelligence brief. The Constitution names the president **commander in chief** of the armed forces—which today means that the president presides over more than 1.4 million active duty military personnel and a massive arsenal of weapons, including nuclear arms.[6] Given this enormous responsibility, the president receives up-to-the-minute information about any pressing military concerns or external threats. So every morning members of the national intelligence community compile information and deliver it to the president and members of the national security team a classified report marked "top secret." Tensions with China, Russian aggression, and the nuclear capabilities of Iran and North Korea regularly fill the pages.[7]

Depending on the content of the intelligence brief, as well as conversations with the director of National Intelligence or the CIA director, the president might convene the national security team in the Situation Room, a secure location in the basement of the White House. As commander in chief, the president makes the decision to authorize military strikes and issues orders to U.S. forces around the world. Although the president consults with a team of experts and military leaders, he or she is the person directing the armed forces to protect American interests.

8:00 AM *Breakfast in the residence—huevos rancheros for Bush, eggs over easy and grits for Obama, nothing for Trump (he doesn't like breakfast), and Special K cereal for Biden.[8]*

Partisan in Chief

8:45 AM *Push Out the Party's Talking Points*

The Constitution doesn't mention political parties. But over time, the president has become the **partisan in chief**, responsible for (1) setting the political party's agenda, (2) communicating that agenda to the public, and (3) raising money for the party and its candidates. The party's political fortunes basically rise and fall with the president. When a president has a high approval rating, that good will on the part of the public can make it easier for the president's party to implement its legislative agenda.[9] Public support for a president can also translate into electoral victory for other members of the party.[10]

On a daily basis, presidents and their staffs work with the national party organization to establish and push out the party's message—typically, a series of talking points that put the president's spin on policy initiatives, major events or crises, and the opposition party's purported failures. There are many ways to do this. Most White Houses rely on daily press briefings to communicate their messages. This venue enables presidents, press secretaries, and other members of the administration to speak with reporters and get their side of any story out to the public. Official press conferences, formal speeches, and remarks at public events provide additional opportunities for presidents to shape and share the party's message.[11]

Donald Trump's White House was an exception. He relied so heavily on social media as a primary way to communicate with the public that his administration ended the practice of the daily press briefing.[12] Instead, Trump tweeted. A lot. Often as much as 50 times a day. Many of the tweets carried the same content that press briefings used to.[13] But Trump's messages to his 84 million Twitter followers were unfiltered by the journalists reporting on the president's statements and actions.[14] President Biden restored the daily press briefing, but also continues to use Twitter, although not as frequently as his predecessor.[15]

Administrator in Chief

9:45 AM   *Hold a Cabinet Meeting*

One of the president's most expansive roles is acting as the **administrator in chief**—the person responsible for implementing the laws that Congress passes. As the U.S. government has increased in size and scope over time, the president has come to rely on a massive federal bureaucracy to fulfill this responsibility. Indeed, the federal bureaucracy manages all major government programs, such as Social Security, student loans, and Medicare. The executive branch also enforces the nation's major laws, including business regulations, civil rights, and environmental and worker safety protections. And when there's a problem with any government program—like yearlong wait times for veterans to get basic health care through the Department of Veterans Affairs or illnesses caused by meat that wasn't properly

Presidents hold regular Cabinet meetings with the leaders of key departments and administration officials. Together, they pursue the administration's policies and priorities, troubleshoot problems that arise, and share advice on domestic and foreign affairs. Cabinet meetings often provide staged photo opportunities to showcase the president as leader of the executive branch.

inspected by the Department of Agriculture—the president has to address it. All told, the president oversees hundreds of federal agencies and more than 3 million employees who work within them.

11:00 AM *"Executive Time"—During this unstructured "free time," presidents can watch a little news, grab a late morning snack prepared by the White House private pastry chef, make some phone calls to close friends and advisers, read policy reports, or just sit back, think, and relax.*

Head of State

12:00 PM *Lunch with a Sports Team*

The president personifies the U.S. government and upon taking the oath of office instantly becomes the most famous person in the world. When people think about the U.S. government, they think about the president. That's largely because the president is the **head of state**—the chief public representative of the country.

The head of state role is multifaceted. One central piece involves ceremonial responsibilities. Presidents tour new schools, hospitals, and

To celebrate Clemson University's NCAA football title, President Trump served the players a variety of fast food from Wendy's, McDonald's, and Domino's. It wasn't an entirely casual affair, though. Waiters in tuxedos served Big Macs on silver trays. President Biden welcomed the Seattle Storm, winners of the 2020 WNBA Championship, to the East Room of the White House, where he accepted a jersey from the players.

military bases; meet with citizens and foreign dignitaries; and attend sporting events, funerals, and awards ceremonies. They invite people to the White House to celebrate their accomplishments. They ring in the major holidays—an Easter egg hunt for children on the White House lawn, the annual pardoning of a Thanksgiving turkey, the lighting of the White House Christmas tree. And they invite championship sports teams to the White House as a way to foster national spirit.

The White House communications team heavily stages most public appearances so that the president gets maximum exposure in the news. The image of an active and engaged leader helps strengthen public respect and admiration for the president, which can carry over into support for a policy agenda and other essential parts of the job.[16]

Another facet of the head of state role is what's become known as "consoler in chief." When there's a natural disaster—a flood, a fire, a hurricane—the president will often travel to the affected area to reassure citizens that the federal government has their back. When there's a mass shooting, collapsed building, or terrorist attack on U.S. soil, the president visits the location of the tragedy or takes to the airwaves to comfort the American people. Ronald Reagan did this when he addressed the nation following the 1986 explosion of the *Challenger* space shuttle on live television. Bill Clinton did it in the wake of the 1995 Oklahoma City bombing that killed 168 people. George W. Bush did it standing upon rubble at the site of the World Trade Center in the aftermath of the attacks on September 11, 2001. And Barack Obama did it through tears at a press conference the day that a mass shooter in Newtown, Connecticut, opened fire at an elementary school and killed 26 people, including 20 first-graders. Donald Trump was the first modern president not to embrace the consoler in chief role,[17] but Joe Biden returned to it when he toured Louisiana in the wake of Hurricane Ida. The 2021 storm left 13 dead and hundreds of thousands without electricity for weeks. Biden told a group of citizens, "Folks, I know you're hurting. . . . I want you to know we're going to be here for you."[18]

Administrator in Chief (again)

1:00 PM   *Meet with Council of Economic Advisers*

Presidents constantly monitor and work to improve the U.S. economy. Ever since President Franklin Roosevelt used the power of the presidency to lift the country out of the Great Depression in the 1930s, shepherding the economy has fallen to the president. And presidents who fall short typically pay a price. Indeed, voters usually identify the economy as the issue that's most important to them. Thus, economic performance is a good predictor of whether a president will win reelection or get booted from the White House.[19]

   To help manage the economy, the president relies on several government agencies and advisers. The Council of Economic Advisers is right down the hall, and its members provide direct and immediate advice on all economic matters. The Treasury secretary is also a top adviser on economic policy. Even with the best advice from experts, though, economic cycles are very unpredictable, and the president has little short-term influence over the economy.[20] That doesn't mean, however, that the president isn't always worried about it and trying to strengthen it.

Legislator in Chief

2:00 PM   *Golf with Members of Congress*

The Constitution grants Congress the power to make the laws. But the president still plays a central role in the lawmaking process.[21] Presidential candidates often propose a large legislative agenda. And the public has increasingly come to expect the president to solve most policy problems. The catch is that the president's legislative agenda must go through Congress—and that's no easy task. Presidents don't even have the power to submit a bill. Instead, all bills must be introduced by a supportive senator or member of the House.

One way presidents fulfill their **legislator in chief** role is by advocating for their preferred legislation with members of Congress. Sometimes they do this through well-publicized meetings in front of the cameras. At other times presidents work the phones, often encouraging members of their own party to remain loyal. Some of them do a lot of schmoozing. They invite legislators to the White House for informal sit-downs or to watch a sporting event.[22] They offer them rides on *Air Force One*.[23] They take in a round of golf with legislators who can introduce their bill or rally the votes for an initiative they support. Regardless of the tactic they employ, presidents must persuade and cooperate with congressional leaders to enact an agenda.

Legislator in Chief (again)

4:00 PM   *Sign an Executive Order*

Presidents' power to legislate isn't limited to pushing laws through Congress. Article II of the Constitution grants the president "executive power" to "take care that the laws shall be faithfully executed." Although it never mentions **executive orders** by name, the Constitution implies that presidents have the authority to issue directives about how to manage the operations of the the federal government—directives that require no congressional approval but still carry the force of law.

Presidents claim authorization to issue executive orders by linking them to a particular provision of the Constitution or statute that grants the executive branch the authority to act. And they've generally had no trouble making these links. President Franklin Roosevelt basically managed the Great Depression through executive order, issuing 3,721 during his presidency.[24] No other president has come close to that number (see Figure 1), but they've issued hundreds of orders pertaining to important policies.[25] Through executive order, Dwight Eisenhower ended school segregation in Arkansas, John F. Kennedy created the Peace Corps, Bill Clinton protected millions of acres of undeveloped land from road-building, mining, and logging, and George W. Bush limited federal funding for stem cell research.[26] With the stroke of a pen, the president can very efficiently change or enact a law without having to work with Congress.[27]

Although issuing executive orders has become a standard practice among modern-day presidents as a way of shaping the policy landscape single-handedly, it's important to keep in mind that executive orders are not very durable. Not only can Congress pass a law to invalidate an executive order, but any president can simply undo a predecessor's executive order with a new one. The Mexico City Policy, also known as

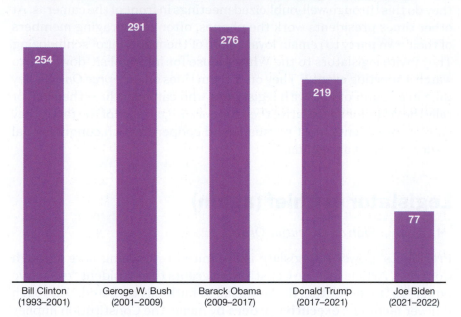

FIGURE 1. Number of Executive Orders Issued by the President

Bill Clinton (1993–2001): 254
Geroge W. Bush (2001–2009): 291
Barack Obama (2009–2017): 276
Donald Trump (2017–2021): 219
Joe Biden (2021–2022): 77

Note: Data represent the total number of executive orders each president signed. For Biden, the number is through August 1, 2022.

Source: "Executive Orders," *Federal Register*.

the Global Gag Rule, is a prime example. First implemented by Ronald Reagan in 1984, the policy prevents foreign organizations that receive any U.S. funding for family planning from providing abortion information, referrals, or services—even with money from other sources.[28] When Democrat Bill Clinton became president in 1993, rescinding the policy was among his first orders. Eight years later, Republican George W. Bush reinstated it. Barack Obama rescinded the order in 2009, only to see Donald Trump reinstate it in 2017. And Joe Biden, like his Democratic predecessors, rescinded it in 2021.

4:20 PM *Head back from the executive order signing ceremony in the Rose Garden, and take a few questions from the White House Press Corps. Arrive at the Oval Office, where several decorated veterans have been invited to receive thanks for their military service.*

5:00 PM *"Executive Time"—Relax before the evening portion of the day begins. Bush worked out; Obama joined his family for dinner; Trump watched the news, talked to friends, and saw his grandchildren; and Biden reads letters he receives from Americans across the country.[29]*

Chief Diplomat

State Dinner

Another of the president's formal roles involves conducting diplomacy and foreign policy to advance American interests. And in the capacity of **chief diplomat**, the president has great freedom to define those interests. Should a representative from the United States meet directly with a foreign dictator like Kim Jong Un of North Korea? It's up to the president. Should we take a hard line on relations with China or Russia? That's the president's call. What about promising military or financial aid to an ally or threatening military action or economic sanctions against a foe? All the president's decision. Some foreign policy actions, particularly those that involve financial assistance or a formal treaty, require input from Congress. But with the largest military and economy in the world at their disposal, presidents have wide latitude and discretion with respect to conducting foreign policy.

Fostering and nurturing diplomatic relationships keeps presidents traveling around the world. During their time in the White House, recent presidents have taken hundreds of trips and visited dozens of countries. George W. Bush and Bill Clinton tie for the gold medal, each having visited 74 different nations during the eight years they served.[30] The most high-profile travel opportunity tends to be the G7 (Group of 7) meeting, at which leaders of the seven democratic nations with the largest economies come together to address global economic and political challenges. The annual G20 meeting expands the group to include the 20 countries with the largest economies. The president also delivers an annual address to the United Nations.

An additional form of diplomacy—one that U.S. presidents tend to reserve for rare occasions—is a state dinner in honor of a foreign leader.

WAR OF WORDS
BIDEN CALLS PUTIN A 'MURDEROUS DICTATOR' AND A 'PURE THUG'

Presidents have a lot of discretion over their foreign policy priorities and principles. President Trump touted his cordial relationship with Russian leader Vladimir Putin, whereas President Biden called Putin a "war criminal" and "murderous dictator" in response to Russia's invasion of Ukraine.

TABLE 1. Roles of the Modern President

Commander in chief: Presides over military personnel and a massive arsenal of weapons.

Partisan in chief: Sets the political party's agenda, communicates it to the public, and raises money for the party.

Administrator in chief: Implements the laws Congress passes, largely by oversight of the massive federal bureaucracy.

Head of state: Serves as the nation's public representative at home and abroad, including as "consoler in chief."

Legislator in chief: Develops and implements a broad legislative agenda, often through executive order.

Chief diplomat: Conducts diplomacy and foreign policy to advance American interests.

These elegant, elaborate black-tie affairs typically include about 120 guests, often among them a celebrity or musician who performs. Elton John, Stevie Wonder, John Legend, Janelle Monáe, and Gwen Stefani are among those who have received coveted invitations to perform and celebrate diplomatic relationships.[31] In recent years, however, the number of state dinners has dwindled.[32]

As the president leaves the state dinner and heads up to the private residence in the White House, it's a time for personal reflection on the jam-packed day. Though not every day involves performing all six key roles of the modern president (see Table 1), most involve exercising quite a few formal and informal powers, all of which fall squarely on the president's shoulders.

11:00 PM *Time for bed. Sleep patterns vary widely by president—George W. Bush and Joe Biden favor 9 P.M. bedtimes, whereas Barack Obama and Donald Trump are night owls.[33]*

DID YOU GET IT?

What does the president do all day?

Short Answer:

- At the end of any given day, the president has filled numerous roles and exercised myriad powers, often more than once.

- Some of the powers are constitutionally granted, while others are more informal.
- Although the Founders were reluctant to grant the president too much power, modern presidents are largely responsible for developing and implementing most major foreign and domestic policies as well as representing the nation in times of crisis, celebration, and on the global stage.

DEVELOPING YOUR SKILLS

Consuming Political Information

Navigate political websites: Most presidential actions are recorded and documented. Visit these reliable sources to learn more about what presidents do and have done.

1. *The Federal Register* (https://www.archives.gov/federal-register/executive-orders /disposition) lists every executive order issued since 1937. Which is *not* an executive order President Obama signed in 2017?

   a. Changing the criteria for issuing a Purple Heart

   b. Recognizing positive actions by the government of Sudan

   c. Providing for an order of succession at the State Department

   d. Changing the designation of the World Organisation for Animal Health

2. If you want to find information about presidential actions with respect to immigration, which types of documents can you access on the official White House website (https://www.whitehouse.gov)?

   a. Presidential memoranda

   b. Campaign speeches

   c. Newspaper articles

   d. Pending legislation

3. The president, as head of state, delivers remarks, speeches, and addresses on a regular basis, including at state dinners. And the American Presidency Project records them. Whom did Donald Trump honor at a state dinner in 2019?

   a. Prime Minister Scott Morrison of Australia

   b. Prime Minister Justin Trudeau of Canada

   c. Chancellor Angela Merkel of Germany

   d. Queen Elizabeth II of the United Kingdom

FIGURE IT OUT

The president's public calendar is available at https://factba.se/calendar. Take a look, and identify one example of the president performing each of the six roles we covered in this segment:

- commander in chief
- partisan in chief
- head of state
- administrator in chief
- legislator in chief
- chief diplomat

For each role, summarize the activity and note the date and time.

Want to Know More?

Many pundits and analysts question whether it's reasonable to expect one person to do such a complex and multifaceted job as president of the United States. One of the best articles about whether it's possible for any president to do the job well is an *Atlantic* magazine piece by John Dickerson. The piece focuses on how the design of the presidency itself makes it unworkable. You can read it here: https://www.theatlantic.com/magazine/archive/2018/05/a-broken-office/556883/

37.
Are faceless bureaucrats out to get you?

#FederalBureaucracy

The alarm buzzes. Still half asleep, you drag yourself out of bed, walk to the bathroom, and fill a glass with water. You don't even think twice about your safety as you gulp it down. Why would you? The water doesn't contain excessive amounts of lead or arsenic because the water company must comply with clean water regulations enforced by the Environmental Protection Agency.[1]

Your head is pounding — you probably didn't need that second shot last night. So you take two Advil. Even though ibuprofen, the main drug in Advil, is quite potent, you don't worry about relying on it for pain. After thorough tests, the Food and Drug Administration approved ibuprofen for over-the-counter sales in 1984.[2] And it required manufacturers to recommend no more than two tablets (400 milligrams) per dose.

You step into a nice hot shower, hoping it'll wake you up. You adjust the water, making it hotter and hotter. The temperature rises slowly and evenly, so you can easily stop turning the knob before the water scalds you. Thank the Consumer Product Safety Commission for that. It handles product complaints about unsafe products, like faulty temperature regulators. It has issued recalls on thousands of products that pose safety risks.[3]

The notion that the government is out to monitor your every move has long concerned not only conspiracy theorists but also many regular Americans. These fears have grown in the era of smart technology and tracking devices.

Feeling a bit more awake, you walk back into your room to get dressed. You decide to wear the new, really soft sweater you received for your birthday. The label says it's 100 percent cashmere. You've never had a cashmere sweater before, but labels don't lie. The Federal Trade Commission enforces the Wool Products Labeling Act, which makes it a crime to label something cashmere when it's really just a rayon/cotton blend.[4]

You're still dragging a little, so you decide to grab a quick coffee on the way to school. You push the ignition button in the car and make your way to Starbucks. The car purrs and the roads are safe. That's because the National Highway Traffic Safety Administration ensures that auto-makers comply with safety standards and that roads provide plenty of space for you to drive comfortably.[5]

At the drive-thru window, you order a venti organic arabica bean coffee with soy milk. You hate that this has become your order. You used to make fun of people who ordered drinks like this. Now you're one of them. But you feel good knowing that there are no insecticides on those beans — coffee or soy. Without the U.S. Department of Agriculture and its team of inspectors, the coffee and milk couldn't be certified as organic.[6]

Back in the car, you're bummed to hear on the radio that the forecast calls for rain. You have big plans for tonight, and bad weather will definitely put a damper on them. It's possible that the forecast is wrong, but it's probably not. The National Weather Service, a part of the National Oceanic and Atmospheric Administration, tends to be pretty accurate.[7]

In the next hour, you're exposed to the Consumer Financial Protection Bureau, which requires banks to post ATM fees;[8] the Department of Education, which enforces the Americans with Disabilities Act to ensure that your school is accessible;[9] and the Occupational Safety and Health Administration, which makes sure that the chemistry lab where you work part-time is asbestos-free and in compliance with cleaning and disinfecting protocols to stop the spread of Covid-19.[10]

In one morning alone, you encountered the work of at least 10 government agencies responsible for implementing rules and overseeing regulations that affect even the most mundane aspects of your day. These agencies are all part of the **federal bureaucracy** — government offices within the executive branch that implement and enforce the law. The more than 2 million people who work in these agencies are federal bureaucrats. The number of federal government employees exceeds 4 million if you include military personnel and postal workers.[11]

Yet for many Americans, bureaucracy is an abstract notion. Most people think little about it and have no idea what it all entails. And when people do think about it, they're usually not envisioning government workers who make lives infinitely safer. Instead, the word "bureaucracy" often conjures up images of a lazy, inefficient, wasteful government where nameless, faceless bureaucrats with no accountability tell you what you can and can't do. Recently, critics have even emphasized the notion of a **deep state** — a derogatory term to describe a group of unelected government officials whom they allege are secretly manipulating and directing national policy.

This segment provides a breakdown of the federal bureaucracy as well as an overview of the millions of people who work within it. In addition to laying out the structure of the executive branch, we clarify the role of the bureaucracy in the U.S. political system and point out some of the general challenges that all large organizations face. You'll see that although critics tend to highlight bureaucratic missteps — and without a doubt, some of those missteps are worthy of criticism — they often overlook the fact that the federal bureaucracy is composed of agencies that enforce vital laws, regulate businesses, and keep Americans safe.

The Federal Bureaucracy: The Largest Organization in the United States

How did we wind up with millions of federal government employees involved in so many aspects of day-to-day life? George Washington got the ball rolling. When he became the first president in 1789, there wasn't really much of a federal government to preside over. The Constitution makes no mention of any specific government agencies. But the Founders surely assumed that in order to carry out the roles of commander in chief and head of state, presidents would need a larger executive branch. Indeed, Article II, Section 2, of the Constitution refers to "principal officers in each of the executive departments," whom the president can appoint "with the advice and consent of the Senate."

And that's what Washington did. With congressional approval, he formally created the Departments of Treasury, War, and State. He then appointed, and the Senate confirmed, the leaders of each department. Over time, this small federal government mushroomed into a sprawling organization comprising dozens of government agencies—almost all created and overseen by Congress but situated within the executive branch.

Describing the organization of any large entity can be tedious. So bear with us as we briefly summarize the structure of the federal bureaucracy. At the top sits the White House Office. Created by President Franklin Roosevelt in the late 1930s, it actually includes 11 offices, including the vice president's. The Office represents the nerve center of the executive branch. It's where the president's closest aides handle the day-to-day operations of the White House, shape the public message, and manage the president's schedule. It's also where the president's top advisers work to develop the administration's positions on the economy, national security, and domestic affairs. In essence, when in need of strategic advice, policy information, or pretty much anything, the president turns to the chief of staff, who runs the White House Office.

Alongside the White House Office, the Cabinet includes 15 departments, each with a particular policy focus, thousands of employees, and a budget in the billions (see Table 1).[12] Three departments have been around since the beginning of the government (the Department of War morphed into the Department of Defense after World War II). The rest emerged to address national concerns or crises. Following World War I, for instance, three government agencies and the Red Cross provided benefits to people who had served in the armed forces. Congress created the Department of Veterans Affairs as a way to merge these efforts and more effectively and efficiently serve veterans. After the terrorist attacks in New York and Washington,

Are faceless bureaucrats out to get you?

TABLE 1. The Cabinet

Department	Created	Mission	Employees	Budget
State	1789	Carries out U.S. foreign policy and international relations.	69,000	$53 billion
Treasury	1789	Manages government revenue by printing money and collecting taxes.	86,049	17 billion
Defense (formerly War)	1789	Coordinates and supervises the armed services and issues of national security.	2,860,000	716 billion
Interior	1849	Manages federal lands and natural resources.	70,003	22 billion
Agriculture	1862	Oversees farming, food, and rural economic development.	105,778	151 billion
Justice	1870	Enforces federal laws.	113,543	33 billion
Commerce	1903	Manages job creation, economic growth, and trade.	43,880	8 billion
Labor	1913	Manages occupational safety, unemployment, and economic statistics.	17,450	42 billion
Veterans Affairs	1930	Provides care to people who served in the military.	377,805	243 billion
Health and Human Services	1953	Protects the health of all Americans.	79,540	1 trillion
Housing and Urban Development	1965	Provides affordable housing and community development.	8,416	48 billion
Transportation	1967	Maintains and modernizes the transportation system and infrastructure.	58,662	89 billion
Energy	1977	Manages energy policy and nuclear safety.	12,944	35 billion
Education	1979	Establishes and administers education laws and policies.	3,912	72 billion
Homeland Security	2002	Provides aviation security, border control, emergency response, and cybersecurity.	229,000	76 billion

Note: Budget and personnel data are from 2021.

Source: U.S. Office of Personnel Management.

D.C., on September 11, 2001, Congress established the Department of Homeland Security, whose mission is to keep the nation safe from domestic and international threats.

At first glance, the size of each department and its budget are jaw-dropping. The Department of Justice, to take just one example, has almost 114,000 employees and a $33 billion annual budget.[13] For what? Well, for a lot, actually. Headed up by the attorney general, the department's job is to enforce federal laws, prevent and control crime, and monitor the federal prison system. To do that, the attorney general oversees nearly 10,000 lawyers who specialize in immigration, civil rights, intellectual property, the environment, taxes, and crime. Beyond lawyers, the department oversees investigative and law enforcement agencies, including the Federal Bureau of Investigation; the Drug Enforcement Administration; the Immigration and Naturalization Service; the Bureau of Alcohol, Tobacco, Firearms and Explosives; and the U.S. Marshals Service. The number of employees and the amount of money required to carry out these responsibilities in a country with more than 320 million people can add up pretty quickly.

Below the top echelon of the bureaucracy are regulatory agencies, independent commissions, and government corporations. Many are embedded within Cabinet departments, whereas others are separate entities. But regardless of where they sit, the vast majority were designed to implement the laws of the United States. The Federal Communications Commission enforces laws pertaining to the airwaves, both TV and radio. The Federal Aviation Administration oversees air travel safety regulations. The Nuclear Regulatory Commission ensures safety rules at nuclear power plants and closely monitors the handling of radioactive materials. The hundreds of other agencies in the federal government— that's not a typo; there are hundreds of them—have similar types of roles and responsibilities.[14] Most are headquartered in Washington, D.C., but many have offices across the country.

Federal Bureaucrats: Some Partisans, but Mostly Public Servants

Given the size and scope of the federal bureaucracy, it's easy to understand why some people assume that it's out to control all aspects of your life. After all, the federal government is, by a substantial margin, the largest employer in America (see Table 2). But unlike people who work for other large employers, like Walmart, Home Depot, or Amazon, government workers must have deep-seated political agendas, right? At least, that's often the assumption.

TABLE 2. Largest 10 Employers in the United States

	Employees
United States Federal Government	2,749,205
Walmart	2,200,000
Amazon.com	1,298,000
Allied Universal	800,000
FedEx Corporation	650,000
Home Depot	505,000
Yum! Brands	450,000
Kroger	438,000
Berkshire Hathaway	391,500
IBM	383,800

Note: Entries are based on the latest available employment statistics. The number of federal government employees does not include military personnel.

Source: "Fortune 500," *Fortune*, 2020.

That was certainly the case for the first 100 years of the U.S. government. Citizens then lived under a **spoils system**. The president got to fill all the jobs in the federal government with **political appointees**—people whose selection for a government position required their full allegiance to the president's party. A successful presidential candidate could turn around and reward family members, friends, colleagues, political donors, and loyal supporters with jobs—from top political positions such as senior adviser or Cabinet secretary to other posts in the bureaucracy, like in the post office or parks department. But as you might imagine, the spoils system compromised the federal government's ability to function. When people are hired based on political loyalty, as opposed to experience and qualifications, incompetence and corruption can quickly follow.

So in 1883, amid rising public pressure, Congress passed and President Chester Arthur signed into law the **Pendleton Act**.[15] The act prevented awarding jobs to unqualified political loyalists and generated stability in the executive branch by establishing two key principles. First, the vast majority of federal employees must be selected based on merit, not political connections. To qualify for most government positions, applicants must take a civil service exam or meet a specific list of qualifications based on a job description. Second, employees cannot be demoted or fired because of their political beliefs. That's why people who hold these positions are typically referred to as "careerists" or "career civil servants."

Congress reaffirmed the principles of the Pendleton Act by passing the **Hatch Act** in 1939. The law prohibits federal employees from working for political candidates or running for partisan offices themselves. It also limits how politically active they can be more generally. Although federal employees can vote, attend political events, volunteer for candidates, and donate to campaigns, they need to do this entirely on their own time. When they're at work, they can't engage in any political activities whatsoever. No campaign signs in their cubicles. No campaign buttons on their coats. No political bumper stickers on government vehicles. No political emails or social media posts while at the office.[16] The goal of the law is clear. Presidents and vice presidents come and go, but federal agencies should be populated with nonpartisan, qualified careerists who can continue the day-to-day operations of the various departments from one presidential administration to the next.

Accordingly, the overwhelming majority of government employees have little or nothing to do with partisan politics. They follow the direction of a leader who was politically appointed—we'll get to that in a minute—but the vast majority don't carry out an explicitly partisan agenda. Instead, they have rather typical jobs and careers. They're lawyers, scientists, engineers, park rangers, accountants, janitors, and administrative assistants. In fact, nearly 80 percent work outside the nation's capital.[17] They're like people who work for any ordinary business. The work they do just happens to be for the federal government.

That's not to say, of course, that political appointees don't fill critical roles. Today, presidents appoint roughly 4,000 people to staff the bureaucracy, including almost all the top leadership positions. These include senior advisers in the White House Office, Cabinet secretaries, and ambassadors. Some appointments have been very controversial—such as when President Kennedy appointed his brother attorney general or when President Trump put his son-in-law Jared Kushner in charge of major policy areas, including the opioid crisis, the Israeli-Palestinian conflict, and the border wall with Mexico.[18] Most appointees don't have family ties, but they do typically have very partisan backgrounds—presidents often select members of Congress or party leaders to fill Cabinet positions and senior roles in the White House Office. About

1,200 of these appointments require Senate confirmation, so the president doesn't have unchecked authority when it comes to naming top policy leaders. But even with these constraints, it's still the president who selects the people to direct the administration's agenda and lead the bureaucracy.[19]

An Overreaching, Inefficient Deep State?

While it's true that mostly nonpartisan federal bureaucrats provide essential services to the American people, no one would argue that the federal government is perfect. The bureaucracy is large and complex. There are multiple layers, thousands of rules and regulations, and millions of employees. It's not surprising that this labyrinth of government agencies generates regular criticism and concern.

Foremost, the bureaucracy can be, well, very bureaucratic. Many agencies are dominated by **bureaucratic proceduralism** (sometimes called red tape)—long processes focused on deadlines and paperwork, not the substance of the work at hand. Many of these processes were implemented with the intention of fairness and thoroughness, but they often result in excessive hurdles and procedures. One study found, for example, that the application process for a loan from the Small Business Administration takes the average person more than 50 hours to complete.[20] FDA approval of a new drug involves dozens of steps and an average 3.5-year wait time.[21] For decades, licensed commercial fishermen were required to report their weekly catches to the Commerce Department, even on weeks when they didn't fish.[22]

Second, with so many governmental units, there's a lot of overlap. Seventeen different agencies gather intelligence regarding foreign and domestic threats.[23] Dozens provide some type of assistance to the poor.[24] This organizational structure is complicated to navigate and not nearly as efficient as it could be. But these problems are not unique to the federal government. Look at the organizational chart of any large college, university, or company, and you'll likely see the same thing. Or ask anyone who has ever needed to get ahold of someone at a health insurance company to ask a question or contest a bill. But given that federal workers are funded by taxpayer dollars, government inefficiency can be particularly irksome.

A third major concern pertains to **bureaucratic discretion**. In implementing the laws—whether in the area of health care, taxes, environmental protection, or immigration—bureaucrats have latitude. Even though laws passed by Congress can be quite lengthy and detailed, bureaucrats regularly use their discretion to issue guidelines, also known as rules, for implementing and enforcing certain provisions of the law. In the average year, bureaucratic agencies establish about 4,000 new rules for carrying out their responsibilities. Many Americans are troubled by the idea of unelected officials—none of whom is directly accountable to the people—creating or implementing anything. Others don't like that some of the rules can seem arbitrary, unfair, and politically motivated.

In 2022, however, the Supreme Court issued a ruling that begins to limit bureaucratic discretion. The crux of the case was the Environmental Protection Agency's (EPA) implementation of a plan to reduce greenhouse gas emissions. Using the Clean Air Act as their guide, the EPA set pollution limits to power plants across the country. Several states objected to the new regulations and sued the EPA. In *West Virginia v. EPA*, the Court sided with the states. The final version of the Clean Air Act—passed by Congress in 1990—does not mention greenhouse gas emissions. And, according to the majority opinion, when a rule devised under bureaucratic discretion addresses a "major question" that has robust "economic and political significance," it must be explicitly authorized by Congress. It cannot be implemented at the discretion of executive agencies.[25]

DID YOU GET IT?
Are faceless bureaucrats out to get you?

Short Answer:

- No. The federal bureaucracy is a sprawling set of departments and agencies, each with responsibilities for developing, regulating, and enforcing particular policies and laws.
- It's made up of mostly career civil servants whose jobs are often nonpolitical and based on merit.
- Political appointees are only a fraction of government workers, although they have leadership positions.

Civic Engagement

Know your rights: Many aspects of daily life involve a government agency, so engaged citizens need to be familiar with the federal bureaucracy. Figure out how to file claims and voice concerns regarding policies that are implemented and enforced by the executive branch.

1. You believe you've been discriminated against at work because of your religion, and you're not going to sit back and take it. Instead, you decide to file a claim with the Equal Employment Opportunity Commission (EEOC), which is responsible for enforcing federal laws that make it illegal to discriminate against a job applicant or employee on the basis of race, sex, religion, national origin, age, or disability. Which of the following steps must you take to file an EEOC charge? (Hint: Visit eeoc.gov and scroll toward the bottom of the home page.)

    a. Contact a lawyer to help with the complaint.

    b. Wait 30 days from the time of the incident before filing the complaint.

    c. Fill out the form on the EEOC public portal.

    d. Visit your local EEOC office to begin the process.

2. Your friend's meddlesome mother regularly emails professors to ask how her daughter is doing in her classes. Your friend has been very clear that she will not give her professors permission to discuss her class performance. But your friend was horrified to learn that her history professor had shared information about two class absences and a "B−" midterm grade. Based on your read of the Student Privacy section on the U.S. Department of Education website (https://studentprivacy.ed.gov/file-a-complaint), does your friend have grounds to file a complaint against the professor?

    a. No. Parents have the right to inquire about their children's grades, even in college.

    b. No. A complaint against a professor or school must be filed within 48 hours of the violation of rights. Your friend found out about it too late.

    c. Yes. The professor clearly violated the Family Educational Rights and Privacy Act (FERPA). Your friend can use the complaint form on the website.

    d. Yes. But your friend must first notify the school.

3. Earlier today, you saw workers at an auto repair shop dump what looked like gallons of oil in a field. You want to file a complaint with the Environmental Protection Agency (EPA). How do you do it?

   a. You can't. The EPA does not investigate environmental crimes.

   b. You must report it to the local police, and they'll contact the EPA.

   c. You can submit a complaint at the "Report Environmental Violations" portal on the EPA's website.

   d. You can submit a complaint right on the home page of the EPA website.

FIGURE IT OUT

Bureaucratic agencies frequently modify the rules they use to implement the laws. But they don't do this alone. For any rule change, the public has the right to comment before the change goes into effect. Regular citizens, in other words, can exercise this right to influence how bureaucrats do their jobs. Give it a try. More specifically:

- Go to regulations.gov and locate a proposed rule with an open comment period. The "Explore" section on the right-hand side of the website lists rules with comments due soon.

- Summarize the proposed rule. Some of them might seem quite technical and complex. Try to find one that's clear or relates to a policy you care about.

- Draft a comment on the rule (and feel free to post your comment online if you want).

Want to Know More?

If this segment sparked your interest in the bureaucracy, then you might be amused by the 1985 movie *Brazil*. The film offers an absurd, futuristic look at a society with bureaucratic governance gone mad. The film begins with a bureaucratic error — a typo — that leads police to arrest the wrong person. A neighbor tries to report the problem, but the bureaucracy makes it almost impossible for her to notify the government. An investigator is assigned to the case, but he too becomes a victim of the bureaucracy he's serving. Too weird for you? Then consider streaming some episodes of *Parks and Recreation*, a comedy that aired from 2009 to 2015. The show stars Amy Poehler as Leslie Knope, a mid-level bureaucrat in the Parks Department in a fictional town in Indiana. Each episode chronicles her attempts to make the town a better place while dealing with a boss who hates the government he works for.

38.
Does it matter who runs the Environmental Protection Agency?

#OversightAndDiscretion

When the U.S. Senate confirmed Lisa Jackson as administrator of the Environmental Protection Agency (EPA), it was a dream come true. Jackson had been "a full-fledged environmentalist" ever since she learned about the Love Canal disaster as a teenager. At that time, as she read about toxic sludge oozing into people's homes in Niagara Falls, New York, her interest in becoming an environmental scientist took shape. "If engineers can invent the processes that create all this waste," Jackson recalled thinking, then "engineers would have to invent the processes to fix it."[1] She became a chemical engineer, earning degrees from Tulane and Princeton.

By the time President Barack Obama appointed Jackson to lead the EPA, she'd been working as an environmental scientist for two decades — first as an engineer at the EPA, where she helped develop hazardous waste cleanup regulations, and then at the New Jersey Department of Environmental Protection, where she oversaw the state's parks, beaches, fish, wildlife, and historic preservation.

Former EPA administrator Lisa Jackson testifies before Congress about the Clean Air Act (left); former administrator Scott Pruitt testifies before the Senate Environment and Public Works Committee (right).

During Jackson's four years as EPA administrator, she worked to combat climate change, establish stricter fuel economy standards, and cut carbon pollution. In the words of President Obama, under Jackson's leadership the EPA took important steps to "protect the air we breathe and the water we drink."[2] Jackson left the agency feeling confident that she had steered the EPA in the "right direction."[3]

But definitely not the direction that Scott Pruitt, President Donald Trump's EPA administrator, had in mind. When Trump appointed Pruitt to lead the EPA in 2017, he had already been an outspoken critic of the agency — first in the Oklahoma State Senate and then as attorney general of Oklahoma. As attorney general, Pruitt had actually sued the EPA more than a dozen times, trying to block environmental regulations he considered to be excessive meddling by the federal government.[4] That's why Trump thought Pruitt was the perfect person to reverse what the president saw as the EPA's "anti-energy agenda that has destroyed millions of jobs."[5]

Upon taking the position, Pruitt promised to run the agency "in a way that fosters both responsible protection of the environment and freedom for American businesses."[6] For Pruitt, keeping his promise meant rolling back regulations on the fossil fuel industry, reducing restrictions on pollutants and chemicals, and relaxing rules for handling pesticides. When Pruitt left the post in 2018, Trump praised him and said he was "reluctant to let him go."[7]

Jackson and Pruitt could not be more different in terms of experience or political views. One a scientist, the other a lawyer. One the perfect choice for Democrats who wanted to protect the environment, the other a Republican who sought to ensure that environmental regulations didn't hamper corporations' economic prosperity. One who considers global warming an existential threat, the other who considers the debate over climate change "far from settled."[8]

These stark differences must matter when it comes to leading the EPA or any government department, right? The person at the helm must play a vital role in carrying out the agency's work? Well, yes and no. This segment examines the relationship between Congress and the bureaucracy and reveals a constant push and pull between the legislative and executive branches. We highlight the many ways that Congress constrains what presidential appointees and the agencies they lead can do. But we also explain the discretion these leaders have in running their departments. By the end, you'll have a better understanding of where and how bureaucrats — even leaders like the administrator of the EPA — can shape government agencies and where they can't.

A Tiny Bit of Background: The Origins of the Environmental Protection Agency

In the 1960s, the consequences of unregulated pollution throughout the United States had become clear. New Yorkers dying from smog pollution. Factories dumping toxic waste into rivers across Appalachia. Pollution in the Great Lakes so extreme that they could no longer sustain marine life. An oil spill in California coating 400 miles of shoreline. Name a state or region of the country, and chances are that it had faced some sort of environmental crisis.

At the time, a hodgepodge of committees and councils established by the federal government addressed these concerns, but not in any centralized way. So in his 1970 State of the Union address, President Richard Nixon laid the groundwork for what would become the Environmental Protection Agency.[9] He told the American people that the "great question of the seventies" was whether we would "make reparations for the damage we have done to our air, to our land, and to our water."[10] Nixon, a Republican, presented to Congress a plan to consolidate many environmental responsibilities under one roof—the EPA. Essentially, he asked Congress to support the creation of an agency that would direct and oversee efforts to promote a safer, healthier, cleaner environment. After a complicated negotiation over the structure of the new agency, Congress approved the proposal in the summer of 1970.[11]

Congressional Oversight: "We'll Be Watching You"

Like the EPA, almost all federal agencies are created through acts passed or ratified by Congress. An act establishing an agency lays out its central mission and the guidelines for how to achieve it. In the case of the EPA, Congress tasked the agency with conducting research on pollutants, monitoring the physical condition of the environment, setting and enforcing standards for air and water quality as well as for waste disposal, and providing financial and technical support for states to develop their own pollution control programs.[12] To carry out these responsibilities, the EPA has a headquarters in Washington, D.C., as well as 10 regional offices around the country.

After creating government agencies, Congress doesn't just leave them alone. Quite the opposite. The House and Senate perform **congressional oversight**—monitoring and investigating whether bureaucratic agencies operate within the bounds of the law. More specifically, Congress oversees the bureaucracy in four ways.[13]

First, Congress has significant **budgetary authority** over all federal agencies, which means that it determines how much money they have to operate—typically by appropriating money to them directly but also by authorizing them to raise funds on their own.[14] The EPA started out in 1970 with a $1.4 billion budget and roughly 5,800 employees, most of whom were engineers and environmental scientists. Throughout the last 50 years, the number of employees has swelled to as many as 18,000, and the budget has topped out at $10 billion. In recent years, however, Republicans in Congress have not been happy with what they see as burdensome regulations the EPA has placed on businesses. So they've slashed the agency's workforce and budget to try to restrict its efforts. Indeed, the 2020 federal budget allocation to the EPA had fallen to just over $9 billion, and the agency employed 20 percent fewer people than it did in its heyday. When the Democrats won back control of Congress in 2021, they authorized a small budgetary increase—but nowhere near the billion dollars required to take the agency back to peak capacity.[15]

Adjusting an agency's responsibilities represents a second facet of congressional oversight. Congress does this by modifying the laws that guide the agency. Indeed, since 1970, Congress has passed more than two dozen major environmental laws—from regulating drinking water to managing waste disposal to protecting endangered species—and assigned their implementation to the EPA.[16] Take the Toxic Substances Control Act as one example. Congress passed this law to give the EPA the authority to require reporting, testing, and restrictions related to

Does it matter who runs the Environmental Protection Agency?

chemical substances.[17] The Oil Pollution Act is another example. Congress passed this legislation in response to a disaster in which an oil tanker ran aground just off the coast of Alaska and spilled more than 11 million gallons of crude oil into the water.[18] The law "streamlines and strengthens the EPA's ability to prevent and respond to catastrophic oil spills."[19] Although the highly partisan nature of the legislative process makes it difficult for Congress to get much done—including passing laws to adjust an agency's responsibilities—the House and Senate have this power, should they choose to use it.

Third, Congress has a say in who runs the bureaucracy.[20] The president has the power to appoint the leaders of government agencies and departments, but the U.S. Senate must confirm them. Overall, roughly 1,200 positions in the federal government require Senate approval. At the EPA, 15 of the agency's more than 14,000 positions fall into this category. It's important to recognize that although the confirmation process can involve contentious hearings and partisan rancor, Congress rarely rejects the president's nominees. In fact, the Senate has voted down only nine Cabinet appointments—ever.[21] Despite their success rate in the Senate, presidents know that the people they nominate—especially for high-profile positions—will face a lot of scrutiny. So when it looks like a nominee might have a rocky road at confirmation, the president often pulls the nomination. During his presidency, Donald Trump pulled more than 60 nominees before the Senate held hearings. In his first year as president, Joe Biden withdrew Neera Tanden's nomination to be director of the Office of Management and Budget. Tanden's history of sending harsh tweets—directed mostly at Republicans—made it impossible to garner more than 49 votes in the Senate, when her confirmation required 51.[22]

Finally, perhaps the most important tool for congressional oversight is a hearing—you know, those boring congressional committee meetings that only insomniacs, policy wonks, and political junkies (like us and hopefully you) watch on C-SPAN3 at 2 A.M. A congressional hearing typically includes members of a congressional committee questioning the leaders of a government agency under oath.[23]

Congress holds hundreds of hearings a year, with some agencies getting more attention than others (see Table 1). Sometimes the hearings are in response to an emerging problem or concern that Congress wants to investigate. When a crisis broke out over lead in the drinking water in Flint, Michigan, for instance, members of Congress called in the head of the EPA to find out what was going on.[24] After the outbreak of the Covid-19 public health crisis in early 2020, the House held hearings on pandemic preparedness and questioned the director of the Centers for Disease Control and Prevention. On the heels of a chaotic withdrawal of U.S. forces from Afghanistan in 2021, the Senate Foreign Relations

TABLE 1. Examples of Congressional Oversight

	Total Budget	Number of Employees	Oversight Hearings
Federal Aviation Administration (FAA)	$18 billion	48,000	43
Internal Revenue Service (IRS)	11.9 billion	78,661	84
Environmental Protection Agency (EPA)	11.2 billion	14,581	118
Federal Bureau of Investigation (FBI)	10.3 billion	35,000	120
Centers for Disease Control and Prevention (CDC)	9.6 billion	18,571	168
Food and Drug Administration (FDA)	6.5 billion	18,000	87
Occupational Safety and Health Administration (OSHA)	612 million	1,850	33

Source: Budget and employee numbers are for 2022 and taken from each agency's Web page. The number of hearings are from 2021 and based on data from govinfo.gov.

Committee summoned Secretary of State Tony Blinken to explain what happened and what went wrong. In all three cases, the hearings drew the public's attention to shortcomings in agency performance.

At other times, the hearings are routine checks on how the agency is functioning. Senators often ask the State Department or the Department of Defense to provide classified briefings on U.S. forces around the world, peace talks, or U.S. tensions with foreign leaders.[25] And at still other times, hearings serve as an opportunity for the agency and Congress to wrangle over the budget. Most of the time, agency leaders try to convince lawmakers that they need more money to carry out their responsibilities and complete projects, like improving the transportation infrastructure or developing new vaccines.[26]

At times, congressional oversight can seem unrelenting. Though she never said it herself, many observers speculated that Lisa Jackson stepped down as administrator because of the continuous battles she faced with Congress during her final two years at the EPA. Republican members of Congress and their allies accused her of implementing "job killing regulations" and waging "regulatory jihad" against major industries.[27] Congressional committees summoned Jackson to testify dozens of times, making it increasingly difficult for her to advance her policy goals. Scott Pruitt also felt the heat from Congress, although for different reasons. He resigned after members of the House and Senate began to investigate some of his suspect behavior as the head of the EPA—he purchased first-class airline tickets, enjoyed low-cost housing provided by a lobbyist, and relied on an undisclosed email address for communication.[28] In the end, both Jackson and Pruitt were fully aware that Congress was taking its oversight responsibility very seriously.

Bureaucratic Discretion: "I Run the Agency and I Can Do What I Want"

Even with multiple tools for oversight, Congress can't monitor everything federal agencies do. Its budgetary authority and power to hold hearings provide incentives for the bureaucracy to comply with Congress's preferences. But administrative leaders do have quite a bit of **bureaucratic discretion**—the power to interpret and implement the laws to support their priorities and preferences. Political scientists often refer to this dynamic as the **principal–agent problem**.[29] When a principal delegates power and authority to an agent, the agent often behaves in a way the principal didn't intend and can't completely control. In this case, Congress is the principal—creating, structuring, and funding the agency—and the EPA is the agent. **Agency drift** can occur when bureaucrats responsible for implementing government policies use their discretion in a way that deviates from the way Congress thinks the agency should be run.

The most basic type of bureaucratic discretion is setting the agency's priorities. Even though Congress establishes the laws surrounding how an agency runs, the laws almost always leave room for administrative leaders to push their own priorities. Look no further than Lisa Jackson and Scott Pruitt. Their lists of goals for the EPA had nothing in common. Other agency and department leaders similarly use their office to advocate for certain policies. President Trump's secretary of Education, Betsy DeVos, used the position to advance charter schools.[30] Miguel Cardona, who holds the post in the Biden administration, prioritizes addressing school achievement disparities between English and non-English-speaking students and helping schools get back on track amid the Covid-19 pandemic.[31]

Bureaucratic discretion also plays out in how an agency implements the law. Indeed, a key tool of any agency is its **rulemaking authority**—the power to set the regulations and guidelines for carrying out laws passed by Congress. Consider the **Clean Air Act**, passed by Congress in 1970 and then amended in 1977 and 1990. The act authorizes the EPA to establish national "air quality standards to protect the public health and welfare and to regulate emissions of hazardous air pollutants."[32] But who leads the EPA—and in particular, whether a Democrat or a Republican is in charge—matters a lot for implementing the law. When it came to fuel efficiency standards, mercury levels, and greenhouse gases, for instance, President Obama's EPA ratcheted up pressure on automakers, power plants, and state governments to monitor and reduce emissions. Trump's EPA considered the Obama administration's rules too stringent and relaxed or abandoned them. The pendulum has swung back with Michael Regan, Biden's EPA director, at the helm (see Table 2). But discretion may be waning. In 2022, the Supreme Court struck down the plans of Biden's EPA, concluding that the Administration's new rules were an overreach of bureaucratic discretion.[33] Future EPA directors appointed by Democratic presidents will have to think about new ways to achieve their goals.

TABLE 2. Implementing the Clean Air Act

	Obama Administration	Trump Administration	Biden Administration
Fuel efficiency standards	Established rule that an auto manufacturer's vehicles must average 46 miles per gallon by 2026.	Changed rule so that an auto manufacturer's vehicles must average 40.4 miles per gallon by 2026.	Ordered auto manufacturers to increase fuel economy to 49 miles per gallon by 2026.
Mercury pollution control	Created the Mercury and Air Toxics Standards rule, which dramatically reduced mercury emissions but cost power plants $3 billion per year to implement.	Changed the rule so that power plants don't have to reduce mercury emissions if it costs anything. They can even increase them.	Reinstated the Obama era standards for mercury pollution.
Greenhouse gas emissions	Implemented the Clean Power Plan (CCP) rule, which required states to meet specific lower greenhouse gas emissions standards.	Replaced the CPP rule with the Affordable Clean Energy rule, which relaxed the emissions standards states must follow.	Proposed a reduction of 1 million tons of methane emissions by 2035, which is more than the amount of carbon dioxide emitted from all U.S. cars and aircraft in 2019.

Source: Veronica Stracqualursi and Gregory Wallace, "Trump Administration to Roll Back Fuel Efficiency Standards Weakening Efforts to Combat Climate Crisis," CNN, March 31, 2020; Ellen Knickmeyer, "Trump EPA Orders Rollback of Obama Mercury Regulation," Associated Press, December 29, 2018; Umair Irfan, "Trump's EPA Just Replaced Obama's Signature Climate Policy with a Much Weaker Rule," Vox, June 29, 2019; Lisa Friedman, "Biden Administration Moves to Limit Methane, a Potent Greenhouse Gas," *New York Times*, November 21, 2021.

EPA administrator Michael Regan (center) and Vice President Kamala Harris speak to Falls Church, Virginia, high school students about the EPA's Clean School Bus Program. The program offers monetary incentives for school districts to replace their existing buses with electric ones.

The EPA, of course, is just one example. Across the spectrum of Cabinet departments and government agencies, different leaders bring substantial discretion to how they implement the same federal program. In 2015, for instance, Secretary of Labor Tom Perez, a Democrat, developed a rule under the Fair Labor Standards Act to change regulations on overtime pay. As a result, almost 5 million workers saw more money in their paychecks.[34] But Perez's Republican successor, Alexander Acosta, thought the rule was too costly for businesses. So he changed it. Only people who earned less than $35,000 per year were eligible for overtime.[35]

Finally, bureaucrats can exercise discretion in how they enforce the law. And the extent to which an agency exercises its enforcement authority often comes down to the political preferences of its leader. Consider the number of civil cases and financial penalties placed on industries that violate pollution laws. When a Democrat leads the EPA— as was the case under the Clinton, Obama, and Biden administrations— the agency tends to issue more fines on polluters than when it's run by Republicans.[36] Similar differences in enforcement by Democratic and Republican administrations are evident in the Occupational Safety and

Health Administration and the Consumer Financial Protection Bureau. The laws Congress passed don't specify goals for how many cases to file or how many fines to levy, so the agencies can prioritize enforcement rules consistent with the director's (and, thus, the president's) preferences.

A Push and Pull between the Two Branches

It should now be clear that agency directors don't have free rein over the agencies they lead. They can't just direct the agency to drop whatever it was doing before they got there, fundamentally reorient the agency's mission, dismantle the agency's infrastructure and field offices, or ignore the law. But it should also be clear that department heads have quite a bit of discretion when it comes to setting priorities, implementing the law, and enforcing it. Still, most don't push too far. If they stray too far from what the president wants, their jobs could be on the line. And if they move the agency too far away from what Congress wants—especially when different political parties control Congress and the executive branch—Congress could threaten their budgets and grill them in public hearings.

DID YOU GET IT?
Does it matter who runs the Environmental Protection Agency?

Short Answer:

- Yes and no.
- Congress exercises substantial oversight in establishing agencies, adjusting their responsibilities, allocating their budgets, and monitoring their behavior through hearings.
- But agency leaders have substantial discretion, including the power to set priorities, develop rules for implementing laws, and decide how to enforce laws.

Consuming Political Information

Navigate government websites: Understanding the federal government's roles and responsibilities requires a familiarity with government agencies. Visit three agency websites whose work you might encounter, and pull some information.

1. The EPA is responsible for implementing many environmental laws. Which of the following acts is *not* one that Congress has tasked the EPA with enforcing?

    a. Clean Water Act

    b. Endangered Species Act

    c. Shark Fin Sales Elimination Act

    d. Nuclear Waste Policy Act

2. The Occupational Safety and Health Administration (OSHA) focuses on protecting workers. Its website lists the topics and sectors it focuses on. Which is one of OSHA's six sectors of focus?

    a. Fast food

    b. Construction

    c. Manufacturing

    d. Retail

3. The Food and Drug Administration (FDA) regulates the safety of — you guessed it — food and drugs. But "food and drug" actually encompasses a lot of different products. According to the FDA's website, which of the following products *doesn't* it regulate?

    a. Cosmetics

    b. Tobacco

    c. Herbal remedies

    d. Medical devices

Knowing some background information about a government agency is often an important part of doing research — it can shed light on why the agency functions like it does as well as the politics involved in the decisions it makes and policies it promotes. Finding this information can be a little tricky, but the EPA website provides a lot of important history about the agency. In the search bar at the top of the site, type in "EPA History." Then navigate the site to answer a series of questions about how the EPA has operated over the last 50 years. More specifically:

- Who was the first administrator of the EPA?

- What example in the "Timeline of Milestones" did you find most important, and why? One or two sentences is fine.

- Can you find evidence on the EPA website that would explain why it's such a controversial agency today? In a couple of sentences, explain how you arrived at your answer.

Want to Know More?

We're not going to lie. Finding engaging and fun material about congressional oversight of the bureaucracy isn't easy. But the 2019 movie *The Report* fits the bill. Adam Driver plays a congressional staffer assigned by his boss (Senator Dianne Feinstein, played by Annette Bening) to lead an investigation into how the CIA detained and interrogated suspected terrorists in the wake of 9/11. *Variety* called the film "sensational."

39.
How does a case get to the Supreme Court?

#JudicialProcess

Supreme Court justice William Brennan, who served on the Court from 1956 to 1990, began each year the same way: he'd ask his new clerks to identify what they thought was the most important law of the land. Answers varied. Some people would say freedom of speech. Others would offer separation of church and state. Still others would conclude that it had to be checks and balances. All wrong answers according to Brennan. The justice — smiling and holding up one hand — would tell each new crop of clerks, "Five." Majority rules on the nine-justice Court, so five justices are all it takes to decide the meaning of a law. In Brennan's words, with five justices voting your way, "You can do anything around here."[1]

It's not only justices who recognize the authority of the Supreme Court. Political activists, senators, and presidents are just as aware of the Court's power to define citizen rights and determine the constitutionality of the nation's laws. As Theodore Roosevelt observed in 1906, "The President and the Congress are all very well in their way. They can say what they think they think, but it rests with the Supreme Court to decide what they have really thought."[2] More than 100 years later, Donald Trump arrived at the same conclusion. At a rally in Cedar Rapids,

Demonstrators gather outside the U.S. Supreme Court as the justices hear arguments in *Young v. UPS*, a pregnancy discrimination case.

Iowa, during his 2016 presidential campaign, Trump told a crowd why they really had no choice but to vote for him: "If you really like Donald Trump, that's great, but if you don't, you have to vote for me anyway. You know why? Supreme Court judges, Supreme Court judges."[3] Trump speculated that the next president would likely fill three, four, or even five Supreme Court vacancies, thereby shaping the future direction of the Court for decades to come. And he was right. He appointed three justices to the Court during his four years as president.

The Supreme Court clearly wields significant power. Indeed, it sits atop the entire judicial branch of government. But below it, a system of federal and state courts works to ensure that citizens have a venue in which to seek justice. To highlight how nine Supreme Court justices ultimately decide the law of the land, this segment tracks the case of Peggy Young, whose dispute with her employer eventually made its way to the Supreme Court.

The Journey through the Court System

Most cases that wind up at the Supreme Court start with real conflicts involving regular people.[4] The story of Peggy Young from Annapolis, Maryland, is one such example. Young had worked as a UPS driver for four years when, in 2006, she became pregnant. Because of the physical labor involved in delivering packages, UPS requested that Young provide a doctor's note authorizing her to continue to do her job. Young presented the letter, which affirmed that she was able to work but stipulated that she should not lift anything heavier than 20 pounds. The job of a UPS driver, however, requires picking up packages that weigh as much as 70 pounds. So UPS requested that Young go on unpaid medical leave for the rest of her pregnancy. Young asked UPS to reconsider the decision, noting that she rarely delivered anything heavier than letters and small packages. More than that, her coworkers had offered to assist her with anything heavier than 20 pounds. UPS management refused her request.

The excitement Young felt about her pregnancy—she and her husband had been trying to conceive a child for quite some time—quickly gave way to anguish and hardship. Forced to go on unpaid leave, Young and her family lost her income and health care benefits. Recalling her treatment by UPS years later, she told the *Washington Post*: "It's all so unreal. . . . Somebody tells you you can't work, when there's nothing wrong with you, you think, 'Really? In this day and age?' I'm not hurt. I'm not disabled. I'm pregnant. I'm having a child. That's it.'"[5]

The more she thought about it, the more unfair Young considered her treatment. She knew that UPS had provided temporary alternative work assignments to employees who couldn't perform their typical duties because of injuries. UPS had even accommodated drivers who'd failed medical exams, lost their driver's licenses, or been in car accidents.[6] So Young sought legal help and, the following year, filed a **civil case** against UPS for violating the Pregnancy Discrimination Act.

Civil cases involve disputes over money between two people or businesses. If the **plaintiff**—the individual who files the lawsuit—wins, then the **defendant**—the party accused of wrongdoing—typically pays monetary damages. Civil cases constitute about 60 percent of those heard in state courts[7] and 80 percent of those heard in the federal court system in the United States.[8] The rest are **criminal cases**, in which the government prosecutes an individual for violating a criminal law—think murder, burglary, kidnapping, assault, dealing drugs. The important thing to keep in mind is that a case can only go to court if there's ample justification of wrongdoing. In a criminal case, the government's prosecuting attorney must present reasonable evidence that a crime occurred. In a civil case, one party must demonstrate plausible evidence of suffering at the hands of the other. Otherwise, a judge will typically not let a case proceed.

Because Young claimed that UPS had violated a federal statute (the U.S. Congress passed the Pregnancy Discrimination Act in 1978), a federal district court in her home state of Maryland heard the case. **District courts** are trial courts—that is, courts where cases are first heard and both parties present their evidence and arguments. These 94 federal district courts, dispersed geographically throughout the country, don't have a choice in deciding which cases to hear. As long as a case pertains to a federal law, the district court must hear it. If Young's case had involved a conflict with a state law, then it would have been taken up by a state court.

Young claimed that UPS had violated the act's disability clause, which requires employers to treat "women affected by pregnancy" in the same way as "other persons not so affected but similar in their ability or inability to work."[9] Moreover, the law specifies that an employer may have to provide "a reasonable accommodation for a disability related to pregnancy."[10] To Young, the case was a no-brainer: UPS had discriminated against her on the basis of her pregnancy and should have to make amends.

The lawyers for UPS disagreed. They argued that the company's long-established policy was to provide alternative work arrangements, such as "light-duty work," only to those who sustained injuries while on the job. Pregnancy didn't fall into this category because it occurred outside the workplace. Deborah Chasanow, the federal judge who presided over the case, ruled against Young, noting that UPS's policy represented a nondiscriminatory "neutral and legitimate business practice" that did not violate the Pregnancy Discrimination Act. Thus, Young did not have the right to sue UPS.

Undeterred, Young appealed her case to a U.S. circuit court. In the federal court system, a circuit court is the first level of **appellate court**. Appellate courts don't hold new trials—that is, they don't review new evidence or hear witnesses. Instead, they review trial court decisions and make sure that, in each case, the lower court applied the law correctly. They either affirm or reverse the lower court's decision. The United States is divided into 12 geographic regions, each served by one circuit court, and each court has between 6 and 29 judges. Rulings are typically issued by randomly selected 3-judge panels, though petitioners can ask the court to hear a case "en banc." In these rare cases, all the judges on the circuit court hear it.

Young appealed to the U.S. Court of Appeals for the Fourth Circuit, which covers Maryland. Her lawyers argued that the district court judge had not interpreted the Pregnancy Discrimination Act correctly. Although the right to appeal a case to a circuit court is guaranteed for a defendant convicted of a crime or a plaintiff who has lost a civil case in trial court, the circuit court often takes years to hear it. Indeed, Young's case didn't get on the docket until the end of 2012, four years after the trial court had issued its ruling. In the meantime, the case had garnered significant national attention, and many interest groups supporting women's rights filed **amicus curiae** briefs urging the court

How does a case get to the Supreme Court?

to support Young's claims. These "friend of the court" briefs provide information that might be useful to the judges as they consider each side's argument. When the circuit court finally handed down its decision in January 2013, it affirmed that UPS's policy had been applied fairly to all workers.[11]

Young's only remaining option was to appeal the case to the U.S. Supreme Court. She and her legal team petitioned for a **writ of certiorari**—an order in which a higher appellate court agrees to review a decision issued by a lower court and requests all documents from the case. To get a "writ of cert" from the Supreme Court, four of the nine justices—in what is called the **rule of four**—must agree to hear the case. If the Supreme Court denies the petition, then the lower court ruling stands.

The path Young's case took through the federal courts—listed step-by-step in the left-hand column of Table 1—represents one of the two ways that the majority of cases reach the Supreme Court. The second route is through the state courts (see the right-hand column of Table 1). The two paths are very similar, although cases moving through the state court system typically have one additional stage of appellate review.

TABLE 1. Paths to the Supreme Court

	Federal Court Path (Two-thirds of cases)	State Court Path (One-third of cases)
Step 1	Conflicts involving a federal law are heard in U.S. district court.	Conflicts involving a state law are heard in state trial court.
Step 2	If you lose, you can appeal the decision to a U.S. circuit court of appeals.	If you lose, you can appeal the decision to the state's intermediate court of appeals.
Step 3	OPTIONAL: If you lose, you can ask the circuit court to rehear your case.	If you lose, you can appeal to the state supreme court.
Step 4	If you lose again, or if the circuit court decides not to rehear the case, you can petition the U.S. Supreme Court.	If you lose, or if the state supreme court decides not to hear your case, you can petition the U.S. Supreme Court.
Step 5	If four justices grant a writ of certiorari, then the U.S. Supreme Court will hear the case.	

Note: If a case involves a dispute between two state governments, then the Supreme Court has original jurisdiction and can opt to hear the case directly.

How the Supreme Court Decides What Cases to Hear

Getting the Supreme Court to hear a case is no easy task. The Court receives thousands of petitions for a writ of certiorari each year and only accepts a small fraction of them. The top panel of Figure 1 charts the number of cases appealed to the Court every year from 1970 to 2020. Notice how dramatically that number has increased throughout the last five decades. In the last decade, the Court has received an average of nearly 7,000 petitions a year, roughly double the number of requests it received in the 1970s. The opposite trend is true in terms of the number of cases the Court chooses to hear. As the number of petitions to the Court has doubled, the number of cases the Court has opted to hear has dropped almost by half (see the bottom panel of Figure 1).[12] In recent years, the Court has accepted only about 80 cases annually, a mere 1 percent of the petitions it receives.

No specific rules or guidelines determine which cases the justices decide to hear, but several types of cases have a better shot than others.[13] The Court tends to select cases when (1) lower appellate court rulings conflict with each other or a prior Supreme Court ruling, (2) the interpretation of a federal law is in dispute, (3) a lower court ruling violates judicial standards or norms, or (4) a major legal or social issue must be resolved.

Young and her lawyers knew the odds were long that the Court would agree to hear her case. Yet on July 1, 2014—more than six years after the case began in district court—the Supreme Court agreed to hear *Young v. UPS*. The justices likely agreed to hear the case because they believed the meaning of a federal law—the Pregnancy Discrimination Act—was unclear. That the outcome of the case would affect the rights of all women in the workforce who are pregnant or might someday become pregnant probably elevated its importance.

When the Supreme Court agrees to hear a case, the justices review the entire written record and all prior legal proceedings and briefs surrounding it. They then typically conduct an hour-long hearing during which lawyers for both sides make **oral arguments**—each side has 30 minutes to present its case, all the while being questioned by the justices. The Court takes several months to consider the arguments, circulate the justices' views internally, and then issue an opinion. In Young's case, the decision was issued on March 25, 2015. The Supreme Court overturned the circuit court's ruling and sided with Young over UPS.

FIGURE 1. Supreme Court Petitions and Decisions, 1960–2020

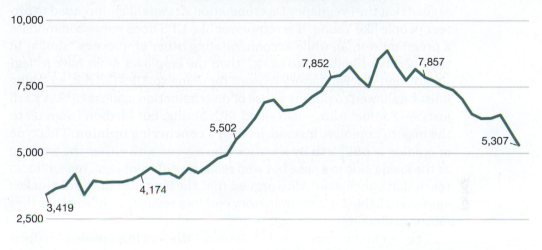

Number of Cases Petitioned to the Court

Number of Cases Argued before the Court

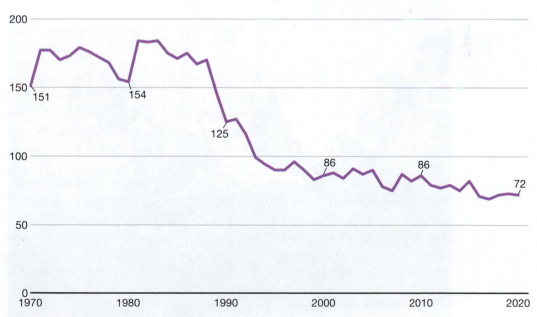

Note: Labels correspond to the years noted along the x axis of each panel. In 1990, for example, 5,502 cases were petitioned to the Court, and the Court chose to hear 125 of them.

Source: Supreme Court of the United States Journal.

Five justices signed on to the **majority opinion**—a document that articulates the final resolution of a case. The majority opinion becomes the law of the land that is to be followed in future cases by judges at all levels of the judiciary. Justice Stephen Breyer, writing for the majority, argued that the Pregnancy Discrimination Act was likely intended to protect people like Young. If an employer like UPS does not accommodate a pregnant woman while accommodating other employees "similar in their ability or inability to work," then the employer must have a "legitimate, non-discriminatory reason" for doing so. UPS did not, so Young must be allowed to pursue a case of discrimination against UPS. A sixth justice—Samuel Alito—also sided with Young, but he didn't sign on to the majority opinion. Instead, he filed a **concurring opinion**. This type of opinion is put forth by a justice who agrees with either the winning or the losing side in a case but who relies on different legal reasoning to reach that conclusion. Alito argued that the language of the act makes employers liable for discriminatory conduct regardless of whether they meant to discriminate or not.

The remaining three justices issued a **dissenting opinion**—a document in which those justices who disagree with the majority and who voted differently on the outcome of the case explain their logic. Although the dissent doesn't become law, it can serve multiple purposes.[14] Justice Ruth Bader Ginsburg, for example, explained that her

Peggy Young addressed reporters after the Supreme Court heard her case. Several months later, the Court issued a ruling and Young learned that she won.

majority opinion in a 1996 case about whether the Virginia Military Institute could deny women admission was "ever so much better than [her] first, second, and at least a dozen more drafts, thanks to Justice Scalia's attention-grabbing dissent."[15] The dissent pushed Ginsburg to sharpen and clarify her argument. Dissenting opinions can also lay out arguments to use in future cases as well as encourage Congress to change a law. In Young's case, the dissenting justices did not believe that the Pregnancy Discrimination Act prohibited denying pregnant women accommodations as long as the denial was based on an "even-handed policy." They argued that the majority opinion went too far and would ultimately force companies to provide all pregnant women with accommodations.

When the Supreme Court announced its decision—so many years after she first provided the doctor's note that set the entire controversy in motion—a satisfied Young told reporters, "It's good to know that we're finally moving in the right direction, where a woman shouldn't have to be forced to choose between starting a family and keeping her job."[16]

DID YOU GET IT?

How does a case get to the Supreme Court?

Short Answer:

- A case starts in a trial court, is appealed to a federal circuit court or state appellate court, and then is appealed again to the Supreme Court.

- Four of the nine Supreme Court justices must vote to issue a writ of certiorari. The justices typically only agree to hear cases involving major controversies or discrepancies in the law.

Quantitative Literacy

Do the math: This segment includes statistics about the trajectory cases follow on their journey to the Supreme Court. Use the data presented in this segment to make some calculations that extend your understanding of the judicial process.

---

1. Based on the information presented in Table 1, if the Supreme Court grants certiorari to 100 cases in a given year, roughly how many more cases will the justices hear that originated in federal district courts than in state courts?

    a. 0 (An equal number of cases come from state and federal courts.)

    b. 33

    c. 50

    d. 66

2. According to Figure 1, which of the following statements is accurate?

    a. Twice as many cases were appealed to the Supreme Court in the 1990s than in the 1970s.

    b. The number of cases heard by the Court was roughly the same in the 1970s as it was in the 1980s.

    c. By 2010, the Supreme Court's caseload was only a little more than half of what it was in 1980.

    d. In 2010, the Supreme Court heard a larger share of cases appealed to it than at any other time since 1970.

3. Calculate the percentage of cases appealed to the Supreme Court that the justices agreed to hear in 1990. You'll need to consider both panels of Figure 1 for this one.

    a. 1.1 percent

    b. 2.3 percent

    c. 12.3 percent

    d. 44.0 percent

Want to Know More?

If you want to learn about any Supreme Court case, we recommend using the website Oyez.org. The site provides a case synopsis, a summary of the key questions at stake in the case, how the justices voted, and a link to the decision. For all decisions since 1955, the site also includes recordings of all oral arguments. If you want to hear how the justices questioned lawyers in *Roe v. Wade* or *Bush v, Gore*, it is all right there.

40.
Are Supreme Court justices too partisan?

#JudicialPolitics

When the Founders met at the Constitutional Convention in 1787, they had to resolve several controversies — the power of the national government, the influence of large versus small states, what to do about slavery, how to protect individual rights. But they were in agreement when it came to the importance of creating the judiciary as the third branch of the government.[1] And they intended for the Supreme Court to be populated by highly qualified, independent-thinking justices. That's why they gave them lifetime appointments. If the justices were insulated from worries about reelection and keeping their jobs, then they could focus on adhering to the law without feeling beholden to any particular leaders or powerful interests. As Alexander Hamilton argued in the *Federalist Papers*, "Nothing can contribute so much to [the judiciary's] firmness and independence as permanency in office."[2]

Most of the 116 people ever to serve on the Supreme Court have taken the mission of judicial independence to heart. John Rutledge, the Court's second chief justice, remarked that "an independent judiciary" was the only way to protect the "interests of the people."[3] Justice Joseph Story, who served for more than 30 years in the

The Supreme Court prides itself on being the most trusted branch of government. But the bruising and partisan confirmation process for justices has called into question whether the Court can act fairly and impartially. In April 2022, Republican senators grilled Ketanji Brown Jackson – the first Black woman nominated to the Court – about critical race theory, the definition of "woman," and her church attendance, all in an attempt to present her as too liberal for the Supreme Court. Jackson was ultimately confirmed to replace retiring justice Stephen Breyer.

early 1800s, recognized that without the impartial administration of the law, "neither our persons, nor our rights, nor our property, can be protected."[4] One hundred years later, Justice Felix Frankfurter, appointed by President Franklin Roosevelt in 1939, argued that "It is hostile to a democratic system to involve the judiciary in the politics of the people."[5] Still today, members of the Court contend that justices must act as fair and impartial jurists. In the words of Justice Ketanji Brown Jackson, "I evaluate the facts, and I interpret and apply the law to the facts of the case before me, without fear or favor, consistent with my judicial oath."[6]

Sounds great, right? There's just one problem: it often seems like the Court doesn't actually operate this way. Look no further than the Supreme Court's decision in *Bush v. Gore*. Nearly six weeks after the 2000 presidential election, there was still no winner. It all came down to Florida, where Republican George W. Bush led Democrat Al Gore by a mere 537 votes out of roughly 6 million cast. Gore's campaign disputed the vote-counting process and requested a recount in several Florida counties. The Bush campaign wanted to avoid a recount at all costs.

Their candidate was ahead, and they wanted to keep it that way. The dispute over the recount worked its way through the court system and eventually reached the Supreme Court. The five conservative justices sided with Bush, while the four more liberal justices sided with Gore.[7] In essence, the conservative justices handed Bush — the conservative candidate — the presidency.

Bush v. Gore is hardly the only seemingly partisan Supreme Court ruling in recent history. In 2010, the Court issued a landmark decision in *Citizens United v. Federal Election Commission*, a campaign finance case. The five conservatives ruled that it's unconstitutional to limit campaign spending by corporations, a view broadly supported by the Republican Party and its major donors. The four more liberal justices, along with most Democrats in Washington, favored spending limits.[8] The same thing happened in 2019, when the conservatives outvoted the liberals and upheld a partisan gerrymandering scheme that helped the Republican Party maintain majority control of the government in several states.[9] It's no surprise that 63 percent of the American public thinks the Supreme Court is "too influenced by politics" or that two-thirds of people view the Court as either too liberal or too conservative.[10]

Is the public right? Is the Supreme Court filled with partisan hacks? Or is it populated with the kinds of independent-minded jurists that many of the Founders envisioned? This segment provides an answer by considering two aspects of judicial politics: (1) the process by which a person becomes a Supreme Court justice and (2) the justices' decision making once they're on the Court. You'll see that the selection process features intense partisan struggles as the president and Senate strive to shape the composition of the Court. But you'll also see that judicial decision making involves more than simply reflecting the values of one political party over the other.

From Borking to Beer: The Increasingly Partisan Confirmation Process

The Constitution lays out a straightforward process for selecting Supreme Court justices. Article II states that the president "by and with the advice and consent of the Senate, shall appoint . . . judges of the Supreme Court." It's a three-part process. First, the president solicits "advice" and suggestions for potential nominees. Second, the president appoints someone. Third, the Senate takes up the nomination, beginning with hearings in the Judiciary Committee and then on the Senate floor. If a majority of senators votes in favor of the nominee, then the Senate has "consented" to the appointment. If not, then the president puts forward another name.

For a long time, the confirmation process ran quite smoothly. Presidents generally nominated qualified individuals who vowed to be independent thinkers, and the Senate typically concluded that the appointees were up to the task. Of the 129 nominees the Senate voted on between 1789 and 1986, it confirmed 91 percent of them. Pretty quickly, too—on average, in less than 25 days from the time the president put forward the name. In several cases, it took the Senate less than a week.[11] Fifty-one percent were confirmed by voice vote, which means the Senate didn't even bother to record how each senator voted; the person's appointment was a foregone conclusion.[12]

That all changed in 1987 when President Ronald Reagan, a Republican, tapped Robert Bork for a seat on the Supreme Court.[13] By all objective measures, Bork was well qualified—a renowned legal scholar, a former high-ranking lawyer in the Justice Department, a federal circuit court judge. But he also articulated very conservative legal and political views in the articles and books he had published. Democrats worried that Bork's confirmation would roll back some of their recent hard-fought gains in civil rights and civil liberties.[14] So on the very day Reagan announced his intention to nominate Bork, Senator Ted Kennedy, a liberal icon, upended the typical confirmation process. He took to the Senate floor to attack the nominee's political beliefs, arguing that "Robert Bork's America is a land in which women would be forced into back-alley abortions, Blacks would sit at segregated lunch counters, rogue police could break down citizens' doors in midnight raids, and school children could not be taught about evolution."[15]

Kennedy's speech set into motion a 130-day confirmation process that resembled a partisan debate over controversial legislation. Dozens of interest groups—some in favor of Bork and some opposed to him—lobbied senators before the vote. Kennedy's strategy of labeling Bork's views as extreme worked. Bork's nomination went down in the Democratic-controlled Senate by a vote of 58 to 42. "Borking" even became a new word, defined by freedictionary.com as "attacking systematically, especially in the media."

The Democrats tried the same tactic when George H. W. Bush nominated Clarence Thomas, a 43-year-old African American conservative, to the Court.[16] Controversy over Thomas's conservative views, however, ended up taking a back seat in the confirmation process. A few days before the Senate was scheduled to vote on the nomination, Anita Hill, a law professor who had worked for Thomas years earlier, accused him of sexual harassment. Throughout two days of riveting televised hearings before the Senate Judiciary Committee, the nation held its breath as Hill uncomfortably testified that Thomas had repeatedly asked her out on dates, called her into his office to discuss pornographic movies, and bragged about his

Protests accompanied the nominations of Robert Bork (1987) and Clarence Thomas (1991) to the Supreme Court.

"sexual prowess."[17] A livid Thomas denied the allegations, famously asserting that the confirmation process had turned into a "a high-tech lynching for uppity blacks who in any way deign to think for themselves."[18]

Despite the drama and uproar, Thomas squeaked through by a largely partisan vote. Ninety-five percent of Republicans supported his confirmation, and 81 percent of Democrats opposed it. The outcome revealed that in a post-Bork world, nothing in a nominee's past was off-limits, but even the most serious allegations would be assessed through a partisan lens.

Fast-forward 27 years to the hearings for Brett Kavanaugh, and the "new normal" of a bitter partisan confirmation process was on clear display. In announcing his 2018 nomination of Kavanaugh, Donald Trump remarked, "This incredibly qualified nominee deserves a swift confirmation and robust bipartisan support."[19] Democrats basically responded with a collective "You've got to be kidding." They were still stewing over Senate Republicans' refusal to begin the confirmation process to replace Supreme Court justice Antonin Scalia following his sudden death in February 2016. Rather than replace Scalia with an Obama appointee who could shift the Court in a liberal direction, Senate Majority Leader Mitch McConnell, a Republican, let the seat remain vacant for the 341 days that remained in Obama's term.[20]

When Kavanaugh's nomination got to the Senate, most Democrats were in no mood to hand the Republicans a victory. And they thought they might be able to defeat Kavanaugh when allegations of sexual assault surfaced. Christine Blasey Ford, a psychology professor, publicly testified that decades earlier at a high school party an inebriated Kavanaugh, along with a friend, had coaxed her into a room, closed the door, held her down, covered her mouth, and laid on top of her. Although she'd managed to break free, Blasey Ford told the Judiciary Committee that the incident caused her years of anxiety.

Brett Kavanaugh's open anger (left) and multiple mentions of beer drinking became fodder for *Saturday Night Live*, on which Matt Damon (right) portrayed an angry, beer-swilling Kavanaugh.

Kavanaugh emphatically denied any wrongdoing, admitting only that he "liked beer" and would occasionally enjoy it with his friends. In his opening statement to the committee, he didn't even try to hide his anger. He told the senators—and the millions of people watching the televised proceedings—that he expected "a good old-fashioned borking," but that the Democrats had gone too far, replacing "advice and consent with search and destroy."[21] He criticized Democrats for going through his high school yearbook looking for dirt and condemned the confirmation process as a "national disgrace" and "a circus."[22] The Senate confirmed Kavanaugh (50–48) in what, until then, had been the most partisan vote in history.

Not all nominees in the post-Bork era have endured confirmation hearings as dramatic and personal as Thomas's and Kavanaugh's (see Table 1).[23] But even in the absence of late-breaking developments and troubling allegations of sexual harassment and sexual assault, no nominee since 2005 has received a majority of votes from senators of both parties. The 2020 vote to confirm Amy Coney Barrett represented the most partisan vote of all time. She squeaked through on a nearly straight party-line 52–48 vote. And for the first time ever, a Supreme Court justice was confirmed with not one vote from the minority party.[24] Things weren't much different in 2022, when Ketanji Brown Jackson, a Biden nominee, squeaked through on a 53–47 vote, though three Republicans did support her nomination. The days of bipartisan confirmation votes for Supreme Court justices appear to be over.

Impartial Thinkers or Partisan Puppets? Judicial Decision Making on the Court

The partisan confirmation process certainly gives the impression that once on the Court, justices do the bidding of the party that put them there. But it turns out that most of the time, justices don't

TABLE 1. Senate Supreme Court Confirmation Votes, 1980–2022

Year	Nominee	Vote	President	Voting to Confirm	
				Republicans	Democrats
1981	Sandra Day O'Connor	99–0	Reagan (R)	100%	100%
1986	Antonin Scalia	98–0	Reagan (R)	100	100
1987	Robert H. Bork	42–58	Reagan (R)	87	4
1987	Anthony M. Kennedy	97–0	Reagan (R)	100	100
1990	David H. Souter	90–9	G. H. W. Bush (R)	100	84
1991	Clarence Thomas	52–48	G. H. W. Bush (R)	95	19
1993	Ruth Bader Ginsburg	96–3	Clinton (D)	93	100
1994	Stephen G. Breyer	87–9	Clinton (D)	78	100
2005	John G. Roberts Jr.	78–22	G. W. Bush (R)	100	50
2005	Samuel A. Alito Jr.	58–42	G. W. Bush (R)	98	9
2009	Sonia Sotomayor	68–31	Obama (D)	23	100
2010	Elena Kagan	63–37	Obama (D)	12	98
2017	Neil M. Gorsuch	54–45	Trump (R)	100	7
2018	Brett Kavanaugh	50–48	Trump (R)	98	2
2020	Amy Coney Barrett	52–48	Trump (R)	98	0
2022	Ketanji Brown Jackson	53–47	Biden (D)	6	100

Note: All nominees were confirmed except for Robert H. Bork. In the 2018 Brett Kavanaugh vote, Republican Lisa Murkowski voted "present," which is not recorded as either a yea or a nay vote.

Source: "Supreme Court Nominations (1789–Present)," U.S. Senate.

automatically make decisions in accord with the party of the president who nominated them. After all, the justices have quite a bit in common, and those similarities cross party lines. There's little in the way of gender or racial diversity, for example, with only six women and four people of color having ever served on the Court. Moreover, the justices have similar educations; eight members of the current Court attended one of two law schools (five Harvard, three Yale). And they share professional experiences. Every justice on today's Court, for instance, previously served as a federal judge. The justices' common backgrounds mean that they've been trained to follow the written law and weigh previous decisions. That's not to say that their personal views never affect their rulings (we'll get to how that happens shortly), but it does suggest that the justices may be less partisan than the confirmation process that got them onto the Court in the first place.

Follow the Law: Bound by the Text of Statutes and the Constitution

The fundamental job of a Supreme Court justice is to decipher the meaning of the written words of the Constitution and federal, state, and local statutes. Although there's often more than one way to interpret the written law—that's often why a case reaches the Supreme Court in the first place—the justices often see eye-to-eye in their reading of the law.[25] In fact, unanimous decisions—those in which all the members of the Supreme Court agree—have historically been the most common rulings (see teal line in Figure 1).[26]

FIGURE 1. Unanimous and Contentious Supreme Court Decisions, 1946–2021

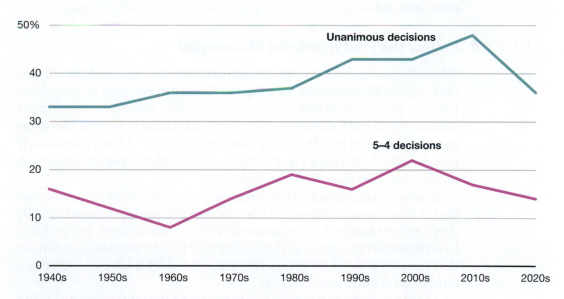

Note: Data presented are the mean number of unanimous and contentious decisions by decade. The 2020s data point only includes 2020 and 2021. Unanimous decisions include all cases that had no dissenting votes.

Source: "The Supreme Court Database," Washington University Law.

Notice that unanimous rulings are far more common than very close decisions (see the purple line), regardless of whether a majority of the justices serving at the time were appointed by Democratic or Republican presidents. Even as the confirmation process has become increasingly partisan, Chief Justice John Roberts has pushed the Court to strive for consensus.[27] This has become more challenging, though, as indicated by the sharp drop in unanimous decisions (29 percent) in the 2021 term.

Follow the Law: Bound by Precedent Cases

The consideration of prior decisions constrains the justices as well. When there's not a directly applicable statute or constitutional provision to consider, justices generally adhere to **precedent**—legal principles established in previous cases. Also known as stare decisis, this is a bedrock principle of judicial behavior in the United States. Whereas elected officials are free to change laws or create news ones whenever they see fit, the justices understand that the Court is meant to provide stability and continuity, so it reverses opinions only in rare circumstances.[28]

Dating back to the 1940s, the Supreme Court has upended precedent—overturned a previous Supreme Court decision—in only 2 percent of the cases it's decided (see Table 2).[29] In the '60s and '70s, the Court overturned more precedents because they heard more cases, but the ratio has been consistent over time, despite increasingly controversial nominees and the partisan confirmation process.

Follow the Party: Judicial Philosophy

When the law is unclear or unsettled, justices have quite a bit of discretion, especially when interpreting the Constitution. And this is where partisan politics, or at least the appearance of it, comes into play. Indeed, a judge's political ideology or past party affiliation is among the strongest predictors of how that judge will rule in a case.[30] This is particularly true in cases involving a clear conservative or liberal policy issue, such as abortion, free speech, or gay rights.[31]

In most cases, though, when judges exercise discretion, it's more complex than a simple partisan calculation. Republican appointees typically don't merely assert, "I'm opposed to same-sex marriage, so I'm going to strike down this state statute legalizing it." Democratic appointees don't usually say, "Gun violence is out of control. This law making it more difficult to acquire a gun is great."

Legal scholars and judges have identified literally dozens of philosophies for how to interpret the law.[32] The most common approaches, however, advocate fundamentally different perspectives on the role of the judiciary. Some justices exercise a **living constitution** approach,

Are Supreme Court justices too partisan?

TABLE 2. The Supreme Court Sometimes Changes Its Mind

	Number of Decisions Overturning Precedent	Percentage of Decisions Overturning Precedent
1940s	11	2.3%
1950s	8	1.0
1960s	44	2.9
1970s	37	2.2
1980s	26	1.6
1990s	25	2.5
2000s	19	2.3
2010s	10	1.5
2020s	2	1.6
Total	**182**	**2.0**

Note: Data include the 8,966 Supreme Court decisions issued from January 1946 through December 2021.

Source: "The Supreme Court Database," Washington University Law.

which means they derive general principles and values from their reading of the Constitution and its history and then apply these principles to modern controversies. In practice, as long as there's a constitutional basis, adherents of this approach are willing to establish citizen rights that are not explicitly stated in the Constitution and invalidate legislative and executive actions they think go against a more current interpretation of the document. Alternatively, other justices prefer a philosophy of **originalism**. They believe that the words in the Constitution should be interpreted as they were understood at the time of the Founding. Justices who exercise this approach consider it beyond the scope of their job to establish new rights or strike down laws they believe are not consistent with contemporary times. That, they think, is a job for lawmakers.

These philosophies might seem a bit abstract. But the 2015 decision in *Obergefell v. Hodges*—which established a constitutional right to same-sex marriage—is a perfect example of the competing approaches in play.

The Constitution never explicitly mentions the right to marriage, same sex or otherwise. But the justices in the majority exercised a more modern and expansive approach when interpreting the Constitution. They believed that marriage is a fundamental liberty and to deny the "right to marry" would be a violation of the equal protection clause of the Fourteenth Amendment. Those in the minority didn't believe that it was the Court's role to create a new right. They argued that the Founders didn't address same-sex marriage and thus the Constitution offers no suggestion for how the judges should rule. Establishing same-sex marriage laws, therefore, should fall to the other two branches of government.

These competing judicial philosophies often link to the views of the political parties. That is, justices appointed by Democrats are often associated with the living constitution approach, which means, for example, that they're more likely to protect and expand civil rights and civil liberties. Those appointed by Republicans are more likely to justify their decisions as consistent with a stricter read of the Constitution. That's why presidents are on the lookout for potential justices who have articulated a clear judicial philosophy—it allows for a pretty good guess as to how the justice will rule on a wide array of issues.

But still, it is important to remember that justices with different philosophies are not constantly at odds with each other. From 2010 to 2020, the Court comprised five justices appointed by Republicans and four appointed by Democrats. Yet the decade saw a higher ratio of unanimous decisions and a lower percentage of 5–4 rulings than the previous decade (see Figure 1). That changed in 2021, when the six conservative justices squared off against the three more liberal justices on controversial decisions about abortion, guns, religion in schools, and the environment. Indeed, partisan 6–3 decisions accounted for 20 percent of the Court's rulings.[33] Court watchers will keep a close eye on the Court in coming years to assess whether this shift away from unanimity persists.

The Bitter Battle for the Supreme Court Is Here to Stay

The increasingly contentious confirmation process is driven by the reality that the Supreme Court is now the final arbiter on a key set of high-profile and enduring issues in U.S. politics. Name a policy issue on which Democrats and Republicans don't agree, and it's likely that the Court will play a central role in shaping the law related to that issue. With lifetime appointments and recent justices serving well into their 80s, both parties realize that any single justice can serve for decades and make consequential decisions that affect the lives of

Are Supreme Court justices too partisan?

millions of Americans. And given the power of precedent, the overwhelming majority of decisions remain, even as the composition of the Court changes. With the stakes being high on many key issues, presidents and senators of both parties do whatever it takes to help advance or sink a nominee.

DID YOU GET IT?
Are Supreme Court justices too partisan?

Short Answer:

- It depends on how you look at it.
- Yes, if you look at the confirmation process, which has become an intensely partisan fight, with Democrats and Republicans seeking to populate the Court with like-minded justices.
- Maybe, in terms of the decisions the Court issues. Competing judicial philosophies do result in what appear to be partisan votes on a host of controversial and high-profile issues.
- No. Supreme Court justices — no matter if they were appointed by Democratic or Republican presidents — have historically been more unified than you might expect given the increasingly partisan confirmation process.

Quantitative Literacy

Interpret the numbers: This segment includes lots of statistics about Senate confirmation votes and Supreme Court decisions. Use the data in the tables and figures we present to draw some conclusions about partisanship on the Court.

1. Based on Table 1, who is the last justice to have received majority support from both parties in the Senate?
   a. Clarence Thomas
   b. Stephen Breyer
   c. John Roberts
   d. Sonia Sotomayor

2. Which is a plausible conclusion to draw based on the data presented in Figure 1?
   a. The percentage of 5–4 rulings over time is consistent with an increasingly divisive confirmation process.
   b. The percentage of unanimous rulings over time is consistent with an increasingly divisive confirmation process.
   c. The increasingly divisive confirmation process is evident in both the percentages of unanimous and 5–4 decisions over time.
   d. The two trend lines in Figure 1 do not appear to be directly related to the increasingly divisive confirmation process.

3. According to Table 2, the percentage of precedent-altering decisions was roughly the same in the 1970s and the 2000s. But the Court actually reversed precedent in nearly twice as many cases during the 1970s. How is this possible?
   a. The Court issued far fewer rulings in the 1970s than in the 2000s.
   b. The Court issued many more rulings in the 1970s than in the 2000s.
   c. It's not possible to compare decisions from the 1970s to decisions in the 2000s.
   d. There is a downward trend in the number of precedent-altering decisions.

FIGURE IT OUT

Given Supreme Court justices' lifetime appointments, the stakes of the confirmation process are especially high. The Pew Research Center analyzed the age at the time of appointment and the length of service of the 104 justices who had served and left the Court by 2017 (see the figure below). Based on Pew's data, answer the following questions:

- What is the most common age range for a Supreme Court nominee?

- In a couple of sentences, summarize the primary point this figure makes.

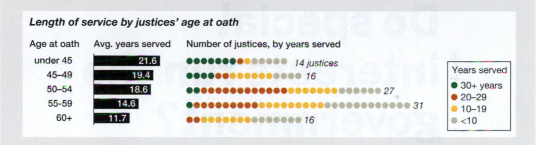

Length of service by justices' age at oath

Age at oath	Avg. years served	Number of justices, by years served
under 45	21.6	14 justices
45–49	19.4	16
50–54	18.6	27
55-59	14.6	31
60+	11.7	16

Years served
- ● 30+ years
- ● 20–29
- ● 10–19
- ● <10

Want to Know More?

If we've piqued your interest in contentious Supreme Court confirmation hearings, then check out *Confirmation*, a 2016 HBO film chronicling the Clarence Thomas nomination. If you'd rather see the real thing, as opposed to Kerry Washington portraying Anita Hill, take a look at *Sex & Justice*, an hour-long documentary narrated by feminist icon Gloria Steinem.

41.
Do special interests run the government?

#Lobbying

In 2008, the United States experienced perhaps its most serious economic crisis since the Great Depression. Although no one factor caused what became known as the Great Recession, the banking industry played a central role. To make a long story short, banks since the 1990s had made billions in profits by taking advantage of loose financial regulations and offering mortgages to people who weren't really qualified to borrow the money.[1] When the housing market began to crash, these people — many of whom were victims of unethical behavior on the part of financial institutions — could no longer afford their mortgage payments. Both the U.S. and the global economy went into a major tailspin. In response, the Democratic-controlled Congress passed legislation regulating the banking industry. The new law touched on everything banks do — from the credit cards, loans, and mortgages they issue to how they invest depositors' money.[2] Needless to say, the banks didn't like the new rules. So they spent hundreds of millions of dollars supporting Republicans who promised to change them.[3] It took a while, but the strategy worked. In 2018, Congress passed a law that rolled back many of the regulations.[4]

By 2040, 50 percent of all new passenger cars and trucks will likely be fully electric.[5] Great news, right? Smooth ride, less pollution, what's

Many Americans — Democrats and Republicans alike — think that members of Congress are bought and paid for by wealthy donors and corporate lobbyists. Meanwhile, politicians regularly deny those allegations. The reality is more complicated.

not to love? A lot, if you ask the gas and oil companies. Every time a vehicle doesn't need gas or oil to run, the $180 billion-a-year oil industry loses money.[6] That's why the American Petroleum Institute — which is funded by oil companies like ExxonMobil — has been working to block electric car initiatives. In Washington, D.C., the institute has lobbied elected officials to oppose subsidies to companies that produce electric cars and to people who buy them. Outside D.C., it has tried to convince state and local governments to stop building the charging stations that electric vehicles rely on to operate.[7] Although the gas and oil industry hasn't been able to kill electric cars, its lobbyists have certainly slowed their rise.

Nearly 60 million Americans (about 20 percent of the U.S. population) can't afford their prescription drugs.[8] One reason is that drug prices in the United States are dramatically higher than they are in other countries.[9] If you live here and need a prescription painkiller or anti-anxiety medication, you'll likely pay 3 times what someone in the United Kingdom will pay for the same drug. You'll spend 6 times what you would on the same medication in Brazil.[10] Why? The issue is complicated, but one factor is that the pharmaceutical industry spends millions trying to persuade Congress not to pursue reforms that would cut into drug companies' profits.[11] And the industry has succeeded. For decades, members of Congress and presidents have proposed many ideas to lower the costs of prescription drugs — from implementing price controls, to allowing Medicare to buy in bulk, to changing patent rules so that generic drugs can make it to market faster. But none of these proposals has mustered sufficient support to become law.

These are just three examples. Name an industry (real estate, defense, insurance, technology) or a cause (abortion, guns, mental health, workers' rights), and we could recount a similar story. From wealthy corporations and businesses to labor unions and public interest groups, **special interests** work to influence the political system to achieve their often narrow goals. Although the term "special interest" is usually viewed as derogatory and associated with self-centered groups that care only about achieving their own goals, the outcomes they push for aren't always nefarious or bad for society. Cleaner air and water, more affordable prescription drugs, and safer bridges and roads are just a few of the societal goods that many special interests push for.

By the end of this segment, you'll see that special interests invest tons of money, adopt multiple tactics, and go to anyone in the government — members of Congress and their staffs, White House officials, federal regulators — to get the laws and policies they want. Although it's tough to determine exactly how successful special interests are, there's no question that they permeate the U.S. political system and work tirelessly to get their way.

How Special Interests Try to Get What They Want

To get what they want, special interests rely on **lobbying**—the practice of trying to influence people in government to pursue a particular policy or action. That might mean encouraging them to adopt a policy, maintain a program, or nix a regulation. Interest groups of all types—Shell Oil, Ford Motor Company, the National Education Association, Google, Planned Parenthood, the U.S. Chamber of Commerce—hire lobbyists. And they pay them a lot. In 2021 alone, special interests spent a total of almost $3.8 billion on lobbying activities in Washington, D.C. Facebook and Amazon each spent around $20 million. Boeing, Comcast, and AT&T came in at roughly $13 million each.[12] Overall, the pharmaceutical industry spent more than $350 million on lobbyists. The electronics and insurance industries spent well over $100 million apiece (see Figure 1).[13]

FIGURE 1. Top 10 Lobbying Industries, 2021

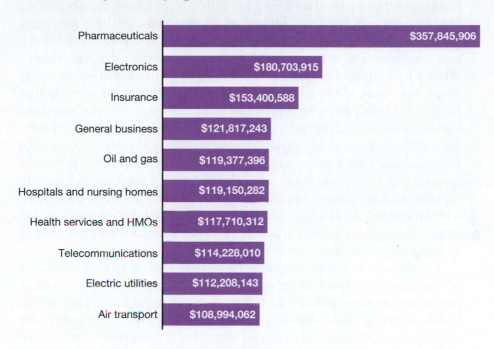

Industry	Amount
Pharmaceuticals	$357,845,906
Electronics	$180,703,915
Insurance	$153,400,588
General business	$121,817,243
Oil and gas	$119,377,396
Hospitals and nursing homes	$119,150,282
Health services and HMOs	$117,710,312
Telecommunications	$114,228,010
Electric utilities	$112,208,143
Air transport	$108,994,062

Note: Figure includes the 10 industries that spent the most on direct federal lobbying in 2021.
Source: "Industries," OpenSecrets.

The lobbying industry is not only well funded but also vast. Lobbyists are so widespread on Capitol Hill that you can't spit on a D.C. street without hitting one. Approximately 12,000 registered lobbyists work in Washington, more than 85 percent of whom work for businesses or corporations.[14] (By law, lobbyists must "register" if they meet with government officials more than once a year, receive more than $3,000 in compensation, and spend at least 20 percent of their time working for a particular client.[15]) To put the 12,000 number in perspective, there are more than 22 registered lobbyists for every member of Congress. And that doesn't account for the thousands of lawyers and support staff who work in lobbying firms but aren't registered themselves. Once these people are included in the count, experts estimate that the number of D.C. lobbyists is more like 90,000 (or 168 per member of Congress).[16]

How does this network of lobbyists influence the government? We break down their tactics into four categories.

Tactic #1: Tell 'Em What You Want

Lobbyists spend a lot of time meeting with White House officials, agency leaders, and members of Congress and their staffs. In these meetings, lobbyists tell government officials the positions they'd like them to take and the courses of action they'd like them to pursue. Although there's often a perception that lobbyists are high-pressure salespeople trying to get members of the government to do what they want come hell or high water, that's not always the case. In fact, in many of these meetings, lobbyists are actually preaching to the choir—that is, speaking with members of the executive and legislative branch who are already on board with their agenda. That's not to say that lobbyists don't also work to persuade government officials to adopt a policy or change a position. But they're usually not spending time convincing people who aren't at least open to their cause.[17] After all, no lobbyist is going to convince President Joe Biden to support cutting corporate taxes, or Senator Ted Cruz to vote to give amnesty to undocumented immigrants.

Lobbyists work their magic by more than merely urging members of Congress to vote a certain way on a piece of legislation or encouraging administration officials to roll back some regulation. They try to build congenial and collaborative relationships with government officials. Every December, for example, members of Congress have to make difficult choices about which lobbyists' holiday parties to attend. If they schedule it just right, they can attend almost 20 lavish affairs across the holiday season (see Figure 2).[18]

Of course, lobbyists don't limit their receptions to the holidays. FRANMAC, the Taco Bell Franchise Management Advisory Council, has been known to host events with 6,000 tacos on Capitol grounds. When members of Congress and their staffers grab a free taco for lunch, they can engage with the company's lobbyists about tax cuts for Taco Bell property maintenance or how to prevent Taco Bell workers from unionizing.[19]

Lobbyists often develop such good working relationships with members of Congress that they're invited right into the legislative process. Many lobbyists, for example, actually write key portions of the bills they want members of Congress to submit. This is increasingly true for members of the House of Representatives. Ever since dramatic cuts to the size of congressional staffs in the 1990s, members have had fewer resources and staff expertise to draft and assess complex legislation.[20] So they're happy to take help from lobbyists. The examples can be eye-popping. Lobbyists for banks helped revise bills regulating the banking industry; they ensured that the taxpayers, not the banks, paid for the bank bailout of 2008.[21] Lobbyists for chemical industry firms wrote provisions of a bill that exempted those companies from regulations and penalties

FIGURE 2. Holiday Parties Hosted by D.C. Lobbyists

SUN	MON	TUE	WED	THU	FRI	SAT
26	27	28	29	30	1	2
			6 pm Motion Picture Association of America holiday reception	*5:30 pm* OCC and Options Industry holiday party		
3	4	5	6	7	8	9
		6 pm Lockheed Martin holiday reception *6 pm* National Retail Federation holiday party *6 pm* CME Group holiday	*4:30 pm* Airlines for America party *6 pm* Microsoft holiday open house *6 pm* Consumer Technology Association party	*5:30 pm* Crop Life America open house *5:30 pm* U.S. Chamber of Commerce holiday reception		
10	11	12	13	14	15	16
		5:30 pm Financial Services holiday celebration *5:30 pm* American Gas Association holiday reception	*5 pm* Tech Net holiday party *5:30 pm* Nuclear Energy Institute congressional reception	*6 pm* National Association of Broadcasters holiday reception *7:30 pm* American Insurance Association reception		

Source: Lee Fang, "Lobbyists Bring Holiday Cheer to Lawmakers and Congressional Staff with Glitzy Parties," The Intercept, December 8, 2017.

for polluting waterways.[22] Lobbyists for an oil company drafted legislation that allowed the company to drill for fossil fuels on environmentally sensitive land.[23] In 2017, lobbyists for health insurance companies bragged when Congress passed a law to limit malpractice lawsuits. And why

In February 2019, the telecommunications industry held a $5,000-per-plate fundraiser for Senator Roger Wicker, a Mississippi Republican. Demonstrators gathered outside the Capital Grille, the D.C. steakhouse where the fundraiser was taking place, to highlight what they saw as the industry's "shameful" lobbying practices.

wouldn't they? The final version of the law looked almost exactly like the bill the insurance industry had proposed.[24] They may have even celebrated in stereotypical lobbyist fashion—with dinner and martinis at a fancy D.C. steakhouse.

Tactic #2: Money, Money, Money

Trying to persuade, cajole, or help government officials to do their job the way you want is all well and good. But money talks, too. And making contributions to the reelection campaign of a member of Congress is a sure way to get his or her attention. Mick Mulvaney, a former congressman from South Carolina, explained to a group of bankers how his congressional office determined whether to meet with a lobbyist: "If you're a lobbyist who never gave us money, I didn't talk to you. If you're a lobbyist who gave us money, I might talk to you."[25] Mulvaney explained that campaign contributions are vital if an industry wants to gain access to a member of Congress and exert influence. After all, he explained, lawmakers "will never know as much about your industry as you do" and won't know what is important "until you tell them." It's not just Mulvaney who behaved this way. Studies have found that members of Congress, state legislators, and senior government officials are more likely to meet with campaign contributors than with people who haven't given to their campaigns.[26]

Despite how unseemly Mulvaney's characterization of who gets access and influence sounds, at least some rules govern lobbyists' behavior. You might be relieved to know that it's illegal to bribe elected officials directly. You can't shower a member of Congress with expensive gifts, meals, or trips. And a lobbyist cannot say, "If you vote for this bill, I'll give $5,000 to your reelection campaign." These are bribes. But the line between illegal bribery and what's permissible is blurry. Meals and gifts are off-limits, but receptions—like those holiday parties—are okay under congressional ethics rules as long as they don't include a sit-down dinner. Campaign contributions are fine, too, as long as the financial support is not contingent on a specific action.[27] So if a lobbyist tells a member of Congress "We really need your vote for this bill" and then, the next day, sends a $5,000 check to the member's campaign office or offers to hold a fundraiser, there's no problem. That's what we might call **legal bribery**. No money was offered in direct exchange for support on a bill. Rather, the lobbyist gave money and just happened to get the desired vote or action. To the lobbyist and the member of Congress, this is business as usual. To the rest of us, it's pretty shady.

Given the relationship between campaign contributions and access, many industries give generously to both Democrats and Republicans. For them, it's not a partisan game. They want to meet with, attempt to influence, and reward anyone willing to support their interests. Heading into the 2022 elections, the securities and investment industry, for example, pretty evenly split its almost $200 million in campaign contributions between the two parties. The finance and health services industries did the same (see Figure 3).[28]

FIGURE 3. Contributions to Federal Campaigns, 2020

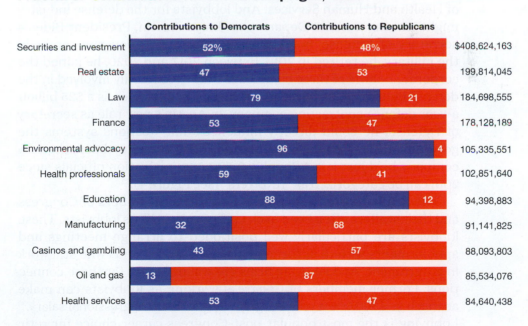

	Contributions to Democrats	Contributions to Republicans	
Securities and investment	52%	48%	$408,624,163
Real estate	47	53	199,814,045
Law	79	21	184,698,555
Finance	53	47	178,128,189
Environmental advocacy	96	4	105,335,551
Health professionals	59	41	102,851,640
Education	88	12	94,398,883
Manufacturing	32	68	91,141,825
Casinos and gambling	43	57	88,093,803
Oil and gas	13	87	85,534,076
Health services	53	47	84,640,438

Note: Figure includes the special interests that contributed at least $80 million to congressional campaigns in 2020. Together, they contributed more than $1.6 billion.

Source: "Top Industries," OpenSecrets.

Some special interests devote their resources to one political party or the other. Law, education, and environmental advocacy groups give mostly to Democrats. Manufacturers and the oil and gas industry mostly fill the campaign coffers of Republicans. And partisan special interests take extra care to make sure they do all they can to support party leaders, committee chairs, and key allies—basically anyone who has disproportionate influence when it comes to introducing a bill and seeing it through the legislative process.[29]

Tactic #3: Trading Places

Special interests are often effective at influencing government officials because many of their lobbyists, board members, and top employees have been in government themselves. In what has become known as the **revolving door**, former government officials often wind up working for lobbying firms or businesses, and former lobbyists and executives frequently start working for the government. Some go back and forth many times.[30]

This practice means that former lobbyists for special interests literally work in the congressional office or government agency implementing the policies they previously tried to shape. Lobbyists for the oil and gas industry might go to work in the Energy Department. Former health corporation executives may take positions in the Department of Health and Human Services. And lobbyists for the defense industry might join the Defense Department. Lloyd Austin, President Biden's secretary of Defense, is a good example. After a lengthy career in the military, he retired in 2016. Between 2017 and 2020, he joined the corporate boards of three companies that were heavily involved in the defense industry. One of them, Raytheon Technologies, is a $25 billion-a-year defense contracting company. In Austin's new role as secretary of Defense, he could directly influence what weapons systems the government bought—including those produced by Raytheon, the very company he'd just left.[31] Roughly 2,500 administration officials since 2001 can be categorized as "revolvers" (see Figure 4).[32]

The revolving door also means that former members of Congress and their staffers often head back up to Capitol Hill as lobbyists. These lobbyists are particularly well positioned to arrange meetings and appointments with their former colleagues and friends who still work in government. And lobbying firms are willing to pay for these connections. Former members of Congress working as lobbyists can make as much as $500,000 a year, roughly 3 times their congressional salary.[33] Lobbying is the most popular post-Congress career choice for retiring members as well as for those defeated in their bids for reelection.[34] In 2021, more than 450 former members of the U.S. House and Senate and more than 1,000 former congressional staffers worked for lobbying

FIGURE 4. The Revolving Door: Lobbyists, Executives, and Corporate Board Members

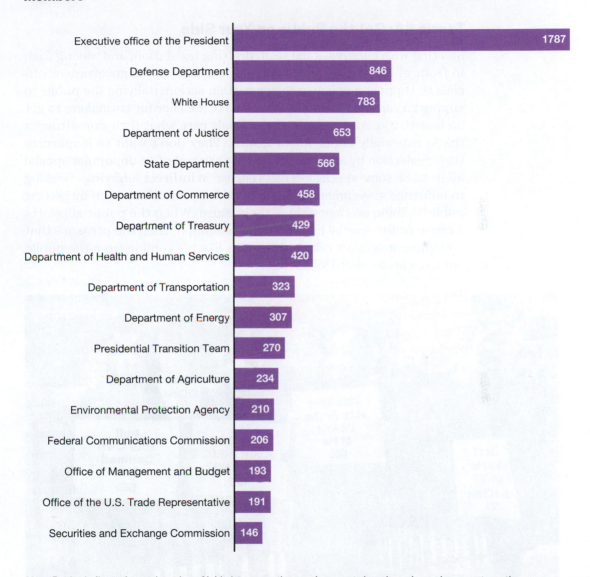

Note: Entries indicate the total number of lobbyists, executives, and corporate board members who were at one time employed by each executive branch office, department, or agency from the mid-1970s to 2022.

Source: "Revolving Door," OpenSecrets.org.

firms. And that number is most certainly an undercount, as it doesn't include former members who "advocate" for special interests but don't formally lobby.

Tactic #4: Get the Public on Your Side

Meeting with congressional staff, drafting legislation, and waving cash in front of lawmakers aren't the only ways to entice government officials to support a policy or take a certain action. Rallying the public to support a cause or an industry can make it easier for lawmakers to get on board, too. After all, elected officials care what their constituents think, especially about major issues. They don't want to jeopardize their reelection by appearing to be the servant of an unpopular special interest. So some special interests engage in **indirect lobbying**—working to influence government officials to take a particular action by getting public opinion on their side of their cause. When the public supports a cause or the special interest championing it, then the pressure that government officials respond to looks like it's coming from the public, not from professional lobbyists.

At the opening ceremony of the 2020 Iditarod race, PETA organized a protest of the event. According to their website, the two-week race forces hundreds of dogs to run 1,000 miles through "biting winds, blinding snowstorms, and subzero temperatures. The race will leave sensitive dogs bloodied, sick, and forever scarred, if they make it back at all."

Do special interests run the government?

These efforts to woo public opinion take many forms: social media ad campaigns, TV and radio commercials, news media appearances, organized rallies. And lots of interests—from wealthy ones to those on a shoestring budget—rely on them to make a case. People for the Ethical Treatment of Animals (PETA), for example, publicizes stories of animal abuse to garner public support for its cause. The Family Research Council, a conservative Christian organization, pushes its "values agenda" by regularly appearing on Fox News.[35] The Brady Campaign, a national gun control advocacy group, takes to the airwaves to educate the public about gun violence. Even powerful corporate interests use indirect lobbying. Energy companies concerned about their image as "greedy fossil fuel polluters" have spent millions on public relations campaigns.[36] They don't want to appear oblivious to concerns over climate change and carbon emissions, so they go to great lengths to assure people that they're doing everything they can to fight pollution. Take a look at the websites of Chevron, Shell, or ExxonMobil, and at first you'll think you've stumbled onto the site of an environmental group.

Reform on the Horizon?

Most people believe that special interests exert too much influence over the government. Seventy percent think the political system favors wealthy interests. More than eight out of ten people believe large corporations have too much power. Three-quarters feel the same way about health insurance companies. And more than 60 percent of citizens contend that banks and tech companies are too powerful.[37]

People blame special interests for major problems in the United States as well. Why are prescription drugs so expensive? Because of the pharmaceutical industry. Why is the gap between the rich and the poor increasing? Because wealthy interests control the tax code. Why do tech companies buy and sell people's personal data without their permission? Because Google and Facebook spend heavily on lobbyists.

Reform proposals to rein in special interest power emerge regularly. Some members of Congress have proposed legislation that bans former members of Congress from ever becoming lobbyists.[38] Others have proposed limiting when former government officials can begin to work for private companies with interests before Congress.[39] Still others have advocated banning lobbyists from holding fundraisers for elected officials.[40] But for the most part, these efforts fail to become law. Hardly surprising, given that powerful special interests work hard to block them.

DID YOU GET IT?

Do special interests run the government?

Short Answer:

- They certainly try. Special interests spend billions of dollars and countless hours trying to ensure that the government advances their often narrow policy goals.
- They rely on direct lobbying, financial contributions, the revolving door, and public relations campaigns to push their agendas.
- Determining whether special interests run the government is difficult, but public opinion and attempts at reform suggest that they have too much influence.

DEVELOPING YOUR SKILLS

Consuming Political Information

Consider the source: There are many claims out there about the power of special interest groups in U.S. politics. Some are based on objective facts and quality journalism, whereas others are more subjective. Separate journalism from opinion when it comes to whether various industries get their way in Washington, D.C. (Hint: If you're unsure about a source after perusing its home page, you might find Media Bias/Fact Check helpful. This organization rates news sources based on ideological perspective and the quality of reporting. You can access it here: https://mediabiasfactcheck.com/.)

1. A *New Yorker* article suggests that the oil industry's influence may be on the decline in the United States. What's the likelihood that the piece offers an objective description of the industry's power?

   a. Very unlikely. *The New Yorker* is a liberal magazine that includes mostly commentary and opinion. Few articles include well-researched facts.

   b. Unlikely. *The New Yorker* is known for superficial reporting, and most of its pieces don't offer in-depth political analysis.

   c. Somewhat likely. *The New Yorker* is known for well-researched journalism, but given its liberal perspective, there might be some bias in how the story is framed.

   d. Very likely. *The New Yorker* is known for ideologically balanced, well-researched journalism.

2. A story on BBC News entitled "Gun Control Advocates Pin Their Hopes on Biden" gives readers an overview of gun control politics in the United States. What type of ideological approach will this article likely offer?

   a. Balanced. The BBC is a well-regarded outlet for objective journalism.

   b. Not balanced. Most BBC articles are commentary, so the perspective of the article will depend on the author.

   c. Not balanced. The BBC is widely regarded as a conservative news outlet.

   d. Not balanced. The BBC is widely regarded as a liberal news outlet.

3. A *Washington Post* op-ed argues that the banking industry is so powerful that it pursues its own interests at the expense of the financial well-being of average citizens. Which assumption can you probably make about the piece?

   a. It's likely balanced ideologically and the product of well-researched journalism.

   b. It's likely left-leaning with little factual basis.

   c. It's likely left-leaning, but because it's a traditional news outlet, an editor would make certain that the op-ed didn't contain false statements.

   d. The *Washington Post* editorial pages are balanced ideologically, so you'd have to read the article to determine its perspective.

FIGURE IT OUT

One of the most prominent tools used to track the influence of special interests is OpenSecrets. Go to the website at https://www.opensecrets.org/ and assess whether the information it presents should be trusted. More specifically:

- List three ways it tracks the influence of special interests.

- For each, summarize the data it uses to monitor special interests.

- Overall, is this a source of information we should trust when analyzing the influence of special interests? Why or why not? A few sentences is fine.

Want to Know More?

For an ominous account of how special interests try to get what they want from the government, take a look at Robert Kaiser's book *So Much Damn Money: The Triumph of Lobbying and the Corrosion of American Government*. The book tracks the rise of the lobbying industry that started in the 1970s. And as a former *Washington Post* reporter and editor, Kaiser writes in a gripping and easy-to-read style.

42.
Is the federal government hopelessly broken?

#PartyPolarization

The government doesn't work! At least that's the consensus if you ask, well, just about anyone.

Ask political leaders — Democrats and Republicans alike. In his 2012 State of the Union address, Barack Obama declared, "Washington is broken." Voters, he went on to say, were justified in expecting another year in which the federal government would "get nothing done."[1] Four years later, Donald Trump, throughout his presidential campaign, regularly referred to government policies and processes as "rigged," "broken," and a "disaster."[2] The government, according to Trump, did almost nothing well. President Joe Biden also doesn't mince words when it comes to government dysfunction. "Everybody is frustrated. That's part of being in government," he told reporters after an unsuccessful series of attempts to reach a deal on an infrastructure bill.[3]

Ask pundits and journalists. You'll be flooded with commentary lamenting the failures of American government. These assessments are so common that it's hard to find an article or book about the U.S. political system that doesn't include the word "broken" or "dysfunctional."

Ask the voters. Roughly 86 percent of them are "very" or "fairly" worried about "the way the government in Washington works." The

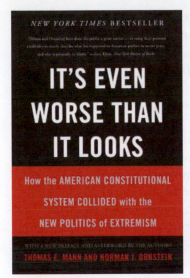
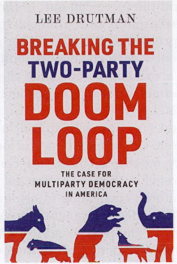
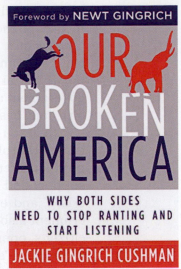

Literally dozens of recent books written by pundits and political scientists lament the way the U.S. government functions — or doesn't.

same proportion worry about the "ability of political leaders to solve the country's biggest problems."[4] In fact, one recent survey found that citizens express more concern about the government's inability to function well than they do about anything else.[5]

So that's it. Is the government hopelessly broken? Yes. Asked and answered.

Except . . . not so fast. This segment takes a broad look at the U.S. federal government's performance and arrives at a somewhat more complex assessment. We debunk the simple narrative that the government is completely broken. Otherwise, it wouldn't be able to carry out the many critical roles and responsibilities it fulfills on a daily basis. But we also make it clear that if you're looking for a government that's nimble, effective, and forward-thinking in how it tackles major problems, you should look elsewhere. The contemporary federal government is dominated by loyal partisans with clear — and often opposing — preferences. Layer this partisanship on top of a legislative process that relies on compromise but gives elected leaders few incentives for bipartisan cooperation, and responsive and effective governance becomes almost impossible.

The Government Isn't Totally Broken

Everyone is a critic. And when you're talking about a federal government comprising more than 2 million civilian employees, a $4 trillion annual budget, and the expectation that it should solve every major problem, it's easy to find things to call out. In fact, the bulk of this segment focuses on the reasons it's often difficult for the government to address the nation's problems. But it's neither accurate nor fair to assess the government's performance by looking only at what it doesn't do well. You also need to consider the breadth of programs the government administers and the resources it provides to Americans on a daily basis.

When you do, it's impossible to conclude that the U.S. government is totally broken. Government institutions and agencies regulate all product safety, monitor all interstate commerce, provide emergency support and relief in the face of natural disasters and public health crises, and enforce thousands of criminal and civil laws. The government also provides retirement benefits and health care to senior citizens, operates the postal service, and manages huge swaths of the country's infrastructure, from highways to railroads to airways (see Table 1).

If this list doesn't impress you, breaking down the numbers might. The U.S. Postal Service delivers 17.7 million pieces of mail *per hour*.[6] The Federal Aviation Administration oversees more than 44,000 flights throughout more than 19,000 airports in the United States *every day*.[7] The Pell Grant program lends money to more than one out of every three students attending college each year.[8] The U.S. military has a presence in roughly 160 countries around the world.[9] Put simply, the federal government makes certain that the country is up and running.

In most cases, the programs the federal government administers began as a response to a major problem in U.S. society. Social

TABLE 1. 12 Things the Federal Government Does Well

- Delivers 188 million pieces of mail every day.
- Issues 64 million Social Security checks every month.
- Issues 150,000 patents every year.
- Prosecutes 165,000 criminal cases each year.
- Awards 6.8 million Pell Grants to college students.
- Guides 16.1 million airline flights each year.
- Processes 150 million citizens' tax returns each year.
- Maintains 294 embassies in 170 countries.
- Maintains 160,000 miles of federal highways.
- Manages 640 million acres of federal land.
- Provides health care to 64 million senior citizens.
- Oversees 1.3 million members of the military.

Security is one example. When the program began in 1935, more than 50 percent of senior citizens' incomes were below the poverty line.[10] Or consider interstate highways. In 1956, the disjointed system of roads and highways made shipping and receiving goods difficult. So the federal government stepped in and funded a national highway system to facilitate travel and interstate commerce.[11] Each of the items listed in Table 1 has a similar story. Throughout history, the federal government has shown itself capable of implementing major changes to advance society.

But the Government Is Pretty Broken

Although the federal government effectively administers many critical programs, it has become easier in recent decades to recount the list of obvious failures than clear triumphs. Serious problems just never seem to get fixed. Health care costs have skyrocketed, and millions of Americans remain uninsured. Stagnant wages characterize millions of workers' paychecks—with no major relief in sight. Battles over immigration fill the airwaves, but legislation hasn't followed. Confusing signals at the beginning of the Covid-19 pandemic led to an all-out public health disaster that the world will be dealing with for years to come. Government shutdowns have almost become business as usual (see Table 2).

How did we get here? Why can't the government figure out how to address pressing issues that confront the population? For at least two fundamental reasons.

TABLE 2. 12 Ways the Federal Government Fails Miserably

- 21 government shutdowns since 1975
- Roughly 11 million undocumented people living in the country
- Income inequality at its highest rates since the 1920s
- Ranks 5th globally in rates of drug overdoses
- National debt of $30 trillion
- 30 million Americans without health insurance
- 40 percent of U.S. highway bridges at or beyond their life span
- Nearly half a million deaths from lead poisoning every year
- 45 million Americans with student loan debt
- One-quarter of all public school buildings in substandard condition
- Ranks 35th globally in life span
- Site of 15 percent of the world's gun deaths

The Growing Divide between Democrats and Republicans

The inability to address major issues often comes down to stalemate and gridlock between Democrats and Republicans. For much of the twentieth century, many Democrats and Republicans in Congress held moderate positions on important issues. In the 1970s, for example, roughly half the Republicans and one-third of the Democrats serving in the House and the Senate were neither ardent liberals nor staunch conservatives. Rather, they took positions that fell in the middle of the liberal-conservative spectrum (see Figure 1).[12] So compromise was possible. Indeed, during this period members of Congress typically voted with the majority of the members of their party just 60 percent of the time. The other 40 percent of the time, they actually went against the majority of their own party and voted with members of the opposition. So on a wide variety of issues, legislation was truly bipartisan—supported by members of both political parties.

But over time, Congress has experienced **party polarization**—the widening gap in political beliefs between Democrats and Republicans, with Democrats moving in a more liberal direction and Republicans moving in a more conservative one. What had been a Congress comprising many members who were willing to cross party lines to craft and pass legislation began to change significantly. By the mid-1990s, the proportion of moderates in each chamber had been cut roughly in half. Fast-forward another 20-plus years, and you're down to a handful of moderate Democrats; moderate Republicans have become nearly extinct. Without moderates, party unity is as strong as ever. Members of Congress vote with their respective party on more than 90 percent of the votes they take. The era of working with the other party, and sometimes voting against your own, is over.[13]

Yet the entire system of government—from checks and balances, to separation of powers, to the bicameral legislature—requires compromise to get anything done. A bill can typically succeed only with support from the president, party leaders, and a majority of members of both chambers of Congress. Given the frequency of **divided government**—a situation in which no one party controls the House, Senate, and White House—building that coalition of support is extraordinarily difficult. Indeed, the U.S. government was divided for 30 of the 42 years from 1980 to 2022. With Democrats and Republicans simultaneously each in control of at least one chamber of Congress or the White House, reaching an agreement on any major issue, regardless of its national importance, has become rare.

The consequences of a polarized political system are most evident in the U.S. Senate, where senators can use the **filibuster**—a Senate rule that

Is the federal government hopelessly broken?

FIGURE 1. The Disappearing Middle in Congress

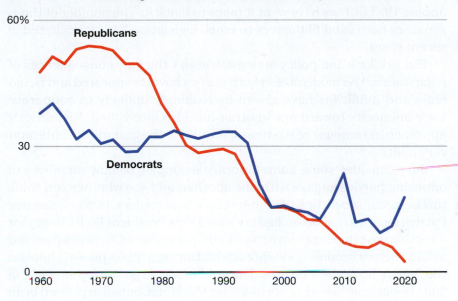

Percentage of moderates in the House of Representatives

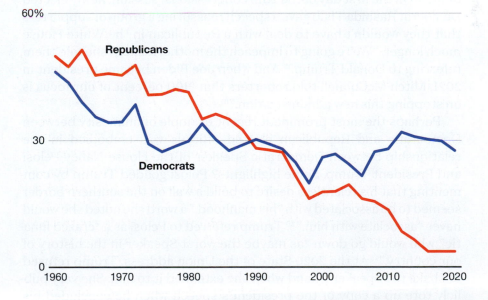

Percentage of moderates in the Senate

Note: The moderate classification is based on whether the member's DW-NOMINATE score fell within the interval of −0.25 and 0.25 in the given Congress.

Source: Voteview.

allows members to deliver speeches of unlimited length with the intent of delaying or killing a bill. To defeat a filibuster, 60 senators must vote for **cloture**. A successful cloture vote means that the bill in question can proceed with a floor vote. As long as 40 members of the minority party oppose the bill, they have what it takes to block it. The number of times senators have used filibusters to block legislation has skyrocketed in recent years.

But gridlock and policy stalemate aren't the only consequences of polarization.[14] As moderates in both parties have disappeared and Democrats and publicans have grown increasingly unlikely to cooperate, their animosity toward one another has also intensified. No tactic or approach, no amount of nastiness, is outside the bounds of contemporary politics.[15]

Just consider some contemporary examples of how members of opposing parties engage with one another, and see whether you think this behavior is befitting of high-level political leaders. In 2004, Senator Patrick Leahy, a Democrat, had criticized Vice President Dick Cheney for directing government contracts to a company where Cheney had served as CEO before becoming vice president. During a "class photo" shoot on the Senate floor, the vice president told Leahy to go "fuck yourself."[16] In 2010, Republican Senate minority leader Mitch McConnell explained in an interview that he refused to cooperate with Democrat Barack Obama—on anything. He told a reporter that "the single most important thing" he wanted to achieve was "for President Obama to be a one-term president."[17] On the first day of the 2019 congressional session, newly elected Democrat Rashida Tlaib gave a speech reassuring a group of supporters that they wouldn't have to deal with a Republican in the White House much longer. "We're going to impeach the motherfucker," she told them, referring to Donald Trump.[18] And when Joe Biden became president in 2021, Mitch McConnell told reporters that "100 percent of our focus is on stopping this new administration."[19]

Perhaps the most prominent recent example of animosity between Democratic and Republican elected officials was embodied in the relationship between Democratic Speaker of the House Nancy Pelosi and President Trump. Some highlights? Pelosi goaded Trump by commenting that his relentless desire to build a wall on the southern border seemed to be associated with "his manhood," a word she noted she would never "associate with him."[20] Trump referred to Pelosi as a "crazed lunatic" who would go down "as maybe the worst Speaker in the history of our country."[21] At the 2020 State of the Union address, Trump refused to shake the Speaker's hand when she extended it to him. She very publicly tore up a copy of the president's speech when he concluded his remarks.[22] Exchanges between Trump and Pelosi had grown so toxic that as the federal government tried to address the Covid-19 pandemic in 2020, the president and Speaker hadn't spoken to each other in more than six months.[23]

These are just a handful of examples of the culture of partisan incivility that embodies Washington, D.C. Although political leaders don't constantly hurl F-bombs at one another, they do regularly engage in mean-spirited insults and often flat-out refuse to work together. That's hardly a recipe for legislative efficiency or effectiveness.

No Incentives for Cooperation

Polarization and a complex legislative process make compromise unlikely. So systematic incentives to encourage political leaders to engage in bipartisanship—especially given the animosity between the two parties—are needed. But few of those incentives exist anymore.

Perhaps most notably, in 2011 the House and Senate banned **earmarks**—any congressionally directed spending or tax regulation that solely benefits a specific state, local community, or congressional district. For years, individual lawmakers would slip into major congressional bills certain goodies just for their state or district. Many were worthy projects, such as commissioning new parks in a congressional district, awarding funds to a state university, giving tax breaks to a business or industry that's important to a particular community. But others often seemed quite frivolous, such as $500,000 to build a museum for teapots in North Carolina,[24] $3.4 million for a safe turtle crossing in Florida,[25] or the so-called Bridge to Nowhere—a $223 million project that would have connected a small city in Alaska to an island with a population of 50 people.[26] When the ban went into effect, Congress was funding, on average, about 10,000 special projects to the tune of a combined $20 billion a year.[27]

While many condemned the annual price tag on earmarks, they did serve a greater purpose. Earmarks provided an incentive for members of Congress to support legislation they didn't really like. Members could agree to vote for a budget proposal, even if they had some reservations, because at least something special for their district had been tucked into it. Members could vote for changes in health care laws, even if they had some qualms, because their support could mean funding for a hospital in their district. They could vote for an imperfect bill but at least brag to their constituents about the good thing they'd brought home to them. To members often obsessed with reelection, this seemed like a good trade-off.

There's no question that negotiating for earmarks was often unbecoming. Members often engaged in backroom deals in which they

To many observers, earmarks look like wasteful spending, often referred to as "pork." To the members of Congress who secure the earmarks, though, they represent new jobs for their districts and states — such as the $4.5 million Congresswoman Maxine Waters (right) secured for a senior citizen center in her California district.

promised to lend support to a bill as long as they could get millions of dollars to fund a project in their district or state. But there's also no question that banning earmarks and bringing more transparency to the legislative process took away a major tool for members to compromise and get things done.[28] Indeed, in 2021, members of both the House and Senate introduced steps to reintroduce "limited" earmarks on spending bills.[29]

An additional feature of congressional politics that reduces incentives for bipartisanship is the **permanent campaign**. Members of Congress start running for reelection the day they're elected—raising money, discouraging potential opponents, trying to please the voters who sent them to Washington. For most members of Congress, the best way to achieve these goals is to stick with their party. Many members live in fear of losing to a primary opponent who claims to be more loyal to the party than they are. This doesn't happen often—roughly 9 out of 10 incumbents who run for reelection win—but that's probably because some high-profile exceptions keep most incumbents running scared.

Democrat Daniel Lipinski, for example, voted with his party's leader—Speaker of the House Nancy Pelosi—96 percent of the time.[30] The Illinois congressman received a paltry score of 13 (out of 100) from the American Conservative Union, a group that rates members based on the extent to which they support conservative principles.[31]

Is the federal government hopelessly broken?

Sounds like a good Democrat. Except that Lipinski opposed abortion rights, and in 2010 he voted against one of the Democrats' signature achievements: the Affordable Care Act. These offenses—one of which was a decade old—were enough for challenger Marie Newman to defeat Lipinski in the 2020 Democratic primary.[32]

Republican Liz Cheney faced a similar fate in Wyoming in 2022.[33] Until 2021, Cheney had been a member of the Republican leadership and was often thought of as a rising star in the party. A reliable conservative, she voted with Donald Trump 93 percent of the time, regularly received the endorsement of the National Rifle Association, and praised the Supreme Court for overturning *Roe v. Wade*.[34] Her crime? She was an outspoken critic of Trump's efforts to overturn the 2020 presidential election and voted to impeach him.[35] She was one of only two Republicans willing to serve on the congressional committee investigating the insurrection on January 6, 2021.[36] So Harriet Hageman, a Trump-endorsed candidate, ran a primary campaign that focused on Cheney's willingness to work with Democrats to take down Trump. It worked. Hageman handily defeated Cheney (66 percent to 29 percent).

The possibility of being challenged and defeated by more loyal partisans, like those who defeated Lipinski and Cheney, leave today's elected officials with little incentive for any sort of bipartisan cooperation. Although the permanent campaign isn't a new feature of American politics, the contemporary electoral environment makes it easy and inexpensive for congressional challengers to take to social media and the internet to paint their opponents as turncoats. Given that voters are more likely to trust politicians who share their preferences,[37] if members of Congress want to get reelected, then they have every incentive to remain loyal to their party.

It's Pretty Hopeless

We'd like to end on a hopeful note. Don't worry—the partisan fever that has taken hold in Washington will pass. Members of Congress from opposing parties will start working together again. It's only a matter of time before the federal government gets its act together and provides comprehensive solutions to big issues like immigration, health care, and income inequality. We'd like to say all these things. Really, we would. But there's just little evidence to warrant such optimism. Although we can rest assured knowing that many government programs function well even amid heightened polarization and gridlock, it's unlikely that elected officials in Washington will come together anytime soon to address all the challenges that remain. And there are lots of them.

DID YOU GET IT?

Is the federal government hopelessly broken?

Short Answer:

- It depends on how you approach the question.
- On the one hand, the government carries out many essential tasks that touch the lives of the more than 300 million people who live in the United States.
- On the other hand, party polarization, a governing structure that demands compromise, and politicians with little incentive to cooperate have increasingly led to a government incapable of addressing many of the nation's most pressing problems.

DEVELOPING YOUR SKILLS

Persuasive Argumentation

Choose a side: Assessing whether the federal government is functioning well or poorly is often a matter of opinion. These questions ask you to build thesis statements to make effective arguments about whether the government is hopelessly broken.

1. If you're writing an essay arguing that the federal government is broken, which thesis statement would be the best way to conclude your introductory paragraph?

   a. The implementation of numerous government programs throughout the last 50 years reveals a government that just does not work.

   b. The contemporary federal government's refusal to tackle health care demonstrates a broken government.

   c. Increasing party polarization in the United States has resulted in a government unable to address many of the biggest problems facing the country.

   d. As public opinion data reveal, most citizens believe that the government is hopelessly broken.

2. If you want to refute much of the conventional wisdom and argue in an essay that the federal government actually functions pretty well, which thesis statement would be the best way to conclude your introductory paragraph?

   a. The federal government must be doing a good job because the United States is a successful country.

   b. Critics of the federal government often ignore the many government programs that keep the nation up and running.

   c. The Social Security program is one of the only examples of a government program that functions very well.

   d. The federal government's failure to address major problems has little to do with the political system's structures, rules, and incentives.

3. If you plan to argue in an essay that the federal government has become increasingly ineffective because of members' refusal to cooperate across party lines, which feature of the political process would be accurate to include?

   a. The increased use of the filibuster

   b. The increase in the number of moderates in the House

   c. The decline in the number of primary challengers

   d. The increased reliance on earmarks

FIGURE IT OUT

Develop your own response to this segment's question — Is the federal government hopelessly broken? — by drafting an introductory paragraph (five or six sentences) for a persuasive essay. More specifically, in the paragraph:

- Draw the reader in by explaining why the topic is important.

- Briefly lay out the competing schools of thought on the topic.

- Conclude with a clear thesis statement that summarizes the central argument for which the rest of the essay will include evidence.

Want to Know More?

If you want to get a real sense of government dysfunction on Capitol Hill, you might enjoy books by a couple of former members of Congress. In *Dead Center: How Political Polarization Divided America and What We Can Do about It*, Democrat Jason Altmire chronicles what it was like to be a moderate in a Congress dominated by strong partisans. For a similar perspective from a Republican, check out Olympia Snowe's *Fighting for Common Ground: How We Can Fix the Stalemate in Congress*.

Contemporary Public Policy

Start Here!

Microsoft founder Bill Gates is an optimist when it comes to the government's role in solving big problems. He believes that government is "uniquely able to provide the resources to make sure solutions reach everyone who needs them."[1] Comedian Groucho Marx, in contrast, was more of a pessimist. "Politics," according to Marx, "is the art of looking for trouble, finding it everywhere, diagnosing it incorrectly, and applying the wrong remedies."[2] Both views are built on a common premise: the government's primary responsibility is to develop and implement plans to solve the nation's problems and improve citizens' lives. How well the government performs is a matter of perspective, but political leaders are expected to formulate **public policy** — the formal actions the government takes, including passing laws and providing funding, to address specific issues or problems.

You've actually already read quite a bit about public policy in the first six sections of this book. By now, you're familiar with how the structure of government shapes where policy debates occur (Section I). You know the criteria the Supreme Court employs to determine whether a policy is constitutional (Section II). You're aware of how public policies affect citizens' political engagement (Section III). You recognize how misinformation works its way into policy debates (Section IV). You're acquainted with how well political leaders represent the American people on key issues (Section V). And you understand how political institutions work together to shape policy (Section VI).

But a complete picture of U.S. politics also requires a basic understanding of the nuts and bolts of key policies and competing perspectives surrounding the most prominent domestic and foreign policy issues of the day. Otherwise, you can't develop a well-reasoned position on an issue, follow debates with a critical eye, or assess the government's performance. As such, this section provides an overview of the policy landscape for six of the most important and enduring domestic and foreign policy issues in U.S. politics.

Although we can't cover every major issue, the six we include in this section receive extensive news coverage, feature prominently in campaigns and elections, and consistently rise to the top of voters' to-do lists for government action. The issues we cover also illustrate the battle among political actors — the parties, the branches of government, and special interests — to determine what policies are enacted and who administers them. Each also demonstrates how the political institutions and processes we've covered throughout the book serve as the mechanisms through which society grapples with major issues or challenges. And they shed light on how we arrive at short- and long-term solutions — or, sometimes, no solution at all.

In summarizing the history and politics of the policies we cover, three patterns emerge:

1 **Partisan politics is a major cause of policy stalemate and inaction.**
The structures of U.S. government — separation of powers and federalism — make enacting major policy changes difficult even in the best circumstances. Throw in the hyper-partisanship of today's politics, and developing the consensus needed to craft and implement comprehensive public policies — around health care, income inequality, or the use of force to fight terrorism — becomes extremely challenging.

2 **Policy solutions require navigating trade-offs and costs.**
Policy debates often boil down to conflicting interests and values. Reducing taxes means less money to spend on health care. Free trade may mean a loss of American jobs. Ending global terrorism could lead to lengthy wars and considerable loss of life. Determining which trade-offs are worth it is part of what makes developing public policy so difficult.

3 **Policy reforms tend to happen when there's a shock to the system or a shift in the political landscape.**
Sometimes these shocks are outside events — such as the 9/11 attacks, which spurred the government to create an enormous apparatus to fight terrorism. Other times they're a consequence of elections. New presidents and changes in congressional party control have ushered in policy change around taxes, trade, and health care.

43.
How can the U.S. government be $32 trillion . . . whoops . . . $33 trillion in debt?

#FiscalPolicy

Hurricane Katrina hit Louisiana in 2005. The devastation was unprecedented. About 80 percent of New Orleans flooded, with much of the city under 10 feet of water. Almost a thousand people died, tens of thousands of residents lost their homes and businesses, and millions of others in the region suffered severe property damage. The storm also wiped out one-fifth of U.S. oil production.[1] The federal government spent more than $120 billion on emergency relief.[2]

In 2008, a global financial crisis threatened the U.S. economy. Reckless banking practices and the crash of the housing market brought large banks and financial institutions to the verge of collapse. If the banks went down, so could the whole economy. To avoid the possibility of another Great Depression, the federal government stepped in with a $700 billion bank bailout. And that was just the beginning. The following year, the

Every year, the White House releases a budget proposal, which serves as a blueprint for Congress to craft a federal budget. Donald Trump's 2021 budget proposal, pictured here, was 138 pages and called for $4.8 trillion in government spending.

government spent another $831 billion to jumpstart the slumping economy with funding for jobs, health care, infrastructure, and education.[3]

In 2020, the world came face-to-face with a terrifying public health crisis. The coronavirus pandemic struck, and for millions of Americans life ground to a halt. At the outset of the pandemic, as citizens stayed at home for weeks and then months to avoid infection, large swaths of the economy shut down. The nation's unemployment rate approached 20 percent, millions of small businesses struggled, and hundreds of thousands of Americans died. Within a few months, the federal government stepped in with a $2 trillion relief package to prop up city and state governments, help businesses stay afloat, pay for medical supplies, and extend unemployment benefits.[4]

In times like these — natural disasters, economic recessions, public health crises — it's nice to know that the U.S. government has enough extra money on hand to help citizens and stabilize the economy. Except for one thing. It doesn't! The U.S. government actually spends more money than it takes in — sometimes by a lot. The **national deficit** — the amount of money the government spends beyond what it raises in a single fiscal year — typically ranges from a few hundred billion to several trillion dollars. With just a handful of exceptions, this has been the case since 1981, when President Ronald Reagan, a Republican, proposed a budget with deficit spending.

It's important to emphasize that this spending isn't coming out of a huge savings account the federal government has accumulated over time. Quite the contrary. The government funds its excess spending by borrowing money. As a result, the **national debt** — the total money the federal government has borrowed — is eye-popping. As of November 2022, the U.S. government was in debt by nearly $32 trillion (see Figure 1).[5] The debt is larger than the economies of China, Germany, and Japan combined. It amounts to about $79,000 for every U.S. citizen and more than $200,000 per taxpayer. It's enough money to pay for a four-year college education for every graduating high school senior in America for the next 50 years. If every household in America contributed $1,000 per month, it would still take more than 18 years to pay off the debt.[6] Okay, okay, you get the picture — it's a lot of dough, and it just keeps rising.

Why is the United States — with the largest economy and the most wealth in the world — drowning in debt? This segment explains how we got here by describing the U.S. government's **fiscal policy** — the way the government raises, spends, and borrows money to manage the economy. You'll come to understand why the national debt is so enormous as well as the consequences of deficit spending.

FIGURE 1. The National Debt, 1950–2022 (in trillions of dollars)

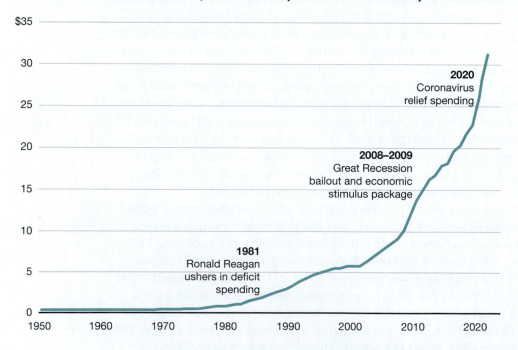

Source: "Historical Debt Outstanding," Treasury Direct. The 2022 point is as of November 10, 2022.

How can the U.S. government be $32 trillion . . . whoops . . . $33 trillion in debt?

How the Federal Government Spends Its Money

The U.S. government spends more money every year than any organization, company, or country in the world. Perhaps not surprising given that the **federal budget**—the government's annual plan for spending and raising money—touches almost every government program and policy. How does Congress provide more money for veterans? By including those changes in the budget. How does it shore up funding for environmental protection or more after-school programs for public school students? By working those items into the budget. How do members of Congress who are worried that we're spending too much on food stamps and housing assistance rein it in? By adjusting the budget. The federal budget is just like any other piece of legislation. The White House can make a proposal, but it's up to members of Congress to introduce, haggle over, and pass an annual budget to send to the president to sign.

In determining spending priorities, the federal government doesn't start from scratch every year. Instead, a large chunk of the budget is accounted for by **mandatory spending** (see Table 1).[7] The spending is mandatory because it funds **entitlement programs** that have already made commitments to citizens. Veterans, for instance, receive guarantees that lifetime health care benefits will be part of their compensation for serving in the military. Senior citizens who retire from

TABLE 1. Federal Government Spending, 2022

	Money Spent	Percentage of Total Spending
Mandatory Spending (Spending on entitlement programs, including Social Security, Medicare, and Medicaid)	$3.7 trillion	65
Discretionary Spending (Defense spending and outlays to fund the rest of the federal government)	$1.7 trillion	30
Interest on the Debt (Payments toward the interest on the money the government borrows)	$319 billion	6
TOTAL	**$5.7 trillion**	**100**

Source: Congressional Budget Office, "The Federal Budget in Office of Management and Budget, "Budget of the U.S. Government: Fiscal Year 2022."

their jobs have been assured that they can count on a Social Security check every month for the rest of their lives. So before negotiations over the federal budget even begin, Congress sets aside money to pay for entitlement programs.

The expansion of entitlement programs, coupled with the fact that people now live longer, means that mandatory spending is becoming an increasingly large share of the budget. Social Security payments alone add up to about $1.2 trillion a year—that's roughly 21 percent of the entire federal budget. Add in $767 billion for Medicare (health care for people aged 65 and older), $409 billion for Medicaid (health care for low-income people and people with disabilities), and more than a trillion for other entitlements, and mandatory spending eats up about two-thirds of the budget. In the 1970s, it accounted for less than a third.[8]

Mandatory spending isn't set in stone. But making changes to payouts for entitlement programs would require the federal government to change the law and, in effect, change the agreements it has made with program recipients. If members of Congress wanted to spend less on Social Security, for example, they could raise the retirement age. If they wanted to reduce the costs of Medicaid, they could adjust the income thresholds to make it harder for low-income people to qualify for government-funded health insurance. But most politicians don't like telling citizens that they aren't going to get the benefits they expect to receive. Although Congress has tweaked mandatory spending from time to time, no federal budget has involved significant cuts to entitlement programs.

When it comes to **discretionary spending**—the parts of the budget that include optional expenses—the federal government has far fewer constraints. Discretionary spending falls into two categories. Defense spending includes all military expenditures—salaries for members of the military, costs of maintaining bases and military equipment around the world, and expenses for procuring new weapons systems. In 2022, defense spending totaled $754 billion. Nondefense discretionary spending—which covers all cabinet departments and federal agencies—came in at around $900 billion.

It's over discretionary spending that members of Congress, the president, and party leaders often find themselves at odds. Raise or reduce spending on military equipment? Expand or trim allocations to the Department of Education, or Justice, or Labor? Increase or decrease personnel stationed on military bases around the globe? Of course, given that discretionary spending amounts to just 30 percent of the overall budget, even significant cuts to particular programs or agencies wouldn't substantially reduce the deficit or debt.

The remainder of government spending—less than 10 percent—goes to pay the interest on the national debt. Just like citizens must pay interest when they borrow money for a home mortgage or to attend college, the government must pay interest when it borrows money to fund its spending. In 2022, the budget set aside $305 billion for interest payments.

Where the Federal Government Gets Its Money

The government clearly spends a lot of money to keep the country up and running. And it gets most of it by taxing citizens. The Sixteenth Amendment to the Constitution, ratified in 1913, gives the federal government the power to "collect taxes on incomes, from whatever source derived." So Congress and the president have created a detailed set of rules for collecting money from citizens.

The rules—compiled into a 2,600-page federal "tax code"—are complicated, but we can break the major streams of government revenue into four categories (see Table 2).[9] The two largest sources of revenue are individual income taxes and payroll taxes. Income taxes are pretty straightforward. If you earn money and clear a certain threshold of income (a little more than $10,000 in 2022), the government will tax it. Payroll taxes come out of your paycheck, too, but they're deductions that go directly toward supporting specific government programs, such

TABLE 2. Federal Government Revenue, 2022

	Revenue Generated	Percentage of Total Revenue
Individual Income Taxes (Taxes on wages, dividends, and interest)	$2 trillion	50
Payroll Taxes (Taxes paid by employers and employees to support Social Security and Medicare)	$1.3 trillion	33
Corporate Income Taxes (Taxes on income made by corporations)	$266 billion	7
Other Taxes (Includes customs duties, tariffs, and estate and gift taxes)	$434 billion	11
TOTAL	**$4 trillion**	**100**

Source: Office of Management and Budget, "Budget of the U.S. Government: Fiscal Year 2022."

as Medicare and Social Security. Income and payroll taxes account for more than 80 percent of the revenue the government takes in.

The next major source of revenue comes from corporations. The government can tax businesses' profits just like it taxes individuals' incomes. Businesses typically pay a lower tax rate than many citizens do, though. So revenue from corporate taxes is only about an eighth of what the government collects from individuals.

Finally, the government relies on a number of other miscellaneous taxes to complete its revenue stream. In 2022, this category totaled $434 billion. Nearly two-thirds of it came from tariffs and customs placed on goods imported from foreign countries and from taxes placed on specific products like alcohol, gas, and cigarettes. Estate and gift taxes—which apply to wealthy people's assets upon their death—accounted for about $21 billion.

How the Federal Government Finances Its Debt

Okay, we spend a lot to run the government, and we raise a lot to pay for it. But if you compare the bottom lines in Tables 1 and 2, you'll see a hefty mismatch. In 2022, the federal government spent about $1.7 trillion more than it took in. To cover the shortfall, the U.S. government borrows money. And every year, as the debt continues to rise, the federal government borrows more and more money. Managing the debt and arranging to finance it falls to the Bureau of Fiscal Service, an agency in the Treasury Department. If we stick with 2022, then the U.S. government owed investors and lenders a little more than $30 trillion.

Who has trillions of dollars to fund this debt? There are four main sources (see Figure 2).[10] U.S. and foreign investors hold almost 60 percent of the national debt. They purchase U.S. treasury notes and receive interest on the money they invest. The interest rates are pretty low—just about 2.5 percent—so this isn't a "get rich quick" scheme. Holding a stake in the debt is considered a very safe investment. China and Japan are the two largest foreign investors. Each nation holds about $1 trillion, or 5 percent of the total national debt.[11]

The next biggest financer of the debt is the federal government. It might seem strange, but yes, the government borrows money from itself. Certain government programs, like Social Security, bring in more money than they need to disburse in any given year. All workers, for example, pay into Social Security, but only retirees draw from it on a monthly basis. So the government borrows from these programs to cover the yearly

How can the U.S. government be $32 trillion ... whoops ... $33 trillion in debt?

FIGURE 2. Who Holds the Nation's Debt?

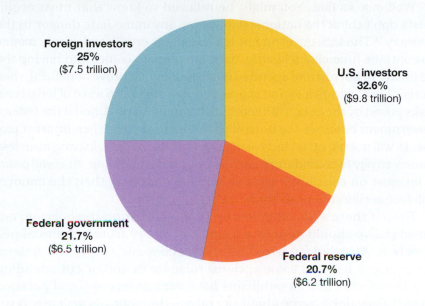

Foreign investors
25%
($7.5 trillion)

U.S. investors
32.6%
($9.8 trillion)

Federal government
21.7%
($6.5 trillion)

Federal reserve
20.7%
($6.2 trillion)

Note: Categories in the chart are based on estimates of who held the debt when it hit $30 trillion in 2021.
Source: "Debt to the Penny," Fiscal Data.

deficit. Currently, the government owes itself almost $3 trillion from Social Security alone.

The smallest of the four lending sources is the **Federal Reserve**. Typically referred to as the Fed, this is the central bank of the U.S. government. Congress created it to manage **monetary policy**—policies that promote economic growth by focusing on the money supply. In particular, the Fed focuses on inflation (an increase in prices) and interest rates (the amount lenders charge for borrowing money). The institution basically works to stabilize the financial system. Owing money to the Fed, however, is a relatively new phenomenon. It holds more than 20 percent of the national debt, but only because it absorbed debt from U.S. banks in the aftermath of the 2008 financial crisis.[12]

Should You Be Worried about the Debt?

Understanding the ins and outs of deficit spending and financing the national debt is a complex endeavor. But a couple things are clear: the federal government spends more than it takes in, and a steady stream of investors and lenders is willing to continue to finance the debt. On its face, the size and accumulation of debt seem problematic. We must be on the brink of economic collapse, right? It's probably time to stockpile food and bottled water and await the destruction of the economy.

Well, not so fast. You might be relieved to know that most economists don't think the national debt poses any immediate danger to the country.[13] The U.S. government has excellent credit and ample means to continue financing a healthy debt for years to come. And having the flexibility to borrow and spend so much money can prove beneficial when a crisis like Covid-19 hits. But the same economists also warn of long-term risks posed by the debt. Ultimately, debts must be paid, and if the federal government continues to borrow at the current pace, then interest payments will gobble up an increasing share of the budget, leaving even less money to pay for mandatory and discretionary spending. At some point, if interest on the debt outpaces economic growth, then the country will face serious financial hardship.[14]

Even if there's no imminent economic threat on the horizon, our fiscal policy should generate a sense of worry from a political perspective. After all, to avoid a future economic crisis, the federal government has two basic options: raise taxes and/or cut spending. But Democrats and Republicans have very different fiscal perspectives.[15] They don't agree about tax rates—Republicans ardently favor lower tax rates on individuals and corporations; Democrats generally believe that corporations and wealthy Americans should pay more in taxes to fund government programs. And they don't agree about spending—whereas Democrats advocate for more spending on health care, social programs, the environment, education, and assistance to the poor, Republicans generally favor cutting almost everything other than defense.[16]

These differences are difficult to overcome, which makes meaningful change to U.S. fiscal policy unlikely. Indeed, yearly partisan battles over the budget have led to 21 government shutdowns since the 1970s. The battle over the budget is sometimes so intense that the parties choose to shut down parts of the government rather than find a compromise. Although the Departments of Defense and Homeland Security always remain open to maintain public safety, government shutdowns can slow air travel, close national parks, and halt site inspections at food, hazardous waste, and chemical plants. They can also result in substantial delays in processing applications for government services—from passports to food stamps to clinical trials for medical research.[17]

And the national debt poses problems not only for fiscal policy. Until Democrats and Republicans can figure out a long-term solution, almost every other domestic policy debate is on hold. Democrats advocate for new investments in college education, health care, and childcare. But

How can the U.S. government be $32 trillion . . . whoops . . . $33 trillion in debt?

with such a large yearly deficit and no viable plan to balance the budget, there's no money to enact these new initiatives. Republicans advocate for a series of individual and corporate tax cuts they believe will spur economic growth. But Democrats fight these tax proposals, viewing them as giveaways to the rich that deplete financial resources for social programs. The mounting national debt—it's literally grown by about $120 million in just the time it took you to read this segment—and stalemate over what to do about it cast a shadow over many other policy debates.

DID YOU GET IT?

How can the U.S. government be $32 trillion . . . whoops . . . $33 trillion in debt?

Short Answer:

- It's simple. We spend substantially more than we take in every year. Government spending, especially on entitlement programs, dramatically outpaces tax revenue.
- The debt keeps increasing because the federal government is able to borrow money whenever it needs to increase spending.
- Although the debt does not pose immediate danger to the nation's economic viability, without some reform, long-term damage to the U.S. economy will likely ensue.

Quantitative Literacy

Make predictions: Understanding the federal budget and assessing whether the national debt poses a major problem requires reading a variety of tables and figures and making projections. Try your hand at this by using the data presented in this segment.

---

1. Take a look at the trend line in Figure 1. Assuming recent trends continue, what is a reasonable estimate of the national debt in 2030?

    a. $25 trillion

    b. $30 trillion

    c. $65 trillion

    d. $90 trillion

2. Based on an analysis of Tables 1 and 2, which action would make the biggest dent in the national deficit?

    a. 10 percent increase in corporate tax revenue

    b. 15 percent increase in individual tax revenue

    c. 20 percent cut in all discretionary spending

    d. 5 percent cut in all mandatory spending

3. Based on the data presented in Figure 2, which of the following would be the biggest threat to the United States' ability to borrow money in the future?

    a. The Federal Reserve refusing to bail out banks in the future

    b. A 50 percent reduction in foreign investment

    c. An increase in the amount of U.S. investment

    d. A one-year freeze in the government lending itself money

FIGURE IT OUT

At first glance, the actual federal budget might look like a maze of numbers. But we hope this segment has equipped you with tools to make sense of it. Spend some time with the table on the next page, which summarizes revenues and spending (outlays) for the 2022 federal budget. The table includes two years prior to the 2022 budget year as well as projections for two years after. Based on the table, answer these questions:

*   How does discretionary spending change after 2022?

*   Compare Medicare spending and Medicare payroll taxes in 2022. What conclusion can you draw from these two figures about the program's financial health heading into the future?

*   Does this table worry you about the national debt? You should answer this question in a couple of sentences, and be sure to refer to specific statistics.

Summary Table S-3 of the 2022 Fiscal Year Federal Budget (in billions of dollars)

	2020	2021	2022	2023	2024
Outlays:					
Discretionary programs:					
Defense	714	735	754	756	778
Non-defense	913	960	913	874	842
Subtotal	1,627	1,696	1,667	1,630	1,621
Mandatory programs:					
Social Security	1,090	1,135	1,196	1,261	1,333
Medicare	769	709	767	842	948
Medicaid	458	521	518	529	563
Other	2,260	2,886	1,255	870	795
Subtotal	4,578	5,251	3,735	3,503	3,533
Net interest	345	303	305	319	365
Total outlays	6,550	7,249	5,707	5,453	5,519
Receipts:					
Individual income taxes	1,609	1,704	2,005	2,174	2,210
Corporation income taxes	212	268	266	367	412
Social insurance and retirement receipts:					
Social Security payroll taxes	965	944	1,032	1,068	1,113
Medicare payroll taxes	292	287	314	326	341
Unemployment insurance	43	55	59	61	60
Other retirement	10	10	11	12	12
Excise taxes	87	74	82	85	90
Estate and gift taxes	18	18	21	22	24
Customs duties	69	85	57	45	45
Deposits of earnings, Federal Reserve System	82	97	102	103	99
Other miscellaneous receipts	36	37	39	40	44
Total receipts	3,421	3,580	3,988	4,304	4,451
Deficit	**3,129**	**3,670**	**1,719**	**1,148**	**1,068**
Net interest	345	303	305	319	365
Primary deficit	2,784	3,367	1,414	829	703
On-budget deficit	3,142	3,597	1,670	1,074	969
Off-budget deficit/surplus (–)	-13	73	48	74	99

Source: "Table S-3. Baseline by Category," Budget of the U.S. Government: Fiscal Year 2022.

Want to Know More?

Do you want to play a game about the national debt? The Committee for a Responsible Federal Budget — a nonpartisan group concerned about the long-term ramifications of U.S. fiscal policy — has a created The Debt Fixer. You can go online and play around with all of the numbers to see if you can get the deficit and debt under control. Increase taxes, cut Social Security spending, adjust defense spending, go nuts. Check it out: http://www.crfb.org/debtfixer/. Or try The Fiscal Ship, another version of a budget game put out by the Brookings Institution: https://fiscalship.org/.

How can the U.S. government be $32 trillion . . . whoops . . . $33 trillion in debt?

44.
Are the rich too rich?

#IncomeInequality

For a high school student in Philadelphia, Pennsylvania, attending the $40,000-a-year private William Penn Charter School is a good bet — nearly every graduate gets into a four-year college. The prospects for students across town at the public South Philadelphia High School are not so bright — only 21 percent are rated college ready.[1]

The average house in Beverly Hills, California, costs more than $6.5 million. Less than a mile outside the famous 90210 zip code, homeless people live in tents and cardboard boxes under highway overpasses.[2]

New York City boasts thousands of restaurants where diners pay an average of $50 for a meal and as much as $300 or more for a fine dining experience. One in five children who live in the city regularly relies on food pantries and soup kitchens for breakfast, lunch, and dinner.[3]

A two-bedroom condo in a newly renovated building in downtown Charlottesville, Virginia, runs in the neighborhood of $1.8 million. The view from the balcony of that condo is a low-income housing project where rent is based on earnings. Some tenants pay as little as $25 a month for their apartments.[4]

Every year — when there's not a global pandemic — roughly 12 percent of Americans head off to Mexico for a vacation, 4 percent cross the Atlantic for a European adventure, and many more travel domestically. The average trip costs $2,037 — an amount far out of reach for the nearly half of Americans who say they can't afford even a night or two away.[5]

The median home price in the United States is $428,700. But wealthy Americans often live in mansions nestled in exclusive neighborhoods — like those pictured here — where they pay tens of millions of dollars for their homes.

We could go on and on. The United States is a land of economic extremes. The **market-based economy** — a system in which supply and demand direct the production and sale of goods and services — produces a wide array of outcomes. The mega-rich can afford palatial homes, fancy schools, expensive meals, and luxury travel, while almost 40 million Americans live in poverty.[6] An economic system so rife with **income inequality** — when a small proportion of the population holds a disproportionately large share of wealth and income — strikes many people as deeply unfair. The racial disparities add an additional layer of concern.

Sounding the alarm bell over the disparities between the rich and the poor has long been a rallying cry of the Democratic Party. Senator Bernie Sanders, a two-time Democratic presidential candidate, is known for proudly carrying the mantle. Dating back to his time as mayor of Burlington, Vermont, in the 1980s, Sanders rarely gives a speech that doesn't include a call to action: "Let us wage a moral and political war against the billionaires and corporate leaders, on Wall Street and elsewhere, whose policies and greed are destroying the middle class of America."[7] During his 2020 campaign, President Joe Biden lamented to a group of wealthy campaign contributors that "when we have income inequality as large as we have in the United States today, it brews and ferments political discord and basic revolution."[8]

But it's not only Democrats who worry about income inequality. Some Republicans have come on board, too. Senator Rand Paul criticized the Obama administration for policies that "allowed the poor to get poorer and the rich to get richer."[9] Former Florida governor and presidential candidate Jeb Bush characterized the Obama years as "pretty good ones for top earners . . . [but] a lost decade for the rest of America."[10]

Are these characterizations accurate? Does the economic system in the United States work really well for the wealthy and not so well for everyone else? Answers to these questions are a matter of perspective, but this segment documents the income and wealth gaps between rich people and poor people. It also introduces you to five prominent policy proposals to address income inequality. You'll see that although there's no shortage of ideas, reform often hinges on changing the tax code or revamping government spending priorities, neither of which is easy to do.

How Rich Are the Rich? A Portrait of Income Inequality in the United States

Extreme wealth and abject poverty are not new to American society. The du Ponts, who made their fortune by manufacturing gunpowder and explosives, were billionaires in the 1800s. So were the Mellons (banking), the Rockefellers (oil), the Strausses (blue jeans), and the Busches (beer).[11] At the same time, millions of Americans worked long hours, lived in shabby housing, and struggled to get by.[12] But even though dramatic economic disparities have always been around, they've been getting worse. Income inequality in 2020 reached its highest point in nearly a century.[13]

The most basic way to illustrate the inequality is to consider how income is distributed across the population. You may have heard of the "top 1 percent"—these are people with the highest incomes. In 2021, a person needed to earn $545,978 to make it into this group. The closer you are to the top 1 percent, the more well-off you are. If your income is in the middle of the distribution, you're probably managing to get by. If it's toward the bottom, then you're probably struggling financially. In the 1970s, the bottom half of all income earners (the "bottom 50 percent") took in about 20 percent of all the income earned in the country. That was more than twice the overall income earned by the top 1 percent (see Figure 1).[14] Startling evidence of income inequality, but nothing compared to today. By 2015, the top 1 percent took in more than 20 percent of all income. The bottom 50 percent? Just 13 percent.

Income inequality is even easier to see when we convert this income distribution into real dollars. The median income in the United States—meaning that half of Americans earn more and half earn less—is approximately $44,225 per year. But many people don't cluster around the median. Rather, almost 13 percent of Americans live at or below the poverty level. In 2022, that equated to an individual yearly income of $13,590 or less. Roughly 6 percent live in "deep poverty," with incomes less than half the poverty level. At the other end of the spectrum, about

FIGURE 1. Share of Total Income Held by the Bottom 50 Percent and Top 1 Percent of Income Earners

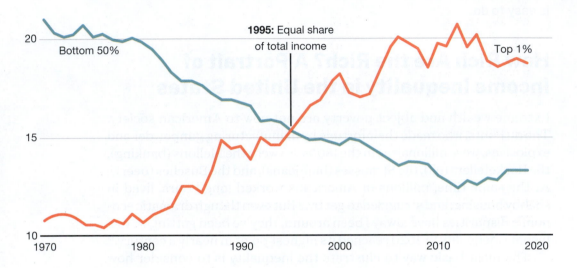

25%

20

15

10

1970   1980   1990   2000   2010   2020

Bottom 50%

1995: Equal share of total income

Top 1%

Source: "Income Inequality, USA, 1913–2020," World Income Inequality Database.

17 percent of working Americans have incomes of at least six figures (see Table 1).[15]

Tracking the size of the "middle class" serves as one more way to gauge income inequality. Typically, you're in the middle class if your household income falls somewhere between 50 percent below and 50 percent above the nation's median household income. In 2022, that was about $74,099 for a family of four. So a household would be categorized as middle class if its wage earners took in between $37,050 and $111,149 that year. Since 1970, the middle class has been steadily shrinking (see Figure 2)—and not because middle-income earners are all moving into upper-income brackets; many are losing ground and moving into lower-income brackets.[16]

Income only tells part of the story, though. People who earn lots of money every year accumulate wealth by buying property, stocks, and bonds that they assume will increase in value or produce income. So there's also a **wealth gap**—an unequal distribution of assets across the population. Indeed, the middle 60 percent of households now hold a

TABLE 1. How Many People Earn a Lot of Money?

Income	Number of People	Percentage of Workforce
$50,000 or more	78,907,083	42.5%
$100,000 or more	28,756,346	16.5
$250,000 or more	4,122,785	2.4
$500,000 or more	913,794	0.5
$1,000,000 or more	330,689	0.2

Note: The entries are based on 2021 data, when the median income was $44,225.

Source: "Income Percentile Calculator for the United States in 2021," DQYDJ.

FIGURE 2. Percentage of Middle-Class American Households, 1970–2020

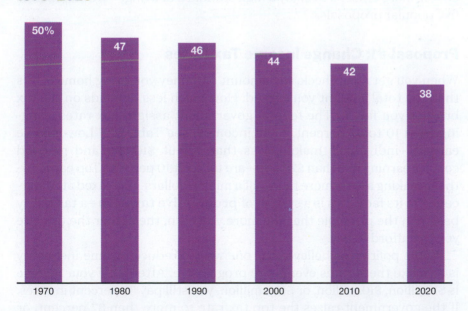

Notes: Bars indicate the percentage of households with annual incomes within 50 percent of the median.

Source: United States Census, "CPS Income Tables, 2020."

smaller share of wealth than the top 1 percent. The wealthiest 50 Americans are worth the same as the poorest 50 percent (that's 165 million people). The six richest Americans—including Tesla founder Elon Musk and Amazon's Jeff Bezos—are each worth more than $100 billion. The combined wealth of these six people exceeds the combined economies of 13 U.S. states.[17]

Policy Proposals to Address Income Inequality

Most contemporary politicians and economists regard income inequality as a problem that requires a policy solution. After all, high income disparities are linked to all sorts of problems—from physical and mental health issues, to higher crime rates, to disengagement from politics, to educational and housing inequities.[18] In addition, a large middle class is critical for a nation's economic success; only when many citizens have money to support themselves and spend in the marketplace can the economy thrive.[19] That's why political leaders, at least rhetorically, have always prioritized developing policies to strengthen the economy and enable more citizens to enjoy a high standard of living.[20] We summarize five popular proposals.

Proposal #1: Change Income Tax Rates

When you get a paycheck, the amount of money you bring home is less than the total amount you earned. How much less depends on the tax bracket you fall in. The federal government assigns tax rates, ranging from 10 to 37 percent, to all incomes (see Table 2).[21] Low-income earners—individuals making less than about $10,000 and married couples earning less than $20,000—are taxed at 10 percent. Top earners—those making a little more than half a million dollars—are taxed at 37 percent. On its face, this is a system of **progressive taxation**—a tax policy based on the principle that the more you earn, the higher the tax rate you can afford to pay.

Some politicians believe that one way to reduce income inequality is to make these rates even more progressive. After all, if your income is $1 million, $10 million, or $100 million, you still pay 37 percent in taxes. If the government raises the top tax rate to more than 37 percent, or creates additional income brackets with higher rates, then the top income earners would pay more in taxes. In a similar vein, a proposal known as the millionaire surtax would impose higher taxes on any income after the first $1 million.

TABLE 2. Federal Income Tax Brackets, 2022

Individuals Filing Singly		Married Couples Filing Jointly	
Taxable Income	**Tax Rate**	**Taxable Income**	**Tax Rate**
Less than $10,275	10%	Less than $20,550	10%
$10,275–$41,775	12	$20,551–$83,550	12
$41,776–$89,075	22	$83,551–$178,150	22
$89,076–$170,050	24	$178,151–$340,100	24
$170,051–$215,950	32	$340,101–$431,900	32
$215,951–$539,900	35	$431,901–$647,850	35
More than $539,900	37	More than $647,850	37

Source: "2022 Tax Brackets," Tax Foundation.

Proposal #2: Raise Taxes on Wealth and Capital Gains

Warren Buffett, the 10th richest person in America, famously asserted in 2007 that he pays taxes at a lower rate than his longtime assistant Debbie Bosanek.[22] How's that possible? It's because Buffett—like most very wealthy people—doesn't make the majority of his money from a salary. Instead, one thing he does is sell assets like stocks, companies, and real estate. Any profits made from selling assets are called capital gains. People have to pay taxes on these profits. But the rate for the **capital gains tax**—the tax on gains beyond $459,750 on any asset owned for more than a year—is set at 20 percent (it's lower for smaller gains). So if Buffett makes $2 million on the sale of stock, he has to pay 20 percent in taxes. Bosanek, meanwhile, might earn a salary of $200,000 per year. (High for an executive assistant for sure, but she does work for a billionaire!) She'll have to pay 32 percent in taxes (see Table 2).[23] Income from salary, in other words, is often taxed at a higher rate than income from selling assets. Because of this aspect of the tax code, analysts sometimes argue that the United States actually has a system of **regressive taxation**, whereby wealthy people pay taxes at a lower rate than lower-income earners do.[24]

To achieve more tax fairness, some politicians and economists support raising the capital gains tax rate, making it similar to the income tax rate. Under this plan, Buffett would pay taxes at the highest rate on the income tax scale (37 percent), similar to the top salary earners at his company. Others advocate for a "wealth tax"—the details vary, but most proposals would require people with tens of millions in assets to pay a 2 or 3 percent tax on them every year.

Proposal #3: Reduce Taxes on High-Income Earners and Corporations

You didn't read that heading wrong. Not all policy proposals designed to create a fairer tax system focus on raising taxes on wealthy Americans. Advocates of **supply-side economics** theorize that lower taxes for everyone, especially the wealthy and corporations, will reduce income inequality. The basic logic is that if you reduce the tax rates on wealthy people, they'll use the money they saved to invest in their businesses. That investment will, in turn, grow their businesses and create more high-paying jobs. And with better jobs, citizens will spend more money on goods and services, which will further strengthen the economy.

Republican presidents have pursued this policy for decades. In the 1980s, Ronald Reagan led the way by advocating for and signing into law two tax bills that dramatically lowered the top income tax rate—from 70 percent down to 28 percent. Twenty years later, after the top rate had been pushed back up, George W. Bush reduced it from nearly 40 percent to 35 percent.[25] And Donald Trump signed a tax law in 2017 that cut taxes on corporate profits substantially, from 35 to 21 percent. Advocates of this approach want to cut the tax rate even further for corporations and top income earners.

Proposal #4: Invest in Improving People's Job Skills

Many advocates of raising taxes on corporations and top income earners are interested in more than simply reducing their wealth and income. They want to generate additional tax revenue to support programs to help low- and middle-income workers make more money and strengthen their financial prospects. The idea is that a focus on **public investments**—money the government spends on things like education, job training, and childcare—can help build a more skilled and talented workforce who can earn a good living.

Proposals for public investment in workforce development vary widely, but many recent plans focus on education and job training. Free community college, for example, would enable people who cannot otherwise afford higher education to receive free access to two additional years of training that might open the door to better jobs with higher pay.[26]

Federal government investment in early childhood education programs might also help, as programs like these at the state level have been shown to increase economic mobility later in life.[27] Advocates also argue that providing job training for public housing residents and public assistance recipients can improve their employment prospects, especially when the training equips people with skills for jobs in the technology sector.[28]

Proposal #5: Increase the Minimum Wage

Almost 60 percent of all workers in the United States are paid on an hourly basis. But employers don't have total freedom in deciding how much to pay their employees. The federal government establishes a national **minimum wage**—the lowest hourly rate any employer may legally pay. Congress passed the first federal minimum wage in 1938—it was just 25 cents an hour. Since then, Congress has raised it 22 times, most recently in 2009 to $7.25 per hour.[29] But 29 states and the District of Columbia have passed minimum wage laws that exceed the federal requirement. In California, for example, workers can't be paid less than $15 per hour. Still, 44 percent of people in the U.S. workforce are classified as "low-wage workers" with a median income of $11.11 per hour.[30] That means that more than 26 million Americans are making about 11 bucks an hour or less.

One proposal to propel more people into the middle class is to pass a law that forces employers to pay higher wages. How much higher is a matter of debate, but many economists and politicians now focus on the concept of a **living wage**—the level of income necessary to provide for a decent standard of living (housing, food, health care, etc.). In some states, the gap between the minimum wage and a living wage is quite dramatic (see Table 3).[31]

In Hawaii, for instance, the minimum wage is only a little more than half of what's required for a single adult to achieve a living wage. For a family of four with two working adults, the minimum wage would need to more than double to move into living wage territory. But even in the states with the lowest gaps, the minimum wage doesn't meet the threshold of a living wage. A common proposal is to raise the national minimum wage to $15 per hour, which would be equal to or more than the living wage for a single adult in 35 states.[32]

Which Policies Will be Adopted?

Short answer: Probably none. Why? Elected officials may agree that income inequality is a problem, but they disagree on the solution. Democratic presidents Bill Clinton and Barack Obama, for example, presided over tax increases—albeit small ones—on the wealthiest Americans. Taxes

TABLE 3. The Gap between the Minimum Wage and a Living Wage

	Minimum Wage	Living Wage (Single adult)	Difference	Living Wage (Each adult in family of four)	Difference
Highest Gap					
Hawaii	$10.10	$19.43	−$9.33	$25.42	−$15.32
Georgia	7.25	15.36	−8.11	19.97	−12.72
North Carolina	7.25	14.72	−7.47	20.90	−13.65
South Carolina	7.25	14.58	−7.33	19.76	−12.51
Utah	7.25	14.52	−7.27	20.31	−13.06
Lowest Gap					
Rhode Island	11.50	14.47	−2.97	21.21	−9.71
Arizona	12.15	14.94	−2.79	19.51	−7.36
Maine	12.15	14.92	−2.77	21.14	−8.99
Washington	13.69	16.34	−2.65	21.67	−7.98
Arkansas	11.00	13.29	−2.29	19.35	−8.35

Note: Information compiled by using MIT's Living Wage website and calculator.

Source: "Living Wage Calculator," MIT.

on the wealthy went down under Republican presidents George W. Bush and Donald Trump. The Democratic House of Representatives passed a bill increasing the minimum wage to $15 per hour in 2019. The Republican Senate never took it up. The parties can't agree when it comes to public investment strategies either. Democrats favor heavy investments in education—both early and post-secondary. Republicans are more inclined to support workforce training programs through partnerships with private companies. Given today's heightened partisanship and increased polarization, any sort of compromise seems unlikely. As a result, income inequality will probably continue to grow.

DID YOU GET IT?

Are the rich too rich?

Short Answer:

- Income inequality is at its highest level in almost 100 years, with more mega-rich citizens than ever before.

- As the top 1 percent of income earners thrive, the middle class is shrinking.

- Although both political parties agree that income equality must be addressed, they disagree on how to do it, making reform difficult.

DEVELOPING YOUR SKILLS

Persuasive Argumentation

Evaluate evidence: Any proposal to reduce income inequality requires making an argument about how different economic policies would best accomplish your goal. Answer these questions about the evidence you'd need to back up particular proposals.

1. Which piece of data is the strongest evidence that income inequality is associated with other inequalities in American society?
   a. The shrinking proportion of citizens categorized as middle class
   b. The record number of billionaires
   c. Lower high school graduation rates for the children of low-wage earners
   d. The dramatic increase in income held by the top 1 percent since 1995

2. Which would advocates of supply-side economics point to as evidence that their approach helps the economy?
   a. An uptick in weekly wages following a corporate tax cut
   b. A slight decline in the size of the middle class following a corporate tax cut
   c. An uptick in weekly wages following an increase in the capital gains tax rate
   d. A slight decline in the size of the middle class following an increase in the capital gains tax rate

3. Based on Table 3, what is the best evidence that a higher minimum wage could propel more citizens into the middle class and move more people toward a living wage?

   a. The five states with the smallest gap between the minimum wage and the living wage rely on the federal minimum wage of $7.25 per hour.

   b. Four of the five states with the highest gap between the minimum wage and the living wage still rely on the federal minimum wage of $7.25 per hour.

   c. Hawaii has a relatively high minimum wage but also a large gap with the living wage.

   d. The state with the highest minimum wage listed has the lowest gap between the minimum wage and the living wage.

FIGURE IT OUT

Determining the best proposal to reduce income inequality requires assembling evidence to show that it works. Defeating a policy proposal that is ineffective also requires evidence — to show that it doesn't work. Assemble these types of evidence for two proposals presented in this segment. More specifically:

- Select the proposal you think would work best to reduce income inequality. Identify two specific pieces of evidence you think would enable you to make the case that the policy reduces income inequality. You don't need to track down actual evidence or data. You just need to describe the kind of evidence you'd need to make your argument.

- Now select a proposal you think wouldn't do much to reduce income inequality. To show that you're right, identify two specific pieces of evidence you'd need.

Want to Know More?

Many books spell out the alarming problems associated with growing income inequality in the United States. Two of the most well-known are Joseph Stiglitz's *The Price of Inequality* and Thomas Piketty's *Capital in the Twenty-First Century*. If movies are more your thing, then *Trading Places* and *Down and Out in Beverly Hills* are two amusing, but undoubtedly politically incorrect, films about income inequality. And for a more recent comedic take on income inequality, you can stream all six seasons of *Schitt's Creek*, where a multimillionaire family finds itself destitute and living in a small-town motel.

45.
Why was your T-shirt made in China?

#TradePolicy

If you ever want to plan an around-the-world trip, the labels on your clothes might make for an interesting travel itinerary. Those socks you put on this morning? They may have come from Bangladesh. Your pants? They might be from Indonesia. Your designer T-shirt probably came from China. Your shoes from India. And that jacket you grabbed on your way out the door? It could have made its way to your closet all the way from Vietnam. Most famous American designers — from Levi's to Nike to Tommy Hilfiger — don't make their products in the United States. Most popular clothing stores — Vans, Gap, Forever 21, Urban Outfitters — don't either. It turns out that the United States imports roughly $90 billion worth of apparel every year.

Have you ever wondered why so many of your clothes come from so far away? Wouldn't it make more sense for designers and clothing companies to produce the items right here in the United States? Nope. It's dramatically cheaper to hire textile workers in other countries (see Figure 1).[1] U.S. garment workers earn nearly 7 times what their Chinese counterparts do. They make 9.5 times what they would for doing the same job in a factory in Bangladesh. With wage disparities like these, it's no wonder that the booming American textile industry of the 1960s is almost completely gone. The simple answer to this segment's question, then? Your T-shirt was made in

549

Workers in a textile factory in Dongguan, China, produce shirts that will be sold under the Hugo Boss label in the United States.

China because it's much cheaper to manufacture it there than in the United States.

But the story is more complicated than that. Your closet is actually a microcosm of **globalization** — the process of growing economic interdependence among countries. Managing the United States' role in this system falls to the federal government. More specifically, Congress and the president develop and manage U.S. **trade policy** — the standards, goals, rules, and regulations that pertain to commerce with foreign countries. The federal government, all in the name of improving our economic standing and stability, decides when to sign trade agreements and with whom, when to reject trade agreements and with whom, and what complex trade negotiations look like.

This segment provides a broad overview of the trade landscape and then introduces you to three approaches to trade policy. You'll come to understand that decisions about which countries to trade with and the rules governing those relationships have a profound impact on American workers' economic prosperity and American consumers' choices. You'll also see that although trade policy is contentious and often divides political leaders, it's one of the few major policy areas not marked by intense partisanship.

FIGURE 1. Monthly Minimum Wage for Garment Workers

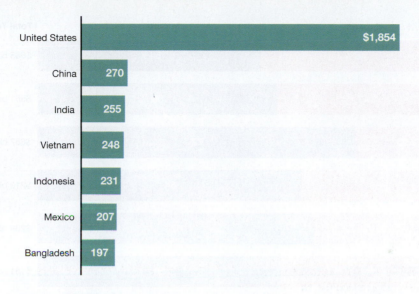

United States	$1,854
China	270
India	255
Vietnam	248
Indonesia	231
Mexico	207
Bangladesh	197

Note: Bars indicate the monthly minimum wage for garment workers in the United States and in the nations from which we import most of our apparel. Together, these six countries manufacture 70 percent of clothing sold in the United States.

Source: Sheng Lu, "Wage Level for Garment Workers in the World," University of Delaware.

A Quick Snapshot of Trade and the Global Economy

Nations have been engaged in commerce with one another from the moment they devised ways to transport goods. Indeed, historians trace the first trade between foreign empires to an exchange of silk for gold more than 5,000 years ago.[2] But the modern era of international trade began in earnest after World War II. In an effort to boost the global economy, 23 nations signed the General Agreement on Tariffs and Trade (GATT) in 1947.[3] The agreement reduced regulations on trade so that all member nations could have freer, more equitable economic relationships.

As communications technology and international shipping capabilities improved, international commerce exploded. By 1994, 125 nations had signed on to GATT. Global trade among them totaled $8.1 trillion in goods and services—from consumer products (cars, clothing, household items) to electronics (phones, computers, office machines) to industrial supplies (oil and chemicals).[4] In 2021, 164 nations engaged in more than $25 trillion in global commerce.[5]

FIGURE 2. Top Seven U.S. Trade Partners

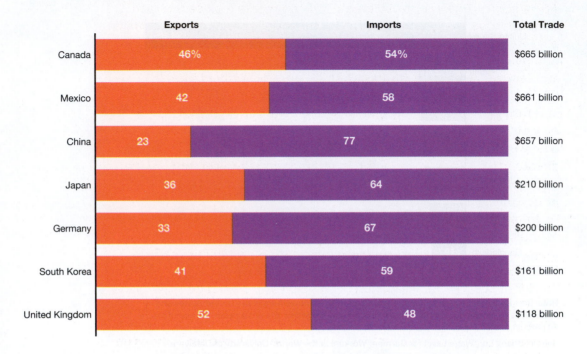

	Exports	Imports	Total Trade
Canada	46%	54%	$665 billion
Mexico	42	58	$661 billion
China	23	77	$657 billion
Japan	36	64	$210 billion
Germany	33	67	$200 billion
South Korea	41	59	$161 billion
United Kingdom	52	48	$118 billion

Note: Bars represent the percentage of exports and imports in the total trade relationship between the United States and its top trade partners in 2021.

Source: U.S. Bureau of the Census, "Top Trading Partners, 2021."

The exponential growth in international commerce has made trade policy a top issue in contemporary politics. The United States alone trades more than $5 trillion in goods every year with 75 foreign countries (Canada, Mexico, and China are the top three—see Figure 2).[6] That's more than 3 times what we traded in the early 1990s. Global trade now accounts for more than one-quarter of all economic activity in the United States.[7]

Although most political leaders and policy makers don't dispute the importance of global trade for economic growth, they don't all agree about how best to manage trade relationships with other countries. Some favor a wide-open system of trade, with unfettered access to goods and services worldwide. Others support heavily regulated trade. And still others have reservations about trade altogether; if they had their way, we'd export and import far fewer goods. In practice, most trade agreements don't comport neatly with any one of these perspectives— they're the product of complex negotiations among countries.

The Free-Trade Perspective

Advocates of **free trade**—international commerce with as few regulations as possible—sit on one end of the trade policy spectrum. In theory, pure free trade means no restrictions or barriers on imports or exports. Companies and corporations are essentially allowed to buy and sell goods and services around the world with little or no government interference. With minimal **tariffs**—taxes placed on imports and exports—American and foreign markets are easier to access. You can see how this might play out by considering the auto industry. In a free-trade world, countries would sell their cars to the highest bidder and let the marketplace dictate prices. With little attention to labor standards or environmental regulations, the countries that manufacture products at the lowest price would succeed.

In practice, though, no trade relationship is entirely "free." When countries negotiate free-trade agreements, they still haggle over tariffs, worker wage and safety regulations, and rules for shipping goods. The United States' largest trade agreement is a case in point. Entered into by President Bill Clinton in 1995, the North American Free Trade Agreement (NAFTA) is a complex, 1,700-page agreement among the United States, Canada, and Mexico. A key feature is the reduction of tariffs on goods traded among the three countries. NAFTA also reduced regulations on transporting goods across borders and eased rules on foreign investment.[8] President Trump renegotiated the deal (more on that shortly), but the point is that NAFTA laid out specific terms to make it easier for the three nations to buy and sell one another's products.

The United States currently participates in 14 free-trade agreements with 20 countries.[9] And most other nations around the world do, too (there are more than 400 active trade agreements). The **World Trade Organization (WTO)**, which replaced GATT in 1995, oversees the system of global free trade. Representatives from 164 member countries—accounting for 98 percent of the world's trade—work together to establish and enforce the rules of international commerce and settle disputes.[10] Expressed simply on the home page of the WTO's website, the organization's main purpose is "to ensure that trade flows as smoothly, predictably, and freely as possible."[11]

Advocates argue that because of free trade, economic circumstances have improved for hundreds of millions of people around the globe. And in wealthier countries like the United States, citizens have much more purchasing power because goods are far more affordable.[12] Conservative *Los Angeles Times* columnist Jonah Goldberg summarizes the argument well: "Free trade has been proven, time and again, as a reliable path to economic development. It pushes the public and private sectors alike

An elaborate network of ports, planes, ships, trains, and trucks facilitates the transport of goods. How else will that T-shirt of yours get to you from China? The port in Los Angeles, California, is the largest in the United States. It ships goods directly to and from Asia, Europe, Africa, South America, and the Caribbean. In 2021 the port moved 10.7 million 20-foot containers of cargo around the world

toward greater accountability and transparency. It lifts people out of poverty."[13] Democrat Robert Reich, an economics professor and President Bill Clinton's secretary of labor, similarly acknowledges that the global economy and free trade "spur economic growth, and . . . lead to lower prices on many goods."[14] Even President Barack Obama generally agrees. Before leaving office, he credited capitalism as being the "greatest driver of prosperity and opportunity the world has ever seen." To those who opposed free trade, Obama asserted, "Trade has helped our economy much more than it has hurt."[15] Indeed, prior to the pandemic in 2020 Americans bought 5 times as much clothing as they did in 1980 yet spent less of their income on clothes.[16] The story was the same for toys, household items, electronic devices, beauty products, and furniture.

The Fair-Trade Perspective

While most political leaders support free-trade principles, they push for trade agreements that emphasize **fair trade**—rules that require countries engaged in commerce to abide by similar labor and environmental standards. You may have seen the words "fair trade" on a package of your coffee or chocolate. The imprint indicates that the workers in the supply chain of the product you're about to drink or eat were treated ethically and paid adequately.[18] Starbucks, for instance, claims that 99 percent of its coffee is "ethically sourced."[18]

Proponents of fair trade aren't only concerned about preventing environmental degradation or worker exploitation. They strive to implement rules and regulations that protect American workers and make the United States competitive in the global marketplace. If we return to our example of the auto industry, you'll see how this works. Autoworkers in the United States earn, on average, $17 per hour. In Canada, they make about $18 per hour. But in Mexico, their average pay is between $5 and $7 per hour.[19] If complete free trade existed among the three nations, then the entire North American auto industry would move to Mexico. With workers there being paid just one-third of what they're paid in the United States, it would be that much cheaper to produce cars. Great news for people who want to buy a car, but a serious problem for the 10 million Americans whose jobs depend on the auto industry.

That's actually part of the reason the Trump administration renegotiated NAFTA—which is now referred to as the United States-Mexico-Canada Agreement (USMCA)—in 2018. The new agreement stipulates that at least 45 percent of the components of any vehicle manufactured in North America must be made by workers earning at least

Donald Trump pressed for trade agreements to include more stipulations that protect American jobs, including those of dairy farmers, autoworkers, and electronics producers.

$16 per hour. This requirement, at least until the pay of Mexican workers increases dramatically, protects U.S. autoworkers' jobs.[20] The Biden administration has emphasized enforcement of the wage requirement as well the agreement's worker rights and environmental protection provisions.[21]

Ensuring that trade agreements serve workers' interests, comply with domestic and international law, and don't cripple specific U.S. industries makes it difficult to hammer out the details. That's why NAFTA was originally 1,700 pages and why the USMCA amendments added another 100 pages. But fair-trade advocates argue that it's worth it. Summarized well by Senator Elizabeth Warren in a 2020 speech, trade policy should "create and defend good American jobs, raise wages and farm income, combat climate change . . . rais[e] living standards worldwide." Engaging in international trade is important, the Democratic senator explained, "but on our terms and only when it benefits American families."[22]

The Protectionist Perspective

Some policy makers are just not convinced that free or fair trade will ever provide economic advantages to the United States. They argue that global trade harms American workers and benefits some countries far more than others. Political leaders with these concerns favor **protectionism**. Protectionists want to shield domestic industries from foreign competition either by prohibiting imports altogether or by imposing severe tariffs on them. This makes foreign products more expensive because producers pass the cost of the tariff on to the consumer. Returning to our auto industry example (last time, we promise), let's say that the United States slapped huge tariffs on cars made in Mexico. That would increase the cost of Mexican-made cars and give the U.S. auto industry the upper hand. After all, U.S.-based companies wouldn't need to pay a tariff, so consumers would buy American cars. The price might be a little higher, but all the money would go to American workers and companies. Or so the argument goes.

Protectionism in its purest form is no longer a viable policy approach. Just ask all those countries that belong to the WTO and whose economies depend on their international trade relationships. Still, many nations impose tariffs, and protectionist rhetoric is on the rise. To justify their position, political leaders with protectionist leanings often cite the loss of domestic manufacturing jobs. Senator Bernie Sanders, for example, considers himself a fair-trade advocate, but his rhetoric is often consistent with protectionist principles. He frequently castigates

NAFTA and its supporters. Indeed, this was one issue that Sanders used to attack Joe Biden in the 2020 Democratic presidential primary. "Joe and I strongly disagree on trade. I helped lead the opposition [to] NAFTA . . . which cost this country over 4 million good-paying jobs," Sanders explained during one of the debates.[23] Similarly, Donald Trump regularly directed harsh words toward China, noting that since China joined the WTO in 2001, "Americans have witnessed the closure of more than 50,000 factories and the loss of tens of millions of jobs."[24] Many American workers—especially those who believe that their formerly well-paying factory jobs have been shipped overseas—embrace protectionist arguments, too.

Although Trump exaggerated the extent of job losses, it is true that as the United States has come to rely increasingly on imports, manufacturing industries have taken a significant hit. The total number of U.S. manufacturing jobs dropped from almost 20 million in 1980 to barely half that by 2020 (see Figure 3).[25] The steel industry is a case in point.

FIGURE 3. The Loss of Manufacturing Jobs and the Growth of Imports, 1970–2021

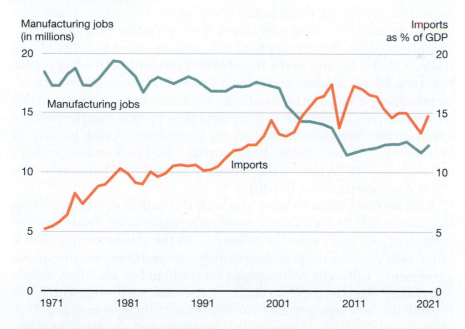

Note: Imports as a percentage of GDP are presented in current dollars.

Source: "Shares of Gross Domestic Product: Imports of Goods and Services," FRED Economic Data, St. Louis Fed, January 27, 2022; "All Employees: Manufacturing," FRED Economic Data, St. Louis Fed, July 2022.

Half as many Americans work in U.S. steel now as did in 1990. So in 2018, President Trump tried to save the industry by announcing substantial tariffs—25 percent for steel and 10 percent for aluminum. The Biden administration has maintained the aluminum tariffs, explaining that they protect American producers struggling to compete with low-priced foreign products.[26]

Supporters of protectionist policies also point to the **trade deficit**—the amount by which a country's imports exceed its exports. Flip back to Figure 2, and you'll see several trade imbalances. The United States' $657 billion relationship with China is a striking example. China sells roughly $506 billion worth of goods to U.S. consumers every year. Chinese consumers buy nowhere near that amount in return. The United States has trade deficits with six of its top trading partners. Protectionists argue that by making it more difficult for consumers and companies to buy foreign products, domestic manufacturing will thrive, trade relationships will exhibit far more balance, and the economy will grow.

Not a Partisan Divide

As you likely noticed, trade policy is one of the few major issues that doesn't break down along party lines. A conservative columnist and a Democratic cabinet secretary both acknowledge some benefits of free trade. A liberal senator and a Republican president both advocate for fair trade. Bernie Sanders and Donald Trump both espouse protectionist principles. It's also an unusual issue because when it comes to broad trade principles, there tends to be general agreement across the political spectrum that foreign trade strengthens the economy. A clear majority of citizens—roughly two-thirds—believes that.[27] And so do most members of Congress. NAFTA passed the Senate by a 73–26 vote. Support for the USMCA was even greater (89–10).

Still, we don't want to leave you with the impression that putting together a trade deal is a simple, cooperative experience. Trade involves millions of jobs and countless industries, so the stakes are high and it often takes years for the president to negotiate and Congress to approve agreements. Different philosophies on trade policy are often deeply entrenched. And the partisan divide on the issue is growing, with fewer Republicans now seeing trade as an opportunity for economic growth.[28] Many free-trade policy proposals, therefore, end up dying in stalemate. But unlike most contemporary policy debates, the gridlock is not primarily the result of typical partisan warfare.[29]

Why was your T-shirt made in China?

DID YOU GET IT?
Why was your T-shirt made in China?

Short Answer:

- In the global economy, disparities in workers' wages make it cheaper to manufacture your T-shirt and many other products thousands of miles away rather than in the United States.
- Global trade is a critical component of U.S. economic growth and stability, so the federal government must develop policies and agreements to conduct international commerce.
- Three central approaches to trade policy — free trade, fair trade, and protectionism — vary in terms of how restrictive trade should be.

DEVELOPING YOUR SKILLS

Persuasive Argumentation

Identify an argument: Many policy debates involve two types of arguments.

- *Normative arguments* are statements of principle that use value judgments to make a case for why a particular policy is good or bad. They are basically arguments for a policy based on what *should* be.
- *Empirical arguments* rely on systematic evidence — often quantitative — to make a case for or against a policy. They are basically arguments for a policy based on what actually *is*. They describe objective, verifiable facts.

These two types of arguments are often at odds, and debates frequently pit a normative argument against an empirical one. Think about how this plays out as you answer these questions about trade policy.

1. Which statement is a *normative argument* in support of protectionism?
   a. The more protectionist policies a country adopts, the higher its median wage.
   b. Countries without protectionist policies sell goods for lower prices.
   c. Countries that rely on protectionist policies are more concerned for their workers' well-being than countries that promote free trade.
   d. Countries without protectionist policies sign more free-trade agreements.

2. Which is the strongest *empirical argument* for pursuing fair-trade policies?

   a. Fair-trade policies are the only ethical way to engage in international commerce.

   b. Fair-trade policies often improve workers' wages.

   c. Fair-trade policies can result in higher prices for consumer goods in poorer countries.

   d. International organizations do not always enforce fair-trade policies.

3. Which thesis statement contains both a normative and an empirical argument in favor of free trade?

   a. Free-trade policies are an ethical way to engage in international commerce, and they improve the standard of living around the world.

   b. Free-trade policies result in lower inflation and fewer carbon emissions.

   c. Free-trade policies limit the economic growth of poorer countries and keep their workers' wages low.

   d. Free-trade policies are an ethical way to engage in international commerce and should be pursued even when they're not in a country's self-interest.

FIGURE IT OUT

The United States is considering entering into a free-trade agreement with three South American countries: Argentina, Brazil, and Ecuador. The agreement will focus on importing agricultural products, alcohol, lumber, and automobiles. What arguments can you make for and against the agreement? More specifically:

- From the perspective of a protectionist, identify two arguments — one normative and one empirical — against this potential agreement. (Each can be just one sentence.)

- Now, from the perspective of an advocate of free trade, identify two arguments — again, one normative and one empirical — for why all four participants would benefit from this agreement. (Each can be just one sentence.)

Your arguments can be based on evidence from the segment or from outside research.

Want to Know More?

There is actually a book that uses the production of T-shirts to explain how international commerce works. *The Travels of a T-Shirt in the Global Economy*, written by Pietra Rivoli, takes you from a cotton field in Texas, to a manufacturing plant in China, back to a store in the United States, to the used-clothing industry in Africa.

46.
Why doesn't everyone have health insurance?

#HealthCarePolicy

You wake up to a phone call from your friend Sarah. She's been in a mountain biking accident. "I'm waiting for X-rays, but it's bad," she tells you. "My ankle looks like it's in the wrong place." No sooner do you hang up the phone than you receive a text from Pablo, whose party you attended the previous night. Along with a photo of a bruised and swollen wrist, he writes, "You left before you had the chance to see me fall down the stairs. Thought it would get better overnight, but no such luck. I think it's broken. On my way to the ER." As you're reading the text, you get a DM from your friend Jerome. He tripped over second base at his softball game and cracked his kneecap. He's smiling in his Instagram post, but photos don't lie. It doesn't look good.

Okay, okay. We know this is a preposterous scenario. What are the odds that anyone has three friends who injure themselves and require an ER visit all on the same weekend? But stick with us for a minute, and you'll see where we're going with it.

When you talk to Sarah on Monday, she's in the best shape — at least in terms of health care. Her mother, an executive at a software company, opted for the top-of-the-line family health insurance plan the company offers. Sometimes referred to as a Cadillac plan, these insurance

The United States pays more per person in health care costs than any country in the world. But due to the convoluted health care system — composed of government and private health insurance, hospitals, doctors, and prescription drug companies — the actual costs of health care can be very difficult to decipher.

policies typically have low deductibles (the amount you have to kick in before the insurance company starts paying) and excellent benefits that cover even the most expensive treatments.[1] And that's certainly true here. Sarah's insurance covers the costs of her emergency room visit, X-rays, surgery to reset her ankle, pain medication, and as much physical therapy as she'll need when her cast comes off. The only costs she'll incur are $15 co-payments for follow-up appointments with her beloved longtime doctor, who will monitor her recovery.

You hear from Pablo and find out that he'll be okay, too. He's more stressed out than Sarah, though, because his trip down the stairs is likely to come with a big price tag. Pablo has insurance — he's on his parents' health care plan. But because they're self-employed, they buy their health coverage directly from an insurance company. Purchasing it that way is super-expensive. Pablo's family can only afford what's known as a silver plan, which means lots of out-of-pocket expenses along the way, starting with a $250 payment at the emergency room. He also has to pay about 30 percent of the costs associated with treating his broken wrist.[2] Pablo will get to see his regular doctor for follow-up care, but each visit will come with a $50 co-pay. And his insurance limits the number of physical therapy sessions it will cover, so at some point he and his parents will have to pay the full cost.

Your pal Jerome? He doesn't sound so good, and it's easy to understand why. He's among the roughly 10 percent of Americans who don't have any health insurance. His parents' joint income of about $50,000 per year means they earn too much to qualify for government-subsidized health care (more on that later) but not enough to afford health insurance for the family.[3] When Jerome arrives at the emergency room with his broken kneecap, the hospital must treat him. Under the law, ERs can't turn anyone away.[4] But he will receive a substantial bill for the visit (surgery to repair a fractured kneecap runs in the neighborhood of $20,000[5]). And that's only the beginning. After surgery, Jerome will have to pay full price for medication. He'll need to find low-cost medical clinics and doctors to help with his follow-up care. Physical therapy will be unlikely unless he can figure out a way to pay for it. Perhaps he can find an online video to learn the exercises necessary for his rehabilitation.

Your hypothetical friends' experiences epitomize the two biggest concerns about health care in the United States. First, not everyone is covered. Second, health care costs — even for many people with insurance — are very high. This is not the case in most other wealthy nations, where the government provides **universal health care** — a policy under which all citizens receive a baseline level of affordable, quality care regardless of their ability to pay for it (see Table 1).

TABLE 1. Types of Universal Health Care Systems in Wealthy Democratic Countries

Single-Payer System	Public/Private Hybrid	Private Insurance Mandate	None
Australia	Austria	Netherlands	United States
Canada	Belgium	Switzerland	
Denmark	France		
England	Germany		
Finland	Japan		
Ireland	Luxembourg		
Italy	South Korea		
New Zealand			
Norway			
Sweden			

Note: Countries listed are the 20 wealthiest members of the Organisation for Economic Cooperation and Development (OECD).

Universal health care takes many forms. Some countries have a **single-payer health system**. Under this system, the government provides or pays for all citizens' health care coverage. There isn't just one way to do this. In some cases, the government directly manages all aspects of the health care system — including employing physicians, setting prices for medical services, and running the hospitals. In others, the government pays private insurance companies to cover everyone. Other countries use a hybrid system — the government relies on a mix of public and private health care providers to make certain that all citizens have a minimum threshold of coverage. A few countries rely entirely on private health insurance, but they require all citizens to purchase it. Because the government negotiates the rates, it's affordable for most people. For those who still can't afford it, the government subsidizes the cost. The United States, by contrast, stands alone. The government does not guarantee access to health care for all citizens. As a result, roughly 26 million Americans have no health insurance.[6]

This segment lays out the health insurance landscape in the United States and walks you through two fundamental challenges involved in providing health care to everyone. You'll see how complicated it can be to enact a major policy with so many different political actors — the president, Congress, special interests, state governments, and the courts — all pushing and pulling in different directions. By the end, you'll have a sense of why health care is such a difficult policy to navigate and why coverage for all Americans isn't on the horizon.

The Health Care Lay of the Land: Who Has It? Who Needs It?

Proposals for universal health care in the United States have been on the table since Theodore Roosevelt ran for president in 1912. His Progressive Party platform called for the "protection of home life against the hazards of sickness, irregular employment, and old age through the adoption of a system of social insurance." Roosevelt lost the election, but future presidents carried the mantle. In a 1947 message to Congress, Harry Truman said that we should strive to make "good health equally available to all citizens." Dwight Eisenhower in the 1950s, John F. Kennedy in the 1960s, and Richard Nixon in the 1970s all advocated for some form of universal health care.[7] And in the early 1990s, Bill Clinton made health care reform a cornerstone of his legislative agenda, famously holding up in an address to Congress the "Health Security" card that would guarantee all citizens health coverage under his plan.[8] These presidents' reform efforts differed substantially in how to deliver health care to citizens. But they had one thing in common: they all crashed and burned in the political process.

Although efforts at universal health care have not met with success, the federal government does guarantee health care to several categories of citizens. In 1965, President Lyndon Johnson signed legislation to guarantee health care to the aged, people with disabilities, and people with limited income.[9] More specifically, people over the age of 65, as well as many people with disabilities, automatically qualify for **Medicare**. Under this program, patients pay nothing for the coverage itself and just a small co-pay for medical treatment and hospitalization. Citizens living near or below the poverty level are also guaranteed health care coverage through **Medicaid**. Jointly administered by the states and the federal government, this program covers almost all medical expenses with a minimal co-pay of typically $4 to $8.[10] Medicare and Medicaid cover about one-third of all Americans.[11]

In the 1990s, the government began guaranteeing health care to all children, too. Congress and the Clinton administration worked together to create the Children's Health Insurance Program (CHIP). It extends coverage to anyone under the age of 18 whose parents earn too much to qualify for Medicaid but cannot afford health insurance.[12] Roughly 10 million children receive health coverage through CHIP every year.[13]

And in 2010, Congress passed the Affordable Care Act (often referred to as Obamacare). The act extended Medicaid coverage to more people, provided subsidies to help citizens who could not afford health insurance to purchase it, allowed young people to stay on their parents' plans until they turned 26, and required citizens who did not get insurance to pay a tax penalty. It also included a provision that prohibited insurance companies from refusing to cover people with pre-existing health problems or charging them more for a policy.[14] All told, the law provided health coverage to more than 20 million Americans who had previously been uninsured.[15] In the words of then–vice president Joe Biden—unaware that a microphone picked him up as he whispered to Barack Obama at the signing ceremony for the new law—"This is a big fucking deal."[16]

And it was a big deal. Obamacare represented the first major expansion of health coverage for adults since the 1960s. But even with the several government programs we've just described, most Americans must still procure and pay for health care on their own. Nearly 50 percent of the overall U.S. population—and almost two-thirds of people between the ages of 18 and 64—get health care through their job (typically sharing the cost with their employer).[17] This leaves many people on precarious footing. The cost and quality of private insurance plans vary dramatically. Some cover all medical expenses at an affordable price. But others are bare bones, with large deductibles, high co-pays, and limitations on medical services. As a result, even people with insurance often find themselves racking up substantial medical bills and debt. The typical family of four with employer-provided health coverage pays roughly $8,100 for medical expenses each year, a figure that analysts expect will continue to rise.[18]

Linking health coverage to employment is also problematic because if you lose your job for any reason, you typically lose your benefits, too.[19] The Covid-19 pandemic that began in 2020 highlights the problem. With many businesses forced to shut down because of the health crisis, millions of Americans found themselves unemployed—some temporarily, some longer-term—at a time when they and their families were particularly susceptible to illness. Four in 10 Americans who lost their jobs or had their hours cut as a result of the pandemic either didn't have insurance or worried about losing it (see Figure 1).[20]

Finally, employment-based health care contributes to substantial societal inequities. People without jobs that provide benefits have less opportunity to access quality health care for themselves and their families. More than half the uninsured are the "working poor"—a designation that means at least one member of a family has a full-time job with pay above the poverty line but below the income needed to afford

FIGURE 1. Health Care Insecurity amid the Covid-19 Pandemic

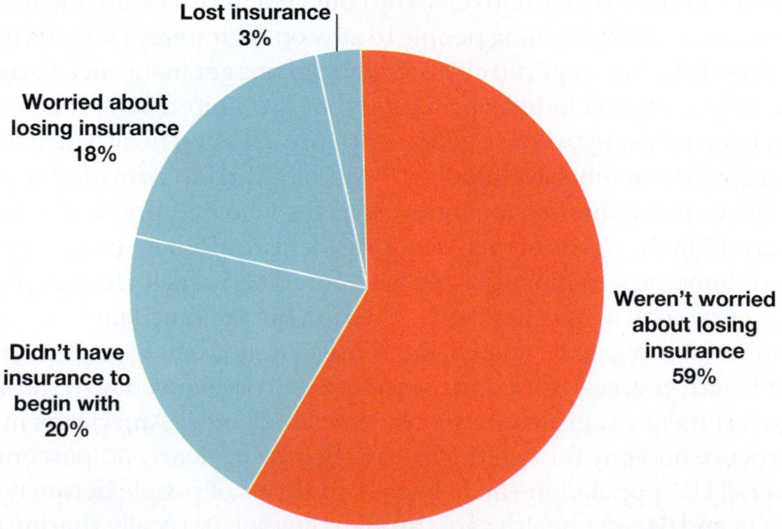

Note: Data are based on adults who lost their jobs or had hours or pay cut because of Covid-19.

Source: Sara R. Collins, Munira Z. Gunja, Gabriella N. Aboulafia, Erin Czyzewicz, and Robyn Rapoport, "New Survey Finds Americans Suffering Health Coverage Insecurity along with Job Losses," The Commonwealth Fund, April 21, 2020.

an insurance policy. The racial disparities are glaring, too, with the burden of being uninsured falling heavily on people of color, particularly Latinos, who are more than twice as likely as White people to lack health coverage.[21] When people without health insurance have health care expenses, it often means accruing medical debt that furthers economic inequality.

Why the U.S. Health Care System Is Unlikely to Change

The challenges associated with an employer-based health care system, as well as the fact that millions of Americans don't have any coverage at all, are well-known. But if history is to serve as a guide, then for two major reasons the prospects of doing anything about it are dim.

Reason #1: Republicans and Democrats Disagree

When the two major political parties diametrically oppose each other on an issue, it's almost impossible to enact major legislation around it. And Democrats and Republicans could not be farther apart on whether to pass a law establishing universal health care or what role the government should play when it comes to health care.

On one side of the debate, most Democrats believe that health care is a human right and the government's responsibility is to make sure every citizen has coverage.[22] They don't all agree on the best approach to covering everyone, though. The more progressive wing of the party—including Senators Bernie Sanders and Elizabeth Warren—advocate for a switch to a single-payer system that would essentially amount to "Medicare for all."[23] Others, including President Biden, support a more moderate approach centered around what is referred to as the public option. This approach would maintain the current private health care system but also create a government-run health insurance program that would be less expensive and compete with private insurance companies. Regardless of the mechanism for delivering care, the Democratic Party platform is clear on the goal: "secure universal health care for the American people for generations."[24]

The modern Republican Party, in contrast, holds the view that universal health care represents too much government intrusion into the economy and people's lives. Many go even further, equating attempts to pass universal health care with a radical socialist takeover of the government. Most Republicans believe it should be up to each person to obtain health insurance. Look no further than the party's website: the statement on health care begins, "Obamacare is a disaster." It goes on to advocate for rolling back regulations that prevent market competition.[25] Nowhere do the Republicans argue for the importance of making sure all citizens have affordable coverage. In fact, Republicans in recent congresses have supported letting private health care insurance companies decide whom to cover and whether to charge people more if they have chronic illnesses.[26]

The vote for or against Obamacare—a policy that doesn't come close to guaranteeing universal health care to all Americans—highlights the partisan divide (see Table 2).[27] The final version of the Affordable Care Act passed without a single Republican vote in Congress. The Democrats

TABLE 2. Democrats and Republicans on Obamacare

Democrats	Republicans
 "Obamacare is a law that every American should be proud of. It's why people with pre-existing conditions are protected in this country." —President Joe Biden	"Doctors are quitting.... Patients are beside themselves. They had a plan [before] that was good. They have no plan now." —President Donald Trump
"We all owe a huge debt to President Obama, who fundamentally transformed health care in America." —Senator Elizabeth Warren	"I would rather drink weed killer than support Obamacare." —Senator John Kennedy
"Under the Affordable Care Act, you have . . . liberty to pursue your happiness." —Former Speaker of the House Nancy Pelosi	"Obamacare was a terrible mistake and we ought to pull it out root and branch." —Senator Mitch McConnell
"I think it's part of a longer-term vision . . . truly guaranteeing health care for all Americans." —Representative Alexandria Ocasio-Cortez	"I would do anything and I will continue to do anything I can to stop the train wreck that is Obamacare." —Senator Ted Cruz

Note: Quotes compiled from a variety of news sources during the decade following the signing of the ACA.

Source: See Note 31 for full source information.

got the bill through the Senate only because they had a 60-seat filibuster-proof majority. And since then, opponents of the law in the House and Senate have held more than 70 votes trying to repeal it.[28] Twelve Republican governors have refused to accept the federal funds provided by the Affordable Care Act to expand Medicaid and, thus, cover more of their citizens.[29] And the battle over health care policy has infiltrated the court system. In 2012, the Supreme Court—by the slimmest of margins—ruled that it's permissible for the government to require most people to maintain a minimum level of health insurance. But other lawsuits challenging the ACA continue to make their way through the court system.[30]

Political leaders are able to dig in their heels around health care because it's easy to inflame citizens' partisan passions. Unlike some policy debates that might seem somewhat obscure to the American people—think corporate tax rates or the war in Ukraine—health care directly affects almost everyone. According to the Centers for Disease Control and Prevention, 60 percent of Americans suffer from a chronic health condition such as diabetes, arthritis, cancer, or heart disease. Forty percent of Americans have two or more chronic conditions.[31] And even people who don't have to deal with these issues themselves certainly know someone close to them who does. So political leaders often make dire predictions and harsh accusations about what their opponents' health care policies will mean for everyday Americans.

Republican candidates and elected officials seek to tap into voters' fears about how universal health care proposals or reforms like Obamacare will lead them to lose their current coverage, and turn medical decisions over to the government. In 2009, former Republican vice-presidential candidate Sarah Palin warned that passing the Affordable Care Act would lead to citizens standing "in front of Obama's 'death panels' so his bureaucrats" can decide who gets care—who lives and who dies.[32] Despite the fact that there was no factual basis whatsoever for that claim—it was just an egregious example of misinformation—five years after the act passed, 29 percent of Republicans still believed that death panels were part of the law.[33]

Democrats also use emotionally charged rhetoric and images to stoke voters' fears. A favorite move is to warn voters that Republican health care reforms will result in substantial cuts to Medicare—in other words, Republicans will take away your grandparents' health care.[34]

Regardless of whether health care-related allegations are true or a caricature of voters' darkest fears, they're sufficient to keep people from breaking with their party's position on health care policy. Indeed, several congressional Democrats who supported Obamacare but represented relatively conservative districts and states lost reelection in

A famous 2012 ad attacking Republican vice-presidential candidate Paul Ryan depicted the congressman taking his grandmother for a walk and then pushing her off a cliff. The ad intended to stoke fears about what health care reform would look like if the Republicans won the election.

part because their Republican opponents portrayed them as out of sync with their constituents on health care.[35]

Reason #2: There's Lots of Money at Stake

The health care industry is enormous. If you consider all the money that goes to hospitals, doctor's offices, insurance companies, pharmaceutical companies, and all the businesses that support health care providers (medical devices, hospital equipment, home health care aides), the industry accounts for almost one-fifth of all economic activity in the country.[36] To put this into perspective, the nation's health care spending is roughly twice that of almost any other wealthy democracy (see Figure 2).[37] What drives some critics of the system crazy is that despite spending all this money, the United States doesn't even have the best health outcomes. The nation lags behind many others in life expectancy and disease rates.[38]

It turns out that all the money flowing into the health care industry helps explain why the United States has never passed a universal coverage law. Think about it this way. Approximately 75 million Americans get health insurance through a private company like UnitedHealth, Kaiser, or Anthem Blue Cross and Blue Shield. Two-thirds of American adults take at least one prescription drug, which generates billions in revenue for pharmaceutical companies like Pfizer, Novartis, and Merck.[39] And doctors in the United States are among the highest paid in the world. The average physician earns more than $350,000 per year; specialists often make upward of half a million dollars.[40] With so much money involved, insurance providers, drug companies, and medical professionals are leery of health care reforms that might affect their bottom line.

Consider how the health care industry reacted to Obamacare. More than 1,750 companies and organizations—including 207 hospitals

FIGURE 2. Average Per Capita Health Care Spending in Wealthy Democracies

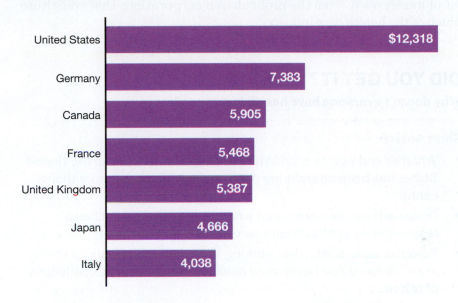

Country	Spending
United States	$12,318
Germany	7,383
Canada	5,905
France	5,468
United Kingdom	5,387
Japan	4,666
Italy	4,038

Note: Bars represent the G7 countries, which are the democracies with the largest economies in the world.
Source: OECD, "Health Spending," 2021.

and 105 insurance companies—hired 4,500 lobbyists and spent well over $1 billion to influence the health care reform bill.[41] At the top of the list of concerns for insurance companies was the requirement that they cover people with pre-existing conditions, such as diabetes, cancer, and asthma. These illnesses often require years, if not a lifetime, of care. Given that these diseases can amount to hundreds of thousands of dollars in expenses, private health insurance companies often don't want to cover people with these conditions—and certainly not if they can't charge more for their coverage. The insurance companies lost this battle. But other entrenched interests fared better. The American Medical Association convinced legislators to strip from the bill any provisions that would amount to less pay for physicians. The American Hospital Association succeeded in limiting Medicaid expansion so that it wouldn't cut too severely into hospitals' profits. Even Burger King took part, successfully fighting to keep out of the final bill a soda tax to help fund health care reform.[42]

The stakes for implementing the kind of single-payer system that many progressive Democrats support are even greater than they were with respect to Obamacare. A single-payer system would likely involve getting rid of most of the private health insurance industry, cutting doctors' salaries, and setting lower drug prices. These changes might be good for the American people—especially those who would be able to access the health care they currently can't afford. But they'd take a lot of money away from the profit-driven corporations that constitute much of the health care industry.

DID YOU GET IT?
Why doesn't everyone have health insurance?

Short Answer:

- Whether and how to provide health care to all citizens in the United States has been an enduring public policy debate for more than a century.
- Deep partisan divisions about whether the government has a responsibility to offer health care make reform difficult.
- Powerful special interests working to protect their financial stake in the billion-dollar health care industry exacerbate the challenges of reform.

DEVELOPING YOUR SKILLS

Quantitative Literacy

Interpret the numbers: Policy debates around health care often focus on how many people are uninsured and how much coverage costs. If you're to gain a complete understanding of the issue, then it's important to be comfortable with the numbers involved.

1. According to census data, about 10 percent of people in the United States do not have health insurance. But in Figure 1, 20 percent of people surveyed reported not having health insurance. How can you explain this discrepancy?
   a. Because of problems with polls, the census number is likely more accurate.
   b. The difference can be attributed to the margin of error in polls.
   c. The census is likely wrong because it's hard to determine who has insurance.
   d. The census measures the entire population, whereas the survey focused on people who were unemployed.

2. Based on the information provided in Table 1, what is the least common way for wealthy nations to deliver universal health care?

   a. Single-payer system

   b. Public/private hybrid

   c. Private insurance mandate

   d. Single-payer and a private insurance mandate are equally uncommon

3. What's the most accurate way to characterize the data presented in Figure 2?

   a. The United States spends two to three times more on health care than other countries do.

   b. The United States spends two to three times more per person on health care than other countries do.

   c. The United States spends roughly 50 percent more on health care than other countries do.

   d. The United States spends roughly 50 percent more per person on health care than other countries do.

FIGURE IT OUT

This segment focused on health care costs and coverage rates. But health policy also requires knowing about health care outcomes: Does the health care system produce good results? Take a look at the table on next page to determine how well the United States fares on this dimension. More specifically:

- Identify one piece of data to support the argument that the U.S. health care system works well.

- Now identify one piece of data to support the argument that the U.S. health care system does not work well.

- Identify one piece of evidence you could interpret as either a positive or a negative outcome of the U.S. health care system. Explain how it can work as evidence in both directions.

Health Outcomes around the Globe

	Average Life Expectancy	Citizens with Chronic Disease	Rates of Obesity	Per Capita Annual Doctor Visits	5-Year Breast Cancer Survival Rate
Australia	82.6	15%	30%	7.7	89.5%
Canada	82.0	22	26	6.8	88.2
France	82.6	18	17	6.1	86.7
Germany	81.1	17	24	9.9	86.0
Netherlands	81.8	14	13	3.8	86.6
New Zealand	81.9	16	32	8.3	87.6
Norway	82.7	16	12	4.5	87.7
Sweden	82.5	18	13	2.8	88.8
Switzerland	83.6	15	11	4.3	86.2
United Kingdom	81.3	14	29	—	85.6
United States	78.6	28	40	4.0	90.2
Average	**81.9**	**17.5**	**22**	**5.8**	**87.6**

Note: Data compiled from the Commonwealth Fund. Health outcomes reflect most recent available data for each measure and vary from 2016 to 2019.

Source: Roosa Tikkanen and Melinda K. Abrams, "U.S. Health Care from a Global Perspective, 2019: Higher Spending, Worse Outcomes?" The Commonwealth Fund, January 30, 2020.

Want to Know More?

Sometimes the best way to understand a policy is to consider how it affects you personally. If you want to get a sense of health insurance prices based on where you live and how much you or your family earn, try out the Kaiser Family Foundation Health Insurance Marketplace Calculator: https://www.kff.org/interactive/subsidy-calculator/. You can see if you're eligible for Medicaid, qualify for an Obamacare subsidy, or will have to pay for private insurance and potentially foot a big bill.

CIVIC
ENGAGEMENT

47.
Are nuclear
weapons still
a problem?

#NonproliferationPolicy

"Drop!" Upon hearing their teacher's command, students quickly dive under their desks and shield their heads and necks. They stay there until the teacher lets them know it's okay to get up. This was America in the 1950s and 1960s. And these "duck and cover" drills were just a routine part of the school day. School districts trained students and teachers to protect themselves from a nuclear bomb explosion. People realized, of course, that hiding under a desk probably wasn't going to save anyone from a nuclear blast. The only reason to crouch under your desk, the joke of the era went, was "to kiss your ass goodbye."[1] But concern about a nuclear attack was genuine, and schools tried to do whatever they could to make children feel prepared and safe.

The threat of nuclear war had become real the moment the Soviet Union tested its first nuclear device at a remote site in Kazakhstan in 1949. Suddenly, two powerful and rival nations had weapons of mass destruction. Policy makers in the United States decided that building up a massive nuclear arsenal was the best way to deter the Soviets from ever using theirs. The Soviets pursued the same strategy. And so began a race to build the most powerful nuclear arsenal in order to project onto the world military and political superiority. This extreme

575

Elementary schools in the 1950s and '60s regularly conducted drills to prepare students for a nuclear bomb attack.

hostility between the United States and the Soviet Union served as the backdrop of global politics for decades.

Referred to as the **Cold War**, the U.S.-Soviet relationship was characterized by propaganda and threats, but it stopped short of actual warfare. Although the history and dynamics of the Cold War are beyond the scope of this segment, suffice it to say that it was rooted in competing political values. Whereas the Soviets opposed capitalism and advocated for a communist system of government, the United States championed free markets and democracy. Both sides were determined to expand their political dominance around the globe, and for nearly half a century the threat of nuclear war between the two nations hung over the world like a dark cloud.

The United States "won" the Cold War when the Soviet Union transitioned away from a completely state-run economy and ultimately collapsed in 1991. Soviet leader Mikhail Gorbachev had adopted a series of economic and political reforms, and the nation's 15 republics devolved into mostly independent countries. Russia, the heart of the Soviet Union, remained a large and powerful nation, but its influence and control across Eastern Europe and the world dissipated substantially.[2]

Are nuclear weapons still a problem?

Posters like these were a regular part of the government's public information campaign to prepare Americans for a nuclear attack.

Gorbachev's negotiations with the Reagan administration also put an end to the nuclear arms race.

But the threat posed by nuclear weapons did not go away. Presidents Clinton, Bush, Obama, Trump, and Biden — all post–Cold War presidents — worked diligently to prevent countries that didn't have nuclear weapons from getting them. Keeping nuclear weapons away from terrorists also became a central concern. Indeed, President Obama warned that terrorists getting their hands on a nuclear bomb posed "the most immediate and extreme threat to global security."[3] And in 2022, when Russia put its nuclear forces on high alert during its invasion of Ukraine, the world was again forced to confront what it means to have nuclear weapons used in war. For the most part, both major political parties agree that **nonproliferation** — the policy of preventing the spread of nuclear weapons — must remain a top foreign policy objective.

This segment provides a broad overview of the nuclear weapons landscape: Who has them? Who has tried to get them? Who still wants them? We then turn to three central foreign policy tools the president and Congress use to deal with hostile foreign adversaries, including those trying to develop nuclear weapons. You'll see that although the Cold War has ended, the threats and challenges associated with nuclear weapons remain intense.

Nuclear Weapons around the World

Only one nation has ever used nuclear weapons in warfare. And it's not Russia, Iran, North Korea, or any of the nuclear hotspots you might hear about in the news. It's actually the United States, which dropped two atomic bombs on the Japanese cities of Hiroshima and Nagasaki toward the end of World War II. The destruction was almost unimaginable. The bomb used on Hiroshima leveled the city and likely killed more than 100,000 people. More than 75,000 people were killed or injured in Nagasaki.[4] And that was with 1940s nuclear technology. Some of today's nuclear weapons are 3,000 times more powerful than the bombs used in World War II.[5]

Given the overwhelming destructive capabilities of nuclear weapons, international efforts have long sought to contain them. Most notably, U.S. policy makers helped negotiate the **Nuclear Nonproliferation Treaty (NPT)**. Adopted in 1968, the treaty allowed the five countries that already had nuclear weapons—the United States, Great Britain, France, China, and the Soviet Union (now Russia)—to keep them, as long as they agreed to two conditions: (1) to work to reduce their own nuclear stockpiles, and (2) to commit not to transfer nuclear weapons or nuclear weapons technology to nonnuclear states.[6] The nonnuclear states that signed the treaty agreed not to develop or acquire nuclear weapons. By 1992, nearly 200 countries had signed. Only India, Pakistan, and Israel refused.

But the treaty has not fully contained the nuclear threat. The five original nuclear states continue to house nuclear arsenals, and China and France have more nuclear weapons today than when they signed the treaty (the United States and Russia have reduced their stockpiles considerably).[7] Moreover, the three nations that refused to sign the NPT have since developed nuclear weapons, as has North Korea, which pulled out of the treaty in 2003. Eight of the nine nations with nuclear weapons capabilities have also tested them (see Table 1).[8] Beyond the nine nations that possess nuclear weapons, 21 additional countries—including South Africa, Taiwan, and Brazil—have tried to develop them. Most have failed or have agreed to dismantle their programs.

TABLE 1. Nuclear Capability and Testing around the World

		Nuclear Warheads	Nuclear Bomb Tests
	Russia	6,255	715
	United States	5,500	1,030
	China	350	47
	France	290	210
	United Kingdom	225	45
	Pakistan	165	6
	India	156	6
	Israel	90	0
	North Korea	40	6

Note: Nuclear warheads numbers are as of 2021, and nuclear bomb tests are since 1945.

Sources: Kelsey Davenport and Kingston Reif, "Nuclear Weapons: Who Has What at a Glance," Arms Control Association, October 2021; "Nuclear Testing Chronology," AtomicArchive.com.

Policy Tools to Stop the Spread of Nuclear Weapons

It's no wonder why so many countries want nuclear weapons. They are a symbol of military power and can be a major bargaining chip in international diplomacy. It's also no wonder why the United States wants to stop their spread. They pose grave risks to citizens worldwide and have the potential to undermine global stability. Given these competing incentives, combating the threat and containing the spread of nuclear weapons is a complex endeavor.

In some cases, the U.S. government operates in a context of **unilateralism**—a policy under which a single nation tries to influence the international relations landscape on its own. In others, the focus is on **multilateralism**—a policy that involves cooperation with allies and international organizations to achieve a common goal. Indeed, the **United Nations**—founded in 1949 and headquartered in New York City—has 193 member nations that pledge to work together to promote political, military, and economic stability around the globe. Part of the UN's mission statement focuses on ultimately eliminating nuclear weapons altogether.[9] In both contexts, U.S. policy makers have come to rely on three primary policy tools, which are not mutually exclusive, to stop the development and spread of nuclear weapons.

Tool #1: Diplomacy — Let's Talk It Out

The United States has a small army of diplomats stationed in Washington, D.C., and around the world whose job is to advocate for U.S. policy

Sometimes diplomacy works and sometimes it doesn't. Ronald Reagan and Mikhail Gorbachev (left) successfully negotiated the end of the U.S. and Soviet arms race in the 1980s. But a deal struck by President Barack Obama and Secretary of State John Kerry (middle) in Iran didn't last. And President Donald Trump and North Korean leader Kim Jong Un couldn't reach a deal at all (right).

Are nuclear weapons still a problem?

interests. Led by the president, U.S. diplomatic efforts rely heavily on the secretary of state, U.S. ambassadors, and foreign service professionals.[10] These diplomats regularly negotiate with their counterparts in foreign countries about international business relationships, global military strategies, political corruption, and human rights abuses. They also play a central role when it comes to nuclear nonproliferation. After all, if you want a country to give up its nuclear weapons program, the first thing you can do is ask it to get rid of it. That's an oversimplification, of course, but diplomacy tends to be what U.S. policy makers use first when they begin their efforts.

In some instances, diplomacy is conducted at the highest levels. President Donald Trump, for example, personally met three times with North Korean leader Kim Jong Un to try to persuade him to dismantle his nuclear weapons program. Jake Sullivan, the national security advisor to Joe Biden, met with China's top diplomat in 2021 to urge Beijing to cease "provocative military activity" and reduce the size of its nuclear arsenal.[11]

In other cases, ambassadors and foreign service professionals take the lead in conducting diplomacy. The U.S. ambassador to the United Nations, for instance, played a pivotal role in developing the 1968 Nuclear Nonproliferation Treaty, and his successors have been responsible for nurturing that agreement for more than half a century.[12] Decades of behind-the-scenes negotiations between Libyan officials and mid-level diplomats from the United States and its allies served as one of several tactics to convince Libya to abandon and destroy its nuclear weapons program.[13] Members of the U.S. diplomatic corps also served as the chief negotiators of the New Strategic Arms Reduction Treaty with Russia in 2010.[14]

But talking a country's government into doing what you want it to do is never easy. So diplomatic failures are part of the landscape, too. Despite nearly 30 years of continued talks aimed at convincing North Korea not to develop nuclear weapons, the nation is now a recognized nuclear power.[15]

Tool #2: Sanctions — Maybe Economic Pain Will Do the Trick

When diplomatic negotiations alone can't get an adversary to cooperate, the U.S. government can impose **sanctions**—actions intended to harm or limit a country's economic activity. Sanctions can be very broad—so broad that they prohibit any economic activity whatsoever with the nation in question. Under these circumstances, an American business can't sell a candy bar to or buy a T-shirt from a business in the sanctioned country. But sanctions can also be more targeted. They can limit the sale of a specific good (like weapons), ban the export of a single product (like oil), or cut off economic activity with specific individuals (like corrupt leaders or criminals).

The response to Russia's invasion of Ukraine in February 2022, for example, was met with widespread sanctions from the United States and the European Union. The United States froze Russian banks' assets and prohibited U.S. citizens from doing business with them; prohibited any new investment in Russian companies; and placed sanctions on Russian oligarchs and elites, including Putin's children. Within the first months following the invasion of Ukraine, more than 600 private sector companies left the Russian market. And the power of the sanctions may grow over time because, as Russia uses its stockpile of planes, tanks, and other military equipment, it will become increasingly difficult for Putin to replace them.[16]

As of 2022, the U.S. government had active sanctions on 23 countries for offenses ranging from violating human rights, to supporting corruption, to disregarding international trade rules, to assisting terrorist organizations (see Table 3).[17]

Sanctions can also play an important role in nonproliferation policy. A nation that has or wants nuclear weapons might very well determine that building up a nuclear arsenal isn't worth the price of a damaged

TABLE 3. Sample of Nations Sanctioned by the U.S. Government

Nation	Stated Reason for Sanction
Central African Republic	Civil war–related violence and atrocities
Iran	Nuclear program; human rights violations; state-sponsored terrorism
Lebanon	Links to terrorist organizations
North Korea	Nuclear program; human rights violations
Russia	Aggression in Ukraine; business with North Korea; U.S. election meddling
Syria	Human rights violations; state-sponsored terrorism
Venezuela	Human rights violations; drug trade; state corruption
Yemen	Financial support of terrorist organizations

Note: Countries listed are among those against which the United States has active sanctions programs as of June 2022.

Source: "Sanctions Programs and Country Information," U.S. Department of the Treasury.

or crippled economy. Consider the case of Iran. In 1984, the U.S. State Department imposed sanctions on Iran for supporting terrorism.[18] They remained in place as Iran ramped up its nuclear weapons program. The sanctions amounted to an almost complete embargo; U.S. companies could not engage in any economic activity with Iran or Iranian-owned businesses. When Iran finally agreed to suspend its nuclear weapons program in 2015, it was in exchange for lifting some of the most debilitating economic sanctions. Although it took a long time (almost 30 years), some analysts believe that sanctions played a key role in bringing Iran to the negotiating table.[19] In fact, even though the Trump administration pulled out of the agreement—often referred to as the Iran nuclear deal—and the Biden administration has not renewed it, Iran continues to comply with many of its stipulations, likely to avoid renewed sanctions.

The U.S. government has also sanctioned countries that support terrorist organizations such as al Qaeda or ISIS. These groups are trying to acquire or build a nuclear bomb, so the United States closely watches any country that supports terrorists financially or militarily. That's among the reasons President Clinton placed sanctions on Sudan in the late 1990s.[20] The economic pain that ensued undoubtedly played some part in convincing the Sudanese government to begin assisting in the fight against global terrorism.[21]

Like diplomacy, though, economic sanctions don't always work.[22] They weren't sufficient for keeping the Syrian government from assisting terrorists or working to develop biological, chemical, and nuclear weapons.[23] Nor did numerous rounds of targeted sanctions deter Pakistan from becoming a nuclear power or providing safe haven to terrorists trying to obtain weapons.[24]

Tool #3: Military Force — The Ultimate Power Play

The most severe foreign policy tool the U.S. government can use to exert its will on another nation is military force. Although the Constitution grants Congress the power to declare war, nowadays, as commander in chief of the armed forces, presidents regularly deviate from the Constitution's intent and initiate military action without a formal declaration of war. Since the 1980s, presidents have ordered air strikes (Bosnia, Sudan, Syria, and Libya), used troops to quash rebellions (Grenada and Haiti), and overseen full-scale military operations with combat troops (Iraq and Afghanistan). In fact, the last time Congress made a formal declaration of war was World War II.[25]

That doesn't mean, however, that Congress plays no role. After two "wars" that were never declared by Congress—the Korean War

FIGURE 1. Countries with the Most U.S. Troops Deployed, 2021

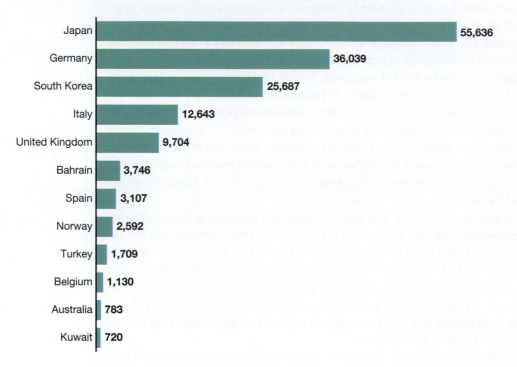

Country	Troops
Japan	55,636
Germany	36,039
South Korea	25,687
Italy	12,643
United Kingdom	9,704
Bahrain	3,746
Spain	3,107
Norway	2,592
Turkey	1,709
Belgium	1,130
Australia	783
Kuwait	720

Note: Bars indicate the number of active U.S. troops in each country as of March 31, 2022.

Sources: "Military and Civilian Personnel by Service/Agency by State/Country," Defense Manpower Data Center, March 2022.

(1950–1953) and the Vietnam War (1961–1975)—Congress tried to reassert its authority by passing the **War Powers Act** in 1973. The law requires the president to notify Congress within 48 hours of deploying the military, and it forbids armed forces from remaining deployed for more than 60 days without congressional authorization.[26] As laid out in the Constitution, Congress must also approve all funding for the military—including for the roughly 175,000 U.S. troops stationed in the Middle East, Europe, and Asia who are ready to respond to terrorist, nuclear, and other threats (see Figure 1).[27]

But even with this law, the president calls most of the shots when it comes to authorizing military action. Indeed, Congress often faces major political constraints in limiting or pushing back against military action launched by the president. Once service members are actively engaged and citizens know there are troops on the ground, members of Congress are reluctant not to authorize or fund the operation, even if it's not an official declaration of war. After all, members don't want to signal—to adversaries, the U.S. military, or the electorate—that they don't support the troops.

Thus, both the president and Congress can use or threaten military force in trying to stop the spread of nuclear weapons. As U.S. policy makers tried to rein in Iran's nuclear aspirations, for instance, U.S. military planners in 2013 let it be known that they were considering a military strike on Iran's nuclear facilities.[28] Prior to President Trump's diplomatic efforts with North Korea in 2018, the United States had also considered a range of military options to deter North Korea's pursuit of nuclear weapons.[29] Although the impact of the threat of military action in these cases is not entirely clear, both nations did come to the bargaining table to negotiate.

But make no mistake, the decision to use force can be costly—and deadly. The one example of the United States pursuing full-blown military action to prevent a country from becoming a nuclear power turned out to be a major foreign policy mistake. Based in part on faulty intelligence suggesting that Iraq had a robust chemical, biological, and nuclear weapons program, President George W. Bush ordered an invasion in 2003.[30] U.S. forces toppled the Iraqi government but never found any weapons of mass destruction. The war dragged on for nine years, cost trillions of dollars, killed and seriously injured thousands of American military personnel and hundreds of thousands of Iraqi civilians, and generated long-term instability in the region.[31]

Nukes and U.S. Politics: An Enduring Challenge

During his 1964 presidential reelection campaign, Democrat Lyndon Johnson attempted to paint his Republican opponent, Senator Barry Goldwater, as a danger to the world. Goldwater, on several occasions, had suggested that nuclear weapons could—even should—be used in war zones.[32] So Johnson ran what became one of the most famous political ads of all time. Entitled "Daisy," the minute-long piece opened with a three-year-old girl happily picking flowers in a field, counting a daisy's petals. It concluded with an ominous countdown to the launch of a nuclear bomb. Upon detonation, the president asserted, "We must either love each other, or we must die. Vote for President Johnson."[33]

Fast-forward to the 2020 presidential election, and concerns about nuclear weapons remained alive and well. Following reports that the Trump administration was considering testing a nuclear device, Democratic presidential candidate Joe Biden didn't mince words: "This is delusional," he said. "A resumption of testing is more likely to prompt other countries to resume militarily significant nuclear testing and undermine our nuclear nonproliferation goals."[34] Reelecting Trump, Biden argued, would pose a grave danger to the United States. His rhetoric was less dire than Johnson's had been 56 years earlier, but Biden's attack showed that concerns over nuclear weapons remain.

Despite all the changes the world has seen since the 1940s—the onset and conclusion of the Cold War, generations of new leaders, tireless unilateral and multilateral efforts aimed at nonproliferation—containing nuclear weapons is still a key part of U.S. foreign policy. And now, concerns over cybersecurity—protecting against cyberattacks into an adversary's financial, political, and military networks (including its nuclear weapons systems)—have become a major defense and foreign policy concern. This has particularly complicated the United States' relationship with Russia. Students may no longer be hiding under their desks, but policy makers—Democrats and Republicans alike—continue to focus on protecting the world from nuclear war and other emerging threats.

DID YOU GET IT?
Are nuclear weapons still a problem?

Short Answer:

- Yes. Containing them has been a challenge since the late 1940s.
- Diplomacy, economic sanctions, and military force are three central foreign policy tools that U.S. policy makers employ to contain the spread of nuclear weapons.
- Though nonproliferation has been a foreign policy priority, the United States has seen mixed success in trying to stop the spread of these weapons.

Civic Engagement

Engage with politics: Becoming politically active around matters of foreign policy can seem daunting. These issues often involve multiple countries, international organizations, and faraway locations. But it is possible to become engaged, and these questions show you how.

1. Perhaps this segment piqued your interest in diplomacy. Or maybe it didn't. Either way, which is a credential you *don't* need to worry about if you want a career as a foreign service officer? (Hint: Start out with the "Job Seekers" tab on the State Department's website.)

    a. Cultural adaptability
    b. Oral communication skills
    c. An advanced educational degree
    d. Quantitative skills

2. If you want to rid the world of nuclear weapons, which organization should you join?

    a. National Council on Foreign Relations
    b. Heritage Foundation
    c. Peace Direct
    d. Global Zero

3. One way to get firsthand exposure to foreign policy issues is to work as an intern at the United Nations. Based on the criteria noted on the organization's website, which statement is true?

    a. Internships are only available at the UN's headquarters in New York.
    b. You must have foreign language expertise.
    c. The internship program is open to college seniors.
    d. You must be a U.S. citizen to intern for the UN.

FIGURE IT OUT

Beyond nuclear weapons, citizens can become active around lots of global issues: human trafficking, land mines, food insecurity, gender equality, international copyright laws, global commerce, climate change — the list goes on and on. Develop a plan to get involved with a global policy issue that interests you. More specifically:

- In a sentence or two, identify the issue and define the problem as you see it. (You might need to conduct a brief internet search to identify your issue of interest.)

- List two organizations you can join or follow to keep abreast of the issue.

- Based on the activities of these organizations, what's one action you can take today to begin working on the issue?

Want to Know More?

If you're interested in seeing different portrayals of the threat of nuclear war, start with President Johnson's famous "Daisy" ad: https://www.youtube.com/watch?v=riDypP1KfOU. After that, maybe try Stanley Kubrick's 1964 dark comedy *Dr. Strangelove or: How I Learned to Stop Worrying and Love the Bomb*, which captures the absurdity and terror of the arms race. For a more contemporary plotline, you can stream Season 2 of *24*, which tracks a counterterrorism agent's attempts to find and disarm a nuclear bomb that's been set to go off in Los Angeles.

48.
Should you worry about terrorist attacks?

#WarOnTerror

U.S. foreign policy changed dramatically on the morning of September 11, 2001. Television networks broke away from their regular programming to report that an airplane had hit Tower 1 of the World Trade Center in New York City. The images were shocking — flames and black smoke engulfing the upper floors of the 110-story building, people jumping out of windows trying to escape the fire, police and firefighters sprinting toward the building trying to save lives. At first, it was unclear what had caused an American Airlines plane — on its way from Boston to Los Angeles — to hit the skyscraper. But 18 minutes later, another plane hit the second tower. Then, 40 minutes after that, a plane crashed into the Pentagon in Washington, D.C. America was under attack. A little more than an hour after the first plane hit, Americans watched in horror as both towers of the World Trade Center crumbled to the ground. Almost 3,000 people died.

Within hours, the nature of the attack began to come into focus. Nineteen foreign nationals had hijacked four commercial airplanes. They were all members of al Qaeda, a violent Islamist organization headquartered in Afghanistan and dedicated to eliminating any Western presence in Muslim countries. The organization's leader, Osama bin

At first glance, this photo might look like a war zone in a foreign country or a bombed-out European city street in World War II. In fact, it's New York City in the aftermath of the September 11, 2001, terrorist attack.

Laden, had issued a decree in 1998 calling for attacks on Americans anywhere in the world.[1] Though the exact details are not known, the hijackers, armed with pocket knives and box cutters, appear to have taken control of the crew and passengers, stormed the cockpits, and deliberately crashed the planes into political and economic landmarks.[2] The fourth plane, apparently headed for the White House, never reached its destination; passengers became aware of what had happened in New York and Washington and fought the hijackers.[3] The plane ultimately crashed in an open field in Pennsylvania, killing all aboard.

The country was in shock. This was the worst attack ever carried out in the United States by a foreign-based terrorist organization. Questions abounded. How did these 19 individuals get into the country? How did they manage to board the planes? Why were they able to bring box cutters on board? Why didn't the FBI and CIA uncover and prevent the plot? Were more attacks on the way? Was the nation now at war? And if so, with whom? From that day forward, preventing a repeat of this event became the U.S. government's prime foreign policy objective.

This segment provides an overview of the **war on terror** — the global effort spearheaded by the United States to destroy terrorist

Should you worry about terrorist attacks?

On the morning of September 11, 2001, a commercial plane hit the World Trade Center. As one tower burned, another plane flew into the second tower. The attacks were carried out by al Qaeda.

organizations and terrorist-supporting regimes that threaten national security and wreak havoc on the global economy.[4] We begin by describing the government's response to the 9/11 terrorist attacks. We then summarize the two ongoing debates in fighting the war on terror: (1) when and how to use military force, and (2) how to strike a balance in protecting national security and citizens' civil liberties. By the end, you'll be in a better position to judge for yourself whether the government's approach to combating terrorism keeps you safe.

Creating an Infrastructure to Fight Terrorism

In response to 9/11, the federal government acted quickly not only to find those who had orchestrated the attacks but also to develop new policies to fight terrorism. President George W. Bush, in an address to the nation nine days after the attacks, assured Americans that "we will direct every resource at our command—every means of diplomacy, every tool of intelligence, every instrument of law enforcement, every financial influence and every necessary weapon of war—to the destruction and to the defeat of the global terror network."[5] Vice President Dick Cheney led the administration's response. Step one, according to Cheney, was to develop "a comprehensive strategy, beginning with far greater homeland security to make the United States a tougher target."[6]

Crafting a policy to combat global terrorism meant acknowledging that existing antiterrorism policies were inadequate. After all, members of violent Islamist groups had had their eyes on U.S. targets for nearly a decade. In some cases, they had succeeded. A truck bomb meant to take down the World Trade Center in 1993 killed six people and wounded 1,000. A car bomb exploded outside a U.S. office in Saudi Arabia, killing five Americans in 1995. Three years later, al Qaeda orchestrated simultaneous bombings of the U.S. embassies in Kenya and Tanzania that resulted in hundreds of deaths. And in 2000, the group bombed a U.S. navy destroyer off the coast of Yemen, killing 17 American sailors. Attacks like these represented a different kind of war—an enemy without uniforms, operating secretly in dozens of countries around the world, willing to target civilians, and prepared to use themselves as weapons and to die for the cause. Summarized well in a report drafted by a bipartisan commission to analyze the events of 9/11, "al Qaeda's new brand of terrorism presented challenges to U.S. governmental institutions that they were not well designed to meet."[7]

Revamping antiterrorism policies meant adopting almost immediate reforms in airport security, border control, and domestic and foreign intelligence gathering.[8] To coordinate these efforts, Congress—at the request of the president—created a new cabinet-level agency, the Department of Homeland Security (DHS). By centralizing national security activities under one roof, the government would be better equipped to share information and coordinate policies. Today, with a more than $98 billion annual budget, DHS manages 22 key agencies in the fight against terrorism, including Customs and Border Protection, the Transportation Security Administration, and the Coast Guard (see Figure 1).[9] Prior to 9/11, these agencies each kept their own watch lists of suspected terrorists, which made it difficult to monitor suspicious individuals comprehensively.[10] Lapses in information sharing were a key reason that the government had been unable to prevent the 9/11 attacks.[11]

The president also sought to reorganize intelligence-gathering and information-sharing activities. President Bush asked Congress to authorize a national intelligence director. Appointed by the president and confirmed by the Senate, the director analyzes U.S. and foreign intelligence, briefs the president, and advises the

FIGURE 1. Department of Homeland Security Budget, 2023

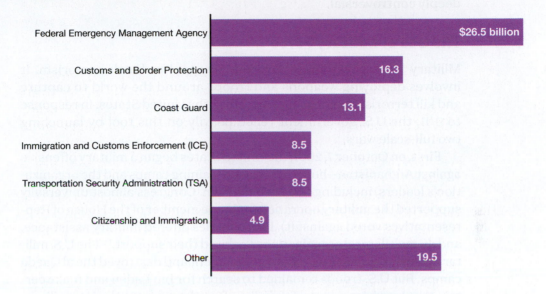

Federal Emergency Management Agency	$26.5 billion
Customs and Border Protection	16.3
Coast Guard	13.1
Immigration and Customs Enforcement (ICE)	8.5
Transportation Security Administration (TSA)	8.5
Citizenship and Immigration	4.9
Other	19.5

Note: The "Other" category includes spending for cybersecurity and infrastructure security, science and technology, countering weapons of mass destruction, federal law enforcement training centers, and domestic nuclear detection programs.

Source: "Budget-in-Brief: Fiscal Year 2023," Department of Homeland Security.

administration about all matters related to national security, especially terrorist threats facing the country. Every president since George W. Bush has continued to rely on the director to serve as the head of the intelligence community.

The government's infrastructure to combat terrorism hasn't been perfect. Each year, roughly 10,000 terrorist attacks continue to result in more than 25,000 deaths worldwide, including on U.S. soil, carried out by individuals pledging allegiance to al Qaeda and similar groups.[12] But decades after its creation, a large government agency remains devoted to the prevention of terrorist plots.

Antiterrorism Policies Are Controversial

An elaborate infrastructure and substantial budget provide a foundation from which to implement the United States' antiterrorism policy. But it's no easy task to track potential threats and actual incidents in the more than 80 countries known to house terrorist cells or among people living in the United States who are affiliated with terrorist groups.[13] Given the complexity of this endeavor, it's no wonder that two central aspects of U.S. antiterrorism policy remain deeply controversial.

The Use of Military Force

Military force is the most severe policy tool to battle terrorism. It involves deploying weapons and troops around the world to capture and kill terrorists before they can attack the United States. In response to 9/11, the U.S. government relied heavily on this tool by launching two full-scale wars.

First, on October 7, 2001, the United States began a military offensive against Afghanistan—home to al Qaeda training camps and the organization's leaders, including Osama bin Laden. Congress almost universally supported the military operation (only one member of the House of Representatives voted against it), 136 countries offered military assistance, and 46 multilateral organizations declared their support.[14] The U.S. military quickly toppled the Afghan government and destroyed the al Qaeda camps. But U.S. troops remained to search for bin Laden and make certain that terrorist groups didn't resurface the moment the U.S. military left. It took 10 years to track down bin Laden. (The U.S. military eventually found him living in a compound in Pakistan and killed him in a nighttime raid.) And it took another 10 years to draw down the U.S. military presence. The last of the U.S. military personnel left Afghanistan in August 2021, but the U.S. government continues to rely on drones, long-range bombers, and spy networks to thwart the resurgence of terrorist cells.[15] A drone attack in Kabul killed al Qaeda leader Ayman al-Zawahiri in July 2022.

The second war was far more controversial from the outset. Although Iraq had not been involved in the 9/11 attacks, the Bush administration argued that the president of Iraq, Saddam Hussein, posed a grave danger because he might supply terrorists with biological, chemical, and nuclear weapons to use against the United States. The administration's true motives for the war are a source of controversy; some argue that protecting U.S. oil interests, demonstrating military strength, or spreading democracy were the reason.[16] Regardless, in March 2003, the U.S. launched a **preventive war**—an attack directed at an adversary to keep that enemy from attacking at a later time. The doctrine of preventive war is very controversial, with many arguing that strikes against a country that is not actively attacking or threatening another nation violate international law.[17] Indeed, only about one-third of the nations that supported the war in Afghanistan—and only a handful of U.S. allies (including Australia, Poland, and the United Kingdom)—actually joined the military operation by providing troops.[18] Many members of Congress were skeptical, too. Although almost all Republicans supported the use of force, a slight majority of Democrats opposed it. The U.S. military ousted Saddam Hussein but never found biological, chemical, or nuclear weapons.

In the end, the question of whether military force to prevent terrorism is worth the cost—in lives, dollars, and global reputation—is a matter of debate. On the one hand, the United States has experienced no attacks close to the scale of 9/11 since 2001. On the other hand, military force has meant risking the lives of hundreds of thousands of military personnel and civilians, not to mention devoting trillions of dollars to the effort. Moreover, close to 1 million U.S. veterans suffer from serious physical and mental health issues as a result of serving in Afghanistan or Iraq (see Table 1).[19]

As policy makers debate the pros and cons of the use of force, presidents continue to rely heavily on it to fight the war on terror. President Obama chose to expand the controversial use of military drones—unmanned aerial vehicles that bomb specific targets and suspects in foreign countries.[20] President Trump ratcheted up military campaigns against terrorist strongholds in Iraq and Syria. Overall, more than 175,000 U.S. troops are deployed around the world, many in places for the purpose of engaging and striking potential terrorist threats.[21]

TABLE 1. The Cost of the Wars in Afghanistan and Iraq

	Afghanistan	Iraq
Length of conflict	19.9 years	8.7 years
Number of military personnel at peak	170,000	130,000
U.S. military deaths	2,448	4,489
Civilian deaths	46,319	185,831
Financial cost	$2.3 trillion	$2.4 trillion
U.S. combat troops remaining	0	2,500

Note: The number of troops remaining in Afghanistan and Iraq are based on estimates as of March 2022.

Sources: "Infographic: U.S. Military Presence around the World," *Al Jazeera*, September 10, 2021; "U.S. Troops Will Likely Be in Iraq for Years to Come, Central Command Boss Says," *Military Times*, March 18, 2022; Neta C. Crawford and Catherine Lutz, "Human Costs of Post-9/11 Wars," Watson Institute, September 1, 2021.

The Tension between Protecting National Security and Individual Freedom

The 19 terrorists who carried out the 9/11 attacks enjoyed and relied on freedoms provided to almost any citizen or traveler to the United States. They lived in the country largely undetected and unobserved as they trained for their mission. They had access to U.S. banks and could use credit cards to cover living expenses and purchase materials. They enrolled in flight training schools with almost no background checks. And they enjoyed ease of phone and internet communications to coordinate with one another and their leaders abroad.

Following the attacks, Congress immediately began to take action to make it easier for intelligence and law enforcement agencies to investigate and thwart suspected terrorists. Less than three months after 9/11, Congress passed and the president signed the **USA PATRIOT Act**. Its central purpose was to deter "terrorist acts in the United States and around the world" by enhancing "law enforcement investigatory tools."[22] The legislation was long and detailed, but it basically made it much easier to obtain search warrants, freeze banking assets, and search people's phone, internet, and bank records without their knowledge.[23] Section 215 of the act, for example, authorized the government to obtain from businesses any records relating to a suspected terrorist.

Although the Patriot Act sailed through Congress with broad bipartisan support, as the war on terror progressed members found themselves amid a fundamental policy debate: How can the government preserve key civil liberties, such as prohibiting unreasonable searches and cruel and unusual punishment, while at the same time doing everything possible to protect the country from future terrorist attacks?

The Bush administration erred on the side of protecting national security. Vice President Cheney pushed what became known as the 1 percent doctrine: law enforcement must investigate and respond to every possible terrorist plot, even if there is just a 1 percent chance it's a legitimate threat.[24] The Bush administration relied on the USA PATRIOT Act to justify violent interrogation methods and prisoner abuse at military prisons, such as the one at Guantánamo Bay, Cuba. Domestically, it used the act to monitor ordinary U.S. citizens' behavior (see Table 2).

Others believed that the fight against terrorism had become marked by serious governmental abuses, including the torture and indefinite detention of suspected terrorists, often to no avail. A U.S. Senate report revealed striking evidence that these methods did not yield

TABLE 2. Controversial Surveillance Provisions of the USA PATRIOT Act

Section 206 Allows the government to tap every device a person uses — landline, cell phone, laptop, and so on — with just one approval from the Foreign Intelligence Surveillance Court.	**Expired**
Section 207 Allows the government to surveil someone who might be engaged in international terrorism, even if the person is not actually connected to any existing terrorist group.	**Expired**
Section 213 Permits "sneak and peek" warrants so that law enforcement can search premises without the owner or occupant's knowledge.	**In effect**
Section 215 Gives the government broad power to demand from businesses records relating to someone who might be involved in terrorism; includes library and phone records.	**Expired**
Section 505 Allows the government to demand communications records from telecom companies without going through the Foreign Intelligence Surveillance Court for approval first.	**In effect**

information to protect against future attacks.[25] Critics also argued that mass surveillance of U.S. citizens had gone too far. The government, for instance, took Section 215 of the Patriot Act to mean it could demand the phone records of every single customer of phone companies including Verizon, the largest cell phone provider in the United States.[26] Collecting this information was shrouded in secrecy, with little or no meaningful oversight. The organizations and companies that held the records could object in secret court hearings, and some did, but the individuals whose information was targeted had little recourse to stop the examination of their records.[27]

Nearly 10 years after the USA PATRIOT Act passed, Senator Ron Wyden, a Democrat from Oregon, took to the Senate floor to raise alarm bells: "When the American people find out how their government has secretly interpreted the Patriot Act, they will be stunned and they will be angry." Congressman Jim Sensenbrenner, a Republican who helped author the law, concluded that the Patriot Act was being abused by the executive branch: "Big Brother is watching. And he is monitoring the phone calls and digital communications of every American."[28] Although many of the controversial provisions of the law have expired, debates around the tension between protecting national security and upholding civil liberties continue to shape U.S. antiterrorism policies.

Where Are We Now?

September 11, 2001, left an indelible mark on our country and reshaped U.S. foreign policy. And as post-9/11 antiterrorism policy enters its third decade, concerns about national security and terrorism continue to affect discussions about border security, immigration, and foreign relations. This will continue to be the case because the fight against global terrorism appears to have no end in sight. Al Qaeda and its offshoots remain active, especially in Afghanistan, the Middle East, North Africa, and South Asia.[29] And even though the war on terror weakened al Qaeda's effectiveness, ISIS—another violent Islamist group whose members are dispersed throughout the world—has filled the vacuum.[30] The Obama and Trump administrations fought the organization for years and ultimately killed its leader, Abu Bakr al-Baghdadi, in a military raid in 2019. But other leaders have since emerged. The Biden administration has been confronted, for example, with ISIS-K fighters in Afghanistan who engage in deadly suicide missions that have killed numerous civilians.[31]

How worried you are about a terrorist attack when you go to bed each night, however, probably depends on your personal psychology. On the one hand, a number of bombings, shootings, and killings linked to terrorist organizations have taken place on U.S. soil.[32] Some of the most deadly and destructive were the bomb blast at the finish line of the Boston Marathon in 2013; the shooting at a gay night club in Orlando, Florida, in 2015; and the 2019 shooting at a Pensacola, Florida, naval air station. It's not surprising, then, that many Americans—40 to 50 percent in most surveys—say they worry that they or someone in their family will likely be the victim of a terrorist attack.[33]

On the other hand, since 9/11 the United States has averaged only six deaths per year at the hands of foreign-born terrorists on U.S. soil. We don't want to make light of these numbers or of the dangers posed by global terrorism. But as far as the extent to which you should worry about attacks like these is concerned, some perspective might be helpful. You're more likely to die in a heat wave or from a random animal attack than from the actions of a foreign-born terrorist. You're several thousand times more likely to choke to death than to lose your life because of the actions of a terrorist who entered the country illegally (see Table 3).[34] And incidents of domestic terrorism—such as at the hands of White supremacists and right-wing extremists—are far more prevalent than those committed by Islamist groups.[35] That's evidence, some would argue, that we're winning the war on terror—even if it has cost countless lives, more than $5 trillion, and some individual freedom. To others, it indicates that many of the government's responses to global terrorism have been disproportionate and overblown.

TABLE 3. Lifetime Odds of Various Causes of Death

Heart disease	1 in 7
Cancer	1 in 7
Diabetes	1 in 53
Motor vehicle accident	1 in 113
Murder	1 in 249
Drowning	1 in 1,183
Choking	1 in 3,409
Plane crash	1 in 9,738
Heat wave	1 in 10,785
Animal attack	1 in 30,167
Foreign-born terrorist	**1 in 45,808**
Illegal immigrant terrorist	**1 in 138,324,873**

Source: Dave Mosher and Skye Gould, "How Likely Are Foreign Terrorists to Kill Americans? The Odds May Surprise You," Business Insider, January 31, 2017.

DID YOU GET IT?
Should you worry about terrorist attacks?

Short Answer:

- As a matter of personal safety, probably not. But as a matter of foreign policy, yes.

- Post 9/11, the federal government created a large infrastructure and developed multiple policies to fight global terrorism. These policies likely prevented a number of attacks, but they're costly.

- Two decades after 9/11, debates regarding the use of military force and protecting individual freedoms remain at the center of antiterrorism policy.

Consuming Political Information

Check the facts: Issues regarding terrorism and policies to address it are susceptible to false claims and misleading information, many of which play into people's fears. Answer these questions by conducting your own internet searches, but be sure to base your answers only on information that comes from credible and reliable websites and sources.

1. Some political leaders claim that since 9/11, thousands of terrorists or suspected terrorists have entered the United States illegally by crossing the southern border. Is this claim true?

    a. Probably not. The government doesn't report every suspected terrorist who gets captured, but information that has been released suggests that it's rare for suspected terrorists to cross the southern border.

    b. Probably, but this information is not public, so we can't know for sure.

    c. Yes. In 2017 alone, nearly 4,000 suspected terrorists were apprehended crossing the southern border.

    d. Yes. Although arrests of suspected terrorists are classified, government reports suggest that at least 10,000 have crossed the southern border illegally and entered the United States since 9/11.

2. Political leaders worldwide often claim that illegal immigrants are most likely to commit acts of terrorism. Is this true?

    a. No. Most attacks are carried out by refugees from countries with a lot of terrorist activity.

    b. No. Most attacks are carried out by foreign-born nationals who are in the country legally.

    c. No. Most attacks are carried out by the country's own citizens who are associated with a foreign-based terrorist organization.

    d. Yes. Most attacks are carried out by foreign-born nationals who are in the country illegally.

3. Many misconceptions circulate about where terrorist attacks occur. Which statement is true about the prevalence of terrorism?

    a. Most attacks occur in Europe.

    b. The United States is among the top 10 countries for attacks.

    c. African nations experience the bulk of attacks.

    d. India, Pakistan, and Afghanistan experience more attacks than the United States or Europe.

Whenever you see a provocative headline or quote, it's probably worth fact-checking it. Determine the accuracy of these two examples:

1. ABC News headline: "Trump Claims '100 percent' of ISIS Caliphate Defeated in Syria."

2. *Wall Street Journal* op-ed written by Mike Pence: "Biden Broke Our Deal with the Taliban."

More specifically, to fact-check these headlines:

- Identify two reliable sources you can turn to in order to assess the accuracy of each headline. In a sentence for each, explain why the source is an appropriate one for fact-checking the claim.
- Determine whether the headline is true, partially true, or completely untrue. Explain in a sentence or two how you arrived at your answer.

Want to Know More?

For an in-depth understanding of what led to the 9/11 attacks, including intelligence failures, be sure to take a look at *The Looming Tower: Al-Qaeda and the Road to 9/11*. The book, written by Lawrence Wright, is also the basis of a Hulu original series of the same name. Mitchell Zuckoff's *Fall and Rise: The Story of 9/11* is another book worth reading. His moment-by-moment account of that fateful day is riveting and terrifying.

Appendix

THE DECLARATION OF INDEPENDENCE

In Congress, July 4, 1776

The unanimous Declaration of the thirteen united States of America,

When in the Course of human events, it becomes necessary for one people to dissolve the political bands which have connected them with another, and to assume among the powers of the earth, the separate and equal station to which the Laws of Nature and of Nature's God entitle them, a decent respect to the opinions of mankind requires that they should declare the causes which impel them to the separation.

We hold these truths to be self-evident, that all men are created equal, that they are endowed by their Creator with certain unalienable Rights, that among these are Life, Liberty and the pursuit of Happiness.—That to secure these rights, Governments are instituted among Men, deriving their just powers from the consent of the governed.—That whenever any Form of Government becomes destructive of these ends, it is the Right of the People to alter or to abolish it, and to institute new Government, laying its foundation on such principles and organizing its powers in such form, as to them shall seem most likely to effect their Safety and Happiness. Prudence, indeed, will dictate that Governments long established should not be changed for light and transient causes; and accordingly all experience hath shewn, that mankind are more disposed to suffer, while evils are sufferable, than to right themselves by abolishing the forms to which they are accustomed. But when a long train of abuses and usurpations, pursuing invariably the same Object evinces a design to reduce them under absolute Despotism, it is their right, it is their duty, to throw off such Government, and to provide new Guards for their future security.—Such has been the patient sufferance of these Colonies; and such is now the necessity which constrains them to alter their former Systems of Government. The history of the present King of Great Britain is a history of repeated injuries and usurpations, all having in direct object the establishment of an absolute Tyranny over these States. To prove this, let Facts be submitted to a candid world.

He has refused his Assent to Laws, the most wholesome and necessary for the public good.

He has forbidden his Governors to pass Laws of immediate and pressing importance, unless suspended in their operation till his Assent should be obtained; and when so suspended, he has utterly neglected to attend to them.

He has refused to pass other Laws for the accommodation of large districts of people, unless those people would relinquish the right of Representation in the Legislature, a right inestimable to them and formidable to tyrants only.

He has called together legislative bodies at places unusual, uncomfortable, and distant from the depository of their public Records, for the sole purpose of fatiguing them into compliance with his measures.

He has dissolved Representative Houses repeatedly, for opposing with manly firmness his invasions on the rights of the people.

He has refused for a long time, after such dissolutions, to cause others to be elected; whereby the Legislative powers, incapable of Annihilation, have returned to the People at large for their exercise; the State remaining in the mean time exposed to all the dangers of invasion from without, and convulsions within.

He has endeavoured to prevent the population of these States; for that purpose obstructing the Laws for Naturalization of Foreigners; refusing to pass others to encourage their migrations hither, and raising the conditions of new Appropriations of Lands.

He has obstructed the Administration of Justice, by refusing his Assent to Laws for establishing Judiciary powers.

He has made Judges dependent on his Will alone, for the tenure of their offices, and the amount and payment of their salaries.

He has erected a multitude of New Offices, and sent hither swarms of Officers to harrass our people, and eat out their substance.

He has kept among us, in times of peace, Standing Armies without the Consent of our legislatures.

He has affected to render the Military independent of and superior to the Civil power.

He has combined with others to subject us to a jurisdiction foreign to our constitution, and unacknowledged by our laws; giving his Assent to their Acts of pretended Legislation:

For Quartering large bodies of armed troops among us:

For protecting them, by a mock Trial, from punishment for any Murders which they should commit on the Inhabitants of these States:

For cutting off our Trade with all parts of the world:

For imposing Taxes on us without our Consent:

For depriving us in many cases, of the benefits of Trial by Jury:

For transporting us beyond Seas to be tried for pretended offences:

For abolishing the free System of English Laws in a neighboring Province, establishing therein an Arbitrary government, and enlarging its Boundaries so as to render it at once an example and fit instrument for introducing the same absolute rule into these Colonies:

For taking away our Charters, abolishing our most valuable Laws, and altering fundamentally the Forms of our Governments:

For suspending our own Legislatures, and declaring themselves invested with power to legislate for us in all cases whatsoever.

He has abdicated Government here, by declaring us out of his Protection and waging War against us.

He has plundered our seas, ravaged our Coasts, burnt our towns, and destroyed the lives of our people.

He is at this time transporting large Armies of foreign Mercenaries to compleat the works of death, desolation and tyranny, already begun with circumstances of Cruelty & perfidy scarcely paralleled in the most barbarous ages, and totally unworthy the Head of a civilized nation.

He has constrained our fellow Citizens taken Captive on the high Seas to bear Arms against their Country, to become the executioners of their friends and Brethren, or to fall themselves by their Hands.

He has excited domestic insurrections amongst us, and has endeavoured to bring on the inhabitants of our frontiers, the merciless Indian Savages, whose known rule of warfare, is an undistinguished destruction of all ages, sexes and conditions.

In every stage of these Oppressions We have Petitioned for Redress in the most humble terms: Our repeated Petitions have been answered only by repeated injury. A Prince whose character is thus marked by every act which may define a Tyrant, is unfit to be the ruler of a free people.

Nor have We been wanting in attentions to our Brittish brethren. We have warned them from time to time of attempts by their legislature to extend an unwarrantable jurisdiction over us. We have reminded them of the circumstances of our emigration and settlement here. We have appealed to their native justice and magnanimity, and we have conjured them by the ties of our common kindred to disavow these usurpations, which, would inevitably interrupt our connections and correspondence. They too have been deaf to the voice of justice and of consanguinity. We must, therefore, acquiesce in the necessity, which denounces our Separation, and hold them, as we hold the rest of mankind, Enemies in War, in Peace Friends.

We, Therefore, the Representatives of the United States of America, in General Congress, Assembled, appealing to the Supreme Judge of the world for the rectitude of our intentions, do, in the Name, and by Authority of the good People of these Colonies, solemnly publish and declare, That these United Colonies are, and of Right ought to be Free and Independent States; that they are Absolved from all Allegiance to the British Crown, and that all political connection between them and the State of Great Britain, is and ought to be totally dissolved; and that as Free and Independent States, they have full Power to levy War, conclude Peace, contract Alliances, establish Commerce, and to do all other Acts and Things which Independent States may of right do. And for the support of this Declaration, with a firm reliance on the protection of divine Providence, we mutually pledge to each other our Lives, our Fortunes and our sacred Honor.

The foregoing Declaration was, by order of Congress, engrossed, and signed by the following members:

John Hancock

New Hampshire
Josiah Bartlett
William Whipple
Matthew Thornton

Massachusetts Bay
Samuel Adams
John Adams
Robert Treat Paine
Elbridge Gerry

Rhode Island
Stephen Hopkins
William Ellery

Connecticut
Roger Sherman
Samuel Huntington
William Williams
Oliver Wolcott

New York
William Floyd
Philip Livingston
Francis Lewis
Lewis Morris

New Jersey
Richard Stockton
John Witherspoon
Francis Hopkinson
John Hart
Abraham Clark

Pennsylvania
Robert Morris
Benjamin Rush
Benjamin Franklin
John Morton
George Clymer
James Smith
George Taylor
James Wilson
George Ross

Delaware
Caesar Rodney
George Read
Thomas M'Kean

Maryland
Samuel Chase
William Paca
Thomas Stone
Charles Carroll, of Carrollton

Virginia
George Wythe
Richard Henry Lee
Thomas Jefferson
Benjamin Harrison
Thomas Nelson, Jr.
Francis Lightfoot Lee
Carter Braxton

North Carolina
William Hooper
Joseph Hewes
John Penn

South Carolina
Edward Rutledge
Thomas Heyward, Jr.
Thomas Lynch, Jr.
Arthur Middleton

Georgia
Button Gwinnett
Lyman Hall
George Walton

Resolved, That copies of the Declaration be sent to the several assemblies, conventions, and committees, or councils of safety, and to the several commanding officers of the continental troops; that it be proclaimed in each of the United States, at the head of the army.

THE CONSTITUTION OF THE UNITED STATES OF AMERICA

[PREAMBLE]

We the People of the United States, in Order to form a more perfect Union, establish Justice, insure domestic Tranquility, provide for the common defence, promote the general Welfare, and secure the Blessings of Liberty to ourselves and our Posterity, do ordain and establish this Constitution for the United States of America.

ARTICLE I

Section 1

[LEGISLATIVE POWERS]

All legislative Powers herein granted shall be vested in a Congress of the United States, which shall consist of a Senate and House of Representatives.

Section 2

[HOUSE OF REPRESENTATIVES, HOW CONSTITUTED, POWER OF IMPEACHMENT]

The House of Representatives shall be composed of Members chosen every second Year by the People of the several States, and the Electors in each State shall have the Qualifications requisite for Electors of the most numerous Branch of the State Legislature.

No Person shall be a Representative who shall not have attained to the Age of twenty five Years, and been seven Years a Citizen of the United States, and who shall not, when elected, be an Inhabitant of that State in which he shall be chosen.

Representatives and *direct Taxes*[1] shall be apportioned among the several States which may be included within this Union, according to their respective Numbers, *which shall be determined by adding to the whole Number of free Persons, including those bound to Service for a Term of Years, and excluding Indians not taxed, three fifths of all other Persons.*[2] The actual Enumeration shall be made within three Years after the first Meeting of the Congress of the United States, and within every subsequent Term of ten Years, in such Manner as they shall by Law direct. The Number of Representatives shall not exceed one for every thirty Thousand, but each State shall have at Least one Representative; *and until such enumeration shall be made, the State of New Hampshire shall be entitled to chuse three, Massachusetts eight, Rhode-Island and Providence Plantations one, Connecticut five, New-York six, New Jersey four, Pennsylvania eight, Delaware one, Maryland six, Virginia ten, North Carolina five, South Carolina five, and Georgia three.*[3]

When vacancies happen in the Representation from any State, the Executive Authority thereof shall issue Writs of Election to fill such Vacancies.

The House of Representatives shall chuse their Speaker and other Officers; and shall have the sole Power of Impeachment.

Section 3

[THE SENATE, HOW CONSTITUTED, IMPEACHMENT TRIALS]

The Senate of the United States shall be composed of two Senators from each State, *chosen by the Legislature thereof,*[4] for six Years; and each Senator shall have one Vote.

Immediately after they shall be assembled in Consequence of the first Election, they shall be divided as equally as may be into three Classes. The Seats of the Senators of the first Class shall be vacated at the Expiration of the second Year, of the second Class at the Expiration of the fourth Year, and of the third Class at the Expiration of the sixth Year, so that one third may be chosen every second Year; *and if Vacancies happen by Resignation, or otherwise, during the Recess of the Legislature of any State, the Executive thereof may make*

---

[1]Modified by Sixteenth Amendment.
[2]Modified by Fourteenth Amendment.
[3]Temporary provision.
[4]Modified by Seventeenth Amendment.

temporary Appointments until the next Meeting of the Legislature, which shall then fill such Vacancies.[5]

No Person shall be a Senator who shall not have attained to the Age of thirty Years, and been nine Years a Citizen of the United States, and who shall not, when elected, be an Inhabitant of that State for which he shall be chosen.

The Vice President of the United States shall be President of the Senate, but shall have no Vote, unless they be equally divided.

The Senate shall chuse their other Officers, and also a President pro tempore, in the Absence of the Vice President, or when he shall exercise the Office of President of the United States.

The Senate shall have the sole Power to try all Impeachments. When sitting for that Purpose, they shall be on Oath or Affirmation. When the President of the United States is tried, the Chief Justice shall preside: And no Person shall be convicted without the Concurrence of two thirds of the Members present.

Judgment in Cases of Impeachment shall not extend further than to removal from Office, and disqualification to hold and enjoy any Office of honor, Trust or Profit under the United States: but the Party convicted shall nevertheless be liable and subject to Indictment, Trial, Judgment and Punishment, according to Law.

Section 4

[ELECTION OF SENATORS AND REPRESENTATIVES]
The Times, Places and Manner of holding Elections for Senators and Representatives, shall be prescribed in each State by the Legislature thereof; but the Congress may at any time by Law make or alter such Regulations, except as to the Places of chusing Senators.

The Congress shall assemble at least once in every Year, and such Meeting shall be on the first Monday in December, unless they shall by Law appoint a different Day.[6]

Section 5

[QUORUM, JOURNALS, MEETINGS, ADJOURNMENTS]
Each House shall be the Judge of the Elections, Returns and Qualifications of its own Members,

and a Majority of each shall constitute a Quorum to do Business; but a smaller Number may adjourn from day to day, and may be authorized to compel the Attendance of absent Members, in such Manner, and under such Penalties as each House may provide.

Each House may determine the Rules of its Proceedings, punish its Members for disorderly Behaviour, and, with the Concurrence of two thirds, expel a Member.

Each House shall keep a Journal of its Proceedings, and from time to time publish the same, excepting such Parts as may in their Judgment require Secrecy; and the Yeas and Nays of the Members of either House on any questions shall, at the Desire of one fifth of those Present, be entered on the Journal.

Neither House, during the Session of Congress, shall, without the Consent of the other, adjourn for more than three days, nor to any other Place than that in which the two Houses shall be sitting.

Section 6

[COMPENSATION, PRIVILEGES, DISABILITIES]
The Senators and Representatives shall receive a Compensation for their Services, to be ascertained by Law, and paid out of the Treasury of the United States. They shall in all Cases, except Treason, Felony and Breach of the Peace, be privileged from Arrest during their Attendance at the Session of their respective Houses, and in going to and returning from the same; and for any Speech or Debate in either House, they shall not be questioned in any other Place.

No Senator or Representative shall, during the Time for which he was elected, be appointed to any civil Office under the Authority of the United States, which shall have been created, or the Emoluments whereof shall have been encreased during such time; and no Person holding any Office under the United States, shall be a Member of either House during his Continuance in Office.

Section 7

[PROCEDURE IN PASSING BILLS AND RESOLUTIONS]
All Bills for raising Revenue shall originate in the House of Representatives; but the Senate may propose or concur with Amendments as on other Bills.

---

[5]Modified by Seventeenth Amendment.
[6]Modified by Twentieth Amendment.

Every Bill which shall have passed the House of Representatives and the Senate, shall, before it become a Law, be presented to the President of the United States: If he approve he shall sign it, but if not he shall return it, with his Objections to that House in which it shall have originated, who shall enter the Objections at large on their Journal, and proceed to reconsider it. If after such Reconsideration two thirds of that House shall agree to pass the Bill, it shall be sent, together with the Objections, to the other House, by which it shall likewise be reconsidered, and if approved by two thirds of that House, it shall become a Law. But in all such Cases the Votes of both Houses shall be determined by yeas and Nays, and the Names of the Persons voting for and against the Bill shall be entered on the Journal of each House respectively. If any Bill shall not be returned by the President within ten Days (Sundays excepted) after it shall have been presented to him, the Same shall be a Law, in like Manner as if he had signed it, unless the Congress by their Adjournment prevent its Return, in which Case it shall not be a Law.

Every Order, Resolution, or Vote to which the Concurrence of the Senate and House of Representatives may be necessary (except on a question of Adjournment) shall be presented to the President of the United States; and before the Same shall take Effect, shall be approved by him, or being disapproved by him, shall be repassed by two thirds of the Senate and House of Representatives, according to the Rules and Limitations prescribed in the Case of a Bill.

Section 8

[POWERS OF CONGRESS]

The Congress shall have Power

To lay and collect Taxes, Duties, Imposts and Excises, to pay the Debts and provide for the common Defence and general Welfare of the United States; but all Duties, Imposts and Excises shall be uniform throughout the United States;

To borrow Money on the credit of the United States;

To regulate Commerce with foreign Nations, and among the several States, and with the Indian Tribes;

To establish an uniform Rule of Naturalization, and uniform Laws on the subject of Bankruptcies throughout the United States;

To coin Money, regulate the Value thereof, and of foreign Coin, and fix the Standard of Weights and Measures;

To provide for the Punishment of counterfeiting the Securities and current Coin of the United States;

To establish Post Offices and post Roads;

To promote the Progress of Science and useful Arts, by securing for limited Times to Authors and Inventors the exclusive Right to their respective Writings and Discoveries;

To constitute Tribunals inferior to the supreme Court;

To define and punish Piracies and Felonies committed on the high Seas, and Offences against the Law of Nations;

To declare War, grant Letters of Marque and Reprisal, and make Rules concerning Captures on Land and Water;

To raise and support Armies, but no Appropriation of Money to that Use shall be for a longer Term than two Years;

To provide and maintain a Navy;

To make Rules for the Government and Regulation of the land and naval Forces;

To provide for calling forth the Militia to execute the Laws of the Union, suppress Insurrections and repel Invasions;

To provide for organizing, arming, and disciplining, the Militia, and for governing such Part of them as may be employed in the Service of the United States, reserving to the States respectively, the Appointment of the Officers, and the Authority of training the Militia according to the discipline prescribed by Congress;

To exercise exclusive Legislation in all Cases whatsoever, over such District (not exceeding ten Miles square) as may, by Cession of particular States, and the Acceptance of Congress, become the Seat of the Government of the United States, and to exercise like Authority over all Places purchased by the Consent of the Legislature of the State in which the Same shall be, for the Erection of Forts, Magazines, Arsenals, dock-Yards, and other needful Buildings;—And

To make all Laws which shall be necessary and proper for carrying into Execution the foregoing Powers, and all other Powers vested by this Constitution in the Government of the United States, or in any Department or Officer thereof.

Section 9

[SOME RESTRICTIONS ON FEDERAL POWER]
The Migration or Importation of such Persons as any of the States now existing shall think proper to admit, shall not be prohibited by the Congress prior to the Year one thousand eight hundred and eight, but a Tax or duty may be imposed on such Importation, not exceeding ten dollars for each Person.[7]

The Privilege of the Writ of Habeas Corpus shall not be suspended, unless when in Cases of Rebellion or Invasion the public Safety may require it.

No Bill of Attainder or ex post facto Law shall be passed.

No Capitation, or other direct, Tax shall be laid, unless in Proportion to the Census or Enumeration herein before directed to be taken.[8]

No Tax or Duty shall be laid on Articles exported from any State.

No Preference shall be given by any Regulation of Commerce or Revenue to the Ports of one State over those of another; nor shall Vessels bound to, or from, one State, be obliged to enter, clear, or pay Duties in another.

No Money shall be drawn from the Treasury, but in Consequence of Appropriations made by Law; and a regular Statement and Account of the Receipts and Expenditures of all public Money shall be published from time to time.

No Title of Nobility shall be granted by the United States: And no Person holding any Office of Profit or Trust under them, shall, without the Consent of the Congress, accept of any present, Emolument, Office, or Title, of any kind whatever, from any King, Prince, or foreign State.

Section 10

[RESTRICTIONS UPON POWERS OF STATES]
No State shall enter into any Treaty, Alliance, or Confederation; grant Letters of Marque and Reprisal; coin Money; emit Bills of Credit; make any Thing but gold and silver Coin a Tender in Payment of Debts; pass any Bill of Attainder, ex post facto Law, or Law impairing the Obligation of Contracts, or grant any Title of Nobility.

No State shall, without the Consent of the Congress, lay any Imposts or Duties on Imports or Exports, except what may be absolutely necessary for executing its inspection Laws: and the net Produce of all Duties and Imposts, laid by any State on Imports or Exports, shall be for the Use of the Treasury of the United States; and all such Laws shall be subject to the Revision and Control of the Congress.

No State shall, without the Consent of Congress, lay any Duty of Tonnage, keep Troops, or Ships of War in time of Peace, enter into any Agreement or Compact with another State, or with a foreign Power, or engage in War, unless actually invaded, or in such imminent Danger as will not admit of delay.

ARTICLE II

Section 1

[EXECUTIVE POWER, ELECTION, QUALIFICATIONS OF THE PRESIDENT]
The executive Power shall be vested in a President of the United States of America. *He shall hold his Office during the Term of four Years, and, together with the Vice President, chosen for the same Term, be elected, as follows*[9]

Each State shall appoint, in such Manner as the Legislature thereof may direct, a Number of Electors, equal to the whole Number of Senators and Representatives to which the State may be entitled in the Congress: but no Senator or Representative, or Person holding an Office of Trust or Profit under the United States, shall be appointed an Elector.

The electors shall meet in their respective States, and vote by ballot for two Persons, of whom one at least shall not be an Inhabitant of the same State with themselves. And they shall make a List of all the Persons voted for, and of the Number of Votes for each; which List they shall sign and certify, and transmit sealed to the Seat of the Government of the United States, directed to the President of the Senate. The President of the Senate shall, in the Presence of the Senate and House of Representatives, open all the Certificates, and the Votes shall then be counted. The Person having the greatest Number of Votes shall be the President, if such

---

[7]Temporary provision.
[8]Modified by Sixteenth Amendment.

[9]Number of terms limited to two by Twenty-Second Amendment.

Number be a Majority of the whole Number of Electors appointed; and if there be more than one who have such Majority, and have an equal Number of Votes, then the House of Representatives shall immediately chuse by Ballot one of them for President; and if no Person have a Majority, then from the five highest on the List the said House shall in like Manner chuse the President. But in chusing the President, the Votes shall be taken by States, the Representation from each State having one Vote; A quorum for this Purpose shall consist of a Member or Members from two thirds of the States, and a Majority of all the States shall be necessary to a Choice. In every Case, after the Choice of the President, the person having the greatest Number of Votes of the Electors shall be the Vice President. But if there should remain two or more who have equal Votes, the Senate shall chuse from them by Ballot the Vice President.[10]

The Congress may determine the Time of chusing the Electors, and the Day on which they shall give their Votes; which Day shall be the same throughout the United States.

No Person except a natural born Citizen, or a Citizen of the United States, at the time of the Adoption of this Constitution, shall be eligible to the Office of President; neither shall any Person be eligible to that Office who shall not have attained to the Age of thirty five Years, and been fourteen Years a Resident within the United States.

In Case of the Removal of the President from Office, or his Death, Resignation, or Inability to discharge the Powers and Duties of the said Office, the Same shall devolve on the Vice President, and the Congress may by Law provide for the Case of Removal, Death, Resignation or Inability, both of the President and Vice President, declaring what Officer shall then act as President, and such Officer shall act accordingly, until the Disability be removed, or a President shall be elected.

The President shall, at stated Times, receive for his Services, a Compensation, which shall neither be increased nor diminished during the Period for which he shall have been elected, and he shall not receive within that Period any other Emolument from the United States, or any of them.

[10]Modified by Twelfth and Twentieth Amendments.

Before he enter on the Execution of his Office, he shall take the following Oath or Affirmation:—"I do solemnly swear (or affirm) that I will faithfully execute the Office of President of the United States, and will to the best of my Ability, preserve, protect and defend the Constitution of the United States."

Section 2

[POWERS OF THE PRESIDENT]

The President shall be Commander in Chief of the Army and Navy of the United States, and of the Militia of the several States, when called into the actual Service of the United States; he may require the Opinion, in writing, of the principal Officer in each of the executive Departments, upon any Subject relating to the Duties of their respective Offices, and he shall have Power to grant Reprieves and Pardons for Offences against the United States, except in Cases of Impeachment.

He shall have Power, by and with the Advice and Consent of the Senate, to make Treaties, provided two thirds of the Senators present concur; and he shall nominate, and by and with the Advice and Consent of the Senate, shall appoint Ambassadors, other public Ministers and Consuls, Judges of the supreme Court, and all other Officers of the United States, whose Appointments are not herein otherwise provided for, and which shall be established by Law: but the Congress may by Law vest the Appointment of such inferior Officers, as they think proper, in the President alone, in the Courts of Law, or in the Heads of Departments.

The President shall have Power to fill up all Vacancies that may happen during the Recess of the Senate, by granting Commissions which shall expire at the End of their next Session.

Section 3

[POWERS AND DUTIES OF THE PRESIDENT]

He shall from time to time give to the Congress Information of the State of the Union, and recommend to their Consideration such Measures as he shall judge necessary and expedient; he may, on extraordinary Occasions, convene both Houses, or either of them, and in Case of Disagreement between them, with Respect to the Time of Adjournment, he may adjourn them to such Time as he shall think proper; he shall receive Ambassadors and other public

Ministers; he shall take Care that the Laws be faithfully executed, and shall Commission all the Officers of the United States.

Section 4
[IMPEACHMENT]
The President, Vice President and all civil Officers of the United States, shall be removed from Office on Impeachment for, and Conviction of, Treason, Bribery, or other high Crimes and Misdemeanors.

ARTICLE III
Section 1
[JUDICIAL POWER, TENURE OF OFFICE]
The judicial Power of the United States, shall be vested in one supreme Court, and in such inferior Courts as the Congress may from time to time ordain and establish. The Judges, both of the supreme and inferior Courts, shall hold their Offices during good Behaviour, and shall, at stated Times, receive for their Services, a Compensation, which shall not be diminished during their Continuance in Office.

Section 2
[JURISDICTION]
The judicial Power shall extend to all Cases, in Law and Equity, arising under this Constitution, the Laws of the United States, and Treaties made, or which shall be made, under their Authority;—to all Cases affecting Ambassadors, other public Ministers and Consuls;—to all Cases of admiralty and maritime Jurisdiction;—to Controversies to which the United States shall be a Party;—to Controversies between two or more States;—*between a State and Citizens of another State;*—between Citizens of different States,—between Citizens of the same State claiming Lands under Grants of different States, *and between a State, or the Citizens thereof, and foreign States, Citizens or Subjects.*[11]

In all Cases affecting Ambassadors, other public Ministers and Consuls, and those in which a State shall be Party, the supreme Court shall have original Jurisdiction. In all the other Cases before mentioned, the supreme Court shall have appellate Jurisdiction, both as to Law and Fact, with such Exceptions, and under such Regulations as the Congress shall make.

The Trial of all Crimes, except in Cases of Impeachment, shall be by Jury; and such Trial shall be held in the State where the said Crimes shall have been committed; but when not committed within any State, the Trial shall be at such Place or Places as the Congress may by Law have directed.

Section 3
[TREASON, PROOF, AND PUNISHMENT]
Treason against the United States, shall consist only in levying War against them, or in adhering to their Enemies, giving them Aid and Comfort. No Person shall be convicted of Treason unless on the Testimony of two Witnesses to the same overt Act, or on Confession in open Court.

The Congress shall have Power to declare the Punishment of Treason, but no Attainder of Treason shall work Corruption of Blood, or Forfeiture except during the Life of the Person attainted.

ARTICLE IV
Section 1
[FAITH AND CREDIT AMONG STATES]
Full Faith and Credit shall be given in each State to the public Acts, Records, and judicial Proceedings of every other State. And the Congress may by general Laws prescribe the Manner in which such Acts, Records and Proceedings shall be proved, and the Effect thereof.

Section 2
[PRIVILEGES AND IMMUNITIES, FUGITIVES]
The Citizens of each State shall be entitled to all Privileges and Immunities of Citizens in the several States.

A Person charged in any State with Treason, Felony or other Crime, who shall flee from Justice, and be found in another State, shall on Demand of the executive Authority of the State from which he fled, be delivered up, to be removed to the State having Jurisdiction of the Crime.

No person held to Service or Labour in one State, under the Laws thereof, escaping into another, shall, in Consequence of any Law or Regulation therein, be discharged from such Service or Labour, but shall be delivered up on Claim of the Party to whom such Service or Labour may be due.[12]

---

[11]Modified by Eleventh Amendment.

[12]Repealed by the Thirteenth Amendment.

Section 3

[ADMISSION OF NEW STATES]

New States may be admitted by the Congress into this Union; but no new State shall be formed or erected within the Jurisdiction of any other State; nor any State be formed by the Junction of two or more States, or Parts of States, without the Consent of the Legislatures of the States concerned as well as of the Congress.

The Congress shall have Power to dispose of and make all needful Rules and Regulations respecting the Territory or other Property belonging to the United States; and nothing in this Constitution shall be so construed as to Prejudice any Claims of the United States, or of any particular State.

Section 4

[GUARANTEE OF REPUBLICAN GOVERNMENT]

The United States shall guarantee to every State in this Union a Republican Form of Government, and shall protect each of them against Invasion; and on Application of the Legislature, or of the Executive (when the Legislature cannot be convened), against domestic Violence.

ARTICLE V

[AMENDMENT OF THE CONSTITUTION]

The Congress, whenever two thirds of both Houses shall deem it necessary, shall propose Amendments to this Constitution, or, on the Application of the Legislatures of two thirds of the several States, shall call a Convention for proposing Amendments, which, in either Case, shall be valid to all Intents and Purposes, as Part of this Constitution, when ratified by the Legislatures of three fourths of the several States, or by Conventions in three fourths thereof, as the one or the other Mode of Ratification may be proposed by the Congress; *Provided that no Amendment which may be made prior to the Year One thousand eight hundred and eight shall in any Manner affect the first and fourth Clauses in the Ninth Section of the first Article;*[13] and that no State, without its Consent, shall be deprived of its equal Suffrage in the Senate.

ARTICLE VI

[DEBTS, SUPREMACY, OATH]

All Debts contracted and Engagements entered into, before the Adoption of this Constitution, shall be as valid against the United States under this Constitution, as under the Confederation.

This Constitution, and the Laws of the United States which shall be made in Pursuance thereof; and all Treaties made, or which shall be made, under the Authority of the United States, shall be the supreme Law of the Land; and the Judges in every State shall be bound thereby, any Thing in the Constitution or Laws of any State to the Contrary notwithstanding.

The Senators and Representatives before mentioned, and the Members of the several State Legislatures, and all executive and judicial Officers, both of the United States and of the several States, shall be bound by Oath or Affirmation, to support this Constitution; but no religious Test shall be required as a Qualification to any Office or public Trust under the United States.

ARTICLE VII

[RATIFICATION AND ESTABLISHMENT]

The Ratification of the Conventions of nine States, shall be sufficient for the Establishment of this Constitution between the States so ratifying the Same.[14]

Done in Convention by the Unanimous Consent of the States present the Seventeenth Day of September in the Year of our Lord one thousand seven hundred and Eighty seven and of the Independence of the United States of America the Twelfth. *In Witness* whereof We have hereunto subscribed our Names,

---

[13]Temporary provision.

[14]The Constitution was submitted on September 17, 1787, by the Constitutional Convention, was ratified by the conventions of several states at various dates up to May 29, 1790, and became effective on March 4, 1789.

G:º WASHINGTON—
Presidt. and deputy from Virginia

New Hampshire
John Langdon
Nicholas Gilman

Massachusetts
Nathaniel Gorham
Rufus King

Connecticut
Wm. Saml. Johnson
Roger Sherman

New York
Alexander Hamilton

New Jersey
Wil: Livingston
David Brearley
Wm. Paterson
Jona: Dayton

Pennsylvania
B Franklin
Thomas Mifflin
Robt. Morris
Geo. Clymer
Thos. FitzSimons
Jared Ingersoll
James Wilson
Gouv Morris

Delaware
Geo: Read
Gunning Bedford jun
John Dickinson
Richard Bassett
Jaco: Broom

Maryland
James McHenry
Dan of St Thos. Jenifer
Danl. Carroll

Virginia
John Blair—
James Madison Jr.

North Carolina
Wm. Blount
Richd. Dobbs Spaight
Hu Williamson

South Carolina
J. Rutledge
Charles Cotesworth
Pinckney
Charles Pinckney
Pierce Butler

Georgia
William Few
Abr Baldwin

AMENDMENTS TO THE CONSTITUTION

Proposed by Congress and Ratified by the Legislatures of
the Several States, Pursuant to Article V of the Original Constitution.

Amendments I–X, known as the Bill of Rights, were proposed by Congress on September 25, 1789, and ratified on December 15, 1791.

AMENDMENT I

[FREEDOM OF RELIGION, OF SPEECH, AND OF THE PRESS]
Congress shall make no law respecting an establishment of religion, or prohibiting the free exercise thereof; or abridging the freedom of speech, or of the press; or the right of the people peaceably to assemble, and to petition the Government for a redress of grievances.

AMENDMENT II

[RIGHT TO KEEP AND BEAR ARMS]
A well regulated Militia, being necessary to the security of a free State, the right of the people to keep and bear Arms, shall not be infringed.

AMENDMENT III

[QUARTERING OF SOLDIERS]
No Soldier shall, in time of peace be quartered in any house, without the consent of the Owner, nor in time of war, but in a manner to be prescribed by law.

AMENDMENT IV

[SECURITY FROM UNWARRANTABLE SEARCH AND SEIZURE]
The right of the people to be secure in their persons, houses, papers, and effects, against unreasonable searches and seizures, shall not be violated, and no Warrants shall issue, but upon probable cause, supported by Oath or affirmation, and particularly describing the place to be searched, and the persons or things to be seized.

AMENDMENT V

[RIGHTS OF ACCUSED PERSONS IN CRIMINAL PROCEEDINGS]
No person shall be held to answer for a capital, or otherwise infamous crime, unless on a presentment or indictment of a Grand Jury, except in cases arising in the land or naval forces, or in the Militia, when in actual service in time of War or in public danger; nor shall any person be subject for the same offence to be twice put in jeopardy of life or limb; nor shall be compelled in any criminal case to be a witness against himself, nor be deprived of life, liberty, or property, without due process of law; nor shall private property be taken for public use, without just compensation.

AMENDMENT VI

[RIGHT TO SPEEDY TRIAL, WITNESSES, ETC.]
In all criminal prosecutions, the accused shall enjoy the right to a speedy and public trial, by an impartial jury of the State and district wherein the crime shall have been committed, which district shall have been previously ascertained by law, and to be informed of the nature and cause of the accusation; to be confronted with the witnesses against him; to have compulsory process for obtaining witnesses in his favor, and to have the Assistance of Counsel for his defence.

AMENDMENT VII

[TRIAL BY JURY IN CIVIL CASES]
In suits at common law, where the value in controversy shall exceed twenty dollars, the right of trial by jury shall be preserved, and no fact tried by a jury, shall be otherwise reexamined in any Court of the United States, than according to the rules of the common law.

AMENDMENT VIII

[BAILS, FINES, PUNISHMENTS]
Excessive bail shall not be required, nor excessive fines imposed, nor cruel and unusual punishments inflicted.

AMENDMENT IX

[RESERVATION OF RIGHTS OF PEOPLE]
The enumeration in the Constitution, of certain rights, shall not be construed to deny or disparage others retained by the people.

AMENDMENT X

[POWERS RESERVED TO STATES OR PEOPLE]
The powers not delegated to the United States by the Constitution, nor prohibited by it to the States, are reserved to the States respectively, or to the people.

AMENDMENT XI

[*Proposed by Congress on March 4, 1794; declared ratified on January 8, 1798.*]
[RESTRICTION OF JUDICIAL POWER]
The Judicial power of the United States shall not be construed to extend to any suit in law or equity, commenced or prosecuted against one of the United States by Citizens of another State, or by Citizens or Subjects of any Foreign State.

AMENDMENT XII

[*Proposed by Congress on December 9, 1803; declared ratified on September 25, 1804.*]
[ELECTION OF PRESIDENT AND VICE PRESIDENT]
The Electors shall meet in their respective states and vote by ballot for President and Vice-President, one of whom, at least, shall not be an inhabitant of the same state with themselves; they shall name in their ballots the person voted for as President, and in distinct ballots the person voted for as Vice-President, and they shall make distinct lists of all persons voted for as President, and of all persons voted for as Vice-President, and of the number of votes for each, which lists they shall sign and certify, and transmit sealed to the seat of the government of the United States, directed to the President of the Senate;—the President of the Senate shall, in presence of the Senate and House of Representatives, open all the certificates and the votes shall then be counted;—The person having the greatest number of votes for President, shall be the President, if such number be a majority of the whole number of Electors appointed; and if no person have such majority, then from the persons having the highest numbers not exceeding three on the list of those voted for as President, the House of Representatives shall choose immediately, by ballot, the President. But in choosing the President, the votes shall be taken by states, the representation from each state having one vote; a quorum for this purpose shall consist of a member or members from two-thirds of the states, and a majority of all the states shall be necessary to a choice. And if the House of Representatives shall not choose a President whenever the right of choice shall devolve upon them, before the fourth day of March next following, then the Vice-President shall act as President, as in the case of the death or other constitutional disability of the President.—The person having the greatest number of votes as Vice-President, shall be the Vice-President, if such number be a majority of the whole number of Electors appointed, and if no person have a majority, then from the two highest numbers on the list, the Senate shall choose the Vice-President; a quorum for the purpose shall consist of two-thirds of the whole number of Senators, and a majority of the whole number shall be necessary to a choice. But no person constitutionally ineligible to the office of President shall be eligible to that of Vice-President of the United States.

AMENDMENT XIII

[*Proposed by Congress on January 31, 1865; declared ratified on December 18, 1865.*]

Section 1

[ABOLITION OF SLAVERY]
Neither slavery nor involuntary servitude, except as a punishment for crime whereof the party shall have been duly convicted, shall exist within the United States, or any place subject to their jurisdiction.

Section 2

[POWER TO ENFORCE THIS ARTICLE]
Congress shall have power to enforce this article by appropriate legislation.

AMENDMENT XIV

[*Proposed by Congress on June 13, 1866; declared ratified on July 28, 1868.*]

Section 1

[CITIZENSHIP RIGHTS NOT TO BE ABRIDGED BY STATES]
All persons born or naturalized in the United States, and subject to the jurisdiction thereof, are citizens of the United States and of the State wherein they reside. No State shall make or enforce any law which shall abridge the privileges or immunities of citizens of the United

States; nor shall any State deprive any person of life, liberty, or property, without due process of law; nor deny to any person within its jurisdiction the equal protection of the laws.

Section 2

[APPORTIONMENT OF REPRESENTATIVES IN CONGRESS]

Representatives shall be apportioned among the several States according to their respective numbers, counting the whole number of persons in each State, excluding Indians not taxed. But when the right to vote at any election for the choice of electors for President and Vice-President of the United States, Representatives in Congress, the Executive and Judicial officers of a State, or the members of the Legislature thereof, is denied to any of the male inhabitants of such State, being twenty-one years of age, and citizens of the United States, or in any way abridged, except for participation in rebellion, or other crime, the basis of representation therein shall be reduced in the proportion which the number of such male citizens shall bear to the whole number of male citizens twenty-one years of age in such State.

Section 3

[PERSONS DISQUALIFIED FROM HOLDING OFFICE]

No person shall be a Senator or Representative in Congress, or elector of President and Vice-President, or hold any office, civil or military, under the United States, or under any State, who, having previously taken an oath, as a member of Congress, or as an officer of the United States, or as a member of any State legislature, or as an executive or judicial officer of any State, to support the Constitution of the United States, shall have engaged in insurrection or rebellion against the same, or given aid or comfort to the enemies thereof. But Congress may by a vote of two-thirds of each House, remove such disability.

Section 4

[WHAT PUBLIC DEBTS ARE VALID]

The validity of the public debt of the United States, authorized by law, including debts incurred for payment of pensions and bounties for services in suppressing insurrection or rebellion, shall not be questioned. But neither the United States nor any State shall assume or pay any debt or obligation incurred in aid of insurrection or rebellion against the United States, or any claim for the loss or emancipation of any slave; but all such debts, obligations and claims shall be held illegal and void.

Section 5

[POWER TO ENFORCE THIS ARTICLE]

The Congress shall have power to enforce, by appropriate legislation, the provisions of this article.

AMENDMENT XV

[*Proposed by Congress on February 26, 1869; declared ratified on March 30, 1870.*]

Section 1

[NEGRO SUFFRAGE]

The right of citizens of the United States to vote shall not be denied or abridged by the United States or by any State on account of race, color, or previous condition of servitude.

Section 2

[POWER TO ENFORCE THIS ARTICLE]

The Congress shall have power to enforce this article by appropriate legislation.

AMENDMENT XVI

[*Proposed by Congress on July 2, 1909; declared ratified on February 25, 1913.*]

[AUTHORIZING INCOME TAXES]

The Congress shall have power to lay and collect taxes on incomes, from whatever source derived, without apportionment among the several States, and without regard to any census or enumeration.

AMENDMENT XVII

[*Proposed by Congress on May 13, 1912; declared ratified on May 31, 1913.*]

[POPULAR ELECTION OF SENATORS]

The Senate of the United States shall be composed of two Senators from each State, elected by the people thereof, for six years; and each Senator shall have one vote. The electors in each State shall have the qualifications requisite for electors of the most numerous branch of the State legislatures.

When vacancies happen in the representation of any State in the Senate, the executive authority of such State shall issue writs of election to fill such vacancies: *Provided,* That the legislature of any State may empower the executive thereof to make temporary appointments until the people fill the vacancies by election as the legislature may direct.

This amendment shall not be so construed as to affect the election or term of any Senator chosen before it becomes valid as part of the Constitution.

AMENDMENT XVIII

[Proposed by Congress December 18, 1917; declared ratified on January 29, 1919.]

Section 1

[NATIONAL LIQUOR PROHIBITION]

After one year from the ratification of this article the manufacture, sale, or transportation of intoxicating liquors within, the importation thereof into, or the exportation thereof from the United States and all territory subject to the jurisdiction thereof for beverage purposes is hereby prohibited.

Section 2

[POWER TO ENFORCE THIS ARTICLE]

The Congress and the several States shall have concurrent power to enforce this article by appropriate legislation.

Section 3

[RATIFICATION WITHIN SEVEN YEARS]

This article shall be inoperative unless it shall have been ratified as an amendment to the Constitution by the legislatures of the several States, as provided in the Constitution, within seven years from the date of the submission hereof to the States by the Congress.[1]

AMENDMENT XIX

[Proposed by Congress on June 4, 1919; declared ratified on August 26, 1920.]

[WOMAN SUFFRAGE]

The right of citizens of the United States to vote shall not be denied or abridged by the United States or by any State on account of sex.

Congress shall have power to enforce this article by appropriate legislation.

AMENDMENT XX

[Proposed by Congress on March 2, 1932; declared ratified on February 6, 1933.]

Section 1

[TERMS OF OFFICE]

The terms of the President and Vice President shall end at noon on the 20th day of January, and the terms of Senators and Representatives at noon on the 3d day of January, of the years in which such terms would have ended if this article had not been ratified; and the terms of their successors shall then begin.

Section 2

[TIME OF CONVENING CONGRESS]

The Congress shall assemble at least once in every year, and such meeting shall begin at noon on the 3d day of January, unless they shall by law appoint a different day.

Section 3

[DEATH OF PRESIDENT-ELECT]

If, at the time fixed for the beginning of the term of the President, the President elect shall have died, the Vice President elect shall become President. If a President shall not have been chosen before the time fixed for the beginning of his term, or if the President elect shall have failed to qualify, then the Vice President elect shall act as President until a President shall have qualified; and the Congress may by law provide for the case wherein neither a President elect nor a Vice President elect shall have qualified, declaring who shall then act as President, or the manner in which one who is to act shall be selected, and such person shall act accordingly until a President or Vice President shall have qualified.

Section 4

[ELECTION OF THE PRESIDENT]

The Congress may by law provide for the case of the death of any of the persons from whom the House of Representatives may choose a President whenever the right of choice shall have devolved upon them, and for the case of the death of any of the persons from whom the Senate may choose a Vice President whenever the right of choice shall have devolved upon them.

Section 5

[AMENDMENT TAKES EFFECT]

Sections 1 and 2 shall take effect on the 15th day of October following the ratification of this article.

Section 6

[RATIFICATION WITHIN SEVEN YEARS]

This article shall be inoperative unless it shall have been ratified as an amendment to the Constitution by the legislatures of three-fourths of the several States within seven years from the date of its submission.

AMENDMENT XXI

[*Proposed by Congress on February 20, 1933; declared ratified on December 5, 1933.*]

Section 1

[NATIONAL LIQUOR PROHIBITION REPEALED]
The eighteenth article of amendment to the Constitution of the United States is hereby repealed.

Section 2

[TRANSPORTATION OF LIQUOR INTO "DRY" STATES]
The transportation or importation into any State, Territory, or Possession of the United States for delivery or use therein of intoxicating liquors, in violation of the laws thereof, is hereby prohibited.

Section 3

[RATIFICATION WITHIN SEVEN YEARS]
This article shall be inoperative unless it shall have been ratified as an amendment to the Constitution by conventions in the several States, as provided in the Constitution, within seven years from the date of the submission hereof to the States by the Congress.

AMENDMENT XXII

[*Proposed by Congress on March 21, 1947; declared ratified on February 27, 1951.*]

Section 1

[TENURE OF PRESIDENT LIMITED]
No person shall be elected to the office of President more than twice, and no person who has held the office of President or acted as President, for more than two years of a term to which some other person was elected President shall be elected to the office of the President more than once. But this Article shall not apply to any person holding the office of President when this Article was proposed by the Congress, and shall not prevent any person who may be holding the office of President, or acting as President, during the term within which this Article becomes operative from holding the office of President or acting as President during the remainder of such term.

Section 2

[RATIFICATION WITHIN SEVEN YEARS]
This article shall be inoperative unless it shall have been ratified as an amendment to the Constitution by the legislatures of three-fourths of the several States within seven years from the date of its submission to the States by the Congress.

AMENDMENT XXIII

[*Proposed by Congress on June 16, 1960; declared ratified on March 29, 1961.*]

Section 1

[ELECTORAL COLLEGE VOTES FOR THE DISTRICT OF COLUMBIA]
The District constituting the seat of Government of the United States shall appoint in such manner as the Congress may direct:

A number of electors of President and Vice President equal to the whole number of Senators and Representatives in Congress to which the District would be entitled if it were a State, but in no event more than the least populous State; they shall be in addition to those appointed by the States, but they shall be considered, for the purposes of the election of President and Vice President, to be electors appointed by a State; and they shall meet in the District and perform such duties as provided by the twelfth article of amendment.

Section 2

[POWER TO ENFORCE THIS ARTICLE]
The Congress shall have power to enforce this article by appropriate legislation.

AMENDMENT XXIV

[*Proposed by Congress on August 27, 1962; declared ratified on January 23, 1964.*]

Section 1

[ANTI-POLL TAX]
The right of citizens of the United States to vote in any primary or other election for President or Vice President, for electors for President or Vice President, or for Senator or Representative of Congress, shall not be denied or abridged by the United States or any State by reason of failure to pay any poll tax or other tax.

Section 2

[POWER TO ENFORCE THIS ARTICLE]

The Congress shall have power to enforce this article by appropriate legislation.

AMENDMENT XXV

[*Proposed by Congress on July 6, 1965; declared ratified on February 10, 1967.*]

Section 1

[VICE PRESIDENT TO BECOME PRESIDENT]

In case of the removal of the President from office or his death or resignation, the Vice President shall become President.

Section 2

[CHOICE OF A NEW VICE PRESIDENT]

Whenever there is a vacancy in the office of the Vice President, the President shall nominate a Vice President who shall take the office upon confirmation by a majority vote of both houses of Congress.

Section 3

[PRESIDENT MAY DECLARE OWN DISABILITY]

Whenever the President transmits to the President pro tempore of the Senate and the Speaker of the House of Representatives his written declaration that he is unable to discharge the powers and duties of his office, and until he transmits to them a written declaration to the contrary, such powers and duties shall be discharged by the Vice President as Acting President.

Section 4

[ALTERNATE PROCEDURES TO DECLARE AND TO END PRESIDENTIAL DISABILITY]

Whenever the Vice President and a majority of either the principal officers of the executive departments, or of such other body as Congress may by law provide, transmit to the President pro tempore of the Senate and the Speaker of the House of Representatives their written declaration that the President is unable to discharge the powers and duties of his office, the Vice President shall immediately assume the powers and duties of the office as Acting President.

Thereafter, when the President transmits to the President pro tempore of the Senate and the Speaker of the House of Representatives his written declaration that no inability exists, he shall resume the powers and duties of his office unless the Vice President and a majority of either the principal officers of the executive department, or of such other body as Congress may by law provide, transmit within four days to the President pro tempore of the Senate and the Speaker of the House of Representatives their written declaration that the President is unable to discharge the powers and duties of his office. Thereupon Congress shall decide the issue, assembling within forty eight hours for that purpose if not in session. If the Congress, within twenty one days after receipt of the latter written declaration, or, if Congress is not in session, within twenty one days after Congress is required to assemble, determines by two-thirds vote of both Houses that the President is unable to discharge the powers and duties of his office, the Vice President shall continue to discharge the same as Acting President; otherwise, the President shall resume the powers and duties of his office.

AMENDMENT XXVI

[*Proposed by Congress on March 23, 1971; declared ratified on July 1, 1971.*]

Section 1

[EIGHTEEN-YEAR-OLD VOTE]

The right of citizens of the United States, who are eighteen years of age or older, to vote shall not be denied or abridged by the United States or by any State on account of age.

Section 2

[POWER TO ENFORCE THIS ARTICLE]

The Congress shall have power to enforce this article by appropriate legislation.

AMENDMENT XXVII

[*Proposed by Congress on September 25, 1789; declared ratified on May 8, 1992.*]

[CONGRESS CANNOT RAISE ITS OWN PAY]

No law varying the compensation for the services of the Senators and Representatives, shall take effect, until an election of representatives shall have intervened.

NO. 10: MADISON

Among the numerous advantages promised by a well constructed Union, none deserves to be more accurately developed than its tendency to break and control the violence of faction. The friend of popular governments never finds himself so much alarmed for their character and fate, as when he contemplates their propensity to this dangerous vice. He will not fail therefore to set a due value on any plan which, without violating the principles to which he is attached, provides a proper cure for it. The instability, injustice, and confusion introduced into the public councils have, in truth, been the mortal diseases under which popular governments have everywhere perished, as they continue to be the favorite and fruitful topics from which the adversaries to liberty derive their most specious declamations. The valuable improvements made by the American constitutions on the popular models, both ancient and modern, cannot certainly be too much admired; but it would be an unwarrantable partiality to contend that they have as effectually obviated the danger on this side, as was wished and expected. Complaints are everywhere heard from our most considerate and virtuous citizens, equally the friends of public and private faith and of public and personal liberty, that our governments are too unstable, that the public good is disregarded in the conflicts of rival parties, and that measures are too often decided, not according to the rules of justice and the rights of the minor party, but by the superior force of an interested and overbearing majority. However anxiously we may wish that these complaints had no foundation, the evidence of known facts will not permit us to deny that they are in some degree true. It will be found, indeed, on a candid review of our situation, that some of the distresses under which we labor have been erroneously charged on the operation of our governments; but it will be found, at the same time, that other causes will not alone account for many of our heaviest misfortunes; and, particularly, for that prevailing and increasing distrust of public engagements and alarm for private rights which are echoed from one end of the continent to the other. These must be chiefly, if not wholly, effects of the unsteadiness and injustice with which a factious spirit has tainted our public administration.

By a faction I understand a number of citizens, whether amounting to a majority or minority of the whole, who are united and actuated by some common impulse of passion, or of interest, adverse to the rights of other citizens, or to the permanent and aggregate interests of the community.

There are two methods of curing the mischiefs of faction: the one, by removing its causes; the other, by controlling its effects.

There are again two methods of removing the causes of faction: the one, by destroying the liberty which is essential to its existence; the other, by giving to every citizen the same opinions, the same passions, and the same interests.

It could never be more truly said than of the first remedy, that it is worse than the disease. Liberty is to faction what air is to fire, an aliment without which it instantly expires. But it could not be a less folly to abolish liberty, which is essential to political life, because it nourishes faction, than it would be to wish the annihilation of air, which is essential to animal life, because it imparts to fire its destructive agency.

The second expedient is as impracticable, as the first would be unwise. As long as the reason of man continues fallible, and he is at liberty to exercise it, different opinions will be formed. As long as the connection subsists between his reason and his self-love, his opinions and his passions will have a reciprocal influence on each other; and the former will be objects to which the latter will attach themselves. The diversity in the faculties of men, from which the rights of property originate, is not less an insuperable obstacle to a uniformity of interests. The protection of these faculties is the first object of Government. From the protection of different and unequal faculties of acquiring property, the possession of different degrees and kinds of property immediately results; and from the influence of these on the sentiments and views of the respective proprietors, ensues a division of the society into different interests and parties.

The latent causes of faction are thus sown in the nature of man; and we see them everywhere brought into different degrees of activity, according to the different circumstances of civil society. A zeal for different opinions concerning religion, concerning Government, and many other points, as well of speculation as of practice; an attachment to different leaders ambitiously contending for pre-eminence and power; or to persons of other descriptions whose fortunes have been interesting to the human passions, have in turn divided mankind into parties, inflamed them with mutual animosity, and rendered them much more disposed to vex and oppress each other, than to co-operate for their common good. So strong is this propensity of mankind to fall into mutual animosities, that where no substantial occasion presents itself, the most frivolous and fanciful distinctions have been sufficient to kindle their unfriendly passions, and excite their most violent conflicts. But the most common and durable source of factions has been the various and unequal distribution of property. Those who hold and those who are without property have ever formed distinct interests in society. Those who are creditors, and those who are debtors, fall under a like discrimination. A landed interest, a manufacturing interest, a mercantile interest, a moneyed interest, with many lesser interests, grow up of necessity in civilized nations, and divide them into different classes, actuated by different sentiments and views. The regulation of these various and interfering interests forms the principal task of modern Legislation, and involves the spirit of party and faction in the necessary and ordinary operations of Government.

No man is allowed to be judge in his own cause, because his interest would certainly bias his judgment and, not improbably, corrupt his integrity. With equal, nay with greater reason, a body of men are unfit to be both judges and parties at the same time; yet what are many of the most important acts of legislation but so many judicial determinations, not indeed concerning the rights of single persons, but concerning the rights of large bodies of citizens; and what are the different classes of legislators but advocates and parties to the causes which they determine? Is a law proposed concerning private debts? It is a question to which the creditors are parties on one side and the debtors on the other. Justice ought to hold the balance between them. Yet the parties are, and must be, themselves the judges; and the most numerous party, or in other words, the most powerful faction must be expected to prevail. Shall domestic manufacturers be encouraged, and in what degree, by restrictions on foreign manufacturers? are questions which would be differently decided by the landed and the manufacturing classes, and probably by neither with a sole regard to justice and the public good. The apportionment of taxes on the various descriptions of property is an act which seems to require the most exact impartiality; yet there is, perhaps, no legislative act in which greater opportunity and temptation are given to a predominant party to trample on the rules of justice. Every shilling with which they overburden the inferior number is a shilling saved to their own pockets.

It is in vain to say that enlightened statesmen will be able to adjust these clashing interests and render them all subservient to the public good. Enlightened statesmen will not always be at the helm. Nor, in many cases, can such an adjustment be made at all without taking into view indirect and remote considerations, which will rarely prevail over the immediate interest which one party may find in disregarding the rights of another or the good of the whole.

The inference to which we are brought is that the *causes* of faction cannot be removed and that relief is only to be sought in the means of controlling its *effects*.

If a faction consists of less than a majority, relief is supplied by the republican principle, which enables the majority to defeat its sinister views by regular vote. It may clog the administration, it may convulse the society; but it will be unable to execute and mask its violence under the forms of the Constitution. When a majority is included in a faction, the form of popular government, on the other hand, enables it to sacrifice to its ruling passion or interest both the public good and the rights of other citizens. To secure the public good and private rights against the danger of such a faction, and at the same time to preserve the spirit and the form of popular government, is then the great object to which our enquiries are directed. Let me add that it is the great desideratum by which alone this form of government can be rescued from the opprobrium under which it has so long labored and be recommended to the esteem and adoption of mankind.

By what means is this object attainable? Evidently by one of two only. Either the existence of the same passion or interest in a majority at the same time must be prevented, or the majority, having such co-existent passion or interest, must be rendered, by their number and local situation, unable to concert and carry into effect schemes of oppression. If the impulse and the opportunity be suffered to coincide, we well know that neither moral nor religious motives can be relied on as an adequate control. They are not found to be such on the injustice and violence of individuals, and lose their efficacy in proportion to the number combined together, that is, in proportion as their efficacy becomes needful.

From this view of the subject it may be concluded that a pure Democracy, by which I mean a Society consisting of a small number of citizens, who assemble and administer the Government in person, can admit of no cure for the mischiefs of faction. A common passion or interest will, in almost every case, be felt by a majority of the whole; a communication and concert results from the form of Government itself; and there is nothing to check the inducements to sacrifice the weaker party or an obnoxious individual. Hence it is that such Democracies have ever been spectacles of turbulence and contention; have ever been found incompatible with personal security or the rights of property; and have in general been as short in their lives as they have been violent

in their deaths. Theoretic politicians, who have patronized this species of Government, have erroneously supposed that by reducing mankind to a perfect equality in their political rights, they would at the same time be perfectly equalized and assimilated in their possessions, their opinions, and their passions.

A Republic, by which I mean a Government in which the scheme of representation takes place, opens a different prospect and promises the cure for which we are seeking. Let us examine the points in which it varies from pure Democracy, and we shall comprehend both the nature of the cure and the efficacy which it must derive from the Union.

The two great points of difference between a Democracy and a Republic are: first, the delegation of the Government, in the latter, to a small number of citizens elected by the rest; secondly, the greater number of citizens and greater sphere of country over which the latter may be extended.

The effect of the first difference is, on the one hand, to refine and enlarge the public views by passing them through the medium of a chosen body of citizens, whose wisdom may best discern the true interest of their country and whose patriotism and love of justice will be least likely to sacrifice it to temporary or partial considerations. Under such a regulation it may well happen that the public voice, pronounced by the representatives of the people, will be more consonant to the public good than if pronounced by the people themselves, convened for the purpose. On the other hand, the effect may be inverted. Men of factious tempers, of local prejudices, or of sinister designs, may, by intrigue, by corruption, or by other means, first obtain the suffrages, and then betray the interests of the people. The question resulting is, whether small or extensive Republics are most favorable to the election of proper guardians of the public weal; and it is clearly decided in favor of the latter by two obvious considerations.

In the first place it is to be remarked that however small the Republic may be, the Representatives must be raised to a certain number in order to guard against the cabals of a few; and that however large it may be they must be limited to a certain number in order to guard against the confusion of a multitude. Hence, the number of Representatives in the two cases not being in proportion to that of the Constituents, and being proportionally greatest in the small Republic, it follows that if the proportion of fit characters be not less in the large than in the small Republic, the former will present a greater option, and consequently a greater probability of a fit choice.

In the next place, as each Representative will be chosen by a greater number of citizens in the large than in the small Republic, it will be more difficult for unworthy candidates to practise with success the vicious arts by which elections are too often carried; and the suffrages of the people being more free, will be more likely to centre on men who possess the most attractive merit and the most diffusive and established characters.

It must be confessed that in this, as in most other cases, there is a mean, on both sides of which inconveniencies will be found to lie. By enlarging too much the number of electors, you render the representative too little acquainted with all their local circumstances and lesser interests; as by reducing it too much, you render him unduly attached to these, and too little fit to comprehend and pursue great and national objects. The Federal Constitution forms a happy combination in this respect; the great and aggregate interests being referred to the national, the local and particular to the State legislatures.

The other point of difference is the greater number of citizens and extent of territory which may be brought within the compass of Republican than of Democratic Government; and it is this circumstance principally which renders factious combinations less to be dreaded in the former than in the latter. The smaller the society, the fewer probably will be the distinct parties and interests composing it; the fewer the distinct parties and interests, the more frequently will a majority be found of the same party; and the smaller the number of individuals composing a majority, and the smaller the compass within which they are placed, the more easily will they concert and execute their plans of oppression. Extend the sphere and you take in a greater variety of parties and interests; you make it less probable that a majority of the whole will have a common motive to invade the rights of other citizens; or if such a common motive exists, it will be more difficult for all who feel it to discover their own strength and to act in unison with each other. Besides other impediments, it may be remarked, that where there is a consciousness of unjust or dishonorable purposes, communication is always checked by distrust in proportion to the number whose concurrence is necessary.

Hence, it clearly appears that the same advantage which a Republic has over a Democracy in controlling the effects of faction is enjoyed by a large over a small republic—is enjoyed by the Union over the States composing it. Does this advantage consist in the substitution of representatives whose enlightened views and virtuous sentiments render them superior to local prejudices and to schemes of injustice? It will not be denied that the representation of the Union will be most likely to possess these requisite endowments. Does it consist in the greater security afforded by a greater variety of parties, against the event of any one party being able to outnumber and oppress the rest? In an equal degree does the increased variety of parties comprised within the Union increase this security? Does it, in fine, consist in the greater obstacles opposed to the concert and accomplishment of the secret wishes of an unjust and interested majority? Here again the extent of the Union gives it the most palpable advantage.

The influence of factious leaders may kindle a flame within their particular States but will be unable to spread a general conflagration through the other States: a religious sect may degenerate into a political faction in a part of the Confederacy; but the variety of sects dispersed over the entire face of it must secure the national Councils against any danger from that source: a rage for paper money, for an abolition of debts, for an equal division of property, or for any other improper or wicked project, will be less apt to pervade the whole body of the Union than a particular member of it; in the same proportion as such a malady is more likely to taint a particular county or district than an entire State.

In the extent and proper structure of the Union, therefore, we behold a republican remedy for the diseases most incident to Republican Government. And according to the degree of pleasure and pride we feel in being republicans ought to be our zeal in cherishing the spirit and supporting the character of federalist.

PUBLIUS
November 22, 1787

NO. 51: MADISON

To what expedient, then, shall we finally resort, for maintaining in practice the necessary partition of power among the several departments as laid down in the constitution? The only answer that can be given is that as all these exterior provisions are found to be inadequate the defect must be supplied, by so contriving the interior structure of the government as that its several constituent parts may, by their mutual relations, be the means of keeping each other in their proper places. Without presuming to undertake a full development of this important idea I will hazard a few general observations which may perhaps place it in a clearer light, and enable us to form a more correct judgment of the principles and structure of the government planned by the convention.

In order to lay a due foundation for that separate and distinct exercise of the different powers of government, which to a certain extent is admitted on all hands to be essential to the preservation of liberty, it is evident that each department should have a will of its own; and consequently should be so constituted that the members of each should have as little agency as possible in the appointment of the members of the others. Were this principle rigorously adhered to, it would require that all the appointments for the supreme executive, legislative, and judiciary magistracies should be drawn from the same fountain of authority, the people, through channels having no communication whatever with one another. Perhaps such a plan of constructing the several departments would be less difficult in practice than it may in contemplation appear. Some difficulties, however, and some additional expense would attend the execution of it. Some deviations, therefore, from the principle must be admitted. In the constitution of the judiciary department in particular, it might be inexpedient to insist rigorously on the principle: first, because peculiar qualifications being essential in the members, the primary consideration ought to be to select that mode of choice which best secures these qualifications; second, because the permanent tenure by which the appointments are held in that department must soon destroy all sense of dependence on the authority conferring them.

It is equally evident that the members of each department should be as little dependent as possible on those of the others for the emoluments annexed to their offices. Were the executive magistrate, or the judges, not independent of the legislature in this particular, their independence in every other would be merely nominal.

But the great security against a gradual concentration of the several powers in the same department consists in giving to those who administer each department the necessary constitutional means and personal motives to resist encroachments of the others. The provision for defence must in this, as in all other cases, be made commensurate to the danger of attack. Ambition must be made to counteract ambition. The interest of the man must be connected with the constitutional rights of the place. It may be a reflection on human nature that such devices should be necessary to control the abuses of government. But what is government itself but the greatest of all reflections on human nature? If men were angels, no government would be necessary. If angels were to govern men, neither external nor internal controls on government would be necessary. In framing a government which is to be administered by men over men, the great difficulty lies in this: You must first enable the government to control the governed; and in the next place oblige it to control itself. A dependence on the people is, no doubt, the primary control on the government; but experience has taught mankind the necessity of auxiliary precautions.

This policy of supplying, by opposite and rival interests, the defect of better motives, might be traced through the whole system of human affairs, private as well as public. We see it particularly displayed in all the subordinate distributions of power, where the constant aim is to divide and arrange the several offices in such a manner as that each may be a check on the other; that the private interest of every individual may be a sentinel over the public rights. These inventions of prudence cannot be less requisite in the distribution of the supreme powers of the State.

But it is not possible to give to each department an equal power of self-defense. In republican government, the legislative authority necessarily predominates. The remedy for this inconveniency is to divide the legislature into different branches; and to render them, by different modes of election and different principles of action, as little connected with each other as the nature of their common functions and their common dependence on the society will admit. It may even be necessary to guard against dangerous encroachments by still further precautions. As the weight of the legislative authority requires that it should be thus divided, the weakness of the executive may require, on the other hand, that it should be fortified. An absolute negative on the legislature appears, at first view, to be the natural defense with which the executive magistrate should be armed. But perhaps it would be neither altogether safe nor alone sufficient. On ordinary occasions it might not be exerted with the requisite firmness, and on extraordinary occasions it might be perfidiously abused. May not this defect of an absolute negative be supplied by some qualified connection between this weaker branch of the stronger department, by which the latter may be led to support the constitutional rights of the former, without being too much detached from the rights of its own department?

If the principles on which these observations are founded be just, as I persuade myself they are, and they be applied as a criterion to the several State constitutions, and to the federal Constitution, it will be found that if the latter does not perfectly correspond with them, the former are infinitely less able to bear such a test.

There are, moreover, two considerations particularly applicable to the federal system of America, which place that system in a very interesting point of view.

First. In a single republic, all the power surrendered by the people is submitted to the administration of a single government; and usurpations are guarded against by a division of the government into distinct and separate departments. In the compound republic of America, the power surrendered by the people is first divided between two distinct governments, and then the portion allotted to each subdivided among distinct and separate departments. Hence a double security arises to the rights of the people. The different governments will control each other, at the same time that each will be controlled by itself.

Second. It is of great importance in a republic not only to guard the society against the oppression of its rulers, but to guard one part of the society against the injustice of the other part. Different interests necessarily exist in different classes of citizens. If a majority be united by a common interest, the rights of the minority will be insecure. There are but two methods of providing against this evil: The one by creating a will in the community independent of the majority—that is, of the society itself; the other, by comprehending in the society so many separate descriptions of citizens as will render an unjust combination of a majority of the whole very improbable, if not impracticable. The first method prevails in all governments possessing an hereditary or self-appointed authority. This, at best, is but a precarious security; because a power independent of the society may as well espouse the unjust views of the major as the rightful interests of the minor party, and may possibly be turned against both parties. The second method will be exemplified in the federal republic of the United States. Whilst all authority in it will be derived from and dependent on the society, the society itself will be broken into so many parts, interests and classes of citizens, that the rights of individuals, or of the minority, will be in little danger from interested combinations of the majority. In a free government the security for civil rights must be the same as that for religious rights. It consists in the one case in the multiplicity of interests, and in the other in the multiplicity of sects. The degree of security in both cases will depend on the number of interests and sects; and this may be presumed to depend on the extent of country and number of people comprehended under the same government. This view of the subject must particularly recommend a proper federal system to all the sincere and considerate friends of republican government: Since it shows that in exact proportion as the territory of the Union may be formed into more circumscribed Confederacies, or States, oppressive combinations of a majority will be facilitated; the best security, under the republican form, for the rights of every class of citizens, will be diminished; and consequently the stability and independence of some member of the government, the only other security, must be proportionally increased. Justice is the end of government. It is the end of civil society. It ever has been and ever will be pursued until it be obtained, or until liberty be lost in the pursuit. In a society under the forms of which the stronger faction can readily unite and oppress the weaker, anarchy may as truly be said to reign as in a state of nature, where the weaker individual is not secured against the violence of the stronger: And as, in the latter state, even the stronger individuals are prompted, by the uncertainty of their condition, to submit to a government which may protect the weak as well as themselves: So, in the former state, will the more powerful factions or parties be gradually induced, by a like motive, to wish for a government which will protect all parties, the weaker as well as the more powerful. It can be little doubted that if the State of Rhode Island was separated from the Confederacy and left to itself, the insecurity of rights under the popular form of government within such narrow limits would be displayed by such reiterated oppressions of factious majorities that some power altogether independent of the people would soon be called for by the voice of the very factions whose misrule had proved the necessity of it. In the extended republic of the United States, and among the great variety of interests, parties, and sects which it embraces, a coalition of a majority of the whole society could seldom take place on any other principles than those of justice and the general good; and there being thus less danger to a minor from the will of the major party, there must be less pretext, also, to provide for the security of the former, by introducing into the government a will not dependent on the latter, or, in other words, a will independent of the society itself.

It is no less certain than it is important, notwithstanding the contrary opinions which have been entertained, that the larger the society, provided it lie within a practicable sphere, the more duly capable it will be of self-government. And happily for the *republican cause*, the practicable sphere may be carried to a very great extent by a judicious modification and mixture of the *federal principle*.

PUBLIUS
February 6, 1788

NO. 78: HAMILTON

To the People of the State of New York:

We proceed now to an examination of the judiciary department of the proposed government.

In unfolding the defects of the existing Confederation, the utility and necessity of a federal judicature have been clearly pointed out. It is the less necessary to recapitulate the considerations there urged, as the propriety of the institution in the abstract is not disputed; the only questions which have been raised being relative to the manner of constituting it, and to its extent. To these points, therefore, our observations shall be confined.

The manner of constituting it seems to embrace these several objects: 1st. The mode of appointing the judges. 2d. The tenure by which they are to hold their places. 3d. The partition of the judiciary authority between different courts, and their relations to each other.

First. As to the mode of appointing the judges; this is the same with that of appointing the officers of the Union in general, and has been so fully discussed in the two last numbers, that nothing can be said here which would not be useless repetition.

Second. As to the tenure by which the judges are to hold their places; this chiefly concerns their duration in office; the provisions for their support; the precautions for their responsibility.

According to the plan of the convention, all judges who may be appointed by the United States are to hold their offices DURING GOOD BEHAVIOR; which is conformable to the most approved of the State constitutions and among the rest, to that of this State. Its propriety having been drawn into question by the adversaries of that plan, is no light symptom of the rage for objection, which disorders their imaginations and judgments. The standard of good behavior for the continuance in office of the judicial magistracy, is certainly one of the most valuable of the modern improvements in the practice of government. In a monarchy it is an excellent barrier to the despotism of the prince; in a republic it is a no less excellent barrier to the encroachments and oppressions of the representative body. And it is the best expedient which can be devised in any government, to secure a steady, upright, and impartial administration of the laws.

Whoever attentively considers the different departments of power must perceive, that, in a government in which they are separated from each other, the judiciary, from the nature of its functions, will always be the least dangerous to the political rights of the Constitution; because it will be least in a capacity to annoy or injure them. The Executive not only dispenses the honors, but holds the sword of the community. The legislature not only commands the purse, but prescribes the rules by which the duties and rights of every citizen are to be regulated. The judiciary, on the contrary, has no influence over either the sword or the purse; no direction either of the strength or of the wealth of the society; and can take no active resolution whatever. It may truly be said to have neither FORCE nor WILL, but merely judgment; and must ultimately depend upon the aid of the executive arm even for the efficacy of its judgments.

This simple view of the matter suggests several important consequences. It proves incontestably, that the judiciary is beyond comparison the weakest of the three departments of power; that it can never attack with success either of the other two; and that all possible care is requisite to enable it to defend itself against their attacks. It equally proves, that though individual oppression may now and then proceed from the courts of justice, the general liberty of the people can never be endangered from that quarter; I mean so long as the judiciary remains truly distinct from both the legislature and the Executive. For I agree, that "there is no liberty, if the power of judging be not separated from the legislative and executive powers." And it proves, in the last place, that as liberty can have nothing to fear from the judiciary alone, but would have every thing to fear from its union with either of the other departments; that as all the effects of such a union must ensue from a dependence of the former on the latter, notwithstanding a nominal and apparent separation; that as, from the natural feebleness of the judiciary, it is in continual jeopardy of being overpowered, awed, or influenced by its co-ordinate branches; and that as nothing can contribute so much to its firmness and independence as permanency in office, this quality may therefore be justly regarded as an indispensable ingredient in its constitution, and, in a great measure, as the citadel of the public justice and the public security.

The complete independence of the courts of justice is peculiarly essential in a limited Constitution. By a limited Constitution, I understand one which contains certain specified exceptions to the legislative authority; such, for instance, as that it shall pass no bills of attainder, no ex-post-facto laws, and the like. Limitations of this kind can be preserved in practice no other way than through the medium of courts of justice, whose duty it must be to declare all acts contrary to the manifest tenor of the Constitution void. Without this, all the reservations of particular rights or privileges would amount to nothing.

Some perplexity respecting the rights of the courts to pronounce legislative acts void, because contrary to the Constitution, has arisen from an imagination that the doctrine would imply a superiority of the judiciary to the legislative power. It is urged that the authority which can declare the acts of another void, must necessarily be superior to the one whose acts may be declared void. As this doctrine is of great importance in all the American constitutions, a brief discussion of the ground on which it rests cannot be unacceptable.

There is no position which depends on clearer principles, than that every act of a delegated authority, contrary to the tenor of the commission under which it is exercised, is void. No legislative act, therefore, contrary to the Constitution, can be valid. To deny this, would be to affirm, that the deputy is greater than his principal; that the servant is above his master; that the representatives of the people are superior to the people themselves; that men acting by virtue of powers, may do not only what their powers do not authorize, but what they forbid.

If it be said that the legislative body are themselves the constitutional judges of their own powers, and that the construction they put upon them is conclusive upon the other departments, it may be answered, that this cannot be the natural presumption, where it is not to be collected from any particular provisions in the Constitution. It is not otherwise to be supposed, that the Constitution could intend to enable the representatives of the people to substitute their will to that of their constituents. It is far more rational to suppose, that the courts were designed to be an intermediate body between the people and the legislature, in order, among other things, to keep the latter within the limits assigned to their authority. The interpretation of the laws is the proper and peculiar province of the courts. A constitution is, in fact, and must be regarded by the judges, as a fundamental law. It therefore belongs to them to ascertain its meaning, as well as the meaning of any particular act proceeding from the legislative body. If there should happen to be an irreconcilable variance between the two, that which has the superior obligation and validity ought, of course, to be preferred; or, in other words, the Constitution ought to be preferred to the statute, the intention of the people to the intention of their agents.

Nor does this conclusion by any means suppose a superiority of the judicial to the legislative power. It only supposes that the power of the people is superior to both; and that where the will of the legislature, declared in its statutes, stands in opposition to that of the people, declared in the Constitution, the judges ought to be governed by the latter rather than the former. They ought to regulate their decisions by the fundamental laws, rather than by those which are not fundamental.

This exercise of judicial discretion, in determining between two contradictory laws, is exemplified in a familiar instance. It not uncommonly happens, that there are two statutes existing at one time, clashing in whole or in part with each other, and neither of them containing any repealing clause or expression. In such a case, it is the province of the courts to liquidate and fix their meaning and operation. So far as they can, by any fair construction, be reconciled to each other, reason and law conspire to dictate that this should be done; where this is impracticable, it becomes a matter of necessity to give effect to one, in exclusion of the other. The rule which has obtained in the courts for determining their relative validity is, that the last in order of time shall be preferred to the first. But this is a mere rule of construction, not derived from any positive law, but from the nature and reason of the thing. It is a rule not enjoined upon the courts by legislative provision, but adopted by themselves, as consonant to truth and propriety, for the direction of their conduct as interpreters of the law. They thought it reasonable, that between the interfering acts of an equal authority, that which was the last indication of its will should have the preference.

But in regard to the interfering acts of a superior and subordinate authority, of an original and derivative power, the nature and reason of the thing indicate the converse of that rule as proper to be followed. They teach us that the prior act of a superior ought to be preferred to the subsequent act of an inferior and subordinate authority; and that accordingly, whenever a particular statute contravenes the Constitution, it will be the duty of the judicial tribunals to adhere to the latter and disregard the former.

It can be of no weight to say that the courts, on the pretense of a repugnancy, may substitute their own pleasure to the constitutional intentions of the legislature. This might as well happen in the case of two contradictory statutes; or it might as well happen in every adjudication upon any single statute. The courts must declare the sense of the law; and if they should be disposed to exercise WILL instead of judgment, the consequence would equally be the substitution of their pleasure to that of the legislative body. The observation, if it prove any thing, would prove that there ought to be no judges distinct from that body.

If, then, the courts of justice are to be considered as the bulwarks of a limited Constitution against legislative encroachments, this consideration will afford a strong argument for the permanent tenure of judicial offices, since nothing will contribute so much as this to that independent spirit in the judges which must be essential to the faithful performance of so arduous a duty.

This independence of the judges is equally requisite to guard the Constitution and the rights of individuals from the effects of those ill humors, which the arts of designing men, or the influence of particular conjunctures, sometimes disseminate among the people themselves, and which, though they speedily give place to better information, and more deliberate reflection, have a tendency, in the meantime, to occasion dangerous innovations in the government, and serious oppressions of the minor party in the community. Though I trust the friends of the proposed Constitution will never concur with its enemies, in questioning that fundamental principle of republican government, which admits the right of the people to alter or abolish the established Constitution, whenever they find it inconsistent with their happiness, yet it is not to be inferred from this principle, that the representatives of the people, whenever a momentary inclination happens to lay hold of a majority of their constituents, incompatible with the provisions in the existing Constitution, would, on that account, be justifiable in a violation of those provisions; or that the courts would be under a greater obligation to connive at infractions in this shape, than when they had proceeded wholly from the cabals of the representative body. Until the people have, by some solemn and authoritative act, annulled or changed the established form, it is binding upon themselves collectively, as well as individually; and no presumption, or even knowledge, of their sentiments, can warrant their representatives in a departure from it, prior to such an act. But it is easy to see, that it would require an uncommon portion of fortitude in the judges to do their duty as faithful guardians of the Constitution, where legislative invasions of it had been instigated by the major voice of the community.

But it is not with a view to infractions of the Constitution only, that the independence of the judges may be an essential safeguard against the effects of occasional ill humors in the society. These sometimes extend no farther than to the injury of the private rights of particular classes of citizens, by unjust and partial laws. Here also the firmness of the judicial magistracy is of vast importance in mitigating the severity and confining the operation of such laws. It not only serves to moderate the immediate mischiefs of those which may have been passed, but it operates as a check upon the legislative body in passing them; who, perceiving that obstacles to the success of iniquitous intention are to be expected from the scruples of the courts, are in a manner compelled, by the very motives of the injustice they meditate, to qualify their attempts. This is a circumstance calculated to have more influence upon the character of our governments, than but few may be aware of. The benefits of the integrity and moderation of the judiciary have already been felt in more States than one; and though they may have displeased those whose sinister expectations they may have disappointed, they must have commanded the esteem and applause of all the virtuous and disinterested. Considerate men, of every description, ought to prize whatever will tend to beget or fortify that temper in the courts: as no man can be sure that he may not be to-morrow the victim of a spirit of injustice, by which he may be a gainer to-day. And every man must now feel, that the inevitable tendency of such a spirit is to sap the foundations of public and private confidence, and to introduce in its stead universal distrust and distress.

That inflexible and uniform adherence to the rights of the Constitution, and of individuals, which we perceive to be indispensable in the courts of justice, can certainly not be expected from judges who hold their offices by a temporary commission. Periodical appointments, however regulated, or by whomsoever made, would, in some way or other, be fatal to their necessary independence. If the power of making them was committed either to the Executive or legislature, there would be danger of an improper complaisance to the branch which possessed it; if to both, there would be an unwillingness to hazard the displeasure of either; if to the people, or to persons chosen by them for the special purpose, there would be too great a disposition to consult popularity, to justify a reliance that nothing would be consulted but the Constitution and the laws.

There is yet a further and a weightier reason for the permanency of the judicial offices, which is deducible from the nature of the qualifications they require. It has been frequently remarked, with great propriety, that a voluminous code of laws is one of the inconveniences necessarily connected with the advantages of a free government. To avoid an arbitrary discretion in the courts, it is indispensable that they should be bound down by strict rules and precedents, which serve to define and point out their duty in every particular case that comes before them; and it will readily be conceived from the variety of controversies which grow out of the folly and wickedness of mankind, that the records of those precedents must unavoidably swell to a very considerable bulk, and must demand long and laborious study to acquire a competent knowledge of them. Hence it is, that there can be but few men in the society who will have sufficient skill in the laws to qualify them for the stations of judges. And making the proper deductions for the ordinary depravity of human nature, the number must be still smaller of those who unite the requisite integrity with the requisite knowledge. These considerations apprise us, that the government can have no great option between fit character; and that a temporary duration in office, which would naturally discourage such characters from quitting a lucrative line of practice to accept a seat on the bench, would have a tendency to throw the administration of justice into hands less able, and less well qualified, to conduct it with utility and dignity. In the present circumstances of this country, and in those in which it is likely to be for a long time to come, the disadvantages on this score would be greater than they may at first sight appear; but it must be confessed, that they are far inferior to those which present themselves under the other aspects of the subject.

Upon the whole, there can be no room to doubt that the convention acted wisely in copying from the models of those constitutions which have established good behavior as the tenure of their judicial offices, in point of duration; and that so far from being blamable on this account, their plan would have been inexcusably defective, if it had wanted this important feature of good government. The experience of Great Britain affords an illustrious comment on the excellence of the institution.

PUBLIUS

Endnotes

HOW DO YOU USE THIS BOOK?

1. David Considine, Julie Horton, and Gary Moorman, "Teaching and Reaching the Millennial Generation through Media Literacy," *Journal of Adolescent & Adult Literacy* 52:6 (2009): 471–81.

2. Jeff Nevid, "Teaching the Millennials," Association for Psychological Science, May 4, 2011, https://www.psychologicalscience.org/observer/teaching-the-millennials (accessed 1/4/21).

3. Louise Hainline, Michael Gaines, Cheryl Long Feather, Elaine Padilla, and Esther Terry, "Changing Students, Faculty, and Institutions in the Twenty-First Century," *Peer Review* 12:3 (Summer 2010), https://www.semanticscholar.org/paper/Changing-Students%2C-Faculty%2C-and-Institutions-in-the-Hainline-Gaines/77bbdc88317db9b7c81bbfc4f2962413ea7f2818 (accessed 2/7/22).

1. WHAT IS THE AMERICAN DREAM?

1. Donald J. Trump, October 29, 2018, https://twitter.com/realDonaldTrump/status/1056919064906469376 (accessed 11/2/18).

2. Ian Schwartz, "Trump to Caravan: Rocks Will Be Considered a Firearm, 'I Hope' Military Won't Shoot," RealClearPolitics, November 1, 2018, https://www.realclearpolitics.com/video/2018/11/01/trump_to_caravan_rocks_will_be_considered_a_firearm_i_hope_military_wont_shoot.html (accessed 11/2/18).

3. Jason Beaubien, "Migrant Caravan: Thousands Move into Guatemala, Hoping to Reach U.S.," National Public Radio, January 18, 2021, https://www.npr.org/2021/01/18/958092745/migrant-caravan-thousands-move-into-guatemala-hoping-to-reach-u-s (accessed 6/16/21).

4. Brian Naylor and Tamara Keith, "Kamala Harris Tells Guatemalans Not to Migrate to the United States," National Public Radio, June 7, 2021, https://www.npr.org/2021/06/07/1004074139/harris-tells-guatemalans-not-to-migrate-to-the-united-states (accessed 6/9/21).

5. Jonas Clark, "In Search of the American Dream," *The Atlantic*, June 2007, https://www.theatlantic.com/magazine/archive/2007/06/in-search-of-the-american-dream/305921/ (accessed 11/2/18).

6. Samantha Smith, "Most Think the 'American Dream' Is within Reach for Them," Pew Research Center, October 31, 2017, https://www.pewresearch.org/fact-tank/2017/10/31/most-think-the-american-dream-is-within-reach-for-them/ (accessed 11/2/18).

7. George Washington, John Clement Fitzpatrick, and David Maydole Matteson, 1776, *The Writings of George Washington from the Original Manuscript Sources, 1745–1799*, p. 479, https://founders.archives.gov/documents/Washington/03-06-02-0100 (accessed 2/7/22).

8. Patrick Henry, "Speech at St. John's Church in Richmond, Virginia," March 23, 1775, http://www.history.org/almanack/life/politics/giveme.cfm (accessed 11/3/18).

9. Data come from the Associated Press (https://apnorc.org/projects/what-americans-think-about-the-economy/), Rasmussen Reports (https://www.rasmussenreports.com/public_content/politics/partner_surveys/82_of_voters_say_religious_liberty_important), Gallup (https://news.gallup.com/poll/357755/socialism-capitalism-ratings-unchanged.aspx), and the Pew Research Center (https://www.pewresearch.org/fact-tank/2016/04/19/5-ways-americans-and-europeans-are-different/ft_16-04-19_americaeurope_speech/; www.pewresearch.org/politics/2012/06/04/partisan-polarization-surges-in-bush-obama-years/; https://www.pewglobal.org/2014/10/09/emerging-and-developing-economies-much-more-optimistic-than-rich-countries-about-the-future/inequality-01/; https://www.pewresearch.org/fact-tank/2016/04/19/5-ways-americans-and-europeans-are-different/ft_16-04-22_usindividualism/; https://www.pewresearch.org/politics/2019/12/17/views-of-the-economic-system-and-social-safety-net/pp_2019-12-17_political-values_3-07/).

10. "Immigration and Americanization, 1880–1930," Digital Public Library of America, https://dp.la/primary-source-sets/immigration-and-americanization-1880-1930 (accessed 11/7/18).

11. Data come from Gallup (https://news.gallup.com/poll/313106/americans-not-less-immigration-first-time.aspx), the Pew Research Center (https://www.opportunityagenda.org/explore/resources-publications/public-opinion-research/public-opinion-meta-analysis; http://www.pewresearch.org/fact-tank/2017/01/19/many-around-the-world-say-womens-equality-is-very-important/; http://www.people-press.org/2018/06/28/shifting-public-views-on-legal-immigration-into-the-u-s/; https://www.pewresearch.org/fact-tank/2020/07/14/most-americans-support-gender-equality-even-if-they-dont-identify-as-feminists/); the *New York Times* (https://www.nytimes.com/2018/06/23/us/immigration-polls-donald-trump.html), and the Roper Center (https://ropercenter.cornell.edu/public-opinion-civil-rights-reflections-civil-rights-act-1964).

12. "Mayflower Compact," The Avalon Project at Yale Law School, https://avalon.law.yale.edu/17th_century/mayflower.asp (accessed 9/9/19).

13. Question wording is as follows: "Some people think the government is trying to do too many things that should be left to individuals and businesses. Others think that government should do more to solve our country's problems. Which comes closer to your own view?"; "In general, do you think there is too much, too little, or about the right amount of government regulation of business and industry?"; and "Do you think the federal government today has too much power, has about the right amount of power, or has too little power?" https://news.gallup.com/poll/27286/government.aspx (accessed 11/5/18); Megan Brenan, "New High 54% Want Government to Solve More Problems in U.S.," Gallup, September 28, 2020, https://news.gallup.com/poll/321041/new-high-government-solve-problems.aspx (accessed 7/15/22).

14. Paul Katzeff, "Top 1%: How Much Income It Takes to Be One of the Richest Americans in Your State," Investor's Business Daily, July 8, 2021, https://www.investors.com/etfs-and-funds/personal-finance/one-percenter-club-how-much-income-it-takes-to-be-one-of-the-richest-americans/ (accessed 7/15/22).

15. Abigial Johnson Hess, "In 2020, Top CEOs Earned 350 Times More than the Typical Worker," CNBC, September 15, 2021, https://www.cnbc.com/2021/09/15/in-2020-top-ceos-earned-351-times-more-than-the-typical-worker.html (accessed 7/15/22).

16. Andrew Kohut, Carroll Doherty, Michael Dimock, and Scott Keeter, "Trends in American Values," Pew Research Center, June 4, 2012, http://www.people-press.org/2012/06/04/section-3-values-about-economic-inequality-and-individual-opportunity/6-4-12-v-48/ (accessed 11/5/18).

17. "Feeling of Alienation among Americans Reaches Highest Point on Record," The Harris Poll, January 20, 2015, https://theharrispoll.com/this-years-midterm-elections-brought-a-bitterly-fought-campaign-across-many-states-soon-after-these-elections-the-harris-poll-revisited-a-long-term-trend-looking-at-how-alienated-americans-feel-th/ (accessed 6/16/21).

18. Maria Hinojosa, "Hate Crimes against Latinos Increase in California," National Public Radio, July 15, 2018, https://www.npr.org/2018/07/15/629212976/hate-crimes-against-latinos-increase-in-california (accessed 11/5/18).

19. "2016 Hate Crime Statistics," U.S. Department of Justice, https://ucr.fbi.gov/hate-crime/2016/topic-pages/victims (accessed 11/5/18).

20. Monica Anderson, "For Black Americans, Experiences of Racial Discrimination Vary by Education Level, Gender," Pew Research Center, May 2, 2019, https://www.pewresearch.org/fact-tank/2019/05/02/for-black-americans-experiences-of-racial-discrimination-vary-by-education-level-gender/ (accessed 6/16/21).

21. Kim Parker and Cary Funk, "Gender Discrimination Comes in Many Forms for Today's Working Women," Pew Research Center, December 14, 2017, http://www.pewresearch.org/fact-tank/2017/12/14/gender -discrimination-comes-in-many-forms-for-todays-working-women/ (accessed 11/5/18).

22. Fiona Hill, "Public Service and the Federal Government," Brookings Institution, May 27, 2020, https://www.brookings.edu/policy2020/votervital /public-service-and-the-federal-government/ (accessed 6/16/21).

2. HOW DID 55 GUYS HAMMER OUT THE CONSTITUTION?

1. Stanton Peele, "Were the Founding Fathers Alcoholics?" Huffington Post, June 15, 2010, https://www.huffingtonpost.com/stanton-peele /alcohol-addiction-were-th_b_610598.html (accessed 9/22/18).

2. Eric W. Nye, "Pounds Sterling to Dollars: Historical Conversion of Currency," https://www.uwyo.edu/numimage/currency.htm (accessed 9/23/18).

3. George Washington, "Letter from the Federal Convention President to the President of Congress, Transmitting the Constitution," September 17, 1787, https://ahp.gatech.edu/letter_constitution_1787.html (accessed 9/21/18).

4. William Peden, *Notes on the State of Virginia* (Chapel Hill: University of North Carolina Press, 1954), http://press-pubs.uchicago.edu/founders /documents/v1ch10s9.html (accessed 9/21/18).

5. Alexander Hamilton, *The Federalist Papers*, No. 17, http://avalon.law.yale .edu/18th_century/fed17.asp (accessed 9/24/18).

6. Hamilton, *The Federalist Papers*, No. 22, http://avalon.law.yale.edu /18th_century/fed22.asp (accessed 9/22/18).

7. "Notes of William Paterson in the Federal Convention of 1787," May 29, 1787, http://avalon.law.yale.edu/18th_century/patterson.asp (accessed 9/21/18).

8. Lee Ann Potter, "Population Estimates Used by Congress during the Constitutional Convention," *Social Education* 70:50 (2006): 270–72.

9. Paul Finkelman, "Garrison's Constitution," *Prologue Magazine (of the National Archives)* 32:4 (2000), https://www.archives.gov/publications /prologue/2000/winter/garrisons-constitution-2.html (accessed 9/21/18).

10. Jonathan Elliot, *The Debates in the Several State Conventions on the Adoption of the Federal Constitution as Recommended by the General Convention at Philadelphia in 1787* (New York: Burt Franklin, 1888), http://press-pubs.uchicago.edu/founders/print_documents/a1_9_1s10 .html (accessed 9/21/18).

11. Phillip Magness, "Alexander Hamilton's Exaggerated Abolitionism," History News Network, June 27, 2015, https://historynewsnetwork.org/blog /153639 (accessed 9/22/18).

12. Potter, "Population Estimates."

13. George Mason, "Speech to the Virginia Ratifying Convention," June 4, 1788, http://teachingamericanhistory.org/library/document/george-mason-speech/ (accessed 9/21/18).

14. James Madison, *The Federalist Papers*, No. 45, http://avalon.law.yale.edu/18th_century/fed45.asp (accessed 9/21/18).

15. Virginia Declaration of Rights, http://avalon.law.yale.edu/18th_century/virginia.asp (accessed 9/21/18).

3. WHICH BRANCH OF GOVERNMENT DID THE FOUNDERS INTEND TO BE THE MOST POWERFUL?

1. Marty Johnson, "Biden Blasts Trump Comments: 'I Am Not Running for Office to Be King of America'," The Hill, April 14, 2020, https://thehill.com/homenews/campaign/492712-biden-blasts-trump-comments-i-am-not-running-for-office-to-be-king-of (accessed 6/15/21).

2. Grace Wyler, "Rand Paul: The Supreme Court Doesn't Get to Decide What's Constitutional," Insider, June 28, 2012, https://www.businessinsider.com/rand-paul-the-supreme-court-doesnt-get-to-decide-whats-constitutional-2012-6 (accessed 6/15/21).

3. Meagan Flynn and Allyson Chiu, "Trump Says His Authority Is 'Total.' Constitutional Experts Have 'No Idea' where He Got That," *Washington Post*, April 14, 2020, https://www.washingtonpost.com/nation/2020/04/14/trump-power-constitution-coronavirus/ (accessed 6/15/21).

4. Alexander Bolton and Jordan Fabian, "Congress Steamrolls Obama's Veto," The Hill, September 28, 2016, https://thehill.com/homenews/senate/298412-congress-votes-to-override-obama (accessed 10/1/18).

5. Adam Cancryn and Sarah Owermohle, "Biden's Agenda Hits Senate Slowdown," Politico, May 26, 2021, https://www.politico.com/newsletters/politico-pulse/2021/05/26/bidens-agenda-hits-senate-slowdown-795565 (accessed 6/15/21).

6. Lucy Connolly, "U.S. Supreme Court Rules Half of Oklahoma Is Native American Land," BBC News, July 10, 2020, https://www.bbc.com/news/world-us-canada-53358330 (accessed 6/15/21).

7. Pete Williams, "In Blow to Trump, Supreme Court Won't Hear Appeal of DACA Ruling," NBC News, February 26, 2018, https://www.nbcnews.com/politics/politics-news/supreme-court-won-t-hear-daca-case-n851186 (accessed 10/1/18).

8. Missy Ryan and Karen DeYoung, "Biden Will Withdraw All U.S. Forces from Afghanistan by September 11, 2021," *Washington Post*, April 13, 2021, https://www.washingtonpost.com/national-security/biden-us-troop-withdrawal-afghanistan/2021/04/13/918c3cae-9beb-11eb-8a83-3bc1fa69c2e8_story.html (accessed 6/15/21).

9. Alexandra Jaffe and Ricardo Alonso-Zaldivar, "Biden Expands 'Obamacare' by Cutting Health Insurance Costs," Associated Press, March 23,

2021, https://apnews.com/article/joe-biden-personal-taxes-ohio
-coronavirus-pandemic-e38fc1b207515b281be23e90b424deb4
(accessed 6/15/21).

10. James Madison, *The Federalist Papers*, No. 51, http://avalon.law.yale
.edu/18th_century/fed51.asp (accessed 10/1/18).

11. "Underage Drinking Laws," https://www.edgarsnyder.com/car-accident
/who-was-injured/teen/underage-drinking-laws.html (accessed
10/1/18).

12. "The Constitution of the United States: A Transcription," National
Archives, https:// www.archives.gov/founding-docs/constitution
-transcript (accessed 10/1/18).

13. The 1984 National Minimum Drinking Age Act, 23 U.S.C. § 158, https://
alcoholpolicy.niaaa.nih.gov/the-1984-national-minimum-drinking
-age-act (accessed 10/1/18).

4. HOW DID THE SUPREME COURT GET ITS POWER?

1. *Gonzales v. O Centro Espírita Beneficente União do Vegetal*, 546 U.S.
418 (2006).

2. *National Federation of Independent Business v. Sebelius*, 567 U.S. 519 (2012).

3. *Trump v. Vance*, 591 U.S. __ (2020).

4. *Marbury v. Madison*, 5 U.S. 137 (1803).

5. For a detailed discussion of the election of 1800, see Edward J. Larson,
*A Magnificent Catastrophe: The Tumultuous Election of 1800, America's
First Presidential Campaign* (New York: Simon & Schuster, 2007).

6. Stacy Conradt, "Martha Washington Called a Visit from Jefferson One of
the Worst Experiences of Her Life," Mental Floss, July 26, 2016, http://
mentalfloss.com/article/82535/why-martha-washington-called-visit
-thomas-jefferson-one-worst-experiences-her-life (accessed 9/8/18).

7. There are numerous academic accounts of the background of the case.
See, for example, Lawrence Goldstone, *The Activist: John Marshall,
Marbury v. Madison, and the Myth of Judicial Review* (New York: Walker
Publishing, 2008); and William E. Nelson, *Marbury v. Madison: The Origins
and Legacy of Judicial Review*, 2nd ed. (Lawrence: University Press of
Kansas, 2018).

8. "Thomas Jefferson's Reaction," Landmark Cases of the U.S. Supreme
Court, https://founders.archives.gov/documents/Adams/99-03-02-1317
(accessed 2/7/22).

9. *Dred Scott v. Sandford*, 60 U.S. 393 (1857).

10. Supreme Court Database, Washington University Law School, http://
scdb.wustl.edu/data.php (accessed 9/8/18); and "Table of Laws Held
Unconstitutional in Whole or in Part by the Supreme Court," Constitution
Annotated, https://constitution.congress.gov/resources/unconstitutional
-laws/ (accessed 6/10/21).

5. WHY IS THE CONSTITUTION SO HARD TO CHANGE?

1. "Measures Proposed to Amend the Constitution," United States Senate, https://www.senate.gov/legislative/MeasuresProposed ToAmendTheConstitution.htm (accessed 2/7/22).

2. "Failed Constitutional Amendments," Election College, http://electioncollege .com/failed-constitutional-amendments/ (accessed 9/11/18).

3. "Proposed Amendments," ConstitutionFacts.com, https://www .constitutionfacts.com/us-constitution-amendments/proposed -amendments/ (accessed 9/11/18).

4. Megan Cloherty, "National Archives Exhibit Shows the 11,000 Ways the Constitution Could Have Changed," WTOP News, March 18, 2016, https://wtop.com/dc/2016/03/national-archives-exhibit -shows-11000-ways-constitution-changed/ (accessed 2/7/22).

5. "Amend the Constitution? Let Us Count the Ways," *New York Times*, August 3, 1987, https://www.nytimes.com/1987/08/03/us/washinton -talk-letters-to-congress-amend-the-constitution-let-us-count-the -ways.html (accessed 9/11/18).

6. "Proposed Amendments," ConstitutionFacts.com.

7. Polling data come from several sources: Paul Herrnson and Kathleen Weldon, "The Public and Proposed Constitutional Amendments: We Love You, You're Perfect, Now Change," Huffington Post, September 15, 2014, https://www.huffingtonpost.com/paul-herrnson/the-public-and -proposed-c_b_5812708.html; "Voters Overwhelmingly Support Term Limits for Congress," McLaughlin & Associates, February 8, 2018, http:// mclaughlinonline.com/2018/02/08/ma-poll-voters-overwhelmingly -support-term-limits-for-congress/; David W. Moore, "Public Favors Voluntary Prayer for Public Schools," Gallup, August 26, 2005, https:// news.gallup.com/poll/18136/Public-Favors-Voluntary-Prayer-Public -Schools.aspx; Joseph Carroll, "Public Support for Constitutional Amendment on Flag Burning," Gallup, June 29, 2006, https://news.gallup.com/poll /23524/Public-Support-Constitutional-Amendment-Flag-Burning.aspx; and Art Swift, "Americans' Support for Electoral College Rises Sharply," Gallup, December 2, 2016, https://news.gallup.com/poll/198917/americans -support-electoral-college-rises-sharply.aspx (accessed 9/13/18).

8. Margot Adler, "Reconstituting the Constitution: How to Rewrite It?" National Public Radio, December 10, 2011, https://www.npr.org/2011/12 /10/143354018/reconstituting-the-constitution-how-to-rewrite-it (accessed 9/11/18).

9. Nicholas Stephanopoulos, "What Jefferson Said," *The New Republic*, November 30, 2008, https://newrepublic.com/article/63773/what -jefferson-said (accessed 9/12/18).

10. The Clean Air Act, H.R. 6518 (July 24, 1963), https://www.govtrack.us /congress/votes/88-1963/h47 (accessed 9/14/18).

11. Immigration Control and Legalization Amendments Act of 1986, H.R. 3810 (October 9, 1986), https://www.congress.gov/bill/99th-congress/house-bill/3810 (accessed 9/14/18).

12. The Personal Responsibility and Work Reconciliation Act of 1996, H.R. 3734 (August 22, 1996), https://www.govtrack.us/congress/votes/104-1996/h331 (accessed 9/14/18).

13. "State Partisan Composition," National Conference of State Legislatures, April 11, 2018, http://www.ncsl.org/research/about-state-legislatures/partisan-composition.aspx (accessed 9/14/18).

14. Evan Andrews, "The Strange Saga of the 27th Amendment," History.com, May 5, 2017, https://www.history.com/news/the-strange-case-of-the-27th-amendment (accessed 9/11/18).

15. James Madison, *The Federalist Papers*, No. 43, http://avalon.law.yale.edu/18th_century/fed43.asp (accessed 9/11/18).

6. DID THE FOUNDERS BELIEVE IN DEMOCRACY?

1. Sarah Hauer, "Paul Ryan Claims the U.S. Is the 'Oldest Democracy' in the World. Is He Right?" PolitiFact, July 11, 2016, https://www.politifact.com/wisconsin/statements/2016/jul/11/paul-ryan/paul-ryan-claims-us-oldest-democracy-world-he-righ/ (accessed 10/13/18).

2. "Full Transcript: Third 2016 Presidential Debate," Politico, October 20, 2016, https://www.politico.com/story/2016/10/full-transcript-third-2016-presidential-debate-230063 (accessed 10/13/18).

3. Kira Bindrim, "Obama Name-Checked Democracy 20 Times in His Farewell Speech, More than the Last 15 Presidents Combined," Quartz, January 11, 2017, https://qz.com/882736/obama-name-checked-democracy-20-times-in-his-farewell-speech-more-than-the-last-15-presidents-combined/ (accessed 10/13/18).

4. Lacey Rose, "Donald Trump on the American Dream," *Forbes*, March 22, 2007, https://www.forbes.com/2007/03/21/donald-trump-dream-oped-cx_lr_dream0307_0322trump.html#63242ed4781b (accessed 10/13/18).

5. Brian Naylor, "Read Trump's January 6 Speech, a Key Part of Impeachment Trial," National Public Radio, February 10, 2021, https://www.npr.org/2021/02/10/966396848/read-trumps-jan-6-speech-a-key-part-of-impeachment-trial (accessed 6/17/21).

6. Pete Williams and Nicole Via y Rada, "Trump's Election Fight Includes over 50 Lawsuits. It's Not Going Well," NBC News, December 10, 2020, https://www.nbcnews.com/politics/2020-election/trump-s-election-fight-includes-over-30-lawsuits-it-s-n1248289 (accessed 6/17/21).

7. Tom Jackman, "Police Union Says 140 Officers Injured in Capitol Riot," *Washington Post*, January 27, 2021, https://www.washingtonpost.com/local/public-safety/police-union-says-140-officers-injured-in-capitol-riot/2021/01/27/60743642-60e2-11eb-9430-e7c77b5b0297_story.html (accessed 6/17/21).

8. Amanda Kaufman, "'Peaceful Patriots': Months after January 6 Insurrection, GOP Members of Congress Attempt to Recast Events of Deadly Attack," *Boston Globe*, May 12, 2021, https://www.bostonglobe.com /2021/05/12/nation/peaceful-patriots-months-after-jan-6-insurrection -gop-members-congress-attempt-revise-events-deadly-attack/ (accessed 6/17/21).

9. 171 Cong. Rec., H2191 (daily ed. May 11, 2021) (statement of Congress-woman Liz Cheney).

10. Libby Cathey, "Biden Says Democracy 'in Peril' in Speech Honoring Fallen Troops," ABC News, May 31, 2021, https://abcnews.go.com /Politics/biden-democracy-worth-dying-speech-honoring-fallen-troops /story?id=78000721 (accessed 6/17/21).

11. Benjamin Rush, *Letters of Benjamin Rush: 1761–1792* (Chicago: American Philosophical Society, 1951).

12. "From John Adams to John Taylor," National Archives, December 17, 1814, https://founders.archives.gov/documents/Adams/99-02-02-6371 (accessed 10/13/18).

13. James Madison, *The Federalist Papers*, No. 51, http://avalon.law.yale .edu/18th_century/fed51.asp (accessed 10/13/18).

14. Max Farrand, ed., *The Records of the Federal Government of 1787*, Rev. ed. (New Haven: Yale University Press, 1937).

15. John Jay, "The Correspondence and Public Papers of John Jay . . . 1794–1826" (New York: G. B. Putnam & Sons, 1890).

16. "Initiative and Referendum States," National Conference of State Legislatures, http://www.ncsl.org/research/elections-and-campaigns /chart-of-the-initiative-states.aspx (accessed 10/13/18).

17. Vann R. Newkirk II, "American Voters Are Turning to Direct Democracy," *The Atlantic*, April 18, 2018, https://www.theatlantic.com/politics /archive/2018/04/citizen-ballot-initiatives-2018-elections/558098/ (accessed 10/13/18).

18. David Crary, "Which Ballot Initiatives Passed? Marijuana, Minimum Wage, and More," *PBS NewsHour*, November 9, 2016, https://www .pbs.org/newshour/politics/ballot-initiatives-passed-marijuana -minimum-wage (accessed 10/13/18).

19. Jo McKeegan, "Evolution of Voting Rights from 1789 to Today Must Continue," FairVote, July 29, 2011, https://www.fairvote.org/evolution -of-voting-rights-from-1789-to-today-must-continue (accessed 10/13/18).

20. "From Thomas Jefferson to John Jay," January 25, 1786, National Archives, https://founders.archives.gov/documents/Jefferson /01-09-02-0190 (accessed 10/13/18).

21. "Extract from Thomas Jefferson to Edward Carrington," January 16, 1787, http://tjrs.monticello.org/letter/1289 (accessed 10/13/18).

22. "From James Madison to George Thomson," June 30, 1825, National Archives, https://founders.archives.gov/documents/Madison/04-03-02-0562 (accessed 10/13/18).

23. "Alien and Sedition Acts," Library of Congress, https://www.loc.gov/rr/program/bib/ourdocs/alien.html (accessed 10/15/18).

24. Ronald G. Shafer, "The Thin-Skinned President Who Made It Illegal to Criticize His Office," *Washington Post*, September 8, 2018, https://www.washingtonpost.com/news/retropolis/wp/2018/09/08/the-thin-skinned-president-who-made-it-illegal-to-criticize-his-office/ (accessed 10/13/18).

25. "Alien and Sedition Acts," Library of Congress.

26. *New York Times Co. v. United States*, 403 U.S. 713 (1971).

27. Don Van Natta Jr., Adam Liptak, and Clifford J. Levy, "The Miller Case: A Notebook, a Cause, a Jail Cell, and a Deal," *New York Times*, October 16, 2005, https://www.nytimes.com/2005/10/16/us/the-miller-case-a-notebook-a-cause-a-jail-cell-and-a-deal.html (accessed 10/14/18).

28. James Risen, "If Donald Trump Targets Journalists, Thank Obama," *New York Times*, December 30, 2016, https://www.nytimes.com/2016/12/30/opinion/sunday/if-donald-trump-targets-journalists-thank-obama.html (accessed 10/14/18).

29. Charlie Savage and Katie Benner, "Trump Administration Secretly Seized Phone Records of Times Reporters," *New York Times*, June 11, 2021, https://www.nytimes.com/2021/06/02/us/trump-administration-phone-records-times-reporters.html (accessed 6/12/21).

7. CAN THE FEDERAL GOVERNMENT TELL THE STATES WHAT TO DO?

1. "What Is a Sanctuary City? And What Happens Now?" CBS News, January 25, 2017, https://www.cbsnews.com/news/what-is-a-sanctuary-city-and-what-happens-now/ (accessed 10/22/18).

2. "Sanctuary City Ordinance," Office of Civic Engagement and Immigrant Affairs, City and County of San Francisco, https://sfgov.org/oceia/sanctuary-city-ordinance-0 (accessed 10/21/18).

3. "Here's Donald Trump's Presidential Announcement Speech," *Time*, June 16, 2015, http://time.com/3923128/donald-trump-announcement-speech/ (accessed 10/19/18).

4. Jerry Shaw, "Local Lawmakers' Quotes Supporting Sanctuary Cities," Newsmax, October 16, 2015, https://www.newsmax.com/FastFeatures/lawmakers-sanctuary-cities-quotes/2015/10/16/id/696493/ (accessed 10/19/18).

5. John Wildermuth, "Oakland Mayor Warns that Immigration Raids May Be Coming This Weekend," *San Francisco Chronicle*, February 24, 2018, https://www.sfgate.com/bayarea/article/Oakland-mayor

-warns-that-immigration-raids-may-be-12706843.php (accessed 10/20/18).

6. Sheriffs Sally Hernandez, Lupe Valdez, Ed Gonzalez, Javier Salazar, and Richard Wiles, "Texas Sheriffs: SB4 Burdens Law Enforcement, Local Taxpayers," *Austin American-Statesman*, April 18, 2017, https://www.statesman.com/news/20170418/texas-sheriffs-sb4-burdens-law-enforcement-local-taxpayers (accessed 10/19/18).

7. "Text of Trump's Executive Order on Interior Immigration Enforcement," Fox News, January 25, 2017, https://www.foxnews.com/politics/text-of-trumps-executive-order-on-interior-immigration-enforcement (accessed 10/20/18).

8. Joseph Tanfani, "Continuing a Fierce Assault on 'Sanctuary' Policies, Sessions Attacks California Bill," *Los Angeles Times*, September 19, 2017, https://www.latimes.com/politics/la-na-pol-sessions-sanctuary-20170919-story.html (accessed 10/19/18).

9. John Myers, "Federal Judge Denies Trump Administration Effort to Block California's 'Sanctuary' Law," *Los Angeles Times*, July 5, 2018, https://www.latimes.com/politics/la-pol-ca-sanctuary-law-ruling-20180705-story.html (accessed 10/20/18).

10. *McCulloch v. Maryland*, 17 U.S. 316 (1819).

11. *Gibbons v. Ogden*, 22 U.S. 1 (1824).

12. Kimberly Amadeo, "Unemployment Rate by Year since 1929 Compared to Inflation and GDP," The Balance, December 8, 2018, https://www.thebalance.com/unemployment-rate-by-year-3305506 (accessed 12/11/18).

13. "Launching the New Deal: FDR and Congress Respond to the Great Depression," National Archives, https://www.archives.gov/legislative/resources/education/new-deal (accessed 9/9/19).

14. "New Deal," History.com, https://www.history.com/topics/great-depression/new-deal (accessed 10/20/18).

15. "Summary Comparison of Total Outlays for Grants to State and Local Governments, 1940–2026," Office of Management and Budget, https://www.whitehouse.gov/omb/historical-tables/ (accessed 6/12/21).

8. WHY CAN YOU SMOKE POT IN COLORADO, BUT COULD GO TO JAIL FOR SMOKING IT IN OKLAHOMA?

1. "State Laws," NORML, http://norml.org/states (accessed 6/12/21).

2. Pub. L. 103-159, 107 Stat. 1536 (November 30, 1993).

3. *Printz v. United States*, 521 U.S. 898 (1997).

4. Danny Heifetz, "The Supreme Court Sports-Gambling Primer," The Ringer, April 16, 2018, https://www.theringer.com/sports/2018/4/16/17231846/sports-gambling-supreme-court-new-jersey-faq (accessed 10/28/18).

5. *Murphy v. National Collegiate Athletic Association*, 584 U.S. __ (2018).

6. Sam Kamin, "Murphy v. NCAA: It's about Much More than Gambling on Sports," The Hill, May 15, 2018, https://thehill.com/opinion/judiciary/387653-murphy-v-ncaa-its-about-much-more-than-gambling-on-sports (accessed 10/27/18).

7. "Drug Scheduling," United States Drug Enforcement Administration, https://www.dea.gov/drug-scheduling (accessed 10/29/18).

8. "State Medical Cannabis Laws," National Conference of State Legislatures, https://www.ncsl.org/research/health/state-medical-marijuana-laws.aspx (accessed 1/26/22).

9. "State Minimum Wages," National Conference of State Legislatures, https://www.ncsl.org/research/labor-and-employment/state-minimum-wage-chart.aspx; "Ohio," Minimum Wage, https://www.minimumwage.com/state/ohio; "How High Are Individual Income Tax Rates in Your State?" Tax Foundation, January 1, 2022, https://files.taxfoundation.org/20220215111110/2022-state-income-tax-rates-and-brackets-2022-state-individual-income-tax-rates-and-brackets-See-income-taxes-by-state-flat-income-taxes.png; "State by State," Death Penalty Information Center, https://deathpenaltyinfo.org/state_by_state; "State Medical Marijuana Laws," National Conference of State Legislatures, https://www.ncsl.org/research/health/state-medical-marijuana-laws.aspx; "Status of State Action on the Medicaid Expansion Decision," Henry J. Kaiser Family Foundation, June 7, 2021, https://www.kff.org/health-reform/state-indicator/state-activity-around-expanding-medicaid-under-the-affordable-care-act/; Caroline Kitchener, Kevin Schaul, N. Kirkpatrick, Daniela Santamariña, and Lauren Tierney, "Abortion Is Now Banned in These States. See here Laws Changed," *Washington Post*, July 12, 2022, https://www.washingtonpost.com/politics/2022/06/24/abortion-state-laws-criminalization-roe/; Bertha Vazquez, "A State-by-State Comparison of Middle School Science Standards on Evolution in the United States," *Evolution: Education and Outreach* 10:5 (2017): Article 5, https://doi.org/10.1186/s12052-017-0066-2; "Nondiscrimination Laws," Movement Advancement Project (MAP), https://www.lgbtmap.org/equality-maps/non_discrimination_laws; "State Political Voting Index," Cook Political Report, https://cookpolitical.com/state-pvis (accessed 6/14/21).

10. "Marriage Age by State, 2021," World Population Review, https://worldpopulationreview.com/state-rankings/marriage-age-by-state (accessed 6/12/21).

11. Kimberly Hiss, "If You Need a Divorce, These States are the Fastest . . . and the Slowest," *Reader's Digest*, April 26, 2021, https://www.rd.com/article/fastest-and-slowest-states-for-divorce/ (accessed 6/12/21).

12. "Driving Age by State, 2021," World Population Review, https://worldpopulationreview.com/state-rankings/driving-age-by-state (accessed 6/12/21).

13. Joe Sneve, "As Noem Scores Points for Her Pro-Liberty Approach to COVID-19, Here's a Look at What She's Done," *Argus Leader*, March 2,

2021, https://www.argusleader.com/story/news/2021/03/02/how
-governor-kristi-noem-handled-covid-19-south-dakota/6876347002/
(accessed 6/13/2021).

14. Hayley Smith, "California Could Lift Most Covid-19 Mask Requirements by June 15, Newsom Says," *Los Angeles Times*, May 12, 2021, https://www.latimes.com/california/story/2021-05-12/newsom-mask-mandate-end-june-15 (accessed 6/13/2021).

15. For the early 2000s data, see Frank Newport and Andrew Dugan, "Partisan Differences Growing on a Number of Issues," Gallup, August 3, 2017, https://news.gallup.com/opinion/polling-matters/215210/partisan-differences-growing-number-issues.aspx (accessed 10/28/18). For 2021 public opinion data on the same issues, see "Amid a Series of Gun Shootings in the U.S., Gun Policy Remains Deeply Divisive," Pew Research Center, April 20, 2021, https://www.pewresearch.org/politics/2021/04/20/amid-a-series-of-mass-shootings-in-the-u-s-gun-policy-remains-deeply-divisive/; Mohamed Younis, "Americans Want More, Not Less, Immigration for the First Time," July 1, 2020, Gallup, https://news.gallup.com/poll/313106/americans-not-less-immigration-first-time.aspx (accessed 6/12/21).

16. State legislative control represents a projection based on election results as of November 13, 2022.

9. WHY CAN'T KIDS PRAY IN PUBLIC SCHOOLS?

1. Jessica Ravitz, "With His Speech, Valedictorian Brings God to Graduation," CNN, June 6, 2013, http://religion.blogs.cnn.com/2013/06/06/hear-what-valedictorian-said-for-cheers/ (accessed 2/9/18).

2. Ravitz, "With His Speech, Valedictorian Brings God to Graduation."

3. General Social Survey, National Opinion Research Council, 1975–2012.

4. General Social Survey, National Opinion Research Council, 1975–2012.

5. Douglas Martin, "Vashti McCollum, 93, Who Brought Landmark Church-State Suit, Is Dead," *New York Times*, August 26, 2006, http://www.nytimes.com/2006/08/26/obituaries/26mccullum.html (accessed 2/9/18).

6. Martin, "Vashti McCollum."

7. *Illinois ex rel. McCollum v. Board of Education of School District Number 71, Champaign County, Illinois*, 333 U.S. 203 (1948).

8. *Zorach v. Clauson*, 343 U.S. 306 (1952).

9. Jeffrey Ohene Darko, "Engel v. Vitale," *PBS American Experience*, https://www.pbs.org/wgbh/americanexperience/features/engel-v-vitale/ (accessed 8/8/18).

10. *Engel v. Vitale*, 370 U.S. 421 (1962).

11. *Lemon v. Kurtzman*, 403 U.S. 602 (1971).

12. *Wallace v. Jaffree*, 472 U.S. 38 (1985).

13. *Lee v. Weisman*, 505 U.S. 577 (1992).

14. *Santa Fe Independent School District v. Doe*, 530 U.S. 290 (2000).

15. *Stone v. Graham*, 449 U.S. 39 (1980).

16. *Florey v. Sioux Falls School District*, 49-5, 619 F.2d 1311 (8th Cir.), 449 U.S. 987 (1980).

17. *Trinity Lutheran Church of Columbia, Inc. v. Comer*, 582 U.S. __ (2017).

18. *Carson v. Makin*, 596 U.S. __ (2022).

19. *Kennedy v. Bremerton School District*, 597 U.S. __ (2022).

10. CAN PEOPLE SAY OFFENSIVE AND HATEFUL THINGS WHENEVER THEY WANT?

1. "From George Washington to Officers of the Army, 15 March 1783," https://founders.archives.gov/documents/Washington/99-01-02-10840 (accessed 1/24/18).

2. Frederick Douglass, "A Plea for Free Speech in Boston," December 9, 1860, https://lawliberty.org/frederick-douglass-plea-for-freedom-of -speech-in-boston/ (accessed 12/9/21).

3. Salman Rushdie, "Excerpts from Rushdie's Address: 1,000 Days 'Trapped inside a Metaphor'," December 12, 1991, http://www.nytimes .com/books/99/04/18/specials/rushdie-address.html (accessed 1/24/18).

4. Pub. L. No. 65–150, 40 Stat. 553 (May 16, 1918).

5. "Nude Dancing Ban Upheld," CBS News, March 29, 2000, https://www .cbsnews.com/news/nude-dancing-ban-upheld/ (accessed 1/24/18).

6. Emily Shapiro and Doug Lantz, "Michelle Carter Sentenced to 2.5 Years for Texting Suicide Case," ABC News, August 3, 2017, http://abcnews .go.com/US/michelle-carter-set-sentenced-texting-suicide-case /story?id=48947807 (accessed 1/24/18).

7. Dane Schiller, "Houston Man Sentenced for 'Crush Videos' of Puppies, Animals Being Killed," *Houston Chronicle*, August 18, 2016, https://www .chron.com/news/houston-texas/article/Man-heads-to-prison-for -making-crush-videos-eos-9171252.php (accessed 6/23/21).

8. *Schenck v. United States*, 249 U.S. 47 (1919).

9. *Brandenburg v. Ohio*, 395 U.S. 444 (1969).

10. Garrett Epps, "Did the President Incite a Riot?" *The Atlantic*, April 5, 2017, https://www.theatlantic.com/politics/archive/2017/04/did-the -president-incite-a-riot/521931/ (accessed 1/30/18).

11. *Hess v. Indiana*, 414 U.S. 105 (1973).

12. *National Socialist Party of America v. Village of Skokie*, 432 U.S. 43 (1977).

13. *Snyder v. Phelps*, 562 U.S. 443 (2011).

14. Michelle Dean, "How Seriously Will the Supreme Court Take Internet Harassment?" Gawker, June 18, 2014, http://gawker.com/how -seriously-will-the-supreme-court-take-internet-hara-1591648347 (accessed 1/30/18).

15. Vauhini Vara, "The Nuances of Threats on Facebook," *New Yorker*, December 3, 2014, https://www.newyorker.com/news/news-desk /nuances-threat-facebook (accessed 1/30/18).

16. *Elonis v. United States*, 575 U.S. __ (2015).

17. 18 U.S.C. § 879 (1982).

18. Josephine Wolff, "The Secret Agents Who Stake Out the Ugliest Corners of the Internet," *The Atlantic*, July 22, 2015, https://www.theatlantic.com /technology/archive/2015/07/secret-service-online-threat-president /399179/ (accessed 1/30/18).

19. Carol Cratty, "North Carolina Man Accused of Twitter Threats to Kill Obama," CNN, September 6, 2012, http://www.cnn.com/2012/09/06 /justice/obama-threat-arrest/index.html (accessed 1/30/18).

20. Melissa Quinn, "Utah Man Indicted for Making Death Threats against Trump," *Washington Examiner*, January 4, 2018, http://www.washingtonexaminer .com/utah-man-indicted-for-making-death-threats-against-trump /article/2645012 (accessed 1/30/18).

21. Sasha Lekach, "Over 12,000 Tweets Are Calling for Trump's Assassination: Here's How the Secret Service Handles It," Mashable, February 2, 2017, https://mashable.com/2017/02/02/threatening-posts-secret-service/ (accessed 1/30/18).

22. Charlie Osborne, "Students Cyberbully Principals; Court Throws Out Cases," ZDNet, January 22, 2012, http://www.zdnet.com/article /students-cyberbully-principals-court-throws-out-cases/ (accessed 1/27/18).

23. Sara Morrison, "How the Law Protects Students Who Cyberbully Their Teachers," Vocativ, May 15, 2017, https://www.vocativ.com/419694 /teachers-victims-cyberbullying-social-media/index.html (accessed 12/9/21).

24. *New York Times Co. v. Sullivan*, 376 U.S. 254 (1964).

25. *Justin E. Fairfax v. CBS Broadcasting Inc.*, 20-1298 (4th Cir. 2021).

26. *Gertz v. Robert Welch, Inc.*, 418 U.S. 323 (1974).

27. *Hustler Magazine, Inc. v. Falwell*, 485 U.S. 46 (1988).

28. Bruce Smith, "Confederate Flag Roils S.C. Neighborhood," *Boston Globe*, October 16, 2010, http://archive.boston.com/news/nation /articles/2010/10/16/confederate_flag_roils_sc_neighborhood/ (accessed 1/28/18).

29. Dave Jamieson, "What It's Like to Be Black and Live under a White Neighbor's Confederate Flag," Huffington Post, June 19, 2015,

https://www.huffingtonpost.com/2015/06/19/charleston-confederate
-flag_n_7624760.html (accessed 1/28/18).

30. Bruce Smith, "S. Carolina Neighbors Wage Battle over Confederate Flag," NBCNews.com, September 26, 2011, http://www.nbcnews.com /id/44667234/ns/us_news-life/t/s-carolina-neighbors-wage-battle -over-confederate-flag/ (accessed 1/28/18).

31. *Tinker v. Des Moines Independent Community School District*, 393 U.S. 503 (1969).

32. *Cohen v. California*, 403 U.S. 15 (1971).

33. "Law and Civil Liberties," PollingReport.com, http://pollingreport.com/law .htm (accessed 1/28/18).

34. *Texas v. Johnson*, 491 U.S. 397 (1989).

35. *United States v. O'Brien*, 391 U.S. 367 (1968).

36. *Virginia v. Black*, 538 U.S. 343 (2003).

37. *City of Erie v. Pap's A.M.*, 529 U.S. 277 (2000).

11. WHAT HAPPENS IF YOU'RE CHARGED WITH A CRIME?

1. Erika Harrell and Elizabeth Davis, "Contacts between the Police and the Public," Bureau of Justice Statistics, December 2020, https://www.bjs .ojp.gov/library/publications/contacts-between-police-and-public-2018 -statistical-tables (accessed 6/23/21).

2. "Traffic Stops," Bureau of Justice Statistics, https://www.bjs.gov/index .cfm?tid=702&ty=tp (accessed 8/8/18).

3. "Estimated Number of Arrests," U.S. Department of Justice, https://ucr .fbi.gov/crime-in-the-u.s/2019/crime-in-the-u.s.-2019/tables/table-29 (accessed 6/23/21).

4. Robert Brame, Michael G. Turner, Raymond Paternoster, and Shawn D. Bushway, "Cumulative Prevalence of Arrest from Ages 8 to 23 in a National Sample," *Pediatrics* 129, no.1 (2012): 21–27.

5. Matthew Friedman, "Just Facts: As Many Americans Have Criminal Records as College Diplomas," Brennan Center for Justice, November 17, 2015, https://www.brennancenter.org/blog/just-facts-many-americans -have-criminal-records-college-diplomas (accessed 8/8/18).

6. Friedman, "Just Facts."

7. *Weeks v. United States*, 232 U.S. 383 (1914).

8. *Wyoming v. Houghton*, 526 U.S. 295 (1999).

9. *Vernonia School District 47J v. Acton*, 515 U.S. 646 (1995).

10. *New Jersey v. T.L.O.*, 469 U.S. 325 (1985).

11. *Safford Unified School District v. Redding*, 557 U.S. __ (2009).

12. *Miranda v. Arizona*, 384 U.S. 436 (1966).

13. *New York v. Quarles*, 467 U.S. 649 (1984).

14. *Gideon v. Wainwright*, 372 U.S. 335 (1963).

15. Bryan Furst, "A Fair Fight: Achieving Indigent Defense Resource Parity," Brennan Center for Justice, September 9, 2019, https://www .brennancenter.org/sites/default/files/2019-09/Report_A%20Fair %20Fight.pdf (accessed 6/23/21).

16. *Escobedo v. Illinois*, 378 U.S. 478 (1964).

17. Ram Subramanian, Léon Digard, Melvin Washington II, and Stephanie Sorage, "In the Shadows: A Review of the Research on Plea Bargaining," Vera Institute of Justice, September 2020, https://www.vera.org /publications/in-the-shadows-plea-bargaining (accessed 6/23/21).

18. Lea Hunter, "What's Wrong with Cash Bail and How to Fix It," Center for American Progress, March 16, 2020, https://www.americanprogress.org /issues/criminal-justice/reports/2020/03/16/481543/ending-cash-bail/ (accessed 6/25/21).

19. Safia Samee Ali, "Illinois Becomes First State to End Cash Bail as Part of Criminal Justice Reform Law," NBC News, February 24, 2021, https:// www.nbcnews.com/news/us-news/illinois-becomes-first-state-end -money-bail-part-massive-criminal-n1258679 (accessed 6/25/21).

20. Debra Cassens Weiss, "Judge Censured for Excessive Bail, Severe Attitude," *ABA Journal*, February 8, 2008, https://www.abajournal.com /news/article/judge_censured_for_excessive_bail_severe_attitude (accessed 2/27/22).

21. "Right to a Speedy Jury Trial," FindLaw, https://criminal.findlaw.com /criminal-rights/right-to-a-speedy-jury-trial.html (accessed 9/13/19).

22. *Mapp v. Ohio*, 367 U.S. 643 (1961).

23. *Rummel v. Estelle*, 445 U.S. 263 (1980).

24. *Gregg v. Georgia*, 428 U.S. 153 (1976).

25. *Furman v. Georgia*, 408 U.S. 238 (1972).

26. *McCleskey v. Kemp*, 481 U.S. 279 (1987).

27. *Roper v. Simmons*, 408 U.S. 238 (1972).

28. *Atkins v. Virginia*, 536 U.S. 304 (2002).

29. *Kennedy v. Louisiana*, 554 U.S. 407 (2008).

12. CAN THE GOVERNMENT REGULATE YOUR SEX LIFE?

1. "Jersey City Man Claims Rite Aid Refused To Sell Emergency Contraception Because of Gender," CBSNewYork, May 30, 2012, https://newyork.cbslocal .com/2012/05/30/jersey-city-man-claims-rite-aid-refused-to-sell -emergency-contraception-because-of-gender/ (accessed 6/2/21).

2. "Jersey City Man" (accessed 8/16/18).

3. Elizabeth Chuck, "Walgreens Pharmacist Refuses to Give Arizona Woman Drug to End Pregnancy," NBC News, June 25, 2018, https:// www.nbcnews.com/news/us-news/walgreens-pharmacist-refuses

-give-arizona-woman-drug-end-pregnancy-n886396 (accessed 6/27/18).

4. CNN Wire, "Woman Slams Walgreens after Pharmacist Refuses to Fill Her Prescription to Induce a Miscarriage," News Channel 3, June 25, 2018, https://wreg.com/2018/06/25/woman-slams-walgreens-after-pharmacist-refuses-to-fill-her-prescription-to-induce-a-miscarriage/ (accessed 6/27/18).

5. Gigi Stone, "Some Pharmacies Refuse to Fill Birth Control Prescriptions," ABC News, August 8, 2008, https://abcnews.go.com/Health/story?id=5542159&page=1 (accessed 6/27/18).

6. "Wis. Pharmacist Asks High Court to Review His Discipline," *Pioneer Press*, November 14, 2015, https://www.twincities.com/2008/04/23/wis-pharmacist-asks-high-court-to-review-his-discipline/ (accessed 8/8/18).

7. J. P. Zenger, "Rape Victim Denied Morning After Pill by Hospital," PennLive.com, July 25, 2006, https://www.dailykos.com/stories/2006/7/25/230517/- (accessed 6/27/18).

8. "Pharmacy Refusals 101," National Women's Law Center, https://nwlc.org/resources/pharmacy-refusals-101/ (accessed 6/23/21).

9. "Refusing to Provide Health Services," Guttmacher Institute, July 1, 2022, https://www.guttmacher.org/state-policy/explore/refusing-provide-health-services# (accessed 7/15/22).

10. Jen Ball, "The Little Understood History of *Griswold v. Connecticut*," Medium, February 9, 2017, https://medium.com/@jballphd/the-little-understood-history-of-griswold-v-connecticut-ba74fa6daf4d (accessed 6/27/18).

11. *Griswold v. Connecticut*, 381 U.S. 479 (1965).

12. *Griswold v. Connecticut*, 381 U.S. 479 (1965).

13. *Eisenstadt v. Baird*, 405 U.S. 438 (1972).

14. *Burwell v. Hobby Lobby Stores*, 573 U.S. 682 (2014).

15. *Roe v. Wade*, 410 U.S. 113 (1973).

16. *Dobbs v. Jackson Women's Health Organization*, 597 U.S. __ (2022).

17. *Dobbs v. Jackson Women's Health Organization*, 597 U.S. __ (2022).

18. Natasha Ishak, "Trigger Laws and Abortion Restrictions, Explained," Vox, June 25, 2022, https://www.vox.com/2022/6/25/23182753/roe-overturned-abortion-access-reproductive-rights-trigger-laws (accessed 7/15/22).

19. "13 States Have Abortion Trigger Bans—Here's What Happens When Roe Is Overturned," Guttmacher Institute, June 6, 2022, https://www.guttmacher.org/article/2022/06/13-states-have-abortion-trigger-bans-heres-what-happens-when-roe-overturned (accessed 7/15/22).

20. Aaron Katersky and Meredith Deliso, "How 3 States Are Moving to Protect Abortion Rights after the Fall of Roe v. Wade," ABC News,

July 2, 2022, https://abcnews.go.com/US/states-moving-protect-abortion-rights-fall-roe-wade/story?id=86061089 (accessed 7/14/22).

21. "After Roe Fell: Abortion Laws by State," Center for Reproductive Rights, https://reproductiverights.org/maps/abortion-laws-by-state/ (accessed 11/15/22).

22. William N. Eskridge, *Dishonorable Passions: Sodomy Laws in America, 1861–2003* (New York: Viking, 2008).

23. *Bowers v. Hardwick*, 478 U.S. 186 (1986).

24. *Lawrence v. Texas*, 539 U.S. 558 (2003).

13. ARE ALL AMERICANS EQUAL UNDER THE LAW?

1. "Transcript: 'This is your victory,' Says Obama," CNN, November 4, 2008, http://edition.cnn.com/2008/POLITICS/11/04/obama.transcript/ (accessed 7/10/18).

2. Adam Nagourney, "Obama Elected President as Racial Barrier Falls," *New York Times*, November 5, 2008, https://www.nytimes.com/2008/11/05/us/politics/05elect.html (accessed 7/10/18).

3. "Representative John Lewis on Obama's Victory," MSNBC, November 4, 2008, https://www.youtube.com/watch?v=Oo-ijYnzn1w (accessed 7/10/18).

4. "Transcript of John McCain's Concession Speech," National Public Radio, November 5, 2008, https://www.npr.org/templates/story/story.php?storyId=96631784 (accessed 7/10/18).

5. "Jim Crow Laws," Smithsonian Institution, http://americanhistory.si.edu/brown/history/1-segregated/jim-crow.html (accessed 8/9/18).

6. *Plessy v. Ferguson*, 163 U.S. 537 (1896).

7. *Brown v. Board of Education of Topeka (1)*, 347 U.S. 483 (1954).

8. Vanessa Romo, "Linda Brown, Who Was at Center of Brown v. Board of Education, Dies," National Public Radio, March 26, 2018, https://www.npr.org/sections/thetwo-way/2018/03/26/597154953/linda-brown-who-was-at-center-of-brown-v-board-of-education-dies (accessed 3/26/18).

9. E. R. Shipp, "Rosa Parks, 92, Founding Symbol of Civil Rights Movement Dies," *New York Times*, October 25, 2005, https://www.nytimes.com/2005/10/25/us/rosa-parks-92-founding-symbol-of-civil-rights-movement-dies.html (accessed 7/13/18).

10. "Civil Rights Martyrs," Southern Poverty Law Center, https://www.splcenter.org/what-we-do/civil-rights-memorial/civil-rights-martyrs (accessed 7/13/18).

11. Christopher Klein, "10 Things You May Not Know about Martin Luther King Jr.," History.com, April 4, 2013, https://www.history.com/news/10-things-you-may-not-know-about-martin-luther-king-jr (accessed 7/13/18).

12. Noah Remnick, "The Civil Rights Act: What JFK, LBJ, Martin Luther King and Malcolm X Had to Say," *Los Angeles Times*, June 28, 2014, http://www.latimes.com/nation/la-oe-civil-rights-quotes-20140629-story.html (accessed 7/13/18).

13. Chris Weston, "Sen. Strom Thurmond Spent a Lifetime in Public Service," *Greenville News*, June 27, 2003, https://www.greenvilleonline.com/story/news/local/greenville-roots/2018/06/26/sen-strom-thurmond-spent-lifetime-public-service/721586002/ (accessed 7/13/18).

14. "Civil Rights Act of 1964," History.com, January 4, 2010, https://www.history.com/topics/black-history/civil-rights-act (accessed 7/13/18).

15. "The Voting Rights Act of 1965," U.S. Department of Justice, https://www.justice.gov/crt/history-federal-voting-rights-laws (accessed 7/13/18).

16. *Shelby County v. Holder*, 570 U.S. 529 (2013).

17. *Loving v. Virginia*, 388 U.S. 1 (1967).

18. "A Look at Voter Suppression Tactics ahead of the Election," National Public Radio, September 13, 2020, https://www.npr.org/2020/09/13/912519039/a-look-at-voter-suppression-tactics-ahead-of-the-election (accessed 6/24/21).

19. Annie Karni and Luke Broadwater, "Biden Signs Law Making Juneteenth a Federal Holiday," *New York Times*, June 17, 2021, https://www.nytimes.com/2021/06/17/us/politics/juneteenth-holiday-biden.html (accessed 6/24/21).

20. "John and Abigail Adams," *PBS American Experience*, https://www.pbs.org/wgbh/americanexperience/features/adams-remember-ladies/ (accessed 7/13/18).

21. Sara M. Evans, *Born for Liberty: A History of Women in America* (New York: Free Press, 1997).

22. *Minor v. Happersett*, 88 U.S. 162 (1874).

23. *Bradwell v. The State*, 83 U.S. 130 (1873).

24. *Goesaert v. Cleary*, 355 U.S. 464 (1948).

25. "Equal Rights Amendment," National Organization for Women, http://now.org/resource/equal-rights-ammendment/ (accessed 7/13/18).

26. *Reed v. Reed*, 404 U.S. 71 (1971).

27. *Craig v. Boren*, 429 U.S. 190 (1976).

28. *United States v. Virginia*, 518 U.S. 515 (1996).

29. *Rostker v. Goldberg*, 453 U.S. 57 (1981).

30. *Michael M. v. Superior Court of Sonoma County*, 450 U.S. 464 (1980).

31. "Campus Sexual Violence: Statistics," Rape, Abuse, and Incest National Network, https://www.rainn.org/statistics/campus-sexual-violence; Haley Ott, "Hundreds Protest Campus Sexual Assault at Universities across the U.S.," CBS News, February 10, 2021, https://www.cbsnews.com/news/college-sexual-assault-us-universities-protests/ (accessed 6/24/21).

32. Jack Drescher, "Out of DSM: Depathologizing Homosexuality," *Behavioral Sciences* 5, no. 4 (2015): 565–75.

33. Joel Engardio, "How Eisenhower's Ban on Gays Backfired," *USA Today*, May 20, 2013, https://www.usatoday.com/story/opinion/2013/05/20 /gay-bashing-like-ike-column/2343963/ (accessed 7/14/18).

34. "Stonewall Riots," History.com, https://www.history.com/topics/the -stonewall-riots (accessed 7/14/18).

35. Employment Non-Discrimination Act of 2007, H.R. Rep. No. 110–406 (2007). https://www.congress.gov/congressional-report/110th-congress /house-report/406/1 (accessed 7/14/18).

36. Dave Umhoefer, "Mark Pocan Says Wisconsin Was the First State to Ban Employment Discrimination against All Gay and Lesbian People," Politifact, June 22, 2014, http://www.politifact.com/wisconsin/statements /2014/jun/22/mark-pocan/mark-pocan-says-wisconsin-was-first-state -ban-empl/ (accessed 7/14/18).

37. *Romer v. Evans*, 517 U.S. 620 (1996).

38. Pub. L. No. 104-199, Defense of Marriage Act (September 21, 1996).

39. Russell Heimlich, "More Americans Supporting Gay Marriage," Pew Research Center, February 23, 2011, http://www.pewresearch.org /fact-tank/2011/02/23/more-americans-supporting-gay-marriage/ (accessed 11/22/19).

40. "Celebrate National Coming Out Day with HRC!" Human Rights Campaign, http://www.hrc.org/resources/national-coming-out-day (accessed 7/15/18).

41. "Ellen DeGeneres Tells *Time* She's a Lesbian," CNN, April 6, 1997, http:// www.cnn.com/SHOWBIZ/9704/06/ellen/ (accessed 7/15/18).

42. "Four-in-Ten Americans Have Close Friends or Relatives Who Are Gay," Pew Research Center, May 23, 2007, http://www.pewsocialtrends. org/2007/05/23/four-in-ten-americans-have-close-friends-or-relatives -who-are-gay/ (accessed 8/13/18).

43. "Remarks by the President and Vice President at Signing of the Don't Ask, Don't Tell Repeal Act of 2010," The White House, December 22, 2010, https://obamawhitehouse.archives.gov/the-press-office/2010 /12/22/remarks-president-and-vice-president-signing-dont-ask -dont-tell-repeal-a (accessed 7/14/18).

44. *Obergefell v. Hodges*, 576 U.S. __ (2015).

45. Justin McCarthy, "Same-Sex Marriage Support Inches Up to New High of 71%," Gallup, June 1, 2022, https://news.gallup.com/poll/393197/same -sex-marriage-support-inches-new-high.aspx (accessed 7/15/22).

46. "LGBTQ Americans Aren't Fully Protected from Discrimination in 29 States," Freedom for All Americans, https://freedomforallamericans.org /states/ (accessed 6/24/21).

47. *Bostock v. Clayton County*, 590 U.S. __ (2020); *R.G. and G.R. Harris Funeral Homes Inc. v. Equal Employment Opportunity Commission*, 590 U.S. __ (2020).

14. IS AMERICA A RACIST COUNTRY?

1. Larry Buchanan, Quoctrung Bui, and Jugal K. Patel, "Black Lives Matter May Be the Largest Movement in U.S. History," *New York Times*, July 3, 2020, https://www.nytimes.com/interactive/2020/07/03/us/george-floyd-protests-crowd-size.html (accessed 6/28/21).

2. Liz Hamel, Audrey Kearney, Ashley Kirzinger, Lunna Lopes, Cailey Muñana, and Mollyann Brodie, "KFF Health Tracking Poll — June 2020," Kaiser Family Foundation, June 26, 2020, https://www.kff.org/racial-equity-and-health-policy/report/kff-health-tracking-poll-june-2020/ (accessed 6/28/21).

3. Associated Press, "Ferguson Police Say Teen Shot by Cop Was Suspect in Robbery; Officer's Identity Revealed," CBS News, August 25, 2014, https://www.cbsnews.com/news/darren-wilson-ferguson-police-officer-who-fatally-shot-michael-brown-identified/ (accessed 7/17/18).

4. Matthew Vann and Erik Ortiz, "Walter Scott Shooting: Michael Slager, Ex-Officer, Sentenced to 20 Years in Prison," NBC News, December 9, 2017, https://www.nbcnews.com/storyline/walter-scott-shooting/walter-scott-shooting-michael-slager-ex-officer-sentenced-20-years-n825006 (accessed 7/17/18).

5. "Timeline: Freddie Gray's Arrest and Death," *Baltimore Sun*, April 12, 2015, http://data.baltimoresun.com/news/freddie-gray/index.html (accessed 6/28/21).

6. Mark Berman, "What the Police Officer Who Shot Philando Castile Said about the Shooting," *Washington Post*, June 21, 2017, https://www.washingtonpost.com/news/post-nation/wp/2017/06/21/what-the-police-officer-who-shot-philando-castile-said-about-the-shooting/ (accessed 7/17/18).

7. Richard A. Oppel Jr., Derrick Bryson Taylor, and Nicholas Bogel-Burroughs, "What to Know about Breonna Taylor's Death," *New York Times*, April 26, 2021, https://www.nytimes.com/article/breonna-taylor-police.html (accessed 6/28/21).

8. "National Exit Polls: How Different Groups Voted," *New York Times*, https://www.nytimes.com/interactive/2020/11/03/us/elections/exit-polls-president.html (accessed 6/28/21).

9. "Race and Ethnicity," PollingReport.com, https://pollingreport.com/race.htm (accessed 6/28/21).

10. "Quick Facts," United States Census Bureau, July 1, 2021, https://www.census.gov/quickfacts/fact/table/US/PST045221 (accessed 7/15/22).

11. Emily A. Shrider, Melissa Kollar, Frances Chen, and Jessica Semeg, "Income and Poverty in the United States: 2020," United States Census Bureau, Report Number P60-273, September 14, 2021, https://www.census.gov/library/publications/2021/demo/p60-273.html; "Status and Trends in the Education of Racial and Ethnic Groups," National Center for Education Statistics, February 2019, https://nces.ed.gov/programs

/raceindicators/indicator_rads.asp; "Home Ownership by Race and Hispanic Origin," United States Census Bureau, https://www.census .gov/data/tables/2000/dec/coh-ownershipbyrace.html; Neil Bhutta, Andrew C. Chang, Lisa J. Dettling, and Joanne W. Hsu, "Disparities in Wealth by Race and Ethnicity in the 2019 Survey of Consumer Finances," Board of Governors of the Federal Reserve System, September 28, 2020, https://www.federalreserve.gov/econres/notes/feds-notes /disparities-in-wealth-by-race-and-ethnicity-in-the-2019-survey-of -consumer-finances-20200928.htm; "How America Banks: Household Use of Banking and Financial Services," Federal Deposit Insurance Corporation, 2019, https://www.fdic.gov/analysis/household-survey /2019appendix.pdf (accessed 7/15/22).

12. "Quick Facts," United States Census Bureau, https://www.census.gov/ quickfacts/fact/table/US/PST045221 (accessed 7/15/22).

13. Andrea Flynn, Dorian T. Warren, Felicia J. Wong, and Susan R. Holmberg, *The Hidden Rules of Race: Barriers to an Inclusive Economy* (New York: Cambridge University Press, 2017).

14. "HHS Poverty Guidelines for 2022," U.S. Department of Health and Human Services, Janaury 12, 2022, https://aspe.hhs.gov/topics /poverty-economic-mobility/poverty-guidelines (accessed 7/15/22).

15. "The State of America's Children, 2021," Children's Defense Fund, https:// www.childrensdefense.org/state-of-americas-children/soac-2021 -child-poverty/ (accessed 6/26/21).

16. Bhutta, Chang, Dettling, and Hsu, "Disparities in Wealth."

17. Jonathan Kozol, "Savage Inequalities: Children in America's Schools," 2015, https://www.jonathankozol.com/media (accessed 7/20/18).

18. Alvin Chang, "White America Is Quietly Self-Segregating," Vox, January 18, 2017, https://www.vox.com/2017/1/18/14296126/white-segregated -suburb-neighborhood-cartoon (accessed 7/22/18).

19. Tracy Hadden Loh, Christopher Coes, and Becca Buthe, "The Great Real Estate Reset," Brookings Institution, December 16, 2020, https://www .brookings.edu/essay/trend-1-separate-and-unequal-neighborhoods -are-sustaining-racial-and-economic-injustice-in-the-us/ (accessed 6/27/21).

20. Nikole Hannah-Jones, "Segregation Now," ProPublica, April 16, 2014, https:// www.propublica.org/article/segregation-now-full-text (accessed 8/13/18); Fermin Leal, "Growing Segregation of Latinos in Public Schools Poses Challenge for Academic Success," Education Writers Association, August 29, 2016, https://www.ewa.org/blog-latino-ed-beat/growing -segregation-latinos-public-schools-poses-challenge-academic -success (accessed 8/13/18).

21. Jason M. Breslow, Evan Wexler, and Robert Collins, "The Return of School Segregation in Eight Charts," *PBS Frontline*, July 15, 2014, https://

www.pbs.org/wgbh/frontline/article/the-return-of-school-segregation-in-eight-charts/ (accessed 7/20/18).

22. Ivy Morgan and Ary Amerikaner, "Funding Gaps 2018," The Education Trust, February 27, 2018, https://edtrust.org/resource/funding-gaps-2018/ (accessed 7/20/18).

23. Lauren Musu-Gillette, Jennifer Robinson, Joel McFarland, Angelina KewalRamani, Anlan Zhang, and Sidney Wilkinson-Flicker, "Status and Trends in the Education of Racial and Ethnic Groups 2016," U.S. Department of Education, August 2016, https://nces.ed.gov/pubs2016/2016007.pdf (accessed 7/20/18).

24. "The Racial Gap in Four-Year High School Graduation Rates," *Journal of Blacks in Higher Education*, March 16, 2020, https://www.jbhe.com/2020/03/the-racial-gap-in-four-year-high-school-graduation-rates/; "College Enrollment Rates," National Center for Education Statistics, May 2021, https://nces.ed.gov/programs/coe/indicator/cpb; Melanie Hanson, "College Graduation Statistics," EducationData.org, February 20, 2021, https://educationdata.org/number-of-college-graduates (accessed 6/27/21).

25. "Fast Facts: SAT Scores," National Center for Education Statistics, 2019, https://nces.ed.gov/fastfacts/display.asp?id=171 (accessed 6/27/21).

26. "Undergraduate Students — All — 2020," Diversity Dashboard, University of Virginia, https://diversitydata.virginia.edu/Home/Details/Undergraduate%20Students (accessed 6/27/21).

27. Meredith Kolodner, "Black Students Are Drastically Underrepresented at Top Public Colleges, Data Show," The Hechinger Report, December 18, 2015, https://hechingerreport.org/black-students-are-drastically-underrepresented-at-top-public-colleges-data-show/ (accessed 7/20/18).

28. "The Economics Daily," Bureau of Labor Statistics, July 23, 2020, https://www.bls.gov/opub/ted/2020/median-weekly-earnings-by-education-second-quarter-2020.htm (accessed 6/27/21).

29. *Regents of the University of California v. Bakke*, 438 U.S. 265 (1978).

30. *Gratz v. Bollinger*, 539 U.S. 244 (2003).

31. Jacob Kang-Brown, Chase Montagnet, and Jasmine Heiss, "People in Jail and Prison in 2020," Vera Institute of Justice, January 2021, https://www.vera.org/publications/people-in-jail-and-prison-in-2020 (accessed 6/28/21).

32. "Quick Facts," United States Census Bureau, http://www.census.gov/quickfacts/fact/table/US/PST045217; John Gramlich, "Black Imprisonment Rate in the U.S. Has Fallen by a Third since 2006," Pew Research Center, May 6, 2020, https://www.pewresearch.org/fact-tank/2020/05/06/share-of-black-white-hispanic-americans-in-prison-2018-vs-2006/ (accessed 7/15/22).

33. "Criminal Justice Facts," The Sentencing Project, http://www.sentencingproject.org/criminal-justice-facts/ (accessed 7/15/22).

34. "A Tale of Two Countries: Racially Targeted Arrests in the Era of Marijuana Reform," American Civil Liberties Union, 2020, https://www.aclu.org/report/tale-two-countries-racially-targeted-arrests-era-marijuana-reform (accessed 6/28/21).

35. Wendy Sawyer, "How Race Impacts Who Is Detained Pretrial," Prison Policy Initiative, October 9, 2019, https://www.prisonpolicy.org/blog/2019/10/09/pretrial_race/ (accessed 6/28/21).

36. "Report to the United Nations on Racial Disparities in the U.S. Criminal Justice System," The Sentencing Project, April 19, 2018, https://www.sentencingproject.org/publications/un-report-on-racial-disparities/ (accessed 6/28/21).

37. "Revoked: How Probation and Parole Feed Mass Incarceration in the United States," Human Rights Watch, July 31, 2020, https://www.hrw.org/report/2020/07/31/revoked/how-probation-and-parole-feed-mass-incarceration-united-states (accessed 6/28/21).

38. "Criminal Justice Fact Sheet," NAACP, https://naacp.org/resources/criminal-justice-fact-sheet (accessed 6/28/21).

39. "Fatal Force Database," *Washington Post*, June 21, 2021, https://www.washingtonpost.com/graphics/investigations/police-shootings-database/ (accessed 6/28/21).

40. Kathy Frankovic, "More African-Americans Fear Victimization by Police than Fear Violent Crime," YouGov, March 15, 2019, https://today.yougov.com/topics/politics/articles-reports/2019/03/15/black-americans-police (accessed 6/28/21).

41. Chloee Weiner, "House Approves Police Reform Bill Named after George Floyd," National Public Radio, March 3, 2021, https://www.npr.org/2021/03/03/973111306/house-approves-police-reform-bill-named-after-george-floyd (accessed 6/28/21).

42. Li Zhou, "The Uncertain Prospects for Police Reform in the Senate, Explained," Vox, April 22, 2021, https://www.vox.com/22388199/george-floyd-police-reform-bill-senate-explained (accessed 6/28/21).

43. Jason Silverstein, "The Only Republican to Vote for George Floyd Police Reform Act Says He 'Accidentally' Pressed the Wrong Button," CBS News, March 4, 2021, https://www.cbsnews.com/news/george-floyd-justice-policing-act-lance-gooden-republican-accident-vote/ (accessed 6/28/21).

44. Felicia Sonmez and Mike DeBonis, "No Deal on Bill to Overhaul Policing in Aftermath of Protests over Killing of Black Americans," *Washington Post*, September 22, 2021, https://www.washingtonpost.com/powerpost/policing-george-floyd-congress-legislation/2021/09/22/36324a34-1bc9-11ec-a99a-5fea2b2da34b_story.html (accessed 7/15/22).

45. Eugene Scott, "Supreme Court Justice Affirms Activists' Fear that Police Can 'Shoot First, and Think Later,'" *Washington Post*, April 3, 2018, https://www.washingtonpost.com/news/the-fix/wp/2018/04/03 /supreme-court-justice-affirms-activists-fears-that-police-can-shoot -first-and-think-later/ (accessed 7/21/18).

46. Cornel West, *Race Matters* (New York: Beacon Press, 1993).

15. WHY DO WOMEN EARN LESS MONEY THAN MEN?

1. John F. Kennedy, "Remarks upon Signing the Equal Pay Act," June 10, 1963, https://www.presidency.ucsb.edu/documents/remarks-upon -signing-the-equal-pay-act (accessed 7/5/18).

2. The Equal Pay Act of 1963, (https://www.eeoc.gov/laws/statutes/epa .cfm (accessed 7/5/18).

3. "Lemonade Stand," Friends of Dan Maffei, https://www.youtube.com /watch?v=Ok_tJO2OwWU (accessed 7/4/18).

4. Data compiled from the U.S. Census Bureau, Catalyst Inc., and a BlackRock survey of investors. See also Arthur Zuckerman, "61 Single Parent Statistics: 2020/2021," CompareCamp, May 26, 2020, https://comparecamp.com/single-parent-statistics/ (accessed 6/23/21).

5. Courtney Connley, "President Biden Says Closing Gender Pay Gap Is 'a Moral Imperative' as House Passes Paycheck Fairness Act," CNBC, April 16, 2021, https://www.cnbc.com/2021/04/16/what-the-paycheck -fairness-act-could-mean-for-women-and-the-pay-gap.html (accessed 6/23/21).

6. Amanda Snell and Anthony B. Kim, "Why Free Market Policies Are Key to Empowering Women," The Daily Signal, November 16, 2018, https://www .dailysignal.com/2018/11/16/why-free-market-policies-are-key-to -empowering-women/ (accessed 11/25/18).

7. "Equal Pay and the Wage Gap," National Women's Law Center, https:// nwlc.org/issue/equal-pay-and-the-wage-gap/ (accessed 11/16/18).

8. Jessica Semega, Melissa Kollar, Emily A. Shrider, and John Creamer, "Income and Poverty in the United States: 2019," United States Census Bureau, September 15, 2020, https://www.census.gov/library/publications /2020/demo/p60-270.html; Amanda Barroso and Anna Brown, "Gender Pay Gap in U.S. Held Steady in 2020," Pew Research Center, May 25, 2021, https://www.pewresearch.org/fact-tank/2021/05/25/gender-pay -gap-facts/ (accessed 12/10/21).

9. Jane Lapidus and Deborah M. Figart, "Remedying Unfair Acts: U.S. Pay Equity by Race and Gender," *Feminist Economics* 4, no.3 (1998): 7–28.

10. "The Simple Truth about the Gender Pay Gap," AAUW, 2021, https:// www.aauw.org/resources/research/simple-truth/ (accessed 6/21/21).

11. The racial double disadvantage is also affected by region, the influx of immigrants, and job opportunities and cultures specific to particular groups. See Leslie McCall, "Sources of Racial Wage Inequality in Metropolitan Labor Markets: Racial, Ethnic, and Gender Differences," *American Sociological Review* 66, no. 4 (2001): 520–41.

12. For a more detailed account of airlines' hiring practices, see Victoria Vantoch, *The Jet Sex: Airline Stewardesses and the Making of an American Icon* (Philadelphia: University of Pennsylvania Press, 2013).

13. "Civil Rights Act of 1964: A Long Struggle for Freedom," Library of Congress, https://www.loc.gov/exhibits/civil-rights-act/civil-rights-act-of-1964.html (accessed 7/8/18).

14. "Equal Pay Act of 1963 and Lilly Ledbetter Fair Pay Act of 2009," U.S. Equal Employment Opportunity Commission, https://www.eeoc.gov/eeoc/publications/brochure-equal_pay_and_ledbetter_act.cfm (accessed 7/8/18).

15. Ariante Hegewisch and Heidi Hartman, "Occupational Segregation and the Gender Wage Gap: A Job Half Done," Institute for Women's Policy Research, January 23, 2014, http://www.iwpr.org/publications/pubs/occupational-segregation-and-the-gender-wage-gap-a-job-half-done (accessed 7/4/18).

16. Katie Shonk, "Women and Negotiation: Narrowing the Gender Gap in Negotiation," Harvard Law School, August 24, 2021, https://www.pon.harvard.edu/daily/business-negotiations/women-and-negotiation-narrowing-the-gender-gap/ (accessed 12/6/21); Linda Babcock and Sarah Laschever, *Women Don't Ask: Negotiation and the Gender Divide* (Princeton, NJ: Princeton University Press, 2003).

17. "Salary Stats: Women vs. Men," *Washington Post*, November 7, 2008, http://www.washingtonpost.com/wp-dyn/content/article/2008/11/06/AR2008110602982.html (accessed 7/4/18).

18. Trevor Wheelwright, "The Top 10 Most Expensive (and Least Expensive) States for Child Care," Move.org, April 13, 2021, https://www.move.org/child-care-cost/ (accessed 6/23/21).

19. Wheelwright, "The Top 10 Most Expensive (and Least Expensive) States for Child Care."

20. Barroso and Brown, "Gender Pay Gap in U.S. Held Steady in 2020."

21. Patrick Boyle, "Nation's Physician Workforce Evolves: More Women, a Bit Older, and toward Different Specialties," Association of American Medical Colleges, February 2, 2021, https://www.aamc.org/news-insights/nation-s-physician-workforce-evolves-more-women-bit-older-and-toward-different-specialties (accessed 6/23/21).

16. DO YOU HAVE TO BAKE A GAY COUPLE'S WEDDING CAKE?

1. Nolan Feeney, "Colorado Says Baker Didn't Discriminate in Refusing to Make Anti-Gay Cake," *Time*, April 6, 2015, https://time

.com/3772884/colorado-baker-refuses-anti-gay-cakes/ (accessed 6/3/21).

2. Alan Gathright and Eric Lupher, "Denver's Azucar Bakery Wins Right to Refuse to Make Anti-Gay Cakes," ABC7, April 23, 2015.

3. Gallup, "LGBT Rights," https://news.gallup.com/poll/1651/gay-lesbian -rights.aspx; American National Election Studies, "Time Series Cumulative File," (accessed 12/10/21).

4. "Religious Landscape Study," Pew Research Center, https://www .pewforum.org/religious-landscape-study/ (accessed 6/24/21).

5. *Obergefell v. Hodges*, 576 U.S. __ (2015).

6. Pamela Danzinger, "Will a Booming Economy Bring a Wedding Market Boom? Not Likely," *Forbes*, February 17, 2018, https://www.forbes.com /sites/pamdanziger/2018/02/17/will-a-booming-economy-bring-a -wedding-market-boom-not-likely/ (accessed 7/26/18).

7. Conor Friedersdorf, "Refusing to Photograph a Gay Wedding Isn't Hateful," *The Atlantic*, March 5, 2014, https://www.theatlantic.com /politics/archive/2014/03/refusing-to-photograph-a-gay-wedding -isnt-hateful/284224/ (accessed 7/26/18).

8. Gene Johnson, "Justices Won't Hear Case of Anti-Gay Florist," *Seattle Times*, June 25, 2018, https://www.seattletimes.com/nation-world /nation-politics/apxjustices-won-t-hear-case-of-anti-gay-marriage -florist/ (accessed 7/26/18).

9. "Vermont Inn Settles Suit over Refusing Lesbian Wedding Reception," *Wisconsin Gazette*, August 23, 2012, https://www.wisconsingazette .com/news/vermont-inn-settles-suit-over-refusing-lesbian-wedding -reception/article_d14e34e4-d12e-5a66-a105-a0cec72760af.html (accessed 7/26/18).

10. Amanda Casanova, "Christian Photographers Close Business to Avoid Shooting Gay Weddings," ChristianHeadlines.com, November 21, 2014, https://www.christianheadlines.com/blog/christian-photographers-close -business-to-avoid-shooting-gay-weddings.html (accessed 7/26/18).

11. Jake Thomas, "Hitching Post Lawsuit Settled by City of Coeur d'Alene," *Inlander*, May 3, 2016, https://www.inlander.com/Bloglander /archives/2016/05/03/hitching-post-lawsuit-settled-by-city-of-coeur -dalene (accessed 7/26/18).

12. Jo Yurcaba, "A 'Troubling Rise' in Business Owners Refusing Gay Couples, Advocates Say," NBC News, April 21, 2021, https://www.nbcnews .com/nbc-out/out-news/troubling-rise-business-owners-refusing-gay -couples-advocates-say-rcna735 (accessed 6/24/21).

13. Michael Paulson, "Can't Have Your Cake, Gays Are Told, and a Rights Battle Rises," *New York Times*, December 16, 2014, https://www.nytimes .com/2014/12/16/us/cant-have-your-cake-gays-are-told-and-a-rights -battle-rises.html (accessed 7/26/18).

14. Julie Compton, "Meet the Couple behind the Masterpiece Cakeshop Supreme Court Case," NBC News, December 6, 2017, https://www.nbcnews.com/feature/nbc-out/meet-couple-behind-masterpiece-cakeshop-supreme-court-case-n826976 (accessed 7/26/18).

15. Adam Liptak, "Cake Is His 'Art.' So He Can Deny One to a Gay Couple?" *New York Times*, September 16, 2017, https://www.nytimes.com/2017/09/16/us/supreme-court-baker-same-sex-marriage.html (accessed 7/26/18).

16. Tony Perkins, "SCOTUS to Hear Masterpiece Cakes Case," The Patriot Post, June 27, 2017, https://patriotpost.us/opinion/49866-scotus-to-hear-masterpiece-cakes-case (accessed 7/26/18).

17. *Masterpiece Cakeshop, Ltd. v. Colorado Civil Rights Commission*, 584 U.S. __ (2018).

18. Howard Fischer, "Arizona Court Rejects Business Owners' Challenge to Same-Sex Wedding Invitations," Tuscon.com, June 7, 2018, https://tucson.com/news/state-and-regional/arizona-court-rejects-business-owners-challenge-to-same-sex-wedding/article_76328a9a-6a6f-11e8-a293-53a3e4f03f10.html (accessed 7/26/18).

19. Brooke Sopelsa, "DOJ Backs Kentucky Photographer Who Won't Do Gay Weddings," NBC News, February 27, 2020, https://www.nbcnews.com/feature/nbc-out/doj-backs-kentucky-photographer-who-won-t-do-gay-weddings-n1144516 (accessed 6/24/21).

20. "Christian School Expels Girl over Sexuality," CBS Sacramento, April 27, 2011, https://sacramento.cbslocal.com/2011/04/27/christian-school-expels-girl-over-sexuality/ (accessed 7/26/18).

21. "Gay Teen Suing School over Expulsion," ABC News, January 7, 2006, https://abcnews.go.com/WNT/story?id=131673 (accessed 7/26/18).

22. Scott Gordon, "High School Senior Kicked Out of Private Colleyville School for Being Gay," 5NBC, October 9, 2020, https://www.nbcdfw.com/news/local/high-school-senior-kicked-out-of-private-colleyville-school-for-being-gay/2458399/ (accessed 6/26/21).

23. Dawn Ennis, "'I'm Doing What Jesus Would Want.' Christian School Headmaster Expelled Gay Athlete for His 'Lifestyle'," SBNation, November 13, 2020, https://www.outsports.com/homophobia/2020/11/13/21562904/gay-track-student-athlete-devin-bryant-expelled-christian-school-civil-rights-texas (accessed 6/26/21).

24. Allie Grasgreen, "Expelled for Sexuality, and Sent a Bill," Inside Higher Education, June 13, 2013, https://www.insidehighered.com/news/2013/06/13/student-expelled-being-gay-and-charged-6000-back-tuition-protests-online-petition (accessed 7/26/18).

25. "Worst List: The Absolute Worst Campuses for LGBTQ Youth," *Campus Pride*, https://campuspride.org/worstlist (accessed 6/24/21).

26. "About Us," Christian Legal Society, https://www.christianlawstudents.org/about/about-us (accessed 7/26/18).

27. Bob Egelko, "Evangelical Law Students Sue Hastings," *San Francisco Chronicle*, October 23, 2004, https://www.sfgate.com/bayarea/article /SAN-FRANCISCO-Evangelical-law-students-sue-2641230.php (accessed 7/26/18).

28. *Christian Legal Society Chapter v. Martinez*, 561 U.S. 661 (2010).

29. *Christian Legal Society Chapter v. Martinez*, 561 U.S. 661 (2010).

30. Peter Schmidt, "Ruling Is Unlikely to End Litigation over Policies on Student Groups," *Chronicle of Higher Education*, June 30, 2010, https://www .chronicle.com/article/ruling-is-unlikely-to-end/66101 (accessed 7/26/18).

31. Page Minemyer, "Number of Catholic Hospitals in US Has Grown 22% Since 2001," Fierce Health Care, May 5, 2016, https://www.fiercehealthcare .com/healthcare/number-catholic-hospitals-us-has-grown-22-since -2001 (accessed 7/26/18).

32. Breana Noble and Kathryn Blackhurst, "Newsmax's Top 100 Evangelical Christian Colleges," Newsmax, October 27, 2015, https://www.newsmax .com/thewire/top-evangelical-christian-colleges/2015/10/26/id /699072/ (accessed 7/26/18).

33. "Statistics about Nonpublic Education in the United States," Department of Education, https://www2.ed.gov/about/offices/list/oii/nonpublic /statistics.html (accessed 7/26/18).

34. Emma Green, "Can Religious Charities Take the Place of the Welfare State?" *The Atlantic*, March 26, 2017, https://www.theatlantic.com /politics/archive/2017/03/budget-religion/520605/ (accessed 6/24/21).

35. *Fulton v. City of Philadelphia*, 593 U.S. __ (2021).

36. *Burwell v. Hobby Lobby Stores*, 573 U.S. 682 (2014).

37. *Roman Catholic Diocese of Brooklyn v. Cuomo*, 592 U.S. __ (2020).

38. Associated Press, "Transgender Student Says He Was Banned by Christian School," *U.S. News & World Report*, October 1, 2017, https://www.usnews .com/news/best-states/new-hampshire/articles/2017-10-01/transgender -student-says-he-was-banned-by-christian-school (accessed 7/26/18); Emanuella Grinberg, "Transgender Teen Fights Back after Suspension for Using 'Wrong' Bathroom," CNN, April 27, 2016, https://www.cnn .com/2016/04/26/health/sc-transgender-student-bathroom-suspension /index.html (accessed 7/26/18).

39. Joellen Kralik, "'Bathroom Bill' Legislative Tracking," National Conference of State Legislatures, July 28, 2017, http://www.ncsl.org/research/education /-bathroom-bill-legislative-tracking635951130.aspx (accessed 7/26/18).

40. Danielle Kurtzleben, "Political Dispute over Transgender Rights Focuses on Youth Sports," National Public Radio, March 11, 2021, https://www.npr .org/2021/03/11/974782774/political-dispute-over-transgender-rights -focuses-on-youth-sports (accessed 6/24/21).

41. Mark Joseph Stern, "Judge: Doctors Have 'Religious Freedom' to Refuse to Treat Trans Patients, Women Who've Had Abortions," Slate, January 3,

2017, http://www.slate.com/blogs/outward/2017/01/03/doctors_may
_refuse_to_treat_transgender_patients_and_women_who_ve_had
_abortions.html (accessed 7/26/18).

42. *Bostock v. Clayton County*, 590 U.S. __ (2020).

17. WHERE DO PEOPLE GET THEIR POLITICAL BELIEFS?

1. "Paul Gosar Is Not Working for You," Brill for Congress, September 22, 2018, https://www.youtube.com/watch?v=1N-m83vYr-Y (accessed 1/4/19).

2. Paul Gosar, September 22, 2018, https://twitter.com/DrPaulGosar/status /1043567335397679105 (accessed 1/9/19).

3. Allan Smith, "Gosar's Siblings Want Their Brother Kicked Out of Congress. They Think Democrats Are Moving Too Slow," NBC News, June 28, 2021, https://www.nbcnews.com/politics/congress/gosar-s-siblings-want -their-brother-kicked-out-congress-they-n1271023 (accessed 7/31/21).

4. "Kennedy Family Members Involved in Politics," Associated Press, February 8, 2017, https://www.chicagotribune.com/news/ct-kennedy -family-members-in-politics-20170208-story.html (accessed 1/4/19).

5. Daniel Nasaw, "The Bush Family Tree," *Wall Street Journal*, June 15, 2015, http://graphics.wsj.com/jeb-bush-family-tree/ (accessed 1/4/19).

6. Robert S. Erikson and Laura Stoker, "Caught in the Draft: The Effects of Vietnam Draft Lottery Status on Political Attitudes," *American Political Science Review* 105, no. 2 (2011): 221–37; Morris Fiorina, *Retrospective Voting in American National Elections* (New Haven, CT: Yale University Press, 1981); Andrew Healy and Neil Malhotra, "Random Events, Economic Losses, and Retrospective Voting: Implications for Democratic Competence," *Quarterly Journal of Political Science* 5, no. 2 (2010): 193–208.

7. M. Kent Jennings, "Political Socialization," in *The Oxford Handbook of Political Behavior*, ed. Russell J. Dalton and Hans-Dieter Klingemann (New York: Oxford University Press, 2007); Virginia Sapiro, "Not Your Parents' Political Socialization: Introduction for a New Generation," *Annual Review of Political Science* 7 (2004): 1–23; Laura Stoker and Jackie Bass, "Political Socialization: Ongoing Questions and New Directions," in *The Oxford Handbook of American Public Opinion and the Media*, ed. Robert Y. Shapiro and Lawrence R. Jacobs (New York: Oxford University Press, 2011).

8. Kathy Frankovic, "Family, Politics, and Thanksgiving," YouGov, December 3, 2014, https://today.yougov.com/topics/politics/articles -reports/2014/12/03/family-thanksgiving-politics (accessed 1/4/19).

9. Molly W. Andolina, Krista Jenkins, Cliff Zukin, and Scott Keeter, "Habits from Home, Lessons from School: Influences on Youth Civic Engagement," *PS: Political Science & Politics* 36, no. 2 (2003): 275–80; M. Kent Jennings and Richard G. Niemi, "The Transmission of Political Values from Parent to Child," *American Political Science Review* 62, no. 1 (1968): 169–84; Sidney Verba, Kay Lehman Schlozman, and Nancy Burns,

"Family Ties: Understanding the Intergenerational Transmission of Political Participation," in *The Social Logic of Politics*, ed. Alan S. Zuckerman (Philadelphia, PA: Temple University Press, 2005); Matthew Tyler and Shanto Iyengar, "Learning to Dislike Your Opponents: Political Socialization in the Era of Polarization," *American Political Science Review*, May 4, 2022, doi:10.1017/S000305542200048X.

10. Jennifer L. Lawless, *Becoming a Candidate: Political Ambition and the Decision to Run for Office* (New York: Cambridge University Press, 2012).

11. Jennifer L. Lawless and Richard L. Fox, *Running from Office: Why Young People Are Turned Off to Politics* (New York: Oxford University Press, 2015).

12. Sarah Shapiro and Catherine Brown, "The State of Civics Education," Center for American Progress, February 21, 2018, https://www.americanprogress.org/issues/education-k-12/reports/2018/02/21/446857/state-civics-education/ (accessed 7/29/21).

13. Rebecca Winthrop, "The Need for Civic Education in 21st Century Schools," Brookings Institution, June 4, 2020, https://www.brookings.edu/policy2020/bigideas/the-need-for-civic-education-in-21st-century-schools/ (accessed 7/29/21); Shelley Billig, Sue Root, and Dan Jesse, *The Impact of Participation in Service-Learning on High School Students' Civic Engagement* (College Park, MD: Center for Information and Research on Civic Learning and Engagement, 2005); David E. Campbell, "Voice in the Classroom: How an Open Classroom Climate Fosters Political Engagement among Adolescents," *Political Behavior* 30, no. 4 (2008): 437–54.

14. D. Sunshine Hillygus, "The Missing Link: Exploring the Relationship between Higher Education and Political Engagement," *Political Behavior* 27, no. 1 (2005): 25–47.

15. Lawless, *Becoming a Candidate*; Jennifer L. Glanville, "Political Socialization or Selection? Adolescent Extracurricular Participation and Political Activity in Early Adulthood," *Social Science Quarterly* 80, no. 2 (1999): 279–90; Daniel Hart, Thomas M. Donnelly, James Youniss, and Robert Atkins, "High School Community Service as a Predictor of Adult Voting and Volunteering," *American Educational Research Journal* 44, no. 1 (2007): 197–219; Daniel A. McFarland and Reuben J. Thomas, "Bowling Young: How Youth Voluntary Associations Influence Adult Political Participation," *American Sociological Review* 71, no. 3 (2006): 401–25.

16. Lawless and Fox, *Running from Office*.

17. Lawless and Fox, *Running from Office*. These findings are consistent with the annual UCLA higher education survey conducted with incoming first-year students. Roughly 20 percent of college students report frequently discussing politics with their friends. See John H. Pryor, Sylvia Hurtado, Linda DeAngelo, Jessica Sharkness, Laura C. Romero, William S. Korn, and Serge Tran, *The American Freshman: National Norms for Fall 2008* (Los Angeles: Higher Education Research Institute, University of California, Los Angeles, 2008).

18. Joe Soss, "Lessons of Welfare: Policy Design, Political Learning, and Political Action," *American Political Science Review* 93, no. 2 (1999): 363–80.

19. Joshua Clinton and Michael Sances, "The Politics of Policy: The Initial Mass Political Effects of Medicaid Expansion in the States," *American Political Science Review* 112, no. 1 (2018): 167–85.

20. Jennifer L. Lawless and Richard L. Fox, "Political Participation of the Urban Poor," *Social Problems* 48, no. 3 (2001): 362–85.

21. Vanessa Williamson, Kris Stella-Trump, and Katherine Einstein, "Black Lives Matter: Evidence that Police-Caused Deaths Predict Protest Activity," *Perspectives on Politics* 16, no. 2 (2018): 400–15.

22. Troy A. Zimmer, "The Impact of Watergate on the Public's Trust in People and Confidence in the Mass Media," *Social Science Quarterly* 59, no. 4 (1979): 743–51.

23. Leonie Huddy and Stanley Feldman, "Americans Respond Politically to 9/11: Understanding the Impact of the Terrorist Attacks and Their Aftermath," *American Psychologist* 66, no. 6 (2011): 455–67.

24. David J. Ciuk, "Americans' Value Preferences Pre-and Post-9/11," *Social Science Quarterly* 97, no. 2 (2016): 407–17.

25. Eitan Hersh, "How Many Republicans Marry Democrats?" FiveThirtyEight, June 28, 2016, https://fivethirtyeight.com/features/how-many-republicans-marry-democrats/ (accessed 1/5/19).

26. Kim Parker, Juliana Menasce Horowitz, Anna Brown, Richard Fry, D'Vera Cohn, and Ruth Igielnik, "Urban, Suburban and Rural Residents' Views on Key Social and Political Issues," Pew Research Center, May 22, 2018, http://www.pewsocialtrends.org/2018/05/22/urban-suburban-and-rural-residents-views-on-key-social-and-political-issues/ (accessed 1/5/19).

18. ARE YOU A DEMOCRAT OR A REPUBLICAN?

1. "Who Is Your Celebrity Soulmate?" Playbuzz, October 16, 2018, https://www.playbuzz.com/hearstdigitalmedia10/who-is-your-celebrity-soulmate (accessed 3/30/19).

2. Joe Robberson, "Which Star Wars Original Trilogy Character Are You?" Zimbio, http://www.zimbio.com/quiz/HslZHIQm8YW/Star+Wars+Original+Trilogy+Character (accessed 3/30/19).

3. "Which Superhero Are You?" Quizony, https://www.quizony.com/which-superhero-are-you/index.html (accessed 3/30/19).

4. Erin LaRosa, "Where Should Your Next Vacation Be?" BuzzFeed, February 2, 2014, https://www.buzzfeed.com/erinlarosa/what-kind-of-vacation-should-you-take (accessed 3/30/19).

5. Sam Stryker and Farrah Penn, "This Quiz Will Tell You the Exact Age You'll Get Married," BuzzFeed, August 4, 2016, https://www.buzzfeed.com/samstryker/this-quiz-will-tell-you-the-exact-age-youll-get-married (accessed 3/30/19).

6. Ashly Perez, "What City Should You Actually Live In?" BuzzFeed, January 16, 2014, https://www.buzzfeed.com/ashleyperez/what-city-should-you-actually-live-in (accessed 3/30/19).

7. "Are You Hot or Not?" GoToQuiz, https://www.gotoquiz.com/are_you_hot_or_not_11 (accessed 3/30/19).

8. "Are You Democratic or Republican?" Quizony, https://www.quizony.com/are-you-democratic-or-republican/ (accessed 3/30/19).

9. Adele Chapin, "Republicans and Democrats Can't Even Agree on Where to Shop," Racked, December 21, 2015, https://www.racked.com/2015/12/21/10633884/shopping-retailers-conservative-liberal (accessed 3/30/19).

10. Lou Ann Hammond, "Are You a Republican or a Democrat? Only Your Car Knows for Sure," Driving the Nation, April 1, 2012, https://www.drivingthenation.com/are-you-a-republican-or-a-democrat-only-your-car-knows-for-sure/ (accessed 3/30/19).

11. Andrew Magnotta, "Queen, the Beatles Most Beloved Bands among Democrats, Republicans," iHeartRadio, May 16, 2018, https://www.iheart.com/content/2018-05-16-queen-the-beatles-most-beloved-bands-among-democrats-republicans/ (accessed 3/30/19).

12. Natalie Andrews and Brian McGill, "What You Like Falls on Party Lines," *Wall Street Journal*, July 18, 2016, http://graphics.wsj.com/elections/2016/facebook-likes/ (accessed 3/30/19).

13. Chris Wilson, "The Most Political Foods in America," *Time*, July 18, 2016, http://time.com/4410194/democratic-republican-bipartisan-political-foods-america/ (accessed 3/30/19).

14. Gary Jacobson, "It's Nothing Personal: The Decline of the Incumbency Advantage in U.S. House Elections," *Journal of Politics* 77, no. 3 (2015): 861–73; Danny Hayes and Jennifer L. Lawless, *Women on the Run: Gender, Media, and Political Campaigns in a Polarized Era* (New York: Cambridge University Press, 2016).

15. Larry M. Bartels, "Partisanship and Voting Behavior, 1956–1996," *American Journal of Political Science* 44, no. 1 (2000): 35–50; Geoffrey L. Cohen, "Party over Policy: The Dominating Impact of Group Influence on Political Beliefs," *Journal of Personality and Social Psychology* 85, no. 5 (2003): 808–22; John Sides and Lynn Vavreck, *The Gamble: Choice and Chance in the 2012 Presidential Election* (Princeton, NJ: Princeton University Press, 2013).

16. Donald Green, Bradley Palmquist, and Eric Schickler, *Partisan Hearts and Minds: Political Parties and the Social Identity of Voters* (New Haven, CT: Yale University Press, 2002); Shanto Iyengar, Guarav Sood, and Yphtach Lelkes, "Affect, Not Ideology: A Social Identity Perspective on Polarization," *Public Opinion Quarterly* 76, no. 3 (2012): 405–31.

17. "Party Affiliation," Gallup, May 3–18, 2021, https://news.gallup.com/poll/15370/party-affiliation.aspx (accessed 7/29/21).

18. Bruce E. Keith, David B. Magleby, Candice J. Nelson, Elizabeth Orr, Mark C. Westlye, and Raymond E. Wolfinger, *The Myth of the Independent Voter* (Berkeley: University of California Press, 1992); John Sides, "Most Political Independents Actually Aren't," Monkey Cage, January 8, 2014, https://www.washingtonpost.com/news/monkey-cage /wp/2014/01/08/most-political-independents-actually-arent/ (accessed 3/30/19).

19. Party identification data come from regular polls conducted by Gallup and the Pew Research Center.

20. Morris P. Fiorina, Samuel J. Abrams, and Jeremy C. Pope, *Culture War? The Myth of a Polarized America*, 3rd ed. (New York: Longman, 2010).

21. "Economy and COVID-19 Top the Public's Policy Agenda for 2021," Pew Research Center, January 28, 2021, https://www.pewresearch.org /politics/2021/01/28/economy-and-covid-19-top-the-publics-policy -agenda-for-2021/ (accessed 8/1/21).

22. "2016 Party Identification Detailed Tables," Pew Research Center, September 13, 2016, https://www.people-press.org/2016/09/13/2016 -party-identification-detailed-tables/ (accessed 3/31/19).

23. Lydia Saad, "U.S. '1%' Is More Republican, but Not More Conservative," Gallup, December 5, 2011, https://news.gallup.com/poll/151310/u.s. -republican-not-conservative.aspx (accessed 3/31/19).

24. Alison Durkee, "Most Voters Want Congress to Pass Stricter Gun Laws, Poll Finds," *Forbes*, May 25, 2022, https://www.forbes.com/sites /alisondurkee/2022/05/25/most-voters-want-congress-to-pass-stricter -gun-laws-poll-finds/?sh=2919f59e1564; Justin McCarthy, "Record High 70% in U.S. Support Same-Sex Marriage," Gallup, June 8, 2021, https:// news.gallup.com/poll/350486/record-high-support-same-sex-marriage .aspx; Justin McCarthy, "Mixed Views among Americans on Transgender Issues," Gallup, May 26, 2021, https://news.gallup.com/poll/350174 /mixed-views-among-americans-transgender-issues.aspx; "Support for Legal Marijuana Holds at Record High of 68%," Gallup, November 4, 2021, https://news.gallup.com/poll/356939/support-legal-marijuana -holds-record-high.aspx; Hannah Hartig, "Wide Partisan Gaps in Abortion Attitudes, but Opinions in Both Parties Are Complicated," Pew Research Center, May 6, 2022, https://www.pewresearch.org/fact -tank/2022/05/06/wide-partisan-gaps-in-abortion-attitudes-but -opinions-in-both-parties-are-complicated/ (accessed 7/17/22).

25. Alex Samuels and Mackenzie Wilkes, "Americans Want the Government to Act on Climate Change. What's The Hold-Up?," FiveThirtyEight, October 8, 2021, https://fivethirtyeight.com/features/americans-want -the-government-to-act-on-climate-change-whats-the-hold-up/ (accessed 1/6/22)

26. Kaiser Family Foundation, "Public Opinion on Single-Payer, National Health Plans, and Expanding Access to Medicare Coverage," October 16, 2020, https://www.kff.org/slideshow/public-opinion-on-single-payer

-national-health-plans-and-expanding-access-to-medicare-coverage/ (accessed 1/6/22).

27. Justin Caffier, "Every Insult the Left Uses to Troll Conservatives, Explained," Vice, February 9, 2017, https://www.vice.com/en_us/article /wn4vvq/every-insult-the-left-uses-to-troll-conservatives-explained (accessed 3/30/19).

19. WHY DOESN'T EVERYONE VOTE?

1. Heidi Parker and Emily Goodin, "MIDTERMS 2022: Voting Time! Selena Gomez, Hailey Bieber, and Katy Perry Urge Fans to Fill Out Their Ballot on Election Day: 'Your Voice Matters!'" *DailyMail.com*, November 8, 2022, https://www.dailymail.co.uk/tvshowbiz/article-11404481/MIDTERMS -2022-Selena-Gomez-Hailey-Bieber-Jennifer-Aniston-urge-fans-vote.html (accessed 11/10/22).

2. Shannon Power, "Celebs Who Voted in the 2022 Midterm Elections: Madonna, Katy Perry, More," *Newsweek*, November 9, 2022, https://www .newsweek.com/celebrities-midterms-voting-votes-madonna-katy -perry-1758177 (accessed 11/10/22).

3. Marisa Losciale, "Eva Longoria, John Legend, and More Celebrities Share Voting Photos Ahead of Election Day," *Parade*, November 7, 2022, https:// parade.com/news/eva-longoria-john-legend-celebrities-share-voting -photos-ahead-of-election-day-2022 (accesed 11/10/22).

4 Lizzy Buczak, "Krispy Kreme Offers Voters a Sweet Deal on Election Day," *Parade*, November 7, 2022, https://parade.com/news/krispy-kreme-free -donut-election-day-2022 (accessed 11/10/22).

5. Howell Raines, "Voting Rights Act Signed by Reagan," *New York Times*, June 30, 1982, https://www.nytimes.com/1982/06/30/us/voting-rights -act-signed-by-reagan.html (accessed 1/16/19).

6. Jose A. DelReal, "Voter Turnout in 2014 Was the Lowest since WWII," *Washington Post*, November 12, 2014, https://www.washingtonpost.com /news/post-politics/wp/2014/11/10/voter-turnout-in-2014-was-the -lowest-since-wwii/ (accessed 1/16/19).

7. Mollie Reilly, "Obama Calls Out Americans' Dismal Voter Turnout: 'Why Are You Staying Home?'" Huffington Post, February 25, 2015, https:// www.huffingtonpost.com/2015/02/25/obama-voter-turnout-immigration_n _6756606.html (accessed 1/16/19).

8. William E. Hudson, *American Democracy in Peril: Seven Challenges to America's Future* (Chatham, NJ: Chatham House, 1995).

9. The figure includes all of the members of the Organisation for Economic Cooperation and Development. Drew Desilver, "In Past Elections, U.S. Trailed Most Developed Countries in Voter Turnout," Pew Research Center, November 3, 2020, https://www.pewresearch.org/fact-tank /2020/11/03/in-past-elections-u-s-trailed-most-developed-countries -in-voter-turnout/ (accessed 8/5/21).

10. Harry Enten, "A Record Number Hold a Strong Opinion of Trump," CNN, May 9, 2020, https://www.cnn.com/2020/05/09/politics/trump-favorable-vs-unfavorable-opinion/index.html (accessed 8/7/21).

11. Lee Drutman, "The High Turnout in 2020 Wasn't Good for American Democracy," Monkey Cage, February 10, 2021, https://www.washingtonpost.com/politics/2021/02/10/high-turnout-2020-wasnt-good-american-democracy/ (accessed 8/5/21).

12. "Voter Turnout," United States Elections Project, https://www.electproject.org/home/voter-turnout/voter-turnout-data (accessed 12/3/21).

13. "2020 Presidential Nomination Contest Turnout Rates," United States Elections Project, http://www.electproject.org/2020p (accessed 1/6/22).

14. Drew Desilver, "Turnout in This Year's U.S. House Primaries Rose Sharply, Especially on the Democratic Side," Pew Research Center, October 3, 2018, http://www.pewresearch.org/fact-tank/2018/10/03/turnout-in-this-years-u-s-house-primaries-rose-sharply-especially-on-the-democratic-side/ (accessed 1/17/19).

15. Michael Finnegan and Ben Welsh, "Tuesday's LA Voter Turnout Was Likely the Lowest Ever, Muddying Garcetti's Historic Reelection Win," *Los Angeles Times*, March 8, 2017, https://www.latimes.com/local/california/la-me-ln-low-turnout-20170308-story.html (access 1/6/22).

16. Rachel White, "Low School Board Election Turnout? Increase the Pool of Eligible Voters," *Education Week*, August 15, 2017, https://blogs.edweek.org/edweek/rick_hess_straight_up/2017/08/low_school_board_election_voter_turnout_increase_the_pool_of_eligible_voters.html (accessed 1/6/22).

17. Asma Khalid, Don Gonyea, and Leila Fadel, "On the Sidelines of Democracy: Exploring Why So Many Americans Don't Vote," National Public Radio, September 10, 2018, https://www.npr.org/2018/09/10/645223716/on-the-sidelines-of-democracy-exploring-why-so-many-americans-dont-vote (accessed 1/17/19).

18. "California Elections, 2020," Ballotpedia, https://ballotpedia.org/California_elections_2020 (accessed 8/5/21).

19. California Secretary of State, "Complete Voter Information Guide," September 14, 2021, https://voterguide.sos.ca.gov/pdf/ (accessed 1/4/21).

20. "Texas Elections, 2018," Ballotpedia, https://ballotpedia.org/Texas_elections,_2018 (accessed 1/16/19).

21. Drew Desilver, "Turnout Soared In 2020 As Nearly Two-Thirds of Eligible U.S. Voters Cast Ballots for President," Pew Research Center, January 28, 2021, https://www.pewresearch.org/fact-tank/2021/01/28/turnout-soared-in-2020-as-nearly-two-thirds-of-eligible-u-s-voters-cast-ballots-for-president/ (accessed 1/6/22).

22. "Voter Registration Deadlines," Vote.org, https://www.vote.org/voter-registration-deadlines/#; "Criminal Disenfranchisement Laws across the United States," Brennan Center for Justice, https://www.brennancenter.org/criminal-disenfranchisement-laws-across-united

-states; "Voter Identification Requirements, Voter ID Laws," National Conference of State Legislatures, July 15, 2021, http://www.ncsl.org/research/elections-and-campaigns/voter-id.aspx#; "State Laws Governing Early Voting," National Conference of State Legislatures, June 11, 2021, https://www.ncsl.org/research/elections-and-campaigns/early-voting-in-state-elections.aspx; "Absentee Ballot Rules," Vote.org, https://www.vote.org/absentee-voting-rules/#oregon; "2020 November General Election Turnout Rates," United States Elections Project, http://www.electproject.org/2020g; "2018 November General Election Turnout Rates," United States Elections Project, http://www.electproject.org/2018g (accessed 8/5/21).

23. Amanda Shendruk, "The Difficulty of Voting in Every U.S. State, Ranked," Quartz, October 27, 2018, https://qz.com/1439299/here-are-the-states-where-its-hardest-to-vote/ (accessed 1/16/19).

24. Christopher Ingraham, "Low Voter Turnout Is No Accident, According to a Ranking of the Ease of Voting in All 50 States," Washington Post, October 22, 2018, https://www.washingtonpost.com/business/2018/10/22/low-voter-turnout-is-no-accident-according-ranking-ease-voting-all-states/ (accessed 2/20/19).

25. Juliette Love, Matt Stevens, and Lazaro Gamio, "Where Americans Can Vote by Mail in the 2020 Elections," New York Times, August 14, 2020, https://www.nytimes.com/interactive/2020/08/11/us/politics/vote-by-mail-us-states.html (accessed 8/7/21).

26. "Elections in America: Concerns over Security, Divisions over Expanding Access to Voting," Pew Research Center, October 29, 2018, http://www.people-press.org/2018/10/29/elections-in-america-concerns-over-security-divisions-over-expanding-access-to-voting/ (accessed 1/16/19).

27. Michael McDonald, "The Competitive Problem of Voter Turnout," Brookings Institution, October 31, 2016, https://www.brookings.edu/opinions/the-competitive-problem-of-voter-turnout/ (accessed 1/16/19).

28. Lydia Saad, "Trump and Clinton Finish with Historically Poor Images," Gallup, November 6, 2016, https://news.gallup.com/poll/197231/trump-clinton-finish-historically-poor-images.aspx (accessed 1/16/19); Scott Clement and Emily Guskin, "Post-ABC Tracking Poll Finds Race Tied, as Trump Opens Up an 8-Point Edge on Honesty," Washington Post, November 2, 2016, https://www.washingtonpost.com/news/the-fix/wp/2016/11/02/tracking-poll-finds-race-tied-as-trump-opens-up-an-8-point-edge-on-honesty/ (accessed 1/16/19); Chris Cillizza, "Hillary Clinton Has a Likability Problem; Donald Trump Has a Likability Epidemic," Washington Post, May 16, 2016, https://www.washingtonpost.com/news/the-fix/wp/2016/05/16/hillary-clintons-long-lingering-likable-enough-problem/ (accessed 1/16/19).

29. "Party Images," Gallup, https://news.gallup.com/poll/24655/party-images.aspx (accessed 8/6/21).

30. "Congress and the Public," Gallup, June 18, 2021, https://news.gallup
.com/poll/1600/congress-public.aspx (accessed 8/6/21).

31. "Do Elected Officials Care about Ordinary Citizens?" Pew Research
Center, February 26, 2020, https://www.pewresearch.org/global
/2020/02/27/attitudes-toward-elected-officials-voting-and-the
-state/pg_2020-02-27_global-democracy_02-1/ (accessed 8/6/21).

32. Ruth Igielnik, "70% of Americans Say U.S. Economic System Unfairly
Favors the Powerful," Pew Research Center, January 9, 2020, https://
www.pewresearch.org/fact-tank/2020/01/09/70-of-americans-say
-u-s-economic-system-unfairly-favors-the-powerful/ (accessed 8/7/21).

33. Steven E. Finkel, "Reciprocal Effects of Participation and Political
Efficacy: A Panel Analysis," *American Journal of Political Science* 29, no. 4
(1985): 891–913.

34. Alyssa Fowers, Atthar Mirza, and Armand Emamdjomeh, "The Votes That
Won Joe Biden the Presidency," *Washington Post*, November 13, 2020,
https://www.washingtonpost.com/graphics/2020/elections/vote
-margin-of-victory/ (accessed 8/5/21).

35. Jim Morrison, Fenit Nirappil, and Gregory S. Schneider, "Virginia Tosses
One-Vote Victory That Briefly Ended GOP Majority in House," *Washington
Post*, December 12, 2017, https://www.washingtonpost.com/local
/virginia-politics/court-tosses-out-one-vote-victory-in-recount-that
-had-briefly-ended-a-republican-majority-in-virginia/2017/12/20/
ed979a70-e5b9-11e7-a65d-1ac0fd7f097e_story.html (accessed 1/16/19).

36. For the People Act of 2021, H.R. 1, 117th Cong. (2021), https://www
.congress.gov/bill/117th-congress/house-bill/1/text (accessed 1/6/22).

37. Betsy Cooper, Daniel Cox, Rachel Lienesch, and Robert P. Jones, "The
Divide over America's Future: 1950 or 2050? Findings from the 2016
American Values Survey," PRRI, October 25, 2016, https://www.prri
.org/research/poll-1950s-2050-divided-nations-direction-post-election/
(accessed 2/26/19).

38. H.R. 1: For the People Act of 2021, GovTrack, March 3, 2021, https://www
.govtrack.us/congress/votes/117-2021/h62 (accessed 8/6/21).

39. Scot Schraufnagel, Michael J. Pomante II, and Quan Li, "Costs of Voting
in the American States: 2020," *Election Law Journal: Rules, Politics, and
Policy* 19, no. 4 (2020): 503–9.

20. WHO PARTICIPATES IN POLITICS?

1. Michelle Ye Hee Lee, "How Small Donations Gave Underdog Democrats
a Fighting Chance for the House," *Washington Post*, November 4, 2018,
https://www.washingtonpost.com/politics/how-small-donations-gave
-underdog-democrats-a-fighting-chance-for-the-house/2018/11/04/
033b99bc-dd1c-11e8-b732-3c72cbf131f2_story.html (accessed 2/1/19).

2. Alexander Burns, Rachel Shorey, and Jugal K. Patel, "Small Donors Fuel
a Big Democratic Lead in 2018 Fundraising," *New York Times*, October 16,

2018, https://www.nytimes.com/interactive/2018/10/16/us/politics/campaign-finance-small-donors.html (accessed 2/1/19).

3. "Thanks to This 9-Year-Old Boy, Snowballs Are Now Legal in Severance, Colorado," Colorado Public Radio, December 4, 2018, http://www.cpr.org/news/story/thanks-to-this-9-year-old-boy-snowballs-are-now-legal-in-severance-colorado (accessed 2/1/19).

4. "Colorado Town Overturns Ban on Snowball Fights Thanks to Nine-Year-Old Boy," CBS News, December 4, 2018, https://www.cbsnews.com/news/severance-colorado-overturns-snowball-ban-dane-best-presentation-arguments-town-board-meeting-today/ (accessed 2/1/19).

5. Eliott C. McLaughlin, "What We Know about Michael Brown's Shooting," CNN, August 15, 2014, https://www.cnn.com/2014/08/11/us/missouri-ferguson-michael-brown-what-we-know/index.html (accessed 2/1/19).

6. Cheryl Corley, "With Ferguson Protests, Twenty-Somethings Become First-Time Activists," National Public Radio, October 24, 2014, https://www.npr.org//2014//10//24//358054785//with-ferguson-protests-20-somethings-become-first-time-activists (accessed 2/1/19).

7. Eyder Peralta and Bill Chappell, "Ferguson Jury: No Charges for Officer in Michael Brown's Death," National Public Radio, November 24, 2014, https://www.npr.org/sections/thetwo-way/2014/11/24/366370100/grand-jury-reaches-decision-in-michael-brown-case (accessed 2/1/19).

8. Gretel Kauffman, "Two Years after Michael Brown Shooting: How Has Ferguson Changed?" *Christian Science Monitor*, August 9, 2016, https://www.csmonitor.com/USA/Justice/2016/0809/Two-years-after-Michael-Brown-shooting-How-has-Ferguson-changed (accessed 2/1/19).

9. "2020 Presidential Voting and Registration Tables," United States Census Bureau, April 29, 2021, https://www.census.gov/newsroom/press-releases/2021/2020-presidential-election-voting-and-registration-tables-now-available.html (accessed 8/2/21).

10. "Voter Turnout in Presidential Elections, 1828–2016," The American Presidency Project, https://www.presidency.ucsb.edu/statistics/data/voter-turnout-in-presidential-elections (accessed 1/6/22).

11. Voter turnout data provided by the United States Elections Project. All other participation data are from the 2020 American National Election Studies (https://www.electionstudies.org).

12. Brooke Auxier, "Activism on Social Media Varies by Race and Ethnicity, Age, Political Party," Pew Research Center, July 13, 2020, https://www.pewresearch.org/fact-tank/2020/07/13/activism-on-social-media-varies-by-race-and-ethnicity-age-political-party/ (accessed 8/2/21).

13. Monica Anderson, Skye Toor, Lee Rainie, and Aaron Smith, "An Analysis of #BlackLivesMatter and Oother Twitter Hashtags Related to Social or Political Issues," Pew Research Center, July 11, 2018, http://www.pewinternet.org/2018/07/11/an-analysis-of-blacklivesmatter-and-other-twitter-hashtags-related-to-political-or-social-issues/ (accessed 2/7/19).

14. Jason Cohen, "#BlackLivesMatter Hashtag Averages 3.7 Million Tweets per Day during Unrest," PCMag, July 20, 2020, https://www.pcmag.com /news/blacklivesmatter-hashtag-averages-37-million-tweets-per-day -during-unrest (accessed 8/2/21).

15. Monica Anderson, Skye Toor, Lee Rainie, and Aaron Smith, "Public Attitudes toward Political Engagement on Social Media," Pew Research Center, July 11, 2018, http://www.pewinternet.org/2018/07/11/public-attitudes -toward-political-engagement-on-social-media/ (accessed 2/1/19).

16. Auxier, "Activism on Social Media."

17. James Dennis, *Beyond Slacktivism: Political Participation on Social Media* (London: Palgrave Macmillan, 2019).

18. Helen Margetts, Peter John, Scott Hale, and Taha Yasseri, *Political Turbulence: How Social Media Shape Collective Action* (Princeton, NJ: Princeton University Press, 2015).

19. Christopher H. Achen and Larry M. Bartels, *Democracy for Realists: Why Elections Do Not Produce Responsive Government* (Princeton, NJ: Princeton University Press, 2016).

20. Voting data come from "Voter Turnout Demographics," United States Elections Project, www.electproject.org/home/voter-turnout/demographics; and Jacob Fabina, "Despite Pandemic Challenges, 2020 Election Had Largest Increase in Voting Between Presidential Elections on Record," United States Census Bureau, April 29, 2021, https://www.census.gov /library/stories/2021/04/record-high-turnout-in-2020-general-election .html (accessed 8/3/21). Data for all activities other than voting are from the 2020 American National Election Study.

21. Sidney Verba, Kay Lehman Schlozman, and Henry E. Brady, *Voice and Equality: Civic Voluntarism in American Politics* (Cambridge, MA: Harvard University Press, 1995).

22. Jan E. Leighley and Jonathan Nagler, *Who Votes Now? Demographics, Issues, Inequality, and Turnout in the United States* (Princeton, NJ: Princeton University Press, 2013).

23. Fabina, "Record High Turnout."

24. Bernard L. Fraga, *The Turnout Gap: Race, Ethnicity, and Political Inequality in a Diversifying America* (New York: Cambridge University Press, 2018).

25. Justin McCarthy, "Mixed Views among Americans on Transgender Issues," Gallup, May 26, 2021, https://news.gallup.com/poll/350174/mixed-views -among-americans-transgender-issues.aspx (accessed 8/5/21).

26. "Economy and COVID-19 Top the Public's Policy Agenda for 2021," Pew Research Center, January 28, 2021, https://www.pewresearch.org /politics/2021/01/28/economy-and-covid-19-top-the-publics-policy -agenda-for-2021/ (accessed 8/4/21).

27. Juliana Menasce Horowitz, Ruth Igielnik, and Rakesh Kochhar, "Most Americans Say There Is Too Much Economic Inequality in the U.S., but Fewer Than Half Call It a Top Priority," Pew Research Center, January 9,

2020, https://www.pewresearch.org/social-trends/2020/01/09/most-americans-say-there-is-too-much-economic-inequality-in-the-u-s-but-fewer-than-half-call-it-a-top-priority/ (accessed 8/5/21).

28. Kat Stafford and Hannah Fingerhut, "AP-NORC Poll: Sweeping Change in US Views of Police Violence," Associated Press, June 17, 2020, https://apnews.com/article/us-news-ap-top-news-racial-injustice-politics-police-728b414b8742129329081f7092179d1f (accessed 8/5/21).

29. Amina Dunn, "Most Americans Support a $15 Federal Minimum Wage," Pew Research Center, April 22, 2021, https://www.pewresearch.org/fact-tank/2021/04/22/most-americans-support-a-15-federal-minimum-wage/ (accessed 8/4/21).

30. Morris P. Fiorina and Samuel J. Abrams, *Disconnect: The Breakdown of Representation in American Politics* (Norman: University of Oklahoma Press, 2009).

21. WHY DO PEOPLE JOIN INTEREST GROUPS?

1. Alexis de Tocqueville, *Democracy in America* (New York: Mentor Books, 1848).

2. *Encyclopedia of Associations: National Organizations of the United States*, 57th ed., http://library.austintexas.gov/database/encyclopedia-associations-national-organizations-us (accessed 2/16/19).

3. Aleksandra Sandstrom and Becka A. Alper, "Americans with Higher Education and Income Are More Likely to Be Involved in Community Groups," Pew Research Center, February 22, 2019, https://www.pewresearch.org/fact-tank/2019/02/22/americans-with-higher-education-and-income-are-more-likely-to-be-involved-in-community-groups/ (accessed 7/31/21).

4. American Cheese Society, https://www.cheesesociety.org/ (accessed 2/16/19).

5. "About: The Reptile Nation," United States Association of Reptile Keepers, https://usark.org/ (accessed 2/16/19).

6. "About," Catfish Farmers of America, http://www.catfishfarmersofamerica.com/about/ (accessed 2/16/19).

7. Elizabeth Flock, "10 Strange Lobbying Groups That We Swear Are Real," *U.S. News & World Report*, January 28, 2013, https://www.usnews.com/news/blogs/washington-whispers/2013/01/28/10-strange-lobbying-groups-that-we-swear-are-real (accessed 2/16/19).

8. "Political Contributions and Lobbying," ExxonMobil, https://corporate.exxonmobil.com/About-us/Policy/Political-contributions-and-lobbying (accessed 2/18/19).

9. "Priorities & Policies," American Bar Association, https://www.americanbar.org/advocacy/governmental_legislative_work/priorities_policy/ (accessed 2/18/19).

10. Peter B. Clark and James Q. Wilson, "Incentive Systems: A Theory of Organization," *Administrative Science Quarterly* 6, no. 2 (1961): 219–66.

11. Mancur Olson, *The Logic of Collective Action: Public Goods and the Theory of Groups* (Cambridge, MA: Harvard University Press, 1965);

Terry M. Moe, *The Organization of Interests* (Chicago: University of Chicago Press, 1980).

12. Robert H. Salisbury, "An Exchange Theory of Interest Groups," *Midwest Journal of Political Science* 13, no. 1 (1969): 1–32.

13. Clark and Wilson, "Incentive Systems: A Theory of Organization."

14. Kristen Purcell and Aaron Smith, "The State of Groups and Voluntary Organizations in America," Pew Research Center, January 18, 2011, https://www.pewresearch.org/internet/2011/01/18/section-1-the-state -of-groups-and-voluntary-organizations-in-america/ (accessed 2/16/19).

15. "Be a Champion for the Environment: Donate Today," Sierra Club, https:// www.sierraclub.org/ (accessed 2/16/19).

16. "Life Membership," National Rifle Association, https://membership.nra.org /Join/Life (accessed 2/16/19).

17. "Your Member Benefits," AARP, https://join.aarp.org/ (accessed 1/5/22).

18. "Benefits Guide," Automobile Association of America, https://midatlantic .aaa.com/membership (accessed 2/16/19).

19. "Letter to the Editor Lunch," https://act.sierraclub.org/events/details? formcampaignid=7010Z000001qqBVQAY&mapLinkHref=https://maps .google.com/maps&daddr=Letter%20to%20the%20Editor%20 Lunch%20(Richmond)@37.544893,-77.44436 (accessed 2/16/19).

SECTION IV: POLITICAL INFORMATION, KNOWLEDGE, AND NEWS

1. "CRAZY NANCY: President Trump UNLOADS on Pelosi and Chuck Schumer," Live Now from Fox, May 23, 2019, https://www.youtube.com /watch?v=EizNtbHmdf4 (accessed 4/4/21).

22. DO PEOPLE KNOW ANYTHING ABOUT U.S. POLITICS?

1. Jason Silverstein, "What Is Pizzagate? An Explainer of the Hillary Clinton Conspiracy Theory That Led to a Shooting in Washington, DC," *New York Daily News*, December 5, 2016, https://www.nydailynews.com/news /politics/pizzagate-clinton-conspiracy-theory-led-dc-shooting-article -1.2899371 (accessed 1/22/19).

2. Spencer S. Hsu, "'Pizzagate' Gunman Says He Was Foolish, Reckless, Mistaken — and Sorry," *Washington Post*, June 14, 2017, https://www. washingtonpost.com/local/public-safety/pizzagate-shooter-apologizes-in -handwritten-letter-for-his-mistakes-ahead-of-sentencing/2017/06/13/ f35126b6-5086-11e7-be25-3a519335381c_story.html (accessed 1/22/19).

3. Amanda Robb, "Anatomy of a Fake News Scandal," *Rolling Stone*, November 16, 2017, https://www.rollingstone.com/politics/politics -news/anatomy-of-a-fake-news-scandal-125877/ (accessed 1/22/19).

4. Craig Silverman, "How the Bizarre Conspiracy Theory behind 'Pizzagate' Was Spread," BuzzFeed, November 4, 2016, https://www.buzzfeed.com /craigsilverman/fever-swamp-election (accessed 1/22/19).

5. *Economist*/YouGov Poll, December 17–20, 2016, https://d25d2506sfb94s .cloudfront.net/cumulus_uploads/document/ljv2ohxmzj/econTabReport .pdf (accessed 1/22/19).

6. Michael E. Miller, "Pizzagate's Violent Legacy," *Washington Post*, February 6, 2021, https://www.washingtonpost.com/dc-md-va /2021/02/16/pizzagate-qanon-capitol-attack/ (accessed 8/22/21).

7. Kevin Roose, "What Is QAnon, the Pro-Trump Viral Conspiracy Theory?" *New York Times*, June 15, 2021, https://www.nytimes.com/article/what -is-qanon.html (accessed 8/22/21).

8. Andrew Romano and Caitlin Dickson, "New Yahoo News/YouGov Poll: Half of Trump Supporters Believe QAnon's Imaginary Claims," Yahoo News, October 20, 2020, https://news.yahoo.com/new-yahoo-news -you-gov-poll-half-of-trump-supporters-believe-q-anons-imaginary -claims-124025042.html (accessed 8/22/21).

9. Scott Timberg, "Bill Maher Tangles with Stephen Colbert," Salon, November 17, 2015, https://www.salon.com/2015/11/17/bill_maher _tangles_with_stephen_colbert_the_late_show_host_brings_out_the _best_and_worst_sides_of_his_complicated_guest/ (accessed 1/22/19).

10. Dana Milbank, "We Are a Deeply Stupid Country," *Washington Post*, July 16, 2018, https://www.washingtonpost.com/opinions/we-are-a-deeply -stupid-country/2018/07/16/1742acdc-893b-11e8-85ae-511bc1146b0b _story.html (accessed 1/22/19); Ted Rall, "Why Are Americans So Stupid — And So Proud of It?" aNewDomain, November 9, 2016, http:// anewdomain.net/why-are-americans-so-stupid-and-proud-of-it-ted-rall -analysis/ (accessed 1/22/19); Robert Strong, "Dumb and Dumber Americans," *Roanoke Times*, August 3, 2021, https://roanoke.com/opinion /columnists/strong-dumb-and-dumber-americans/article_e5bbceea -ee2d-11eb-a203-5feb5f206238.html (accessed 8/23/21); Michael A. Cohen, "The Era of Stupid," *Boston Globe*, May 16, 2020, https://www .bostonglobe.com/2020/05/16/opinion/era-stupid/ (accessed 8/23/21).

11. "Doh! Americans Know 'The Simpsons' Better than First Amendment," Live Science, March 1, 2006, https://www.livescience.com/7069-doh -americans-simpsons-amendment.html (accessed 1/24/19).

12. Petr H., "25 Unbelievable Things Americans Believe," List25, March 26, 2015, https://list25.com/25-unbelieavable-things-americans-believe/ (accessed 1/24/19).

13. "Seven Dwarfs vs. Supreme Court Justices," United Press International, August 14, 2006, https://www.upi.com/Odd_News/2006/08/14/Seven -Dwarfs-vs-Supreme-Court-justices/14791155596541/ (accessed 1/24/19).

14. Matthew Kendrick, "34% of Americans Can Find Ukraine on a Map. They're More Likely to Support an Aggressive Posture Against Russia," MorningConsilt.com, February 9, 2022, https://morningconsult .com/2022/02/09/can-americans-find-ukraine-on-a-map/ (accessed 7/19/22).

15. Patrick Riccards, "Woodrow Wilson Foundation Finds Only One State Can Pass U.S. Citizenship Exam," Real Clear Politics, https://www.realclearpublicaffairs.com/public_affairs/2020/05/27/woodrow_wilson_foundation_finds_only_one_state_can_pass_us_citizenship_exam_494368.html (accessed 8/15/21).

16. Michael X. Delli Carpini, "An Overview of the State of Citizens' Knowledge about Politics," Annenberg School of Communication, January 1, 2005, https://repository.upenn.edu/asc_papers/53/ (accessed 1/22/19).

17. "Political Engagement, Knowledge and the Midterms," Pew Research Center, April 25, 2018, https://www.people-press.org/2018/04/26/10-political-engagement-knowledge-and-the-midterms/10_6/; "2016 Civics Battery," Annenberg Public Policy Center, http://cdn.annenbergpublicpolicycenter.org/wp-content/uploads/Constitution_Day_2016_Civics_Appendix.pdf; Philip Bump, "Barely Half of Americans Know the Political Party of Their Representative," *Washington Post*, July 24, 2014, https://www.washingtonpost.com/news/the-fix/wp/2014/07/24/barely-half-of-americans-know-the-political-party-of-their-representative; Chris Cillizza, "People Hate Congress. But Most Incumbents Get Reelected. What Gives?" *Washington Post*, May 9, 2013, https://www.washingtonpost.com/news/the-fix/wp/2013/05/09/people-hate-congress-but-most-incumbents-get-re-elected-what-gives; "What the Public Knows — in Pictures, Words, Maps, and Graphs," Pew Research Center, April 28, 2015, https://www.people-press.org/2015/04/28/what-the-public-knows-in-pictures-words-maps-and-graphs/; Dustin Cable, "And Now the 96%," Weldon Cooper Center for Public Service, September 25, 2012, http://statchatva.org/2012/09/25/and-now-the-96-percent/; Bianca DiJulio, Jamie Firth, and Mollyann Brodie, "Data Note: Americans' Views on the U.S. Role in Global Health," Kaiser Family Foundation, January 23, 2015, https://www.kff.org/global-health-policy/poll-finding/data-note-americans-views-on-the-u-s-role-in-global-health/ (accessed 1/24/19); and data from Danny Hayes and Jennifer L. Lawless's module in the 2016 Cooperative Congressional Election Survey.

18. Charles Pope, "Poll: Nearly 50 Percent of Republicans Believe Health Care Reform Includes Death Panel," *The Oregonian*, August 20, 2009, https://www.oregonlive.com/politics/index.ssf/2009/08/poll_nearly_50_percent_of_repu.html (accessed 1/24/19).

19. "Half of Americans Are Unsure about Popular Vaccine Misinformation," Rutgers Today, August 13, 2021, https://www.rutgers.edu/news/half-americans-are-unsure-about-popular-vaccine-misinformation (accessed 8/23/21).

20. "Immigration," Gallup, https://news.gallup.com/poll/1660/immigration.aspx (accessed 5/26/19).

21. Anna Flagg, "Is There a Connection between Undocumented Immigrants and Crime?" *New York Times*, May 13, 2019, https://www.nytimes.com

/2019/05/13/upshot/illegal-immigration-crime-rates-research.html (accessed 5/26/19).

22. Chris Bell, "The People Who Think 9/11 May Have Been an 'Inside Job'," BBC, February 1, 2018, https://www.bbc.com/news/blogs-trending -42195513 (accessed 9/22/19).

23. Rebecca Jennings, "Many People Believe the Moon Landing Was Fake. But Who's Profiting?" Vox, June 24, 2019, https://www.vox .com/the-goods/2019/6/24/18692080/moon-landing-50th-anniversary -steph-curry-conspiracy-theory-hoax (accessed 9/22/19).

24. Toby Bolsen, James N. Druckman, and Fay Lomax Cook, "The Influence of Partisan Motivated Reasoning on Public Opinion," *Political Behavior* 36, no. 2 (2014): 235–62.

25. Data come from an *Economist*/YouGov poll conducted December 17–20, 2016, https://d25d2506sfb94s.cloudfront.net/cumulus_uploads /document/ljv2ohxmzj/econTabReport.pdf and a CNN poll conducted September 4–8, 2015, http://i2.cdn.turner.com/cnn/2015/images/09/12 /iranpoll.pdf.

26. Caitlin Dickson, "Poll: Two-Thirds of Republicans Still Think the 2020 Election Was Rigged," Yahoo! News, August 4, 2021, https://news.yahoo .com/poll-two-thirds-of-republicans-still-think-the-2020-election-was -rigged-165934695.html (accessed 8/23/21).

27. "Yahoo! News Covid-19 Vaccination Survey," YouGov, July 30–August 2, 2021, https://docs.cdn.yougov.com/40k9knkv6y/20210803_yahoo _vaccine_tabs.pdf (accessed 8/23/21).

28. Ashley Parker and Steve Eder, "Inside the Six Weeks Donald Trump Was a Non-Stop 'Birther'," *New York Times*, July 2, 2016, https://www.nytimes .com/2016/07/03/us/politics/donald-trump-birther-obama.html (accessed 1/24/19).

29. Julia Glum, "Some Republicans Still Think Obama Was Born in Kenya As Trump Resurrects Birther Conspiracy Theory," *Newsweek*, December 11, 2017, https://www.newsweek.com/trump-birther-obama-poll-republicans -kenya-744195 (accessed 8/15/21).

30. Michael E. Miller, "JFK Assassination Conspiracy Theories: The Grassy Knoll, Umbrella Man, LBJ, and Ted Cruz's Dad," *Washington Post*, October 27, 2017, https://www.washingtonpost.com/news /retropolis/wp/2017/10/24/jfk-assassination-conspiracy-theories -the-grassy-knoll-umbrella-man-lbj-and-ted-cruzs-dad/ (accessed 1/24/19).

31. Matthew Yglesias, "Vince Foster's Death and Subsequent Conspiracy Theories, Explained," Vox, May 25, 2016, https://www.vox.com /2016/5/25/11761128/vince-foster (accessed 1/24/19).

32. Joseph E. Uscinski and Joseph M. Parent, *American Conspiracy Theories* (New York: Oxford University Press, 2014).

23. SHOULD YOU BELIEVE THE POLLS?

1. Cara Korte, "Most American Say Climate Change Is a Crisis, New Study Shows," CBS News, October 27, 2021, https://www.cbsnews.com/news/climate-change-crisis-poll/ (accessed 7/19/22).

2. "Most Parents Don't Want Their Schools to Require COVID-19 Vaccination, but Most Favor Requiring Masks for Unvaccinated Children and Staff," Kaiser Family Foundation, August 11, 2021, https://www.kff.org/coronavirus-covid-19/press-release/most-parents-dont-want-their-schools-to-require-covid-19-vaccination-but-most-favor-requiring-masks-for-unvaccinated-children-and-staff/ (accessed 7/19/22).

3. Fox News poll, August 7–10, 2021. N = 1,002 adults nationwide. Margin of error ± 3. https://pollingreport.com/budget.htm (accessed 8/16/21).

4. Caroline Vakil, "Two-Thirds in New Poll Favor 'Stricter Gun Control Laws'," The Hill, June 29, 2022, https://thehill.com/blogs/blog-briefing-room/3540964-two-thirds-in-new-poll-favor-stricter-gun-control-laws/ (accessed 7/19/22).

5. ABC News/*Washington Post* poll, June 27–30, 2021. N = 907. Margin of error ± 3.5. https://pollingreport.com/politics.htm (accessed 8/16/21).

6. Gallup poll, July 6–21, 2021. N = 1,007. Margin of error ± 4.0. https://pollingreport.com/afghan.htm (accessed 8/16/21).

7. "Latest 2020 State Presidential Election Polls," Real Clear Politics, https://www.realclearpolitics.com/epolls/latest_polls/state_president/ (accessed 8/16/21).

8. Steven Shepard, "Oprah 2020 Gets Low Ratings from Voters," Politico, January 17, 2018, https://www.politico.com/story/2018/01/17/oprah-winfrey-2020-poll-343096 (accessed 8/16/21).

9. David Lublin, "Quality, Not Quantity: Strategic Politicians in U.S. Senate Elections, 1952–1990," *Journal of Politics* 56, no. 1 (1994): 228–41.

10. Audrey Hayes, Paul-Henri Gurian, and Michael H. Crespin, "The Calculus of Concession: Media Coverage and the Dynamics of Winnowing in Presidential Nominations," *American Politics Research* 32, no. 3 (2004): 310–37.

11. Anneke Ball, Brittany Stephanis, and Robert Leslie, "Election Polls Aren't Getting Any Less Accurate, but the Public Trusts Them Less and Less. Here's Why," Insider, February 1, 2021, https://www.insider.com/election-polls-accuracy-donald-trump-2021-1 (accessed 8/16/21).

12. "State Primary Election Types," National Conference of State Legislatures, June 26, 2018, http://www.ncsl.org/research/elections-and-campaigns/primary-types.aspx (accessed 5/21/19).

13. "Population Distribution by Age," Kaiser Family Foundation, https://www.kff.org/other/state-indicator/distribution-by-age (accessed 5/21/19).

14. "Polling Memo: Americans' Views on Social Security," Social Security Works, March 2019, https://socialsecurityworks.org/2019/03/26/social -security-polling/ (accessed 5/21/19).

15. Michael R. Kagay, "Poll on Doubt of Holocaust Is Corrected," *New York Times*, July 8, 1994, https://www.nytimes.com/1994/07/08/us/poll-on -doubt-of-holocaust-is-corrected.html (accessed 5/21/19).

16. CBS News poll, May 3–6, 2018. $N = 1,101$ adults nationwide. Margin of error ± 3.

17. CNN poll conducted by SSRS, May 2–5, 2018. $N = 1,015$ adults nation-wide. Margin of error ± 3.6.

18. CNN poll conducted by Opinion Research Corporation, January 21–23, 2011. $N = 1,012$ adults nationwide. Margin of error ± 3.

19. "Writing Survey Questions," Pew Research Center, https://www.pewresearch .org/methods/u-s-survey-research/questionnaire-design/ (accessed 5/23/19).

20. Gallup poll, May 3–18, 2021. $N = 1,016$ adults nationwide. Margin of error ± 4. https://news.gallup.com/poll/244709/pro-choice-pro-life-2018 -demographic-tables.aspx (accessed 8/16/21).

21. "Abortion," Gallup, https://news.gallup.com/poll/1576/abortion.aspx (accessed 7/19/22).

22. Ruth Igielnik, "Many Americans Say They Voted, but Did They?" Pew Research Center, March 10, 2016, https://www.pewresearch.org/fact -tank/2016/03/10/many-americans-say-they-voted-but-did-they/ (accessed 5/23/19).

23. Justin McCarthy, "Less Than Half in U.S. Would Vote for a Socialist for President," Gallup, May 9, 2019, https://news.gallup.com/poll/254120 /less-half-vote-socialist-president.aspx (accessed 5/23/19).

24. Daniel J. Hopkins, "No More Wilder Effect, Never a Whitman Effect: Why and When Polls Mislead about Black and Female Candidates," *Journal of Politics* 71, no. 3 (2009): 769–81.

25. Steven Shepard, "GOP Insiders: Polls Don't Capture Secret Trump Vote," Politico, October 28, 2016, https://www.politico.com/story/2016/10 /donald-trump-shy-voters-polls-gop-insiders-230411 (accessed 8/17/21).

26. "Majority Disapprove Overturning Roe," Monmouth University, June 28, 2022, https://www.monmouth.edu/polling-institute/reports/monmouthpoll _us_062822/ (accessed 7/19/22).

27. "Presidential Approval Ratings — Joe Biden," January–June 2022, Gallup, https://news.gallup.com/poll/329384/presidential-approval -ratings-joe-biden.aspx (accessed 8/4/22).

28. "FiveThirtyEight's Pollster Ratings," FiveThirtyEight , March 25, 2021, https://projects.fivethirtyeight.com/pollster-ratings/ (accessed 3/16/22).

29. Frank Newport, "American Public Opinion and Guns," Gallup, December 4, 2015, https://news.gallup.com/opinion/polling-matters/187511 /american-public-opinion-guns.aspx (accessed 5/23/19).

30. Michael Andrea Strebel and Marco R. Steenbergen, "The Impact of the November 2015 Terrorist Attacks in Paris on Public Opinion: A Natural Experiment," ResearchGate, https://www.researchgate.net/publication /321666668_The_impact_of_the_november_2015_terrorist_attacks _in_Paris_on_public_opinion_a_natural_experiment (accessed 5/23/19).

31. Nate Silver, "How FiveThirtyEight Calculates Pollster Ratings," FiveThirtyEight, September 25, 2014, https://fivethirtyeight.com /features/how-fivethirtyeight-calculates-pollster-ratings/ (accessed 5/23/19).

24. WHY DO YOU HEAR MORE ABOUT POLITICIANS' SEX SCANDALS THAN THE BILLS THEY PROPOSE?

1. David Maurasse, *A Future for Everyone: Innovative Social Responsibility and Community Partnerships* (New York: Routledge, 2004).

2. Joel Achenbach, "Did the News Media, Led by Walter Cronkite, Lose the War in Vietnam?" *Washington Post*, May 25, 2018, https://www.washingtonpost .com/national/did-the-news-media-led-by-walter-cronkite-lose-the-war -in-vietnam/2018/05/25/a5b3e098-495e-11e8-827e-190efaf1f1ee_story .html (accessed 4/8/19).

3. Louis Harris, "A Respectful Farewell to Walter Cronkite as CBS Anchor- man," The Harris Survey, March 9, 1981, https://theharrispoll.com/wp -content/uploads/2017/12/Harris-Interactive-Poll-Research-A-RESPECTFUL -FAREWELL-TO-WALTER-CRONKITE-AS-CBS-ANCHORMAN-1981-03.pdf (accessed 4/8/19).

4. "Carl Bernstein: The Golden Age of Investigative Journalism Never Existed," Big Think, August 9, 2010, https://bigthink.com/the-voice -of-big-think/carl-bernstein-the-golden-age-of-investigative-journalism -never-existed; John Sexton, "New Biography: Walter Cronkite Biased, Unethical," Breitbart, May 21, 2012, https://www.breitbart.com /the-media/2012/05/21/new-biography-reveals-cronkite-was-biased -unethical/ (accessed 4/8/19).

5. "Democracy on Deadline: Who Owns the Media?" PBS, https://www.pbs .org/independentlens/documentaries/democracyondeadline/ (accessed 9/23/19).

6. James T. Hamilton, *All the News That's Fit to Sell: How the Market Transforms Information into News* (Princeton, NJ: Princeton University Press, 2004).

7. Markus Prior, *Post-Broadcast Democracy: How Media Choice Increases Inequality in Political Involvement and Polarizes Elections* (New York: Cambridge University Press, 2007).

8. Danny Hayes and Jennifer L. Lawless, *News Hole: The Demise of Local Journalism and Political Engagement* (New York: Cambridge University Press, 2021).

9. Jack Shafer and Tucker Doherty, "The Media Bubble Is Worse Than You Think," Politico, April 25, 2017, https://www.politico.com/magazine /story/2017/04/25/media-bubble-real-journalism-jobs-east-coast -215048 (accessed 4/13/19).

10. Mark Jurkowitz, "The Growth in Digital Reporting," Pew Research Center, March 26, 2014, https://www.journalism.org/2014/03/26/the-growth-in -digital-reporting/ (accessed 6/11/19).

11. "NBA, DMX, Gabby Petito Stand Out on Google's 2021 Year in Search Trends," ABC7 News, December 8, 2021, https://https://abc7ny.com /google-searches-2021-top-trends-trending-year-in-search/11311750/; Michelle Butterfield, "Year in Review: The Most Viral News Stories of 2021," Global News, December 31, 2021, https://globalnews.ca /news/8481259/year-in-review-2021-viral-news-stories/ (accessed 8/4/22).

12. Julia McCoy, "New Outbrain Study Says Negative Headlines Do Better than Positive," March 15, 2014, https://www.business2community.com /blogging/new-outbrain-study-says-negative-headlines-better-positive -0810707 (accessed 4/10/19).

13. Ap Dijksterhuis and Henk Aarts, "On Wildebeests and Humans: The Preferential Detection of Negative Stimuli," *Psychological Science* 14 (2003): 14–18.

14. Thomas E. Patterson, "News Coverage of Donald Trump's First 100 Days," Shorenstein Center on Media, Politics, and Public Policy, May 18, 2017, https://shorensteincenter.org/news-coverage-donald-trumps-first-100 -days/ (accessed 8/18/21).

15. Carolyn L. Todd, "Why You Love the Real Housewives' Iconic Fights, According to Psychologists," Bustle, December 14, 2017, https://www .bustle.com/p/why-you-love-the-real-housewives-iconic-fights -according-to-psychologists-7547646 (accessed 4/13/19).

16. Lynn Letukas, *Primetime Pundits: How Cable News Covers Social Issues* (London: Lexington Books, 2014).

17. "Horserace Coverage Dominates," Pew Research Center, June 21, 2010, https://www.journalism.org/2010/06/21/horserace-coverage-dominates/ (accessed 4/13/19).

18. Jack Shafer, "Why Horse-Race Political Journalism Is Awesome," Politico, January 9, 2019, https://www.politico.com/magazine/story/2019/01/09 /why-horse-race-political-journalism-awesome-223867 (accessed 4/13/19).

19. Dannagal G. Young, "Stop Covering Politics as a Game," NiemanLab, https://www.niemanlab.org/2017/12/stop-covering-politics-as-a-game/ (accessed 4/13/19).

20. Thomas E. Patterson, "A Tale of Two Elections: CBS and Fox News' Portrayal of the 2020 Presidential Campaign," Shorenstein Center on Media, Politics, and Public Policy, December 17, 2020, https://

shorensteincenter.org/patterson-2020-election-coverage/ (accessed 8/17/21).

21. Eli Watkins, "'Bigfoot Erotica' Takes Center Stage in Virginia Congressional Race," CNN, July 30, 2018, https://www.cnn.com/2018/07/30/politics/bigfoot-erotica-virginia/index.html (accessed 4/13/19).

22. Matthew Yglesias, "The Virginia House Race at the Center of the 'Bigfoot Erotica' Controversy, Explained," Vox, July 30, 2018, https://www.vox.com/2018/7/30/17629580/riggleman-cockburn-bigfoot-erotica (accessed 9/23/19).

23. "Candidate Pepper Sprays Himself in Ad," Huffington Post, June 14, 2018, www.huffpost.com/entry/congressional-candidate-pepper-sprays-himself-in-ad_n_5b20441fe4b086050ad1f33d (accessed 4/13/19).

24. Ricky Young, "Congressman Spent Campaign Funds for Rabbit Air Travel," San Diego Union-Tribune, January 3, 2017, www.sandiegouniontribune.com/news/watchdog/sd-me-hunter-rabbits-20170103-story.html (accessed 4/13/19).

25. Pete Brown, "Pushed Even Further: U.S. Newsrooms View Mobile Alerts as a Standalone Platform," Columbia Journalism Review, December 20, 2018, https://www.cjr.org/tow_center_reports/newsrooms-view-mobile-alerts-as-standalone-platform.php (accessed 8/17/21).

26. Joe Concha, "Michael Avenatti Has Appeared on CNN and MSNBC 108 Times since March 7, Says Free Beacon," The Hill, May 11, 2018, https://thehill.com/homenews/media/387325-michael-avenatti-has-appeared-on-cnn-and-msnbc-108-times-since-march-7-says (accessed 4/13/19).

27. "Pop Goes the Weiner," New York Post, August 29, 2016, https://nypost.com/cover/covers-for-august-29-2016/ (accessed 4/7/22).

28. "Meet Carlos Danger," New York Post, July 24, 2013, https://nypost.com/list/anthony-weiner-our-best-covers-headlines/ (accessed 4/7/22).

29. "Says Sexy Pic Might be Him, But He Didn't Send it . . . HUH? Weiner's Pickle," Daily News, July 2, 2011.

30. Anna North, "Revenge Porn, Biphobia, and Alleged Relationships with Staffers: The Complicated Story around Rep. Katie Hill, Explained," Vox, October 28, 2019, https://www.vox.com/identities/2019/10/23/20928700/katie-hill-congresswoman-resigns-leaked-red-state (accessed 8/18/21).

31. David Bauder, "Poll: Americans Want More of What Journalists Want to Report," Associated Press, June 11, 2018, https://apnews.com/article/journalists-north-america-donald-trump-ap-top-news-journalism-2dba8dfe5d93459f80ef08f9db58ac67; Erik Sass, "Americans Sick of Gossip, Sports in News Coverage, Want More Substance," Media Daily News, October 21, 2014, https://www.mediapost.com/publications

/article/236675/americans-sick-of-gossip-sports-in-news-coverage
.html (accessed 3/17/22).

32. Joel Ericsen and Jeffry Gottfried, "Partisans Disagree on Media's Best,
Worst Traits," Pew Research Center, September 29, 2016, https://www
.pewresearch.org/fact-tank/2016/09/29/news-media-best-worst-traits/
(accessed 4/13/19).

25. HOW DO YOU KNOW IF YOU'RE READING FAKE NEWS?

1. Elisa Shearer, "More than 8 in 10 Americans Get News from Digital
Devices," Pew Research Center, January 12, 2021, https://www
.pewresearch.org/fact-tank/2021/01/12/more-than-eight-in-ten
-americans-get-news-from-digital-devices/; Mason Walker and
Katerina Eva Matsa, "News Consumption across Social Media in 2021,"
Pew Research Center, September 20, 2021, https://www.pewresearch
.org/journalism/2021/09/20/news-consumption-across-social-media
-in-2021/ (accessed 8/4/22).

2. Amy Mitchell, Jeffrey Gottfried, Michael Barthel, and Elisa Shearer,
"Pathways to News," Pew Research Center, July 7, 2016, https://www
.journalism.org/2016/07/07/pathways-to-news/ (accessed 4/23/19).

3. "Verification and Accuracy," American Press Institute, https://www
.americanpressinstitute.org/journalism-essentials/verification
-accuracy/ (accessed 4/23/19).

4. Bill Kovach and Tom Rosenstiel, *The Elements of Journalism: What
Newspeople Should Know and the Public Should Expect* (New York:
Three Rivers Press, 2007).

5. Tony Room, "Congress Adopts $1.9 Trillion Stimulus, Securing First
Major Win for Biden," *Washington Post*, March 10, 2021, https://www
.washingtonpost.com/us-policy/2021/03/10/house-stimulus-biden
-covid-relief-checks/ (accessed 8/19/21).

6. Andrew Duehren and Kristina Peterson, "House Passes $1.9 Trillion
Covid-19 Stimulus Bill; Biden to Sign Friday," *Wall Street Journal*, March 10,
2021, https://www.wsj.com/articles/house-set-to-approve-covid-19
-relief-bill-11615372203 (accessed 8/19/21).

7. Arthur Delaney and Tara Golshan, "Thanks to the Covid-19 Relief Bill,
Parents Could Soon Be Getting Regular Checks," Huffington Post,
March 9, 2021, https://www.huffpost.com/entry/child-tax-credit-monthly
-payments_n_604674cac5b6e29350b24bb0 (accessed 8/19/21).

8. Wendell Husebo, "Democrats Want Covid Welfare Provisions to Last
Well beyond the Pandemic Itself," Breitbart, March 15, 2021,
https://www.breitbart.com/economy/2021/03/15/politico-democrats
-want-covid-welfare-provisions-last-well-beyond-pandemic/ (accessed
8/19/21).

9. Jeffrey Rodack, "Dems' Covid Bill Dedicates $36 Billion Subsidy to
Obamacare," Newsmax, March 4, 2021, https://www.newsmax.com

/politics/covid-bill-obamacare-subsidy/2021/03/04/id/1012512/
(accessed 8/19/21).

10.   Roman Chiarello, "Toomey Calls Out Covid Relief Bill's 'Litany of Outrageous Items,'" Fox News, March 8, 2021, https://www.foxnews.com /politics/toomey-litany-outrageous-items-covid-relief-bill-indefensible (accessed 8/19/21).

11.   "Donald Trump to CNN Reporter: You Are Fake News," CNBC, January 11, 2017, https://www.youtube.com/watch?v=veZs75jlAlw (accessed 4/23/19).

12.   Angie Drobnic Holan, "The Media's Definition of Fake News versus Donald Trump's," Politifact, October 18, 2017, https://www.politifact.com /truth-o-meter/article/2017/oct/18/deciding-whats-fake-medias -definition-fake-news-vs/ (accessed 4/23/19).

13.   Summer Meza, "'Fake News' Named Word of the Year," *Newsweek*, November 2, 2017, https://www.newsweek.com/fake-news-word-year -collins-dictionary-699740 (accessed 4/23/19).

14.   Amanda Seitz and Beatrice Dupuy, "Not Real News: A Look at What Didn't Happen This Week," Associated Press, April 19, 2019, https:// news.yahoo.com/not-real-news-look-didnt-happen-week-191728628 .html (accessed 4/23/19).

15.   Ben Gilbert, "The 10 Most Viewed Fake News Stories on Facebook in 2019 Were Just Revealed in a New Report," Insider, November 6, 2019, https://www.businessinsider.com/most-viewed-fake-news-stories -shared-on-facebook-2019-2019-11 (accessed 8/18/21).

16.   Melissa Holzberg, "Facebook Banned 1.3 Billion Accounts over Three Months to Combat 'Fake' and 'Harmful' Content," *Forbes*, March 22, 2021, https://www.forbes.com/sites/melissaholzberg/2021/03/22/facebook -banned-13-billion-accounts-over-three-months-to-combat-fake-and -harmful-content/ (accessed 8/20/21).

17.   Ryan J. Foley, "'Fake News' Smear Takes Hold among Politicians at All Levels," *PBS NewsHour*, March 11, 2018, https://www.pbs.org/newshour/politics/fake -news-smear-takes-hold-among-politicians-at-all-levels (accessed 4/23/19).

18.   Julia Manchester, "Trump Tweet about 'Very Civil Conversation' with Australian PM Resurfaces after Transcript Leaked," The Hill, August 3, 2017, https://thehill.com/homenews/administration/345181-trump-tweet -about-very-civil-conversation-with-australian-leader (accessed 4/23/19); Tamara Keith, "President Trump's Description of What's 'Fake' Is Expanding," National Public Radio, September 2, 2018, https://www.npr .org/2018/09/02/643761979/president-trumps-description-of-whats -fake-is-expanding (accessed 4/23/19).

19.   "Congressman Mo Brooks Rebuts Vicious and Scurrilous Fake News Media and Socialist Democrat Attacks," January 12, 2021, https://brooks .house.gov/media-center/news-releases/congressman-mo-brooks -rebuts-vicious-scurrilous-fake-news-media-and (accessed 8/18/21).

20. Betsy Z. Russell, "Residency Questions Raised about Controversial North-Central Idaho Lawmaker," *Spokesman-Review*, September 18, 2017, http://www.spokesman.com/stories/2017/sep/18/residency -questions-raised-about-controversial-nor/ (accessed 4/23/19).

21. Scott Maxwell, "Commentary: Candidate Caught with Fake Diploma Calls It 'Fake News'—until She's Forced to Exit Race," *Orlando Sentinel*, August 14, 2018, https://www.orlandosentinel.com/opinion/os-melissa-howard -fake-diploma-scott-maxwell-20180814-story.html (accessed 4/23/19).

22. Paul Glader, "10 Journalism Brands Where You Find Real Facts Rather than Alternative Facts," *Forbes*, February 1, 2017, https:// www.forbes.com /sites/berlinschoolofcreativeleadership/2017/02/01/10-journalism -brands-where-you-will-find-real-facts-rather-than-alternative-facts /#688fddeee9b5 (accessed 4/23/19).

23. Bill McCarthy, "GOP Candidates Take Page from Trump Playbook in Bashing Media," Poynter Institute, January 29, 2019, https://www.poynter .org/ethics-trust/2019/gop-candidates-take-page-from-trump-playbook -in-bashing-media/ (accessed 4/23/19).

26. WHY DO FOX NEWS AND CNN VIEWERS SEE POLITICS SO DIFFERENTLY?

1. Lee Moran, "CNN's Don Lemon and Chris Cuomo Shred Fox News' Tucker Carlson over Racist Rhetoric," Huffington Post, December 19, 2018, https://www.huffpost.com/entry/cnn-don-lemon-chris-cuomo-tucker -carlson_n_5c19f52de4b08db99058f60f (accessed 5/4/19).

2. Lee Moran, "Fox News' Sean Hannity: CNN Gives World a 'Perverted' View of America," Huffington Post, March 12, 2019, https://www.huffpost .com/entry/fox-news-sean-hannity-cnn-perverted-view-country_n _5c875ff0e4b0ed0a0016b3a1 (accessed 5/4/19).

3. Jessica Estepa and Gregory Korte, "Obama Tells David Letterman: People No Longer Agree on What Facts Are," *USA Today*, January 12, 2018, www.usatoday.com/story/news/politics/onpolitics/2018/01/12 /obama-weighs/1027893001/ (accessed 5/4/19).

4. Ted Koppel, *Lights Out: A Cyberattack, a Nation Unprepared, Surviving the Aftermath* (New York: Crown, 2015).

5. Bill Keveney, "Cable News Race: Fox Holds onto Top Spot in Rating after Post-Election Dip," *USA Today*, June 30, 2021, https://www.usatoday .com/story/entertainment/tv/2021/06/30/fox-news-leads-ratings-after -falling-behind-cnn-post-election/7801577002/ (accessed 8/20/21).

6. Dennis T. Lowry, Tarn Ching, Josephine Nio, and Dennis W. Leitner, "Setting the Public Fear Agenda: A Longitudinal Analysis of Network TV Crime Reporting, Public Perceptions of Crime, and FBI Crime Statistics," *Journal of Communication* 53, no. 1 (2003): 61–73.

7. For the original media priming study, see Shanto Iyengar, Donald Kinder, Mark Peters, and Jon Krosnick, "The Evening News and Presidential

Evaluations," *Journal of Personality and Social Psychology* 46, no. 4 (1984): 778–87. For a more recent take, see Austin Hart and Joel A. Middleton, "Priming under Fire: Reverse Causality and the Classic Media Priming Hypothesis," *Journal of Politics* 76, no. 2 (2014): 581–92.

8. Charlie Smart, "The Differences in How CNN, MSNBC, and Fox Cover the News," The Pudding, https://pudding.cool/2018/01/chyrons/ (accessed 5/4/19).

9. *Anderson Cooper 360°*, June 4, 2020, https://transcripts.cnn.com/show /acd/date/2020-06-04/segment/01; *Cuomo Prime Time*, June 5, 2020, http://us.cnn.com/TRANSCRIPTS/2006/05/CPT.01.html; *CNN Tonight*, April 13, 2021, http://edition.cnn.com/TRANSCRIPTS/2104/13/cnnt.02 .html; *Tucker Carlson Tonight*, November 10, 2020, https://www.foxnews .com/transcript/tucker-how-defund-the-police-movement-backfired-on -democrats; *Hannity*, June 29, 2021, https://www.foxnews.com/transcript /hannity-on-crime-surge-debates-over-defunding-the-police; *The Ingraham Angle*, June 5, 2020, https://www.foxnews.com/transcript/push-to -dismantle-us-police-based-on-lies-and-false-data (accessed 8/25/21).

10. Markus Prior, *Post-Broadcast Democracy: How Media Choice Increases Inequality in Political Involvement and Polarizes Elections* (New York: Cambridge University Press, 2007).

11. Kathleen Hall Jamieson and Joseph N. Cappella, *Echo Chamber: Rush Limbaugh and the Conservative Media* (New York: Oxford University Press, 2008).

12. Farhad Manjoo, *True Enough: Learning to Live in a Post-Fact Society* (Hoboken, NJ: Wiley, 2008).

13. Cass Sunstein, *Republic.com 2.0* (Princeton, NJ: Princeton University Press, 2007).

14. Mark Jurkowitz, Amy Mitchell, Elisa Shearer, and Mason Walker, "U.S. Media Polarization and the 2020 Election: A Nation Divided," Pew Research Center, January 24, 2020, https://www.pewresearch.org /journalism/2020/01/24/u-s-media-polarization-and-the-2020-election -a-nation-divided/ (accessed 8/24/21).

15. "Republicans and Democrats Agree: They Can't Agree on Basic Facts," Pew Research Center, August 23, 2018, https://www.pewresearch.org /fact-tank/2018/08/23/republicans-and-democrats-agree-they-cant -agree-on-basic-facts/ft_18-08-23_basicfacts_large-majorities-both -parties/ (accessed 5/4/19).

16. Matthew Levendusky and Neil Malhotra, "Does Media Coverage of Partisan Polarization Affect Political Attitudes?" *Political Communication* 33, no. 2 (2016): 283–301; Matthew Levendusky, "Partisan Media Exposure and Attitudes toward the Opposition," *Political Communication* 30, no. 4 (2013): 565–81.

17. "The Partisan Landscape and Views of the Parties," Pew Research Center, October 10, 2019, https://www.pewresearch.org/politics/2019/10/10 /the-partisan-landscape-and-views-of-the-parties/ (accessed 8/24/21).

18. Matthew S. Levendusky, "Why Do Partisan Media Polarize Viewers?" *American Journal of Political Science* 57, no. 3 (2013): 61–23.

27. WHO WILL YOU PROBABLY VOTE FOR?

1. "Reeve Doubted Embryonic Stem Cell Research," WND, October 13, 2004, https://mobile.wnd.com/2004/10/26992/#22O8slWqxeFRQc4i.99 (accessed 6/8/19).

2. "Kucinich's Speech at the Congresso Was Profound," Daily Kos, October 11, 2007, https://www.dailykos.com/stories/2007/10/11/396923 /-Kucinich-s-Speech-at-the-Congresso-Was-Profound (accessed 6/8/19).

3. Gina Sunseri, "Newt Gingrich Proposes Moon, Mars Flights: A Reality Check," ABC News, January 26, 2012, https://abcnews.go.com /Technology/newt-gingrich-promises-moon-base-flights-mars-reality /story?id=15449425 (accessed 6/8/19).

4. Adam Martin, "The 15 Craziest Politician Promises," Complex, September 4, 2012, https://www.complex.com/pop-culture/2012/09 /the-15-craziest-politician-campaign-promises/rick-santorum-ban -hard-core-pornography (accessed 6/8/19).

5. Jason Linkins, "Herman Cain Would Impose Bizarre Three-Page Limit on Legislation," Huffington Post, August 8, 2011, https://www.huffpost.com /entry/herman-cain-three-page-limit-legislation_n_873128 (accessed 6/8/19).

6. "Here's Donald Trump's Presidential Announcement Speech," *Time*, June 16, 2015, https://time.com/3923128/donald-trump-announcement -speech/ (accessed 6/8/19).

7. Larry M. Bartels, "Partisanship and Voting Behavior, 1956–1996," *American Journal of Political Science* 44, no. 1 (2000): 35–50; Geoffrey L. Cohen, "Party over Policy: The Dominating Impact of Group Influence on Political Beliefs," *Journal of Personality and Social Psychology* 85, no. 5 (2003): 808–22; David C. King and Richard E. Matland, "Sex and the Grand Old Party: An Experimental Investigation of the Effect of Candidate Sex on Support for a Republican Candidate," *American Politics Research* 31, no. 6 (2003): 595–612; John Sides and Lynn Vavreck, *The Gamble: Choice and Chance in the 2012 Presidential Election* (Princeton, NJ: Princeton University Press, 2013).

8. Arthur Lupia, "Shortcuts versus Encyclopedias: Information and Voting Behavior in California Insurance Reform Elections," *American Political Science Review* 88, no. 1 (1994): 63–76.

9. "U.S. National Election Day Exit Polls," Roper, https://ropercenter .cornell.edu/exit-polls/us-national-election-day-exit-polls; "2016 Exit Polls," CNN, https://www.cnn.com/election/2016/results/exit-polls; "2020 Exit Polls," CNN, https://www.cnn.com/election/2020/exit-polls /president/national-results (accessed 10/1/21).

10. "Exit Polls," CNN, https://www.cnn.com/election/2016/results/exit-polls (accessed 6/8/19).

11. "Exit Polls," CNN, https://www.cnn.com/election/2018/exit-polls (accessed 9/9/21); "2022 Exit Polls," CNN, https://www.cnn.com/election/2022/exit-polls/national-results/house (accessed 11/9/22).

12. "Political Independents: Who They Are, What They Think," Pew Research Center, March 14, 2019, https://www.people-press.org/2019/03/14/political-independents-who-they-are-what-they-think/ (accessed 6/8/19).

13. Beatrice Jin and Caitlin Oprysko, "Here's Where the Democratic Candidates Stand on the Biggest 2020 Issues," Politico, April 25, 2019, https://www.politico.com/interactives/2019/04/25/2020-democratic-presidential-candidates-take-stands-issues/ (accessed 6/9/19).

14. Michael Tesler, "Priming Predispositions and Changing Policy Positions: An Account of When Mass Opinion Is Primed or Changed," *American Journal of Political Science* 59, no. 4 (2015): 806–24.

15. Megan Brenan, "One in Four Americans Consider Abortion a Key Voting Issue," Gallup, July 7, 2020, https://news.gallup.com/poll/313316/one-four-americans-consider-abortion-key-voting-issue.aspx (accessed 9/9/21).

16. Jackson Hogan, "Young Candidates to Duke It Out in Jefferson County School Board Elections," The Bulletin, May 4, 2019, https://www.bendbulletin.com/localstate/7132345-151/young-candidates-to-duke-it-out-in-jefferson (accessed 6/8/19).

17. Lydia Saad and Megan Brenan, "Americans' Intensity Running High Before U.S. Midterms," Gallup, July 8, 2022, https://news.gallup.com/poll/394628/americans-intensity-running-high-midterms.aspx (accessed 7/21/22).

18. Hannah Fingerhut, "What Voters Want in a President Today, and How Their Views Have Changed," Pew Research Center, February 12, 2016, https://www.pewresearch.org/fact-tank/2016/02/12/what-voters-want-in-a-president-today-and-how-their-views-have-changed/ (accessed 6/9/19).

19. "What Traits Do Voters Prefer in a President?" Sachs Media Group, July 7, 2018, https://sachsmedia.com/news/poll-younger-older-voters-seek-different-things-in-president/ (accessed 6/9/19).

20. Danny Hayes, "Has Television Personalized Voting Behavior?" *Political Behavior* 31, no. 2 (2009): 231–60.

21. "Election 2020 Favorability Ratings," Real Clear Politics, https://www.realclearpolitics.com/epolls/other/president/trumpbidenfavorability.html; Lydia Saad, "Trump and Clinton Finish with Historically Poor Images," Gallup, November 8, 2016, https://news.gallup.com/poll/197231/trump-clinton-finish-historically-poor-images.aspx (accessed 4/21/22).

22. "Voters Would Rather Have a Beer with Bush," Independent Online, October 18, 2000, https://www.iol.co.za/mercury/world/voters-would-rather-have-a-beer-with-bush-49676 (accessed 6/9/19).

23. "Would You Rather Have a Beer with Clinton or Trump?" Rasmussen Reports, June 15, 2016, https://www.rasmussenreports.com/public_content/politics/elections/election_2016/would_you_rather_have_a_beer_with_clinton_or_trump (accessed 6/11/19).

24. "Biden or Trump: Who Would You Rather Have a Beer With?" Ranker, https://blog.ranker.com/drink-a-beer-with-biden-or-trump (accessed 9/9/21).

25. Danny Hayes and Jennifer L. Lawless, *Women on the Run: Gender, Media, and Political Campaigns in a Polarized Era* (New York: Cambridge University Press, 2016).

26. Kira Sanbonmatsu, "Gender Stereotypes and Vote Choice," *American Journal of Political Science* 46, no. 1 (2002): 20–34.

27. Richard L. Fox, "Congressional Elections: Women's Candidacies and the Road to Gender Parity," in *Gender and Elections*, 5th ed., ed. Susan J. Carroll and Richard L. Fox (New York: Cambridge University Press, 2022); Danny Hayes and Jennifer L. Lawless, "The Contingent Effects of Sexism in Primary Elections," *Political Research Quarterly*, September 2021, doi:10.1177/10659129211043134; Jennifer L. Lawless and Kathryn Pearson, "The Primary Reason for Women's Under-Representation: Re-Evaluating the Conventional Wisdom," *Journal of Politics* 70, no. 1 (2008): 67–82; Dawn Langan Teele, Joshua Kalla, and Frances Rosenbluth, "The Ties That Double Bind: Social Roles and Women's Underrepresentation in Politics," *American Political Science Review* 112, no. 3 (2018): 525–41.

28. Tasha S. Philpot and Hanes Walton Jr., "One of Our Own: Black Female Candidates and the Voters Who Support Them," *American Journal of Political Science* 51, no. 1 (2007): 49–62; Yanna Krupnikov, Spencer Piston, and Nichole M. Bauer, "Saving Face: Identifying Voter Responses to Black Candidates and Female Candidates," *Political Psychology* 37, no. 2 (2016): 253–73.

29. Monika L. McDermott, "Religious Stereotyping and Voter Support for Evangelical Candidates," *Political Research Quarterly* 62, no. 2 (2008): 340–54.

28. HOW DO DEMOCRATS AND REPUBLICANS FIGHT TO CONTROL THE GOVERNMENT?

1. James Arkin, "Latino Victory Fund Launches Effort to Draft Gallego for Arizona Senate in 2020," Politico, September 13, 2018, https://www.politico.com/story/2018/09/13/gallego-arizona-senate-2020-786127 (accessed 11/25/19).

2. James Arkin, "Crowd of Democrats Jockey over Arizona Senate Special," Politico, December 25, 2018, https://www.politico.com/story/2018/12/25/arizona-senate-special-election-democrats-1075107 (accessed 11/25/19).

3. Kevin Robillard, "Mark Kelly's Arizona Senate Run Could Spark a Clash with the Left," Huffington Post, February 13, 2019, https://www.huffpost

.com/entry/mark-kellys-arizona-senate-run-could-spark-a-clash-with-the-left_n_5c6316bae4b0a8731aead328 (accessed 11/25/19).

4. Yvonne Wingett Sanchez, "Retired Astronaut Mark Kelly Running for U.S. Senate as Democrat to Take on McSally," *Arizona Republic*, February 12, 2019, https://www.azcentral.com/story/news/politics/arizona/2019/02/12/arizona-us-senate-astronaut-mark-kelly-announces-run-congressional-bid-gabby-giffords/2845417002/ (accessed 11/25/19).

5. Clarice Silber, Jonathan J. Cooper, and Alan Fram, "Democrats Lean away from Leftward Swing in Crucial Senate Races," *Christian Science Monitor*, July 22, 2019, https://www.csmonitor.com/USA/Politics/2019/0722/Democrats-lean-away-from-leftward-swing-in-crucial-Senate-races (accessed 11/25/19).

6. "Mark Kelly for Senate," Federal Election Commission, https://www.fec.gov/data/committee/C00696526/?cycle=2020 (accessed 9/8/21); Zach Montellaro, "Campaigns Spend Inefficiently, Too Little on Digital," Politico, March 22, 2019, https://www.politico.com/newsletters/morning-score/2019/03/22/campaigns-spend-inefficiently-too-little-on-digital-554740 (accessed 11/25/19); "Tiernan Donahue," LinkedIn, https://www.linkedin.com/in/tiernan-donohue-b59853a7/ (accessed 11/25/19); "50 Politicos to Watch: Fundraisers," Politico, https://www.politico.com/news/stories/0711/59945_Page3.html (accessed 9/8/21); "Who We Work With," Run the World Digital, https://runtheworlddigital.com/clients/ (accessed 11/25/19); "Our Clients," Aisle 518, https://aisle518.com/#our-clients (accessed 11/25/19); "Clients," Greenberg, Quinlan, Rosner Research, https://www.gqrr.com/clients/ (accessed 11/25/19).

7. "My Next Mission," Mark Kelly for Senate, February 12, 2019, https://www.youtube.com/watch?v=Ts9iXe0Te24 (accessed 9/8/21).

8. Alexander Burns, "Mark Kelly to Run for Senate in Arizona," *New York Times*, February 12, 2019, https://www.nytimes.com/2019/02/12/us/politics/mark-kelly-senate-mccain.html (accessed 11/25/19).

9. James Arkin, "Democrats Could Dodge Messy Arizona Primary after Gallego Passes on Senate Bid," Politico, March 25, 2019, https://www.politico.com/story/2019/03/25/arizona-primary-gallego-senate-bid-1292907 (accessed 11/25/19).

10. "Arizona Senate Election Results 2020," NBC News, February 10, 2021, https://www.nbcnews.com/politics/2020-elections/arizona-senate-results (accessed 9/8/21).

11. "Democratic National Committee," Ballotpedia, https://ballotpedia.org/Democratic_National_Committee (accessed 11/30/19).

12. "Republican National Committee—2015," Democracy in Action, http://www.p2016.org/parties/rnc15.html (accessed 11/30/19).

13. "Consultant Directory," Campaigns & Elections, https://www.campaignsandelections.com/politicalpages/categories/pollsters-analysis (accessed 11/30/19).

14. Robin Kolodny and Angela Logan, "Political Consultants and the Extension of Party Goals," *PS: Political Science & Politics* 31, no. 2 (1998): 155–59.

15. Daniel M. Butler and Eleanor Neff Powell, "Understanding the Party Brand: Experimental Evidence on the Role of Valence," *Journal of Politics* 76, no. 2 (2014): 492–505.

16. David Winston, "The Contract with America's Legacy," *Roll Call*, September 25, 2019, https://www.rollcall.com/news/opinion/contract-americas-legacy (accessed 11/30/19).

17. "GOP Tries to Frame Democrats as Socialists ahead of Elections," Associated Press, April 29, 2019, https://www.marketwatch.com/story/gop-tries-to-frame-democrats-as-socialists-ahead-of-elections-2019-04-29 (accessed 11/30/19).

18. Bob Bryan, "The Midterm Elections Cemented Obamacare's Legacy and Showed Democrats Can Actually Win on Healthcare," Business Insider, November 7, 2018, https://www.businessinsider.com/2018-midterm-election-results-obamacare-healthcare-big-winner-2018-11 (accessed 11/30/19).

19. Tim Reid, "'The Supreme Court Did Us a Favor': Democrats Seize on Abortion Ruling as Midterm Lifeline," Reuters, July 20, 2022, https://www.reuters.com/world/us/the-supreme-court-did-us-favor-democrats-seize-abortion-ruling-midterm-lifeline-2022-07-20/ (accessed 7/25/22).

20. Cherie D. Maestas, L. Sandy Maisel, and Walter J. Stone, "National Party Efforts to Recruit State Legislators to Run for the U.S. House," *Legislative Studies Quarterly* 30, no. 2 (2005): 277–300.

21. Hans J. G. Hassell, "Party Control of Party Primaries: Party Influence in Nominations for the U.S. Senate," *Journal of Politics* 78, no. 1 (2016): 75–87.

22. Ben Kesling, "Democrats Recruit Veterans as Candidates in Bid to Retake the House," *Wall Street Journal*, October 24, 2018, https://www.wsj.com/articles/democrats-seek-to-win-with-help-from-military-veteran-candidates-1540373406 (accessed 11/30/19).

23. Lynn Vavreck, "Unable to Excite the Base? Moderate Candidates Still Tend to Outdo Extreme Ones," *New York Times*, May 8, 2018, https://www.nytimes.com/2018/05/08/upshot/unable-to-excite-the-base-moderate-candidates-still-tend-to-outdo-extreme-ones.html (accessed 11/30/19).

24. Steve Peoples, "No Senate Run for Arizona Gov. Ducey, Blow to GOP Recruiting," AP News, March 3, 2022, https://apnews.com/article/2022-midterm-elections-arizona-doug-ducey-mitch-mcconnell-congress-2806c5b5d6dfcf9f658de0adf0657c26 (accessed 7/25/22).

25. Jason Lemon, "McConnell Says He Only Cares About Winning, Fine with Pro-Trump Republicans," *Newsweek*, April 1, 2022, https://www.newsweek.com/mcconnell-fine-pro-trump-republicans-1694145 (accessed 7/25/22).

26. Michael Scherer, Colby Itkowitz, and Josh Dawsey, "Candidate Challenges, Primary Scars Have GOP Worried about Senate Chances," *Washington Post*, July 10, 2022, https://www.washingtonpost.com /politics/2022/07/10/republicans-senate-midterms/ (accessed 7/25/22).

27. Data compiled by OpenSecrets. "Political Parties," OpenSecrets, November 14, 2022, https://www.opensecrets.org/parties/ (accessed 11/14/22).

28. Burgess Everett, "Top Dem Senate Super PAC Pulls Out of Colorado in Sign of Confidence," Politico, October 16, 2020, https://www .politico.com/news/2020/10/16/senate-majority-pac-colorado-429886 (accessed 9/8/21).

29. "Expenditures For and Against Candidates: Democratic Senatorial Campaign Committee," OpenSecrets, https://www.opensecrets.org /parties/indexp.php?cycle=2018&cmte=DSCC (accessed 12/2/19).

30. "Expenditures For and Against Candidates: National Republican Congressional Committee," OpenSecrets, https://www.opensecrets.org /parties/indexp.php?cycle=2018&cmte=NRCC (accessed 12/2/19).

31. Gary C. Jacobson and Jamie L. Carson, *The Politics of Congressional Elections*, 9th ed. (New York: Rowman and Littlefield, 2015).

29. IS THERE TOO MUCH MONEY IN ELECTIONS?

1. Sara Fischer, "White House Stumbles Explaining Soap Opera Producer as Ambassador," CNN, December 3, 2014, https://www.cnn.com/2014 /12/02/politics/soap-opera-producer-ambassador-to-hungary/ (accessed 6/15/19).

2. Tamara Keith, "When Big Money Leads to Diplomatic Posts," National Public Radio, December 3, 2014, https://www.npr.org/2014/12/03 /368143632/obama-appoints-too-many-big-donors-to-ambassadorships -critics-say (accessed 6/15/19).

3. "Obama Fundraiser Noah Mamet Appointed U.S. Envoy to Argentina," *Haaretz*, December 3, 2014, https://www.haaretz.com/world-news /1.629776#! (accessed 6/15/19).

4. Samantha Lachman, "Obama Nominee for Ambassador to Argentina Has Never Actually Been There," Huffington Post, February 7, 2014, https://www.huffingtonpost.com/2014/02/07/ambassador -argentina-nominee_n_4747108.html (accessed 6/15/19).

5. Emily R. Siegel, Andrew W. Lehren, Brandy Zadrozny, Dan De Luce, and Vanessa Swales, "Donors to the Trump Inaugural Committee Got Ambassador Nominations. But Are They Qualified?" NBC News, April 3, 2019, https://www.nbcnews.com/politics/donald-trump /donors-trump-inaugural-committee-got-ambassador-nominations -are-they-qualified-n990116 (accessed 6/15/19).

6. Rafael Bernal, "Ambassador Nominee: Bahamas a U.S. Protectorate for All Intents and Purposes," The Hill, August 2, 2017, https://thehill

.com/homenews/senate/345060-ambassador-nominee-bahamas
-a-us-protectorate-for-all-intents-and-purposes (accessed 6/15/19).

7. Tamba François Koundouno, "Trump Reappoints David Fischer as US Ambassador to Morocco," Morocco World News, January 26, 2019, https://www.moroccoworldnews.com/2019/01/264486/trump -david-fischer-us-ambassador-morocco/ (accessed 6/15/19).

8. Todd Neikirk, "14 Trump Ambassador Nominees Donated Large Sums to His Inaugural Fund," The Hill, April 7, 2018, https://hillreporter.com /14-trump-ambassador-nominees-donated-large-sums-to-his -inaugural-fund-30043 (accessed 6/15/19).

9. Isaac Arnsdorf, "Trump Rewards Big Donors with Jobs and Access," Politico, December 27, 2016, https://www.politico.com/story/2016/12 /donald-trump-donors-rewards-232974 (accessed 9/14/21).

10. Bradley Jones, "Most Americans Want to Limit Campaign Spending, Say Big Donors Have Greater Political Influence," Pew Research Center, May 8, 2018, https://www.pewresearch.org/fact-tank/2018/05/08/most -americans-want-to-limit-campaign-spending-say-big-donors-have -greater-political-influence/; Ipsos, "Americans Report a Bipartisan Desire for Transparent Political Financing Laws," February 18, 2019, https://www.ipsos.com/sites/default/files/ct/news/documents/2019-02 /press_release_2_18_19_0.pdf (accessed 10/15/21).

11. Aamer Madhani and Brian Slodysko, "Biden Taps Major Donors for Argentina and Switzerland Envoys," Associated Press, August 6, 2021, https://apnews.com/article/joe-biden-europe-switzerland-argentina -b42e0aa9e53be08862d9095e1b813488 (accessed 9/16/21).

12. Niall McCarthy, "How Much Does Money Matter in U.S. Presidential Elections?" Forbes, July 28, 2016, https://www.forbes.com/sites /niallmccarthy/2016/07/28/how-much-does-money-matter-in-u-s -presidential-elections-infographic/#3a79615a6a6a (accessed 6/16/19).

13. "Total Cost of Election, (1998–2020)," OpenSecrets, https://www .opensecrets.org/elections-overview/cost-of-election (accessed 10/15/21).

14. "Incumbent Advantage," OpenSecrets, https://www.opensecrets.org /elections-overview/incumbent-advantage (accessed 9/14/21).

15. Karl Evers-Hillstrom, "Most Expensive Ever: 2020 Election Cost $14.4 Billion," OpenSecrets, February 11, 2021, https://www.opensecrets.org /news/2021/02/2020-cycle-cost-14p4-billion-doubling-16/ (accessed 9/14/21).

16. "2020 Voter Registration Data," New Mexico Secretary of State, https://www .sos.state.nm.us/voting-and-elections/data-and-maps/voter-registration -statistics/2020-voter-registration-statistics/ (accessed 9/14/21).

17. Evers-Hillstrom, "Most Expensive Ever."

18. McCarthy, "How Much Does Money Matter in U.S. Presidential Elections?"

19. "Did Money Win?" OpenSecrets, https://www.opensecrets.org/elections
-overview/winning-vs-spending?cycle=2020; "2020 Presidential Race,"
OpenSecrets, https://www.opensecrets.org/2020-presidential-race
(accessed 9/14/21).

20. "Contribution Limits," Federal Election Commission, https://www.fec
.gov/help-candidates-and-committees/candidate-taking-receipts
/contribution-limits/ (accessed 9/14/21).

21. "Top Self-Funding Candidates," OpenSecrets, https://www.opensecrets
.org/elections-overview/top-self-funders (accessed 9/14/21).

22. "*SpeechNow.org v. FEC*," June 24, 2015, https://campaignlegal.org
/cases-actions/speechnoworg-v-fec (accessed 6/19/19).

23. *Citizens United v. Federal Election Commission*, 558 U.S. 310 (2010).

24. "Outside Spending," OpenSecrets, https://www.opensecrets.org
/outsidespending/fes_summ.php (accessed 9/14/21).

25. Josh Dunbar, "The 'Citizens United' Decision and Why It Matters," Center
for Public Integrity, October 18, 2012, https://publicintegrity.org/politics
/the-citizens-united-decision-and-why-it-matters/ (accessed 6/15/19).

26. Doyle McManus, "For the GOP, It's the Billionaires' Primary," *Los Angeles
Times*, April 21, 2015, https://www.latimes.com/opinion/op-ed/la-oe
-0422-mcmanus-politics-megadonors-koch-20150422-column.html
(accessed 6/15/19).

27. "Campaign Finance Laws and Policies," Virginia Department of Elections,
https://www.elections.virginia.gov/candidatepac-info/regulation-and
-policies/; "Campaign Finance," Florida Division of Elections, https://dos
.myflorida.com/elections/candidates-committees/campaign-finance/;
"Laws and Rules," Ohio Secretary of State, https://www.ohiosos.gov
/campaign-finance/laws-and-rules/; "Contribution Limits," Washington
Public Disclosure Admission, https://www.pdc.wa.gov/rules-enforcement
/guidelines-restrictions/contribution-limits (all accessed 10/15/21).

28. "State-by-State Comparison of Campaign Finance Requirements,"
Ballotpedia, https://ballotpedia.org/State-by-state_comparison_of
_campaign_finance_requirements (accessed 6/19/19).

29. "Campaign Finance Laws: An Overview," National Conference of State
Legislatures, July 17, 2015, http://www.ncsl.org/research/elections-and
-campaigns/campaign-finance-an-overview.aspx (accessed 6/19/19).

30. Philip Bump, "Bernie Sanders Keeps Saying His Average Donation Is
$27, But His Own Numbers Contradict That," *Washington Post*, April 18,
2016, https://www.washingtonpost.com/news/the-fix/wp/2016/04/18
/bernie-sanders-keeps-saying-his-average-donation-is-27-but-it-really
-isnt/ (accessed 6/15/19).

31. "Bernie Sanders," OpenSecrets, https://www.opensecrets.org/2020
-presidential-race/bernie-sanders/candidate?id=N00000528 (accessed
9/15/21).

32. "Donald Trump," OpenSecrets, https://www.opensecrets.org/2020 -presidential-race/donald-trump/candidate?id=N00023864 (accessed 9/15/21).

33. "What Does It Cost to Run for City Council (and Win)?" Campaign in a Box, January 28, 2018, https://www.campaigninabox.us/blog/2018/1/28 /what-does-it-cost-to-run-for-city-council-and-win (accessed 6/20/19).

34. "Election Overview," FollowTheMoney.org, https://www.followthemoney .org/tools/election-overview?s=MT&y=2020 (accessed 9/15/21).

35. "Charting the U.S. Top 50 Advertising Spenders," HowMuch.net, https:// howmuch.net/articles/worlds-top-50-biggest-advertising-spenders (accessed 9/15/21).

36. "Who Are the Biggest Donors?" OpenSecrets, https://www.opensecrets .org/elections-overview/biggest-donors (accessed 9/15/21).

37. "Top Industries," OpenSecrets, https://www.opensecrets.org/elections -overview/industries (accessed 9/15/21).

38. Joshua Kalla and David E. Broockman, "Campaign Contributions Facilitate Access to Congressional Officials: A Randomized Field Experiment," *American Journal of Political Science* 60, no. 3 (2016): 545–58.

39. Lynda W. Powell, *The Influence of Campaign Contributions in State Legislatures* (Ann Arbor: University of Michigan Press, 2012).

40. Aaron Smith and Maeve Duggan, "Presidential Campaign Donations in the Digital Age," Pew Research Center, October 25, 2012, https://www .pewinternet.org/2012/10/25/presidential-campaign-donations -in-the-digital-age/ (accessed 6/15/19).

41. "Donor Demographics," OpenSecrets, https://www.opensecrets.org /elections-overview/donor-demographics (accessed 9/15/20).

42. Jennifer L. Lawless and Richard L. Fox, *Women, Men & U.S. Politics: 10 Big Questions* (New York: Norton, 2017).

43. Donors include all contributors who gave more than $200 to a federal candidate, PAC, or party. "Donor Demographics," OpenSecrets.

44. Lawless and Fox, *Women, Men & U.S. Politics*.

30. WHAT IS THE ELECTORAL COLLEGE ANYWAY?

1. Patrick J. Kiger, "10 Countries besides the U.S. That Have Electoral Colleges," HowStuffWorks, February 1, 2019, https://people .howstuffworks.com/10-countries-besides-us-have-electoral-colleges .htm (accessed 6/29/19).

2. Bradley Jones, "Majority of Americans Continue to Favor Moving Away from Electoral College," Pew Research Center, January 27, 2021, https:// www.pewresearch.org/fact-tank/2021/01/27/majority-of-americans -continue-to-favor-moving-away-from-electoral-college/ (accessed 9/13/21).

3.   Allen Guelzo and James Hulme, "In Defense of the Electoral College," *Washington Post*, November 15, 2016, https://www.washingtonpost.com/posteverything/wp/2016/11/15/in-defense-of-the-electoral-college/ (accessed 7/3/19).

4.   James Madison, *The Federalist Papers*, No. 10, http://avalon.law.yale.edu/18th_century/fed10.asp (accessed 6/29/19).

5.   "2024 Presidential Election Interactive Map," 270towin.com (accessed 10/15/21).

6.   "Who Are Some of the Members of the Electoral College?" CBS News, December 15, 2016, https://www.cbsnews.com/news/who-are-some-of-the-members-of-the-electoral-college/ (accessed 7/1/19).

7.   Robert W. Bennett, *Taming the Electoral College* (Stanford, CA: Stanford University Press, 2006).

8.   "Exploring the Beliefs and Behaviors of American Voters," Democracy Fund, https://www.voterstudygroup.org/ (accessed 6/30/19).

9.   *Baker v. Carr*, 369 U.S. 186 (1962); *Reynolds v. Sims*, 377 U.S. 533 (1964).

10. Kim Parker, Juliana Menasce Horowitz, Anna Brown, Richard Fry, D'Vera Cohn, and Ruth Igielnik, "Demographic and Economic Trends in Urban, Suburban and Rural Communities," Pew Research Center, May 22, 2018, https://www.pewresearch.org/social-trends/2018/05/22/demographic-and-economic-trends-in-urban-suburban-and-rural-communities (accessed 11/21/19).

11. "Party Affiliation by State," Pew Research Center, https://www.pewforum.org/religious-landscape-study/compare/party-affiliation/by/state/ (accessed 9/13/21).

12. "Map of General-Election Campaign Events and TV Ad Spending by 2020 Presidential Candidates," National Popular Vote, https://www.nationalpopularvote.com/map-general-election-campaign-events-and-tv-ad-spending-2020-presidential-candidates (accessed 9/12/21).

13. "Map of General-Election Campaign Events and TV Ad Spending by 2020 Presidential Candidates," National Popular Vote.

14. Robert M. Hardaway, *The Electoral College and the Constitution: The Case for Preserving Federalism* (New York: Praeger, 1994).

15. Daniel McGraw, "What If We Did Have a Popular Vote for President?" The Bulwark, April 4, 2019, https://thebulwark.com/what-if-we-did-have-a-popular-vote-for-president/ (accessed 7/3/19).

16. "Presidential Results," CNN, https://www.cnn.com/election/2020/results/president (accessed 9/18/21).

17. Alison Durkee, "Supreme Court Kills Last Trump Election Lawsuit," *Forbes*, March 8, 2021, https://www.forbes.com/sites/alisondurkee/2021/03/08/supreme-court-kills-last-trump-election-lawsuit/ (accessed 9/18/21).

18. Andy Sullivan and Michael Martina, "In Recorded Call, Trump Pressures Georgia Official to 'Find' Votes to Overturn Election," Reuters, January 3, 2021, https://www.reuters.com/article/us-usa-election-trump/in-recorded-call-trump-pressures-georgia-official-to-find-votes-to-overturn-election-idUSKBN2980MG (accessed 9/18/21).

19. Brett Samuels, "Stephen Miller: 'Alternate' Electors Will Keep Trump Election Challenge Alive," The Hill, December 14, 2020, https://thehill.com/homenews/campaign/530092-stephen-miller-alternate-electors-will-keep-trump-challenge-alive-post (accessed 9/18/21).

20. "It's Official: The Election Was Secure," Brennan Center for Justice, December 11, 2020, https://www.brennancenter.org/our-work/research-reports/its-official-election-was-secure (accessed 9/19/21).

21. "Watch: Video Shows Capitol Mob Calling for the Death of the Vice President," *PBS Newshour*, February 10, 2021, https://www.pbs.org/newshour/politics/watch-video-shows-capitol-mob-calling-for-the-death-of-the-vice-president-plaskett-says (accessed 9/18/21).

22. "Counting of Electoral College Votes, Part 3," CSPAN, https://www.c-span.org/video/?507663-5/joint-session-congress-certifies-joe-biden-us-president (accessed 9/18/21).

31. HOW DO YOU RUN FOR PRESIDENT?

1. "I Am Not Going to Get into Politics: George Clooney," *Indian Express*, May 15, 2019, https://indianexpress.com/article/entertainment/hollywood/george-clooney-not-entering-politics-5729019/ (accessed 9/9/21).

2. Kate Hogan and Elizabeth Leonard, "George Clooney's Activism in Photos," *People*, December 2, 2020, https://people.com/movies/george-clooney-career-in-photos/ (accessed 9/9/21).

3. Judy Kurtz, "George Clooney: Just Put a F — — — Mask On," The Hill, December 16, 2020, https://thehill.com/blogs/in-the-know/in-the-know/530458-george-clooney-just-put-a-f-ing-mask-on; Andrea Mandell, "George Clooney Talks Trump, Twins, and Racial Politics in 'Suburbicon'," *USA Today*, September 10, 2017, https://www.usatoday.com/story/life/movies/2017/09/10/toronto-film-festival-george-clooney-talks-racial-politics-suburbicon/650946001 (accessed 4/22/22).

4. Nicole Weaver, "Oprah Winfrey and More Celebrities Who Might Run for President in 2020," Showbiz CheatSheet, March 1, 2019, https://www.cheatsheet.com/entertainment/celebrities-who-might-run-for-president-in-2020.html/ (accessed 7/13/19).

5. Cheyenne Haslett and Soo Rin Kim, "Which States Will Have Kanye West on the Ballot Now That Access Deadlines Have Passed?" ABC News, September 5, 2020, https://abcnews.go.com/Politics/states-kanye-west-ballot-now-access-deadlines-passed/story?id=72825469 (accessed 9/9/21).

6. Maane Khatchatourian, "George Clooney Voted Celebrity Best Fit to Be U.S. President," *Entertainment Weekly*, July 24, 2012, https://ew.com /article/2012/07/24/george-clooney-voted-celebrity-best-fit-president (accessed 7/13/19).

7. "George Clooney Testifies before Congress on Sudan," CBS News, March 14, 2012, https://www.cbsnews.com/news/george-clooney -testifies-before-congress-on-sudan/ (accessed 7/13/19).

8. Marty Cohen, David Karol, Hans Noel, and John Zaller, *The Party Decides: Presidential Nominations before and after Reform* (Chicago: University of Chicago Press, 2008).

9. John Sides and Lynn Vavreck, *The Gamble: Choice and Chance in the 2012 Presidential Election* (Princeton, NJ: Princeton University Press, 2013); Michael J. Goff, *The Money Primary: The New Politics of the Early Presidential Nomination Process* (New York: Rowman and Littlefield, 2004).

10. Bob Fredericks, "Clinton's Campaign Staff Is Five Times the Size of Trump's," *New York Post*, October 7, 2016, https://nypost.com/2016/10/07 /clintons-campaign-staff-is-five-times-the-size-of-trumps/ (accessed 7/13/19).

11. Wendy L. Patrick, "Voting with Our Eyes: Attractive Candidates Get More Votes," *Psychology Today*, July 3, 2016, https://www.psychologytoday .com/us/blog/why-bad-looks-good/201607/voting-our-eyes-attractive -candidates-get-more-votes (accessed 7/13/19).

12. "Barack Obama: Yes We Can," https://www.youtube.com/watch?v= Fe751kMBwms (accessed 9/18/19).

13. Daniella Diaz and Gregory Krieg, "Elizabeth Warren Took Selfies for 4 Hours after Her New York Rally. It's Part of Her Plan," CNN, September 17, 2019, https://www.cnn.com/2019/09/17/politics /elizabeth-warren-selfie-line-new-york-four-hours-plan/index.html (accessed 9/18/19).

14. Harry Stevens and Adrian Blanco, "Only Two Recent Major Party Nominees Have Lost Both Iowa and New Hampshire," *Washington Post*, February 13, 2020, https://www.washingtonpost.com/politics /2020/02/13/only-two-recent-major-party-nominees-have-lost-both -iowa-new-hampshire/ (accessed 9/9/21); "Race for the White House," Democracy in Action, https://www.p2016.org/chrniowa/iavisits15r.html (accessed 7/13/19); "Presidential Candidate Campaign Travel, 2020," Ballotpedia, https://ballotpedia.org/Presidential_candidate_campaign _travel,_2020 (accessed 9/9/21).

15. Stephen Battaglio, "President Trump's Acceptance Speech Draws 23.8 Million TV Viewers, Trailing the Audience for Biden," *Los Angeles Times*, August 28, 2020, https://www.latimes.com /entertainment-arts/business/story/2020-08-28/trump-acceptance -speech-21-6-million-viewers-republican-national-convention-biden (accessed 9/9/21).

16. Benjamin Mullin, "Democratic Convention Draws over 24.6 Million Viewers as Biden Accepts Nomination," *Wall Street Journal*, August 21, 2020, https://www.wsj.com/articles/democratic-convention-draws -more-than-21-million-tv-viewers-as-biden-accepts-nomination -11598035719 (accessed 9/9/21).

17. D. Sunshine Hillygus and Simon Jackman, "Voter Decision Making in Election 2000: Campaign Effects, Partisan Activation, and the Clinton Legacy," *American Journal of Political Science* 47, no. 4 (2003): 583–96.

18. Ezra Klein, "Hillary Clinton's 3 Debate Performances Left the Trump Campaign in Ruins," Vox, October 19, 2016, https://www.vox.com /policy-and-politics/2016/10/19/13340828/hillary-clinton-debate -trump-won (accessed 7/13/19).

19. "2024 Presidential Election Interactive Map," 270towin.com (accessed 10/15/21).

20. Donald P. Green and Alan S. Gerber, *Get Out the Vote: How to Increase Voter Turnout*, 4th ed. (Washington, DC: Brookings Institution Press, 2019).

21. Donald P. Green and Michael Schwam-Baird, "Mobilization, Participation, and American Democracy: A Retrospective and Postscript," *Party Politics* 22, no. 2 (2016): 158–64.

32. IF EVERYONE HATES CONGRESS, WHY DO SO MANY MEMBERS GET REELECTED?

1. These are the results of a NexisUni search conducted on July 26, 2022.

2. "Congress and the Public," Gallup, https://news.gallup.com/poll/1600 /congress-public.aspx (accessed 9/12/21).

3. Jennifer L. Lawless and Richard L. Fox, *Running from Office: Why Young Ameri-cans Are Turned Off to Politics* (New York: Oxford University Press, 2015).

4. Data are from a Public Policy Polling survey of 830 registered voters conducted from January 3 to January 6, 2013.

5. "Congress and the Public," Gallup, https://news.gallup.com/poll/1600 /congress-public.aspx; "Reelection Rates Over the Years," OpenSecrets, https://www.opensecrets.org/elections-overview/reelection-rates (accessed 10/15/21); "U.S. Congress Approval Rating," YouGov, November 5, 2022, https://today.yougov.com/topics/politics/trackers /us-congress-approval-rating (accessed 11/14/22).

6. The congressional reelection rate for 2023 assumes that, in the 13 races that remain uncalled as of November 14, 2022, the candidate who is in the lead will win the race. See "Path to 128: Tracking the Remaining House Races," *New York Times*, November 14, 2022, https://www .nytimes.com/interactive/2022/11/10/us/elections/results-house-seats -elections-congress.html?action=click&pgtype=Article&state=default &module=election-results&context=election_recirc&region=NavBar (accessed 11/14/22).

7. Scott J. Basinger, "Scandals and Congressional Elections in the Post-Watergate Era," *Political Research Quarterly* 66, no. 2 (2013): 385–98.

8. "Release: Congressional Management Foundation Names Khanna Best Office for Constituent Services of 435 House Offices," Office of Congressman Ro Khanna, May 30, 2019, https://khanna.house.gov /media/press-releases/release-congressional-management-foundation -names-khanna-best-office (accessed 8/18/19).

9. Sara Bondioli, "Here's What Your Member of Congress Can Actually Do for You," Huffington Post, October 6, 2015, https://www.huffpost .com/entry/ask-congress-for-help_n_56099706e4b0af3706dd57d9 (accessed 8/18/19).

10. "Life in Congress: The Member Perspective," Congressional Management Foundation, https://www.congressfoundation.org/projects/life-in -congress/the-member-perspective (accessed 8/18/19).

11. Roger H. Davidson, Walter J. Oleszek, and Frances E. Lee, *Congress and Its Members*, 13th ed. (Washington, DC: Congressional Quarterly Press, 2012), p. 131.

12. Mark Weiner, "How Effective Is U.S. Rep. Dan Maffei? Opponent John Katko Says He's a Dud," Syracuse.com, October 6, 2014, https://www .syracuse.com/news/2014/10/how_effective_is_us_rep_dan_maffei _opponent_john_katko_says_hes_a_dud.html (accessed 8/18/19).

13. "New York's 24th Congressional District," Ballotpedia, https://ballotpedia .org/New_York%27s_24th_Congressional_District (accessed 8/18/19).

14. "House Data from 1973–2020," Center for Effective Lawmaking, https://thelawmakers.org/data-download (accessed 9/12/21).

15. "Rep. Katko Named among Most Effective Lawmakers in Congress," Office of Congressman John Katko, March 4, 2019, https://katko.house .gov/media-center/press-releases/rep-katko-named-among-most -effective-lawmakers-congress (accessed 8/18/19); Robert Harding, "Rep. John Katko Rated One of the Most Effective Lawmakers in Congress," *The Citizen,* March 5, 2019, https://auburnpub.com/blogs /eye_on_ny/rep-john-katko-rated-one-of-most-effective-lawmakers-in /article_9cf00404-8d71-5649-891c-9364171ffc98.html (accessed 8/18/19); "Newsletters," Office of Congressman John Katko, https:// katko.house.gov/media-center/newsletters (accessed 8/18/19).

16. Sean McMinn, "House Members Send Mail on Taxpayer's Dime, Vulnerable Ones Do It Much More," *Atlanta Journal-Constitution*, August 12, 2016, https://www.ajc.com/news/house-members-send -mail-taxpayer-dime-vulnerable-ones-much-more/grryMApyngGhg Bsh6FnEFJ/ (accessed 8/19/19).

17. Danny Hayes and Jennifer L. Lawless, *Women on the Run: Gender, Media, and Political Campaigns in a Polarized Era* (New York: Cambridge University Press, 2016); Danny Hayes and Jennifer L. Lawless, "As Local News Goes, So Goes Citizen Engagement: Media, Knowledge, and

Participation in U.S. House Elections," *Journal of Politics* 77, no. 2 (2015): 447–62.

18. "Cathy McMorris Rodgers," OpenSecrets, https://www.opensecrets.org/members-of-congress/cathy-mcmorris-rodgers/summary?cid=N00026314&cycle=2020 (accessed 9/16/21).

19. "Political Parties," OpenSecrets, https:/opensecrets.org/politicalparties/ (accessed 10/24/22).

20. "Incumbent Advantage," OpenSecrets, https://www.opensecrets.org/elections-overview/incumbent-advantage (accessed 9/12/21).

21. Matthew Hay Brown, "Though He Says He Was Helped by His Father's Reputation, John Sarbanes Says He Wants to Forge His Own Political Path," *Baltimore Sun*, January 5, 2007, https://www.baltimoresun.com/news/bs-xpm-2007-01-05-0701050055-story.html (accessed 8/18/19).

22. "John Sarbanes," Ballotpedia, https://ballotpedia.org/John_Sarbanes (accessed 9/12/21).

23. "Redistricting Criteria," National Conference of State Legislatures, http://www.ncsl.org/research/redistricting/redistricting-criteria.aspx (accessed 8/18/19).

24. "U.S. House Election Results," *New York Times*, https://www.nytimes.com/interactive/2022/11/08/us/elections/results-house.html?action=click&pgtype=Article&state=default&module=election-results&context=election_recirc&region=NavBar (accessed 11/9/22).

25. See David Canon, *Actors, Athletes, and Astronauts: Political Amateurs in the United States Congress* (Chicago: University of Chicago Press, 1990) and Gary Jacobson, "Strategic Politicians and the Dynamics of U.S. House Elections, 1946–86," *American Political Science Review* 83, no. 3 (1989): 773–93.

26. Hayes and Lawless, *Women on the Run*.

27. Jacqueline Thomsen, "Supreme Court Finds That Courts Can't Rule on Partisan Gerrymandering Cases," The Hill, June 27, 2019, https://thehill.com/regulation/court-battles/450623-supreme-court-rules-that-courts-cant-rule-in-political-partisan (accessed 8/18/19).

33. ARE THIRD PARTIES DOOMED TO FAIL IN THE UNITED STATES?

1. "Partisan Composition of State Legislatures," Ballotpedia, https://ballotpedia.org/Partisan_composition_of_state_legislatures (accessed 9/8/21).

2. Jeffrey M. Jones, "Support for Third U.S. Political Party at High Point," Gallup, February 15, 2021, https://news.gallup.com/poll/329639/support-third-political-party-high-point.aspx (accessed 9/8/21).

3. "Massachusetts Registered Voter Enrollment: 1948–2021," Website of the Secretary of the Commonwealth of Massachusetts, https://www.sec.state.ma.us/ele/eleenr/enridx.htm (accessed 9/8/21).

4. "The Worst Ballot Access Laws in the United States," FairVote, January 13, 2015, https://www.fairvote.org/the-worst-ballot-access-laws-in-the-united-states (accessed 7/31/19).

5. "List of Political Parties in the United States," Ballotpedia, https://ballotpedia.org/List_of_political_parties_in_the_United_States (accessed 11/10/22).

6. Edward A. Hinick, ed., *Televised Presidential Debates in a Changing Media Environment* (Santa Barbara, CA: Praeger, 2018).

7. "The Commission on Presidential Debates: An Overview," The Commission on Presidential Debates, https://www.debates.org/about-cpd/overview/ (accessed 9/8/21).

8. Fawn Johnson, "Gary Johnson's Biggest Challenge Is Getting Noticed," *Morning Consult*, July 21, 2016, https://morningconsult.com/2016/07/21/gary-johnsons-biggest-challenge-getting-noticed (accessed 7/31/19).

9. Maurice Duverger, *Political Parties: Their Organization and Activity in the Modern State* (London: Science Editions Publishers, 1954).

10. William H. Riker, "The Two-Party System and Duverger's Law: An Essay on the History of Political Science," *American Political Science Review* 76, no. 4 (1982): 753–66; Bernard Grofman, André Blais, and Shaun Bowler, *Duverger's Law of Plurality Voting* (New York: Springer, 2009).

11. "The 1992 Elections: State by State," *New York Times*, November 5, 1992, https://www.nytimes.com/1992/11/05/us/the-1992-elections-state-by-state-northeast.html (accessed 8/7/19).

12. "No Red Scare Here: Americans Are Firmly Anti-Communist," Rasmussen Reports, November 9, 2017, http://www.rasmussenreports.com/public_content/politics/general_politics/november_2017/no_red_scare_here_americans_are_firmly_anti_communist (accessed 7/31/19).

13. Alec Tyson, "How Important Is Climate Change to Voters in the 2020 Election?" Pew Research Center, October 6, 2020, https://www.pewresearch.org/fact-tank/2020/10/06/how-important-is-climate-change-to-voters-in-the-2020-election/ (accessed 9/8/21).

14. Kevin Uhrmacher and Kevin Schaul, "Where Democrats Stand," *Washington Post*, April 8, 2020, https://www.washingtonpost.com/graphics/politics/policy-2020/climate-change/green-new-deal (accessed 9/8/21).

15. Benjy Sarlin, "Anti-Trump Forces Have Few Options for Third Party Alternative," MSNBC, March 4, 2016, http://www.msnbc.com/msnbc/anti-trump-forces-have-few-options-third-party-alternative (accessed 8/2/19).

16. Bill Scher, "Nader Elected Bush: Why We Shouldn't Forget," RealClearPolitics, May 31, 2016, https://www.realclearpolitics.com/articles/2016/05/31

/nader_elected_bush_why_we_shouldnt_forget_130715.html (accessed 8/2/19).

17. Eli Watkins, "How Gary Johnson and Jill Stein Helped Elect Donald Trump," CNN, November 25, 2016, https://www.cnn.com/2016/11/10 /politics/gary-johnson-jill-stein-spoiler/index.html (accessed 8/2/19).

18. Ian Schwartz, "Obama: If You Don't Vote, That's a Vote for Trump," RealClearPolitics, September 28, 2016, https://www.realclearpolitics .com/video/2016/09/28/obama_a_vote_for_a_third-party_candidate _is_a_vote_for_trump_if_you_dont_vote_thats_a_vote_for_trump.html (accessed 8/7/19).

34. HOW WELL DOES CONGRESS SERVE THE AMERICAN PEOPLE?

1. Jennifer E. Manning, "Membership of the 117th Congress: A Profile," Report No. R46705 Congressional Research Service, https://crsreports .congress.gov/product/pdf/R/R46705; For median net worth, see: Jennifer E. Manning, "Membership of the 116th Congress: A Profile," Report No. R45583 Congressional Research Service, https://sgp.fas .org/crs/misc/R45583.pdf (accessed 5/25/22).

2. Robert Weissberg, "Collective versus Dyadic Representation in Congress," *American Political Science Review* 72, no. 2 (1978): 535–47; Robert S. Erickson, Michael B. Mackuen, and James A. Stimson, *The Macro Polity* (New York: Cambridge University Press, 2002).

3. Erickson, Mackuen, and Stimson, *The Macro Polity*.

4. Kim Parker, Rich Morin, and Juliana Menasce Horowitz, "Retirement, Social Security, and Long-Term Care," Pew Research Center, March 21, 2019, https://www.pewresearch.org/social-trends/2019/03/21/retirement -social-security-and-long-term-care/ (accessed 10/9/21).

5. John Gramlich, "Few Americans Support Cuts to Most Government Programs, Including Medicaid," Pew Research Center, May 26, 2017, https://www.pewresearch.org/fact-tank/2017/05/26/few-americans -support-cuts-to-most-government-programs-including-medicaid/ (accessed 10/23/19).

6. "Will Medicare Run Out of Money?" Bipartisan Policy Center, March 16, 2021, https://bipartisanpolicy.org/event/will-medicare-run-out-of-money/ (accessed 10/9/21); Thomas Franck, "Social Security Trust Funds Now Expected to Run Out of Money Sooner than Expected due to Covid, Treasury Says," CNBC, August 31, 2021, https://www.cnbc.com/2021/08/31 /social-security-trust-funds-set-to-be-depleted-sooner-than-expected .html (accessed 10/9/21).

7. Eli Yokley, "Voters Are Nearly United in Support for Expanded Background Checks," Morning Consult, March 10, 2021, https:// morningconsult.com/2021/03/10/house-gun-legislation-background -checks-polling/ (accessed 10/10/21).

8. Data for Progress and Vox Survey, January 29–February 1, 2021. N = 1,124. Margin of error ± 2.9. https://www.filesforprogress.org/datasets /2021/2/dfp-vox-biden-immigration-agenda.pdf (accessed 10/9/21).

9. NPR/PBS NewsHour/Marist Poll, July 15–17, 2019. N = 1,346. Margin of error ± 3.5. https://pollingreport.com/budget.htm (accessed 10/10/2021).

10. "Daily Kos Elections' Statewide Election Results by Congressional and Legislative Districts," Daily Kos, March 23, 2021, https://www.dailykos .com/stories/2013/07/09/1220127/-Daily-Kos-Elections-2012-election -results-by-congressional-and-legislative-districts#NY (accessed 10/9/21).

11. "2021 Full Downloadable PVI State and District List," Cook Political Report, April 15, 2021, https://cookpolitical.com/analysis/national/pvi /2021-pvi-full-downloadable-state-and-district-list (accessed 10/9/21).

12. "2021 Fully Downloadable PVI State and District List," Cook Political Report.

13. "Congressional District Urban/Rural Characteristics," ProximityOne, http://proximityone.com/cd113_2010_ur.htm (accessed 10/9/21).

14. "Sponsors and Cosponsors," Congress.gov (accessed 10/9/21); and "Download the Data," Center for Effective Lawmaking, https:// thelawmakers.org/data-download (accessed 10/9/21).

15. Alexandra Villareal, "White Male Minority Rule Pervades Politics across the U.S., Research Shows," *The Guardian*, May 26, 2021, https://www .theguardian.com/us-news/2021/may/26/white-male-minority-rule-us -politics-research (accessed 10/9/21).

16. Hanna F. Pitkin, *The Concept of Representation* (Berkeley: University of California, 1967).

17. Karl Evers-Hillstrom, "Majority of Lawmakers in 116th Congress Are Millionaires," OpenSecrets, April 23, 2020, https://www.opensecrets .org/news/2020/04/majority-of-lawmakers-millionaires/ (accessed 10/9/21).

18. Center for American Women and Politics, "History of Women in the U.S. Congress," https://cawp.rutgers.edu/facts/levels-office/congress /history-women-us-congress (accessed 10/9/21).

19. Katherine Schaeffer, "Racial, Ethnic Diversity Increases Yet Again with the 117th Congress," Pew Research Center, January 28, 2021, https:// www.pewresearch.org/fact-tank/2021/01/28/racial-ethnic-diversity -increases-yet-again-with-the-117th-congress/ (accessed 10/9/21).

20. Richard L. Fox, "Congressional Elections: Women's Candidacies and the Road to Gender Parity," in *Gender and Elections*, 5th ed., ed. Susan J. Carroll and Richard L. Fox (New York: Cambridge University Press, 2021).

21. For evidence of gender-neutral outcomes in congressional primaries, see Jennifer L. Lawless and Kathryn Pearson, "The Primary Reason for

Women's Under-Representation: Re-Evaluating the Conventional Wisdom," *Journal of Politics* 70, no. 1 (2008): 67–82. For more on women and men's performance in general elections, see Barbara Burrell, *Gender in Campaigns for the U.S. House of Representatives* (Ann Arbor: University of Michigan Press, 2014).

22. Benjamin Highton, "White Voters and African American Candidates for Congress," *Political Behavior* 26, no. 1 (2004): 1–25; Tasha S. Philpot and Hanes Walton, "One of Our Own: Black Female Candidates and the Voters Who Support Them," *American Journal of Political Science* 51, no. 1 (2007): 49–62; Daniel J. Hopkins, "No More Wilder Effect, Never a Whitman Effect: When and Why Polls Mislead about Black and Female Candidates," *Journal of Politics* 71, no. 3 (2009): 769–81.

23. Jennifer L. Lawless and Richard L. Fox, *It Still Takes a Candidate: Why Women Don't Run for Office* (New York: Cambridge University Press, 2010).

24. Jennifer L. Lawless and Richard L. Fox, *Men Rule: The Continued Under-Representation of Women in U.S. Politics* (Washington, DC: Women & Politics Institute, 2012); Richard L. Fox and Jennifer L. Lawless, "Uncovering the Origins of the Gender Gap in Political Ambition," *American Political Science Review* 108, no. 3 (2014): 499–519; Jennifer L. Lawless and Richard L. Fox, "The Gender Gap in Political Ambition: Everything You Need to Know in 10 Charts," Center for Effective Lawmaking, University of Virginia, Working Paper, March 2022, https://thelawmakers .org/wp-content/uploads/2022/03/Gender-Gap-in-Political-Ambitions _Report_Final-Jen-Lawless-2022-3-1.pdf (accessed 8/9/22).

25. Claudine Gay, "The Effect of Black Congressional Representation on Participation," *American Political Science Review* 95, no. 3 (2001): 589–602; Claudine Gay, "Spirals of Trust? The Effect of Descriptive Representation on the Relationship between Citizens and Their Government," *American Journal of Political Science* 46, no. 4 (2002): 717–32; Sue Thomas, "Introduction: Women and Elective Office: Past, Present, and Future," in *Women and Elective Office*, 2nd ed., ed. Sue Thomas and Clyde Wilcox (New York: Oxford University Press, 2005).

26. Jane Mansbridge, "Should Blacks Represent Blacks and Women Represent Women? A Contingent 'Yes'," *Journal of Politics* 61, no. 3 (1999): 628–57.

27. Nancy Burns, Kay Lehman Schlozman, and Sidney Verba, *The Private Roots of Public Action: Gender, Equality, and Political Participation* (Cambridge, MA: Harvard University Press, 2001); Susan B. Hansen, "Talking about Politics: Gender and Contextual Effects on Political Proselytizing," *Journal of Politics* 59, no. 1 (1997): 73–103; David E. Campbell and Christina Wolbrecht, "See Jane Run: Women Politicians as Role Models for Adolescents," *Journal of Politics* 68, no. 2 (2006): 233–47; Christina Wolbrecht and David E. Campbell, "Role Models Revisited: Youth, Novelty, and the Impact of Female Candidates," *Politics, Groups, and Identities* 5, no. 3 (2017): 418–34.

28. Christian R. Grose, *Congress in Black and White: Race and Representation in Washington and at Home* (New York: Cambridge University Press, 2011); John D. Griffin, "When and Why Minority Legislators Matter," *Annual Review of Politics* 17 (2014): 327–336.

35. HOW DOESN'T A BILL BECOME A LAW?

1. Rob Stein, "Surgeon General Warns Youth Vaping Is Now an 'Epidemic,'" National Public Radio, December 18, 2018, https://www.npr.org/sections /health-shots/2018/12/18/677755266/surgeon-general-warns-youth -vaping-is-now-an-epidemic (accessed 1/30/20).

2. Rob Stein, "Teen Vaping Soared in 2018," National Public Radio, December 17, 2018, https://www.npr.org/sections/health-shots /2018/12/17/676494200/teen-vaping-soared-in-2018 (accessed 1/30/20).

3. Sally Hawkins, Knez Walker, Ashley Riegle, and Anthony Rivas, "Teen Who Was Put on Life Support Says, 'I Didn't Think of Myself as a Smoker,'" ABC News, September 11, 2019, https://abcnews.go.com /US/teen-put-life-support-vaping-didnt-smoker/story?id=65522370 (accessed 5/11/22).

4. David Jackson, "Trump Moves to Ban Flavored Vaping Products to Discourage Young People from e-Cigarettes," *USA Today*, September 11, 2019, https://www.usatoday.com/story/news/politics/2019/09/11 /donald-trump-wants-to-ban-flavored-vapes-discourage-young-people -from-e-cigarettes/2284270001/ (accessed 1/30/20).

5. Roxanne Roberts, "Vivek Murthy Wants to Fix Our Mental Health Crisis. But How Much Can He Do?" *Washington Post*, June 27, 2022, https:// www.washingtonpost.com/lifestyle/2022/06/27/vivek-murthy-surgeon -general/ (accessed 7/27/22).

6. Laura Bach, "States and Localities That Have Restricted the Sale of Flavored Tobacco Products," Campaign for Tobacco-Free Kids, April 19, 2022, https://www.tobaccofreekids.org/assets/factsheets/0398.pdf (accessed 5/27/22).

7. "Statistics and Historical Comparison," GovTrack.us, https://www .govtrack.us/congress/bills/statistics (accessed 10/4/21).

8. Barbara Sprunt, "READ: $2 Trillion Coronavirus Relief Bill," National Public Radio, March 25, 2020, https://www.npr.org/2020/03/25 /820759545/read-2-trillion-coronavirus-relief-bill (accessed 4/14/20).

9. Kelsey Snell, "The Infrastructure Bill Includes Upgrades to Roads, Bridges, and . . . Salmon Recovery?" National Public Radio, August 3, 2021, https://www.npr.org/2021/08/03/1024338460/the-infrastructure -bill-includes-upgrades-to-roads-bridges-and-salmon-recovery (accessed 10/4/21).

10. Danielle Kurtzleben, "Just Because a Bill Is Long Doesn't Mean It's Bad," National Public Radio, March 11, 2017, https://www.npr.org

/2017/03/11/519700465/when-it-comes-to-legislation-sometimes
-bigger-is-better (accessed 5/11/22).

11. Ella Nilsen, "House Democrats Have Passed Nearly 400 Bills. Trump and Republicans Are Ignoring Them," Vox, November 29, 2019, https://www
.vox.com/2019/11/29/20977735/how-many-bills-passed-house
-democrats-trump (accessed 1/30/20).

12. Mitch McConnell, May 8, 2019, https://twitter.com/senatemajldr
/status/1126154769641480193 (accessed 1/30/20).

13. Louis Jacobson, "Rep. Lynn Jenkins Blames Harry Reid for 'Do-Nothing Senate'," PolitiFact, August 6, 2014, https://www.politifact.com
/truth-o-meter/statements/2014/aug/06/lynn-jenkins/rep-lynn
-jenkins-blames-harry-reid-do-nothing-sena/ (accessed 1/31/20).

14. Karyn Moyer, "The U.S. Produces over 70% of the World's Mint," AgHires, December 22, 2017, https://blog.aghires.com/u-s-produces-70-worlds
-mint/ (accessed 1/31/20).

15. Jesse Rifkin, "Members Literally Don't Have Enough Time to Read Some Bills before a Vote Is Held. This Change Would Require They Do," GovTrack.us, March 29, 2018, https://govtrackinsider.com/members
-literally-dont-have-enough-time-to-read-some-bills-before-a-vote-is
-held-e8691c86c91d (accessed 5/11/22).

16. David M. Herszenhorn, "Senator's 15-Hour Filibuster Gains 'Path Forward' on Gun Control Measures," *New York Times*, June 16, 2016, https://www.nytimes.com/2016/06/17/us/politics/senate-filibuster
-gun-control.html (accessed 2/5/20).

17. Abby Ohlheiser, "Watch Ted Cruz Read Every Word of 'Green Eggs and Ham' on the Senate Floor," *The Atlantic*, September 24, 2013, https://
www.theatlantic.com/politics/archive/2013/09/watch-ted-cruz-read
-every-word-green-eggs-and-ham-senate-floor/310674/ (accessed
2/5/20).

18. "Cloture Motions," U.S. Senate, https://www.senate.gov/legislative
/cloture/clotureCounts.htm (accessed 10/4/21).

19. Alex Tausanovitch and Sam Berger, "The Impact of the Filibuster on Federal Policymaking," Center for American Progress, December 5, 2019, https://
www.americanprogress.org/issues/democracy/reports/2019/12/05/478199
/impact-filibuster-federal-policymaking/ (accessed 2/6/20).

20. "Vital Statistics on Congress," Brookings Institution, February 2021, https://www.brookings.edu/multi-chapter-report/vital-statistics-on
-congress/ (accessed 10/4/21).

21. Josh M. Ryan, "The Disappearing Conference Committee: The Use of Procedures by Minority Coalitions to Prevent Conferencing," *Congress & the Presidency* 38, no. 1 (2011): 101–25.

22. "Presidential Vetoes," U.S. House of Representatives, January 21, 2021, https://history.house.gov/Institution/Presidential-Vetoes/Presidential
-Vetoes/ (accessed 10/4/21).

23. Barbara Sinclair, *Unorthodox Lawmaking: New Legislative Processes in the U.S. Congress*, 5th ed. (Washington, DC: CQ Press, 2016).

36. WHAT DOES THE PRESIDENT DO ALL DAY?

1. "President Bush Delivers Farewell Address to the Nation," The White House, January 15, 2009, https://georgewbush-whitehouse.archives .gov/news/releases/2009/01/20090115-17.html (accessed 12/13/19).

2. Alan Connor, "No Time to Think?" BBC News Magazine, July 29, 2008, http://news.bbc.co.uk/2/hi/uk_news/magazine/7530594.stm (accessed 12/13/19).

3. Dan Berman, "Trump: 'I Thought It Would be Easier,'" CNN, April 28, 2017, https://www.cnn.com/2017/04/28/politics/donald-trump-president -easier/index.html (accessed 12/13/19).

4. "Biden Cracks Joke When Asked about What It's Like in White House Now," CNN, https://www.youtube.com/watch?v=m3MrXiwnqo8 (accessed 10/6/21).

5. "Trump's Daily Schedule v Obama and Bush," BBC News, January 9, 2018, https://www.bbc.com/news/world-us-canada-42610275 (accessed 11/15/19); Sean Neumann, "What Joe Biden's Daily Work Routine Looks Like 1 Month In," *People*, February 26, 2021, https:// people.com/politics/what-joe-bidens-daily-work-routine-has-looked -like-one-month-in-a-normal-white-house/ (accessed 10/6/21).

6. "Military Size by Country, 2022," World Population Review, https:// worldpopulationreview.com/country-rankings/military-size-by-country (accessed 3/24/22).

7. Carol D. Leonnig, Shane Harris, and Greg Jaffe, "Breaking with Tradition, Trump Skips President's Written Intelligence Report and Relies on Oral Briefings," *Washington Post*, February 9, 2018, https://www .washingtonpost.com/politics/breaking-with-tradition-trump-skips -presidents-written-intelligence-report-for-oral-briefings/2018/02/09 /b7ba569e-0c52-11e8-95a5-c396801049ef_story.html (accessed 11/15/19).

8. Kat Kinsman, "All the Presidents Ranked in Order of How Much They Loved Breakfast," Extra Crispy, February 13, 2018, https://www.myrecipes.com /extracrispy/all-the-presidents-ranked-in-order-of-how-much-they-loved -breakfast; Emily Heil and Tom Sietsema, "Diner-in-Chief: How the Bidens Might Entertain In and Out of the White House," *Washington Post*, October 20, 2020, https://www.washingtonpost.com/food/2020/10/20/diner-in -chief-how-bidens-would-dine-entertain-white-house/ (accessed 10/6/21).

9. Brandice Canes-Wrone and Scott de Marchi, "Presidential Approval and Legislative Success," *Journal of Politics* 64, no. 2 (2002): 491–509.

10. James E. Campbell and Joe A. Sumners, "Presidential Coattails in Senate Elections," *American Political Science Review* 84, no. 2 (1990): 513–24.

11. Samuel Kernell, *Going Public*, 4th ed. (Washington, DC: CQ Press, 2010).

12. Aren Yourish and Jasmine C. Lee, "The Demise of the White House Press Briefing under Trump," *New York Times*, January 28, 2019, https://www.nytimes.com/interactive/2019/11/02/us/politics/trump-twitter-presidency.html (accessed 11/15/19).

13. Timothy Macafee, Bryan McLaughlin, and Nathan Shae Rodriguez, "Winning on Social Media: Candidate Social-Mediated Communication and Voting during the 2016 US Presidential Election," *Social Media + Society*, 5, no. 1 (2019); Chris Wells, Dhavan V. Shah, Jon C. Pevehouse, JungHwan Yang, Ayellet Pelled, Frederick Boehm, Josephine Lukito, Shreenita Ghosh, and Jessica L. Schmidt, "How Trump Drove Coverage to the Nomination: Hybrid Media Campaigning," *Political Communication* 33, no. 4 (2016): 669–76.

14. Michael D. Shear, Maggie Haberman, Nicholas Confessore, Karen Yourish, Larry Buchanan, and Keith Collins, "How Trump Reshaped the Presidency in over 11,000 Tweets," *New York Times*, November 2, 2019, https://www.nytimes.com/interactive/2019/11/02/us/politics/trump-twitter-presidency.html (accessed 11/15/19).

15. Jenni Fink, "Biden Tweets Less but Gains More Followers than Trump in First 100 Days," *Newsweek*, April 29, 2021, https://www.newsweek.com/biden-tweets-less-gains-more-followers-trump-first-100-days-1587302 (accessed 7/28/22).

16. Martha Joynt Kumar, *Managing the President's Message* (Baltimore, MD: Johns Hopkins University Press, 2007).

17. Tom McCarthy, "Consoler-in-Chief? Lacking Empathy, Trump Weighs the Economic Costs, Not the Human Ones," *The Guardian*, April 22, 2020, https://www.theguardian.com/us-news/2020/apr/22/trump-consoler-in-chief-coronavirus-crisis (accessed 5/27/22).

18. Jim Tankersley, "Biden Tours Hurricane Ida Damage in New Orleans," *New York Times*, September 10, 2021, https://www.nytimes.com/2021/09/03/us/politics/biden-louisiana-hurricane-ida.html (accessed 10/6/21).

19. Michael Lewis-Beck and Charles Tien, "The Political Economy Model: 2016 U.S. Election Forecasts," *PS: Political Science & Politics* 49, no. 4 (2016): 661–63.

20. Neil Irwin, "Presidents Have Less Power over the Economy Than You Might Think," *New York Times*, January 17, 2017, https://www.nytimes.com/2017/01/17/upshot/presidents-have-less-power-over-the-economy-than-you-might-think.html (accessed 11/17/19).

21. William G. Howell, Saul P. Jackman, and Jon C. Rogowski, *Executive Influence and the Nationalizing Politics of Threat* (Chicago: University of Chicago Press, 2013); Andrew Rudalevige, *Managing the President's Program* (Princeton, NJ: Princeton University Press, 2002).

22. Jeff Zeleny, "Obama Woos G.O.P. with Attention, and Cookies," *New York Times*, February 4, 2009, https://www.nytimes.com/2009/02/05/us/politics/04web-zeleny.html (accessed 11/17/19).

23. Anna Palmer and John Bresnahan, "Air Force One Charm Offensive Takes Off," Politico, February 9, 2015, https://www.politico.com/story /2015/02/barack-obama-air-force-one-charm-offensive-115004 (accessed 11/17/19).

24. "Executive Order 7034: Creating Machinery for the Works Progress Administration," The American Presidency Project, https://www .presidency.ucsb.edu/documents/executive-order-7034-creating -machinery-for-the-works-progress-administration (accessed 11/17/19).

25. "Executive Orders," Federal Register, https://www.federalregister.gov /presidential-documents/executive-orders (accessed 10/5/21).

26. "Executive Order 10730: Desegregation of Central High School (1957)," National Archives, https://www.ourdocuments.gov/doc.php?flash=false &doc=89 (accessed 11/17/19); "Executive Order 10924: Establishment and Administration of the Peace Corps in the Department of State," The American Presidency Project, https://www.presidency.ucsb.edu /documents/executive-order-10924-establishment-and-administration -the-peace-corps-the-department (accessed 11/17/19); David E. Sanger with Sam Howe Verhovek, "Clinton Proposes Wider Protection for U.S. Forests," New York Times, October 14, 1999, https://www.nytimes .com/1999/10/14/us/clinton-proposes-wider-protection-for-us-forests .html (accessed 11/17/19); "Executive Order 13435: Expanding Approved Stem Cell Lines in Ethically Responsible Ways," The American Presidency Project, https://www.presidency.ucsb.edu/documents/executive -order-13435-expanding-approved-stem-cell-lines-ethically-responsible -ways (accessed 11/17/19).

27. Kenneth R. Mayer, "Executive Orders and Presidential Power," Journal of Politics 61, no. 2 (1999): 445–66; Jeffrey A. Fine and Adam L. Warber, "Circumventing Adversity: Executive Orders and Divided Government," Presidential Studies Quarterly 42, no. 2 (2012): 256–74.

28. "The Mexico City Policy: An Explainer," Kaiser Family Foundation, January 28, 2021, https://www.kff.org/global-health-policy/fact-sheet /mexico-city-policy-explainer/ (accessed 10/6/21).

29. John Haltiwanger, "How Trump's Daily White House Schedule Full of 'Executive Time' Compares with the Schedules of Obama, Bush, and Clinton," Business Insider, February 4, 2019, https://www.businessinsider .com/trumps-executive-time-compared-to-obama-bush-clinton-daily -schedules-2019-2 (accessed 11/15/19); Michael D. Shear, "Obama after Dark: The Precious Hours Alone," New York Times, July 2, 2016, https:// www.nytimes.com/2016/07/03/us/politics/obama-after-dark-the -precious-hours-alone.html (accessed 11/15/19); Sarah Friedmann, "Photos of Trump and His Grandchildren Show Them Tagging Along at Presidential Events," Bustle, October 13, 2018, https://www.bustle.com/p /photos-of-trump-his-grandchildren-show-them-tagging-along-at -presidential-events-11965985 (accessed 11/15/19). Kevin Liptak, "Inside the New President's Routine: Oval Office Fires and Early Bedtimes,"

CNN, February 16, 2021, https://www.cnn.com/2021/02/15/politics /joe-biden-presidential-routine/index.html (accessed 10/6/21).

30. "Travels Abroad of the President," Office of the Historian, https:// history.state.gov/departmenthistory/travels/president/obama-barack (accessed 11/15/19).

31. Alan Taylor, "Photos from State Dinners Past," *The Atlantic*, April 22, 2018, https://www.theatlantic.com/photo/2018/04/photos-from-state -dinners-past/558578/; Hilary Weaver, "The Obamas Have Outdone Themselves with Star-Studded Parties," *Vanity Fair*, January 13, 2017, https://www.vanityfair.com/style/2017/01/obama-white-house-parties -over-the-years (accessed 3/24/22).

32. "Trump Hosts Second State Dinner," CNN, September 20, 2019, https:// www.cnn.com/2019/09/20/politics/gallery/trump-state-dinner /index.html (accessed 11/17/19).

33. Katie Dangerfield, "Donald Trump Sleeps 4–5 Hours Each Night; He's Not the Only Famous 'Short Sleeper'," Global News, January 17, 2018, https://globalnews.ca/news/3970379/donald-trump-sleep-hours-night/ (accessed 11/17/19).

37. ARE FACELESS BUREAUCRATS OUT TO GET YOU?

1. "New Testing Method for Lead and Arsenic in Contaminated Soil Saves Money and Protects Public Health," U.S. Environmental Protection Agency, https://www.epa.gov/sciencematters/new-testing-method -lead-and-arsenic-contaminated-soil-saves-money-and-protects-public (accessed 10/31/19).

2. Irvin Molotsky, "Agency Approves Painkiller for Over-the-Counter Sales," *New York Times*, May 19, 1984, https://www.nytimes.com/1984/05/19/us /agency-approves-painkiller-for-over-the-counter-sales.html (accessed 10/31/19).

3. "Recall List," U.S. Consumer Product Safety Commission, https://www .cpsc.gov/Recalls (accessed 10/31/19).

4. "Wool Products Labeling Act," Federal Trade Commission, https://www .ftc.gov/node/119457 (accessed 10/31/19).

5. "Road Safety," U.S. Department of Transportation, https://www.nhtsa .gov/road-safety (accessed 10/31/19).

6. "USDA Organic," U.S. Department of Agriculture, https://www.usda.gov /topics/organic (accessed 10/31/19).

7. "The National Weather Service (NWS)," National Oceanic and Atmospheric Administration, https://www.weather.gov/about/ (accessed 10/31/19).

8. Peter Jackson, "Check the Screen for ATM Fees," Consumer Financial Protection Bureau, March 21, 2013, https://www.consumerfinance.gov /about-us/blog/check-the-screen-for-atm-fees/ (accessed 10/31/19).

9. "Protecting Students with Disabilities," U.S. Department of Education, https://www2.ed.gov/about/offices/list/ocr/504faq.html (accessed 10/31/19).

10. "Occupational Safety and Health Administration: Asbestos," U.S. Department of Labor, https://www.osha.gov/SLTC/asbestos/; "Protecting Workers: Guidance on Mitigating and Preventing the Spread of COVID-19 in the Workplace," U.S. Department of Labor, https://www.osha.gov/coronavirus/safework (accessed 10/4/21).

11. Julie Jennings and Jared C. Nagel, "Federal Workforce Statistics Sources: OPM and OMB," Congressional Research Service, June 24, 2021, https://sgp.fas.org/crs/misc/R43590.pdf (accessed 10/4/21).

12. "A-Z Index of U.S. Government Departments and Agencies," USA.gov, https://www.usa.gov/federal-agencies (accessed 3/24/22).

13. "FY 2021 Budget Request at a Glance," U.S. Department of Justice, August 20, 2021, https://www.justice.gov/doj/page/file/1246841/download (accessed 10/4/21).

14. "A–Z Index of U.S. Government Departments and Agencies," USA.gov, https://www.usa.gov/federal-agencies/ (accessed 11/1/19).

15. Sean M. Theriault, "Patronage, the Pendleton Act, and the Power of the People," *Journal of Politics* 65, no. 1 (2005): 50–68.

16. "The Hatch Act: Political Activity and the Federal Employee," U.S. Food and Drug Administration, https://www.fda.gov/about-fda/ethics/hatch-act-political-activity-and-federal-employee (accessed 11/7/19).

17. Mike Maciag, "Federal Employees by State," Governing, October 3, 2013, https://www.governing.com/gov-data/federal-employees-workforce-numbers-by-state.html (accessed 11/8/19).

18. Sean Illing, "The Most Powerful Person in the White House Not Named Donald Trump," Vox, June 13, 2020, https://www.vox.com/policy-and-politics/2020/6/13/21265067/jared-kushner-trump-white-house-andrea-bernstein (accessed 10/7/21).

19. B. Dan Wood and Richard Waterman, "The Dynamics of Political Control of the Bureaucracy," *American Political Science Review* 85, no. 3 (1991): 801–28.

20. Eric Pianin, "Tale of the Red Tape: $22 Billion in Savings from Cutting Ridiculous Regulations," The Fiscal Times, August 19, 2015, http://www.thefiscaltimes.com/2015/08/19/Tale-Red-Tape-22-Billion-Savings-Cutting-Ridiculous-Regulations (accessed 11/8/19).

21. Zachary Brennan, "New FDA Generic Drug Reports Tabulate Approval Times," Regulatory Focus, March 14, 2018, https://www.raps.org/news-and-articles/news-articles/2018/3/new-fda-generic-drug-reports-tabulate-approval-tim (accessed 11/8/19).

22. Pianin, "Tale of the Red Tape."

23. Nona Agrawal, "There's More than the CIA and FBI: The 17 Agencies that Make Up the U.S. Intelligence Community," *Los Angeles Times*, January

17, 2017, https://www.latimes.com/nation/la-na-17-intelligence-agencies-20170112-story.html (accessed 11/7/19).

24. "Government Agencies," Center for Poverty & Inequality Research, https://poverty.ucdavis.edu/government-agencies (accessed 11/7/19).

25. *West Virginia v. Environmental Protection Agency*, 597 U.S. ___ (2022).

38. DOES IT MATTER WHO RUNS THE ENVIRONMENTAL PROTECTION AGENCY?

1. Guy Lasnier, "EPA Administrator Speaks of Commitment to Environmental Justice," UC Santa Cruz NewsCenter, June 13, 2011, https://news.ucsc.edu/2011/06/jackson-commencement.html (accessed 4/5/20).

2. Darren Samuelsohn and Erica Martinson, "Jackson's EPA Tenure Parsed," Politico, December 27, 2012, https://www.politico.com/story/2012/12/epa-administrator-lisa-jackson-resigns-085530 (accessed 4/5/20).

3. John M. Broder, "EPA Chief Set to Leave; Term Fell Shy of Early Hope," *New York Times*, December 27, 2012, https://www.nytimes.com/2012/12/28/science/earth/lisa-p-jackson-of-epa-to-step-down.html (accessed 4/5/20).

4. Dominique Mosbergen, "Scott Pruitt Has Sued the Environmental Protection Agency 13 Times. Now He Wants to Lead It," Huffington Post, January 17, 2017, https://www.huffpost.com/entry/scott-pruitt-environmental-protection-agency_n_5878ad15e4b0b3c7a7b0c29c (accessed 4/5/20).

5. Oliver Milman, "Scott Pruitt's EPA: A Dream for Oil and Gas Firms Is Nightmare for Environment," *The Guardian*, December 8, 2016, https://www.theguardian.com/us-news/2016/dec/08/scott-pruitt-trump-administration-epa-oil-gas-environment (accessed 4/5/20).

6. Brendan McDermid, "Trump to Nominate Pruitt to Lead EPA: Statement," Reuters, December 8, 2016, https://www.reuters.com/article/us-usa-trump-epa-idUSKBN13X15S (accessed 4/5/20).

7. Coral Davenport, Lisa Friedman, and Maggie Haberman, "EPA Chief Scott Pruitt Resigns under a Cloud of Ethics Scandals," *New York Times*, July 5, 2018, https://www.nytimes.com/2018/07/05/climate/scott-pruitt-epa-trump.html (accessed 4/5/20).

8. Scott Pruitt and Luther Strange, "The Climate-Change Gang," *National Review*, May 17, 2016, https://www.nationalreview.com/2016/05/climate-change-attorneys-general/ (accessed 4/5/20).

9. Lily Rothman, "Here's Why the Environmental Protection Agency Was Created," *Time*, March 22, 2017, https://time.com/4696104/environmental-protection-agency-1970-history/ (accessed 4/5/20).

10. "January 22, 1970: State of the Union Address," Miller Center, https://millercenter.org/the-presidency/presidential-speeches/january-22-1970-state-union-address (accessed 4/13/20).

11. Terry M. Moe, "The Politics of Bureaucratic Structure," in *Can the Government Govern?*, ed. John E. Chubb and Paul E. Peterson (Washington, DC: Brookings Institution, 1989), pp. 267–329; "The Origins of EPA," U.S. Environmental Protection Agency, https://www.epa.gov/history/origins-epa (accessed 4/5/20).

12. "The Origins of EPA."

13. Joshua D. Clinton, David E. Lewis, and Jennifer L. Selin, "Influencing the Bureaucracy: The Irony of Congressional Oversight," *American Journal of Political Science* 58, no. 2 (2014): 387–40; Linda L. Fowler, *Watchdogs on the Hill: The Decline of Congressional Oversight of U.S. Foreign Relations* (Princeton, NJ: Princeton University Press, 2015); Joel D. Aberbach, *Keeping a Watchful Eye* (Washington, DC: Brookings Institution, 1990); Matthew D. McCubbins and Thomas Schwartz, "Congressional Oversight Overlooked: Police Patrol versus Fire Alarm," *American Journal of Political Science* 28, no. 1 (1984): 165–77.

14. E. Scott Adler, *Why Congressional Reforms Fail: Reelection and the House Committee System* (Chicago: University of Chicago Press, 2002); Jeffrey S. Banks and Barry R. Weingast, "The Political Control of Bureaucracies under Asymmetric Information," *American Journal of Political Science* 36, no. 2 (1992): 509–24; Morris P. Fiorina, *Congress: Keystone of the Washington Establishment* (New Haven, CT: Yale University Press, 1977).

15. "EPA's Budget and Spending," U.S. Environmental Protection Agency, https://www.epa.gov/planandbudget/budget (accessed 10/8/21).

16. "Laws and Executive Orders," U.S. Environmental Protection Agency, https://www.epa.gov/laws-regulations/laws-and-executive-orders (accessed 10/8/21).

17. 15 U.S.C. § 2601 et seq. (1976).

18. Stephen Leahy, "Exxon Valdez Changed the Oil Industry Forever — But New Threats Emerge," *National Geographic*, March 22, 2019, https://www.nationalgeographic.com/environment/2019/03/oil-spills-30-years-after-exxon-valdez/ (accessed 4/11/20).

19. 33 U.S.C. § 2701 et seq. (1990).

20. David E. Lewis, *The Politics of Presidential Appointments: Political Control and Bureaucratic Performance* (Princeton, NJ: Princeton University Press, 2008).

21. "Cabinet Nominations Rejected, Withdrawn, or No Action Taken," U.S. Senate, https://www.senate.gov/legislative/Nominations RejectedorWithdrawn.htm (accessed 10/8/21).

22. Nandita Bose and Jeff Mason, "Biden Withdraws Tanden's Nomination to Be White House Budget Chief," Reuters, March 2, 2021, https://www.reuters.com/article/us-usa-biden-omb/biden-withdraws-tandens-nomination-to-be-white-house-budget-chief-idUSKCN2AU2TL (accessed 10/8/21).

23. Robert J. McGrath, "Congressional Oversight Hearings and Policy Control," *Legislative Studies Quarterly* 38, no. 3 (2013): 349–76.

24. Elizabeth Chuck, "Lawmakers Call for EPA Chief Gina McCarthy, Michigan Governor to Resign over Flint," NBC News, March 17, 2016, https://www.nbcnews.com/storyline/flint-water-crisis/representatives -call-epa-chief-gina-mccarthy-michigan-governor-resign-over-n540806 (accessed 4/11/20).

25. Robbie Gramer and Jack Detsch, "Pandemic Stymies Congressional Check on Trump's Foreign Policy," FP Foreign Policy, April 8, 2020, https://foreignpolicy.com/2020/04/08/pandemic-coronavirus-stymies -congressional-check-oversight-trump-foreign-policy-afghanistan -iran-iraq-classified-briefings/ (accessed 4/11/20).

26. Michael Laris, "Trump Administration Proposes Billions in Transporta- tion Cuts — and New Spending," *Washington Post*, February 10, 2020, https://www.washingtonpost.com/local/trafficandcommuting /trump-administration-proposes-billions-in-transportation-cuts — and -new-spending/2020/02/10/85153096-4c5c-11ea-b721-9f4cdc90bc1c _story.html (accesed 4/11/20); Lisette Voytko, "Health Secretary Asks for Emergency Coronavirus Funding while Trump Calls for 16% Cut to CDC Budget," *Forbes*, February 26, 2020, https://www.forbes.com/sites /lisettevoytko/2020/02/26/health-secretary-asks-for-emergency -coronavirus-funding-while-trump-calls-for-16-cut-to-cdc-budget/ (accessed 4/11/20).

27. John M. Broder, "EPA Head Lisa Jackson to Step Down," *Boston Globe*, December 28, 2012, https://www.bostonglobe.com/news /nation/2012/12/28/epa-head-lisa-jackson-step-down/j5QiH2qu ADLMWu1GsWM5zK/story.html (accessed 4/11/20).

28. Jeremy Diamond, Eli Watkins, and Juana Summers, "EPA Chief Scott Pruitt Resigns amid Scandals, Citing 'Unrelenting Attacks'," CNN, July 5, 2018, https://www.cnn.com/2018/07/05/politics/scott-pruitt -epa-resigns/index.html (accessed 4/11/20).

29. Matthew McCubbins, Roger Noll, and Barry Weingast, "Administrative Procedures as Instruments of Political Control," *Journal of Law, Economics, and Organization* 3:2 (1987): 243–77.

30. "Secretary of Education Betsy DeVos Announces New Initiative to Support Opening and Expanding Charter Schools in Opportunity Zones," U.S. Department of Education, October 10, 2019, https://www.ed.gov /news/press-releases/secretary-education-betsy-devos-announces -new-initiative-support-opening-and-expanding-charter-schools -opportunity-zones (accessed 4/13/20).

31. Omar Erez, "Secretary of Education Dr. Miguel Cardona Stands Out from His Predecessor," *Boston Political Review*, May 6, 2021, https://www .bostonpoliticalreview.org/post/secretary-of-education-dr-miguel -cardona-stands-out-from-his-predecessor (accessed 10/8/21).

32. 42 U.S.C. § 7401 et seq. (1970).

33. Adam Liptak, "Supreme Court Limits E.P.A.'s Ability to Restrict Power Plant Emissions," *New York Times*, July 1, 2022, https://www.nytimes.com/live/2022/06/30/us/supreme-court-epa (accessed 7/29/22).

34. Dave Jamieson, "Labor Secretary Says New Overtime Rule Will Help Millions 'Get Back into the Middle Class'," Huffington Post, July 3, 2015, https://www.huffpost.com/entry/tom-perez-overtime_n_7721398 (accessed 4/5/20).

35. Jeff Stein, "Trump Administration Releases New Rules on Overtime Pay," *Washington Post*, March 7, 2019, https://www.washingtonpost.com/us-policy/2019/03/08/trump-administration-releases-new-overtime-rules/ (accessed 4/5/20).

36. "Civil Cases and Settlements," U.S. Environmental Protection Agency, https://cfpub.epa.gov/enforcement/cases/ (accessed 3/24/22).

39. HOW DOES A CASE GET TO THE SUPREME COURT?

1. S. M., "Why the Supreme Court Is Slowing Down," *The Economist*, May 9, 2016, https://www.economist.com/blogs/democracyinamerica/2016/05/fit-be-tied (accessed 10/3/21).

2. Theodore Roosevelt, *Presidential Addresses and State Papers: April 14, 1906 to January 14, 1907* (Whitefish, MT: Literary Licensing, LLC, 2014), p. 763.

3. Jesse Byrnes, "Trump: Republicans 'Have No Choice' but to Vote for Me," The Hill, July 28, 2016, http://thehill.com/blogs/blog-briefing-room/news/289716-trump-republicans-have-to-vote-for-me-because-of-supreme-court (accessed 10/3/21).

4. Lee J. Epstein, Jeffrey A. Segal, Harold J. Spaeth, and Thomas G. Walker, *The Supreme Court Compendium: Data, Decisions, and Developments*, 6th ed. (Thousand Oaks, CA: CQ Press, 2015).

5. Brigid Schulte, "Former UPS Driver at Center of Pregnancy Discrimination Case before the Supreme Court," *Washington Post*, November 30, 2014, https://www.washingtonpost.com/local/former-ups-driver-at-center-of-pregnancy-discrimination-case-before-supreme-court/2014/11/30/5a08c048-7787-11e4-bd1b-03009bd3e984_story.html (accessed 10/3/21).

6. Joseph U. Leonoro, "U.S. Supreme Court Tackles Pregnancy Discrimination in the Workplace," *National Law Review*, April 2, 2015, https://www.natlawreview.com/article/us-supreme-court-tackles-pregnancy-discrimination-workplace (accessed 10/3/21).

7. "State Court Caseload Statistics," Court Statistics Project, https://www.courtstatistics.org/other-pages/statecourtcaseloadstatistics (accessed 10/3/21).

8. "Federal Judicial Caseload Statistics 2017," U.S. Courts, March 31, 2017, https://www.uscourts.gov/statistics-reports/federal-judicial-caseload-statistics-2017 (accessed 10/3/21).

9. *Young v. UPS*, 575 U.S. ___ (2015).

10. The Pregnancy Discrimination Act of 1978, https://www.eeoc.gov/laws/statutes/pregnancy.cfm (accessed 10/3/21).

11. Whitney Benns, "Young v. UPS: A Backgrounder and Case Review," OnLabor, March 25, 2015, https://onlabor.org/young-v-ups-a-backgrounder-and-case-review/ (accessed 10/3/21).

12. Journal of the Supreme Court of the United States, https://www.supremecourt.gov/orders/journal.aspx (accessed 10/3/21).

13. Charles M. Cameron, Jeffrey A. Segal, and Donald Songer, "Strategic Auditing in a Political Hierarchy: An Informational Model of the Supreme Court's Certiorari Decisions," *American Political Science Review* 94, no. 1 (2000): 101–16; H. W. Perry Jr., *Deciding to Decide: Agenda Setting in the United States Supreme Court* (Cambridge, MA: Harvard University Press, 1994).

14. Melvin Urofsky, *Dissent and the Supreme Court: Its Role in the Court's History and the Nation's Constitutional Dialogue* (New York: Vintage, 2015).

15. Ruth Bader Ginsburg, "Lecture: The Role of Dissenting Opinions," *Minnesota Law Review* 95, no. 1 (2010): 1–8.

16. Robert Barnes and Brigid Schulte, "Justices Revive Case Claiming UPS Discriminated against Pregnant Worker," *Washington Post*, March 25, 2015, https://www.washingtonpost.com/national/justices-revive-case-claiming-ups-discriminated-against-pregnant-worker/2015/03/25/217223aa-d317-11e4-a62f-ee745911a4ff_story.html (accessed 10/3/21).

40. ARE SUPREME COURT JUSTICES TOO PARTISAN?

1. Edgar B. Herwick III, "Why Did the Framers Give Lifetime Tenure to Supreme Court Justices?" 89.7 WGBH, October 2, 2018, https://www.wgbh.org/news/politics/2018/10/02/why-did-the-framers-give-lifetime-tenure-to-supreme-court-justices (accessed 1/14/20).

2. Alexander Hamilton, *The Federalist Papers*, No. 78, https://avalon.law.yale.edu/18th_century/fed78.asp (accessed 1/14/20).

3. Irving R. Kaufman, "Maintaining Judicial Independence: A Mandate to Judges," *American Bar Association Journal* 66, no. 4 (1980): 470–72.

4. Joseph Story, "Commentaries on the Constitution," University of Chicago, http://press-pubs.uchicago.edu/founders/documents/preambles21.html (accessed 1/14/20).

5. "Justices Uphold Partisan Lines in Redistricting," *New York Times*, July 1, 1986, https://www.nytimes.com/1986/07/01/us/justices-uphold-partisan-lines-in-redistricting.html (accessed 1/14/20).

6. Seung Min Kim, Ann E. Marimow, and Aaron C. Davis, "Ketanji Brown Jackson Pledges Independence and Neutrality in Supreme Court Confirmation Hearing," *Washington Post*, March 21, 2022, https://www.washingtonpost.com/politics/2022/03/21/jackson-opening-statement (accessed 5/27/22).

7. *Bush v. Gore*, 531 U.S. 98 (2000).

8. *Citizens United v. Federal Election Commission*, 558 U.S. 310 (2010).

9. *Rucho v. Common Cause*, 588 U.S. ___ (2019).

10. "Nearly 7 In 10 Favor a Limit on How Long SCOTUS Justices Can Serve," Quinnipiac Poll, May 18, 2022, https://poll.qu.edu/poll-release?releaseid =3846 (accessed 8/9/22).

11. Tom Murse, "How Long It Takes to Confirm U.S. Supreme Court Nominees," ThoughtCo., November 4, 2019, https://www.thoughtco.com/confirming -u-s-supreme-court-nominees-3879361 (accessed 1/14/20).

12. "Supreme Court Nominations (1789–Present)," U.S. Senate, https://www .senate.gov/legislative/nominations/SupremeCourtNominations 1789present.htm (accessed 1/14/20).

13. Lee Epstein, René Lindstädt, Jeffrey A. Segal, and Chad Westerland, "The Changing Dynamics of Senate Voting on Supreme Court Nominees," *Journal of Politics* 68, no. 2 (2006): 296–307.

14. Kenneth B. Noble, "New Views Emerge of Bork's Role in Watergate Dismissals," *New York Times*, July 26, 1987, https://www.nytimes .com/1987/07/26/us/new-views-emerge-of-bork-s-role-in-watergate -dismissals.html (accessed 1/14/20).

15. Senator Edward Kennedy, "Robert Bork's America," C-SPAN, July 1, 1987, https://www.c-span.org/video/?c4594844/senator-kennedy-opposes -bork-nomination (accessed 1/14/20).

16. "We're Going to Bork Him, NOW Declares," *Seattle Times*, July 6, 1991, https://archive.seattletimes.com/archive/?date=19910706&slug =1292925 (accessed 1/14/20).

17. Julia Jacobs, "Anita Hill's Testimony and Other Key Moments from the Clarence Thomas Hearings," *New York Times*, September 20, 2018, https://www.nytimes.com/2018/09/20/us/politics/anita-hill-testimony -clarence-thomas.html (accessed 1/14/20).

18. Jacobs, "Anita Hill's Testimony."

19. "Remarks by President Trump Announcing Judge Brett M. Kavanaugh as the Nominee for Associate Justice of the Supreme Court of the United States," July 9, 2018, https://trumpwhitehouse.archives.gov /briefings-statements/remarks-president-trump-announcing -judge-brett-m-kavanaugh-nominee-associate-justice-supreme -court-united-states/ (accessed 10/7/21).

20. Mike DeBonis and Paul Kane, "Republicans Vow No Hearings and No Votes for Obama's Supreme Court Pick," *Washington Post*, February 23, 2016, https://www.washingtonpost.com/news/powerpost/wp/2016/02/23 /key-senate-republicans-say-no-hearings-for-supreme-court-nominee/ (accessed 1/14/20).

21. "Brett Kavanaugh's Opening Statement: Full Transcript," *New York Times*, September 26, 2018, https://www.nytimes.com/2018/09/26/us/politics

/read-brett-kavanaughs-complete-opening-statement.html (accessed 1/14/20).

22. "Brett Kavanaugh's Opening Statement."

23. "Supreme Court Nominations (1789–Present)," U.S. Senate, https://www.senate.gov/legislative/nominations/SupremeCourtNominations1789present.htm (accessed 4/30/22).

24. Lisa Mascaro, "Barrett Confirmed As Supreme Court Justice in Partisan Vote," Associated Press, October 26, 2020, https://apnews.com/article/election-2020-donald-trump-virus-outbreak-ruth-bader-ginsburg-amy-coney-barrett-82a02a618343c98b80ca2b6bf9eafe07 (accessed 10/9/21).

25. Abbe R. Gluck and Richard A. Posner, "Statutory Interpretation on the Bench: A Survey of Forty-Two Judges on the Federal Courts of Appeals," *Harvard Law Review* 131, no. 5 (2018): 1298–1373.

26. "The Supreme Court Database," Washington University Law, http://scdb.wustl.edu/data.php?s=1 (accessed 10/9/21).

27. "Chief Justice Says His Goal Is More Consensus on Court," *New York Times*, May 21, 2006, https://www.nytimes.com/2006/05/22/washington/22justice.html (accessed 1/19/20).

28. Jack S. Knight and Lee Epstein, "The Norm of Stare Decisis," *American Journal of Political Science* 40, no. 4 (1996): 1018–35; Jeffrey Segal and Howard Spaeth, "The Influence of Stare Decisis on the Votes of United States Supreme Court Justices," *American Journal of Political Science* 40, no. 4 (1996): 971–1003.

29. "The Supreme Court Database."

30. Daniel R. Pinello, "Linking Party to Judicial Ideology in American Courts: A Meta-Analysis," *Justice System Journal* 20, no. 3 (1999): 219–54.

31. Jeffrey A. Segal and Harold J. Spaeth, *The Supreme Court and the Attitudinal Model* (New York: Cambridge University Press, 1993).

32. Lackland H. Bloom, *Methods of Interpretation: How the Supreme Court Reads the Constitution* (New York: Oxford University Press, 2009).

33. Angie Gou, "As Unanimity Declines, Conservative Majority's Power Runs Deeper than the Blockbuster Cases," ScotusBlog, July 3, 2022, https://www.scotusblog.com/2022/07/as-unanimity-declines-conservative-majoritys-power-runs-deeper-than-the-blockbuster-cases/ (accessed 7/30/22).

41. DO SPECIAL INTERESTS RUN THE GOVERNMENT?

1. Eric Rauchway, "The 2008 Crash: What Happened to All That Money?" History.com, February 1, 2019, https://www.history.com/news/2008-financial-crisis-causes (accessed 3/4/20).

2. Kimberly Amadeo, "What Is the Dodd-Frank Wall Street Reform Act?" The Balance, October 30, 2020, https://www.thebalance.com /dodd-frank-wall-street-reform-act-3305688 (accessed 10/5/21).

3. Pete Schroeder, "Banks Spent Record Amounts on Lobbying in Recent Election," Reuters, March 8, 2017, https://www.reuters.com/article /us-usa-banks-lobbying/banks-spent-record-amounts-on-lobbying -in-recent-election-idUSKBN16F26P (accessed 3/4/20).

4. Aaron Klein, "No, Dodd-Frank Was Neither Repealed Nor Gutted. Here's What Really Happened," Brookings Institution, May 25, 2018, https://www.brookings.edu/research/no-dodd-frank-was-neither -repealed-nor-gutted-heres-what-really-happened/ (accessed 3/4/20).

5. Peter Valdes-Dapena, "By 2040, More than Half of New Cars Will Be Electric," CNN, September 6, 2019, https://www.cnn.com /2019/05/15/business/electric-car-outlook-bloomberg/index.html (accessed 3/4/20).

6. "Oil and Gas Industry Revenue in the United States from 2010 to 2018 (in Million U.S. Dollars)," Statista, https://www.statista.com/statistics /294614/revenue-of-the-gas-and-oil-industry-in-the-us/ (accessed 3/4/20).

7. Gavin Bade, "The Oil Industry vs. the Electric Car," Politico, September 16, 2019, https://www.politico.com/story/2019/09/16/oil-industry -electric-car-1729429 (accessed 3/5/20).

8. "ICYMI: 58 Million American Adults Can't Afford Prescription Drugs," Chuck Grassley news release, November 12, 2019, https://www.grassley .senate.gov/news/news-releases/icymi-58-million-american-adults -can-t-afford-prescription-drugs (accessed 3/5/20).

9. "Comparison of U.S. and International Prices for Top Medicare Part B Drugs by Total Expenditures," U.S. Department of Health and Human Services, October 25, 2018, https://aspe.hhs.gov/system/files /pdf/259996/ComparisonUSInternationalPricesTopSpending PartBDrugs.pdf (accessed 3/5/20).

10. Ben Hirschler, "How the U.S. Pays 3 Times More for Drugs," Reuters, October 13, 2015, https://www.scientificamerican.com/article/how -the-u-s-pays-3-times-more-for-drugs/ (accessed 3/5/20).

11. Susan Scutti, "Big Pharma Spends Record Millions on Lobbying amid Pressure to Lower Drug Prices," CNN, January 24, 2019, https://www.cnn .com/2019/01/23/health/phrma-lobbying-costs-bn/index.html (accessed 3/5/20).

12. "Top Spenders," OpenSecrets, https://www.opensecrets.org/federal -lobbying/top-spenders (accessed 3/5/20).

13. "Industries," OpenSecrets, https://www.opensecrets.org/federal -lobbying/industries (accessed 7/31/22).

14. Tala Hadavi, "Lobbying in Q1 Topped a Record $938 Million, but Lobbyists Say Their Profession is Misunderstood," CNBC, October 5, 2020, https://www.cnbc.com/2020/10/05/q1-lobbying-spend-was-record-938-million-but-lobbyists-decry-stereotype.html (accessed 10/5/21).

15. Tom Murse, "What Does a Lobbyist Do?" ThoughtCo., January 15, 2020, https://www.thoughtco.com/what-does-a-lobbyist-do-3367609 (accessed 3/5/20).

16. "Factbox — How Many Lobbyists Are There in Washington?" Reuters, September 13, 2009, https://www.reuters.com/article/obama-lobbying/factbox-how-many-lobbyists-are-there-in-washington-idUSN1348032520090913 (accessed 3/12/20).

17. Jeffrey Birnbaum, *The Lobbyists: How Influence Peddlers Work Their Way in Washington* (repr., New York: Three Rivers Press, 2015).

18. Lee Fang, "Lobbyists Bring Holiday Cheer to Lawmakers and Congressional Staff with Glitzy Parties," The Intercept, December 8, 2017, https://theintercept.com/2017/12/08/congress-lobbyist-holiday-parties/ (accessed 3/12/20).

19. John Hendrickson, "What Is Congress Going to Do with 6,000 Tacos?" *Esquire*, April 22, 2015, https://www.esquire.com/news-politics/news/a34549/congress-six-thousand-tacos/ (accessed 3/12/20).

20. Lee Drutman and Steven M. Teles, "Why Congress Relies on Lobbyists Instead of Thinking for Itself," *The Atlantic*, March 10, 2015, https://www.theatlantic.com/politics/archive/2015/03/when-congress-cant-think-for-itself-it-turns-to-lobbyists/387295/ (accessed 4/15/20).

21. Eric Lipton and Ben Protess, "Banks' Lobbyists Help in Drafting Financial Bills," *New York Times*, May 23, 2013, https://dealbook.nytimes.com/2013/05/23/banks-lobbyists-help-in-drafting-financial-bills/ (accessed 3/5/20).

22. "The Chemical Lobby Writes Its Own Law," RepresentUs, https:///bulletin.represent.us/the-chemical-lobby-writes-its-own-law/ (accessed 3/5/20).

23. Jimmy Williams, "I Was a Lobbyist for More than 6 Years. I Quit. My Conscience Couldn't Take It Anymore," Vox, January 5, 2018, https://www.vox.com/first-person/2017/6/29/15886936/political-lobbying-lobbyist-big-money-politics (accessed 3/10/20).

24. Kimberly Kindy, "In Trump Era, Lobbyists Boldly Take Credit for Writing a Bill to Protect Their Industry," *Washington Post*, August 1, 2017, https://www.washingtonpost.com/powerpost/in-trump-era-lobbyists-boldly-take-credit-for-writing-a-bill-to-protect-their-industry/2017/07/31/eb299a7c-5c34-11e7-9fc6-c7ef4bc58d13_story.html (accessed 3/5/20).

25. Renae Merle, "Mulvaney Discloses 'Hierarchy' for Meeting Lobbyists, Saying Some Would Be Seen Only If They Paid," *Washington Post*, April 25, 2018, https://www.washingtonpost.com/news/business

/wp/2018/04/25/mick-mulvaney-faces-backlash-after-telling-bankers
-if-you-were-a-lobbyist-who-never-gave-us-money-i-didnt-talk-to-you/
(accessed 3/5/20).

26.   Joshua Kalla and David E. Broockman, "Campaign Contributions Facilitate Access to Congressional Officials: A Randomized Field Experiment," *American Journal of Political Science* 60, no. 3 (2016): 545–58; Lynda W. Powell, *The Influence of Campaign Contributions in State Legislatures* (Ann Arbor: University of Michigan Press, 2012).

27.   Williams, "I Was a Lobbyist."

28.   "Top Industries," OpenSecrets, https://www.opensecrets.org /industries/index.php?ind=A&cycle=2018 (accessed 3/10/20); "Political Parties, 2022 Election Cycle," OpenSecrets, https://www.opensecrets .org/parties/ (accessed 10/21/22).

29.   Michael Beckel, "Business Targets Campaigns of Key Committee Members," OpenSecrets, April 13, 2011, https://www.opensecrets .org/news/2011/04/business-targets-campaigns-of-key/ (accessed 3/10/20); Marie Hojnacki and David C. Kimball, "Organized Interests and the Decision of Whom to Lobby in Congress," *American Political Science Review* 92, no. 4 (1998): 775–90.

30.   Joshua McCrain, "Revolving Door Lobbyists and the Value of Congressional Staff Connections," *Journal of Politics* 80, no. 4 (2018): 1369–83.

31.   Alyce McFadden, "Employment History, Austin Lloyd," OpenSecrets, March 9, 2021, https://www.opensecrets.org/revolving/rev_summary .php?id=82688 (accessed 7/31/22).

32 . "Revolving Door," OpenSecrets, https://www.opensecrets.org /revolving (accessed 8/5/22).

33.   Russell Berman, "An Exodus from Congress Tests the Lure of Lobbying," *The Atlantic*, May 1, 2018, https://www.theatlantic.com/politics /archive/2018/05/lobbying-the-job-of-choice-for-retired-members-of -congress/558851/ (accessed 3/5/20).

34.   Berman, "An Exodus."

35.   "Washington Update," Family Research Council, https://www.frc.org/ (accessed 3/11/20).

36.   Patrick Galey, "Energy Giants Spend $1 Billion on Climate Lobbying, PR since Paris," Phys.org, March 22, 2019, https://phys.org/news/2019 -03-energy-giants-spent-1bn-climate.html (accessed 3/12/20).

37.   Ruth Igielnik, "70% of Americans Say U.S. Economic System Unfairly Favors the Powerful," Pew Research Center, January 9, 2020, https:// www.pewresearch.org/fact-tank/2020/01/09/70-of-americans-say-u-s -economic-system-unfairly-favors-the-powerful/ (accessed 3/8/20).

38.   Francine McKenna, "Warren Proposes Lifetime Ban on Members of Congress Becoming Lobbyists," Market Watch, August 21, 2018, https:// www.marketwatch.com/story/warren-proposes-lifetime-ban-on

-members-of-congress-becoming-lobbyists-2018-08-21 (accessed 3/8/20).

39. Francine McKenna, "Sen. Baldwin, Rep. Cummings to Introduce Bill to Reduce Revolving-Door Conflicts," MarketWatch, July 14, 2015, https://www.marketwatch.com/story/sen-baldwin-rep-cummings-to -introduce-bill-to-reduce-revolving-door-conflicts-2015-07-14 (accessed 3/8/20).

40. "Fighting Special Interest Lobbyist Power over Public Policy," Center for American Progress, September 27, 2017, https://www.americanprogress .org/issues/democracy/reports/2017/09/27/439675/fighting-special -interest-lobbyist-power-public-policy/ (accessed 3/8/20).

42. IS THE FEDERAL GOVERNMENT HOPELESSLY BROKEN?

1. "Pres. Obama: Washington Is Broken," Associated Press, January 24, 2012, https://www.youtube.com/watch?v=tnHYoqqg0dI (accessed 3/21/20).

2. Gregory Krieg, "Trump Says EVERYTHING Is Broken, Rigged, Awful, a Disaster," CNN, October 15, 2016, https://www.cnn.com/2016/10/15 /politics/donald-trump-broken-disaster/index.html (accessed 3/21/20).

3. "Everybody Is Frustrated, Biden Says amid Democratic In-Fighting over His Agenda," CBS News, October 4, 2021, https://www.cbsnews.com /news/biden-democrats-agenda-frustration/ (accessed 10/6/21).

4. Kim Parker, Rich Morin, and Juliana Menasce Horowitz, "Worries, Priorities, and Potential Problem-Solvers," Pew Research Center, March 21, 2019, https://www.pewsocialtrends.org/2019/03/21/worries -priorities-and-potential-problem-solvers/ (accessed 3/21/20).

5. Parker, Morin, and Horowitz, "Worries, Priorities, and Potential Problem-Solvers."

6. "1 Day in the Postal Service," U.S. Postal Service, https://facts.usps .com/one-day/ (accessed 10/6/21).

7. "Air Traffic by the Numbers," Federal Aviation Administration, https:// www.faa.gov/air_traffic/by_the_numbers/ (accessed 3/21/20).

8. "Federal Grant Aid," Urban Institute, http://collegeaffordability.urban .org/financial-aid/federal/#/pell_grants (accessed 10/6/21).

9. Mohammed Hussein and Mohammed Haddad, "Infographic: US Military Presence around the World," Al Jazeera, September 10, 2021, https://www.aljazeera.com/news/2021/9/10/infographic-us-military -presence-around-the-world-interactive (accessed 10/6/21).

10. Lukas Pleva, "Texas Congresswoman Eddie Bernice Johnson Says Social Security Slashed Poverty among the Elderly," PolitiFact, August 17, 2010, https://www.politifact.com/factchecks/2010/aug/17/eddie-bernice -johnson/texas-congresswoman-eddie-bernice-johnson-says-soc/ (accessed 3/26/20).

11. Richard F. Weingroff, "Federal-Aid Highway Act of 1956: Creating the Interstate System," *Public Roads*, Summer 1996, https://www.fhwa.dot.gov /publications/publicroads/96summer/p96su10.cfm (accessed 3/26/20).

12. Voteview.com

13. Shawn Zeller, "No Quarter for Centrists in House: 2020 Vote Studies," *Roll Call*, March 3, 2021, https://www.rollcall.com/2021/03/03/no -quarter-for-centrists-in-house-2020-vote-studies/ (accessed 10/6/21).

14. James A. Thurber and Antoine Yoshinaka (eds.), *American Gridlock: The Sources, Character, and Impact of Political Polarization* (New York: Cambridge University Press, 2015); Sarah A. Binder, "The Dynamics of Legislative Gridlock, 1947–96," *American Political Science Review* 93, no. 3 (1999): 519–33; Jesse Richman, "Parties, Pivots, and Policy: The Status Quo Test," *American Political Science Review* 105, no. 1 (2011): 151–65; Barbara Sinclair, *Party Wars: Polarization and the Politics of National Policy Making* (Norman: University of Oklahoma Press, 2006); Sean M. Theriault, *Party Polarization in Congress* (New York: Cambridge University Press, 2008); Jamie L. Carson, Michael H. Crespin, Charles J. Finocchiaro, and David W. Rohde, "Redistricting and Party Polarization in the U.S. House of Representatives," *American Politics Research* 35, no. 6 (2007): 878–90; Kirby Goidel, *America's Failing Experiment: How We the People Have Become the Problem* (Lanham, MD: Rowman and Littlefield, 2013).

15. Thomas Zittel, "The Bright and Dark Sides of Party Polarization," Social Science Research Council, February 20, 2018, https://items.ssrc.org /democracy-papers/the-dark-and-bright-sides-of-party-polarization/ (accessed 3/26/20).

16. "Dick Cheney: Telling Patrick Leahy 'F — k Yourself' Was 'Sort of the Best Thing I Ever Did'," Huffington Post, June 23, 2010, https://www .huffpost.com/entry/dick-cheney-patrick-leahy-fuck-yourself_n_549100 (accessed 3/28/20).

17. Glenn Kessler, "When Did McConnell Say He Wanted to Make Obama a 'One-Term President'?" *Washington Post*, September 25, 2012, https:// www.washingtonpost.com/blogs/fact-checker/post/when-did -mcconnell-say-he-wanted-to-make-obama-a-one-term-president /2012/09/24/79fd5cd8-0696-11e2-afff-d6c7f20a83bf_blog.html (accessed 3/28/20).

18. Brian Manzullo and Todd Spangler, "Rashida Tlaib on Donald Trump: We Will Impeach the Mother****er," *Detroit Free Press*, January 4, 2019, https://www.freep.com/story/news/politics/2019/01/04/rashida -tlaib-curses-donald-trump-video/2480451002/ (accessed 3/28/20).

19. Allan Smith, "McConnell Says He's '100 Percent' Focused on 'Stopping' Biden's Administration," NBC News, May 5, 2021, https://www.nbcnews .com/politics/joe-biden/mcconnell-says-he-s-100-percent-focused -stopping-biden-s-n1266443 (accessed 10/6/21).

20. Shelby Black, "These Nancy Pelosi Quotes about Donald Trump Throw Shade in a Subtle Way," Elite Daily, February 24, 2019, https://www.elitedaily.com/p/these-nancy-pelosi-quotes-about-donald-trump-throw-shade-in-a-subtle-way-15960914 (accessed 3/28/20).

21. Ian Schwartz, "Trump: Pelosi Has Become a 'Crazed Lunatic,' Will Go Down as the Worst Speaker in History," RealClearPolitics, January 10, 2020, https://www.realclearpolitics.com/video/2020/01/10/trump_pelosi_has_become_a_crazed_lunatic_will_go_down_as_the_worst_speaker_in_history.html#! (accessed 3/28/20).

22. Sheryl Gay Stolberg, "Trump and Pelosi Exchange Snubs at the State of the Union Address," *New York Times*, February 4, 2020, https://www.nytimes.com/2020/02/04/us/politics/pelosi-trump-handshake.html (accessed 3/29/20).

23. Manu Raju, "Pelosi and Trump Haven't Spoke in Five Months," CNN, March 24, 2020, https://www.cnn.com/2020/03/24/politics/nancy-pelosi-trump-talks/index.html (accessed 3/29/20).

24. Michael Grunwald, "A 'Bridge to Nowhere', an Overstuffed Highway Bill, a Teapot Museum, Pork by Any Other Name," *Washington Post*, April 30, 2006, https://www.washingtonpost.com/archive/opinions/2006/04/30/a-bridge-to-nowhere-an-overstuffed-highway-bill-a-teapot-museum-span-classbankheadpork-by-any-other-name-span/b4038a46-632a-40f8-85c5-87c3d286d325/ (accessed 3/27/20).

25. Scott Mayerowitz and Nathalie Tadena, "Stimulus Waste? The $3.4 Million Turtle Crossing," ABC News, July 9, 2009, https://abcnews.go.com/Business/Economy/story?id=8045022&page=1 (accessed 3/27/20).

26. Steve Quinn, "Alaska's 'Bridge to Nowhere' Project Finally Scrapped," Reuters, October 23, 2015, https://www.reuters.com/article/us-alaska-bridge/alaskas-bridge-to-nowhere-plan-finally-scrapped-idUSKCN0SI00120151024 (accessed 3/26/20).

27. Madian Khabsa and Joe Walsh, "Data Science for Social Good," http://www.dssgfellowship.org/2014/07/02/shining-a-light-on-earmarks/ (accessed 10/6/21).

28. John Hudak, "Congress in 2019: Why the First Branch Should Bring Back Earmarks," Brookings Institution, December 27, 2018, https://www.brookings.edu/blog/fixgov/2018/12/27/congress-in-2019-why-the-first-branch-should-bring-back-earmarks/ (accessed 3/26/20).

29. John Hudak, "Earmarks Are Back, and Americans Should Be Glad," Brookings Institution, March 17, 2021, https://www.brookings.edu/blog/fixgov/2021/03/17/earmarks-are-back-and-americans-should-be-glad/ (accessed 10/6/21).

30. "Head to Head: Compare Voting Records," ProPublica, https://projects.propublica.org/represent/members/P000197-nancy-pelosi/compare-votes/L000563-daniel-lipinski/116 (accessed 3/26/20).

31. "Federal Legislative Ratings," American Conservative Union, http://acuratings.conservative.org/acu-federal-legislative-ratings/?year1=2018&chamber=11&state1=0&sortable=7 (accessed 3/26/20).

32. Sheryl Gay Stolberg, "Marie Newman Beats Dan Lipinski, Democratic Incumbent, in Illinois House Primary," *New York Times*, March 18, 2020, https://www.nytimes.com/2020/03/18/us/politics/marie-newman-dan-lipinski-illinois.html (accessed 3/26/20).

33. Isabella Murray, "Who Is Harriet Hageman, the Trump-Backed Candidate Who Beat Liz Cheney?" ABC News, August 16, 2022, https://abcnews.go.com/Politics/harriet-hageman-trump-backed-candidate-beat-liz-cheney/story?id=88410864 (accessed 10/20/22).

34. "Your Vote Defends Freedom," National Rifle Association of America, Political Victory Fund, https://www.nrapvf.org/emails/2020/wyoming/liz-cheney-wy-al-general/ (accessed 10/20/22).

35. "Congress Minutes," Politico, June 24, 2022. https://www.politico.com/minutes/congress/06-24-2022/ (accessed 10/20/22).

36. Luke Broadwater, "House Panel Requests McCarthy's Phone Records Be Preserved in January 6 Inquiry," *New York Times*, September 2, 2021, https://www.nytimes.com/2021/09/02/us/politics/liz-cheney-jan-6-committee.html (accessed 10/20/22).

37. Joseph Bafumi and Michael C. Herron, "Leapfrog Representation and Extremism: A Study of American Voters and Their Members in Congress," *American Political Science Review* 104, no. 3 (2010): 519–42; Luke Keele, "The Authorities Really Do Matter: Party Control and Trust in Government," *Journal of Politics* 67, no. 3 (2005): 873–86; Joseph S. Nye Jr., Philip Zelikow, and David C. King, eds., *Why People Don't Trust Government* (Cambridge, MA: Harvard University Press, 1997).

SECTION VII: CONTEMPORARY PUBLIC POLICY

1. Dana Goldstein, "5 Questions for Bill Gates: The Full Interview," Daily Beast, July 14, 2017, https://www.thedailybeast.com/5-questions-for-bill-gates-the-full-interview (accessed 8/30/20).

2. Ed O'Connor, "From Groucho to W.C. Fields to Rodney... Some Quotes to Live By," *Press & Journal*, January 29, 2020, https://www.pressandjournal.com/stories/from-groucho-to-wc-fields-to-rodney-some-quotes-to-live-by-ed-oconnor,81737 (accessed 8/30/20).

43. HOW CAN THE U.S. GOVERNMENT BE $32 TRILLION ... WHOOPS ... $33 TRILLION IN DEBT?

1. Minerals Management Service, "Pipeline Damage Assessment from Hurricanes Katrina and Rita in the Gulf of Mexico," Det Norske Veritas, https://www.bsee.gov/sites/bsee.gov/files/tap-technical-assessment-program//581aa.pdf (accessed 5/3/20).

2. Allison Plyer, "Facts for Features: Katrina Impact," The Data Center, August 26, 2016, https://www.datacenterresearch.org/data-resources/katrina/facts-for-impact/ (accessed 5/3/20).

3. H.R. 1 (111th): American Recovery and Reinvestment Act of 2009, https://www.govtrack.us/congress/bills/111/hr1/summary (accessed 5/4/20).

4. Kelsey Snell, "What's Inside the Senate's $2 Trillion Coronavirus Aid Package," National Public Radio, March 26, 2020, https://www.npr.org/2020/03/26/821457551/whats-inside-the-senate-s-2-trillion-coronavirus-aid-package (accessed 10/23/21).

5. "Historical Debt Outstanding," Treasury Direct, https://www.treasurydirect.gov/govt/reports/pd/histdebt/histdebt_histo5.htm (accessed 5/3/20).

6. "U.S. National Debt Clock," https://www.usdebtclock.org/ (accessed 11/10/22); "The National Debt Is Now More than $24 Trillion. What Does That Mean?" Peter G. Peterson Foundation, https://www.pgpf.org/infographic/the-national-debt-is-now-more-than-24-trillion-what-does-that-mean (accessed 5/3/20).

7. Office of Management and Budget, "Budget of the U.S. Government: Fiscal Year 2022," https://www.whitehouse.gov/wp-content/uploads/2021/05/budget_fy22.pdf (accessed 6/28/22).

8. Veronique de Rugy and Jason J. Fichtner, "Growth in Entitlements Means Less Money to Budget," Mercatus Center, January 14, 2013, https://www.mercatus.org/publications/financial-markets/growth-entitlements-means-less-money-budget (accessed 5/4/20).

9. Office of Management and Budget, "Budget of the U.S. Government: Fiscal Year 2022."

10. "Debt to the Penny," Fiscal Data, https://fiscaldata.treasure.gov/datasets/debt-to-the-penny (accessed 6/28/22).

11. Drew Desilver, "5 Facts about the National Debt," Pew Research Center, July 24, 2019, https://www.pewresearch.org/fact-tank/2019/07/24/facts-about-the-national-debt/; Kimberly Amadeo, "Who Owns the U.S. National Debt?" The Balance, April 18, 2020, https://www.thebalance.com/who-owns-the-u-s-national-debt-3306124 (accessed 5/4/20).

12. Louise Sheiner and David Wessel, "Where Is the U.S. Government Getting All the Money It's Spending in the Coronavirus Crisis?" Brookings Institution, March 25, 2020, https://www.brookings.edu/blog/up-front/2020/03/25/where-is-the-u-s-government-getting-all-the-money-its-spending-in-the-coronavirus-crisis/ (accessed 5/4/20).

13. Ryan Cooper, "There Is No Reason to Worry about the National Debt Right Now," The Week, April 22, 2020, https://theweek.com/articles/909794/there-no-reason-worry-about-national-debt-right-now; David Wessel, "How Worried Should You Be about the Federal Deficit and Debt?" Brookings Institution, October 15, 2019, https://www.brookings.edu/policy2020/votervital/how-worried-should-you-be-about-the-federal-deficit-and-debt/; William D. Lastrapes, "Why the National

Debt Doesn't Matter — or How I Learned to Stop Worrying and Love Treasuries," The Conversation, March 19, 2015, https://theconversation .com/why-the-national-debt-doesnt-matter-or-how-i-learned-to-stop -worrying-and-love-treasuries-38775 (accessed 5/5/20).

14. James McBride, Andrew Chatzky, and Anshu Siripurapu, "The National Debt Dilemma," Council on Foreign Relations, April 30, 2020, https:// www.cfr.org/backgrounder/national-debt-dilemma; Irina Ivanova, "5 Problems with a $22 Trillion National Debt," CBS News, February 14, 2019, https://www.cbsnews.com/news/22-trillion-national-debt-is-it-a -looming-crisis/ (accessed 5/5/20).

15. George Krause, "Partisan and Ideological Sources of Fiscal Deficits in the United States," *American Journal of Political Science* 44, no. 3 (2000): 541–59.

16. "Republican Platform," Republican National Committee, https://www .gop.com/platform/restoring-the-american-dream/; "Democratic Party Platform," Democratic National Committee, https://democrats.org /where-we-stand/the-issues/jobs-and-the-economy/; "How Republicans and Democrats View Federal Spending," Pew Research Center, April 11, 2019, https://www.people-press.org/2019/04/11/how-republicans -and-democrats-view-federal-spending/ (accessed 5/5/20).

17. "Q&A: Everything You Should Know about Government Shutdowns," Committee for a Responsible Federal Budget, September 17, 2020, http://www.crfb.org/papers/qa-everything-you-should-know-about -government-shutdowns#Whatis (accessed 2/5/21).

44. ARE THE RICH TOO RICH?

1. "William Penn Charter School," https://www.penncharter.com/; "District Scorecard," School District of Philadelphia Performance Office, https://www.philasd.org/performance/programsservices/school -progress-reports/district-scorecard/#AG1_college_career (accessed 5/17/20).

2. Hannah Miet, "Submarket Snapshot: Single-Family Homes in Beverly Hills," The Real Deal, February 26, 2016, https://therealdeal.com/la /2016/02/26/submarket-snapshot-single-family-homes-in-beverly-hills/; Joel Grover and Amy Corral, "Homeless People Are without Toilets and Going in the Streets. We Asked the Mayor of LA Why," NBC4, February 19, 2020, https://www.nbclosangeles.com/investigations/homeless -people-are-without-toilets-and-going-in-the-streets-we-asked-the -mayor-of-la-why/2311759/ (accessed 5/17/20).

3. Heather Cross, "9 Most Expensive New York City Restaurants," TripSavvy, June 26, 2019, https://www.tripsavvy.com/most -expensive-new-york-city-restaurants-1613415 (accessed 5/17/20); "NYC by the Numbers: Food Pantries and Soup Kitchens," Hunter College Food Policy Center, https://www.nycfoodpolicy.org/nyc-by-the -numbers-food-insecure-households-pantries/ (accessed 10/19/21).

4. "Residences at 218," https://www.residencesat218.com/; "Friendship Court," https://affordablehousingonline.com/housing-search/Virginia /Charlottesville/Friendship-Court/10006481 (accessed 10/19/21).

5. Daniel Avery, "A Record Number of Americans Are Traveling Abroad," *Newsweek*, March 28, 2019, https://www.newsweek.com/record -number-americans-traveling-abroad-1377787; "Americans to Spend Record $101.7 Billion on Summer Vacation in 2019," *Lodging*, July 8, 2019, https://lodgingmagazine.com/americans-to-spend-record-101-7-billion -on-summer-vacation-in-2019/ (accessed 5/17/20); Sarah Fielding, "Nearly Half of Americans Can't Afford a Vacation, According to New Research," BestLife, August 16, 2019, https://bestlifeonline.com /americans-cant-afford-vacation-survey/ (accessed 5/17/20).

6. "What Is the Current Poverty Rate in the United States?" Center for Poverty & Inequality Research, University of California–Davis, https:// poverty.ucdavis.edu/faq/what-current-poverty-rate-united-states (accessed 5/17/20).

7. U.S. senator Bernie Sanders's Facebook feed, https://www.facebook .com/senatorsanders/photos/let-us-wage-a-moral-and-political-war -against-the-billionaires-and-corporate-lea/10150951109247908/ (accessed 5/17/20).

8. Paul Waldman, "Biden's Comments about Segregationists and the Rich Are Deeply Problematic," *Washington Post*, June 19, 2019, https://www.washingtonpost.com/opinions/2019/06/19/bidens -comments-about-segregationists-rich-are-deeply-problematic/ (accessed 5/17/20).

9. "Rand Paul on Welfare & Poverty," OnTheIssues.org, https://www .ontheissues.org/economic/Rand_Paul_Welfare_+_Poverty.htm (accessed 5/17/20).

10. Catherine Rampell, "Republicans Have Started to Care about Income Inequality," *Washington Post*, January 22, 2015, https://www.washingtonpost .com/opinions/catherine-rampell-republicans-have-started-to-care -about-income-inequality/2015/01/22/f1ee7686-a276-11e4-903f -9f2faf7cd9fe_story.html (accessed 5/17/20).

11. Katia Savchuk, "America's Oldest Billion-Dollar Family Fortunes," *Forbes*, July 1, 2015, https://www.forbes.com/sites/katiasavchuk/2015 /07/01/americas-oldest-billion-dollar-family-fortunes/ (accessed 5/17/20).

12. Lily Rothman, "How American Inequality in the Gilded Age Compares to Today," *Time*, February 5, 2018, https://time.com/5122375/american -inequality-gilded-age/ (accessed 5/17/20).

13. Juliana Menasce Horowitz, Ruth Igielnik, and Rakesh Kochhar, "Trends in Income and Wealth Inequality," Pew Research Center, January 9, 2020, https://www.pewresearch.org/social-trends/2020/01/09/trends -in-income-and-wealth-inequality/ (accessed 10/19/21).

14. "Income Inequality, USA, 1913–2020," World Inequality Database, https://wid.world/country/usa/ (accessed 10/1/21).

15. "Income Percentile Calculator for the United States in 2021," DQYDJ, https://dqydj.com/income-percentile-calculator/ (accessed 10/5/21).

16. Alan Krueger, "A Shrinking Middle Class Means a Shrinking Economy," Reuters, January 13, 2012, https://www.reuters.com/article /idUS328380449020120113 (accessed 5/17/20); U.S. Census, "CPS Income Tables, 2020," https://www.census.gov/topics/income-poverty /income/data/tables/cps.html; Jeffrey B. Wenger and Melanie A. Zaber, "Most Americans Consider Themselves Middle Class. But Are They?" RAND Corporation, May 14, 2021, https://www.rand.org/blog/2021/05 /most-americans-consider-themselves-middle-class-but.html (accessed 10/19/21).

17. Alexandre Tanzi and Mike Dorning, "Top 1% of U.S. Earners Now Hold More Wealth than All of the Middle Class," Bloomberg News, October 8, 2021, https://www.bloomberg.com/news/articles/2021-10-08/top -1-earners-hold-more-wealth-than-the-u-s-middle-class; Ben Steverman and Alexandre Tanzi, "The Richest 50 Americans Are Worth the Same as the Poorest 165 Million," Bloomberg News, October 8, 2020, https://www.mercurynews.com/2020/10/08/the-50-richest-americans- are-worth-as-much-as-the-poorest-165-million/; Grace Dean, "The 6 Richest Americans Are Worth More than the GDP of 13 US States Combined, Including Delaware, Maine, and Hawaii," Insider, April 15, 2021, https://www.businessinsider.com/richest-americans-gdp-states -billionaires-centibillionaires-jeff-bezos-elon-musk-2021-4 (accessed 10/19/21).

18. Richard G. Wilkinson and Kate E. Pickett, "Income Inequality and Social Dysfunction," *Annual Review of Sociology* 35, no. 1 (2009): 493–511; David J. Peters, "American Income Inequality across Economic and Geographic Space, 1970–2010," *Social Science Research* 42, no. 6 (2013): 1490–1504.

19. Jim Tankersley, "The 100% Economy: Why the U.S. Needs a Strong Middle Class to Thrive," *The Atlantic*, May 18, 2012, https://www.theatlantic.com /business/archive/2012/05/the-100-economy-why-the-us-needs-a -strong-middle-class-to-thrive/257385/ (accessed 5/17/20).

20. "The Blue-Collar Presidency," Trump White House Archives, October 30, 2020, https://trumpwhitehouse.archives.gov/articles/blue-collar -presidency/ (accessed 10/19/21).

21. Tax Foundation, "2022 Tax Brackets," November 10, 2021, https:// taxfoundation.org/2022-tax-brackets/ (accessed 6/28/22).

22. Rachel Tiede, "Clinton Correct Buffett Claimed to Pay a Lower Tax Rate than His Secretary," PolitiFact, October 18, 2016, https://www.politifact .com/factchecks/2016/oct/18/hillary-clinton/clinton-correct-buffett -claimed-pay-lower-tax-rate/ (accessed 5/18/20).

23. Tom Wheelwright, "5 Ways That Billionaire Warren Buffett Pays a Lower Tax Rate than His Secretary," Entrepreneur, August 30, 2019, https://www.entrepreneur.com/article/338189 (accessed 5/18/20).

24. Greg Rosalsky, "Is the American Tax System Regressive?" National Public Radio, October 29, 2019, https://www.npr.org/sections/money /2019/10/29/774091313/is-the-american-tax-system-regressive (accessed 5/18/20).

25. David Wessel, "What We Learned from Reagan's Tax Cuts," Brookings Institution, December 8, 2017, https://www.brookings.edu/blog/up -front/2017/12/08/what-we-learned-from-reagans-tax-cuts/; (accessed 5/18/20); Emily Horton, "The Legacy of the 2001 and 2003 'Bush' Tax Cuts," Center on Budget and Policy Priorities, October 23, 2017, https:// www.cbpp.org/research/federal-tax/the-legacy-of-the-2001-and-2003 -bush-tax-cuts (accessed 5/18/20).

26. Robert Farrington, "These States Offer Tuition-Free Community College," Forbes, March 25, 2020, https://www.forbes.com/sites/robertfarrington /2020/03/25/these-states-offer-tuition-free-community-college (accessed 5/19/20).

27. John A. Powell, "Six Policies to Reduce Economic Inequality," Othering and Belonging Institute, University of California–Berkeley, https:// belonging.berkeley.edu/six-policies-reduce-economic-inequality (accessed 5/19/20).

28. Lucy Tianxiaoshan Yu, "How Does Vocational Education Impact Income Gaps?" Chicago Policy Review, November 26, 2018, https:// chicagopolicyreview.org/2018/11/26/how-does-vocational-education -impact-income-gaps/ (accessed 5/19/20).

29. "What Is the History of the Minimum Wage?" Center for Poverty & Inequality Research, University of California–Davis, https://poverty .ucdavis.edu/faq/what-history-minimum-wage (accessed 5/18/20).

30. Nicole Bateman and Martha Ross, "The Pandemic Hurt Low Wage Workers the Most — And So Far, the Recovery Has Helped Them the Least," Brookings Institution, July 28, 2021, https://www.brookings .edu/research/the-pandemic-hurt-low-wage-workers-the-most -and-so-far-the-recovery-has-helped-them-the-least/ (accessed 10/20/21).

31. "Living Wage Calculator," https://livingwage.mit.edu/ (accessed 5/17/20). These calculations are based on county-level data that are aggregated at the state level. They don't represent the living wage for any one individual in a given state.

32. Alex Valdes, "The 'Living Wage' in Every State in 2021," Money Talks News, April 8, 2021, https://www.moneytalksnews.com/slideshows /how-much-is-really-a-living-wage-in-every-state/ (accessed 10/20/21).

45. WHY WAS YOUR T-SHIRT MADE IN CHINA?

1. Sheng Lu, "Wage Level for Garment Workers in the World," University of Delaware, https://shenglufashion.com/2018/03/04/wage-level-for-garment-workers-in-the-world-updated-in-2017/ (accessed 5/30/20).

2. Heather Whipps, "How Ancient Trade Changed the World," Live Science, February 18, 2008, https://www.livescience.c23-ancient-trade-changed-world.html (accessed 6/2/20).

3. Douglas Irwin, *Clashing over Commerce: A History of U.S. Trade Policy* (Chicago: University of Chicago Press, 2017).

4. "Value of Exported Goods and Services, 1960 to 2017," Our World in Data, https://ourworldindata.org/grapher/exports-of-goods-and-services-constant-2010-us?country=DEU~JPN~GBR~USA~MEX~CAN~NGA~OWID_WRL (accessed 6/1/20).

5. Karin von Abrams, "Global Ecommerce Forecast, 2021," eMarketer, July 7, 2021, https://www.emarketer.com/content/global-ecommerce-forecast-2021 (accessed 10/24/21).

6. "Countries & Regions," Office of the United States Trade Representative, https://ustr.gov/countries-regions (accessed 6/3/20); Erin Duffin, "Ranking of the Top Trading Partners of the United States for Trade Goods in 2019, by Export Value," Statista, March 17, 2020, https://www.statista.com/statistics/186592/ranking-of-the-largest-trading-partners-for-us-exports-in-2010/ (accessed 5/30/20); U.S. Bureau of the Census, "Top Trading Partners, 2021," https://www.census.gov/foreign-trade/statistics/highlights/top/top2112yr.html (accessed 6/28/22).

7. "Value of Exported Goods and Services," Our World in Data; Kimberly Amadeo, "What Does the United States Trade with Foreign Countries?" The Balance, February 18, 2020, https://www.thebalance.com/u-s-imports-and-exports-components-and-statistics-3306270 (accessed 6/2/20).

8. "NAFTA Key Provisions," https://www.iatp.org/sites/default/files/NAFTA_Key_Provisions.htm (accessed 5/31/20).

9. "Free Trade Agreements," International Trade Administration, https://www.trade.gov/free-trade-agreements (accessed 10/24/21).

10. "The WTO," World Trade Organization, https://www.wto.org/english/thewto_e/thewto_e.htm (accessed 10/24/21).

11. "Home," World Trade Organization, https://www.wto.org/ (accessed 10/24/21).

12. "International Trade Policy," Cato Institute, https://www.cato.org/trade-policy (accessed 10/24/21).

13. Jonah Goldberg, "First Things First: Fix Mexico," Jewish World Review, April 12, 2006, http://jewishworldreview.com/cols/jonah041206.asp (accessed 5/30/20).

14. Quoted in Johanna Hanfeld, *Globalization and Public Health* (London: McGraw-Hill, 2014), p. 46.

15. Barack Obama, "The Way Ahead," *The Economist*, October 8, 2016, https://www.economist.com/by-invitation/2016/10/08/the-way-ahead (accessed 6/5/20).

16. Odessa Denby, "The Cost of Modern Fashion," Medium, July 22, 2020, https://medium.com/live-your-life-on-purpose/the-cost-of-modern-fashion-383737da3a20 (accessed 10/24/21).

17. Amy Shoenthal, "What Exactly Is Fair Trade, and Why Should We Care?" *Forbes*, December 14, 2018, https://www.forbes.com/sites/amyschoenberger/2018/12/14/what-exactly-is-fair-trade-and-why-should-we-care/ (accessed 5/30/20).

18. Julie Craves, "Starbucks Claims 99% 'Ethically Sourced' Coffee, But What Does That Even Mean?" *Roast Magazine*, May 15, 2015, https://dailycoffeenews.com/2015/05/15/starbucks-claims-99-ethically-sourced-coffee-but-what-does-that-even-mean/ (accessed 6/3/20).

19. "Automotive Worker Salary," Zip Recruiter, October 2021, https://www.ziprecruiter.com/Salaries/Automotive-Worker-Salary; "Automotive Industry Average Salary in Canada, 2021," Talent.com, https://ca.talent.com/salary?job=automotive+industry; "Only 269,000 Mexicans Earn More than US $16 per Hour, or 308 Pesos," Mexico News Daily, August 30, 2018, https://mexiconewsdaily.com/news/only-269000-mexicans-earn-more-than-16-per-hour/ (accessed 10/24/21).

20. Amanda M. Countryman, "USMCA: The 3 Most Important Changes in the New NAFTA and Why They Matter," The Conversation, December 11, 2019, https://theconversation.com/usmca-the-3-most-important-changes-in-the-new-nafta-and-why-they-matter-128735 (accessed 10/24/21).

21. "FACT SHEET: Biden Administration Reaches Agreement with Mexico on GM Silao Rapid Response Action and Delivers Results for Workers," Office of the United States Trade Representative, July 2021, https://ustr.gov/about-us/policy-offices/press-office/fact-sheets/2021/july/fact-sheet-biden-administration-reaches-agreement-mexico-gm-silao-rapid-response-action-and-delivers (accessed 10/24/21).

22. Elizabeth Warren, "Trade — On Our Terms," Medium, July 29, 2019, https://medium.com/@teamwarren/trade-on-our-terms-ad861879feca (accessed 6/3/20).

23. The Fix Team, "Transcript: The Third Democratic Debate," *Washington Post*, September 12, 2019, https://www.washingtonpost.com/politics/2019/09/13/transcript-third-democratic-debate/ (accessed 10/24/21).

24. "President Trump Rally in Louisville, Kentucky," C-SPAN, March 20, 2017, https://www.c-span.org/video/?425711-1/president-trump-promises-pass-health-care-bill-in-form (accessed 10/24/21).

25. "Shares of Gross Domestic Product: Imports of Goods and Services," FRED Economic Data, St. Louis Fed, January 27, 2022, https://fred

.stlouisfed.org/series/B021RE1A156NBEA; "All Employees: Manufacturing," FRED Economic Data, St. Louis Fed, July 2022, https://fred.stlouisfed .org/series/MANEMP (accessed 7/15/22).

26. Ana Swanson, "Biden Reinstates Aluminum Tariffs in One of His First Trade Moves," *New York Times*, February 2, 2021, https://www.nytimes .com/2021/02/02/business/economy/biden-aluminum-tariffs.html (accessed 10/25/21).

27. Mohamed Younis, "Sharply Fewer in U.S. View Trade as Opportunity," Gallup, March 31, 2021, https://news.gallup.com/poll/342419 /sharply-fewer-view-foreign-trade-opportunity.aspx (accessed 10/24/21).

28. Younis, "Sharply Fewer in U.S. View Trade as Opportunity."

29. David Karol, "Divided Government and U.S. Trade Policy: Much Ado about Nothing?" *International Organization* 54, no. 4 (2000): 825–44.

46. WHY DOESN'T EVERYONE HAVE HEALTH INSURANCE?

1. Margot Sanger-Katz, "Is My Health Plan a Cadillac? Why Are We Comparing Health Insurance to Cars?" *New York Times*, July 20, 2019, https://www.nytimes.com/2019/07/20/upshot/explaining-cadillac -health-plans.html (accessed 10/19/21).

2. Sarah Goodell, "Silver Plan," WebMD, June 9, 2019, https://www.webmd .com/health-insurance/terms/silver-plan (accessed 7/28/20).

3. "Eligibility," Medicaid.gov, https://www.medicaid.gov/medicaid/eligibility /index.html (accessed 7/28/20).

4. "Emergency Medical Treatment & Labor Act," Centers for Medicare & Medicaid Services, https://www.cms.gov/Regulations-and-Guidance /Legislation/EMTALA (accessed 7/28/20).

5. "ORIF Kneecap Fracture," MDSave, https://www.mdsave.com/procedures /orif-kneecap-fracture/d586fac8 (accessed 7/28/20).

6. Amanda Seitz, "Number of Uninsured Americans Drops to an All-Time Low," *PBS Newshour*, August 2, 2022, https://www.pbs.org/newshour /health/number-of-uninsured-americans-drops-to-an-all-time-low (accessed 8/4/22).

7. "Progressive Party Platform of 1912," The American Presidency Project, https://www.presidency.ucsb.edu/documents/progressive-party -platform-1912; Sheila Mulrooney Eldred, "When Harry Truman Pushed for Universal Health Care," History.com, November 20, 2019, https:// www.history.com/news/harry-truman-universal-health-care; Peter Ubel, "A Surprising Early Supporter of Obamacare: Eisenhower?" *Forbes*, January 21, 2014, https://www.forbes.com/sites/peterubel/2014/01/21 /a-surprising-early-supporter-of-obamacare-eisenhower/; "John F. Kennedy Argues for Universal Healthcare," Films for Action, May 20, 1962, https://www.filmsforaction.org/watch/john-f-kennedy-argues

-for-universal-healthcare/; "President Richard Nixon's Special Message to the Congress Proposing a Comprehensive Health Insurance Plan," Kaiser Health News, February 6, 1974, https://khn.org/news/nixon -proposal/ (accessed 6/12/22).

8. "Clinton's Health Plan: Transcript of President's Address to Congress on Health Care," *New York Times*, September 23, 1993, https://www .nytimes.com/1993/09/23/us/clinton-s-health-plan-transcript-president -s-address-congress-health-care.html (accessed 7/28/20).

9. Tom van der Voort, "In the Beginning: Medicare and Medicaid," Miller Center, University of Virginia, July 24, 2017, https://millercenter.org /issues-policy/us-domestic-policy/beginning-medicare-and-medicaid (accessed 7/28/20).

10. "Cost Sharing Out of Pocket Costs," Medicaid.gov, https://www .medicaid.gov/medicaid/cost-sharing/cost-sharing-out-pocket-costs /index.html (accessed 7/30/20).

11. "Health Insurance Coverage of the Total Population," Kaiser Family Foundation, 2019, https://www.kff.org/other/state-indicator/total -population/?currentTimeframe=0&sortModel=%7B%22colId%22: %22Location%22,%22sort%22:%22asc%22%7D (accessed 10/19/21).

12. "The Children's Health Insurance Program," Georgetown University Health Policy Institute, February 6, 2017, https://ccf.georgetown.edu /2017/02/06/about-chip/ (accessed 7/28/20).

13. "Total Number of Children Ever Enrolled in CHIP Annually," Kaiser Family Foundation, https://www.kff.org/other/state-indicator/annual-chip -enrollment/?currentTimeframe=0&sortModel=%7B%22colId%22: %22Location%22,%22sort%22:%22asc%22%7D (accessed 10/19/21).

14. "Can I Get Coverage If I Have a Pre-Existing Condition?" U.S. Depart- ment of Health and Human Services, https://www.hhs.gov/answers /affordable-care-act/can-i-get-coverage-if-i-have-a-pre-existing -condition/index.html (accessed 8/9/20).

15. "Chart Book: Accomplishments of Affordable Care Act," Center on Budget and Policy Priorities, March 19, 2019, https://www.cbpp.org /research/health/chart-book-accomplishments-of-affordable-care-act (accessed 7/28/20).

16. "Joe Biden to Obama: 'This Is a Big Fucking Deal'," https://www.youtube .com/watch?v=HHKq9tt50O8 (accessed 7/28/20).

17. "How Many Americans Get Health Insurance from Their Employer?" eHealth, December 6, 2019, https://www.ehealthinsurance.com /resources/small-business/how-many-americans-get-health-insurance -from-their-employer (accessed 7/28/20).

18. Ashley Joyce, "The Real Cost of Health Care: Interactive Calculator Estimates Both Direct and Hidden Household Spending," Kaiser Family Foundation, February 21, 2019, https://www.kff.org/health-costs/press -release/interactive-calculator-estimates-both-direct-and-hidden

-household-spending/; Darla Mercado, "Your Health Insurance Costs Are about to Go Up in 2020," CNBC, September 26, 2019, https://www.cnbc .com/2019/09/26/your-health-insurance-costs-are-about-to-go -up-in-2020.html (accessed 6/12/22).

19. Jonathan R. Goodman, "Fear over Healthcare Locks Americans in Jobs — and Throttles Creativity," *The Guardian*, November 13, 2017, https://www.theguardian.com/commentisfree/2017/nov/13/fear-over -healthcare-locks-americans-jobs-throttles-creativity (accessed 7/28/20).

20. Sara R. Collins, Munira Z. Gunja, Gabriella N. Aboulafia, Erin Czyzewicz, and Robyn Rapoport, "New Survey Finds Americans Suffering Health Coverage Insecurity along with Job Losses," The Commonwealth Fund, April 21, 2020, https://www.commonwealthfund.org/blog/2020/new -survey-finds-americans-suffering-health-coverage-insecurity-job -losses (accessed 7/28/20).

21. Jennifer Tolbert, Kendal Orgera, and Anthony Damico, "Key Facts about the Uninsured Population," Kaiser Family Foundation, November 6, 2020, https://www.kff.org/uninsured/issue-brief/key-facts-about -the-uninsured-population/ (accessed 10/19/21).

22. Dylan Scott, "On Health Care, There Are 3 Types of Democrats Running for President," Vox, July 30, 2019, https://www.vox.com/2019/7/30/20747974 /democratic-debate-health-care-medicare-for-all (accessed 7/28/20).

23. Benjy Sarlin, "Why 'Medicare for All' Wrecked Elizabeth Warren but Not Bernie Sanders," NBC News, March 5, 2020, https://www.nbcnews.com /politics/2020-election/why-medicare-all-wrecked-elizabeth-warren -not-bernie-sanders-n1150691 (accessed 7/28/20).

24. "Health Care," Democratic National Committee, https://democrats.org /where-we-stand/the-issues/health-care/ (accessed 7/28/20).

25. "Health Care," Republican National Committee, https://prod-cdn-static. gop.com/static/home/data/platform.pdfhttps://www.gop.com/issue /health-care/ (accessed 7/28/20).

26. Paul Waldman, "Republicans Keep Trying to Strip Protections for Preexisting Conditions," *Washington Post*, September 5, 2018, https:// www.washingtonpost.com/blogs/plum-line/wp/2018/09/05/republicans -keep-on-trying-to-strip-protections-for-pre-existing-conditions/ (accessed 7/28/20).

27. M. J. Lee, "10 Best Pro & Con Health Care Quotes," Politico, March 29, 2012, https://www.politico.com/story/2012/03/10-best-pro-con-health -care-quotes-074638; Matt Fuller and Jeffrey Young, "Progressives Support Shoring Up ACA before Tackling Medicare for All," Huffington Post, March 27, 2019, https://www.huffpost.com/entry/trump-aca -democrats-array-ocasio-cortez-health-care-medicare_n_5c9bc 9f9e4b072a7f603a718; Mary Rechtoris, "8 Donald Trump Quotes on Health Care — 'Repeal It, Replace It, Get Something Great'," Becker's Hospital Review, August 16, 2016, https://www.beckershospitalreview .com/hospital-management-administration/8-striking-donald-trump

-quotes-on-healthcare-repeal-it-replace-it-get-something-great. html; Josh Levin, "The Likely Next U.S. Senator from Louisiana Can't Stop Talking about Drinking Weed Killer," *Slate*, October 14, 2016, https://slate.com/news-and-politics/2016/10/john-kennedy-and -weed-killer-a-political-love-story.html (accessed 8/1/20); Andrew Prokop, "Mitch McConnell: Repeal Obamacare, Except Maybe Keep Everything It Does in Kentucky," *Vox*, May 29, 2014, https://www.vox .com/2014/5/29/5761140/mitch-mcconnell-repeal-obamacare-except -maybe-keep-everything-it-does; Jose Delreal, "Ted Cruz: 'I Would Do Anything'," *Politico*, October 17, 2013, https://www.politico.com /story/2013/10/ted-cruz-i-would-do-anything-098508; Dylan Scott, "How Elizabeth Warren Has Stayed Out of the Medicare-for-All Fray," *Vox*, September 16, 2019, https://www.vox.com/policy-and-politics /2019/9/16/20869090/elizabeth-warren-2020-medicare-for-all-voxcare (accessed 6/12/22).

28. Chris Riotta, "GOP Aims to Kill Obamacare Yet Again after Failing 70 Times," *Newsweek*, July 29, 2017, https://www.newsweek.com/gop -health-care-bill-repeal-and-replace-70-failed-attempts-643832 (accessed 8/2/20).

29. Selena Simmons-Duffin, "12 Holdout States Haven't Expanded Medicaid, Leaving 2 Million People in Limbo," National Public Radio, July 1, 2021, https://www.npr.org/sections/health-shots/2021/07/01/1011502538 /12-holdout-states-havent-expanded-medicaid-leaving-2-million -people-in-limbo (accessed 10/19/21).

30. Tammy Luhby, "Challenges to the Affordable Care Act Aren't Over," CNN, June 17, 2021, https://www.cnn.com/2021/06/17/politics /affordable-care-act-challenges/index.html (accessed 10/19/21).

31. "About Chronic Diseases," Centers for Disease Control and Prevention, https://www.cdc.gov/chronicdisease/about/index.htm (accessed 8/1/20).

32. Ben Cosman, "'Death Panels' Will Be Sarah Palin's Greatest Legacy," *The Atlantic*, May 30, 2014, https://www.theatlantic.com/politics /archive/2014/05/death-panels-will-be-sarah-palins-greatest-legacy /371888/ (accessed 8/1/20).

33. Paige Winfield Cunningham, "The Health 202: Republicans Kill Obamacare's Controversial 'Death Panel'," *Washington Post*, February 9, 2018, https://www.washingtonpost.com/news/powerpost/paloma /the-health-202/2018/02/09/the-health-202-republicans-kill-obamacare -s-controversial-death-panel/5a7c601d30fb041c3c7d76c7/ (accessed 8/1/20).

34. Kenneth Rapoza, "In Attack Ad, Paul Ryan Kills Grandma in Wheelchair," *Forbes*, August 12, 2012, https://www.forbes.com/sites/kenrapoza/2012 /08/12/liberal-group-throws-granny-off-cliff-again/ (accessed 8/1/20).

35. Brendan Nyhan, Eric McGhee, John Sides, Seth Masket, and Steven Greene, "One Vote Out of Step? The Effects of Salient Roll Call Votes in the 2010 Election," *American Politics Research* 40, no. 5 (2012): 844–79.

36. "Historical," Centers for Medicare & Medicaid Services, https://www
    .cms.gov/Research-Statistics-Data-and-Systems/Statistics-Trends
    -and-Reports/NationalHealthExpendData/NationalHealthAccounts
    Historical (accessed 7/29/20).

37. "Health Spending," OECD, 2021, https://data.oecd.org/healthres/health
    -spending.htm (accessed 8/5/22).

38. Roosa Tikkanen and Melinda K. Abrams, "U.S. Health Care from a
    Global Perspective, 2019: Higher Spending, Worse Outcomes?" The
    Commonwealth Fund, January 30, 2020, https://www.commonwealthfund
    .org/publications/issue-briefs/2020/jan/us-health-care-global-perspective
    -2019 (accessed 8/3/20).

39. "Prescription Drugs," Health Policy Institute, Georgetown University,
    https://hpi.georgetown.edu/rxdrugs/# (accessed 7/29/20).

40. Lindsay Wilcox, "Physician Salary Report 2021: Compensation Steady
    Despite COVID-19," Weatherby Healthcare, May 26, 2021, https://
    weatherbyhealthcare.com/blog/annual-physician-salary-report
    (accessed 10/19/21).

41. Joe Eaton and M. B. Pell, "Lobbyists Swarm Capitol to Influence
    Health Reform," Center for Public Integrity, February 24, 2010, https://
    publicintegrity.org/health/lobbyists-swarm-capitol-to-influence
    -health-reform/ (accessed 7/29/20).

42. Christine Spolar and Joe Eaton, "The Food Lobby's War on a Soda Tax,"
    Center for Public Integrity, November 4, 2009, https://publicintegrity
    .org/health/the-food-lobbys-war-on-a-soda-tax/ (accessed 10/24/21).

47. ARE NUCLEAR WEAPONS STILL A PROBLEM?

1. Stephanie Buck, "Fear of Nuclear Annihilation Scarred Children
   Growing Up in the Cold War, Studies Later Showed," Medium, August 29,
   2017, https://timeline.com/nuclear-war-child-psychology-d1ff491b5fe0
   (accessed 7/1/20).

2. Archie Brown, "The Gorbachev Revolution and the End of the Cold War,"
   in The Cambridge History of the Cold War, ed. Melvyn P. Leffler and Odd
   Arne Westad (Cambridge: Cambridge University Press, 2010), pp. 244–66.

3. Matthew Bunn, "Reducing the Greatest Risks of Nuclear Threat and
   Terrorism," Daedalus 1 (Fall 2009): 112–23.

4. "Hiroshima and Nagasaki Death Toll," Children of the Atomic Bomb,
   http://www.aasc.ucla.edu/cab/200708230009.html (accessed 7/5/20).

5. Jay Bennett, "Here's How Deadlier Today's Nukes Are Compared to
   World War II A-Bombs," Popular Mechanics, December 13, 2020, https://
   www.popularmechanics.com/military/a23306/nuclear-bombs-powerful
   -today/ (accessed 10/19/21).

6. "Treaty on the Non-Proliferation of Nuclear Weapons (NPT)," United
   Nations Office for Disarmament Affairs, https://www.un.org/disarmament
   /wmd/nuclear/npt/text (accessed 10/19/21).

7. Michael E. O'Hanlon, Robert Einhorn, Steven Pifer, and Frank A. Rose, "Experts Assess the Nuclear Non-Proliferation Treaty, 50 Years after It Went into Effect," Brookings Institution, March 3, 2020, https://www.brookings.edu/blog/order-from-chaos/2020/03/03/experts-assess-the-nuclear-non-proliferation-treaty-50-years-after-it-went-into-effect/ (accessed 10/19/21).

8. Kelsey Davenport, Kingston Reif, and Daryl Kimball, "Nuclear Weapons: Who Has What at a Glance," Arms Control Association, October 2021, https://www.armscontrol.org/factsheets/Nuclearweaponswhohaswhat; "Nuclear Testing Chronology," AtomicArchive.com, https://www.atomicarchive.com/almanac/test-sites/testing-chronology.html (accessed 10/19/21).

9. "United Nations Conference to Negotiate a Legally Binding Instrument to Prohibit Nuclear Weapons, Leading towards Their Total Elimination," United Nations, 2017, https://www.un.org/disarmament/tpnw/submissions-ngos.html (accessed 7/8/20).

10. "Representing America in a Career that Matters," U.S. Department of State, https://careers.state.gov/ (accessed 7/8/20).

11. "Biden Aide to Meet with Top Chinese Diplomat amid Tensions," Al Jazeera, October 5, 2021, https://www.aljazeera.com/news/2021/10/5/biden-aide-to-meet-top-chinese-diplomat-amid-tensions (accessed 10/19/21).

12. Eleni Zervos, "The United States Celebrates 50 Years of the Treaty on the Nonproliferation of Nuclear Weapons," U.S. Department of State Archive, March 5, 2020, https://2017-2021.state.gov/the-united-states-celebrates-50-years-of-the-treaty-on-the-nonproliferation-of-nuclear-weapons/index.html (accessed 10/19/21).

13. Kelsey Davenport, "Chronology of Libya's Disarmament and Relations with the United States," Arms Control Association, January 2018, https://www.armscontrol.org/factsheets/LibyaChronology (accessed 7/8/20).

14. "New START Treaty," U.S. Department of State, https://www.state.gov/new-start/ (accessed 7/8/20).

15. Rebeccah L. Heinrichs, "Now There's No Denying It: Obama's Failed Iran Deal Wasn't Worth the Cost," The Hill, December 22, 2017, https://thehill.com/opinion/national-security/366197-now-theres-no-denying-it-obamas-failed-iran-deal-wasnt-worth-the (accessed 7/8/20).

16. "Fact Sheet: United States, G7, and EU Impose Severe and Immediate Costs on Russia," The White House, April 6, 2022, https://www.whitehouse.gov/briefing-room/statements-releases/2022/04/06/fact-sheet-united-states-g7-and-eu-impose-severe-and-immediate-costs-on-russia/ (accessed 6/28/22).

17. "Sanctions Programs and Country Information," U.S. Department of the Treasury, https://www.treasury.gov/resource-center/sanctions/programs/pages/programs.aspx (accessed 6/28/22).

18. "The Iran Primer," United States Institute of Peace, October 11, 2010, https://iranprimer.usip.org/resource/us-sanctions (accessed 7/8/20).

19. Tom O'Connor, "Do U.S. Sanctions Hurt Iran? Yes, and It's Everyday People Who Suffer Most," *Newsweek*, November 5, 2018, https://www.newsweek.com/do-us-sanctions-hurt-iran-everyday-people-suffer-most-1201954 (accessed 7/8/20).

20. "Sudan: What You Need to Know about U.S. Sanctions," U.S. Department of the Treasury, July 25, 2008, https://home.treasury.gov/policy-issues/financial-sanctions/sanctions-programs-and-country-information/sudan-and-darfur-sanctions (accessed 10/19/21).

21. Carol Morello, "U.S. Lifts Sanctions on Sudan, Ending Two Decades of Embargo," *Washington Post*, October 6, 2017, https://www.washingtonpost.com/world/national-security/us-lifts-sanctions-on-sudan-ending-two-decades-of-embargo/2017/10/06/aac1bd22-86d5-434e-9a21-1e0d57a72cb0_story.html (accessed 7/8/20).

22. Nikolay Marinov, "Do Economic Sanctions Destabilize Country Leaders?" *American Journal of Political Science* 49, no. 3 (2005): 564–76.

23. "Syria War: New U.S. Sanctions Target Assad Government's Foreign Backers," BBC, June 17, 2020, https://www.bbc.com/news/world-middle-east-53076994; Kelsey Davenport and Kingston Reif, "Nuclear Weapons: Who Has What at a Glance," Arms Control Association, October 2021, https://www.armscontrol.org/factsheets/Nuclearweaponswhohaswhat (accessed 6/12/22).

24. Shubhangi Pandey, "U.S. Sanctions on Pakistan and Their Failure as Strategic Deterrent," Observer Research Foundation, August 1, 2018, https://www.orfonline.org/research/42912-u-s-sanctions-on-pakistan-and-their-failure-as-strategic-deterrent/ (accessed 7/8/20).

25. "About Declarations of War by Congress," U.S. Senate, https://www.senate.gov/about/powers-procedures/declarations-of-war.htm (accessed 10/19/21).

26. War Powers Resolution, Pub. L. No. 93-148, 87 Stat. 555 (November 7, 1973).

27. "Military and Civilian Personnel by Service/Agency by State/Country," Defense Manpower Data Center, March 2022, https://dwp.dmdc.osd.mil/dwp/api/download?fileName=DMDC_Website_Location_Report_2203.xlsx&groupName=milRegionCountry (accessed 7/15/22).

28. Barbara Starr, "U.S. Military Plans against Iran Being Updated," CNN, April 18, 2010, https://www.cnn.com/2010/POLITICS/04/18/us.iran/index.html (accessed 7/10/20).

29. Van Jackson, "Want to Strike North Korea? It's Not Going to Go the Way You Think," Politico Magazine, January 12, 2018, https://www.politico.com/magazine/story/2018/01/12/north-korea-strike-nuclear-strategist-216306 (accessed 7/10/20).

30. Jason M. Breslow, "Colin Powell: U.N. Speech 'Was a Great Intelligence Failure'," *Frontline*, May 17, 2016, https://www.pbs.org/wgbh/frontline

/article/colin-powell-u-n-speech-was-a-great-intelligence-failure/
(accessed 7/11/20).

31. Philip Bump, "15 Years after the Iraq War Began, the Death Toll Is Still Murky," *Washington Post*, March 20, 2018, https://www.washingtonpost .com/news/politics/wp/2018/03/20/15-years-after-it-began-the-death -toll-from-the-iraq-war-is-still-murky/ (accessed 7/10/20).

32. Bart Barnes, "Barry Goldwater, GOP Hero, Dies," *Washington Post*, May 30, 1998, https://www.washingtonpost.com/wp-srv/politics/daily /may98/goldwater30.htm (accessed 7/9/20).

33. "Daisy" ad, https://www.youtube.com/watch?v=riDypP1KfOU (accessed 7/1/20).

34. "Biden Calls Trump Nuclear Testing Discussion Reckless, Dangerous," Reuters, May 28, 2020, https://www.reuters.com/article/us-usa -election-biden-nuclear/biden-calls-trump-nuclear-testing-discussion -reckless-dangerous-idUSKBN2342GK (accessed 7/10/20).

48. SHOULD YOU WORRY ABOUT TERRORIST ATTACKS?

1. Kate Zernike and Michael T. Kaufman, "The Most Wanted Face of Terrorism," *New York Times*, May 2, 2011, https://www.nytimes.com /2011/05/02/world/02osama-bin-laden-obituary.html (accessed 6/14/20).

2. "The 9/11 Tapes: The Story in the Air," *New York Times*, September 7, 2011, http://archive.nytimes.com/www.nytimes.com/interactive/2011/09/08 /nyregion/911-tapes.html; "9/11: Voices from the Doomed Planes," *The Telegraph*, September 10, 2011, https://www.telegraph.co.uk/news /worldnews/september-11-attacks/8754395/911-Voices-from-the -doomed-planes.html (accessed 6/13/20).

3. "Flight 93 Hijacker: 'Shall We Finish It Off?'" CNN, July 23, 2004, https://www.cnn.com/2004/US/07/22/911.flight.93/index.html (accessed 6/13/20).

4. Brenda J. Lutz and James M. Lutz, *Globalization and the Economic Consequences of Terrorism* (London: Palgrave Macmillan, 2017).

5. "Text: President Bush Addresses the Nation," *Washington Post*, September 20, 2001, https://www.washingtonpost.com/wp-srv/nation /specials/attacked/transcripts/bushaddress_092001.html (accessed 10/20/21).

6. "Transcript of Dick Cheney's Remarks on National Security," CNN, https://www.cnn.com/2009/POLITICS/05/21/cheney.transcript/ (accessed 6/19/20).

7. "The 9/11 Commission Report," National Commission on Terrorist Attacks upon the United States, https://govinfo.library.unt.edu/911/report /911Report_Exec.htm (accessed 6/14/20).

8. "The 9/11 Commission Report."

9. "Budget-in-Brief: Fiscal Year 2023," Department of Homeland Security, https://www.dhs.gov/sites/default/files/2022-03/22-%201835%20 -%20FY%202023%20Budget%20in%20Brief%20FINAL%20with%20 Cover_Remediated.pdf (accessed 8/5/22).

10. Steven Brill, "Is America Any Safer?" *The Atlantic*, September 2016, https://www.theatlantic.com/magazine/archive/2016/09/are-we-any -safer/492761/ (accessed 6/14/20).

11. "A Brief History of the Information Sharing Environment," Office of the Director of National Intelligence, October 2015, https://www .dni.gov/index.php/who-we-are/organizations/ise/ise-archive/ise -blog/2461-a-brief-history-of-the-information-sharing-environment (accessed 6/24/20).

12. Hannah Ritchie, Joe Hasell, Cameron Appel, and Max Roser, "Terrorism," Our World in Data, November 2019, https://ourworldindata.org/terrorism #all-charts-preview (accessed 6/12/20).

13. "Where Are ISIS's Foreign Fighters Coming From?" National Bureau of Economic Research, June 2016, https://www.nber.org/digest/jun16 /w22190.html (accessed 6/18/20).

14. "The Global War on Terrorism: The First 100 Days," U.S. Department of State Archive, https://2001-2009.state.gov/s/ct/rls/wh/6947.htm (accessed 6/18/20).

15. Eric Schmitt and Helene Cooper, "How the U.S. Plans to Fight from Afar after Troops Exit Afghanistan," *New York Times*, April 15, 2021, https:// www.nytimes.com/2021/04/15/us/politics/united-states-al-qaeda -afghanistan.html (accessed 10/20/21).

16. Robert Draper, *To Start a War: How the Bush Administration took America into Iraq* (New York: Penguin Press, 2020).

17. David J. Garren, "Preventive War: Shortcomings Classical and Contemporary," *Journal of Military Ethics* 18, no. 3 (2019): 204–22.

18. "Q&A: What Is the 'Coalition of the Willing'?" *New York Times*, March 28, 2003, https://archive.nytimes.com/www.nytimes.com/cfr/international /slot1_032803.html (accessed 2/7/21).

19. Neta C. Crawford and Catherine Lutz, "Human Cost of Post-9/11 Wars," Watson Institute, Brown University, September 2021, https://watson .brown.edu/costsofwar/figures/2021/WarDeathToll; For the number of military personnel, see: "A Timeline of U.S. Troop Levels in Afghanistan since 2001," Military Times, July 6, 2016, https://www.militarytimes.com/news /your-military/2016/07/06/a-timeline-of-u-s-troop-levels-in-afghanistan -since-2001/ and Miriam Berger, "Invaders, Allies, Occupiers, Guests: A Brief History of U.S. Military Involvement in Iraq," *Washington Post*, January 11, 2020, https://www.washingtonpost.com/world/2020/01/11 /invaders-allies-occupiers-guests-brief-history-us-military-involvement -iraq/. For deaths and financial costs, see: Watson Institute for International and Public Affairs, "Costs of War," https://watson.brown.edu/costsofwar/.

And for the number of troops remaining as of 2021, see: "US Combat Forces to Leave Iraq by End of Year," BBC, July 27, 2021, https://www.bbc.com/news/world-us-canada-57970464 (accessed 7/5/22).

20. Jessica Purkiss and Jack Serle, "Obama's Covert Drone War in Numbers: Ten Times More Strikes than Bush," Bureau of Investigative Journalism, January 17, 2017, https://www.thebureauinvestigates.com/stories/2017-01-17/obamas-covert-drone-war-in-numbers-ten-times-more-strikes-than-bush (accessed 6/22/20).

21. Hussein and Haddad, "Infographic: U.S. Military Presence around the World," *Al Jazeera*, September 10, 2021, https://www.aljazeera.com/news/2021/9/10/infographic-us-military-presence-around-the-world-interactive; Meghann Myers, "U.S. Troops Will Likely Be in Iraq for Years to Come, Central Command Boss Says," Military Times, March 18, 2022, https://www.militarytimes.com/news/pentagon-congress/2022/03/18/us-troops-will-likely-be-in-iraq-for-years-to-come-central-command-boss-says/ (accessed 6/28/22).

22. H.R. 3162 — Uniting and Strengthening America by Providing Appropriate Tools Required to Intercept and Obstruct Terrorism (USA PATRIOT ACT) Act of 2001.

23. Eric Rosenbach and Aki J. Peritz, "The USA Patriot Act," Belfer Center for Science and International Affairs, July 2009, https://www.belfercenter.org/publication/usa-patriot-act (accessed 6/19/20).

24. Ron Suskind, *The One-Percent Doctrine: Deep Inside America's Pursuit of Its Enemies since 9/11* (New York: Simon & Schuster, 2006).

25. Spencer Ackerman, Dominic Rushe, and Julian Borger, "Senate Report on CIA Torture Claims Spy Agency Lied about 'Ineffective' Program," The Guardian, December 9, 2014, https://www.theguardian.com/us-news/2014/dec/09/cia-torture-report-released (accessed 2/7/21).

26. Dara Lind, "Everyone's Heard of the Patriot Act. Here's What It Actually Does," Vox, June 2, 2015, https://www.vox.com/2015/6/2/8701499/patriot-act-explain (accessed 6/19/20).

27. "Are They Allowed to Do That? A Breakdown of Selected Government Surveillance Programs," Brennan Center for Justice, https://www.brennancenter.org/sites/default/files/analysis/Government%20Surveillance%20Factsheet.pdf (accessed 2/7/21).

28. Jim Sensenbrenner, "This Abuse of the Patriot Act Must End," *The Guardian*, June 9, 2013, https://www.theguardian.com/commentisfree/2013/jun/09/abuse-patriot-act-must-end (accessed 6/19/20).

29. Peter Bergen and David Sterman, "Jihadist Terrorism 17 Years after 9/11," New America Foundation, September 10, 2018, https://www.newamerica.org/international-security/reports/jihadist-terrorism-17-years-after-911/ (accessed 10/20/21).

30. Peter Bergen and David Sterman, "Terrorism in America 18 Years after 9/11," New America Foundation, September 18, 2019, https://www

.newamerica.org/international-security/reports/terrorism-america
-18-years-after-911/ (accessed 10/20/21).

31. Natasha Bertrand, Katie Bo Williams, and Zachary Cohen, "Biden
Promised ISIS-K Will 'Pay.' Having No Troops in Afghanistan Makes
That Harder," CNN, September 5, 2021, https://www.cnn.com
/2021/09/05/politics/afghanistan-counterterrorism-challenges/index
.html (accessed 10/20/21),

32. "U.S. Terrorist Attacks Fast Facts," CNN, September 2, 2021, https://
www.cnn.com/2013/04/18/us/u-s-terrorist-attacks-fast-facts/index
.html (accessed 10/20/21).

33. "Terrorism," Gallup, https://news.gallup.com/poll/4909/Terrorism
-United-States.aspx (accessed 6/12/20).

34. Dave Mosher and Skye Gould, "How Likely Are Foreign Terrorists to Kill
Americans? The Odds May Surprise You," Business Insider, January 31,
2017, https://www.businessinsider.com/death-risk-statistics-terrorism
-disease-accidents-2017-1 (accessed 6/19/20).

35. Domestic Terrorism Prevention Act of 2019, S. 894, March 27, 2019,
https://www.congress.gov/116/bills/s894/BILLS-116s894is.xml
(accessed 2/7/21).

Credits

ART

Section 5
p. 354: Kiss Me I'm Polish
p. 390: Mapping Specialists

Section 6
p. 501: Kiss Me I'm Polish

TEXT

Segment 17
Table 1: "Table: Political Engagement in Young People's Families" from *Running from Office Why Young Americans are Turned Off to Politics* by Jennifer L. Lawless and Richard L. Fox. © 2015 Oxford University Press. Reproduced with permission of the Licensor through PLSclear.

Segment 44
Table 3: Data from the MIT Living Wage Calculator adapted by permission of Dr. Amy Glasmeier and Massachusetts Institute of Technology. MIT Living Wage Calculator © 2022 Dr. Amy K. Glasmeier and the Massachusetts Institute of Technology.

Segment 45
Figure 3: "Imports of goods and services (current US$)" from *World Bank national accounts data, and OECD National Accounts data files*. Used under a Creative Commons Attribution 4.0 International License (CC BY 4.0) https://creativecommons.org/licenses/by/4.0/

PHOTO

How Do You Use This Book?
p. 7: Author photos Courtesy of Richard L. Fox and Courtesy of Jennifer L. Lawless

Segment 1
p. 13: Iv'n S'nchez / picture-alliance / dpa / AP Images

Segment 2
p. 24: dbtravel / Alamy Stock Photo

Segment 3
p. 36: By permission of Gary Varvel and Creators Syndicate, Inc.
p. 38: (left to right) AP Photo / Lawrence Journal-World, Mike Yoder; Beer glass: boule13 / Getty Images; Artwork: Daniel Essrow

Segment 4
p. 48: Supreme Court of the United States
p. 51: (left to right) World History Archive / Alamy Stock Photo; Art Reserve / Alamy Stock Photo; IanDagnall Computing / Alamy Stock Photo; IanDagnall Computing / Alamy Stock Photo; Sarin Images / The Granger Collection

Segment 5
p. 57: Sueddeutsche Zeitung Photo / Alamy Stock Photo

Segment 6
p. 66: Samuel Corum / Getty Images
p. 73: (left to right) MPI / Getty Images; THE NEW YORK TIMES / Redux

Segment 7
p. 78: AP Photo / Charles Reed / U.S. Immigration and Customs Enforcement
p. 79: (left to right) Kevork Djansezian / Getty Images; AP Photo / Jeff Chiu

Segment 8
p. 89: (left to right) agefotostock / Alamy Stock Photo; MediaNews Group / Inland Valley Daily Bulletin via Getty Images
p. 95: (left to right) Emanuel Tanjala / Alamy Stock Photo ; AP Photo / Scott Sonner

Segment 9
p. 101: Richard Graulich / The Palm Beach Post / ZUMA Wire / Alamy Live News

Segment 10
p. 110: Samuel Corum / Anadolu Agency / Getty Images
p. 112: Mark Reinstein / Corbis via Getty Images
p. 116: Contraband Collection / Alamy Stock Photo

Segment 11
p. 121: David Stephenson / ZUMAPRESS.com / Alamy Stock Photo

Segment 12
p. 133: www.STUS.com
p. 136: (left to right) Craig Hudson for The Washington Post via Getty Images; Allison Bailey / NurPhoto via AP
p. 139: The Magazine of the Year, Feb 1948.

Segment 13
p. 144: (left to right) Alpha Historica / Alamy Stock Photo; Bettmann / Getty Images; Theo Wargo / Getty Images
p. 146: (left to right) AP Photo / Bill Hudson; (right) PictureLux / The Hollywood Archive / Alamy Stock Photo; (bottom) Black Star / Alamy Stock Photo
p. 149: (left to right) Everett Collection / Shutterstock; Niday Picture Library / Alamy Stock Photo
p. 152: (left) AP Photo; (right) Leonard Fink / The LGBT Community Center National History Archive

Segment 14
p. 158: Michael B. Thomas / Getty Images

Segment 15
p. 170: Courtesy of the John F. Kennedy Presidential Library and Museum
p. 174: The Advertising Archives

Segment 16
p. 182: Bumble Dee / Alamy Stock Photo
p. 187: Courtesy of Austin Wallis

Segment 17
p. 195: Leigh Green / Alamy Stock Photo
p. 197: Melinda Lee Patelli

Segment 18
p. 207: Tim Graham / Alamy Stock Photo

Segment 19
p. 220: Montinique Monroe / Getty Images

Segment 20
p. 233: Courtesy of Sara Knuth / Greeley Tribune
p. 236: (left to right) JannHuizenga / Getty Images; Jeff Swensen / Getty Images

Segment 21
p. 245: (left to right) AP Photo / J.B. Forbes; Andrew Harrer / Bloomberg via Getty Images
p: 250: (top left to right) Daniel Acker / Bloomberg via Getty Images; Melinda Lee Patelli; (bottom left to right) Patti McConville / Alamy Stock Photo; Melinda Lee Patelli

Segment 22
p. 257: Michael E. Miller / The Washington Post via Getty Images
p. 263: snopes.com

Segment 23
p. 267: MSNBC
p. 278: Fox News
p. 279: OZY.com

Segment 24
p. 282: (left to right) WBZ Channel 4; Fox News
p. 287: (left to right) MSNBC; Fox News
p. 289: (left to right) MSNBC; Fox News; CNN

Segment 25
p. 294: Fox News
p. 297: CNN; photos used in ad: Hannah Beier / Bloomberg via Getty Images; Kevin Dietsch / Getty Images; Nathan Howard / Getty Images; AP Photo / Ted Jackson
p. 301: (logos courtesy of the respective sources)
p. 303: LifeZette.com; FamVeld / Shutterstock

Segment 26
p. 306: Cleobie Impang
p. 308: CNN; FoxNews
p. 309: Fox News; CNN
p. 311: FoxNews; CNN

Segment 27
p. 321: Chip Somodevilla / Getty Images
p. 324: (left to right) Chuck Nacke / Alamy Stock Photo; Kristin Callahan / Everett Collection / Alamy Live News; Ed Lefkowicz / Alamy Live News; SOPA Images Limited / Alamy Stock Photo
p. 327: (top left to right) CBS ; Justin Sullivan / Getty Images; (bottom left to right) Official White House Photo by Pete Souza; NBC

Segment 28
p. 331: (left to right) MSNBC; CSPAN
p. 334: (left to right) Republican National Committee; Democratic National Committee; AP Photo / Carolyn Kaster
p. 335: NRCC

Segment 29
p. 342: Rob Rogers © 2014 Reprinted by permission of ANDREWS MCMEEL SYNDICATION. All rights reserved.

Segment 30
p. 357: (left to right) NBC; CNN

Segment 31
p. 368: (left to right) Jason Merritt / Getty Images; FABRICE COFFRINI / AFP / Getty Images
p. 374: Sanders, Romney, Yang: Chip Somodevilla / Getty Images; Harris, Clinton: Justin Sullivan / Getty Images; Trump: Win McNamee / Getty Images

Segment 32
p. 384: Joe Raedle / Getty Images
p. 388: Greene.house.gov; SAUL LOEB / AFP via Getty Images

Segment 33
p. 396: Bruce Bolinger / Cartoon Stock
p. 401: (logos courtesy of the respective sources)

Segment 34
p. 409: Jeff Brown

Segment 35
p. 420: ABC News
p. 422: (left to right) shooter / Alamy Stock Photo; Richard Levine / Alamy Stock Photo
p. 424: (top left to right) Abaca Press / Alamy Stock Photo; The Photo Access / Alamy Stock Photo; (bottom left to right) REUTERS / Alamy Stock Photo; Tom Williams / Roll Call / Getty Images
p. 427: (left to right) CNN; CSPAN

Segment 36
p. 435: (left to right) PAUL J.RICHARDS / AFP via Getty Images; BRENDAN SMIALOWSKI / AFP via Getty Images; james cheadle / Alamy Stock Photo; Photo Pool Maxpix / Alamy Stock Photo
p. 438: Drew Angerer / Getty Images
p. 439: (left to right) dpa picture alliance / Alamy Stock Photo; Drew Angerer / Getty Images
p. 443: (left to right) Kremlin Pool / Alamy Stock Photo; aNews.com

Segment 37
p. 448: Nate Beeler, courtesy of Cagle Cartoons

Segment 38
p. 460: (left to right) AP Photo / Pablo Martinez Monsivais; AP Photo / Charles Dharapak
p. 467: Jemal Countess / UPI / Bloomberg via Getty Images

Segment 39
p. 472: Win McNamee / Getty Images
p. 478: Jonathan Ernst / Reuters / Alamy Stock Photo

Segment 40
p. 483: Pat Bagley, courtesy of Cagle Cartoons
p. 486: (left to right) Steve Liss / The LIFE Images Collection via Getty Images; LUKE FRAZZA / AFP via Getty Images
p. 487: (left to right) Win Mcnamee / CNP / ZUMA Wire / Alamy Live News; NBC

Segment 41
p. 497: Clay Bennett Editorial Cartoon used with permission of Clay Bennett, the Washington Post Writers Group and the Cartoonist Group. All rights reserved
p. 502: Courtesy of Fight for the Future
p. 506: Lance King / Getty Images

Segment 42
p. 511: (all) Melinda Lee Patelli
p. 518: Jeff Malet Photography / Newscom; Waters.House.gov

Segment 43
p. 525: AP Photo / J. Scott Applewhite

Segment 44
p. 538: (left to right) Mint Images / Getty Images; Shutterstock / Frank Fennema

Segment 45
p. 550: Qilai Shen / Getty Images
p. 554: AP Photo / Dean Musgrove
p. 555: Win McNamee / Getty Images

Segment 46
p. 562: Jeff Koterba, courtesy of Cagle Cartoons
p. 568: (each row, left to right) White House Photo; IanDagnall Computing / Alamy Stock Photo; Michael Brochstein / Alamy Live News; Sipa USA / Alamy Stock Photo; UPI / Alamy Stock Photo; The Photo Access / Alamy Stock Photo; Douglas Christian / ZUMA Wire / Alamy Live News; World History Archive / Alamy Stock Photo
p. 570: (both) Agenda Project Action Fund

Segment 47
p. 576: GraphicaArtis / Getty Images
p. 577: (left to right) swim ink 2 / Corbis via Getty Images; Jim Heimann Collection / Getty Images
p. 579: (flags) Color_dreams / Shutterstock; charnsitr / Shutterstock; oxameel / Shutterstock; T. Lesia / Shutterstock; MATULEE / Shutterstock; nortongo / Shutterstock; charnsitr / Shutterstock; Ola.Nia / Shutterstock; G7 Stock / Shutterstock
p. 580: (left to right) Bettmann / Getty Images; Olivier Douliery-Pool / Getty Images; Planetpix / Alamy Live News

Segment 48
p. 590: Larry Towell / Magnum Photos
p. 591: Spencer Platt / Getty Images

Glossary/Index

general election, 377–78, *378*
media coverage of, 318
raising and spending money for, *337*, 337–38
to secure nomination, 375
campaign chair, *370*
campaign contributions, by lobbyists, 502–4, *503*
campaign financing, 341–52
argument against, 349–50
argument in support of, 348–49
contribution to own campaign as, *345*, *346*
by corporations and unions, 346, *347*, 484
federal laws governing, *345*, 345–47
future of, 350
by individual donations, 345, *345*, 346, *347*, 348, 350
by political action committees (PACs), 345, *345*, 346, *347*
and political favors, 341–42, 349–50
by political parties, *337*, 337–38
public, 350
public attitudes about, 342, *343*
quick overview of, 343–44, *344*
reporting system for, 345–46, 347
state laws governing, 347, *347*
by Super PACs, *345*, 346
and winning elections, 344
Campaign in a Box, 348
campaign manager, *370*
campaign message, 369–71
campaign offices, 372
campaign promises, 320–21
Campaigns & Elections website, 332
campaign staff, 369, *370*
campaign trail, 371–73
Campus Pride, 186
candidates, identifying and recruiting, 335–36
Cantwell, Maria, *427*

capital gains tax, 543–44 Taxes on profits from the sale of assets, such as stocks, bonds, and real estate.

capital punishment, *94*, 129
Cardona, Miguel, 465
"career civil servants," 454
"careerists," 454
Carlson, Tucker, 307
cars, warrantless searches of, 123

casework, 386 The direct help that members of Congress provide to citizens living in their district or state.

casinos, campaign contributions by, *503*
Castile, Philando, 158

categorical grants, 85 Federal funding given to states to run federal programs; they include very specific instructions for how to spend the federal money.

Catholicism, on being gay as sin, 183

caucuses, 373 Political meetings where voters gather to select a candidate for president; voters typically listen to speeches from representatives of each candidate's campaign before indicating which candidate they support.

CBS (network), 114
census, 355
Center for American Progress, 254
Center for Effective Lawmaking, 387
Centers for Disease Control and Prevention (CDC), *463*, *464*
Central African Republic, sanctions on, *582*
ceremonial responsibilities, 438–39, *439*

challengers, 319 Candidates who run against incumbents.

Challenger space shuttle disaster, *439*
character traits, in voting choice, 322–23, 326, *327*
Charlottesville, Va., Unite the Right rally in, *110*
charter schools, 465
Chasanow, Deborah, 474
Chauvin, Derek, 157

checks and balances, 26, 42–44, *43* Measures ensuring that each branch of government is able to prevent another branch, or an elected leader, from becoming too powerful.

chemical industry, lobbying by, 500–501
Cheney, Dick, 516, 592, 596
Cheney, Liz, 66–67, 519
Chevron, 507

chief diplomat, 443–444, *444* Presidential role of conducting diplomacy and foreign policy to advance the nation's interests.

chief strategist, for presidential campaign, *370*
childcare cost, pay gap due to, *177*, 177–78
Children's Health Insurance Program (CHIP), 565
China
and nuclear weapons, 578, *579*, 581
trade policy with, 557, 558
Christian Legal Society (CLS), 186–87
Christian Legal Society v. Martinez (2004), 187–88
church, separation of state and, 101
chyrons, *289*, 309, *309*

CIA director, 436
circuit court, 474, *475*
citizen engagement, 6, 236–37
citizenship, as requirement for federal officeholder,
68–69, *69*
Citizenship and Immigration, *593*
citizenship test, 259

**Citizens United v. Federal Election Commission,
346,** 484 The 2010 Supreme Court case that struck
down limits on how much corporations and unions
can spend on federal elections.

City Tavern (Philadelphia), 23–24
civics class, 198–99

civic skills, 199, 238 Communication skills,
knowledge of the political system, and critical
thinking; people with these skills are more likely
than people who lack them to participate politically.

civil case, 473 A legal dispute between two people
or businesses, typically over financial or monetary
issues.

civil liberties, 98 Basic freedoms that protect
citizens from undue government intrusion into their
lives; many are enumerated in the Bill of Rights.
  clashes regarding, 99
  and evolving social norms and new technologies,
    99
  extended to all citizens, 99
  vs. national security, 596–97, *597*

civil rights, 98–99 Basic protections from unfair or
unequal treatment based on demographic characteristics, such as race, ethnicity, sex, or gender
identity; generally grounded in the equal protection
clause of the Fourteenth Amendment.
  for African Americans, 17, *17*, 143–44, *144*, 145–48
  clashes regarding, 99
  different frameworks for applying, 153–54
  and evolving social norms and new technologies,
    99
  extended to all citizens, 99
  for LGBTQ people, 151–53
  for women, *144*, 148–50

Civil Rights Act of 1964, 147 Landmark federal legislation that prohibited segregation on the grounds
of race, sex, religion, or national origin and banned
discrimination in all places of "public accommodation"; barred discrimination in hiring and employment; and created the Equal Employment
Opportunity Commission.
  and gender equality, 149, 150, 153
  and pay gap, 175

people's attitudes toward, 17, *17*
and racial justice, 158
civil rights movement, *144, 146,* 146–47
civil service exam, 454

Civil War amendments, 61, **144,** 145 Three amendments to the Constitution that established the
legal foundation for equality after the Civil War.
They abolish slavery (Thirteenth Amendment), make
formerly enslaved persons citizens and guarantee
them equal protection under the law (Fourteenth
Amendment), and grant the right to vote to all citizens regardless of race (Fifteenth Amendment).

classified briefings, 464

Clean Air Act, 60, 456, **465–66** Passed in 1970 and
amended in 1977 and 1990; authorizes the Environmental Protection Agency to establish national
air quality standards and regulate emissions of
hazardous pollutants.

Clean Energy, 251
Clean School Bus Program, *467*
clear and present danger, 111
climate change, and party identification, 214
Clinton, Bill
  diplomacy by, 443
  executive orders by, 441, 442, *442*
  fake news about, 263–64
  and gay rights, 151, 152
  and gun control, 91
  on health care reform, 564, 565
  and income inequality, 545
  and nuclear weapons, 577
  and Oklahoma City bombing, 439
  political appointments by, 467
  presidential election of, 400
  sanctions by, 583
  and sensationalism in media, 288
  trade policy of, 553, 554
Clinton, Hillary
  conspiracy theories about, 263–64
  and democracy, 65
  as elector, 356
  fake news about, 293, 307
  likability of, 326, *327*
  and negative partisanship, 322–23
  and Pizzagate, 256–58, *257*
  popular *vs.* electoral votes for, 353, 359, *359*
  presidential campaign of, 372, *374, 375*
  public opinion about, 227
  and third parties, 402
  Donald Trump's defeat of, 232
closed-door negotiations, 431

cloture, 428, 516 A legislative procedure in which a minimum of 60 votes ends a Senate filibuster and requires the chamber to vote on the bill.

CLS (Christian Legal Society), 186–87
CNN (media outlet)
    accusations of "fake news" on, 74, 299
    agenda setting by, 307–8, *308*
    conflict on, 286, *286*
    criticism on Fox of, 305
    framing by, 310–11, *311*
    history of, 283
    news alerts on, 288, 293
    as news source, straight news *vs.* punditry on, 297, *297*
    priming by, 308–9, *309, 310*
    selective exposure to, 311–13, *313*
    shaping of news by, *306,* 306–7
coalition building, 513
Coast Guard, 592, *593*
Cohen v. California (1965), 116
Colbert, Stephen, *327*

Cold War, 575–77, **576,** *576* The period of extreme hostility between the United States and the former Soviet Union after World War II; the relationship was characterized by propaganda and threats, but stopped short of actual warfare.

collective action problem, 249 A situation in which everyone benefits from a group's efforts regardless of whether they join, so individuals may be tempted not to join the group because they will benefit anyway.

collective representation, 410–411 The degree to which policies and actions taken by Congress reflect the views of a majority of the U.S. population.

college(s)
    political socialization in, 199
    religious freedom *vs.* gay rights in, 186–87
college education, racial inequities in, 162–63
Colorado, campaign financing laws in, 347
Comcast, 498
Comet Ping Pong pizzeria, 256–58, *257*

commander in chief, 436, *444* Presidential role of presiding over and directing military personnel and the nation's arsenal of weapons.

commerce, power to regulate, 81

commerce clause, 81 A provision of Article I, Section 8, of the Constitution that gives Congress the power to regulate interstate commerce.

Commerce Department, 455
Commission on Presidential Debates, 399
committee chair, 423
committee hearings, 423–24
committee system, in Congress, 423–25, *431*
communications director
    for presidential campaign, *370*
    and reelection to Congress, 388
Communist Party USA, 401, *401*
compromise, 513

compulsory voting, 221 Voting that is required by law; failure to do so results in penalties or fines.

concession speech, 379

concurrent powers, 82, *82* Governing responsibilities held by both the federal and the state governments.

concurring opinion, 478 A judicial opinion that agrees with either the majority or the dissenting opinion but relies on different legal reasoning to reach that conclusion.

Confederate flag, 115

conference committee, 428–29 A committee comprising members of the House of Representatives and Senate whose role is to iron out differences in the House and Senate versions of a bill that passed in each chamber.

confirmation, of Supreme Court justices, 483, *483,* 484–87, *488*
conflict, in news, 285–87
Congress
    budgetary authority of, 462
    checks and balances on and by, 42–44, *43*
    collective representation in, 410–11
    constituent representation in, 412–14, *413, 414*
    descriptive representation in, 414–16, *415*
    diversity in, 408–9, *409, 410*
    enumerated powers of, 38, 39–42, *40*
    and federal bureaucracy, 459–68
    limiting number of terms in, 57, *58*
    and military action, 583–85
    public opinion of, 383–85, *384, 385*
    reelection to (*See* reelection to Congress)
    relative power of, 36, 37–44
congressional districts, 389–92, *390*
congressional elections, cost of, 343, *344*
congressional hearings, 463–65, *464*
Congressional Management Foundation, 386

D.C. (District of Columbia)
    electors for, 356
    voting rights for, 71, *71*
DCCC (Democratic Congressional Campaign
    Committee), *333, 337,* 389
death panels, 261, 569
death penalty, *94,* 129
debates
    exclusion of third-party candidates from,
        399–400
    floor, 426–28, *431*
    in presidential campaign, 371–72, 377
Debs, Eugene V., 110
debt, national. *See* national debt
deductibles, 562

deep state, 449, 455–56 A derogatory term to
describe a group of unelected government officials
who are alleged to manipulate and direct national
policy.

defendant, 473 The party accused of wrongdoing in
a civil or criminal case.

Defense Department, 450, *451,* 464, 504, *505,* 532
defense industry, lobbying by, 504
Defense of Marriage Act (1996), 152–53
defense spending, 528
deficit spending, 526, 531–33
DeGeneres, Ellen, 152

delegates, 373–374 Individuals who have been
selected to represent their state's party at the
nominating convention.

democracy, 65–76, **67** A system of government in
which power is derived from the people.
    amendments on expanding, 61
    challenges posed by Electoral College to,
        358–62, *359–61*
    direct, 67, 355
    Founders on, 67–74, *69, 71*
    and free press, 72–74
    and January 6, 2021, attack on Capitol, 65–67
    and open and direct elections, 68–70, *69*
    representative, 67, 68, 409
    and voting rights, 70–72, *71*

Democrat(s), 206–18
    base voters of, 210
    belief in conspiracy theories by, 258, 262, *262*
    coexistence of Republicans and, 216
    cultural differences and, 206–7, *208*
    diversity and inclusion and, 214–15, *215*
    economic policies of, 212, *213*
    fiscal policy of, 532–33

on health insurance, 567–70, *568*
identification with, 208–10, *209, 211*
and income inequality, 538, 545–46
labels for, 215–16
media sources for, 312–13, *313*
money raised by, *337,* 337–38
and party polarization (*See* party polarization)
platform of, 210–12
social and domestic policies of, 213–14, *214*
and state policies, 93–95, *94*
voting choice by, 321–23, *322*
Democratic Congressional Campaign Committee
    (DCCC), *333, 337,* 389
Democratic National Committee (DNC), 332–33,
    333, 335, *337*
Democratic-Republican Party, 49
Democratic Senatorial Campaign Committee
    (DSCC), *333, 337*
demographic characteristics, and descriptive
    representation, 414–16, *415*
Department of Agriculture, 448, *451, 505*
Department of Commerce, *451*
Department of Defense, 450, *451,* 464, 504,
    505, 532
Department of Education, 449, *451*
Department of Energy, *451,* 504, *505*
Department of Health and Human Services, 422,
    451, 504
Department of Homeland Security (DHS), 450–52,
    451, 532, 592, *593*
Department of Housing and Urban Development, *451*
Department of Justice, *451,* 452, *505*
Department of Labor, *451*
Department of State, 450, *451,* 464, *505*
Department of the Interior, *451*
Department of the Treasury, 450, *451, 505*
Department of Transportation, *451, 505*
Department of Veterans Affairs, 450, *451*
Department of War, 450, *451*

descriptive representation, 414–416, *415* The
degree to which elected officials reflect citizens'
demographic characteristics.

desegregation, racial, 145–47
detention, indefinite, 596

devolution, 84–85 A transfer of governing responsibilities from the federal government to state and
local governments.

DeVos, Betsy, 465
DHS (Department of Homeland Security), 450–52,
    451, 532, 592, *593*
diplomacy, 443–44, *444*
    and nuclear weapons, *580,* 580–81

direct democracy, 67, 355 A system of government in which citizens make their preferences known by voting on specific issues and policies.

Director of National Intelligence, 436

discretionary spending, *527, ***528** The portion of the federal government's annual budget that includes optional expenses, which fall into two categories: defense spending and nondefense spending.

discrimination, 20
    reverse, 163
dismissal of case, 129

dissenting opinion, 478–79 A judicial opinion that disagrees with the majority opinion; explains the logic of the justices who voted in the minority.

district court, 473–74, *475* A trial court where most civil and criminal cases are first heard.

District of Columbia (D.C.)
    electors for, 356
    voting rights for, 71, *71*
diversity
    and American Dream, 17, *17,* 20
    in Congress, 408–9, *409, 410*
    and party identification, 214–15, *215*

divided government, 513 A situation in which no one political party controls the House, Senate, and White House.

divorce laws, different state policies on, 93–94, *94*
DNC (Democratic National Committee), 332–33, *333, 335, 337*
Dobbs v. Jackson Women's Health Organization (2022), 136–38
domestic policies, and party identification, 213–14, *214*
domestic terrorism, 598
Dominguez, Travis Luke, 113
Donnelly, Joe, 338
donors and donations, 341–52
    argument against, 349–50
    argument in support of, 348–49
    in deciding to run for president, 369
    federal laws governing, *345,* 345–47
    future of, 350
    and political favors, 341–42, 349–50
    as political participation, 236
    public attitudes about, 342, *343*
    state laws governing, 347, *347*
"don't ask, don't tell" policy, 151, 152

double jeopardy, 128 Being tried again for a crime you've already been acquitted of; prohibited by the Fifth Amendment.

Douglas, William, 135
Douglass, Frederick, 109
draft cards, burning of, 110, *116,* 117
draft registration, 150
"dreamers," 411, 513, 519

***Dred Scott v. Sandford,* 52** The 1857 Supreme Court case that struck down the Missouri Compromise.

drinking age, national, 37–44
driving, different state policies on, 94
Drudge Report, 276
Drug Enforcement Administration, 452
drug-related crimes, racial disparities in, 163–64
DSCC (Democratic Senatorial Campaign Committee), *333, 337*

dual federalism, 83 A system of federalism in which federal and state governments exercise their powers independently and without interference from one another.

due process, 124, 134 The idea that one's constitutional rights cannot be infringed on arbitrarily by the state or national government; this clause is referenced in the Fifth and Fourteenth Amendments.

duPonts, 539
Duverger, Maurice, 400

Duverger's Law, 400 The theory that countries with single-member districts and plurality voting almost always wind up with a strong two-party system.

early childhood education programs, 545
early contests, 373–75

earmarks, 517–518 A spending allocation or tax regulation included in a piece of legislation that solely benefits a specific state, local community, or congressional district.

"echo chamber," 312
e-cigarettes, 419–31
economic advisers, 440
economic injustice, racial, 159–61, *160*
economic policies, and party identification, 212, *213*
economic recessions, fiscal policy and, 524–25, 532
economic sanctions, and nuclear weapons, 581–83, *582*

education
  and political participation, *239*, 240
  public investments in, 544–45, 546
  racial inequities in, 161–63, *162*
educational interest groups, campaign contributions by, *503*
Education Appropriations Subcommittee, *424*
Edwards, John, 327
Eighteenth Amendment, *57*, 61
Eighth Amendment, 98, *122*, 127, 128
Eilish, Billie, 219
Eisenhower, Dwight D., 151, *435*, 442, 564
elected positions, too many, 224–25
election(s)
  fundamental challenges to "democratic," 319
  general, 319
  horse race coverage of, 287
  media coverage of, 318
  midterm, 221–23, *223*
  money and power in, 319
  nonpartisan, 323
  open and direct, 68–70, *69*
  partisanship and, 319
  primary, 223, 319, 373–75
  special, 224
  too many, 224–25
  voting choice in, 320–29
  winning, 319
election day, 379
election fraud, conspiracy theories about, 262, *262*, 363
elector(s), 355, 356
  number of, 356, *358*
  slate of, 356–57

Electoral College, 353–66, **355** A system for selecting the president laid out in Article II, Sections 2 and 3, of the Constitution; voters in each state choose electors to decide which presidential and vice-presidential candidates the state supports.
  and 2020 election, 354, 362–64
  amendment to, *58*, 61
  challenges to democracy posed by, 358–62, *359–61*
  creation of, 69
  fragility of, 364
  history of, 354–55
  and "one person, one vote," 360, *360*
  and popular vote *vs.* electoral vote, 353, 356–57, 359, *359*
  process of, *356*, 356–58, *358*
  and safe *vs.* swing states, *354*, 360–62, *361*
  and small states, 355, 362
  and unequal representation, 71–72
  voting for members of, 69
  winner-take-all system in, 357, 360

electoral districts, 389–92, *390*
electoral system, 68–70, *69*

electoral vote(s), 356 Allocated to each state based on the size of the state's congressional delegation (the number of representatives in the House plus the two senators); the winner of the statewide popular vote for president typically receives all of that state's electoral votes.
  allocation of, *356*, 356–57, *358*
  certification of, 357–58, 363–64
  number of, 356, *358*
  popular *vs.*, 353, 356–58, 359, *359*

electorate
  misinformed, 261–64, *262*
  poorly informed, 258–61, *260*
electric vehicles, 467, 496–97
electronics industry, lobbying by, 498, *499*
Ellsberg, Daniel, 73
Elmo, *424*
Elonis, Anthony, 112–13
Elonis v. United States (2015), 113
Emancipation Proclamation, 145
embargo, 583
emergency contraception, 132, 133
emissions, regulation of, 466, *466*
employment-based health insurance, 565–67
Energy and Commerce Committee, 423
energy companies, lobbying by, 507
Energy Department, *451*, 504, *505*
Engel, Steven, 103
Engel v. Vitale (1959), 103–5

entitlement programs, *527,* **527**–528 Programs that require the federal government to make payments to any person who meets the program's eligibility criteria established by law (such as Social Security, Medicare, and veterans' benefits).

enumerated powers, 38, 39–42, *40* The powers of each branch of government as specifically listed in the Constitution.

environmental advocacy groups, campaign contributions by, *503*, 504
environmental interest groups, 248
environmental laws, 462–63
environmental policy, and party identification, 214
environmental protection, 402
Environmental Protection Agency (EPA)
  background of, 461
  budget of, 462
  bureaucratic discretion in, 465–68, *466*
  clean water regulations of, 447
  congressional oversight over, 462–65, *464*

FDA (Food and Drug Administration), 419, 447, 455, *464*

federal agencies
  adjusting responsibilities of, 462–63
  agency drift of, 465
  budgetary authority over, 462
  bureaucratic discretion in, 465–68, *466*
  congressional oversight of, 462–65, *464*
  creation of, 461, 462
  enforcement of law by, 467–68
  hearings for, 463–65, *464*
  implementation of law by, 465–67, *466*
  leadership of, 459–61, 463
  principal-agent problem in, 465
  rulemaking authority of, 465–68, *466*
  setting priorities of, 465
Federal Aviation Administration (FAA), 452, *464*, 512
federal banks, 80

federal budget, *525, 527,* **527**–529 The federal government's annual plan for spending and raising money.

federal bureaucracy, 447–58, **449** Government offices within the executive branch that implement and enforce the law.
  Congress and, 459–68
  and deep state, 449, 455–56
  examples of, 447–49
  history of, 450
  partisans *vs.* public servants in, 452–55
  scope of, 450–52, *451*
  size of, *451, 452, 453*

Federal Bureau of Investigation (FBI), 452, *464*
federal campaign financing laws, *345,* 345–47
Federal Communications Commission, 452, *505*
federal courts, *475*
federal district courts, 473–74
Federal Election Campaign Act (1971), 345
Federal Emergency Management Agency, *593*
federal government
  powers of, 81–83, *82*
  strength of, 25–26
  supremacy of, 77–87
federal government revenue, *529,* 529–30
federal grant money, *84,* 84–85

federalism, 26, 79 A system in which the national and state governments share power.
  cooperative, 83
  and different state policies, 93–95, *94*
  dual, 83
  evolution of, 83–85, *84*
  and marijuana laws, 88–91, *91, 93, 94,* 95
  and Tenth Amendment, 91–93

Federalist(s), 31, 49–50

***Federalist Papers,* 31,** 482 A series of essays written after the Constitutional Convention that advocated for ratification of the Constitution and tried to reassure skeptics about the soundness of the structure and features of the government the Founders designed.

federal judgeships, 49–52
federal officeholders, requirements for, 68–69, *69*

Federal Reserve, 531 The central bank of the U.S. government that focuses on managing monetary policy; typically referred to as the Fed.

federal system, state powers in, 81–83, *82*
Federal Trade Commission, 448
#FeeltheBern, *372*
Ferguson, Missouri
  racial justice in, 233
  racial profiling in, 164–65
Fifteenth Amendment, 61, 70, 144, 147
Fifth Amendment, *122,* 124, 128, 135

filibuster, 427–428, **514–16** A Senate rule that allows members to deliver speeches of unlimited length on the Senate floor with the intent of delaying a vote on a bill or killing it altogether.

finance director, for presidential campaign, *370*
finance industry, lobbying by, 503, *503*
financial resources, of incumbents, 388–89
financing
  of campaigns (*See* campaign financing)
  of national debt, 530–31, *531*
First Amendment, 73–74, 98, 101
  and freedom of expression, 110, 111, 115
  and political participation, 234
  and religious freedom *vs.* gay rights, 185
  and right to privacy, 135
  and separation of church and state, 101, 102, 103

fiscal policy, 524–36, **526** How the federal government raises, spends, and borrows money to manage the economy.
  and concerns about national debt, 531–33
  of Democrats *vs.* Republicans, 532–33
  and discretionary spending, *527,* 528
  and economic recessions, 524–25
  and entitlement programs, *527,* 527–28
  and federal budget, *527,* 527–29
  and federal government revenue, *529,* 529–30
  and financing of national debt, 530–31, *531*
  and interest on debt, *527,* 529
  and mandatory spending, *527,* 527–28

fiscal policy (*continued*)
  and national debt, 526, *526*
  and national deficit, 524, 525–26
  and natural disasters, 524, 525
  and public health crises, 525

flag burning, *58,* 117
Flint, Mich., drinking water in, 463
floor, moving bill to, 425–26, *431*
floor debate, 426–28, *431*
Florida, campaign financing laws in, *347*
Floyd, George, 157–58, *158,* 237, 310–11
George Floyd Justice in Policing Act, 165
Flynn, Michael, 309
Foley, Mark, 288
Food and Drug Administration (FDA), 419, 447, 455, *464*
Ford, Christine Blasey, 422, 486–87
Ford Motor Company, 498
foreign investors, in financing of national debt, 530, *531*

formal powers, 435 Powers of the president that are explicitly stated in Article II of the Constitution.

form letters, as political participation, 236
For the People Act, 229
Foster, Vince, 263–64
foster parents, same-sex couples as, 188
Founders, 10
  on constitutional amendments, 57–58
  and Constitutional Convention, 23–24
  on democracy, 67–74, *69, 71*
  and Electoral College, 354–55
  and federalism, 26
  on free press, 72–74
  and individuals' rights, 31–32
  on open and direct elections, 68–70, *69*
  on separation of powers, 36, 38, 41–42
  and slavery, 29–31, *30*
  on states' rights, 79
  on voting rights, 70–72, *71*
4chan, 257–58
Fourteenth Amendment, 143–56
  equal protection clause of, 98–99, 144
  and frameworks to assess claims of unequal treatment, 153–54
  and gender equality, 148–50
  due process clause of, 134
  and racial equality, 145
  and same-sex marriage, 153, 184, 492
  and slavery, 61, 144
Fourth Amendment, 98, *122,* 123, 128, 135
Fox News
  agenda setting by, 307–8, *308*
  conflict on, 286

criticism of other media outlets by, 305
framing by, 310–11, *311*
history of, 283
ideological news on, 298
polls by, 276
priming by, 308–9, *309, 310*
selective exposure to, 311–13, *313*
sensationalism of, 288
shaping of news by, *306,* 306–7

framing, 310–311, *311* The media's power to provide the context of an issue so as to emphasize certain aspects over others.

France, and nuclear weapons, 578, *579*
Franchise Management Advisory Council (FRANMAC), 500
Frankfurter, Felix, 483
franking privilege, 387, *388*
Franklin, Benjamin, 23, 29, 72
Franklin, Tim, 113
freedom, 14, 15–16, *16*

freedom of expression, 110 A clause of the First Amendment that establishes citizens' right to hold and freely communicate opinions; often referred to as the right of free speech.
  as First Amendment right, 110
  and imminent lawless action, 111–13
  and libel and slander, 113–15
  limits to, 110
  and symbolic speech, 115–17

freedom of religion
  attitudes toward, 15, *16*
  as First Amendment right, 98, 100–108
  and illegal substances, 47
  and prayer in public schools, 100–108, *102, 104*
freedom of speech, 109–19
  as First Amendment right, 98, 109–10
  and imminent lawless action, 111–13
  and libel and slander, 113–15
  limits to, 110
  and symbolic speech, 115–17
freedom of the press, 72–74
Freedom Riders, 146

free exercise clause, 101 A clause of the First Amendment stating that there shall be no laws "prohibiting the free exercise" of religion, thus broadly granting citizens the right to practice whatever religion they choose, or none at all.

free market system, 15, *16,* **212** An economic system in which privately owned businesses operate without government interference.

free ride, 249 To benefit from a group's efforts without joining the group.

free trade, 553–554 An approach to international commerce that favors minimal restrictions on exports and imports. In theory, pure free trade means no restrictions or barriers on imports or exports.

"friend of the court" briefs, 474–75
friends, political socialization by, 199–200, *200*
fuel efficiency standards, 466, *466*
fundraising, *337*, 337–38
    by incumbents, 388–89
    for presidential campaign, 372

G7 (Group of 7), 443
G20 (Group of 20), 443
Gaetz, Matt, *282*
Gallego, Ruben, 330–31, 336
Gallup polls, 274, *274*
gambling
    and campaign contributions, *503*
    sports, 92
García Zárate, José Ines, 77
Gardner, Cory, 338
Garner, Tyrone, 139
Gates, Bill, 522
GATT (General Agreement on Tariffs and Trade), 551, 553
gay citizens
    changing attitudes toward, 182–83, *183*
    and same-sex sodomy laws, 138–40
gay pride parade, 151
gay rights
    vs. free speech, 112, *112*
    pride parades and, *144*
    religious freedom *vs.,* 181–91
    struggle for, 151–53
Geekvape, 423
gender, and descriptive representation, 414–16, *415*
gender-based discrimination
    and American Dream, 20
    and party identification, 214–15, *215*
    Supreme Court on, 479
gender equality, *144*, 148–50
    in wages (*See* pay gap)
gender preferences, in voting choice, 327
General Agreement on Tariffs and Trade (GATT), 551, 553
general business, lobbying by, *499*

general election, 319 Contests that typically feature candidates from opposing parties squaring off to determine who will win the elective office.

general election campaign, 377, 378, *378*
Georgia, special election for U.S. Senate seat in, 285
Gerry, Elbridge, 68

gerrymandering, 389–92, *390*, 391, 484

Gertz v. Welch (1974), 114

get out the vote (GOTV), 378 A strategic initiative in which campaigns sift through each state or district's list of registered voters and use every means possible (phone calls, door-knocking, email, offers of rides to the polls) to encourage potential supporters to cast a ballot. Also known as the ground game.

Gibbons, Thomas, 81

***Gibbons v. Ogden,* 80–81** The 1824 Supreme Court case that affirmed the supremacy clause in the application of the commerce clause.

Giddings, Priscilla, 300
Gideon, Clarence, 125
Gideon v. Wainwright (1963), *122*, 125
Giffords, Gabby, 330
gifts, by lobbyists, 502–3
gift taxes, 530
Gingrich, Newt, 320
Ginsburg, Ruth Bader, 105, 478–79, *488*
global economy, trade and, 551–52, *552*
Global Gag Rule, 442

globalization, 550 The process of growing economic interdependence among countries.

Goldberg, Jonah, 553–54
"golden age of journalism," 282–83
Goldin, Frances, *144*
Goldwater, Barry, 585
golfing, by presidents, *435*, 440–41
Gomez, Selena, 219
Goode, Virgil, 402
Google, 498, 507
Google News, 283, *284*, 284–85, 293, 297
Gorbachev, Mikhail, 576, 577, *580*
Gore, Al, 322, 353, 402, 483–84
Gorsuch, Neil M., 188, *488*
Gosar, Paul, 194–96
GOTV (get out the vote) effort, 378

government, 10 Institutions, rules, and procedures that organize and structure a group of citizens.
    creation of, 10–11
    framework of, 11
    limited, 14, 18–19, *19*
    political socialization by, 200–201
    representative, 11
    self-, 18

government corporations, 452
government functioning, amendments on, 61
government shutdowns, 513, 532
Grace University, religious freedom *vs.* gay rights in, 186
grants
    block, 85
    categorical, 85
    federal, *84,* 84–85
grassroots support, 348
Gray, Freddie, 158
Gray Wolf Recovery, 251
Great Britain, and nuclear weapons, 578, *579*

Great Compromise, 28 The plan adopted at the Constitutional Convention that established a legislative branch with two chambers: the House of Representatives, and the Senate, in which a state's representation would be based on its population, in which each state — regardless of size — would have two members.

Great Depression, 83–84, 440, 442
Great Recession, and lobbying by banking industry, 496
Green, Marjorie Taylor, *388*
greenhouse gas emissions, 456, 466, *466*
"Green New Deal," 402
Green Party, 209, *399, 401,* 402, 403
Greenshields, Bill, *116*
Gregg v. Georgia (1976), *122,* 129
Grenada, military action in, 583
Griswold, Estelle, 134–35
Griswold v. Connecticut (1965), 135, 139
ground game, in presidential campaign, 378
Group of 7 (G7), 443
Group of 20 (G20), 443
Guantánamo Bay military prison, 596
guilty finding, 128–29
gun control, 91–92
    Congress and, 406, 427
    different state policies on, 95
    and election season of 2022, 335
    floor debate on, 427
    lobbying for, 507
    and mass shootings, 406, 439–40, 598
    and party identification, 213, *214*
    and party polarization, 513
    support for, 411
    Tenth Amendment and, 91–93
Gun Owners of America, 247
Guttmacher Institute, 137

habeas corpus, 126 A protection requiring that a person who has been placed under arrest be brought before a judge to determine whether there is just cause for the arrest and detainment; established in Article I of the Constitution.

Hageman, Harriet, 519
Haiti, military action in, 583
Hamilton, Alexander, 26, 29, 482
Hannity, Sean, 305
Hardwick, Michael, 138–39
Harris, Kamala, 13, 78, 364, *374, 467*
Harrison, Jaime, *331*
Hart, Gary, 288
hashtags, 4
    political participation via, 237
    in presidential campaigns, 372
Hastings College of the Law, religious freedom *vs.* gay rights in, 187–88

Hatch Act, 454 Passed in 1939, a law that limits the political activities of federal employees, preventing them from working for political candidates or running for partisan offices themselves.

hate crimes, 20
Hawaii, Republicans *vs.* Democrats in, 93

head of state, 438–440, *444* Presidential role of serving as the country's public face.

Health, Education, Labor, and Pensions Committee, 423, 425
health care
    federal grant money for, 84
    party politics on, 334
health care costs, 513
health care industry, 570–72, *571*
health care insecurity, and Covid-19 pandemic, 566, *566*
health care policy, and party identification, 214
health care reform
    Congress and, 411, 427–28
    Democrats *vs.* Republicans on, 567–70, *568*
    history of attempts at, 564–67, *566*
    money at stake for, 570–72, *571*
health care spending, 570–72, *571*
health corporation executives, 04
health insurance, 47, 561–74
    and Affordable Care Act (Obamacare), 565, *568,* 568–70, 571
    and Children's Health Insurance Program, 565
    and chronic health conditions, 569, 571
    during Covid-19 pandemic, 566, *566*
    current state of, 564–67, *566*
    deductibles in, 562
    Democrats *vs.* Republicans on, 567–70, *568*
    employment-based, 565–67
    and health care spending, 570–72, *571*
    and Medicaid, 565, 569

and Medicare, 565
misinformation about, 261
overview of, 561–64, *563*
and poverty, 566–67
and pre-existing conditions, 569, 571
private, 568
private insurance mandate, *563*, 564
and public option, 567
public/private hybrid system, *563*, 564
racial disparities in, 567
and single-payer health system, *563*, 564, 567, 571–72
and universal health care, *563*, 563–64, 567–68
health insurance industry, lobbying by, 498, *499*, 501–2, 507
health professionals, campaign contributions by, *503*
"Health Security" card, 564
health services industry, lobbying by, 503, *503*
hearing(s)
on confirmation of Supreme Court justices, 483, *483*, 484–87, *486*, 487
Congressional, 463–65, *464*
preliminary, 126–27
by Supreme Court, 476–79, *477*
Henry, Patrick, 15
Herman, Simah, *420*
Herrell, Yvette, 344
highway system, 513
Hill, Anita, *485*, 485–86
Hill, Katie, 289–90
Hiroshima, atomic bomb dropped on, 578
hoasca tea, 47
holiday(s), president's role in, 439
holiday parties, hosted by lobbyists, 500, *501*, 503
Holocaust, public opinion poll on, *270*, 270–71
home ownership, racial inequality in, 160, *160*
homosexuality
and gay rights under the law, 151–53
and same-sex sodomy laws, 138–40

horse race coverage, 287 News stories that focus on the competition involved in an election rather than details of the candidates' policy positions.

hospitals, lobbying by, *499*
Houghton, Sandra, 123
House Financial Services Committee, *424*
House Foreign Affairs Subcommittee, *424*
House of Representatives
cost of election to, 343, *344*
electoral process for, 69, *69*
Howard, Melissa, 300
Huffington Post, 275–76, 298
Human Rights Campaign, 152

Hurricane Ida, 440
Hurricane Katrina, 524
Hussein, Saddam, 594–95
Hustler v. Falwell (1988), 114–15

ICE (Immigration and Customs Enforcement Agency), 77–78, *593*
ideological news sources, 298–99, *299*, 312
"I Have a Dream" speech (King), *144*, 147
ImMasche, Sonia, 232, 238
immigrants and immigration
attitudes toward, 17, *17*
border wall to stop, 78, 215, *215*
and melting pot, 17
misinformation about, 261
undocumented, 17, *17*, 79, 402, 411, 513, 519
Immigration and Customs Enforcement Agency (ICE), 77–78, *593*
Immigration and Naturalization Service, 452
immigration reform, 60, 411, 513, 519
imminent lawless action, free speech and, 111–13

implied powers, 44 Powers not explicitly granted to Congress or the president in the Constitution, but that derive from a broad interpretation of the necessary and proper clause and the take care clause.

imports
tariffs on, 553
trade policy and, *557*, 557–58
#I'mWithHer, 372
incarceration rate, racial disparities in, 163–64, *164*
incentives, for cooperation, 517–19
inclusion, and party identification, 214–15, *215*
income
median, 539
and political participation, 238, *239*, 240
income distribution, 539–42, *540*, *541*

income inequality, 537–48, 538 Circumstance in which a small proportion of the population holds a disproportionately large share of income and wealth.
capital gains tax and, 543–44
and education, 537
examples of, 537, *538*
and health insurance, 566–67
and housing, 537, *538*
and income distribution, 539–42, *540*, *541*
income tax rates and, 542, *543*
and market-based economy, 538
and median income, 539
minimum wage *vs.* living wage and, 545, *546*
overview of, 537–39
and party identification, 212
policy proposals to address, 542–46, *543*, *546*

income inequality (*continued*)

    public investments and, 544–45

    racial, 159–60, *160*

    regressive taxation and, 543

    supply-side economics and, 544

    in United States, 539–42, *540, 541*

    and wealth gap, 540–42

income security, federal grant money for, 84

income tax(es), 82

    corporate, *529,* 530

    different state policies on, 93–94, *94*

    individual, 529, *529*

income tax rates, and income inequality, 542, *543*

incumbency, and descriptive representation, 415

incumbents, 319, 335 Candidates who already hold a position and are seeking reelection.

    reelection of (*See* reelection to Congress)

Independent, 209, 323 An individual who doesn't affiliate with either of the two major political parties.

independent commissions, 452

independent expenditures, 337–38 Spending in an election that is not coordinated with a candidate's campaign.

Independent Party, *399,* 400

India, and nuclear weapons, 578, *579*

indigenous people, voting rights for, 71

indirect lobbying, 506–7 Lobbyists' practice of working to influence government officials to take a particular action by getting public opinion on their side of their cause.

individual donation, 345, *345,* 346, 348, 350

individual freedom

    vs. national security, 596–97, *597*

    and party identification, 213, *214*

individual income taxes, 529, *529*

individualism, 15, *16,* 19–20 In political culture, a value that embodies personal liberty, resourcefulness, and self-reliance.

individual mandate, 47

individuals' rights, 31–32

inflation, 335

informal powers, 435 Powers of the president that lack an explicit constitutional basis but still allow for considerable influence over the political system.

information, consuming political, 5

infrastructure bills, 419, 421

Inhofe, James, *427*

inside strategies, 251–52 An approach to lobbying in which groups build broad support for their cause by having members engage directly with people at the center of power; tactics include meetings with, and financial contributions to, elected officials.

Instagram

    news stories on, 283

    Donald Trump and, 373

institutions, knowledge of, *260*

insurance industry, lobbying by, 498, *499,* 501–2

integration, racial, 145–47

intelligence brief, 436

interest, on national debt, *527,* 529

interest group(s), 244–53. *See also* special interests

    in America, 245–48

    benefits of membership in, 248–50

    political, 246–47, *247*

    as political participation, 236–37

    public, *245, 247,* 247–48

    role as member of, 251–52

intermediate scrutiny, 153 A standard of judicial scrutiny when assessing cases of unequal treatment under the law; assumes a law is unconstitutional unless there is an "important governmental reason" for the disparate treatment.

Internal Revenue Service (IRS), *464*

internet

    misinformation on, 261–64, *262*

    news stories on, 283, *284,* 284–85

    and political participation, 235–38, *237*

interracial marriage, 148

interrogation methods, 596

interstate highways, 513

investors, in financing of national debt, 530, *531*

Iowa, caucuses in, 373, *374,* 374–75

Iran, sanctions on, *582,* 583

Iran nuclear deal, 583

Iraq, military action in, 583, 585, 594–95, *595*

IRS (Internal Revenue Service), *464*

ISIS, 583, 598

ISIS-K, 598

Israel, and nuclear weapons, 578, *579*

issues

    in presidential campaign, 369–71

    in voting choice, 323–26, *324, 325*

Jack, William, 181–82

Jackson, Ketanji Brown, 483, *483,* 487, *488*

Jackson, Lisa, 459–61, *460,* 464–65, 468

lawmaking activity, 413, *413*
Lawrence, John, 139
Lawrence v. Texas (2003), 139–40
law special interest groups, campaign contributions by, 504
lawyer, right to, *122*, 125–26
Leahy, Patrick, 516
leaking, to press, 74
Lebanon, sanctions on, *582*
Lilly Ledbetter Fair Pay Act (2009), 175
left-leaning, 216
left-wing, 216

legal bribery, 503 The practice of lobbyists offering financial or other support to politicians without the explicit expectation that the politician will act in the lobbyists' interests.

Legend, John, 219, 444
legislative branch
    checks and balances on and by, 42–44, *43*
    enumerated powers of, 38, 39–42, *40*
    and executive branch, 459–68
    relative power of, 36, 37–44
legislative process, 419–33
    committee system in, 423–25, *431*
    floor debate and vote in, 426–28, *431*
    getting bill to floor in, 425–26, *431*
    introduction of bill in, 420–23, *431*
    number of bills introduced *vs.* enacted in, 420, *421*
    reconciling House and Senate versions of bill in, 428–29, *431*
    regular order in, 420
    signing bill into law or vetoing by president in, 429–30, *430, 431*
    summary of, 430, *431*
    unorthodox legislating in, 430–31
legislative record, and reelection to Congress, 387–88

legislator in chief, 440–42, *444* Presidential role of initiating legislation to address issues facing the nation.

Lemon, Don, 305

Lemon Test, *104,* **104**–105 A standard developed in *Lemon v. Kurtzman* that outlines a three-pronged test to determine whether a law is permissible under the establishment clause.

Lemon v. Kurtzman (1971), 104, 106
lesbian citizens
    changing attitudes toward, 182–83, *183*
    equality for, 151–53
Lewis, John, 143

LGBTQ citizens
    changing attitudes toward, 182–83, *183*
    equality for, 151–53
LGBTQ rights
    and equality under the law, *144*
    free speech *vs.*, 112, *112*
    religious freedom *vs.*, 181–91
    struggle for, 151–53

libel, 113–15 False written statements that damage a person's reputation; not protected by the First Amendment.

liberal(s), 215, 216

liberal political philosophy, 215 Favors an expansive role for government in promoting economic and social equality and fair treatment among citizens; an outlook generally embraced by Democrats.

Libertarian Party
    identification with, 209
    party platform of, 401, *401*
    and political debates, *399,* 399–400
    as spoiler, 403

liberty, 14, **15**–16, *16,* 19–20 The freedom from excessive government restrictions imposed on one's political views or way of life.
    civil, 98

Libya, military action against, 583
Licensing Act (193), 81
likability, in voting choice, 322–23, 326, *327*
Limbaugh, Rush, 283

limited government, 14, **18**–19, *19,* 20 The principle that written laws serve as the basis for governmental authority.

Lincoln, Abraham, 145
Lipinski, Daniel, 518–19
literacy tests, *147,* 147–48

living constitution, 490–92 An approach to interpreting the Constitution in which justices derive general principle and values from their reading of the Constitution and its history and then apply those principles to modern controversies.

living wage, 545, *546* The level of income necessary to provide for a decent standard of living (housing, food, health care, etc.).

lobbying, 496–509, 498 The practice of trying to influence people in government to pursue a particular policy or action.

media consultant, for presidential campaign, *370*
median household income, racial inequality in, 159, *160*
median income, 539
media strategy
    of presidential campaign, 372
    and reelection to Congress, 387–88

Medicaid, 565 A government program, begun in 1965, that provides health care to those living near or below the poverty level.
    different state policies on, *94*
    as entitlement program, 528
    federal grant money for, 84

Medicare, 565 A government program, begun in 1965, that provides health care to people over the age of 65 as well as to many people with disabilities.
    as entitlement program, 528
    federal grant money for, 84
    support for, 411

Medicare for all, 567
Meet the Press (television show), 297
Mellons, 539

melting pot, 17 A term to describe the diversity of the more than 15 million European immigrants who came to the country between 1880 and the early 1900s.

Mendez, John, 79
mercury levels, 466, *466*
message
    development of winning, 333–35
    for presidential campaign, 369–71
methane emissions, *466*
#MeToo, 237
Mexican border, migrant caravan at, 12–13
Mexico City Policy, 441–42
Meyers, Seth, 295
middle class, 540, *541*, 542
"midnight appointments," 50

midterm election, 221–223, *223* A national election that takes place two years into a president's term.

migrant caravan, 12–13
military, gay people serving in, 151, 152
military force
    to battle terrorism, 594–95, *595*
    and nuclear weapons, 583–85, *584*
Miller, Carina, 325
Miller, Judith, 74

Miller, Lucas, 56
millionaire surtax, 542
Minhaj, Hasan, *424*

minimum wage, 545, 546, *546* The lowest hourly rate any employer may legally pay.
    different state policies on, 93, *94*
    and trade policy, 549–50, *551*

minority leader, 426
Miranda, Ernesto, 124
Miranda, Lin-Manuel, 219
Miranda v. Arizona (1966), *122*, 124

Miranda warning, 124–125 A rule that those placed under arrest must be informed of their constitutional rights before police interrogation; established by the Supreme Court in *Miranda v. Arizona.*

misinformed electorate, 261–64, *262*
misoprostol, 132–33

Missouri Compromise (1857), 52 A federal law that sought to maintain the balance of power between free states and slave states.

Monáe, Janelle, 444
Mondale, Walter, 322
monetary damages, 473

monetary policy, 531 Policies that promote economic growth by focusing on the money supply.

money
    for campaigns (*See* campaign financing)
    in elections, 319
Montana, campaign financing laws in, 347
moon landing, conspiracy theories about, 261
Morris, Gouverneur, 28
Moses, Casandra, 325
motion to dismiss case, 128
MSNBC (media outlet)
    conflict on, 286
    criticism on Fox of, 305
    history of, 283
    polls by, 275–76
    shaping of news by, 294, 306
Mueller, Robert, 309
Mulinix, David, 357
Mullins, David, 185

multilateralism, 580 A policy under which countries cooperate with other nations and international organizations to achieve a common foreign policy goal.

and income inequality, 538, 545
on leaks to media, 74
likability of, *327*
on media effects, 305, 307
and nuclear weapons, 577, *580*
and party polarization, 510
political appointments by, 459, 466, 467
political favors by, 341
presidential schedule of, 434, 436, 444
and racial equality, 143–44
on social media, 372
and terrorism, 598
on third parties, 402
threat to assassinate, 113
trade policy of, 554
and voter turnout, 220, 221
Obamacare (2010)
background of, 565
Democrats *vs.* Republicans on, *568*, 568–70
and fake news, 261
and federal-state relations, 84
filibuster on, 427–28
health care industry and, 571
party polarization and, 519
passage of, 47
public opinion on, 411
Obergefell v. Hodges (2015), 152–53, 491–92

objectivity, 282–283 A principle of news organizations that requires journalists to present information in a nonbiased, balanced, fair way.

O'Brien, David, 117
Ocasio-Cortez, Alexandria, 300, *568*
Occupational Safety and Health Administration (OSHA), 449, *464*, 467–68
occupational segregation, 174–75, *176*
O'Connor, Sandra Day, *488*
Office of Management and Budget, 463, *505*
Office of the U.S. Trade Representative, *505*
Ogden, Aaron, 81
Ohio, campaign financing laws in, *347*
oil and gas industry, lobbying by, 497, *499*, 501, *503*, 504
Oil Pollution Act, 463
Oklahoma, Republicans *vs.* Democrats in, 93
Oklahoma City bombing, 439
1 percent doctrine, 596
"one person, one vote," 360, *360*

open seats, 319 Positions for which there are no incumbents seeking reelection.

oral arguments, 476 The part of a Supreme Court hearing during which lawyers present their cases while being questioned by the justices.

originalism, 491–492 An approach to interpreting the Constitution motivated by the belief that the words in the Constitution should be interpreted as they were understood at the time of the Founding.

original jurisdiction, 51 A court's authority to hear a case for the first time; applies to the Supreme Court only in cases involving "ambassadors, other public ministers and consuls, and those in which a state shall be a party."

Orlando, Florida night club mass shooting, 598
OSHA (Occupational Safety and Health Administration), 449, *464*, 467–68
Ossoff, Jon, 344
Oswald, Lee Harvey, 263

outside strategies, 251 An approach to lobbying in which groups build broad support for their cause by rallying their members to pressure elected officials; such tactics include letter-writing and email campaigns, protests and rallies, and information campaigns.

override, of veto, 429–30, *430, 431*

PACs (political action committees), 345, *345*, 346
Pakistan
    and nuclear weapons, 578, *579*
    and terrorism, 594
Parks, Rosa, 146
partisan(s), in federal bureaucracy, 452–55

partisan gerrymandering, 389–92, *390, 391* The process of drawing electoral district boundaries that make it easier for one political party than the other to win an election.

partisan in chief, 436–37, *444* Presidential role of serving as the leader of the party and directing the party's agenda, communicating that agenda to the public, and raising money for the party and its candidates.

partisan match, *412*, 412–13
partisan mismatch, *412*, 412–13
partisan news, 298–99, *299*, 312
partisan politics, and policy stalemate and inaction, 523
partisanship
    and conspiracy theories, 262, *262*
    and elections, 319
    negative, 322–23
    and political participation, 238, *239*, 240
partisan warfare, 383
party convention, 376–77
    delegates to, 373–74

party identification, 196, 208–10 The political party a person affiliates with.
    by demographic groups, 210, *211*
    and political participation, 238, *239,* 240
    of registered voters, *209,* 209–10
    and voting choice, 321–23, *322*

party nomination, for president, 375, 376

party platform(s), 210–12, 332, 376 A formal document passed by the political parties every four years at the presidential nomination convention; articulates a party's positions on key policy issues, underlying principles, and goals for the future.
    of third parties, 400–402, *401*

party polarization, 510–21, 514 The widening gap in political beliefs between Democrats and Republicans, with Democrats moving in a more liberal direction and Republicans moving in a more conservative one.
    and animosity, 516–17
    and disappearing moderates in Congress, 514, *515*
    and divided government, 514
    and earmarks, 517–18
    and filibuster, 514–16
    future of, 519
    government failures due to, *513,* 513–19
    and incentives for cooperation, 517–19
    overview of, 510–11
    and permanent campaign, 518–19
    vs. things that government does well, 511–13, *512*

party politics, 330–40
    developing winning message in, 333–35
    identifying and recruiting candidates in, 335–36
    limits of party influence in, 338
    political party organizations and, *332,* 332–33
    raising and spending money in, *337,* 337–38
Paterson, William, 26
Patriot Act, 596–97, *597*
Paul, Rand, 35, 538

pay gap, 169–80, 171 The difference between men's and women's wages.
    current status of, 169–71
    and Equal Pay Act, 169, 171
    due to exorbitant cost of childcare, *177,* 177–78
    due to gender and occupational segregation, 174–75, *176*
    and Lilly Ledbetter Fair Pay Act, 175
    measuring, 171–74, *172*
    and party identification, 214
    prospects for closing, 178

payroll taxes, 529, *529*
Pell Grant program, 512
Pelosi, Nancy
    fake news about, 254–55
    on health care reform, *568*
    and January 6 insurrection, 66
    messaging campaign against, *335*
    and reelection campaigns, 518
    and Donald Trump, 516–17
Pence, Mike, 336, 363, 364

Pendleton Act, 453–54 Passed in 1883, a law that prevented the president from awarding jobs to unqualified political loyalists; required the vast majority of federal employees to be selected based on merit, not political connections.

Pensacola, Florida naval air station mass shooting, 598

Pentagon Papers, 73 A classified report about U.S. involvement in the Vietnam War published by the *New York Times* and the *Washington Post;* it revealed a long history of U.S. leaders lying to the public about prospects for winning the war in Vietnam.

People of the Ethical Treatment of Animals (PETA), *506,* 507
Perez, Tom, 467
Perkins, Tony, 185

permanent campaign, 518–519 When elected officials start campaigning and fundraising for their next election as soon as they are elected.

Perot, Ross, *397,* 400
Perry, Katy, 219
personal freedom, and party identification, 213, *214*
personal image, in voting choice, 322–23, 326, *327*
"personal infosphere," 312
persuasive argumentation, 5–6
PETA (People of the Ethical Treatment of Animals), *506,* 507
petitions, as political participation, 235, 236, 238
Pew Research Center, 419
pharmaceutical industry, lobbying by, 497–98, *499,* 507
Phiede, Amanda, 133
Phillips, Jack, 185
Pinckney, Charles, 28
Pizzagate, 256–58, *257*

plaintiff, 473 An individual who files a lawsuit.

Planned Parenthood, 134, 498
platforms, 210–12, 332, 376
    of third parties, 400–402, *401*

plea bargain, 126 An arrangement in which a defendant pleads guilty to a lesser crime in exchange for a reduced sentence.

Pledge of Allegiance, 101
Plessy, Homer, 145

***Plessy v. Ferguson,* 145** The 1896 Supreme Court case that established the "separate but equal" doctrine; equal protection under the law did not require racial integration.

polarization, affective, 312–13
police
    arrest by, 124–25
    questioning by, 125–26
    racial profiling by, 164–65
    searches and seizures by, 123
police brutality, 157–58, 165
policy advisers, for presidential campaign, *370*
policy positions, in voting choice, 323–26, *324, 325*

political action committees (PACs), 345, *345,* 346 Organizations that exist for the sole purpose of influencing elections, both by endorsing candidates and by donating to their campaigns.
    Super PACs, *345,* 346

political appointees, 453, 454–55 People whose selection for a government position requires their allegiance to the president's political party.

political consultants, 332–33

political culture, 13–14 The general set of beliefs, attitudes, and values on which a political system is based.

political efficacy, 228 The belief among citizens that their voices will be taken seriously by political leaders and can influence the government.

political engagement, 192–93
    core themes of, 193
    defined, 192
    in families, 196–97, *198*
    interest groups as, 244–53
    party identification as, 206–18
    political participation as, 232–43
    political socialization and, 194–205
    resources and, 193
    voting as, 219–31
political favors, 341–42, 349–50
political information, 254–55
    consuming, 5

political institutions, 406–407 The central components of government with the power to craft, implement, and review the nation's laws.

political interest group, 246–247, *247* An official association of people with similar concerns who seek to influence public policy.

political issues, knowledge of, *260*

political knowledge, 256–65 What citizens know about politics and government.
    and conspiracy theories, 256–58, *257,* 261–64, *262*
    defined, **258**
    key components of, 259–60, *260*
    and misinformed electorate, 261–64, *262*
    and poorly informed electorate, 258–61, *260*
    and public opinion polls, 271

political participation, 232–43, 234 The ways in which citizens actively engage with their government and make their voices heard in the political system.
    demographics of, 238–40, *239*
    methods of, 234–38, *235, 237*
    and responsiveness of elected leaders, 238–40
    via social media, 235–38, *237*

political parties, 206–18
    base voters of, 210
    coexistence of, 216
    cultural differences and, 206–7, *208*
    diversity and inclusion and, 214–15, *215*
    economic policies of, 212, *213*
    identification with, 208–10, *209, 211*
    knowledge of, *260*
    labels for, 215–16
    money raised by, *337,* 337–38
    platform of, 210–12
    polarization of, *207*
    social and domestic policies of, 213–14, *214*
    third (See third party)
political party organizations, *332,* 332–33

political representation, 234 The way in which the political system reflects the demographics, preferences, and priorities of all the people it represents.

political socialization, 194–205, 196 The process by which people acquire their political beliefs and values, including whether to participate and be politically engaged.
    early, 201–2
    by family, 196–97, *198*

their party's candidates to decide who competes in the general election.

primary opponent, losing to, 518–19

priming, 308–309, *310* The media's power to establish the criteria by which people assess political candidates, elected officials, and issues.

principal-agent problem, 465 A situation that occurs when a principal (Congress) delegates power and authority to an agent (the bureaucracy) and the agent behaves in a way the principal didn't intend and can't completely control.

Printz v. United States, 92
priorities, in voting choice, *325,* 325–26

prior restraint, 73 Government action that prohibits the press from reporting potentially harmful information.

privacy, right to. *See* right to privacy
private insurance mandate, for health insurance, *563,* 564
processes, knowledge of, *260*
Professional and Amateur Sports Protection Act (1992), 92
professional associations, as interest groups, 246–47, *247*
profile pictures, political participation via, 237
progressives, 216

progressive taxation, 542, *543* A tax policy based on the principle that the more you earn, the higher the tax rate you pay.

Prohibition amendment, *57,* 61
"pro-life" voting record, 519

proportional representation, 28 A system in which the number of representatives a state sends to the national legislature is determined by that state's population.

protectionism, 556–558, *557* An approach to international commerce that shields domestic industries from foreign competition by prohibiting imports altogether or imposing severe tariffs on them.

Pruitt, Scott, *460,* 460–61, 465, 468
public appearances, 439
public defenders, court-appointed, 125–26
public figures, knowledge of, *260*
public financing, 350
public health crises, fiscal policy and, 525

public interest group, *245, 247,* **247**–248 A citizen group that is open to anyone to join; it mobilizes citizens to take action around a particular policy area.

public investments, 544–45, 546 Money the government spends on programs including education, job training, and childcare.

public opinion, lobbying and, 506–7

public opinion polls, 266–80, **268** Surveys of citizens that gauge the preferences and beliefs of the U.S. population or a subset of it.
    accuracy of, 267–68
    actual beliefs *vs.* answers to, 271–72
    on Congressional approval, 383–85, *384, 385*
    evaluating, 276
    knowledge of people polled in, 271
    margin of error for, 273–74, *274*
    pervasiveness of, 266–67
    in presidential campaign, 369, *370*
    random sampling for, 269
    representative sample for, 269
    sample for, 268
    sample size for, 269–70
    social desirability bias in, 272–73, *273*
    timing of, 276
    trustworthy source for, *275,* 275–76
    weighting in, 269
    wording of questions in, *270,* 270–71

public option, for health insurance, 567

public policy, 522 The formal actions the government takes, including passing laws and providing funding, to address specific issues or problems.
    knowledge of, *260*
    overview of, 522–23
    partisan politics and, 523
    shocks to system and, 523
    trade-offs and costs and, 523

Public Policy Polling survey, 394
public/private hybrid system, for health insurance, *563,* 564
"public safety exception," 124–25
public schools
    political socialization in, 198–99
    racial inequities in, 161–62, *162*
    racial segregation in, 145–46
    religion in, *58,* 100–106, *102, 104*
    warrantless searches of, 123
public servants, in federal bureaucracy, 452–55

pundits, 296–297, *297* Commentators — typically social critics, policy experts, former political leaders, or people who work in politics — who share their opinions about the news of the day and tell citizens how to interpret the latest political headlines and events.

punishment, cruel and unusual, 98, *122*, 128–29
Purdue, 344

purposive benefit, 248–249 The sense of reward or purpose associated with joining an interest group and achieving its goals.

Putin, Vladimir, 309, *443*, 582

QAnon, 257–58
quantitative literacy, 6

race
 and descriptive representation, 414–16
 discrimination based on, 20
Race Matters (West), 166
racial disparities, in health insurance, 567
racial equality, 145–48
 attitudes toward, 17, *17*
 and *Brown v. Board of Education,* 145–46
 and Civil Rights Act (1964), 147
 and civil rights movement, *144,* 145–48, *146*
 and election of Obama, 143–44
 and Emancipation Proclamation, 145
 and Freedom Riders, 146–47
 and Jim Crow laws, 145
 and party identification, 214–15, *215*
 and *Plessy v. Ferguson,* 145
 and "separate but equal" doctrine, 145–46
 and Voting Rights Act (1965), 147–48
racial inequities, 157–68
 in criminal justice system, 157–58, 163–65, *164*
 economic, 159–61, *160*
 educational, 161–63, *162*
 and party identification, 214–15, *215*
 and road to racial justice, 158–59, 166

racial justice, 158 Fair and equal treatment for people of all races.
 and disparities in criminal justice system, 157–58, 163–65, *164*
 and economic injustice, 159–61, *160*
 and educational inequities, 161–63, *162*
 road to, 158–59, 166

racial preferences, in voting choice, 327

racial profiling, 164–165 The practice of using race or ethnicity to make assumptions about an individual's possible criminal behavior.

racial segregation, 145–47, 161

racism, 157–68
 in criminal justice system, 157–58, 163–65, *164*
 and economic injustice, 159–61, *160*
 and educational inequities, 161–63, *162*
 and party identification, 214, *215*
 and road to racial justice, 158–59, 166
rallies, in presidential campaign, 378
Rand, Jonas, 224

random digital dialing, 269 A technique for selecting a random sample in which a computer generates every possible 10-digit phone number in the United States and then randomly chooses which numbers to call.

random sampling, 269 A technique for assembling a sample in which each member of the larger population has an equal chance of being chosen.

rape, statutory, 150
ratification, of amendments, 59, *59,* 60

ratification process, 31–32 Two-thirds of the states — 9 out of 13 — had to approve the Constitution in their legislatures for it to become law.

rational basis test, 153 A standard of judicial scrutiny when assessing cases of unequal treatment under the law; assumes a law is constitutional if it treats people differently as long as it meets a "legitimate government interest."

Raytheon Technologies, 504
Reagan, Ronald
 appointment of Supreme Court justices by, 485
 as consoler in chief, 439
 executive orders by, 442
 and flag burning, 117
 on immigration reform, 60
 and national deficit, 526
 and nuclear weapons, 577, *580*
 and party identification, 322
 and supply-side economics, 544
 and Voting Rights Act, 220
Real Time (television show), 258
receptions, hosted by lobbyists, 500, *501,* 503
recessions, fiscal policy and, 524–25, 532
recidivism, 129

redistricting, 389–92, *390, 391* A process that happens every 10 years when state governments redraw congressional districts' lines to reflect population shifts.

Redmond, Norene, 127
red tape, 455

Reed v. Reed (1971), 150
reelection to Congress, 383–94
    access to big money and, 388–89
    advantages of incumbents and, 385–91
    constituent services (casework) and, 386
    gerrymandering and, 389–92, *390*
    legislative record and, 387–88
    and permanent campaign, 518–19
    public approval *vs.*, 383–85, *384, 385*
Reform Party, 209, *399*, 402
Regan, Michael, 466, *467*
Regents of the University of California v. Bakke
    (1978), 163

regressive taxation, 543 A tax policy that results in wealthy people paying a lower tax rate than lower-income earners.

regular order, 420 The conventional multistep legislative process.

regulatory agencies, 452
Rehnquist, William, 124–25
Reich, Robert, 554
Reid, Harry, 422
religion, in public schools, *58*, 100–106, *102, 104*
religious decorations, in public schools, 105
religious documents, in public schools, 105
religious education, in public schools, 102–3

religious freedom, 182 The right to exercise one's religious beliefs; protected by the First Amendment; increasingly controversial as religious freedom and conflict with the civil rights of gay and lesbian citizens.
    attitudes toward, 15, *16*
    as First Amendment right, 98, 100–108
    gay rights *vs.*, 181–91
    and illegal substances, 47
    vs. marriage equality, 181–82, 184–86
    and prayer in public schools, 100–108, *102, 104*
    in schools, 186–88

religious preferences, in voting choice, 327
religious schools, state funding for, 105
reporting, balanced, 298–99
representation, 408–18
    collective, 410–11
    constituent, 412–14, *413, 414*
    descriptive, 414–16, *415*
    proportional, 28
    slavery and, 28–31, *30*

representative democracy, 67, *67*, 68, **409** A system of government in which voters select leaders to advocate on behalf of their interests.

representative government, 11

representative sample, 269 A microcosm of the population whose demographic and political characteristics — such as gender, race, age, income, religion, and party affiliation — reflect the population whose opinions the pollster is trying to measure.

republic, 68
Republican(s), 206–18
    base voters of, 210
    belief in conspiracy theories by, 258, 262, *262*
    coexistence of Democrats and, 216
    cultural differences and, 206–7, *208*
    diversity and inclusion and, 214–15, *215*
    economic policies of, 212, *213*
    fiscal policy of, 532–33
    on health insurance, 567–70, *568*
    identification with, 208–10, *209, 211*
    and income inequality, 538, 544, 546
    labels for, 215–16
    media sources for, 312–13, *313*
    money raised by, *337*, 337–38
    and party polarization (*See* party polarization)
    platform of, 210–12
    social and domestic policies of, 213–14, *214*
    and state policies, 93–95, *94*
    voting choice by, 321–23, *322*
Republican National Committee (RNC), 332–33, *333, 337*

reserved powers, 91–93 The states' authority to do anything that is not specifically delegated to the federal government or prohibited to the states by the Constitution.

residency, as requirement for federal officeholder, 68–69, *69*
resources, of incumbents, 387–89, *388*

retrospective voting, *325*, **325**–326 Making voting decisions based on whether you're better or worse off now than you were the last time you voted.

revenue, federal government, *529*, 529–30
"reverse discrimination," 163

revolving door, 504–506, *505* The practice of former government officials subsequently becoming lobbyists and former lobbyists subsequently working for the government.

Richards, Kevin, 325
Riggleman, Denver, 288
right(s)
    civil (*See* civil rights)
    of individuals, 31–32

right-leaning, 216
rights of the accused, 120–31
    in Bill of Rights, 122
    on cruel and unusual punishment, *122*, 128–29
    Miranda warning as, 124–25
    preliminary hearing as, 126–27
    due process as, 124
    during questioning at police station, 125–26
    on right to an attorney, *122*, 125–26
    on self-incrimination, *122*, 124–25
    and statistics on crime, 121–22
    Supreme Court on, 121–29, *122*
    during trial, 127–28
    on unlawful search and seizure, *122*, 123
right to an attorney, *122*, 125–26
Right to Life Party, *401*

right to privacy, 135 Based on the Supreme Court's interpretation of the First, Fifth, Fourth, Third, and Ninth Amendments, this concept establishes that citizens have a right to make intimate and personal decisions free from government intervention.
    and abortion, 132–33, 135–38, *138*
    Bill of Rights and, 98
    and birth control, 132, 133–35
    and consensual sex, 138–40
    Supreme Court on, 135

right-wing, 216
right-wing extremists, 598
RNC (Republican National Committee), 332–33, *333, 337*
Roberts, John G., Jr., 105, 391, *488*, 490
Rockefellers, 539

Roe v. Wade, 49, **135**–138, *136, 273*, 519 The 1973 Supreme Court case establishing that the right to privacy applies to the decision to terminate a pregnancy.

Romney, Mitt, *374*
Roosevelt, Franklin Delano, 83, 440, 442, 450, 483
Roosevelt, Theodore, 471, 564
Roper poll, *270*, 270–71
Rossi, Leslie, *236*
Rostker v. Goldberg (1980), 150

rulemaking authority, 465–467, *466* The power of the bureaucracy to set the regulations and guidelines (often referred to as rules) for carrying out laws passed by Congress.

rule of four, 475 Process for how the Supreme Court determines whether to hear a case; at least four of the nine justices must agree to hear it.

Rules Committee, 425
Rummel, William, 129
Rush, Benjamin, 67
Rushdie, Salman, 109
Russell, Richard, 147
Russert, Tim, *357*
Russia
    and cybersecurity, 586
    and nuclear weapons, 576, 577, 578, *579*, 581
    sanctions on, 582, *582*
Rutledge, John, 482
Ryan, Paul, 65

safe states, 361, *378* States where the outcome of a presidential election is typically not in doubt.

same-sex marriage
    and party identification, 213, *214*
    religious freedom *vs.*, 181–82, 184–86
    struggle for, 152–53
    Supreme Court ruling on, 152–53, 491–92
same-sex sodomy, 138–40

sample, 268 The group of people whose responses to a poll are used to estimate the views of the population the pollster is interested in.
    representative, 269

sample size, 269–70 The total number of people in a sample; represented by the letter *N*.

sampling, random, 269

sanctions, 581–583, *582* Actions taken by a nation or international organization intended to harm or limit another nation's economic activity.

sanctuary city, 77–79 A city with an ordinance directing local law enforcement officers not to assist federal law enforcement officials with the deportation of people living in the country illegally.

sanctuary state, 79, *79*
Sanders, Bernie
    on campaign contributions, 348
    campaigning by, 372, *374*
    on health insurance, 567
    on income inequality, 538
    policy positions of, 323, *324*
    on trade policy, 556–57, 558
San Francisco, as sanctuary city, 77–78
Santorum, Rick, 320
Sarbanes, John, 389–91
savings, racial inequality in, 160, *160*, 161
Saylor, Violet, 115
Scalia, Antonin, 92, 479, 486, *488*

single-issue voters, 324 Citizens who vote on the basis of a candidate's position on one particular policy.

single-payer health system, *563,* **564,** 567, 571–72 A system in which the government pays for all citizens' health care coverage.

Situation Room, 436
Sixteenth Amendment, 529
Sixth Amendment, *122,* 125, 127

slacktivism, 238 A somewhat derogatory term for political participation that takes place through social media; requires less effort or commitment than most traditional forms of political participation.

slander, 113–15 False spoken statements that damage a person's reputation; not protected by the First Amendment.

slavery
    amendments related to, 61, 144
    and *Dred Scot v. Sandford,* 52
    and Emancipation Proclamation, 145
    and representation, 28–31, *30*
    and U.S. Constitution, 28–31, *30*
    and voting rights, 70, *71*
slogan, for presidential campaign, 369–71
Small, Xochitl Torres, 344
Small Business Administration, 455
small states, Electoral College and, 355, 362
Snead, Courtney, 325

social desirability bias, 272–273, *273* A condition in which survey respondents think there's a "right" or socially acceptable answer to the question posed, so they provide that answer — whether they believe it or not — to avoid feeling like they'll be judged negatively by the pollster.

socialism, 334
Socialist Party USA, 401–2
social media
    campaigns and elections in, 318
    fake news stories on, 300
    misinformation on, 261–64, *262*
    news stories on, 283
    political participation via, 235–38, *237*
    in presidential campaign, 369, 372–73
    selective exposure to, 312
    Donald Trump's use of, 437
social policies, and party identification, 213–14, *214*

Social Security program
    as entitlement program, 528
    and federal debt financing, 530–31
    and federal-state relations, 83
    goal of, 419, 512–13
    public opinion on, 411
sodomy, 138–40

solidary benefits, 249 The friendships, networking opportunities, and camaraderie that people get by joining a group and associating with like-minded people.

Sotomayor, Sonia, 105, 137, *488*
Souter, David H., *488*
South Africa, and nuclear weapons, 578
Southern Poverty Law Center, 146
Soviet Union, and nuclear weapons, 575–77, *576, 578, 579, 580*

Speaker of the House, 422, 425 The leader of the U.S. House of Representatives, voted in by the majority party in the chamber.

special election, 224 An election that is called to fill a vacancy.

special interests, 496–509, **498** Groups that work to influence the political system to achieve their often narrow goals. *See also* interest group(s)
    campaign contributions by, 502–4, *503*
    examples of, 496–98
    lobbying by, 498–507, *499, 501*
    reforming of, 507
    revolving door between government and, 504–6, *505*
    wooing public opinion by, 506–7

speech
    freedom of (*See* freedom of speech)
    symbolic, 115–17
spending
    defense *vs.* nondefense, 528
    deficit, 526, 531–33
    discretionary, *527,* 528
    mandatory, *527,* 527–28
spending cuts, and national debt, 532
"split" state legislatures, 95

spoils system, 453 A system in place during the first 100 years of the U.S. government in which the president had the power to fill all the jobs in the federal bureaucracy with political appointees.

sponsoring, of bills, 413, *413*
sports gambling, 92

standards of living
    and party identification, 212
    racial inequality in, 159–61, *160*

standing, 51 Direct involvement in a legal dispute that grants a person the right to sue in a particular court.

standing committees, 423 Permanent congressional committees that focus on specific policy areas and hold regularly scheduled meetings.

Starbucks, 555
state(s)
    federal grant money to, 84, *84*
    influence of large *vs.* small, 26–28, *27*
    powers of, 81–83, *82*
    reserved powers of, 91–93
    separation of church and, 101
state campaign financing laws, 347, *347*
state court(s), 474, *475*
state court of appeals, *475*
State Department, 450, *451*, 464, *505*
state dinners, 443–44
state legislatures, "split," 95
state policies
    federalism and, 88–97
    on marijuana, 88–91, *91*, 93, *94*, 95
    and Tenth Amendment, 91–93
    widely different, 93–95, *94*
states' rights, 78–87
    and basis for federal supremacy, 80–81
    and cooperative federalism, 83–85, *84*
    and federalism, 79–80
    and sanctuary cities, 77–79
    and state powers in federal system, 81–83, *82*
state supreme court, *475*
state trial court, *475*
statutory rape, 150
steel industry, trade policy and, 557–58
Stefani, Gwen, 444
Stein, Jill, 402
stem cell research, 441
Stewart, Potter, 73–74
Steyer, Tom, 346
Stonewall Inn, 151, *152*
Story, Joseph, 482–83
Strausses, 539

strict scrutiny, 153 The highest standard of judicial scrutiny when assessing claims of unequal treatment under the law; assumes a law is unconstitutional unless the government can demonstrate that the law serves a "compelling interest" and is narrowly tailored to suit that interest.

Stutzman, Barronelle, 184
Sudan
    military action against, 583
    sanctions on, 583
Sullivan, Jake, 581
Sullivan, L. B., 114

Super PACs, *345*, *346* Political action committees that can accept unlimited contributions from individuals, unions, and corporations.

Super Tuesday, 375 A day in March during a presidential election year when a dozen or so states hold their primaries or caucuses.

supply-side economics, 544 The theory that the economy will flourish with lower taxes and regulations on businesses and corporations, resulting in more economic prosperity for people at all income levels.

supremacy clause, 80 A provision of the Constitution that suggests that federal laws consistent with the Constitution supersede state or local laws.

Supreme Court
    on abortion, 135–38, *136*
    on birth control, 134–35
    on campaign financing, 346, 350
    checks and balances on and by, 42–44, *43*
    concurring opinion in, 478
    on consensual sex, 138–40
    decision to hear cases by, 476–79, *477*
    on different frameworks for applying civil rights, 153–54
    dissenting opinion in, 478–79
    on free speech, 111–17
    on gay rights, 151–53
    on gender equality, 149, *150*
    on greenhouse gas emissions, 456
    on gun control, 92
    on health care policy, 569
    journey through court system to, 472–75, *475*
    judicial review by, 42, 44
    majority opinion in, 478–79
    oral arguments in, 476
    on partisan gerrymandering, 391
    powers of, 41–42, 471–72
    on racial equality, 145, 148, 158, 161, 163, 165
    of religious freedom *vs.* LGBTQ rights, 184–88
    on rights of the accused, 121–29, *122*
    rule of four in, 475
    on separation of church and state, 102–6, *104*
    on sports gambling, 92
    on voting rights, 148
    writ of certiorari to, 475

unilateralism, 580 A policy under which a nation tries to influence the international relations landscape by taking action on its own.

United Nations (UN), 580, 581 Founded in 1949 and headquartered in New York City; comprises 193 member nations that pledge to work together to promote political, military, and economic stability around the globe.

universal health care, 563–572 A system in which the government guarantees all citizens a baseline level of health care regardless of their ability to pay for it.

unorthodox legislating, 430–31 Shaping or passing legislation by circumventing the traditional legislative process and not following regular order.

unreasonable searches and seizures, 98, *122,* **123** Searches of private property by government officials or police without an approved warrant; prohibited by the Fourth Amendment.

USA PATRIOT Act, 596–597, *597* A law enacted after 9/11; designed to deter terrorism in the United States by making it easier for the federal government to obtain search warrants, freeze assets, and search people's phone, internet, and bank records without their knowledge.

veto, 42, **429**–430, *430, 431* To reject a bill passed by Congress; also, a power granted to the president by the Constitution.

Watergate scandal, 201
Waters, Maxine, *518*

weak party system, 338 A system in which political parties exert only loose control over the candidate selection process.

wealth. *See also* income inequality
    racial inequality in, 160, *160*

wealth gap, 540–42 An unequal distribution of assets across the population.

wealth tax, 544
weapons of mass destruction, 585, 594–95. *See also* nuclear weapons
wedding-related services, for same-sex marriages, 184–86
Weeks v. United States (1914), *122*

weighting, 269 Adjusting poll responses to ensure that the sample accurately reflects the characteristics of the population. Weighting doesn't involve changing the answers to any survey questions, but it does involve counting some people's responses more heavily and others' less.

Weiner, Anthony, *282,* 289
Welch, Edgar Maddison, 256–57
welfare, federal grant money for, 85
welfare reform, 60
West, Cornel, 166
Westboro Baptist Church, 112, *112*
West Virginia v. EPA (2022), 456
White, Byron, 138–39
White, John, 389
White House, and lobbyists, *505*
White House communications team, 439
White House Office, 450, 454
White House Press Corps, 442
white nationalists, *110*
White supremacists, 598
Will & Grace (television show), 152
Wilson, James, 30
Wilson, Woodrow, *435*
winner-take-all system
    for awarding delegates to party convention, 373
    in Electoral College, 357, 360
    and third parties, 400

winning message, development of, 333–35
witnesses, at trial, 127–28
women, voting rights for, 70–71, *71*
women's equality, *144,* 148–50, *149*
    in wages (*See* pay gap)
Women's Equality Party, *401*
women's rights
    and party identification, 214–15, *215*
    public opinion on, 17, *17*
women's suffrage, 148–49, *149*
Wonder, Stevie, 444
Woodard, Jeffrey, 186
Wool Products Labeling Act, 448
workforce development, 544–45, 546
Working Class Party, *399*
Working Families Party, *399, 401*
World Trade Center attack. *See* September 11, 2001, terrorist attack

World Trade Organization (WTO), 553, 556, 557 An international organization comprising 164 member nations that work together to establish and enforce the rules of international commerce and ensure that trade flows smoothly.

World War II, use of nuclear weapons in, 578

writ of certiorari, 475, *475,* 476 An order in which an appellate court agrees to review a decision issued by a lower court and requests all documents from the case.

writ of mandamus, 50 An order issued by a court directing a government official to take a particular action.

Wyden, Ron, 597

Yahoo News, 283, 297
Yang, Andrew, *374*
Yemen, sanctions on, *582*
"Yes We Can" speech, 372
Young, Peggy, *472, 472*–78
Young v. UPS, 472, 472–78
YouTube, 372

Zangwill, Israel, 17
Zorach v. Clauson (1952), 103
Zuckerberg, Mark, *424*